# MANAGERIAL FINANCE

## THEORY AND TECHNIQUES

# MANAGERIAL

## THEORY AND TECHNIQUES

**Dennis J. O'Connor**

*California State University, Fullerton*

**Alberto T. Bueso**

*California State University, Fullerton*

PRENTICE-HALL, INC., ENGLEWOOD CLIFFS, NEW JERSEY 07632

# FINANCE

*Library of Congress Cataloging in Publication Data*

O'CONNOR, DENNIS J (DATE)
    Managerial finance.

    Includes bibliographies and index.
      1. Corporations—Finance.  2. Business enter-
prises—Finance.  I.  Bueso, Alberto T., joint
author.  II. Title.
HG4026.027      658.1′5      80-24933
ISBN 0-13-550269-1

To Our Mothers
Eleanor Lococo
Nelly Bueso

Printed in the United States of America

10  9  8  7  6  5  4  3  2  1

**MANAGERIAL FINANCE: THEORY AND TECHNIQUES**
Dennis J. O'Connor and Alberto T. Bueso

*Editorial/production supervision by Pam Wilder*
*Interior and cover design by Walter Behnke*
*Manufacturing buyer: Gordon Osbourne*

PRENTICE-HALL INTERNATIONAL, INC., *London*
PRENTICE-HALL OF AUSTRALIA PTY. LIMITED, *Sydney*
PRENTICE-HALL OF CANADA, LTD., *Toronto*
PRENTICE-HALL OF INDIA PRIVATE LIMITED, *New Delhi*
PRENTICE-HALL OF JAPAN, INC., *Tokyo*
PRENTICE-HALL OF SOUTHEAST ASIA PTE. LTD., *Singapore*
WHITEHALL BOOKS LIMITED, *Wellington, New Zealand*

# CONTENTS

# 3

## THE USE OF PRESENT- AND FUTURE-VALUE TABLES IN FINANCIAL DECISION MAKING

# 4

## RISK AND THE VALUE OF COMMON STOCK

# 5

## THE ACQUISITION OF DEBT CAPITAL AND STOCKHOLDER WEALTH

# 12

## ASSET MANAGEMENT IN AN INTERNATIONAL CONTEXT

# 13

## THE ASSET-SPECIFIC COST OF CAPITAL: ESTIMATING THE WEIGHTS

# 14

## THE ASSET-SPECIFIC COST OF CAPITAL: COMPONENT COST

**PART THREE    THE ACQUISITION OF CAPITAL    379**

# 15

## CAPITAL MARKETS: AN OVERVIEW

# 16

## SHORT-TERM CAPITAL ACQUISITION

# 17

## LONG-TERM DEBT CAPITAL

# 18

## EQUITY CAPITAL: RETAINED EARNINGS AND NEW COMMON STOCK

## PART FOUR    FINANCIAL ANALYSIS    491

# 19

## ANALYSIS OF THE FIRM'S FUTURE FINANCIAL PROSPECTS

## EPILOGUE

## INDEX

# PREFACE

It has long been recognized by educators and businessmen that every business administration student, regardless of his/her specific area of concentration, should have an understanding of the principles of financial management. Accordingly, almost every business administration program in the United States requires completion of a basic course in financial management. This book, *Managerial Finance: Theory and Techniques*, is an introductory text for use in the first financial management course. It is designed specifically to show how all business decision makers and the firm will benefit from a sound understanding of the principles of finance.

The first objective of the book is to get you to look at every decision alternative open to the firm in terms of its risk-return characteristics. We then show how risk and return are related to the welfare of the firm's owners. The main objective of the book is to help you develop a conceptually correct view of financial management. We hope that after you have completed the course, you will look at the management of the firm differently.

The second objective of *Managerial Finance: Theory and Techniques* is to examine the wide range of techniques currently used by financial managers. We look at each technique and indicate the possible situations in which it can be used and exactly how the technique can help in the evaluation of the risk-return implications of each alternative. We also stress the roles played by the various types of managers (production, marketing, and finance) in properly implementing these techniques and the key business judgments that are involved. When you have completed this text you will better appreciate the excitement and "artistry" involved in financial decision making.

*Managerial Finance: Theory and Techniques*, while having an analytical focus, does not require a high level of mathematical or statistical competence. Only simple algebra and very simple statistical concepts are used in the book. The materials have been extensively class tested over two academic years, and to our knowledge, not one student of the several hundreds involved in the test ever mentioned having undue difficulties with the math. You should also be aware of the fact that the end of chapter questions and problems provide a convenient way for review and study. Each question and problem is related to a specific concept covered in the chapter.

## ADDITIONAL STUDY MATERIALS

Many students may find it helpful to use the book, *A Self-Correcting Approach to Managerial Finance: Theory and Techniques*, which was specifically designed for use with *Managerial Finance: Theory and Techniques*. This self-correcting book takes you through the most difficult concepts and computations on a step-by-step basis. Difficult situations are broken into a number of simpler problems and later combined. We have had great success using this teaching and learning device in the past. In addition to the self-correcting activities, the book also includes a list of concepts you should learn for each chapter and an extensive array of problems and objective questions with answers that will enable you to test how well you understand the material *before* you take a classroom test. This supplementary text will help you use study time more efficiently and is likely to improve the understanding and retention of the materials.

## ACKNOWLEDGMENTS

We received many detailed and specific suggestions for improvements in every chapter of the book. We are deeply indebted to the following individuals for their suggestions and comments on the original manuscript: Dalton Bandy (California State University, Fullerton), David Cole (Ohio State University), Donald Crane (California State University, Fullerton), Larry Dann (University of Oregon), Perry Dodds (California State University, Fresno), J. R. Ezzell (The Pennsylvania State University), Adam K. Gehr, Jr. (University of Missouri, Columbia), Charles P. Jones (North Carolina State University, Raleigh), John Lindvall (California Polytechnic State University, San Luis Obispo), Gilbert McKee (California State Polytechnic, Pomona), W. Gerald Platt (San Francisco State University), Michael Rozeff (University of Iowa), G. Robert Sanderson (San Jose State University), Perry J. Stickels (California State University, Fullerton), John Stowe (University of Missouri, Columbia), and Tony R. Wingler (University of North Carolina, Greensboro).

    The School of Business Administration & Economics and the Department of Finance at California State University, Fullerton, provided logistical support to this project. Their help in reproducing the manuscript enabled us to use it in class situations. Our students provided us with invaluable assistance by correcting mathematical errors and improving the explanation of various topics. It is not an exaggeration to state that without their contributions, the project could not have reached this stage of development. We also owe a debt of gratitude to Gail Champion and Janet Gerhard for their help in typing the manuscript.

We also are indebted to the people at Prentice-Hall for their support. David C. Hildebrand guided us through the "mysteries" in the publishing world. Ernest C. Hursh gave us a better understanding of proper marketing techniques. Rita DeVries performed an excellent editing job on our original manuscript. Last, and in this case certainly not least, Gerry Johnson was instrumental in our signing with Prentice-Hall. As the California State University, Fullerton campus representative for Prentice-Hall, her powers of persuasion encouraged us to select Prentice-Hall as the publisher for our book.

# THE THEORY
# OF FINANCE

# Introduction to PART ONE

Part One provides the students with an overview of financial decision making. We have developed a simplified conceptual framework that emphasizes the risk and return for each decision alternative. Decisions related to the acquisition of assets and the financing of such assets are evaluated within the context of stockholder wealth maximization. It should be noted that Part One emphasizes concepts rather than computations. We are trying to develop a general understanding of finance. Specific techniques related to this conceptual framework are discussed in Parts Two, Three, and Four of the book.

# MAXIMIZATION OF STOCKHOLDER WEALTH AS A GUIDE FOR FINANCIAL DECISION MAKING

## 1

## INTRODUCTION

Today, the management of even a small corporation is a complex and difficult task. Each year, thousands of decisions must be made, most of which will affect, to a greater or lesser degree, the financial status of the corporation. Some of these decisions can improve that financial situation; others can be a detriment to it.

What are these decisions? How do they affect the financial well-being of the corporation? What criteria should the manager use for making these decisions?

Within the confines of one book, it is impossible to review every possible decision—or even every type of decision—made by managers. It is possible, however, to develop general analytical and methodological frameworks that managers can use when making decisions.

The seven chapters of this part are devoted to the development of an analytic framework (called the *theory of finance*) for evaluating the financial effects of corporate decisions. The theory of finance represents a simplified picture of the relationship between corporate management and corporate owners. The objective of the simplification is to permit us to focus on the most important aspects of the decision-making process. The theoretical structure developed in the first part of this book will permit both the student and the manager to attack and solve a broad range of corporate financial problems.

The remainder of the book is devoted to the development of specific methodologies that can be applied to specific problems. We have been careful to show how these recommended methodologies are consistent with the analytical-theoretical framework developed in Part I. The selection of the methodologies for inclusion in this book and the depth of their coverage was influenced by several factors.

First, methodologies that are applied to relatively important decision-making situations tend to be covered in the greatest detail. Second, because we have seen that some of the methodologies currently employed by management are only marginally consistent with best practice, this book emphasizes the best technique and minimizes the presentation of the less satisfactory.

For the book as a whole, then, there is a general theoretical framework that can be applied to all corporate financial situations and a selection of the most important techniques that can be applied to specific problems.

## FINANCIAL ASPECTS OF CORPORATE DECISIONS

Management must, of course, decide on the type and quantity of products to be produced by the firm. In a general sense, these are marketing-related decisions. However, their financial implications, like those of all marketing decisions, are significant to the firm. For example, a marketing study may reveal an opportunity for the development of a new product and for entry into a new market. Among the many questions that will have to be answered before the firm undertakes such a project, of the first importance are, What will be the production cost? and, How many units can be sold at various prices? Thus, although the decision is primarily a marketing one, the criteria for acceptance or rejection will be financial. The decision will be based on management's evaluation of the effect of the marketing alternative on the financial well-being of the firm. As a general rule, marketing alternatives are always selected on the basis of their financial consequences.

Management must also decide how its products will be produced.

Decisions in this area may be called production-related decisions: Should the firm replace old machinery? Should a new technology be introduced? Should an old facility be expanded, or a new one constructed? Although technical or engineering expertise is required for answering these questions, management usually makes the final decision. Management considers not only the technical aspects but also the possible effects of various alternatives on the firm's financial health. In the final analysis, the choice among production alternatives is based upon financial considerations.

In addition to marketing-related and production-related decisions, management is also required to make "pure" financing decisions. These are decisions that relate to the right side of the balance sheet: Should the firm use short- or long-term debt? Should earnings be retained? Should new common stock be sold? Again, management chooses among the numerous alternatives open to it on the basis of the estimated effect on the financial well-being of the firm. In fact, every major decision, be it marketing-, production-, or financing-related, should be scrutinized in terms of its financial results to the firm.

## STOCKHOLDER-WEALTH MAXIMIZATION

What do we mean when we speak of the financial well-being of the corporation? How does the manager know when the well-being of the corporation has been maximized? Thus far, we have been deliberately vague on these points. Now let us become more specific.

The objective of the modern corporation is and should be the maximization of *stockholder wealth*. Stockholder wealth maximization means simply this:

1. Since the wealth of stockholders is determined by the value of their assets, and common stock is a stockholder asset,
2. And since the price of common stock is determined by the expected future payments that will be paid to the owner of the stock and by the uncertainty attached to such payments,
3. Then management should choose those business alternatives that maximize expected future payments to stockholders with a minimum of uncertainty. Such actions will maximize the value of common stock and, by definition, stockholder wealth.

The central point of this chapter is that management should and does make choices among decision alternatives on the basis of the estimated results of the various alternatives on common-stock price and stockholder wealth. The security market, which has thousands of participants, impersonally evaluates decisions made by management and arrives at a consensus market price for the stock on the basis of this evaluation. This idea will be developed in greater detail in the sections that follow.

## PROFIT MAXIMIZATION vs. STOCKHOLDER-WEALTH MAXIMIZATION

The concept of earnings or profit maximization is basically a single-period or, at the most, a short-run concept. It is usually interpreted to mean the maximization of earnings within a given period of time. However, stockholders are interested in future as well as present profits. Stocks usually sell at many times current earnings, suggesting that the stockholder is interested in developments beyond the present period.

Stock price is a better basis for the evaluation of management. In a relatively competitive stock market such as that in the United States, the prospects of the corporation's future are constantly being evaluated. In establishing a price for the stock of a given corporation, the stock market considers not only profits in the current period but future profits and dividends, extending well beyond the present.

For example, consider the case of Comsat, a quasi-government corporation whose purpose was to develop and operate communications statellites. At the time the original shares were sold to the public, the corporation had no profits, and no prospect of profits, much less dividends, for years into the future. But despite the absence of current income, the stock was easily sold, owing to the public's expectations of future profits. Purchasers of common stock certainly look at the performance of the corporation during the current period, but they also evaluate the expectation of its future profits.

The implications of this for management are clear. Decision alternatives facing the corporation must be evaluated not only in terms of their effect on current profits but also in terms of their earnings potential. The objective of stock-price maximization introduces a long-term dimension into corporate decision making. The market will minimize the importance of short-term developments that temporarily "puff up" profits. It will respond positively to corporate decisions that make the long-term earnings and dividends picture more attractive.

The preceding discussion illustrates two critical differences between the possible corporate goals of profit maximization and stock-price maximization. The first difference relates to the time horizon of benefits. The goal of stock-price maximization implies that management should take a longer-run point of view. The second important difference is that the pursuit of stock-price maximization implies that corporate management is continuously being evaluated by impersonal stock-market forces. Thus, management must consider the psychological, informational, and institutional forces at work in the market. The profit-maximization goal either ignores this market-evaluation phenomenon or assumes that the market will evaluate the firm on the basis of current earnings alone. As we shall see in the following chapters, management should always keep an eye on the market forces that determine the price of the firm's common stock.

It would be incorrect, however, to say that profit maximization and stockholder-wealth maximization are totally different objectives. Stockholder-wealth maximization is in reality an expanded, more detailed version of the profit-maximizing principle. The following aspects of the two may help bring this idea into sharper focus:

1. Stockholder-wealth maximization focuses on the stockholder rather than the firm. Profit maximization focuses on the firm and assumes that what is good for the firm is good for the stockholder.
2. The profit-maximization principle abstracts from time. Stockholder-wealth maximization places a heavy emphasis on future events.
3. The concept of stockholder-wealth maximization introduces the idea that a capital market evaluates the firm's activities and establishes a price for common stock. This idea is not specified in the usual formulation of the profit-maximizing principle (although it could be).
4. The principle of profit maximization emphasizes accounting profits, whereas stockholder-wealth maximization emphasizes cash payments to stockholders. Even though in the long run this difference may not be great, we will see that evaluating decisions on a cash basis as distinct from a profit basis can lead to significantly different results.
5. By emphasizing the importance of future developments on the price of common stock, the concept of stockholder-wealth maximization stresses the risk and uncertainty associated with corporate decision alternatives. It implies that management must concern itself with the risk implications of decisions, since the stock market is likely to pay lower prices for more risky stocks (other things being equal).

Thus, the objective of stockholder-wealth maximization spells out things that may or may not be assumed by the user of the profit-maximizing objective.

An outline of the relationship between profit maximization and stockholder-wealth maximization is presented in Figure 1–1. This schematic presentation emphasizes the fact that current profits are only one of several factors that contribute to stockholder wealth. The diagram also shows the importance of the security market's reaction to corporate decisions, an importance that will become more apparent as we proceed through this book.

## FORCES GENERATING STOCKHOLDER-WEALTH MAXIMIZATION

Why should corporate management attempt to maximize stockholder wealth? As we shall see, because it is in management's interest to do so. Such behavior is consistent with the desire of management for secure positions with high compensation. There are a number of forces at work that might jeopardize the tenure of a management group that fails to pursue a policy of stockholder-wealth maximization.

The first and perhaps least-powerful force to consider is the combined preference of individual stockholders. Stockholders, like almost everyone

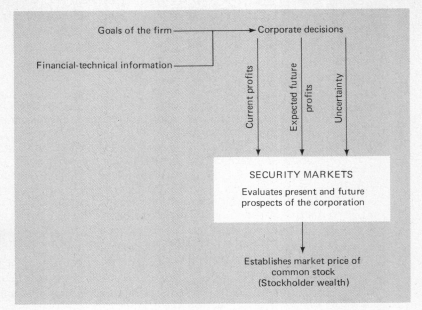

Goals of the firm ──────────────► Corporate decisions

Financial-technical information ───┘

Current profits

Expected future profits

Uncertainty

SECURITY MARKETS

Evaluates present and future
prospects of the corporation

Establishes market price of
common stock
(Stockholder wealth)

**FIGURE 1–1**

Profit maximization
and
stockholder-wealth
maximization

else, prefer more income and consumption rather than less. They are happier when management pursues policies that allow them to achieve as high a level of satisfaction as possible. Management groups that consistently frustrate the stockholders' desire for more income and consumption risk the possibility of a revolt by the stockholders, with perhaps the result that the current management will be replaced.

In the real world, such revolts do take place, but they are rarely successful. On occasion, a group of disenchanted stockholders does challenge management. However, for the challenge to be successful, voting proxies from a large number of stockholders must be obtained. Management can use corporate funds to distribute information and obtain voting proxies, whereas the challengers must use private funds. Not only is a challenge very expensive, but stockholders as a group are usually inclined to continue with the known, even if less than satisfactory, management group. It appears that management usually has little to fear from a revolt by stockholders.

There are more powerful forces at work. The prospect of a corporate raid is one such force. A corporation with unrealized potential for stock-price growth may find itself a target of a takeover raid from another corporation. In such a case, the aggressor corporation makes a "tender offer" in an attempt to gain control of the firm. The "tender offer" price is usually above the current market price, and the offer is made contingent on the acquisition of a sufficient number of shares to gain control of the target corporation. Should an insufficient number of shares be tendered, the offer is withdrawn. Management's best defense against a raid of this type is the maintenance of a high stock price that is consistent with stockholder-wealth maximization.

Institutional investors also exert some pressure on corporate managers. Mutual funds, pension funds, and trust departments of commercial banks may be in a position to exercise direct control on corporate management. In many instances, the common-stock holdings of just a few financial institutions would be enough to force changes in management. Of course, actions of this type are rare. Perhaps financial institutions are satisfied with corporate management performance, or perhaps they are unwilling to take an active part in the management of the corporation. One must conclude, however, that these concentrations in stock ownership exert at least indirect pressure on management to maximize stockholder wealth.

In recent years, management compensation has been tied to performance with increasing frequency. For example, the extensive use of stock options to motivate management to keep stock prices high also represents a force in the direction of stockholder-wealth maximization. In such cases, top managers are given the option to buy a specific number of common stock shares at or near the market price of the stock on the date the option is given. They pay nothing for the option. If the price of the stock goes up, the manager can simultaneously exercise the option (at the earlier, lower price) and sell the stock (at the current, higher price). The difference between the old and the new prices represents a profit for the manager. Such options are given so that the possibility of such profits will encourage corporate management to base its decisions on their effect on the stock price and stockholder wealth.

## CONSTRAINTS ON STOCKHOLDER-WEALTH MAXIMIZATION

The phrase *stockholder-wealth maximization* is overdramatic and, in a sense, misleading. The mention of such a goal brings to mind an image of greedy little corporate managers, engaged in activities designed to enrich themselves and the stockholders at the expense of all others. A picture like that can cause people in today's society to feel that management shouldn't maximize stockholder wealth—to say, "Sure, some profits are acceptable, but firms don't have to *maximize* profits!"

First, we must recognize that in the real world, management does not squeeze out the last penny of profit. The objective of stockholder-wealth maximization is what can be called a constrained objective. There is a complicated set of social forces that may restrict the activities of corporate management in its pursuit of higher stock prices and stockholder wealth.

First of all, the law constrains corporate stockholder-wealth maximization behavior. To start with the ridiculous, the law prohibits corporate management from murdering competitors or sabotaging their facilities, even if such actions should increase the price of common stock of the corporation.

Equally obvious are laws prohibiting collusion among competitors, stock-price manipulation, pollution, false or misleading advertising, and other activities of this kind. Less obvious but very important legal constraints are child labor laws, building and zoning codes, minimum-wage laws, antidiscrimination laws, and the like. One can only conclude that the alternatives open to management to pursue the maximization of stockholder wealth are greatly restricted by the legal environment.

Then, there are forces other than legal that constrain corporate management. The concept that business has a social responsibility in addition to legal obligations is widely recognized by both business leaders and scholars. This ethic of social responsibility often leads to the adoption of corporate policies that appear to be inconsistent with stockholder-wealth maximization. Corporations are expected to retain workers when they are ill, minimize nuisances (noise, dust, and so on), improve the appearance of their facilities, make financial contributions to worthy causes and in all ways be model citizens. To be sure, the consequences of failing to accept this social responsibility are not immediate fines or imprisonment. They may, however, include the passage of unfavorable legislation in the future. The fact is that pressures do exist, and management does respond to them. The adoption of social policies that appear to counter the stockholder-wealth-maximization goal may in fact not do so.

Technological factors may also restrict corporate management in its pursuit of greater stockholder wealth. Owing to technology, the modern corporation requires an amount of equity capital that usually exceeds that available from a small group of individual investors. When corporate ownership is spread over a large number of people, the entire group of owners is unable to participate in the managment of corporate affairs. So a management group evolves—a group with interests that may differ from those of the stockholders. Some observers believe, for example, that the separation of ownership and managerial control in the modern corporation has resulted in management's pursuit of policies that lead neither to profit nor to stockholder-wealth maximization. Management is sometimes viewed as attempting to maximize sales, its own salaries, or its security.

The approach taken in this book recognizes that corporate management does not pursue stockholder-wealth maximization at all costs. There are a host of organizational, social, and legal forces that restrict management. These forces are usually natural and reasonable; they should not be viewed as perversions of a sacred ideal. All social institutions, of which corporations are one type, are restricted in many ways. That is the nature of social organization. This book assumes that the goal of management is to maximize the wealth of the stockholders *subject to those constraints imposed by society*. The word *maximization* is not meant to imply that business pursues its objectives to the exclusion of broad societal goals and objectives.

Another aspect of stockholder-wealth maximization is worth a brief review. As you recall from your courses in economics, the American economic system operates on market principles. There is no central planning authority that allocates investment funds to various firms and industries. To a large extent, investors make the decision as to who gets investment funds. If, for example, investors perceive the petroleum industry as a good investment, they provide funds to that industry; if they perceive the petroleum industry negatively, they withhold their investment funds and place them somewhere else. Thus, the firms that receive capital are those that promise high returns to investors. That is the way the system works.

In addition, it is likely that the firms providing those services most demanded by society will be most able to furnish the highest returns to stockholders. Thus, the firm's pursuit of stockholder-wealth maximization is good not only for the firm's stockholders but also for society as a whole, since high returns to stockholders are most often an indication of high social preference. By pursuing the goal of stockholder-wealth maximization, management permits consumers (speaking through market behavior) to direct investors to the most preferred investment alternatives. A management failing to give investors the proper signal fails to attract investment funds and fails to satisfy the expressed needs of society.

This is not to say that the market operates with 100 percent efficiency. Almost everyone agrees that, at least occasionally, firms in their search for high profits operate in a fashion inconsistent with the best interest of the general public. Traditionally, in the United States, the public has responded by enforcing new legal or social constraints on management behavior. Detrimental corporate practices are presumed to be minimized in this fashion.

Of course, some people argue that the whole system of markets should be abandoned and some new (usually unspecified) system adopted. However attractive these new systems are, they are not likely to become a reality in the near future. Until they are, the only way investment funds can be allocated is on the basis of expected stockholder benefit. Thus, management should pursue stockholder-wealth maximization because it is central to an efficient allocation of investment funds, which is essential if our economic system is to function in an efficient fashion.

## SMALLER BUSINESSES

The concepts and illustrations used in this book apply most directly to the financial-management situation of relatively large, publicly owned corporations. However, most of the material included is also applicable to financial management in smaller corporations, partnerships, and single proprietorships. When different rules apply, special presentation of material will be made.

In smaller businesses, stockholder-wealth maximization can be translated to mean owner-wealth maximization. The forces generating owner-wealth maximization in a small business are related to the forces of competition in the economy. Remember also that there is little separation of ownership and control in a small firm. Thus, the objectives of the small business are not very different from those of the large corporation.

## ORGANIZATION OF THE BOOK

This book is designed to provide the manager with general guidelines for making financial decisions. The techniques presented are specifically tied to the goal of stockholder-wealth maximization.

### PART ONE: THE THEORY OF FINANCE

The intent of the first seven chapters that make up Part One of *Managerial Finance: Theory and Techniques* is to provide a simplified picture of financial decision making. This simplified picture, called the theory of finance, is designed to show how various decisions are related to each other and how all decisions should be related to stockholder wealth. The emphasis in Part One is on concept rather than techniques. It presents a way of looking at problems rather than a means of solving them.

### PART TWO: THE ACQUISITION OF ASSETS

Chapters 8 through 14 (Part Two) deal with the specific techniques used to evaluate decision alternatives in asset-acquisition situations. In a general sense, the topics covered in this section relate to the left-hand side of the balance sheet. How should the firm go about making decisions relating to the acquisition of a new machine, a new subsidiary, increases in inventory, or increases in accounts receivable? These questions are answered in Part Two. The emphasis here is on computations and decisions. All the techniques presented, however, are evaluated in terms of their compatibility with the theory of finance and stockholder-wealth maximization.

### PART THREE: THE ACQUISITION OF CAPITAL

Chapter 15 through 18 (Part Three) deal with the acquisition of the funds needed to conduct the activities of the firm. Generally, the topics covered in this section relate to the right-hand side of the balance sheet. Should the firm retain earnings, sell new common stock, sell new bonds? Should it use inventories as collateral for a short-term loan, or attempt to obtain an unsecured loan? What types of funds are available from commercial banks, insurance companies, and finance companies? These are the questions answered in the third part of the book. The suggested techniques and solutions are evaluated in terms of their consistency with the theory of finance and stockholder wealth.

## PART FOUR: FINANCIAL ANALYSIS

The fourth part of the book contains one chapter, which deals with the evaluation of the firm. This important topic is reserved for last because the techniques of evaluation make more sense once the objectives and recommended courses of action for the firm are better understood.

The book as a whole should provide the student or manager with both a frame of reference and a useful package of techniques for financial decision-making situations. The book is more than a catalog of techniques. It provides a conceptual framework that can be applied to many different problems in a changing business world. It is a financial-management book for both the manager of today and tomorrow's managers.

**QUESTIONS FOR DISCUSSION**

1. Explain the difference between profit maximization and stockholder-wealth maximization.
2. Explain how common-stock prices are related to stockholder wealth.
3. What is a stockholder revolt? How is the possibility of such a revolt apt to affect management policies?
4. Review the last few weeks of *The Wall Street Journal* or *Business Week* and find an illustration of a corporate takeover in progress. What are the motives of the aggressor firm? What pressure is put on the target firm?
5. Evaluate the strength of the forces that encourage management to pursue stockholder-wealth maximization as the goal of the firm.
6. Why is the objective of stockholder-wealth maximization known as a constrained objective?
7. List some of the legal and social constraints that affect the management of General Motors Corporation.
8. In what way is the phrase "stockholder-wealth maximization" overdramatic?
9. How does the objective of stockholder-wealth maximization relate to the well-being of American society?
10. Discuss the relationship between stockholder-wealth maximization and the maximization of owner wealth in small businesses.

**BIBLIOGRAPHY**

Since the topics of the first seven chapters are so closely related, one comprehensive bibliography covering all seven chapters is included at the end of Part One.

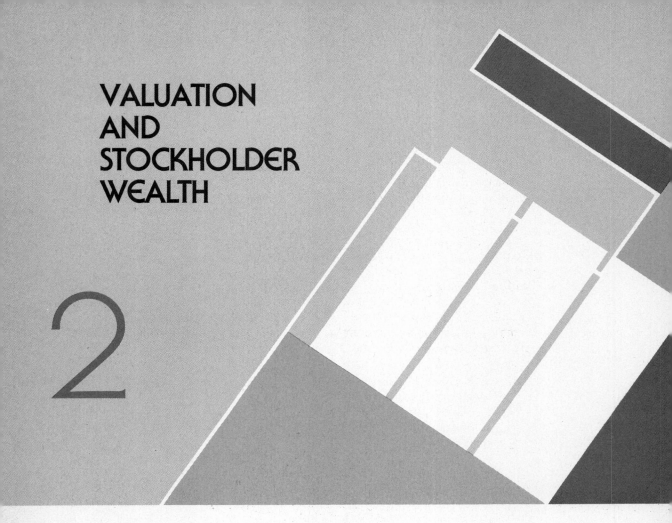

# VALUATION AND STOCKHOLDER WEALTH

## 2

## INTRODUCTION

In this chapter, we will examine the relationship between the cash flows expected by stockholders and stockholder wealth. Other things being equal, the higher the expected cash flows associated with a common stock, the higher the value of that stock. In addition, stocks for which cash flows are expected at or near the present time are valued more highly than stocks with identical cash flows expected in the distant future. We shall focus on the logic employed by market participants as they process information on the amount and timing of cash flows, and thus establish values for common stocks. A discussion of the effect of risk differences on common-stock price will be postponed until Chapter 4. The process of stock-price and stockholder-wealth determination is outlined in Figure 2–1.

For reasons that will become obvious as we proceed through this chapter, it is easier to explain the relationship between cash flows and security prices if bonds, rather than stocks, are used for purposes of illustration. Thus, the first part of the chapter will analyze the relation of expected cash flows to the market price of bonds. Only after the process of bond-price determination is developed will we discuss the determination of common-stock prices. Remember, our intent is not to develop realistic examples of bond-price determination (which will be discussed in a later chapter), but to develop some general principles of security-price determination that can be used to evaluate the effect of expected cash flows on common-stock price and stockholder wealth.

## THE NATURE OF MARKET VALUE

The market value of a real asset reflects the possible cash flows associated with that asset. Assets that are associated with relatively high possible cash flows are considered valuable. A large diamond ring, for example, is considered valuable because the owner of the ring can dispose of it for a large amount of money. An apartment house or office complex is valuable if it can generate large cash flows. On the other hand, when we talk of a worn-out automobile as having a low market value, we are recognizing the fact that renting or selling that automobile will produce only a small amount of money. Thus, money flows and market values are two sides of the same coin. A high market value implies high possible money flows, and vice versa.

The market value of financial assets, such as stocks and bonds, is similarly related to possible cash flows. Other things being equal, a common stock associated with high possible dividend payments would be more valuable than one with lower possible dividend payments.[1] This is the nature of market value.

---

[1] It is assumed here that there is no difference in the riskiness associated with the different cash flows. This assumption will be set aside in Chapter 4.

## TIME VALUE OF MONEY

The value of an asset is related not only to the amount of possible cash flows, but also to the length of time that must elapse before such cash flows will be received. Assume that you own two U.S. savings bonds. There are no regular interest payments associated with either bond, and at maturity, the federal government will redeem each bond for $100. Assume further that the first bond (bond X) will mature today, and the second bond (bond Y) one year from now. Which bond is more valuable? Obviously, the first.[2] As a general rule, people prefer to receive cash flows as soon as possible. Assets associated with cash flows received in the future have a lower value than assets associated with cash flows occurring at the present (other things being equal). This phenomenon, by which people value present over future cash flows, is known as the *time value of money*. The fact that money has a time value means that a dollar received now is worth more than a dollar to be received in the future.

Precisely why is bond X worth more than bond Y? The answer to this question is simply that a person will be able to attain a superior comsumption pattern if bond X is chosen. If, for example, you want current consumption, $100 is immediately available when you choose bond X. If, on the other hand, you prefer to postpone consumption until next year, that $100 can be "saved" for a year, and at the end of the year, you will have a larger amount ($100 plus one year's interest). This is what makes bond X the superior alternative.

The logic incorporated in the example above is familiar to most Americans. It revolves around the idea that when money is "saved" (that is, invested at a positive rate of interest), the future value or compound value will be greater than the present value. For example, for every dollar placed in a savings account paying interest, more than one dollar can be withdrawn at the end of one year.

It is a relatively simple matter to compute the amount that can be withdrawn in the future (future value) for each dollar deposited in such an account today. Assume, for example, that you deposit $1,000 in a savings account paying 5 percent interest per annum. What will be the value of this $1,000 one year from now (future value)? At the end of one year, you will be permitted to withdraw the principal amount, $1,000, plus the interest of $50, for a total of $1,050, as shown in Table 2–1.

If you decided to leave the money in the account for an additional year,

---

[2]U.S. savings bonds are sold at an amount below maturity value. The difference between the salesprice and the maturity value represents the interest earned by the purchaser of the bond. Usually, the bonds are held for ten or more years. The rate of interest is set by the Treasury. In the examples used in this chapter, maturities are much shorter than the maturities of actual U.S. savings bonds, and the interest rates tend to be higher than those set by the Treasury.

**TABLE 2-1**

### FUTURE VALUE AT THE END OF ONE YEAR

| | |
|---|---:|
| Principal (amount deposited at the beginning of period 1) | $1,000 |
| Dollar interest paid for period 1 (5% of $1,000) | 50 |
| Amount available in one year (future value) | $1,050 |

the amount available to you in two years would be even greater. As shown in Table 2–2, the dollar interest payment for year 2 ($52.50) is greater than the dollar interest payment for year 1 ($50.00), even though the interest rate remained at 5 percent. This higher dollar interest results from the fact that during the second year, interest is paid not only on the original $1,000 deposit, but also on the $50 interest earned during the first year. The payment of interest on principal and prior-earned interest is known as compounding (compound interest). (In the example above, interest is compounded annually, so that each period equals one year. Where interest is compounded more frequently, each period would be of a shorter time. For example, quarterly compounding involves three-month periods.)

**TABLE 2-2**

### FUTURE VALUE AT THE END OF TWO YEARS

| | |
|---|---:|
| Principal (amount in the account at the beginning of year 2) | $1,050 |
| Dollar interest paid in year 2 (5% of $1,050) | 52.50 |
| Amount available at the end of year 2 (future value) | $1,102.50 |

The future value, or compound value, can be expressed in a convenient algebraic formula:[3]

$$FV_n = PV_0(1 + i)^n \qquad (2\text{-}1)$$

where FV = the future value

$PV_0$ = the present value

$i$ = the interest rate per period that could be earned elsewhere on comparable investments (an opportunity cost)

$n$ = the number of periods that the funds are invested

---

[3]The derivation of this equation is presented in Appendix 2A.

In our example, the future value at the end of one year can be easily computed as follows:

$$FV_1 = PV_0 (1+i)^n$$

$$= \$1,000(1+0.05)^1 = \$1,050$$

It is only slightly more difficult to compute future values for more distant future times. For example, the future value of $1,000, earning 5 percent per annum in a savings account for two or five years, would be computed as follows:

*Future Value at the end of two years*

$$FV_2 = PV_0(1+i)^2$$

$$= \$1,000(1.05)(1.05) = \$1,000(1.1025)$$

$$= \$1,102.50$$

*Future Value at the end of five years*

$$FV_5 = PV_0(1+i)^5$$

$$= \$1,000(1.05)(1.05)(1.05)(1.05)(105)$$

$$= \$1,000(1.27628)$$

$$= \$1,276.28$$

Let's go back to our choice between savings bond X ($100 today) and savings bond Y ($100 one year from now). If bond X is chosen, $100 will be received today. If that $100 can earn 5 percent per year, it will have a future value of $105 at the end of one year. So when Bond X is chosen, money will be received earlier, and it can be invested and earn an additional return.

In this example, we "proved" bond X superior to bond Y by comparing wealth at a *future* point in time. That is, if bond Y is chosen, we will have $100 *one year from now*; if bond X is chosen, we will have $105 *one year from now*. Note that the comparison was based on wealth at exactly the same point in time, *one year from now*. This fact is of crucial importance.

Assume, for example, that you are forced to choose between U.S. savings bonds P and Q. If you choose bond P, you will receive $1,000 today. If you choose bond Q, you will receive $1,150 two years from now. In order to make a rational decision, you must compare the value of these bonds at the same point in time. Assume that you select bond P, and your money can earn 10 percent per year. At the end of two years, you would have:

$$FV_2 = PV_0(1+i)^2$$

$$= \$1,000(1.10)(1.10) = \$1,000(1.21)$$

$$= \$1,210$$

Your choice of bond P would result in greater wealth two years from now ($1,210) than if you had chosen bond Q ($1,150). Note that for a rational decision, the wealth effects at the *same point in time* were compared.

## PRESENT VALUE

Typically, the present time rather than a future time is generally used as the point of reference for choices among alternatives. Instead of computing the contribution of bond P to wealth at a future point, we usually compute the contribution of bond Q to present wealth. Since bond Q will pay $1,150 in two years, we know that it is worth less than $1,150 today. In order to compute the exact contribution of bond Q to present wealth, a procedure called *discounting* is used. Discounting reduces higher future values to lower present values, and permits wealth comparison at the present moment. *Discounting may be thought of as the process of computing unknown present values from known future values.*

The procedures used in discounting (computing present values) are closely related to the procedures used in compounding (computing future values). A simple mathematical manipulation turns the equation for future value into an equation for present value:

If

$$FV_n = PV_0(1+i)^n$$

and both sides of the equation are divided by $(1+i)^n$, then:

$$PV_0 = \frac{FV_n}{(1+i)^n} \tag{2-2}$$

Using equation 2-2, we can compute the present value of bond Q. The computation would be as follows:

$$PV_0 = \frac{FV_2}{(1+0.10)^2} = \frac{\$1,150}{(1.10)(1.10)} = \frac{\$1,150}{1.21} = \$950.41$$

We can now compare the present values of bonds P and Q. Our present wealth would be greater if we choose bond P ($1,000) rather than bond Q ($950.41). The rational person would make the same choice whether the comparison is made at year 2 (compounding) or at the present time (discounting). The methods are equivalent, but discounting or present value is used much more extensively in finance.

Let's go back and look at the significance of the present value of $950.41 of bond Q. What exactly does this value represent? *The present value is the amount that must be invested today in order to duplicate a predetermined future value.* If we invest $950.41 at a 10 percent annual rate of interest for two years, we will have $1,150 at the end of two years. The computation would be as follows:

$$FV_2 = PV_0(1 + i)^2 = \$950.41(1.10)(1.10) = \$950.41(1.21) = \$1,150$$

Present values can be computed for any number of expected future payments. Assume that you would like to know the present value of a U.S. government bond (bond W) that will pay $70 in interest every year for the next three years. At the end of year 3, the principal amount of $1,000 will also be repaid. Also assume that your money could earn a 10 percent return in similar investment opportunities. The series of payments received is illustrated in Figure 2–2, where we see that there are three future values

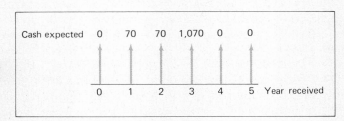

**FIGURE 2–2**

Time Line for Cash Flows (Bond W)

involved ($FV_1 = \$70$, $FV_2 = \$70$, and $FV_3 = \$1,070$ in annual interest and principal). The present value of bond W would be equal to the sum of the present values of the three future values. The computation of the present value of bond W would be as follows:

$$PV_0 = \frac{FV_1}{(1+i)^1} + \frac{FV_2}{(1+i)^2} + \frac{FV_3}{(1+i)^3}$$

$$= \frac{\$70}{(1.10)} + \frac{\$70}{(1.10)(1.10)} + \frac{\$1,070}{(1.10)(1.10)(1.10)}$$

$$= \frac{\$70}{(1.10)} + \frac{\$70}{(1.21)} + \frac{\$1,070}{(1.331)} = \$63.64 + \$57.85 + \$803.91$$

$$= \$925.40$$

Thus, the present value of bond W is $926.

Seen from another angle, the cash flows described in Figure 2–2 could be duplicated exactly if $925.40 were invested at an annual rate of return of 10 percent. Let us assume that $925.40 is deposited at a commercial bank paying 10 percent annual interest (where interest is *not* compounded daily, but yearly). At the end of the first year, $70 will be withdrawn from the bank. The same withdrawal would be made at the end of the second year. As shown in Table 2–3, you would be able to duplicate the cash flows shown in Figure 2–2.

TABLE 2-3

## DEPOSITING $925.40 AT A COMMERCIAL BANK (10%)

| Year | Funds at the beginning of the year | + | Interest earned during the year | = | Amount available at the end of the year | − | Withdrawal | = | Funds at the end of the year |
|------|------|---|------|---|------|---|------|---|------|
| 1 | $925.40 | + | $92.54 | = | $1,017.94 | − | $70.00 | = | $947.94 |
| 2 | $947.94 | + | $94.79 | = | $1,042.73 | − | $70.00 | = | $972.73 |
| 3 | $972.73 | + | $97.27 | = | $1,070.00 | − | $1,070.00 | = | 0 |

## A DIVERSION—EXPANDING THE $(1 + i)^n$ TERM

Present values can be computed for any number of future payments or periods. The only annoying part is expanding the $(1 + i)^n$ term. For example, the computation of the present value of $100,000 received 20 years from now would require 19 multiplications in order to arrive at the value of $(1 + i)^{20}$. There is nothing difficult about this; it is simply tedious. In order to save time and reduce frustrations, tables that eliminate the need for the multiplication of the $(1 + i)^n$ term have been developed. An abbreviated version of such a table is presented in Table 2–4. The numbers in the body of the table

TABLE 2-4

### EXPANSION OF $(1 + i)^n$ TERM[a]

#### (Future-Value Coefficients)

| Time Period (n) | Interest Rates (i) | | | |
|------|------|------|------|------|
| | 5% | 10% | 15% | 20% |
| 1 | 1.050 | 1.100 | 1.150 | 1.200 |
| 2 | 1.102 | 1.210 | 1.322 | 1.440 |
| 3 | 1.158 | 1.331 | 1.521 | 1.728 |
| 4 | 1.216 | 1.464 | 1.749 | 2.074 |
| 5 | 1.276 | 1.611 | 2.011 | 2.488 |

[a]The numbers in this table have been rounded to three decimal places.

represent the products of the expansion multiplication. For example, if you want to know the value of $(1 + 0.15)^4$, find the intersection of period 4 and 15 percent, and you will see that the answer is 1.749.

This technique can simplify the computations required to solve the numerical illustrations presented in this chapter. Thus, if you want to find the future value of $1,000 invested for three years at a rate of return of 15 percent you could solve the problem using equation 2–1 as follows:

$$FV_3 = PV_0(1+i)^3$$

$$= \$1,000(1+0.15)^3$$

From Table 2–4, the value of $(1 + 0.15)^3$ can be found by locating the intersection of period 3 and 15 percent. Thus;

$$FV_3 = \$1,000(1.521) = \$1,521$$

Table 2–4 can also be used to determine present values. For example, what is the present value of $1,000 received five years from now, if your money could earn a 20 percent return in similar investment opportunities? You could answer this problem using equation 2–2 as follows:

$$PV_0 = \frac{FV_5}{(1+i)^5} = \frac{\$1,000}{(1+0.20)^5}$$

From Table 2-4, the value of $(1+0.20)^5$ can be found by locating the intersection of period 5 and 20 percent. Thus:

$$PV_0 = \frac{\$1,000}{(2.488)} = \$401.93$$

Table 2–4 does not present any new concepts. Its only purpose is to facilitate the computation of problems presented in this chapter. We will expand this table and present others in the next chapter.

## SIZE OF CASH FLOWS AND PRESENT VALUE

There is a positive relationship between the size of cash flows and the present value of a security. That is, other things being equal, securities with higher cash flows will have higher present values. For purposes of illustration, look at two U.S. savings bonds; bond F will pay $500 and bond G $600 at the end of five years. Assuming a discount rate of 15 percent and using Table 2–4, the respective present values can be easily computed:

| Bond F | Bond G |
|---|---|

$$PV_F = \frac{FV_5}{(1+i)^5} = \frac{\$500}{(2.011)} \qquad PV_G = \frac{FV_5}{(1+i)^5} = \frac{\$600}{(2.011)}$$

$$= \$248.63 \qquad\qquad\qquad = \$298.36$$

As you can see from the computations, the bond with the larger cash flows has the higher present value. Both bonds have the same maturity (five years) and are discounted at the same rate (15 percent). The only difference between these two bonds is the size of their respective cash flows.

## TIMING OF CASH FLOWS AND PRESENT VALUE

The timing of cash flows will also affect the present value of securities. Other things being equal, securities associated with cash flows received near the present time will have higher present values than securities that are expected to yield cash flows in the more distant future. Figure 2–3 shows cash-flow information for bonds A and B. Notice that the total cash flows over the two-year period are the same for both bonds ($1,100). However, the present value of bond A is greater than the present value of bond B. The reason is that the cash flows of bond A are received earlier than those of bond B.

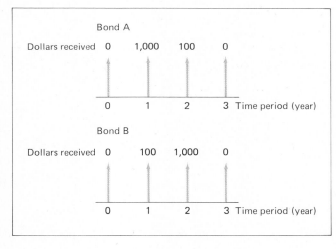

**FIGURE 2–3**

Time Lines for Cash Flows of Bonds A and B

This point can be verified by computing the present values. We will assume that 5 percent could be earned elsewhere on the funds to be employed, and we will use Table 2–4 to get the appropriate coefficients. As you can see, bond B has a lower present value, because the large $1,000 payment is received relatively late. Timing as well as amount of cash flows is an important determinant of the values of securities.

$$\text{Bond A}$$

$$PV_A = \frac{FV_1}{(1+i)^1} + \frac{FV_2}{(1+i)^2}$$

$$= \frac{1,000}{1.05} + \frac{100}{1.102} = \$1,033.12$$

$$\text{Bond B}$$

$$PV_B = \frac{FV_1}{(1+i)^1} + \frac{FV_2}{(1+i)^2}$$

$$PV_B = \frac{100}{1.05} + \frac{1,000}{1.102} = \$1,002.68$$

23

CHAP. 2   Valuation and Stockholder Wealth

## DISCOUNT RATE AND PRESENT VALUE

The present value of the cash flows associated with a security is inversely related to the discount rate. High discount rates will be associated with relatively low present values. In order to simplify the presentation, make the assumption that high-risk securities will have relatively high discount rates. This relationship between risk and discount rate is developed more fully in chapters 4, 5, and 6. At this point, we want to stress the mathematical or mechanical aspects of the relationship between discount rate and present value. This can best be accomplished through example.

Assume that there are two bonds, each with an expected cash flow of $1,000 at the end of five years. Bond J is issued by a firm that is having serious financial difficulty. The security market evaluates the firm and decides that it will not purchase securities unless a minimum rate of 20 percent is earned. Thus, the security market establishes a discount rate of 20 percent for bond J. Similarly, the security market assigns a discount rate of 10 percent to bond K. As expected, the present value of bond K (lower discount rate) is greater than the present value for bond J (higher discount rate). Observe also that the relationship between discount rate and present value is nonlinear. Thus, doubling the discount rate *does not* halve the present value. The present value for each discount rate must be computed separately:

<table>
<tr><td align="center">*Bond J*</td><td align="center">*Bond K*</td></tr>
</table>

$$PV_J = \frac{FV_5}{(1+.20)^5} = \frac{\$1,000}{2.488}$$

$$PV_K = \frac{FV_5}{(1+.10)^5} = \frac{\$1000}{1.611}$$

$$= \$401.93$$

$$= \$620.73$$

Although we are avoiding a detailed discussion of the discount rate at this point, you should by this time have some idea about what it is and what it isn't. The discount rate reflects the rate at which funds will earn interest *if they are employed elsewhere* in a comparable investment. For example, one might consider investments in short-term U.S. securities and deposits in insured savings accounts as comparable investments, since there is little risk in either case. Thus, in computation of the present value of the U.S. security, the rate of interest on the savings deposit is used as the discount rate. This discount rate is not derived from the security for which the present value is computed. In computing present values, the discount rate reflects the cost of opportunities foregone by the investor.

## PRESENT VALUE OF A PERPETUITY

Thus far we have been examining the relationship between the present value of a financial security and three factors: the size of cash flows, the timing of cash flows, and the discount rate employed. Even though our ultimate objective is to examine the factors affecting common-stock price and stockholder wealth, we have used bonds as the basis for our discussions concerning these crucial relationships. Bonds serve as a convenient illustration because they possess two simplifying characteristics: First, they usually have a fixed term or maturity date. Second, most bonds carry a fixed interest payment.

In this section, we will discuss the present value of perpetuities. Perpetuities have the second but not the first characteristic of bonds. That is, they have fixed dollar payments but do not have a fixed term. The fixed dollar payments go on forever, hence the designation *perpetuity*. In the next section, we will show that common stocks have neither of the characteristics of bonds noted above. That is, common stocks do not have a fixed maturity date *and* they do not have a fixed dollar payment. But for now, let's examine the procedures used to establish the present value of a perpetuity.

One type of perpetuity is known as a perpetual bond. Such bonds carry a fixed interest payment but have no maturity. The issuer of the bond is committed to the payment of interest on the bonds forever. Such bonds have been issued in the past but are extremely rare today. However, if perpetual bonds were in circulation, how could the present value of such bonds be established? The dilemma becomes clearer upon examination of equation 2–3:

$$PV_{pb} = \frac{I_1}{(1 + k_d)^1} + \frac{I_2}{(1 + k_d)^2} + \ldots + \frac{I_\infty}{(1 + k_d)^\infty} \qquad (2\text{-}3)$$

where $PV_{pb}$ = the present value of the perpetual bond

$\quad I$ = the interest payment received in every period

$\quad k_d$ = the interest rate per period that could be earned elsewhere on comparable investments (the opportunity cost)

$\quad n$ = the period in which payment is made

This equation differs from our earlier present-value formula in that we could go on and on with the $I/(1 + k_d)^n$ terms. There seems to be no end.

Fortunately, there is a way. When the dollar payments are fixed, the mathematics of limits permits us to simplify equation 2–3 into the form presented in equation 2–4:[4]

$$PV_{pb} = \frac{I}{k_d} \qquad (2\text{-}4)$$

Equation 2–4 makes the computation of the present value of a perpetual bond a simple matter. For example, assume that a perpetual bond has a $60-per-year interest payment and that comparable investment opportunities yield 8 percent. The present value can be computed as follows:

---

[4]This derivation is presented in Appendix 2B.

$$PV_{pb} = \frac{I}{k_d} = \frac{\$60}{0.08} = \$750$$

Preferred stock is a security issued with some frequency by American corporations, and under usual conditions, preferred stocks are perpetuities, since they carry fixed dollar dividend payments and have no maturity.[5] The present value of a preferred stock can be computed using the equation developed for perpetuities:

$$PV_{ps} = \frac{D_p}{k_p}$$

(2-5)

where $PV_{ps}$ = the present value of the preferred stock

$D_p$ = the fixed periodic cash flow received—in this case, the preferred dividend

$k_p$ = the rate of return that could be earned elsewhere on comparable investments (the opportunity cost)

In order to illustrate equation 2–5, assume that the preferred stock of Alice Corporation has an annual dividend of $100 and that comparable investments yielding 12 percent are available. The present value of the Alice Corporation's preferred stock is $833.33:

$$PV_{ps} = \frac{D_p}{k_p} = \frac{\$100}{.12} = \$833.33$$

This section has taken us a further step in our examination of the factors affecting common-stock price and stockholder wealth. We have shown that the principles of valuation applying to financial securities with fixed maturities also apply to securities with no maturity date (preferred stock). In both cases, the size of the cash flow and the discount rate are primary determinants of present value. Note, however, that the timing of the cash flows was not relevant to our discussion of perpetuities, since all payments were assumed to be fixed at the same amount.

## PRESENT VALUE OF COMMON STOCK

Common stock differs from both bonds and preferred stock in that the size of the dividend expected by the common stockholder is not specified by contract. The dividend to be received by the owner of a share of common stock is established periodically (usually each year) by the corporation's

---

[5]In most but, not all cases, preferred stock carries a fixed dividend and no maturity. Unlike common stockholders, preferred stockholders typically do not participate in the election of corporate officials. In most cases, preferred stock is more like bonds than like common stock.

board of directors.[6] The dividends change from year to year; they may be much higher or lower than those anticipated at the time the stock was purchased.

The conceptual approach to computing the present value of common stock is no different from that used to compute present values of bonds or preferred stocks. The conceptual approach is presented in equation 2–6:

$$PV_s = \frac{D_1^s}{(1 + k_s)^1} + \frac{D_2^s}{(1 + k_s)^2} + \ldots + \frac{D_\infty^s}{(1 + k_s)^\infty} \qquad (2\text{-}6)$$

where $PV_s$ = the present value of the common stock

$\quad\quad D_n^s$ = the cash flow (dividend) anticipated in period $n$

$\quad\quad k_s$ = the rate of return that could be earned elsewhere on

$\quad\quad\quad$ comparable investments (the opportunity cost)

Since the dividends ($D_{si}$) are expected to vary over time, it is not possible to simplify the equation as we did in the case of perpetuities. There is no way out of this dilemma. Therefore, it is impossible to compute present values into infinity.

As so frequently happens in finance and economics, the problem is resolved through the use of assumption. The first assumption, the "no-growth" assumption, treats common-stock dividends as being fixed at the present level, or some other level determined by careful analysis of the firm. This procedure rests on the assumption that changes in common-stock dividends will be small, and the present value of these slightly variable dividends can be approximated through the use of an equivalent fixed dividend. The "no-growth" assumption reduces the present-value procedure for common stock to that of a perpetuity:

$$PV_s \text{ (no growth)} = \frac{D_e^s}{k_s} \qquad (2\text{-}7)$$

where $PV_s$ (no growth) = the present value of common stock, assuming that dividends are constant

$\quad\quad D_e^s$ = the constant common-stock dividend

$\quad\quad k_s$ = the rate of return that could be earned elsewhere on comparable investments (the opportunity cost)

To illustrate equation 2–7, assume that the Ann Corporation is expected to pay a fixed dividend of $25. In addition, it is assumed that comparable investments yielding 20 percent are available.

---

[6]Annual dividends are usually paid in four quarterly installments. We will ignore this factor and treat dividends as if they were received at the end of the year.

$$PV_s \text{ (no growth)} = \frac{\$25}{.20} = \$125$$

Thus, the present value of Ann Corporation's stock is $125 per share.

The "no-growth" assumption is frequently unrealistic, so an alternate assumption is frequently made in its place. The "constant-growth" approach assumes that dividends will increase at a constant rate over time. For example, if present dividends are $20 per year and are expected to grow at a rate of 10 percent a year, next year's dividend will be $22 ($20 × 1.10), and the year after that, the dividend will be $24.20 ($22 × 1.10). The "constant-growth" assumption is that this process goes on and on into infinity. Equation 2–8 is a mathematical representation of this idea:

$$PV_s \text{ (constant growth)} = \frac{D_0^s(1 + g)}{(1 + k_s)} + \frac{D_0^s(1 + g)^2}{(1 + k_s)^2} + \ldots + \frac{D_0^s(1 + g)^\infty}{(1 + k_s)^\infty} \tag{2-8}$$

where $PV_s$ (constant growth) = the present value of common stock, assuming that dividends grow at a constant rate

$D_0^s$ = the present (period 0) level of dividends on common stock

$g$ = the growth rate in dividends

$k_s$ = the rate of return that could be earned elsewhere on comparable investments (comparable to $k_d$ in bond examples)

Of course, equation 2-8 is not useful for computation. It can, however, be simplified into equation 2-9:[7]

$$PV_s \text{ (constant growth)} = \frac{D_1}{k_s - g} \tag{2-9}$$

where $D_1$ = the dividend to be received next year [$D_0(1 + g)$]

To illustrate, assume that Bridge Corporation will pay a dividend of $10 next year, that dividends are expected to grow at a rate of 5 percent, and that comparable investments have rates of return of 8 percent. In this case, the present value of the common stock is equal to $333.33:

$$PV_s \text{ (constant growth)} = \frac{D_1}{k_s - g} = \frac{\$10}{.08 - .05} = \$333.33$$

This example also brings to light an important limitation of the constant-growth equation. The equation is valid only if the rate of growth (g)

---

[7]The derivation is presented in Appendix 2C.

is less than the rate of return on comparable investments ($k_s$). For example, if the rate of growth had been 10 rather than 5 percent, the term ($k_s - g$) would have been negative. The results of the equation then become absurd.

**The Expected Growth in Dividends.** The expected future growth in dividends affects the market price of the stock of the firm. Other things being equal, the greater the expected growth rate in dividends, the higher the stock price. This point can be illustrated by comparing the prices of common stock of two firms (A and B) with different expectations of dividend growth. Assume that both firms A and B are currently paying a dividend ($D_0$) of $2 per share and that the market discounts the expected dividends of both firms ($k_s$) at the rate of 20 percent. However, the dividends of firm A are expected to remain constant, whereas those of firm B are expected to grow at a constant annual rate of 5 percent for the foreseeable future. The price of the common stock for each firm can be computed as follows:

$$\text{Stock A} \qquad\qquad \text{Stock B}$$

$$\text{PV}_s(A) = \frac{D_1}{k_s - g} = \frac{\$2.00}{0.2 - 0.0} = \$10 \qquad \text{PV}_s(B) = \frac{\$2.10}{0.20 - 0.05} = \$14$$

These results are reasonable, since people would be willing to pay a higher price to receive higher expected future benefits. The expected dividends for stock B (from year 1 to infinity) are expected to be greater than the expected dividends of A (constant $2 per year). Thus, the price of B will be higher than the price of A, other things being equal.

As expectations of growth in dividends change, so does the price of common stock. For example, assume that firm B makes a significant discovery in the energy field and the future dividends of the firm are expected to grow at a *new* constant annual rate of 10 percent. The price of the stock of firm B will change to:

$$\text{PV}_s(B) = \frac{\$2.20}{0.20 - 0.10} = \$22$$

In general, good financial news will have a positive effect on the value of the stock of the firm. But if new information causes the market to lower its expectations as to the growth rate in dividends, the stock price will fall. For example, if the expected growth rate of the dividends of firm B is reduced to 2 percent, the market price of B will decline to:

$$\text{PV}_s(B) = \frac{\$2.04}{0.20 - 0.02} = \$11.33$$

Figure 2–4 illustrates the expected growth rates of various types of firms. The expected dividends of some firms are declining, while others are increasing at a "normal" growth rate (usually estimated as 4 percent per year). A word of caution is in order. It is almost impossible to sustain a very high annual growth rate in dividends for a very long period of time. For

CHAP. 2 Valuation and Stockholder Wealth

example, the dividends of a firm with an expected growth rate of 20 percent will increase from $1.00 to $38.32 over a 20-year period.

$$(FV_{20} = PV(1 + i)^n = \$1(1 + .20)^{20} = \$38.32)$$

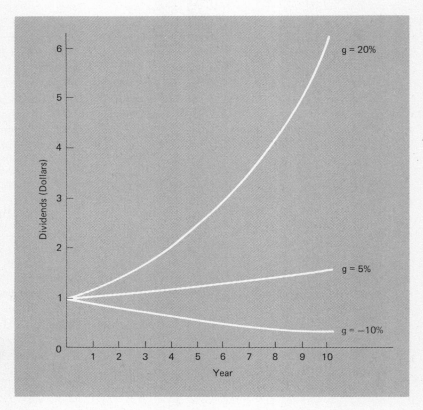

FIGURE 2–4

Growth Rates in
Dividends

**A Misconception About Common-Stock Cash Flows.**

Many students become confused when examining the cash flows associated with a common stock. They look at common stock as being held by the investor for a fixed term. Cash inflows are perceived as being of two types: the dividends received during the holding period, and the money that would result from the sale of the stock at the end of the period. Thus, the student concludes that it is not only expected dividends but also the expected stock price that should be included in the present-value/price computation. On occasion, we hear statements such as, "I don't care what the dividends of the stock are. I want a stock that will increase in price."

Although many people perceive stocks as having two distinctly different types of cash flows, there is in fact only one cash flow, dividends, that affects the present value and therefore the price of common stock. For purposes of illustration, let us assume that an investor purchases one share of common stock and plans to sell it two years from now. The expected cash flows to the investor are equal to the dividends that will be paid over the next two years plus the market price of the stock two years from now. In order to simplify the problem, assume that the first dividend will be paid exactly one year from now.

$$PV_s = \frac{D_1}{(1 + k_s)} + \frac{D_2}{(1 + k_s)^2} + \frac{P_2}{(1 + k_s)^2} \qquad (2\text{-}10)$$

where $D_1$ = the expected dividend one year from now

$D_2$ = the expected dividend two years from now

$P_2$ = the expected price two years from now

What will be the market price ($P_2$) at which the investor will be able to sell the stock two years from now? The buyer will pay a price for the stock that is dependent on expected future cash flows at that time. If the new investor has a holding period of two years and we assume that the $k_s$ is the same, the price two years from now should be as follows:

$$PV_s^2 = P_2 = \frac{D_3}{(1 + k_s)} + \frac{D_4}{(1 + k_s)^2} + \frac{P_4}{(1 + k_s)^2} \qquad (2\text{-}11)$$

where $D_3$ = the expected dividend in year 3

$D_4$ = the expected dividend in year 4

$P_4$ = the expected price in year 4

We can substitute the value obtained for the price in year 2 ($P_2$) in equation 2-11, into equation 2-10. The result would be:

$$PV_s = P_0 = \frac{D_1}{(1 + k_s)} + \frac{D_2}{(1 + k_s)^2} + \frac{1}{(1 + k_s)^2} \left[ \frac{D_3}{(1 + k_s)^1} + \frac{D_4}{(1 + k_s)^2} + \frac{P_4}{(1 + k_s)^2} \right]$$

$$= \frac{D_1}{(1 + k_s)} + \frac{D_2}{(1 + k_s)^2} + \frac{D_3}{(1 + k_s)^3} + \frac{D_4}{(1 + k_s)^4} + \frac{P_4}{(1 + k_s)^4} \qquad (2\text{-}12)$$

What will be the market price ($P_4$) in year 4? Again, the new buyer will pay a price for the stock that depends on the expected cash flows over the holding period. If we assume a two-year holding period and the same $k_s$, $P_4$ can be computed as follows:

$$PV_s^4 = P_4 = \frac{D_5}{(1 + k_s)} + \frac{D_6}{(1 + k_s)^2} + \frac{P_6}{(1 + k_s)^2} \qquad (2\text{-}13)$$

Now the $PV_s^4$ can be substituted for $P_4$ in equation 2–12. The process can go on and on, with substitutions for $P_6$, $P_8$, and so forth. Eventually we are left with the first equation presented in this discussion of common-stock value, equation 2–6:

$$PV_s = P_0 = \frac{D_1}{(1 + k_s)} + \frac{D_2}{(1 + k_s)^2} + \frac{D_3}{(1 + k_s)^3} + \ldots + \frac{D_\infty}{(1 + k_s)^\infty}$$

What we have done is to show that dividends are the only relevant cash flows for the process of common-stock valuation. Future stock prices are not independent cash flows. In point of fact, future stock prices are present values of future dividends. Future stock prices will be higher only if dividend expectations are higher (assuming a constant $k_s$).

## THE IMPLICATIONS FOR MANAGEMENT OF PRESENT VALUE AND PRICE

This book emphasizes that the objective of management is and should be to maximize the wealth of stockholders. Management can accomplish this task by pursuing policies that increase the price of common stock, which is an asset held by stockholders. The process through which price is determined was presented in Figure 2–1, and it is shown in a slightly altered form as Figure 2–5. The implications of this figure are important. A competitive market evaluates common stocks and establishes a present value for the stock. The price of the stock is identical to the present value established by the impersonal competitive market forces.

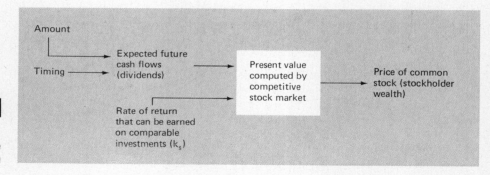

**FIGURE 2–5**

The Process of
Present-Value/Stock-Price
Determination

The implications for management are clear. Management, in its quest for stockholder-wealth maximization, should examine business decision alternatives in terms of their effect on the present value/price of common stock. At issue here are the importance of the size of cash flows and the timing of cash flows in determining stock price and therefore stockholder wealth.

## SUMMARY OF PRESENT VALUE

The concept of present value is central to almost every aspect of the discipline of finance. The student of finance must have a clear understanding of the meaning of present value and the factors that affect it. Since many students have difficulty with this, we have attempted to show that *present value is the amount that must be invested now in order to generate a specific pattern of future cash flows*—the present worth of future receipts. The concept of present value is closely related to the amount that should be paid for security that will yield a specific pattern of cash flows.

Three important factors affect the present value of a security:

1. *The size of the cash flows expected in the future.* Other things being equal, the larger the expected cash flows, the higher the present value.
2. *The timing of the cash flows.* Other things being equal, securities with cash flows that are expected soon will have higher present values than securities with cash flows expected later.
3. *The discount rate employed.* The conceptual problems related to this point will be discussed in substantial detail in later chapters, but the mathematical principal has already been established. A higher discount rate results in a lower present value, and vice versa.

## VALUATION OF SMALLER BUSINESSES

The present value of owners' equity in closely held corporations, proprietorships, or partnerships is determined in the same fashion as is the present value of common stock. As indicated in equation 2–14, the price or market value of smaller businesses may be thought of as the present value of the net cash flows to the owners.[8] As suggested by the equation, the price at which a business can be sold will be reflected in the size of the expected cash flows to owners and the discount rate employed. Although it is not specified to equation 2–14, the timing of the cash flows is also important.

$$\text{Price}_{sb} = \frac{\text{NCF}}{k_{sb}}$$

(2-14)

where Price $_{sb}$ = price of the small business

NCF = net cash flows to the owners

$k_{sb}$ = the rate of return that could be earned elsewhere on comparable investments (the opportunity cost)

These ideas are confirmed by real-world practices. For example, the prices paid for apartment complexes and office buildings are based upon cash-flow estimates. In fact, the price of most small businesses is usually computed as some multiple of the expected annual cash flows. In addition, both federal and state courts use the concept embodied in equation 2–14 in establishing the values of non–publicly owned businesses.

---

[8]Equation 2–14 corresponds to the no-growth situation presented in equation 2–7. Equation 2–14 could be modified to accommodate expected growth in the net cash flows to the owners.

One difference between the valuation of publicly traded common stock and the valuation of smaller businesses relates to the markets in which these assets are sold. Common stocks are typically sold in large national markets that are competitive. Smaller firms are typically sold in local markets. The implication of this difference will be discussed in the following chapters. At this point, it is important to recognize that the value of both smaller firms and the stockholder equity in large, publicly owned corporations is affected by the expected amount of the cash flows to the owners and the timing of such cash flows, discounted at the appropriate rate.

QUESTIONS FOR DISCUSSION

1. Why are the following assets considered valuable?
   a. A prime parcel of ocean-front property
   b. A painting by Rembrandt
   c. 100 shares of IBM common stock
2. Why is $1,000 received today worth more than $1,000 received five years from now?
3. Give a verbal explanation (not a numerical example) of how compounding works.
4. Give a verbal explanation (not a numerical example) of how discounting works.
5. Why is it more convenient to use present value than future value when comparing the attractiveness of assets?
6. Why must comparisons among asset-acquisition alternatives be made at the same point in time?
7. Describe the mathematical relationship between future and present value.
8. Give a verbal description of the following time line for cash flows:

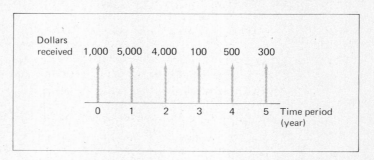

9. Explain how the number 2.074 was derived in Table 2–4.
10. Using present-value equations, "prove" the following:
   a. The size of cash flows affects present value
   b. The timing of cash flows affects present value
   c. The discount rate employed affects present value
11. Discuss the three important factors affecting the value of securities.
12. Explain the meaning of the following terms:
   a. $PV_s$ (no growth)
   b. $PV_s$ (constant growth)

13. How do the perpetuity examples used in the book differ from the bond examples?

14. What are the implications of present-value techniques to the management of the firm?

15. "Dividends are the only relevant cash flows for the process of stock-price determination." Explain, and show why future stock prices are dependent on dividends.

16. What are the determinants of the market value of smaller businesses?

17. Explain how the growth rate in dividends affects the market price of common stock.

**PROBLEMS**   *Use Table 2–4 in solving these problems.*

1. Calculate the future value of investing today $1,000 for a three-year period at a rate of return of:
   a. 5%    b. 10%    c. 15%

2. Calculate the present value of receiving $1,000 every year for three years:
   a. Given a discount rate of 5%
   b. Given a discount rate of 10%
   c. Given a discount rate of 15%

3. Calculate the present value of receiving $500 three years from now:
   a. Given a discount rate of 5%
   b. Given a discount rate of 10%
   c. Given a discount rate of 15%

4. Without the use of tables, calculate the future value of investing today $100 for a two-year period at a rate of return of:
   a. 5% paid annually
   b. 10% paid annually
   c. 15% paid annually

5. Without the use of tables, calculate the present value of receiving $100 two years from now, given a discount rate of:
   a. 5%    b. 10%    c. 15%

6. Which of the following alternatives would have a higher present value if the discount rate is 10%?
   a. Receiving $100 two years from now
   b. Receiving $150 five years from now

7. What should be the price of a perpetuity if the annual interest received is $100, and the $k_d$ of the bondholder is 8%?

8. What should be the price of a share of common stock if the expected dividend next year is $10, the $k_s$ of the stockholders is 15%, and the expected growth rate of the corporation is a constant 5% for the foreseeable future?

9. What would be the effect on the market price of the common stock described in Problem 8, if the market's expectation of the growth in dividends for the firm (g) changes to:
   a. no growth (0%)    b. 10%

10. Ten years ago, an investor purchased a perpetuity paying an annual interest of $50. The investor paid $1,000 for this perpetuity.
    a. What was the interest rate that could be earned on comparable investments *at the date of the original purchase?*
    b. What would be the current market price of the perpetuity if the *current* interest rate on comparable investment opportunities is:
        i. 3%    ii. 10%    iii. 15%

11. Calculate the current market price of a share of preferred stock paying an annual dividend of $8 per share, if the rate of return that can be earned on comparable investments is:
    a. 6%    b. 8%    c. 10%

12. The dividends paid on the common stock of the Reliance Corporation have grown in the past at an annual rate of 10%. This growth rate is expected to continue in the future. The dividend paid today ($D_o$) is $2.00, and the $k_s$ of the stockholders is 12%.
    a. What should be the market price of a share of common stock of the Reliance Corporation?
    b. Assuming that the market expects the future growth rate in dividends to be only *half* the past growth rate, what will be the market price?

# APPENDIX 2A
## Derivation of the Future Value of a Single Sum

The equation used to compute the future value of a single sum is:

$$FV_n = PV_0(1 + i)^n$$

where FV = the future value

$PV_0$ = the present value

$i$ = the interest rate per period that could be earned elsewhere on comparable investments (the opportunity cost)

$n$ = the number of periods that the funds are invested

The logic of this equation is demonstrated as follows:

$$FV_1 = \begin{array}{c} \text{Original deposit at} \\ \text{the beginning of year 1} \end{array} + \begin{array}{c} \text{Interest earned during} \\ \text{the year} \end{array}$$

$$= PV_0 + iPV_0 = PV_0(1 + i) \qquad (2A\text{-}1)$$

For period 2, the future value will be equal to:

$$FV_2 = FV_1 + iFV_1 = FV_1(1 + i) \qquad (2A\text{--}2)$$

Since $FV_1 = PV_0(1 + i)$, equation 2A–2 can be rewritten as:

$$FV_2 = PV_0(1 + i)(1 + i) = PV_0(1 + i)^2$$

For period 3, the future value will be equal to:

$$FV_3 = FV_2 + iFV_2 = FV_2(1 + i) \qquad (2A\text{--}3)$$

Since $FV_2 = PV_0(1 + i)^2$, equation 2A–3 can be rewritten as:

$$FV_3 = PV_0(1 + i)^2(1 + i) = PV_0(1 + i)^3$$

Therefore, the future value for any period $n$ will be equal to:

$$FV_n = PV_0(1 + i)^n \qquad (2\text{-}1)$$

# APPENDIX 2B
## Present Value of a Perpetuity

The value of a perpetuity is equal to the present value of all future cash flows discounted at the appropriate discount rate. For example, the value of a perpetual bond paying a constant annual interest of $I$ can be expressed mathematically as follows:

$$PV_{pb} = \frac{I}{(1 + k_d)} + \frac{I}{(1 + k_d)^2} + \cdots + \frac{I}{(1 + k_d)^\infty} \qquad (2B\text{-}1)$$

We can multiply both sides of an equality by the same amount, thus maintaining the equality. If we multiply equation 2B-1 by $(1 + k_d)$, the equality will be maintained:

$$(1 + k_d)PV_{pb} = I + \frac{I}{(1 + k_d)} + \cdots + \frac{I}{(1 + k_d)^{\infty-1}} \qquad (2B\text{-}2)$$

We can subtract the same amount from each side of an equality, and the equality will be maintained. Therefore, equation 2B-2 minus equation 2B-1 will be:[9]

$$(1 + k_d)PV_{pb} - PV_{pb} = I - \frac{I}{(1 + k_d)^\infty} \qquad (2B\text{-}3)$$

However, if we multiply a number greater than 1 by itself an infinite number of times, the product will approach infinity. A constant number divided by infinity will be equal to zero. Given a positive value for $k_d$:

---

[9]Note that the second term in equation 2B–2 is identical to the first term in equation 2B–1; thus they will cancel out, and so on.

$$\frac{I}{(1 + k_d)^\infty} \to O$$

Thus, equation 2B-3 will be equal to:

$$(1 + k_d)PV_{pb} - PV_{pv} = I$$

$$PV_{pb} + k_d PV_{pb} - PV_{pb} = I$$

$$K_d PV_{pb} = I$$

$$PV_{pb} = \frac{I}{k_d}$$

This equation is the same as equation 2-4 in the body of the chapter.

# APPENDIX 2C
## The Value of Common Stock with a Constant Annual Growth Rate in Dividends

The value of common stock is equal to the present value of all expected dividends discounted at the appropriate discount rate. Thus, the value of common stock will be equal to:

$$PV_s = \frac{D_1}{(1 + k_s)} + \frac{D_2}{(1 + k_s)^2} + \ldots + \frac{D_\infty}{(1 + k_s)^\infty} \qquad (2C\text{-}1)$$

Given that dividends are expected to grow at a constant annual growth rate of g:

$$D_1 = D_0(1 + g)$$

$$D_2 = D_0(1 + g)^2$$

$$\vdots \qquad \vdots$$

$$D^\infty = D_0(1 + g)^\infty$$

Substituting these values in equation 2C-1, the value of common stock is equal to:

$$PV_s = \frac{D_0(1 + g)}{(1 + k_s)} + \frac{D_0(1 + g)^2}{(1 + k_s)^2} + \ldots + \frac{D_0(1 + g)^\infty}{(1 + k_s)^\infty} \qquad (2C\text{-}2)$$

Multiplying both sides of the equation by $\dfrac{(1 + k_s)}{(1 + g)}$ , we would obtain:

$$PV_s \frac{(1 + k_s)}{(1 + g)} = D_0 + \frac{D_0(1 + g)}{(1 + k_s)} + \ldots + \frac{D_0(1 + g)^{\infty - 1}}{(1 + k_s)^{\infty - 1}} \qquad (2C\text{-}3)$$

Equation 2C-3 minus equation 2C-2 will equal:

$$PV_s \frac{(1 + k_s)}{(1 + g)} - PV_s = D_0 - \frac{D_0(1 + g)^\infty}{(1 + k_s)^\infty} \qquad (2C\text{-}4)$$

If we assume that $k_s$ is greater than g:

$$\frac{D_0(1 + g)^\infty}{(1 + k_s)^\infty} \rightarrow O$$

Thus, equation 2C-4 will simplify to:

$$\frac{PV_s(1 + k_s) - PV_s(1 + g)}{(1 + g)} = D_0$$

$$PV_s + k_s PV_s - PV_s - g PV_s = D_0(1 + g) = D_1$$

$$PV_s(k_s - g) = D_1$$

$$PV_s = \frac{D_1}{k_s - g}$$

This equation is the same as equation 2-9 in the body of the chapter.

**BIBLIOGRAPHY**   Since the topics of the first seven chapters are so closely related, one comprehensive bibliography covering all seven chapters is included at the end of Part 1.

# THE USE OF PRESENT-
AND FUTURE-
VALUE TABLES
IN FINANCIAL
DECISION MAKING

3

## INTRODUCTION

As we saw in Chapter 2, present and future values are important concepts in the valuation of corporate securities. And because these concepts appear in virtually every chapter of this book, we will devote this chapter to an explanation of how present and future values can be computed. The procedures will utilize a series of tables that significantly reduce computation time. It is important that students understand both the meaning of these tables and the large number of ways in which they can be used.

# THE TABLES

## COEFFICIENTS FOR FUTURE VALUES OF SINGLE AMOUNTS

Table 3–1, the Table of Coefficients for Future Values of Single Amounts, is nothing but an expanded version of the $(1 + i)^n$ table (Table 2–4), whose entries all appear in Table 3–1.[1] For example, the future-value coefficient for a cash flow occurring at the end of the fourth year and assuming an interest rate of 15 percent is 1.749. This number can be found in either table, or it can be computed by expanding $(1 + .15)$ to the fourth power. It is the *coefficient* that when multiplied by the present amount will yield the future value.

Table 3–1 greatly reduces required computations. For example, assume that you are depositing $20,000 in a savings account that pays 8 percent annual interest, and that you plan to let the principal and interest accumulate for 18 years. The amount in the account at the end of 18 years can easily be computed by using Table 3–1. Note that the procedure calls for multiplying the present sum ($20,000) by the future-value coefficient specified by the problem. (Coefficients from Table 3–1 are identified by "1 Coef.")

$$FV_n^i = PV(1\ Coef._n^i)$$

$$FV_{18}^{8\%} = \$20,000(1\ Coef._{18}^{8\%})$$

$$= \$20,000(3.996)$$

$$= \$79,920$$

Once Table 3–1 has been mastered, computational time will be measured in seconds rather than minutes. Although the underlying concept is relatively simple, there are some problems in implementation. The first problem relates to the meaning of Table 3–1 as compared to other tables. The coefficients in Table 3–1 are used to compute the future value of a single "deposit" made today. As we proceed through a discussion of other tables, we will continually show how they differ from Table 3–1 in this respect. A second problem relates to the time at which cash flows are received. In Table 3–1, and in all the tables in this chapter, cash flows occur at the end of the year, and in the real world, this is not always the case. A third problem relates to the units of measurement employed in the table. Only a selection of time points and rates are included. For example, assume that you are interested in computing the future value of $10,000 held for 21 years in an account paying 7¼ percent interest. There is no simple way to adapt Table 3–1 to this problem. However, more detailed tables, identical in concept to

---

[1] Tables 3–1, 3–2, 3–3, and 3–4 also appear in the back of the book as Appendix I.

TABLE 3–1

## COEFFICIENTS FOR FUTURE VALUES OF $1

A-3

$$1 \text{ Coef.} = (1 + i)^n$$

Interest Rate

| To be held until the end of Period | 1% | 2% | 3% | 4% | 5% | 6% | 7% |
|---|---|---|---|---|---|---|---|
| 1 | 1.010 | 1.020 | 1.030 | 1.040 | 1.050 | 1.060 | 1.070 |
| 2 | 1.020 | 1.040 | 1.061 | 1.082 | 1.102 | 1.124 | 1.145 |
| 3 | 1.030 | 1.061 | 1.093 | 1.125 | 1.158 | 1.191 | 1.225 |
| 4 | 1.041 | 1.082 | 1.126 | 1.170 | 1.216 | 1.262 | 1.311 |
| 5 | 1.051 | 1.104 | 1.159 | 1.217 | 1.276 | 1.338 | 1.403 |
| 6 | 1.062 | 1.126 | 1.194 | 1.265 | 1.340 | 1.419 | 1.501 |
| 7 | 1.072 | 1.149 | 1.230 | 1.316 | 1.407 | 1.504 | 1.606 |
| 8 | 1.083 | 1.172 | 1.267 | 1.369 | 1.477 | 1.594 | 1.718 |
| 9 | 1.094 | 1.195 | 1.305 | 1.423 | 1.551 | 1.689 | 1.838 |
| 10 | 1.105 | 1.219 | 1.344 | 1.480 | 1.629 | 1.791 | 1.967 |
| 11 | 1.116 | 1.243 | 1.384 | 1.539 | 1.710 | 1.898 | 2.105 |
| 12 | 1.127 | 1.268 | 1.426 | 1.601 | 1.796 | 2.012 | 2.252 |
| 13 | 1.138 | 1.294 | 1.469 | 1.665 | 1.886 | 2.133 | 2.410 |
| 14 | 1.149 | 1.319 | 1.513 | 1.732 | 1.980 | 2.261 | 2.579 |
| 15 | 1.161 | 1.346 | 1.558 | 1.801 | 2.079 | 2.397 | 2.759 |
| 16 | 1.173 | 1.373 | 1.605 | 1.873 | 2.183 | 2.540 | 2.952 |
| 17 | 1.184 | 1.400 | 1.653 | 1.948 | 2.292 | 2.693 | 3.159 |
| 18 | 1.196 | 1.428 | 1.702 | 2.026 | 2.407 | 2.854 | 3.380 |
| 19 | 1.208 | 1.457 | 1.754 | 2.107 | 2.527 | 3.026 | 3.617 |
| 20 | 1.220 | 1.486 | 1.806 | 2.191 | 2.653 | 3.207 | 3.870 |
| 25 | 1.282 | 1.641 | 2.094 | 2.666 | 3.386 | 4.292 | 5.427 |
| 30 | 1.348 | 1.811 | 2.427 | 3.243 | 4.322 | 5.743 | 7.612 |

| Period | 8% | 9% | 10% | 12% | 14% | 15% | 16% |
|---|---|---|---|---|---|---|---|
| 1 | 1.080 | 1.090 | 1.100 | 1.120 | 1.140 | 1.150 | 1.160 |
| 2 | 1.166 | 1.186 | 1.210 | 1.254 | 1.300 | 1.322 | 1.346 |
| 3 | 1.260 | 1.295 | 1.331 | 1.405 | 1.482 | 1.521 | 1.561 |
| 4 | 1.360 | 1.412 | 1.464 | 1.574 | 1.689 | 1.749 | 1.811 |
| 5 | 1.469 | 1.539 | 1.611 | 1.762 | 1.925 | 2.011 | 2.100 |
| 6 | 1.587 | 1.677 | 1.772 | 1.974 | 2.195 | 2.313 | 2.436 |
| 7 | 1.714 | 1.828 | 1.949 | 2.211 | 2.502 | 2.660 | 2.826 |
| 8 | 1.851 | 1.993 | 2.144 | 2.476 | 2.853 | 3.059 | 3.278 |
| 9 | 1.999 | 2.172 | 2.358 | 2.773 | 3.252 | 3.518 | 3.803 |
| 10 | 2.159 | 2.367 | 2.594 | 3.106 | 3.707 | 4.046 | 4.411 |
| 11 | 2.332 | 2.580 | 2.853 | 3.479 | 4.226 | 4.652 | 5.117 |
| 12 | 2.518 | 2.813 | 3.138 | 3.896 | 4.818 | 5.350 | 5.926 |
| 13 | 2.720 | 3.066 | 3.452 | 4.363 | 5.492 | 6.153 | 6.886 |
| 14 | 2.937 | 3.342 | 3.797 | 4.887 | 6.261 | 7.076 | 7.988 |
| 15 | 3.172 | 3.642 | 4.177 | 5.474 | 7.138 | 8.137 | 9.266 |
| 16 | 3.426 | 3.970 | 4.595 | 6.130 | 8.137 | 9.358 | 10.748 |
| 17 | 3.700 | 4.328 | 5.054 | 6.866 | 9.276 | 10.761 | 12.468 |
| 18 | 3.996 | 4.717 | 5.560 | 7.690 | 10.575 | 12.375 | 14.463 |
| 19 | 4.316 | 5.142 | 6.116 | 8.613 | 12.056 | 14.232 | 16.777 |
| 20 | 4.661 | 5.604 | 6.728 | 9.646 | 13.743 | 16.367 | 19.461 |
| 25 | 6.848 | 8.623 | 10.835 | 17.000 | 26.462 | 32.919 | 40.874 |
| 30 | 10.063 | 13.268 | 17.449 | 29.960 | 50.950 | 66.212 | 85.850 |

| To be held until the end of: Period | Interest Rate | | | | | |
|---|---|---|---|---|---|---|
| | 18% | 20% | 24% | 28% | 32% | 36% |
| 1 | 1.180 | 1.200 | 1.240 | 1.280 | 1.320 | 1.360 |
| 2 | 1.392 | 1.440 | 1.538 | 1.638 | 1.742 | 1.850 |
| 3 | 1.643 | 1.728 | 1.907 | 2.067 | 2.300 | 2.515 |
| 4 | 1.939 | 2.074 | 2.364 | 2.684 | 3.036 | 3.421 |
| 5 | 2.288 | 2.488 | 2.932 | 3.436 | 4.007 | 4.653 |
| 6 | 2.700 | 2.986 | 3.635 | 4.398 | 5.290 | 6.328 |
| 7 | 3.185 | 3.583 | 4.508 | 5.629 | 6.983 | 8.605 |
| 8 | 3.759 | 4.300 | 5.590 | 7.206 | 9.217 | 11.703 |
| 9 | 4.435 | 5.160 | 6.931 | 9.223 | 12.166 | 15.917 |
| 10 | 5.234 | 6.192 | 8.594 | 11.806 | 16.060 | 21.647 |
| 11 | 6.176 | 7.430 | 10.657 | 15.112 | 21.199 | 29.439 |
| 12 | 7.288 | 8.916 | 13.215 | 19.343 | 27.983 | 40.037 |
| 13 | 8.599 | 10.699 | 16.386 | 24.759 | 36.937 | 54.451 |
| 14 | 10.147 | 12.839 | 20.319 | 31.961 | 48.757 | 74.053 |
| 15 | 11.974 | 15.407 | 25.196 | 40.565 | 64.359 | 100.712 |
| 16 | 14.129 | 18.488 | 31.243 | 51.923 | 84.954 | 136.97 |
| 17 | 16.672 | 22.186 | 38.741 | 66.461 | 112.14 | 186.28 |
| 18 | 19.673 | 26.623 | 48.039 | 85.071 | 148.02 | 253.34 |
| 19 | 23.214 | 31.948 | 59.568 | 108.89 | 195.39 | 344.54 |
| 20 | 27.393 | 38.338 | 73.864 | 139.38 | 257.92 | 468.57 |
| 25 | 62.669 | 95.396 | 216.542 | 478.90 | 1033.6 | 2180.1 |
| 30 | 143.371 | 237.376 | 634.820 | 1645.5 | 4142.1 | 10143. |

| Period | 40% | 50% | 60% | 70% | 80% | 90% |
|---|---|---|---|---|---|---|
| 1 | 1.400 | 1.500 | 1.600 | 1.700 | 1.800 | 1.900 |
| 2 | 1.960 | 2.250 | 2.560 | 2.890 | 3.240 | 3.610 |
| 3 | 2.744 | 3.375 | 4.096 | 4.913 | 5.832 | 6.859 |
| 4 | 3.842 | 5.062 | 6.544 | 8.352 | 10.498 | 13.032 |
| 5 | 5.378 | 7.594 | 10.486 | 14.199 | 18.896 | 24.761 |
| 6 | 7.530 | 11.391 | 16.777 | 24.138 | 34.012 | 47.046 |
| 7 | 10.541 | 17.086 | 26.844 | 41.034 | 61.222 | 89.387 |
| 8 | 14.758 | 25.629 | 42.950 | 69.758 | 110.200 | 169.836 |
| 9 | 20.661 | 38.443 | 68.720 | 118.588 | 198.359 | 322.688 |
| 10 | 28.925 | 57.665 | 109.951 | 201.599 | 357.047 | 613.107 |
| 11 | 40.496 | 86.498 | 175.922 | 342.719 | 642.684 | 1164.902 |
| 12 | 56.694 | 129.746 | 281.475 | 582.622 | 1156.831 | 2213.314 |
| 13 | 79.372 | 194.619 | 450.360 | 990.457 | 2082.295 | 4205.297 |
| 14 | 111.120 | 291.929 | 720.576 | 1683.777 | 3748.131 | 7990.065 |
| 15 | 155.568 | 437.894 | 1152.921 | 2862.421 | 6746.636 | 15181.122 |
| 16 | 217.795 | 656.84 | 1844.7 | 4866.1 | 12144. | 28844.0 |
| 17 | 304.914 | 985.26 | 2951.5 | 8272.4 | 21859. | 54804.0 |
| 18 | 426.879 | 1477.9 | 4722.4 | 14063.0 | 39346. | 104130.0 |
| 19 | 597.630 | 2216.8 | 7555.8 | 23907.0 | 70824. | 197840.0 |
| 20 | 836.683 | 3325.3 | 12089.0 | 40642.0 | 127480. | 375900.0 |
| 25 | 4499.880 | 25251. | 126760.0 | 577060.0 | 2408900. | 9307600.0 |
| 30 | 24201.432 | 191750. | 1329200. | 8193500.0 | 45517000. | 230470000.0 |

CHAP. 3 The Use of Present- and Future-Value Tables in Financial Decision Making

this one but specifying time and rate in very small units, are available.[2] Thus, one must conclude that Table 3–1 can be used in only a limited number of situations and must be used with care.

## COEFFICIENTS FOR PRESENT VALUES OF SINGLE AMOUNTS

As we demonstrated earlier, the present value of a single future amount can be computed using the expansion of the $(1 + i)^n$ term:

$$PV = \frac{FV_n}{(1 + i)^n}$$

Since Table 3–1 contains expansions of this term, it can be used to compute present values. For example, assume you are asked to compute the present value of a financial asset that will yield a single payment of $10,000 at the end of 30 years, and that assets with similar risks are currently earning 14 percent. The coefficients in Table 3–1 can be used for purposes of computing this present value:

$$PV_{30}^{14\%} = \frac{FV}{(1\ Coef._{30}^{14\%})} = \frac{\$10,000}{50.950} = \$196.27$$

That is, if $196.27 is invested for 30 years at 14 percent, the resulting sum will be $10,000 ($196.27 $\times$ 50.950).

Table 3–2 is an alternate table of coefficients for computing present values. The coefficients in Table 3–2 are nothing more than the reciprocals of the coefficients in Table 3–1.[3] The nature of these reciprocals can best be understood by looking at equation 3–1 and solving a problem.

$$PV = \frac{FV}{(1 + i)^n} = FV \left[ \frac{1}{(1 + i)^n} \right] \tag{3-1}$$

For purposes of illustration, assume that a financial asset will yield one payment of $17,000 at the end of 11 years and that assets of similar risk are yielding 9 percent. Using equation 3–1 and Table 3–1, we can solve this problem. As you can see, dividing by a number gives the same result as multiplying by the reciprocal of that number.

$$PV_{11}^{9\%} = \frac{FV}{(1\ Coef._{11}^{9\%})} = \frac{17,000}{2.580} = \$6,589$$

$$= FV \left( \frac{1}{1\ Coef._{11}^{9\%}} \right) = 17,000 \left( \frac{1}{2.580} \right) = \$17,000(.3876) = \$6,589$$

---

[2]For example, David Thorndike, *The Thorndike Encyclopedia of Banking and Finance Tables* (Boston: Warren, Gorham & Lamont, 1973).
[3] $1/_n$ is the reciprocal of n.

TABLE 3–2

## COEFFICIENTS FOR PRESENT VALUE OF $1

A⁻¹

$$2 \text{ Coef.} = \frac{1}{(1 + i)^n}$$

| To be received at the end of: Period | 1% | 2% | 3% | 4% | 5% | Discount Rate 6% | 7% | 8% | 9% | 10% | 12% | 14% | 15% |
|---|---|---|---|---|---|---|---|---|---|---|---|---|---|
| 1 | .990 | .980 | .971 | .962 | .952 | .943 | .935 | .926 | .917 | .909 | .893 | .877 | .870 |
| 2 | .980 | .961 | .943 | .925 | .907 | .890 | .873 | .857 | .842 | .826 | .797 | .769 | .756 |
| 3 | .971 | .942 | .915 | .889 | .864 | .840 | .816 | .794 | .772 | .751 | .712 | .675 | .658 |
| 4 | .961 | .924 | .889 | .855 | .823 | .792 | .763 | .735 | .708 | .683 | .636 | .592 | .572 |
| 5 | .951 | .906 | .863 | .822 | .784 | .747 | .713 | .681 | .650 | .621 | .567 | .519 | .497 |
| 6 | .942 | .888 | .838 | .790 | .746 | .705 | .666 | .630 | .596 | .564 | .507 | .456 | .432 |
| 7 | .933 | .871 | .813 | .760 | .711 | .665 | .623 | .583 | .547 | .513 | .452 | .400 | .376 |
| 8 | .923 | .853 | .789 | .731 | .677 | .627 | .582 | .540 | .502 | .467 | .404 | .351 | .327 |
| 9 | .914 | .837 | .766 | .703 | .645 | .592 | .544 | .500 | .460 | .424 | .361 | .308 | .284 |
| 10 | .905 | .820 | .744 | .676 | .614 | .558 | .508 | .463 | .422 | .386 | .322 | .270 | .247 |
| 11 | .896 | .804 | .722 | .650 | .585 | .527 | .475 | .429 | .388 | .350 | .287 | .237 | .215 |
| 12 | .887 | .788 | .701 | .625 | .557 | .497 | .444 | .397 | .356 | .319 | .257 | .208 | .187 |
| 13 | .879 | .773 | .681 | .601 | .530 | .469 | .445 | .368 | .326 | .290 | .229 | .182 | .163 |
| 14 | .870 | .758 | .661 | .577 | .505 | .442 | .388 | .340 | .299 | .263 | .205 | .160 | .141 |
| 15 | .861 | .743 | .642 | .555 | .481 | .417 | .362 | .315 | .275 | .239 | .183 | .140 | .123 |
| 16 | .853 | .728 | .623 | .534 | .458 | .394 | .339 | .292 | .252 | .218 | .163 | .123 | .107 |
| 17 | .844 | .714 | .605 | .513 | .436 | .371 | .317 | .270 | .231 | .198 | .146 | .108 | .093 |
| 18 | .836 | .700 | .587 | .494 | .416 | .350 | .296 | .250 | .212 | .180 | .130 | .095 | .081 |
| 19 | .828 | .686 | .570 | .475 | .396 | .331 | .276 | .232 | .194 | .164 | .116 | .083 | .070 |
| 20 | .820 | .673 | .554 | .456 | .377 | .312 | .258 | .215 | .178 | .149 | .104 | .073 | .061 |
| 25 | .780 | .610 | .478 | .375 | .295 | .233 | .184 | .146 | .116 | .092 | .059 | .038 | .030 |
| 30 | .742 | .552 | .412 | .308 | .231 | .174 | .131 | .099 | .075 | .057 | .033 | .020 | .015 |

| Period | 16% | 18% | 20% | 24% | 28% | 32% | 36% | 40% | 50% | 60% | 70% | 80% | 90% |
|---|---|---|---|---|---|---|---|---|---|---|---|---|---|
| 1 | .862 | .847 | .833 | .806 | .781 | .758 | .735 | .714 | .667 | .625 | .588 | .556 | .526 |
| 2 | .743 | .718 | .694 | .650 | .610 | .574 | .541 | .510 | .444 | .391 | .346 | .309 | .277 |
| 3 | .641 | .609 | .579 | .524 | .477 | .435 | .398 | .364 | .296 | .244 | .204 | .171 | .146 |
| 4 | .552 | .516 | .482 | .423 | .373 | .329 | .292 | .260 | .198 | .153 | .120 | .095 | .077 |
| 5 | .476 | .437 | .402 | .341 | .291 | .250 | .215 | .186 | .132 | .095 | .070 | .053 | .040 |
| 6 | .410 | .370 | .335 | .275 | .227 | .189 | .158 | .133 | .088 | .060 | .041 | .029 | .021 |
| 7 | .354 | .314 | .279 | .222 | .178 | .143 | .116 | .095 | .059 | .037 | .024 | .016 | .011 |
| 8 | .305 | .266 | .233 | .179 | .139 | .108 | .085 | .068 | .039 | .023 | .014 | .009 | .006 |
| 9 | .263 | .226 | .194 | .144 | .108 | .082 | .063 | .048 | .026 | .015 | .008 | .005 | .003 |
| 10 | .227 | .191 | .162 | .116 | .085 | .062 | .046 | .035 | .017 | .009 | .005 | .003 | .002 |
| 11 | .195 | .162 | .135 | .094 | .066 | .047 | .034 | .025 | .012 | .006 | .003 | .002 | .001 |
| 12 | .168 | .137 | .112 | .076 | .052 | .036 | .025 | .018 | .008 | .004 | .002 | .001 | .001 |
| 13 | .145 | .116 | .093 | .061 | .040 | .027 | .018 | .013 | .005 | .002 | .001 | .001 | .000 |
| 14 | .125 | .099 | .078 | .049 | .032 | .021 | .014 | .009 | .003 | .001 | .001 | .000 | .000 |
| 15 | .108 | .084 | .065 | .040 | .025 | .016 | .010 | .006 | .002 | .001 | .000 | .000 | .000 |
| 16 | .093 | .071 | .054 | .032 | .019 | .012 | .007 | .005 | .002 | .001 | .000 | .000 | |
| 17 | .080 | .060 | .045 | .026 | .015 | .009 | .005 | .003 | .001 | .000 | .000 | | |
| 18 | .069 | .051 | .038 | .021 | .012 | .007 | .004 | .002 | .001 | .000 | .000 | | |
| 19 | .060 | .043 | .031 | .017 | .009 | .005 | .003 | .002 | .000 | .000 | | | |
| 20 | .051 | .037 | .026 | .014 | .007 | .004 | .002 | .001 | .000 | .000 | | | |
| 25 | .024 | .016 | .010 | .005 | .002 | .001 | .000 | .000 | | | | | |
| 30 | .012 | .007 | .004 | .002 | .001 | .000 | .000 | | | | | | |

As reciprocals of the $(1 + i)^n$ term, all coefficients in Table 3–2 can be derived from the coefficients in Table 3–1 by dividing them into the number 1. In the sense that multiplication is a less difficult task than division, Table 3–2 simplifies present-value computations. For example, it is relatively easy to compute the present value of $62,000 received 16 years from now, assuming that investments of similar risk are earning 15 percent:

$$PV_{16}^{15\%} = FV(2\ Coef._{16}^{15\%}) = 62,000(.107) = \$6,634$$

Notice that the notation "2 Coef." is used to identify coefficients from Table 3–2.

Remember that even though it is easier to use Table 3–2, present values can always be computed using Table 3–1 or by expanding the $(1 + i)^n$ term. Also, note that the coefficients in Table 3–2 are less than 1. This is consistent with the idea that present values are lower than future values. Money has a time value.

## COMPUTING FUTURE AND PRESENT VALUES FOR MULTIPLE AMOUNTS

Thus far, the presentation has focused on single amounts; we have computed the present value for a single amount received in the future and the future value of a single amount received at the present. Many problems are not this simple. Situations are frequently encountered in which multiple amounts are received or paid out at several different times. For example, consider the situation in which a financial asset will yield $4,000 at the end of the fifth year, $7,000 at the end of the tenth year, and $11,000 at the end of the fifteenth year. Assume that investments of similar risk have interest rates of 12 percent. The present value of these multiple payments can be computed by (1) computing a separate present value for each amount, and (2) adding the three separate present values to get a total present value for the series of payments:

$$PV_n^{\%} = FV(2\ Coef._n^{\%})$$

$$PV_5^{12\%} = (\$4,000)(.567)\ = \$2,268$$

$$PV_{10}^{12\%} = (\$7,000)(.322)\ =\ 2,254$$

$$PV_{15}^{12\%} = (\$11,000)(.183) = \underline{\ 2,013}$$

$$\text{Total present value} = \$6,535$$

The point to remember is that present and future values of multiple amounts can always be computed by proceding on an amount-by-amount basis and then adding the individual present or future values.

## COEFFICIENTS FOR PRESENT VALUES OF ANNUITIES

An annuity is defined as a series of equal payments. For example, one of the prizes in the New York State lottery calls for a payment at the time the prize is awarded and 19 additional annual payments of $50,000. These 19 equal annual payments constitute a 19-year annuity. For those of us interested in computing present values, it is fortunate that a separate table has been developed that greatly simplifies the computation by eliminating the need for year-by-year present-value computations.

Table 3–3 makes computations for computing present values for annuities a simple matter. For example, if a 10 percent interest rate is applied to the New York State lottery example, the present value can be computed as follows ("3 Coef." is used to identify coefficients from Table 3–3):

$$PVA_n^\% = A(3\ Coef._n^\%)$$

where $A$ = amount of periodic annuity payment

$PVA$ = present value of the annuity

$$PVA_{19}^{10\%} = \$15,000(8.365)(\text{from Table 3-3}) = \$418,250$$

The coefficients appearing in Table 3–3 are simply sums of the coefficients included in Table 3–2. This important fact is shown mathematically in equations 3–2 and 3–3.

$$PVA_n^i = A_1 \left[ \frac{1}{(1+i)^1} \right] + A_2 \left[ \frac{1}{(1+i)^2} \right] + \ldots + A^n \left[ \frac{1}{(1+i)^n} \right] \qquad (3\text{-}2)$$

Since $A_1 = A_2 = \ldots = A_n$:

$$PVA_n^i = A \left[ \frac{1}{(1+i)^1} + \frac{1}{(1+i)^2} + \ldots + \frac{1}{(1+i)^n} \right]$$

$$= A \sum_{n=1}^{n} \frac{1}{(1+i)^n} \qquad (3\text{-}3)$$

The coefficients appearing in Table 3-3 are mathematically described as:

$$\sum_{n=1}^{n} \frac{1}{(1+i)^n}$$

In more practical terms, they are the summation of the coefficients in Table 3–2. For purposes of illustration, consider a three-year $1,000 annuity and an interest rate of 5 percent. If we compute the present value of the annuity on a year-by-year basis, we can use Table 3–2.

TABLE 3–3

## COEFFICIENTS FOR PRESENT VALUE OF A $1 ANNUITY

$$3 \text{ Coef.} = \sum_{n=1}^{n} \frac{1}{(1+i)^n}$$

A-2

| Received at the end of each period for: Period | Discount Rate 1% | 2% | 3% | 4% | 5% | 6% | 7% | 8% | 9% | 10% |
|---|---|---|---|---|---|---|---|---|---|---|
| 1 | 0.990 | 0.980 | 0.971 | 0.962 | 0.952 | 0.943 | 0.935 | 0.926 | 0.917 | 0.909 |
| 2 | 1.970 | 1.942 | 1.913 | 1.886 | 1.859 | 1.833 | 1.808 | 1.783 | 1.759 | 1.736 |
| 3 | 2.941 | 2.884 | 2.829 | 2.775 | 2.723 | 2.673 | 2.624 | 2.577 | 2.531 | 2.487 |
| 4 | 3.902 | 3.808 | 3.717 | 3.630 | 3.546 | 3.465 | 3.387 | 3.312 | 3.240 | 3.170 |
| 5 | 4.853 | 4.713 | 4.580 | 4.452 | 4.329 | 4.212 | 4.100 | 3.993 | 3.890 | 3.791 |
| 6 | 5.795 | 5.601 | 5.417 | 5.242 | 5.076 | 4.917 | 4.766 | 4.623 | 4.486 | 4.355 |
| 7 | 6.728 | 6.472 | 6.230 | 6.002 | 5.786 | 5.582 | 5.389 | 5.206 | 5.033 | 4.868 |
| 8 | 7.652 | 7.325 | 7.020 | 6.733 | 6.463 | 6.210 | 5.971 | 5.747 | 5.535 | 5.335 |
| 9 | 8.566 | 8.162 | 7.786 | 7.435 | 7.108 | 6.802 | 6.515 | 6.247 | 5.995 | 5.759 |
| 10 | 9.471 | 8.983 | 8.530 | 8.111 | 7.722 | 7.360 | 7.024 | 6.710 | 6.418 | 6.145 |
| 11 | 10.368 | 9.787 | 9.253 | 8.760 | 8.306 | 7.887 | 7.499 | 7.139 | 6.805 | 6.495 |
| 12 | 11.255 | 10.575 | 9.954 | 9.385 | 8.863 | 8.384 | 7.943 | 7.536 | 7.161 | 6.814 |
| 13 | 12.134 | 11.348 | 10.635 | 9.986 | 9.394 | 8.853 | 8.358 | 7.904 | 7.487 | 7.103 |
| 14 | 13.004 | 12.106 | 11.296 | 10.563 | 9.899 | 9.295 | 8.745 | 8.244 | 7.786 | 7.367 |
| 15 | 13.865 | 12.849 | 11.938 | 11.118 | 10.380 | 9.712 | 9.108 | 8.559 | 8.060 | 7.606 |
| 16 | 14.718 | 13.578 | 12.561 | 11.652 | 10.838 | 10.106 | 9.447 | 8.851 | 8.312 | 7.824 |
| 17 | 15.562 | 14.292 | 13.166 | 12.166 | 11.274 | 10.477 | 9.763 | 9.122 | 8.544 | 8.022 |
| 18 | 16.398 | 14.992 | 13.754 | 12.659 | 11.690 | 10.828 | 10.059 | 9.372 | 8.756 | 8.201 |
| 19 | 17.226 | 15.678 | 14.324 | 13.134 | 12.085 | 11.158 | 10.336 | 9.604 | 8.950 | 8.365 |
| 20 | 18.046 | 16.351 | 14.877 | 13.590 | 12.462 | 11.470 | 10.594 | 9.818 | 9.128 | 8.514 |
| 25 | 22.023 | 19.523 | 17.413 | 15.622 | 14.094 | 12.783 | 11.654 | 10.675 | 9.823 | 9.077 |
| 30 | 25.808 | 22.397 | 19.600 | 17.292 | 15.373 | 13.765 | 12.409 | 11.258 | 10.274 | 9.427 |

| Period | 12% | 14% | 16% | 18% | 20% | 24% | 28% | 32% | 36% |
|---|---|---|---|---|---|---|---|---|---|
| 1 | 0.893 | 0.877 | 0.862 | 0.847 | 0.833 | 0.806 | 0.781 | 0.758 | 0.735 |
| 2 | 1.690 | 1.647 | 1.605 | 1.566 | 1.528 | 1.457 | 1.392 | 1.332 | 1.276 |
| 3 | 2.402 | 2.322 | 2.246 | 2.174 | 2.106 | 1.981 | 1.868 | 1.766 | 1.674 |
| 4 | 3.037 | 2.914 | 2.798 | 2.690 | 2.589 | 2.404 | 2.241 | 2.096 | 1.966 |
| 5 | 3.605 | 3.433 | 3.274 | 3.127 | 2.991 | 2.745 | 2.532 | 2.345 | 2.181 |
| 6 | 4.111 | 3.889 | 3.685 | 3.498 | 3.326 | 3.020 | 2.759 | 2.534 | 2.339 |
| 7 | 4.564 | 4.288 | 4.039 | 3.812 | 3.605 | 3.242 | 2.937 | 2.678 | 2.455 |
| 8 | 4.968 | 4.639 | 4.344 | 4.078 | 3.837 | 3.421 | 3.076 | 2.786 | 2.540 |
| 9 | 5.328 | 4.946 | 4.607 | 4.303 | 4.031 | 3.566 | 3.184 | 2.868 | 2.603 |
| 10 | 5.650 | 5.216 | 4.833 | 4.494 | 4.193 | 3.682 | 3.269 | 2.930 | 2.650 |
| 11 | 5.938 | 5.453 | 5.029 | 4.656 | 4.327 | 3.776 | 3.335 | 2.978 | 2.683 |
| 12 | 6.194 | 5.660 | 5.197 | 4.793 | 4.439 | 3.851 | 3.387 | 3.013 | 2.708 |
| 13 | 6.424 | 5.842 | 5.342 | 4.910 | 4.533 | 3.912 | 3.427 | 3.040 | 2.727 |
| 14 | 6.628 | 6.002 | 5.468 | 5.008 | 4.611 | 3.962 | 3.459 | 3.061 | 2.740 |
| 15 | 6.811 | 6.142 | 5.575 | 5.092 | 4.675 | 4.001 | 3.483 | 3.076 | 2.750 |
| 16 | 6.974 | 6.265 | 5.669 | 5.162 | 4.730 | 4.033 | 3.503 | 3.088 | 2.758 |
| 17 | 7.120 | 5.373 | 5.749 | 4.222 | 4.775 | 4.059 | 3.518 | 3.097 | 2.763 |
| 18 | 7.250 | 6.467 | 5.818 | 5.273 | 4.812 | 4.080 | 3.529 | 3.104 | 2.767 |
| 19 | 7.366 | 6.550 | 5.877 | 5.316 | 4.844 | 4.097 | 3.539 | 3.109 | 2.770 |
| 20 | 7.469 | 6.623 | 5.929 | 5.353 | 4.870 | 4.110 | 3.546 | 3.113 | 2.772 |
| 25 | 7.843 | 6.873 | 6.097 | 5.467 | 4.948 | 4.147 | 3.564 | 3.122 | 2.776 |
| 30 | 8.055 | 7.003 | 6.177 | 5.517 | 4.979 | 4.160 | 3.569 | 3.124 | 2.778 |

$$PVA_{\overline{3}}^{5\%} = \$1{,}000(0.952) + \$1{,}000(0.907) +$$
$$\$1{,}000(0.864) \text{ (from Table 3-2) } = \$2{,}723$$

Using Table 3-3, we can obtain the same answer:

$$PVA_{\overline{3}}^{5\%} = FV(3 \text{ Coef.}_{\overline{3}}^{5\%})$$

$$= \$1{,}000(2.723) = \$2{,}723$$

Note the relationship among the coefficients $(0.952 + 0.907 + 0.864 = 2.723)$.

Thus, Table 3–3 is nothing more than a special type of expansion of the $(1 + i)^n$ term. The basic logic of present and future values is fully incorporated in this table. The only advantage of Tables 3–2 and 3–3 is that they simplify computations. Managers striving for stockholder-wealth maximization can be assured that the tables provide a conceptually correct procedure for adjusting cash flows received in the future to equivalent present values.

**Computation for Special Annuity Problems.** Table 3–3 can be used to compute the present value of a series of *equal* periodic payments. Series of *unequal* payments present additional difficulties. For example, consider the following series of unequal payments, and assume that a 10 percent discount rate should be used to compute the present value of the series:

| Year | Amount Received |
|:----:|:---------------:|
| 1 | $1,000 |
| 2 | $1,000 |
| 3 | $ 500 |
| 4 | $1,000 |
| 5 | $1,000 |

The present value of these payments can be expressed mathematically as follows:

$$PV_{\overline{5}}^{10\%} = \frac{1{,}000}{(1 + 0.10)^1} + \frac{1{,}000}{(1 + 0.10)^2} + \frac{500}{(1 + 0.10)^3} + \frac{1{,}000}{(1 + 0.10)^4} + \frac{1{,}000}{(1 + 0.10)^5}$$

The annuity table (Table 3–3) cannot be easily applied in this situation, because the $1,000 cannot be factored out of the equation.

It is possible to modify the computational procedures involving the annuity tables (Table 3–3) in order to accommodate these unorthodox situations. Consider the case of an annuity that begins at some point after year 1 (called a delayed annuity). For purposes of illustration, let us compute the present value of receiving $1,000 at the end of each year from year 4 through year 20, using a discount rate of 8 percent. Table 3–2 could be used, but this would require 17 multiplications and addition of the results. The coefficients shown in Table 3–3 can be modified to achieve the solution to this problem. Mathematically, the problem can be expressed as follows:

$$PV_{4-20}^{8\%} = \$1,000 \left[ \frac{1}{(1 + 0.08)^4} + \frac{1}{(1 + 0.08)^5} + \ldots + \frac{1}{(1 + 0.08)^{20}} \right]$$

The coefficients in Table 3–3 represent the present value of an annuity with the first payment taking place in year 1. The present value of an annuity with payments from years 4 through 20 is equal to that of an annuity from years 1 through 20 *less* the present value of an annuity from years 1 through 3. Mathematically, this can be expressed as follows:

$$PVA_{4-20}^{8\%} = \$1,000(3 \text{ Coef.}_{20}^{8\%}) - \$1,000(3 \text{ Coef.}_{3}^{8\%})$$

$$= \$1,000(3 \text{ Coef.}_{20}^{8\%} - 3 \text{ Coef.}_{3}^{8\%})$$

$$= \$1,000(9.818 - 2.577) = \$7,241$$

Thus, the coefficient for a delayed annuity can be computed by subtracting the coefficient of the period of delay from the coefficient that would apply if the annuity began at year 1. This adjusted coefficient can be used to compute the present value of delayed annuities.

There are other unorthodox situations to which Table 3–3 can be applied. For example, consider a financial asset that will yield $1,000 from years 1 through 5, and $2,000 from years 6 through 10. This situation is depicted in Figure 3–1. The present value of this series of payments can be computed in several ways. The present value of the first five $1,000 cash inflows could be computed as a simple annuity, using Table 3–3. The present value of the second five cash inflows (in years 6 through 10) of $2,000 could be computed as the present value of a delayed annuity. The total present value of the entire ten cash inflows is equal to the sum of the two five-year annuities. The present-value computations, based on an 8 percent discount rate, would be as follows:

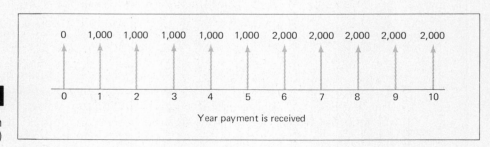

Time Line for Cash Flows (in dollars)

$$PVA_{5}^{8\%} = \$1,000(3 \text{ Coef.}_{5}^{8\%}) = \$1,000(3.993) \qquad = \$3,993$$

$$PVA_{6-10}^{8\%} = \$2,000(3 \text{ Coef.}_{10}^{8\%} - 3 \text{ Coef.}_{5}^{8\%}) = \$2,000(6.710 - 3.993) = \underline{\ 5,434}$$

Total present value $\qquad = \$9,427$

## COEFFICIENTS FOR FUTURE VALUE OF ANNUITIES

On occasion, it may be necessary to compute the future value of an annuity (a series of equal payments). For example, you may be interested in knowing how much you will have in a savings account at the end of ten years if you deposit $1,000 one year from today ($t_1$) and nine more payments of $1,000 at the end of each year thereafter. We will assume that 12 percent per annum can be earned on the deposits. The time line for the cash flows is presented in Figure 3–2. Note that in this situation, the first $1,000 deposit will earn interest for nine years, the second for eight years, and so on.

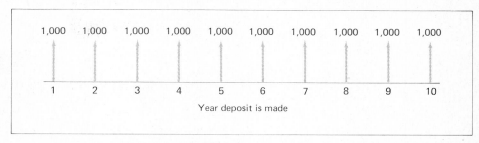

**FIGURE 3–2**

Time Line for Cash Flows Deposited in a Savings Account (in dollars)

It is possible to use Table 3–1 to compute the future value of each deposit separately. But this would require ten different computations, and Table 3–4 permits us to shorten the computational procedure to only one step. It should be noted that the coefficients in Table 3–4 are nothing more than a different presentation of the coefficients in Table 3–1. The future value of the annuity in question can be computed as follows:

$$FVA_n^\% = A(4 \text{ Coef.}_n^\%)$$

$$FVA_{10}^{12\%} = \$1,000(17.549) = \$17,549$$

That is, if $1,000 is deposited each year for ten years and interest is paid at the rate of 12 percent per year, the value of the account at the end of the ten years will be $17,549.

## COMPOUND PERIODS OTHER THAN ONE YEAR

Thus far, we have assumed that interest is paid at the end of each year. However, many savings institutions offer interest paid daily, quarterly, or semiannually. The tables shown in the previous pages can be used in such cases, but slight adjustments in procedures must be introduced. To illustrate the problem, let us use a numerical example. We already know that if you

TABLE 3–4

## COEFFICIENTS FOR FUTURE VALUE OF ANNUITIES

A-4

$$4 \text{ Coef.}^{\%}_{n} = \sum_{n=0}^{n-1} (1-i)^n$$

| To be Deposited each Period | 1% | 2% | 3% | 4% | 5% | 6% |
|---|---|---|---|---|---|---|
| 1 | 1.000 | 1.000 | 1.000 | 1.000 | 1.000 | 1.000 |
| 2 | 2.010 | 2.020 | 2.030 | 2.040 | 2.050 | 2.060 |
| 3 | 3.030 | 3.060 | 3.091 | 3.122 | 3.152 | 3.184 |
| 4 | 4.060 | 4.122 | 4.184 | 4.246 | 4.310 | 4.375 |
| 5 | 5.101 | 5.204 | 5.309 | 5.416 | 5.526 | 5.637 |
| 6 | 6.152 | 6.308 | 6.468 | 6.633 | 6.802 | 6.975 |
| 7 | 7.214 | 7.434 | 7.662 | 7.898 | 8.142 | 8.394 |
| 8 | 8.286 | 8.583 | 8.892 | 9.214 | 9.549 | 9.897 |
| 9 | 9.369 | 9.755 | 10.159 | 10.583 | 11.027 | 11.491 |
| 10 | 10.462 | 10.950 | 11.464 | 12.006 | 12.578 | 13.181 |
| 11 | 11.567 | 12.169 | 12.808 | 13.486 | 14.207 | 14.972 |
| 12 | 12.683 | 13.412 | 14.192 | 15.026 | 15.917 | 16.870 |
| 13 | 13.809 | 14.680 | 15.618 | 16.627 | 17.713 | 18.882 |
| 14 | 14.947 | 15.974 | 17.086 | 18.292 | 19.599 | 21.051 |
| 15 | 16.097 | 17.293 | 18.599 | 20.024 | 21.579 | 23.276 |
| 16 | 17.258 | 18.639 | 20.157 | 21.825 | 23.657 | 25.673 |
| 17 | 18.430 | 20.012 | 21.762 | 23.698 | 25.840 | 28.213 |
| 18 | 19.615 | 21.412 | 23.414 | 25.645 | 28.132 | 30.906 |
| 19 | 20.811 | 22.841 | 25.117 | 27.671 | 30.539 | 33.760 |
| 20 | 22.019 | 24.297 | 26.870 | 29.778 | 33.066 | 36.786 |
| 25 | 28.243 | 32.030 | 36.459 | 41.646 | 47.727 | 54.865 |
| 30 | 34.785 | 40.568 | 47.575 | 56.805 | 66.439 | 79.058 |

| Period | 7% | 8% | 9% | 10% | 12% | 14% |
|---|---|---|---|---|---|---|
| 1 | 1.000 | 1.000 | 1.000 | 1.000 | 1.000 | 1.000 |
| 2 | 2.070 | 2.080 | 2.090 | 2.100 | 2.120 | 2.140 |
| 3 | 3.215 | 3.246 | 3.278 | 3.310 | 3.374 | 3.440 |
| 4 | 4.440 | 4.506 | 4.573 | 4.641 | 4.770 | 4.921 |
| 5 | 5.751 | 5.867 | 5.985 | 6.105 | 6.353 | 6.610 |
| 6 | 7.153 | 7.336 | 7.523 | 7.716 | 8.115 | 8.536 |
| 7 | 8.654 | 8.923 | 9.200 | 9.487 | 10.089 | 10.730 |
| 8 | 10.260 | 10.637 | 11.028 | 11.436 | 12.300 | 13.233 |
| 9 | 11.978 | 12.488 | 13.021 | 13.579 | 14.776 | 16.085 |
| 10 | 13.816 | 14.487 | 15.193 | 15.937 | 17.549 | 19.337 |
| 11 | 15.784 | 16.645 | 17.560 | 18.531 | 20.655 | 23.044 |
| 12 | 17.888 | 18.977 | 20.141 | 21.384 | 24.133 | 27.271 |
| 13 | 20.141 | 21.495 | 22.953 | 24.523 | 28.029 | 32.089 |
| 14 | 22.550 | 24.215 | 26.019 | 27.975 | 32.393 | 37.581 |
| 15 | 25.129 | 27.152 | 29.361 | 31.772 | 37.280 | 43.842 |
| 16 | 27.888 | 30.324 | 33.003 | 35.950 | 42.753 | 50.980 |
| 17 | 30.840 | 33.750 | 36.974 | 40.545 | 48.884 | 59.118 |
| 18 | 33.999 | 37.450 | 41.301 | 45.599 | 55.750 | 68.394 |
| 19 | 37.379 | 41.446 | 46.018 | 51.159 | 63.440 | 78.969 |
| 20 | 40.995 | 45.762 | 51.160 | 57.275 | 72.052 | 91.025 |
| 25 | 63.249 | 73.106 | 84.701 | 98.347 | 133.334 | 181.871 |
| 30 | 94.461 | 113.283 | 136.308 | 164.494 | 241.333 | 356.787 |

| Period | 16% | 18% | 20% | 24% | 28% | 32% |
|---|---|---|---|---|---|---|
| 1 | 1.000 | 1.000 | 1.000 | 1.000 | 1.000 | 1.000 |
| 2 | 2.160 | 2.180 | 2.200 | 2.240 | 2.280 | 2.320 |
| 3 | 3.506 | 3.572 | 3.640 | 3.778 | 3.918 | 4.062 |
| 4 | 5.066 | 5.215 | 5.368 | 5.684 | 6.016 | 6.362 |
| 5 | 6.877 | 7.154 | 7.442 | 8.048 | 8.700 | 9.398 |
| 6 | 8.977 | 9.442 | 9.930 | 10.980 | 12.136 | 13.406 |
| 7 | 11.414 | 12.142 | 12.916 | 14.615 | 16.534 | 18.696 |
| 8 | 14.240 | 15.327 | 16.499 | 19.123 | 22.163 | 25.678 |
| 9 | 17.518 | 19.086 | 20.799 | 24.712 | 29.369 | 34.895 |
| 10 | 21.321 | 23.521 | 25.959 | 31.643 | 38.592 | 47.062 |
| 11 | 25.733 | 28.755 | 32.150 | 40.238 | 50.399 | 63.122 |
| 12 | 30.850 | 34.931 | 39.580 | 50.985 | 65.510 | 84.320 |
| 13 | 36.786 | 42.219 | 48.497 | 64.110 | 84.853 | 112.303 |
| 14 | 43.672 | 50.818 | 59.196 | 80.496 | 109.612 | 149.240 |
| 15 | 51.660 | 60.965 | 72.035 | 100.815 | 141.303 | 197.997 |
| 16 | 60.925 | 72.939 | 87.442 | 126.011 | 181.87 | 262.36 |
| 17 | 71.673 | 87.068 | 105.931 | 157.253 | 233.79 | 347.31 |
| 18 | 84.141 | 103.740 | 128.117 | 195.994 | 300.25 | 459.45 |
| 19 | 98.603 | 123.414 | 154.740 | 244.033 | 385.32 | 607.47 |
| 20 | 115.380 | 146.628 | 186.688 | 303.601 | 494.21 | 802.86 |
| 25 | 249.214 | 342.603 | 471.981 | 898.092 | 1706.8 | 3226.8 |
| 30 | 530.312 | 790.948 | 1181.882 | 2640.916 | 5873.2 | 12941.0 |

| Period | 36% | 40% | 50% | 60% | 70% | 80% |
|---|---|---|---|---|---|---|
| 1 | 1.000 | 1.000 | 1.000 | 1.000 | 1.000 | 1.000 |
| 2 | 2.360 | 2.400 | 2.500 | 2.600 | 2.700 | 2.800 |
| 3 | 4.210 | 4.360 | 4.750 | 5.160 | 5.590 | 6.040 |
| 4 | 6.725 | 7.104 | 8.125 | 9.256 | 10.503 | 11.872 |
| 5 | 10.146 | 10.846 | 13.188 | 15.810 | 18.855 | 22.370 |
| 6 | 14.799 | 16.324 | 20.781 | 26.295 | 33.054 | 41.265 |
| 7 | 21.126 | 23.853 | 32.172 | 43.073 | 57.191 | 75.278 |
| 8 | 29.732 | 34.395 | 49.258 | 69.916 | 98.225 | 136.500 |
| 9 | 41.435 | 49.153 | 74.887 | 112.866 | 167.983 | 246.699 |
| 10 | 57.352 | 69.814 | 113.330 | 181.585 | 286.570 | 445.058 |
| 11 | 78.998 | 98.739 | 170.995 | 291.536 | 488.170 | 802.105 |
| 12 | 108.437 | 139.235 | 257.493 | 467.458 | 830.888 | 1444.788 |
| 13 | 148.475 | 195.929 | 387.239 | 748.933 | 1413.510 | 2601.619 |
| 14 | 202.926 | 275.300 | 581.859 | 1199.293 | 2403.968 | 4683.914 |
| 15 | 276.979 | 386.420 | 873.788 | 1919.869 | 4087.745 | 8432.045 |
| 16 | 377.69 | 541.99 | 1311.7 | 3072.8 | 6950.2 | 15179.0 |
| 17 | 514.66 | 759.78 | 1968.5 | 4917.5 | 11816.0 | 27323.0 |
| 18 | 700.94 | 1064.7 | 2953.8 | 7868.9 | 20089.0 | 49182.0 |
| 19 | 954.28 | 1491.6 | 4431.7 | 12591.0 | 34152.0 | 88528.0 |
| 20 | 1298.8 | 2089.2 | 6648.5 | 20147.0 | 58059.0 | 159350.0 |
| 25 | 6053.0 | 11247.0 | 50500.0 | 211270.0 | 824370.0 | 3011100.0 |
| 30 | 28172.0 | 60501.0 | 383500.0 | 2215400.0 | 11705000.0 | 56896000.0 |

deposit $1,000 in a savings account, and if the interest paid is 8 percent compounded annually, the account will contain $1,080 at the end of one year. However, if the savings institution pays and compounds interest quarterly, the account will contain more than $1,080 at the end of one year. In this case, it is best to view the institution as paying 2 percent per quarter rather than 8 percent per annum. The quarterly compounding process will be as follows:

Amount at the end of quarter 1 = $1,000.00 + $20.00 = $1,020.00

Amount at the end of quarter 2 = $1,020.00 + $20.40 = $1,040.40

Amount at the end of quarter 3 = $1,040.40 + $20.81 = $1,061.21

Amount at the end of quarter 4 = $1,061.21 + $21.22 = $1,082.43

You can observe from this example that the future value will be greater if quarterly rather than annual compounding is used. The reason for this difference is that with quarterly compounding, interest is earned on previously earned interest during the year. Table 3–1 can be used to determine the future value if a few adjustments are made. These adjustments can be expressed mathematically as follows:

<table>
<tr><td>Unadjusted</td><td>Adjusted</td></tr>
<tr><td>$FV = PV(1 + i)^n$</td><td>$FV = PV(1 + i/m)^{mn}$</td></tr>
</table>

where $m$ = the number of times per year compounding occurs

In our example, $i$ would be 8 percent, $m$ would be 4, and $i/m$ would be 2 percent. Since $n$ equals 1, $mn$ equals 4. If we adjust the interest rate to 2 percent and the number of periods to 4, we can use Table 3–1 to compute the future value:

$$FV_4^{2\%} = \$1,000(1 \text{ Coef.}_4^{2\%}) = \$1,000(1.082) = \$1,082$$

A similar procedure can be used to deal with semiannual, monthly, weekly, or even daily compounding. The simple annual interest rate is adjusted by the number of periods per year compounding takes place. The $n$ term is increased by multiplying the number of years by the number of times compounding takes place each year.

## DISCOUNT PERIODS OTHER THAN ONE YEAR

Another common problem relates to the computation of present values when the cash flows occur with a frequency other than annually. For example, assume that we want to compute the present value of $1,200 received during a one-year period. Further assume that the discount rate that reflects the riskiness of the asset is 12 percent, and that *the cash flows are received at the end of the year.* The present value is computed as follows:

$$PV_1^{12\%} = \$1,200(2 \; Coef._1^{12\%}) = \$1,200(0.893) = \$1,071.60$$

But the assumption that the cash flow is received at the end of the year may not be reasonable. A machine, for example, generates cash flows during the entire year, not only at the end of the year. If the cash flows are generated evenly throughout the year, it may be desirable to treat the $1,200 cash flow as a 12-payment ($100 per month) annuity. Table 3–3 can be used to compute the present value of this monthly annuity. We must make adjustments to Table 3–2 similar to those we made when making our future-value computations. That is, the annual rate is divided by the number of periods, and the number of years is multiplied by the number of periods payments are received during one year. For our example, the computations would be as follows:

$$PVA_{12}^{1\%} = \$100(3 \; Coef._{12}^{1\%}) = \$100(11.255) = \$1125.50$$

Reducing the discount period reflects the fact that cash flows are received earlier than the end of the year. This increases the present value of the cash flows. If, for example, we go through the same process using weekly discounting, the present value will be increased.[4]

## SELECTED APPLICATIONS OF THE TABLES

### BOND VALUES

Tables 3–2 and 3–3 can be used to compute the value of bonds. For illustration, let us compute the present value of a ten-year bond with a par value of $1,000. Assume further that the bond was issued two years ago and thus has a remaining life of eight years before maturity. At the time the bond was issued, the competitive securities market established the required rate of return to the bondholders as 8 percent. Thus, the fixed annual interest payment associated with the bond is $80 per year, and this interest is paid at the end of each year. The expected cash flows associated with the bond are depicted in Figure 3–3. The cash flow in year 8 represents the interest paid for the year plus the repayment of the $1,000 par value upon maturity of the bond.

As conditions in the security market change, so will the current market value of the bond. This new value will be reflected in the bond's price in the secondary bond market. Assume, for example, that market interest rates have shifted in such a fashion that market participants now have a required rate of return of 10 percent for this hypothetical bond.[5] That is, bonds with identical risk characteristics are currently required to return 10 percent to debt suppliers. This will result in a new price for the bond in the secondary

---

[4]The tables presented in this book do not contain sufficient detail for weekly discounting.
[5]Factors affecting the required rate of return of a security are discussed in greater detail in Chapter 4.

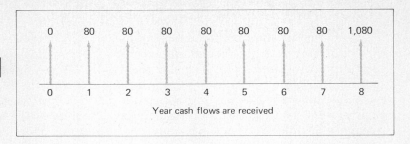

**FIGURE 3–3**

Expected Annual Cash Flows associated with Hypothetical Bond (in dollars)

market. This new price can be computed using Tables 3–2 and 3–3. The present value of an eight-year $80 annuity can be computed using Table 3–3. The present value of the single amount of $1,000 received at the end of year 8 can be computed using Table 3–2. A 10 percent discount rate, *which reflects the current market evaluation*, is used as the discount rate. The computation is as follows:

$$PVA_8^{10\%} = \$80(3 \ Coef._8^{10\%}) = \$80(5.335) \qquad = \$426.80$$

$$PV_8^{10\%} = \$1,000(2 \ Coef._8^{10\%}) = \$1,000(0.467) = \underline{467.00}$$

Total present value and market price of the bond   = $893.80

As expected, the current market price of the bond is lower than the par value. This reduction in price reflects the increase in the required rate of return to the bondholders caused by the shift in market interest rates. The present value of fixed dollar cash flows is reduced as the discount rate is increased.

In actuality, most bonds pay interest semiannually rather than annually. A bond with an annual interest return of $80 will actually make a $40 interest payment every six months. A new time line for semiannual cash flows is presented in Figure 3–4. The cash flows are depicted as a 16-period $40 annuity, and a single amount of $1,000 due to be received at the end of period 16 (eight years from now).

**FIGURE 3–4**

Time Line for Semiannual Cash Flows for Hypothetical Bond (in dollars)

Bond-market participants have detailed tables that permit them to compute the value of bonds when interest is paid semiannually. These bond tables are nothing more than specialized versions of the present-value tables

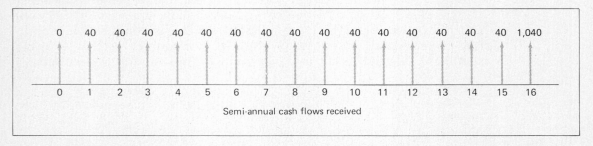

PART ONE: The Theory of Finance

described in this chapter. Thus, as you can see, present value is used in the "real world."

## PAYMENTS ON TERM LOANS

A loan granted by a bank may require repayment of both interest and principal in a certain number of equal annual payments. For example, assume that a bank makes a $10,000 loan at a 10 percent annual interest rate, and requires that the loan be repaid in five equal annual installments. Table 3–3 and the present-value-of-an-annuity technique can be used to compute the annual installment payments. In this case, the annuity payment is unknown. We do know the appropriate coefficient and thus the present value of the annuity. By adjusting our procedure and solving for the $A$ term, we can compute the installment payments as follows:

$$PVA_5^{10\%} = A(3 \text{ Coef.}_5^{10\%})$$

$$\$10,000 = A(3.791)$$

$$A = \frac{\$10,000}{3.791} = \$2,637.83$$

Thus, five annual payments of $2,637.83 are just sufficient to repay the entire $10,000 loan *plus* the annual interest of 10 percent on the unpaid balance. Table 3–5 shows how the five equal annual payments amortize (pay back) the loan. Note that in the early years, a relatively large portion of the fixed annual payment constitutes interest. As the principal outstanding (unpaid balance) declines, so does the interest payment.

### TABLE 3–5

#### LOAN-AMORTIZATION SCHEDULE

| Year | Payment | Interest[a] | Principal Repayment | Debt Outstanding |
|------|---------|-------------|---------------------|------------------|
| 1 | $2,637.83 | $1,000.00 | $1,637.83 | $8,362.17 |
| 2 | $2,637.83 | $836.22 | $1,801.61 | $6,560.56 |
| 3 | $2,637.83 | $656.06 | $1,981.77 | $4,578.79 |
| 4 | $2,637.83 | $457.88 | $2,179.95 | $2,398.84 |
| 5 | $2,637.83 | $239.88 | $2,397.95 | $0.89[b] |

[a]Interest is always 10% of the debt outstanding at the end of the preceding year.

[b]The outstanding balance was not reduced to zero owing to the rounding errors in Table 3-3.

Institutions that regularly extend term loans use detailed loan-amortization tables. These tables are simply specialized versions of the tables presented in this chapter. Again, present-value techniques have applications in the "real world."

Table 3–2 can be used to compute the annual rate of growth on a single future amount. For example, assume that the Champion Corporation had earnings per share of $2.00 in 1969, and ten years later the earnings per share have increased to $2.96. The techniques associated with Table 3–2 can be used to compute the true annual compound rate of growth of the earnings per share of the Champion Corporation. The computation would be as follows:

$$PV = FV^?_{10}(2 \text{ Coef.}^?_{10})$$

$$2.00 = 2.96(2 \text{ Coef.}^?_{10})$$

$$(2 \text{ Coef.}^?_{10}) = \frac{2.00}{2.96} = 0.676$$

In this case, the present value and future value are both known. With this information, the *2 Coef.* can be computed. Now we have the coefficient and the number of years. The annual rate of growth can be found by referring to the 10-year line in Table 3–2 and searching for the coefficient. The 10-year coefficient of 0.676 is found in the 4 percent column. Therefore, this 4 percent is the annual rate of growth of the earnings per share of the Champion Corporation. The procedure involves computing the coefficient, and then searching in Table 3–2 at a known period in order to find the correct interest or growth rate.

Keep in mind that the growth rate is a compound annual growth rate and differs from a simple growth rate. A simple growth rate is often computed by taking the percentage change in amounts over the period in which the change took place (ten years, in this case). Here, the 10-year simple growth is equal to 4.8 percent (48%/10). Many people compute a simple—and incorrect—annual growth rate by dividing the multiyear percentage increase by the number of years. In our case, some people might conclude that the earnings per share of the Champion Corporation have increased at a 4.8 percent annual rate. This procedure is incorrect, since the compounding effect is not introduced.

Table 3–6 shows the growth of $2.00 earnings per share at a 4 and a 4.8 percent true annual growth. You can observe from the table that if a 4.8 percent annual growth rate is used, the earnings per share at the end of ten years will be $3.20, not $2.96. This illustration is designed to show that true annual growth rates can be computed *only* if compounding is incorporated into the analysis. Table 3–2 can be used for this purpose.[6]

The same procedure can be used to compute the true annual rate of return of an investment. For example, assume that $120,000 can be invested

---

[6]The procedure to determine the true annual growth rate could be modified in such a way that Table 3–1 could also be used.

TABLE 3-6

### GROWTH IN EARNINGS PER SHARE

| Year | At a 4% annual growth rate | At a 4.8% annual growth rate |
|------|----------------------------|------------------------------|
| 1969 | $2.00 | $2.00 |
| 1970 | $2.08 | $2.10 |
| 1971 | $2.16 | $2.20 |
| 1972 | $2.25 | $2.30 |
| 1973 | $2.34 | $2.41 |
| 1974 | $2.43 | $2.53 |
| 1975 | $2.53 | $2.65 |
| 1976 | $2.63 | $2.78 |
| 1977 | $2.74 | $2.91 |
| 1978 | $2.85 | $3.05 |
| 1979 | $2.96 | $3.20 |

today in such a manner that 20 years from today the investor will receive $465,116. The true annual rate of return to the investor can be computed by first computing the *2 Coef.*, and then searching Table 3–2 on the 20-year line for that coefficient. In our example, the *2 Coef.* is computed as follows:

$$PV = FV_{20}^{?}(2\ Coef._{20}^{?})$$

$$\$120,000 = \$465,116(2\ Coef._{20}^{?})$$

$$(2\ Coef._{20}^{?}) = \frac{\$120,000}{\$465,116} = 0.258$$

On the 20-year line in Table 3–2, this coefficient is associated with a 7 percent discount rate. Thus, 7 percent is the true annual rate of return of the investment.

## RATES OF RETURN FOR ANNUITIES

Investments often yield returns to the investor in the form of equal annual payments. Assume, for example, that we wish to compute the true annual rate of return on a $6,418 investment made today. The investor will receive a $1,000 cash return at the end of every year for years 1 through 10. Within the notational framework developed in this chapter, the annual rate of return can be computed as follows:

$$PVA_{10}^{?} = A(3\ Coef._{10}^{?})$$

$$\$6,418 = \$1,000(3\ Coef._{10}^{?})$$

$$(3\ Coef._{10}^{?}) = \frac{\$6,418}{\$1,000} = 6.418$$

Since the equal annual payments ($1,000) and the present value ($6,418) are known, it is a simple matter to compute the *3 Coef*. The next step is to search Table 3–3 along the 10-year line. The coefficient of 6.418 is found in the 9 percent column. That is, the true annual rate of return for this annuity type of investment is 9 percent.

SUMMARY

The pursuit of stockholder-wealth maximization requires that management be able to analyze and compare cash flows occurring at different times. As demonstrated in Chapter 2, both future- and present-value techniques facilitate the comparison of different cash-flow streams. In this chapter we have shown the availability of tables that permit management to address a broad range of problems involving present and future values with a minimum amount of difficulty. These tables make it possible for management to evaluate the implications of cash flows many years in the future. With the tables, it is a relatively simple matter to compare present values for annuities and bond values. In addition, the tables serve as a basis for computing such things as loan amortization, rates of return, and rates of growth.

These are only some of the uses to which the tables can be put; there are many others. And in practice, business has more detailed tables available for specialized problems: detailed present- and future-value tables, bond tables, amortization tables, and tables of many other types.

The student should remember two very important things about these tables. First, all of them are designed to adjust cash flows for differences in timing. Second, such adjustments for differences in timing are required if stockholder wealth is to be maximized.

QUESTIONS
FOR
DISCUSSION

1. Give a verbal explanation of the relationship among Tables 3–1, 3–2, 3–3, and 3–4.
2. Describe how we might construct a table for use in computing future values compounded daily. Use Table 3–1 as a starting point in your description.
3. Explain why a loan-amortization table contains declining interest payments and rising principal repayments.
4. "If profits increase 50% over a five-year period, the annual rate of growth in profits is 10%." True or false? Explain your answer and illustrate.
5. Why are future- and present-value tables used by management?
6. Describe some of the different ways in which the present- and future-value tables can be used by management.
7. How do present-value tables relate to stockholder-wealth maximization?

PROBLEMS

1. Calculate the number of dollars you would have in a savings account five years from now if you invest $1,000 today, given that:
   a. The interest paid is 8% compounded annually.
   b. The interest rate is 10% compounded annually.

c. The interest rate is 8% compounded quarterly.

d. The interest rate is 8% compounded semiannually.

2. Calculate the present value, discounted at 10%, of receiving:

   a. $1,000 at the end of year 5

   b. $100 at the end of year 3, and $200 at the end of year 4

   c. $100 at the end of year 8, and $100 at the end of year 10

3. A rich uncle gives you two options, each with the same level of risk. Option A is to receive $5,000 five years from now. Option B is to receive $3,000 today. Which option would most increase your wealth, if investment alternatives of similar risk are currently yielding an 8% return?

4. Calculate the present value of the following future benefits, given a discount rate of 6%:

   a. $5,000 every year, for years 1 through 10

   b. $10,000 every year, for years 5 through 20

   c. $5,000 every year for years 1 through 5, *plus* $10,000 every year for years 6 through 10

   d. $1,000 every year for years 1 through 3, *nothing* in year 4, then $2,000 every year for years 5 through 8

5. Calculate the present value of a bond with a par value of $1,000, a coupon interest rate of 8% paid semiannually ($40 every six months), and a maturity of ten years. The market discounts similar risk bonds at:

   a. 4%    b. 8%    c. 10%

   d. What is the relationship between the present value of the bonds and the market discount rate?

6. A commercial bank is willing to make you a loan of $100,000. The bank asks an 8% interest rate, and requires ten equal annual payments to repay both interest and principal. What will be the dollar amount of the annual payment?

7. What has been the annual growth rate of dividends for a firm that paid a $5.00 dividend in 1970 and a $13.85 dividend in 1979?

8. What is the annual rate of return of investing $56,500 today and receiving $10,000 every year for years 1 through 10?

9. You have two alternative investment opportunities. Alternative A is a bond paying 8% a year (paid annually) for 20 years with a par value of $10,000. The market discounts similar risk bonds at a 10% rate. Alternative B is investing in a project that will return $2,000 every year for years 1 through 10. The market discounts similar risk investments at a 20% rate.

   a. Calculate the present value of each alternative.

   b. Which alternative is riskier? Explain your answer.

   c. Assuming you were given the choice of receiving one of the alternatives as a gift, which would you prefer if:

      i. There was no possibility of selling either alternative investment.

      ii. There was a ready market for both alternative investments.

10. Calculate the present value of a $1,000-par-value bond. The coupon interest rate is 8% paid annually, and the maturity of the bond is 20 years. The required rate of return of the bondholders is:

    a. 8%    b. 6%    c. 10%

    d. What will be the present value of the bond in parts *a* through *c* if the maturity of the bond was one year instead of 20 years? What is the relationship between the volatility in the present value of bonds and the number of years to maturity?

11. Jack Sanders, now 55 years old, is interested in saving for retirement. Mr. Sanders plans to deposit $5,000 every year for the next ten years at a commercial bank. The first deposit will be exactly one year from today. Calculate the amount that Mr. Sanders will have in his checking account if the bank pays an annual interest rate of:
    a. 6%    b. 8%    c. 10%

12. Jane Doe desires to accumulate $20,000 for her retirement, which is eight years away. Ms. Doe prefers to deposit her savings at a savings and loan association in her community. The savings and loan pays 8% per annum. How many dollars would Ms. Doe have to deposit each year for eight years (assuming equal deposits each year, the first deposit to be made exactly one year from now) in order to reach her goal of $20,000?

**BIBLIOGRAPHY**    Since the topics of the first seven chapters are so closely related, one comprehensive bibliography covering all seven chapters is included at the end of Part One.

# RISK
# AND THE VALUE
# OF
# COMMON STOCK

4

## INTRODUCTION

The purchaser of common stock advances money for the stock with the expectation that the corporation will pay him or her future dividends. The dividends actually received may exceed those expected or, on the other hand, may fall short of expectations. It is the uncertainty with respect to the receipt of future dividends that reflects the riskiness of owning a particular common stock. Needless to say, some stocks are more risky than others because of differences in the degree of certainty attached to them.

This chapter is devoted to the development of general principles that govern the relationship between the riskiness of common stock and the price or value of that stock. The material is directed toward answering three questions:

1. What is the nature of the risk associated with holding a common stock?
2. What factors affect this risk?
3. How does the risk affect the price of common stock?

As you will see, we use an intuitive approach to answer these questions.

## THE MEANING OF RISK

*Risk* is one of those words that has many shades of meaning in everyday usage. We all think we know the meaning of the word, but most of us have difficulty developing a precise definition. If you think about the definitional problem for a moment, you will probably conclude that risky actions or alternatives are those with a relatively high probability of unpleasant consequences. There are many examples of risky actions or alternatives in our everyday lives. Skiing is considered risky because the possibility of injury is relatively great. Driving while hazardous conditions such as snow prevail is risky because of the relatively high possibility of personal injury and/or damage to the automobile. Risk and the possibility of unpleasant consequences go hand in hand.

The risk associated with the purchase of common stock is related to the possibility of unpleasant financial consequences. One possible unpleasant consequence is that *actual dividends will be lower than the dividends expected at the time the stock is purchased*. Those stocks for which we have substantial uncertainty about future dividend payments are considered more risky than those stocks associated with relatively certain cash flows to stockholders.[1] For example, the stock of American Telephone and Telegraph Corporation (AT&T) is less risky than the stock of Trans World Airlines (TWA). The telephone business is relatively stable and does not suffer from extreme fluctuations in revenues, costs, and, most important, dividends paid to stockholders; the airline industry is subject to greater fluctuations in revenues, costs, and dividends. Therefore, AT&T is perceived to be less risky than TWA.

## THE SOURCES OF RISK

The factors that affect the riskiness of a corporation's cash flows may be divided into two broad categories. *Business-risk factors* are those that affect the operating cash flows of the firm. This category includes literally thousands of factors that affect revenues, cost of sales, and administrative

---

[1]Statistical techniques for the measurement of risk are discussed in Appendix 4A.

costs. *Financial-risk factors* are those that are introduced by the type of financing used by the corporation.

Some business-risk factors are beyond the control of management—for example, inflation. When inflation affects revenues more than costs, the corporation's net cash flows are increased; and of course, vice versa. Business conditions, international conflicts, technological changes, changes in government policies, and many other factors are beyond the control of management. Management can only attempt to minimize such risks through the use of accurate forecasts and contingency planning.

Other business-risk factors are more amenable to control by management. Labor disputes, managerial turnover, equipment breakdowns, new-product development—these are business-risk factors because they affect the operating cash flows of the firm, but these can, to some extent, be controlled by the firm.

Financial-risk factors are related to the type of financing used by the firm. When the corporation finances itself through the use of debt rather than equity, the riskiness of the cash flows is increased. When debt is used, interest and principal repayment are fixed by contract with the creditors of the firm. Should the corporation be unable to meet these contractual obligations, creditors can take legal recourse against the firm. The failure to meet debt obligations can result in the imposition of limits upon management, replacement of management, or even liquidation of the company. The maturity of the debt obligations add another dimension to the financial risk. From the corporation's point of view, short-term debt is usually riskier than long-term debt, because the firm is obligated to repay the principal amount at an earlier date. It may have difficulties in refinancing or may experience higher interest costs upon refinancing. These points will be given greater attention at a later point in this book.

To summarize, the modern corporation is in a position of having uncertain future cash flows. The uncertainty of future cash flows of the corporation makes the cash flows to the stockholders uncertain. The riskiness associated with future cash flows is caused by many factors, both business and financial, and is the natural state of affairs in an uncertain world. As we will see in this chapter, such business and financial risk have an effect on the market price of common stock.

## RISK AVERSION

Most people try to avoid risk, especially when there is the possibility of large financial loss. For example, assume that you are asked to select one of the following opportunities. Which one would you choose?

- *Opportunity A:* At no cost, you can receive an asset that will provide either $50,000 or $0 at the end of one year. There is an 80% chance that you will receive $50,000. There is a 20% chance that you will receive nothing.

- *Opportunity B*: At no cost, you can receive an asset that will provide $35,000 at the end of one year. The payment is guaranteed by the U.S. government. It has a 100% chance of being paid.

Most of us would choose opportunity B, because we would be sure of receiving $35,000. Most of us would view the possibility of receiving the $50,000 as being too low compared to the certainty of receiving $35,000. Or, looked at from another angle, the possibility of receiving zero dollars is too great to make opportunity A attractive. Most of us try to minimize the possibility of the unpleasant consequence of our choice.

But believe it or not, some people would choose A rather than B. These people are atypical; they are less risk-averse than most of us. They see the chance of receiving an additional $15,000 as being sufficient to undertake the risk of receiving nothing.

It should be noted that everyone is risk-averse to some extent. For example, we could modify opportunity A in such a way that virtually no one would make that selection. Even the greatest risk taker would think long and hard before choosing opportunity A if the possibility of receiving $50,000 were 1 percent and the possibility of receiving nothing were 99 percent.

Risk aversion has important implications for the value of common stocks and bonds. *Other things being equal*, people are averse to riskier stocks and bonds. The greater the corporation's business and financial risk, the more uncertain the dividends associated with common stock, the more risky the stock, and the greater the investor's desire to avoid that stock.

The phenomenon of risk aversion does not imply that people will never take risks. What it does imply is that people will purchase riskier common stocks only if they are compensated for taking that risk. Investors will demand higher returns on a more-risky as compared to a less-risky security. Compare, for example, bonds issued by the U.S. Treasury and Chrysler Motors Corporation. The risk associated with Treasury bonds is minimal. Chrysler bonds, on the other hand, are relatively risky; Chrysler Motors has substantial business and financial risk, reflecting the fact that the firm has had difficulty maintaining its market share and has had its profits fluctuate considerably over the years. The prospects for this auto maker are cloudy. Bond buyers will not choose Chrysler bonds over Treasury bonds unless Chrysler provides a higher rate of return than Treasury bonds. Chrysler can and does sell bonds to the public, but only if higher returns are promised. Bondholders take a risk only if compensation for it is forthcoming.

## INVESTOR STRATEGIES FOR AVERTING RISK

Investors avert risk in two ways. First, some investors try to select securities that have relatively certain cash flows, hence a lower risk.[2] Those of us that are extremely risk-averse choose U.S. government securities, because such

---

[2]Hereinafter, the word *securities* signifies common stock, bonds, etc.

securities have no risk of default. The U.S. government could, if all else fails, simply create the money required to pay interest and principal on such securities. Those of us with little aversion to risk (usually called risk takers) may be willing to purchase common stock in a new high-technology firm. Such investment may have a high probability that no dividends will be paid in the future and that the stock may become worthless.

The second way the investor may reduce risk exposure is through a diversification strategy. In practice, very few investors are willing to place all their available funds in one investment, unless such an investment has a very low risk level. Intuitively, investors realize that "putting all their eggs in one basket" is a risky strategy. They spread their risk over a number of securities in order to minimize the effect of a negative event on a single security. For example, General Motors is a well-managed, financially strong corporation. But despite its good reputation, GM is susceptible to a number of unforeseen events that could impair the corporation's ability to pay dividends and/or interest. A sustained oil embargo, imposition of stringent auto pollution-control requirements, and other possibilities could adversely affect GM sales and thus cash flows. Thus, most investors are unwilling to hold just one single security, whether it be GM common stock or the security of any other organization.

Diversification does not eliminate risk; it is merely a *risk-minimization strategy*. One portion of the risk associated with holding common stock (referred to as *diversifiable* risk) can be eliminated through diversification, but another portion (nondiversifiable risk) cannot. Nondiversifiable risk is the risk common to all common stocks. If the economy moves into a severe depression, for example, the cash flows of most U.S. corporations would be negatively affected to some extent. Regardless of the diversification strategy pursued, the investor would expect to incur losses under such adverse conditions.

Risks particular to a single firm or a small group of firms may be diversified by the investor pursuing proper strategy. For example, the owner of a portfolio consisting of common stocks of many different corporations is relatively certain that managerial turnover will have only a limited effect on expected returns. Someone holding a portfolio of 50 different common stocks expects that the management situations of some companies may deteriorate, but also that those of other firms in the portfolio may improve—and that the unforeseen deterioration in one management situation will be offset by unforeseen improvement in others. The expectations will cancel each other out, and the investor has minimized the possible volatility of expected cash flows owing to management performance. The same situation applies to unforeseen changes in sales, costs, technological innovations, and many other factors. The holder of a well-diversified portfolio has to worry less about such factors than does the investor whose entire investment is committed to only one firm.

The investor attempting to minimize risks through the creation of a portfolio of common stock must apply some common sense in the selection of the stocks to include in the portfolio. As a general rule, the investor attempts to avoid the stocks of closely related corporations. Since firms in the same industry are likely to be affected in the same way by certain events (oil embargos, for instance), the risk-averting investor avoids concentrating the entire portfolio in one industry. Other factors too, such as corporate size and location, seem to have an effect on the performance of common stock, so the risk-averse portfolio would avoid concentration on firms of equal size and similar location. In the final analysis, diversifiable risks can best be minimized through the construction of a portfolio made up of the common stocks of corporations not closely related to each other.

For example, consider the two portfolios of common stocks presented in Table 4–1. Portfolio B has a relatively high degree of diversification and a relatively low level of risk. The group of stocks in portfolio A is more likely to be affected by a single unforeseen event (an airline strike, perhaps). This makes portfolio A relatively risky.

**TABLE 4–1**

PORTFOLIOS OF COMMON STOCKS AND DIVERSIFICATION

| Portfolio A (low diversification of risk) | Portfolio B (relatively high diversification of risk) |
| --- | --- |
| Braniff International | Braniff International |
| Pan American World Airways | General Motors |
| Trans World Corporation | Safeway Stores |
| American Airlines | BankAmerica Corporation |
| Eastern Air Lines | General Foods |

The discussion up to this point has tended to emphasize the positive aspects of portfolios—that is, that large losses may be avoided through the construction of a diversified portfolio. But we must also recognize that the possibility of large unforeseen gains is also reduced through portfolio construction. Some of the stocks in a diversified portfolio may very well exhibit dramatic increases in value. However, these "higher performers" will be offset, in all likelihood, by other stocks that have disappointing performances. The "winners" may be partially offset by the "losers," and vice versa. It is not possible to have one without the other. The minimization of risk through portfolio construction may result in lower returns than if a single high-growth stock had been selected. Portfolio holders settle for an average gain and a relatively low risk.

## COMPETITIVE-MARKET EVALUATION OF RISK

Even though investors are risk-averse, they frequently purchase risky securities in order to gain an extra measure of return. How much additional compensation do investors demand for additional risk undertaken? What is the price the market must pay in order to induce investors to take risk? Before developing a specific procedure for evaluating the price of risk, it is best to make a general reconnaissance flight over the ground to be covered and the underlying assumptions of the analysis.

The rate at which investors are compensated for taking risk—that is, the price of risk—is determined in a competitive market. Among certain other important attributes, the competitive market for securities has two salient features:[3]

1. In the competitive securities market of the United States, there are a large number of buyers and sellers of securities. This implies that individual transactions have no influence on price. Individuals or small groups of individuals are not able to manipulate the market for securities to their advantage, since they constitute only a very small part of the entire market.

2. In the competitive market for securities in the United States, information about particular securities is accurate, easily accessible, and rapidly disseminated. This implies that no one market participant has an informational advantage over others.

In short, the market for common stocks in the United States is a competitive market. The price established for an individual stock is an equilibrium price that clears the market. At this equilibrium price, there are no unsatisfied buyers or sellers. It is the price that best reflects the market participants' perception of the value of that stock. The price is not manipulated or controlled by a small group. It is established by informed and impersonal market forces. Monopoly profits on stock transactions are virtually nonexistent.

Another very important characteristic of the competitive stock market in the United States is its assumption that stocks are held in portfolios—that is, that stockholders hold portfolios of stocks. These portfolio holders are assumed to have eliminated all diversifiable risk in their respective portfolios. The competitive market for stocks will compensate stockholders for the nondiversifiable risk associated with holding a stock. No compensation is paid for the diversifiable risk associated with a stock, since our portfolio-holding stockholder has no such risk.

The equilibrium price of a common stock sold in the competitive stock market will be inversely related to the nondiversifiable risk of that stock. As suggested in Chapter 2, the market price of common stock can be viewed as the present value of future expected dividends. The more the nondiversifiable risk in the stock, the higher the discount rate used in computing the present value of future dividends, and the lower the stock price.

The discount rate used to compute the present value of the expected

---

[3]A more complete description of competitive markets is presented in Chapter 13.

*discount rate*

dividends from a specific common stock is known as the *required rate of return of the stockholders* ($k_s$). In finance, we talk about risky stocks as having relatively high required rates of return, and vice versa. Security-market participants will require relatively high compensation for taking relatively high nondiversifiable risks. Since the required rate of return of the stockholders becomes the discount rate in computing the present value of stock, high-nondiversifiable-risk stocks have high discount rates and low prices (assuming other things are equal).[4]

## REQUIRED RATES OF RETURN

The rate of return required by the competitive market ($k$) may be viewed as comprising a risk-free rate and a risk premium. The risk-free rate is the rate of return that security-market participants will demand in the absence of risk. That is, even when market participants are *perfectly certain* of future expected cash flows, they will demand a positive rate of return, the risk-free rate. This follows from the fact that present consumption has a greater utility than future consumption, and people demand compensation for the postponement of consumption. In a sense, the required risk-free rate of return represents the price of time, or the price of consumption postponement, and is independent of any uncertainty as to future cash flows.

Thus, the required rate of return may be expressed as follows:

$$k = \text{RFR (risk-free rate)} + \text{RP (risk premium)} \qquad (4\text{--}1)$$

Equation 4–1 helps us understand how required rates of return of individual securities are determined. For example, Table 4–2 contains information on four hypothetical common stocks traded in the competitive market. Note that the required rates of return are different for each of these stocks. This reflects the fact that the stocks possess different amounts of risk, and thus the market assesses different risk premiums. Note that the risk-free rate is the same for each stock, since it represents the "price of consumption postponement" at a given time and has nothing to do with the riskiness of individual stocks.

Using equation 4–1 as a frame of reference, we can now develop a general conceptual framework that will help us understand the factors involved in the security market's determination of the required rate of return for a specific security. Remember that this required rate of return is used as the discount rate in estimating security prices. The management of the corporation must understand these factors in order to maximize stockholder wealth.

---

[4]The mechanical relationship between discount rate and price has been discussed in Chapter 2. A more complete discussion of diversification is presented in Appendix 7A.

TABLE 4–2

### REQUIRED RATES OF RETURN FOR HYPOTHETICAL STOCKS

$$k_s = \text{RFR} + \text{RP}_s$$

| Stock | Risk-Free Rate (RFR) | Risk Premium (RP) | Required Rate of Return ($k_s$) |
|-------|------------------------|---------------------|-----------------------------------|
| D | 6% | 12% | 18% |
| E | 6% | 6% | 12% |
| F | 6% | 9% | 15% |
| G | 6% | 15% | 21% |

## RISK PREMIUMS

As we have seen, portfolios "average out" both the returns and the level of risk associated with holding securities (stocks, bonds, and so on). If an investor had many millions of dollars, the ultimate diversification could be achieved by the construction of a portfolio comprising a selection of all the securities available. The portfolio would consist of all the securities in the market, risky and less risky, and the amount invested in each security would be proportionate to the relative size of each issue. All diversifiable risk could be eliminated in this fashion, and the investor would earn a rate of return equal to the average return of the market.

Remember, however, that even the large market portfolio has some risk. Since the cash flows are not perfectly certain, the portfolio as a whole will have a risk premium. This situation is summarized in equation 4–2, in which $k_m$ is the required rate of return *of the market portfolio*.

$$k_m = \text{Risk-free rate (RFR)} + \text{Risk premium of market portfolio (RP}_m) \tag{4–2}$$

It is important to note that $\text{RP}_m$ exists because certain risks are nondiversifiable. For example, a severe depression would make the cash flows of all securities less certain, thus affecting the value of the entire portfolio. $\text{RP}_m$ represents compensation for nondiversifiable risk only, since the market portfolio has by definition no diversifiable risk. The relationship between the required rate of return of the market portfolio and nondiversifiable risk is summarized in Figure 4–1. Using the notation in the figure, equation 4–2 can be rewritten as follows:

$$k_m = \text{RFR} + (k_m - \text{RFR}) \tag{4–3}$$

The term $(k_m - \text{RFR})$ is the risk premium for the market portfolio, the compensation paid by the competitive market for the nondiversifiable risk.

The level of risk (and the risk premium) for the market portfolio reflects the fact that it is an average. Individual securities may have more or less

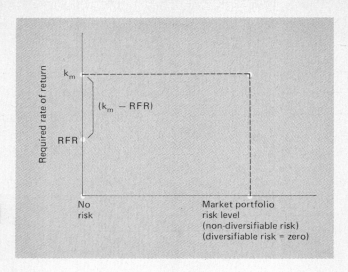

FIGURE 4-1

Market-Portfolio Risk
Premium

nondiversifiable risk than the market portfolio. For example, the electric utility industry is relatively insensitive to changes in economic conditions. During a depression, consumers continue to buy electricity, and the cash flows of electric utilities remain relatively constant. Thus, we would conclude that the risk premium for electric utilities is lower than that of the market portfolio. On the other hand, firms that manufacture machine tools are likely to be more sensitive to an economic depression. Cash flows of machine-tool firms are apt to be less certain than those of the market portfolio, resulting in a risk premium greater than the risk premium of the market portfolio.

## BETA—A MEASURE OF THE RELATIVE RISKINESS OF SECURITIES

Equation 4–4 provides the framework that will be employed to estimate the required rate of return of individual securities. Note that this equation is merely a more detailed version of equation 4–1.

$$k = RFR + (k_m - RFR)\beta \qquad (4\text{-}4)$$

where $(k_m - RFR)$ = the risk premium of the market portfolio

$\beta$ = the relative nondiversifiable riskiness of a security. It may be thought of as equal to:

$$\frac{\text{nondiversifiable risk of a security}}{\text{Risk of the market portfolio}}$$

$(k_m - RFR)\beta$ = the risk premium for *the individual security*

The β term in equation 4–4 is called *beta*. The concept of β is widely used in financial management and portfolio management.

For purposes of illustrating the meaning of equation 4–4, assume that the security market is such that the risk-free rate of return (RFR) is 6 percent, and the risk premium of the market portfolio ($k_m$ − RFR) is 10 percent. In such circumstances, a security with a beta of 2.0 (twice the nondiversifiable risk of the market portfolio) will have a required rate of return (k) of 26% [k = 6% + (10%)2]. A security with a beta of 0.5 (half the nondiversifiable risk of the market portfolio) will have a required rate of return of 11 percent [k = 6% + (10%)0.5]. If the nondiversifiable risk of a security is exactly equal to the risk of the market portfolio (β = 1), the stock will have a required rate of return of 16 percent [k = 6% + (10%)], which is the same as the required rate of return of the market portfolio.

Following the idea suggested by equation 4–4, we will proceed with the explanation of the required rate of return of specific securities by focusing on the following three factors:

1. The beta for a particular security. This is a measure of the riskiness of a specific security *relative* to the riskiness of the market portfolio.
2. The risk-free rate of return. This is the price of the postponement of current consumption.
3. The risk premium of the market portfolio ($k_m$ − RFR). This represents the degree to which the market is risk-averse.

Thus far, we know that high risk will be associated with high betas, high required rates of return, and low market prices for securities (other things being equal). But why do some securities have high betas (high risk) and others low betas (low risk)?

The nondiversifiable risk of a security is related to two factors:

1. The total variability of the expected returns associated with a particular security *relative* to the variability of the expected returns of the market portfolio ($\sigma_s/\sigma_m$), and
2. The correlation of the returns of the security to the returns of the market portfolio ($r_{s,m}$).[5]

The first source of relative riskiness ($\sigma_s/\sigma_m$) is relatively easy to understand. The standard deviation ($\sigma$) is a measure of variability. When $\sigma_s > \sigma_m$, the expected variability of the individual security ($\sigma_s$) is greater than the expected variability of the market portfolio ($\sigma_m$). Other things being equal, the higher this ratio, the greater the riskiness of the particular security.[6]

The second factor ($r_{s,m}$), while more difficult to understand, is equally

---

[5]The symbol r denotes the correlation coefficient; the symbol $\sigma$ denotes standard deviation; s and m refer to the specific security and the market respectively.

[6]The computation of the standard deviation and the correlation coefficient are discussed in Appendix 4A.

important. The relative riskiness of a security (β) is also a function of the correlation of the expected returns of the specific security with the expected return of the market portfolio. This relationship can best be demonstrated through the use of simple numerical examples.

Consider the relationship between two fictional stocks, U.S. Automobile Corporation and Central Motors Corporation. The expected returns of both stocks are sensitive to the price and availability of oil. Assume that you are planning to purchase two shares of stock. The alternatives open to you are to (1) purchase two shares of U.S. Auto, (2) purchase two shares of Central Motors, or (3) purchase one share of U.S. Auto and one share of Central Motors. The returns associated with each of the stocks are presented in Table 4–3. Note that the cash flows are related to the oil situation in exactly the same manner for each of the stocks. Furthermore, these stocks have the same expected cash flows and expected variability (σ).

**TABLE 4–3**

U.S. AUTOMOBILE CORPORATION AND CENTRAL MOTORS CORPORATION:
Expected Cash Flows per Share of Common Stock

| Oil Situation[a] | Cash Flows of U.S. Auto | Cash Flows of Central |
|---|---|---|
| Plentiful | $75 | $75 |
| Normal | $50 | $50 |
| Scarce | $25 | $25 |

[a]In this illustration, it is assumed that each situation has exactly the same probability of occurrence.

Since riskiness is related to the uncertainty associated with expected cash flows, the cash flows of each of the three possible portfolios can be computed as in Table 4–4, where we see that the expected cash flows are *exactly* the same for each of the possible portfolios. The reason we cannot reduce risk through diversification is that the returns of U.S.A. and C.M. have a perfect positive correlation. When two stocks are expected to behave in *exactly* the same way in given situations, diversification does not reduce the overall risk of the investment. The participants in a competitive market would have no preference for any of the three possible portfolios.

**TABLE 4–4**

U.S. AUTOMOBILE CORPORATION AND CENTRAL MOTORS CORPORATION:
Expected Cash Flows of Possible Portfolios

| Oil Situation | Two of U.S.A. | Two of C.M. | One of Each |
|---|---|---|---|
| Plentiful | $150 | $150 | $150 |
| Normal | $100 | $100 | $100 |
| Scarce | $50 | $50 | $50 |

Now consider the relationship between two stocks, U.S. Automobile and the Tempe Bicycle Manufacturing Corporation. Both these stocks are sensitive to the price and availability of petroleum. Assume that when gasoline is expensive and difficult to obtain, bicycle sales will increase and auto sales will decrease. The expected returns on the stocks of U.S. Auto and Tempe Bicycle are shown in Table 4–5. Note that although the stocks are related to the oil situation in opposite ways, each has the same expected cash flows and the same amount of expected variability ($\sigma$).

### TABLE 4–5

U.S. AUTOMOBILE AND TEMPE BICYCLE MANUFACTURING CORPORATIONS:
Expected Cash Flows per Share of Common Stock

| Oil Situation[a] | Cash Flows of U.S. Auto | Cash Flows of Tempe Bicycle |
|---|---|---|
| Plentiful | $75 | $25 |
| Normal | $50 | $50 |
| Scarce | $25 | $75 |

[a]In this illustration, it is assumed that each situation has the same probability of occurrence.

Table 4–6 illustrates what is really a remarkable phenomenon. The combination of two risky stocks can create a portfolio that has *absolutely no risk*. That is, a portfolio comprising one share of U.S. Auto and one share of Tempe Bicycle has no uncertainty in the expected cash flows. The investment will return $100 regardless of the oil situation. Therefore, the investor has been able to eliminate risk through diversification.

### TABLE 4–6

U.S. AUTOMOBILE AND TEMPE BICYCLE MANUFACTURING CORPORATIONS:
Expected Cash Flows of Possible Portfolios

| Oil Situation | Two of U.S. Auto | Two of Tempe | One of Each |
|---|---|---|---|
| Plentiful | $150 | $50 | $100 |
| Normal | $100 | $100 | $100 |
| Scarce | $50 | $150 | $100 |

In combination, Tables 4–4 and 4–6 tell us something that is even more important. The ability of a portfolio to diversify away risk will depend on the relationship between the expected cash flows of the stocks in the portfolio. If the returns on the stocks in the portfolio have a perfectly positive correlation, no risk is eliminated. If the returns on the stocks in the portfolio have a perfectly negative correlation, all risk can be eliminated through diversification. Of course, neither of these situations occurs with any frequency in the real world, but the information thus obtained can serve as a basis for a general statement about the correlation of expected cash flows and risk: *The higher the correlation between securities, the less of the total riskiness can be diversified away.*

This general statement is illustrated in Table 4–7. The expected returns of U.S. Auto and Central Motors were perfectly positively correlated (+1); therefore, no benefits were obtained through diversification. A moderate positive correlation occurs when the returns of stocks are expected to move in the same direction, but not in a systematic fashion. A moderate positive correlation will reduce some of the risks of a portfolio. A situation in which the returns were uncorrelated (tended to move independently) would result in even greater risk reduction. Negative correlation (returns expected to move in opposite directions) tends to reduce portfolio risks to even lower levels. Finally, the portfolio can be riskless if the expected returns of the stocks are perfectly negatively correlated, as was the case for U.S. Auto and Tempe Bicycle.

**TABLE 4–7**

CORRELATION AND DIVERSIFICATION OF RISK

| Nature of correlation among returns of securities | Amount of total risk that can be reduced through diversification |
|---|---|
| Perfect positive correlation (+1) | NONE |
| Moderate positive correlation | |
| Uncorrelated (0) | |
| Moderate negative correlation | |
| Perfect negative correlation (−1) | ALL |

The implications of this discussion for the relative riskiness of a particular security ($\beta$) are reasonably straightforward. A security whose returns are not closely correlated with the returns of other securities in the market (the market portfolio) will have a relatively small amount of risk, other things being equal. This low correlation (a low $r_{s,m}$) indicates that the forces affecting the uncertainty of the specific security are different (or of a different magnitude) from the forces affecting all other securities in the market (the market portfolio).

In summary, beta is a measure of the relative riskiness of a particular security. It is affected by the variability of the expected returns of a security relative to the expected returns of the market portfolio and the correlation of those expected returns. Mathematically, beta can be expressed as follows:

$$\beta = (r_{s,m}) \frac{\sigma_s}{\sigma_m}$$

(4-5)

The value of beta has been obtained for many securities. Most of the empirical work done on betas applies to common stocks. Table 4–8 shows the beta values of various common stocks traded in major exchanges. The data in this table reinforce intuitive notions as to the riskiness of different stocks. Public utilities are commonly considered less risky than airline companies. You can observe from the table that the riskiness of AT&T stock ($\beta = 0.75$) is lower than that of Eastern Air Lines stock ($\beta = 1.35$).[7]

### TABLE 4–8

VALUE OF BETAS FOR SELECTED COMMON STOCKS

| Corporation | Beta ($\beta$) |
|---|---|
| Amerada Hess | 1.00 |
| American Express | 1.35 |
| American Telephone & Telegraph | 0.75 |
| Atlantic Richfield | 0.90 |
| Bank of New York Co. | 0.70 |
| Boise Cascade | 1.30 |
| Caesars World | 1.25 |
| Control Data | 1.65 |
| Denny's Inc. | 1.45 |
| Eastern Air Lines | 1.35 |
| General Motors | 1.00 |
| Prentice-Hall | 0.85 |
| IBM | 1.05 |

Source: *The Value Line Investment Survey*, July 13, 1979.

## THE SECURITY-MARKET LINE

The concept that the required rate of return of a security is equal to the risk-free rate of return plus a risk premium has been summarized in equation 4–4:

$$k = RFR + (k_m - RFR)\beta$$

It is important to note that this is an equation for a straight line.[8] That is, the required rate of return for a security is assumed to be a linear function of the risk-free rate of return and the risk premium of the market portfolio ($k_m - RFR$).[9] Equation 4–4 can also be expressed in the form of a security-market line, as shown in Figure 4–2. Note that the relationship between a change in the required rate of return ($\Delta k$) and a change in beta ($\Delta\beta$) is constant over the entire range of beta. That is, a change of given size in the

[7]The procedures for computing beta are discussed in Appendix 14A.
[8]The general form for an equation of a straight line is $y = a + bx$. $a$ is the intercept in the $y$ axis—that is, the value of $y$ when $x$ is equal to zero; $b$ is the slope of the line—that is, the change in $y$ for every unit change in $x$.
[9]The linearity of the relationship is the subject of considerable debate. In this introductory text, we will assume the relationship to be linear.

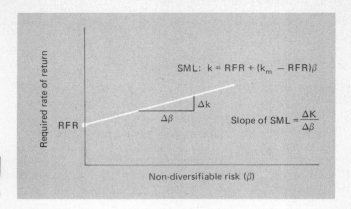

**FIGURE 4-2**

Security-Market Line

beta will have the same effect on the required rate of return regardless of the initial value of beta. This relationship ($\Delta k/\Delta \beta$), which is the slope of the line, may be viewed as the price of risk. That is, it shows how much the required rate of return increases as risk ($\beta$) increases.

The security-market line (SML) is widely used in finance and portfolio management. It is a convenient way of making a number of statements about the conditions in the competitive market at a given time. For example, the slope of the SML ($\Delta k/\Delta \beta$) indicates the extent to which the market is risk-averse. A higher price of risk (slope) indicates that market participants demand more compensation for taking on an additional unit of risk—that is, they are more risk-averse. This situation is depicted in Figure 4–3. In Figure 4–3(a), increases in $\beta$ are associated with relatively small increases in the required rate of return; the price of risk is relatively low (flat slope). In Figure 4–3(b), increases in $\beta$ are associated with relatively high increases in the required rate of return (steep slope); the price of risk is greater than that indicated by Figure 4–3(a).

The extent to which the market is risk-averse changes over time. In

**FIGURE 4-3**

Security-Market Lines
Reflecting Different
Levels of Risk
Aversion

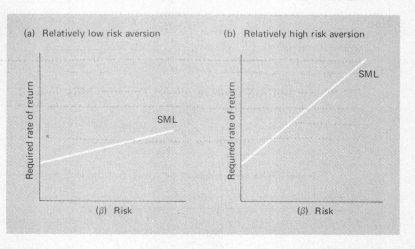

some years, the market is not very concerned about risk and demands a relatively low risk premium, as in Figure 4–3(a). At other times, the market is very risk-averse as in Figure 4–3(b), and thus demands a relatively high risk premium. Demographic factors, recent experiences, expectations about future economic conditions, and other social, political, and economic factors are responsible for such changes in the risk aversion of the market. The important point to remember is that the risk aversion of the market may change over time. Increases in risk aversion would result in an increase in the required rate of return, even though the risk of the security remains unchanged. It is also important to realize that the degree of risk aversion of the market is beyond the control of corporate management, even though it is a market phenomenon that affects the corporation.

To repeat, the risk-free rate of return (RFR) is equal to the rate of return on a riskless security. It represents the compensation for the postponement of consumption. In terms of the security-market line, the risk-free rate is the value of $k$ when $\beta$ equals zero (the y intercept).

In actual, "real-world" security markets, substantial volatility in security prices is introduced by changes in the risk-free rate of return. This is one of the key factors creating instability in bond and stock prices. The variability of the risk-free rate of return is illustrated in Table 4–9, where the rate of return of U.S. Treasury bills is used as a proxy for the risk-free rate, since Treasury bills are virtually risk-free.[10] As is shown, the "T-Bill" rate has substantial volatility from year to year, month to month, and even week to week. For example, the yearly average rate increased from 4.071 in 1972 to 7.041 in 1973.

Thus, in the real world, the risk-free rate of return changes frequently, causing shifts in the SML. Assuming that the price of risk remains constant (slope of the SML), an increase in the risk-free rate will shift the entire SML upward, thus increasing the required rate of return of the various securities in the market. Figure 4–4 illustrates the effect of a change in the risk-free rate on the required rate of return. $SML_0$ represents the original security-market line. The risk-free rate is 8 percent, and thus the required rate of return of the market portfolio ($\beta = 1$) is 12 percent. Now let us assume that the risk-free rate increases to 12 percent. Investors will recognize that they can earn the same rate (12 percent) both in Treasury bills and with the market portfolio. The Treasury bills, however, have lower risk. Therefore, investors will sell the market portfolio and purchase Treasury bills. Equilibrium in the market will not be restored until the rate of return of the market portfolio is greater than the risk-free rate. The difference between these two rates ($k_m$ − RFR) will be the price of risk for the market portfolio.

---

[10]Treasury bills are short-term debt issues of the U.S. government and have no default risk, since the U.S. government has the power to create money. In addition, there is an excellent secondary market for these securities. The short maturity of the bills minimizes price fluctuations that are due to changes in interest rates. The sole risk of these securities is the possibility of purchasing-power loss owing to inflation. Treasury bills are discussed in greater detail in Chapter 11.

TABLE 4–9

### VOLATILITY IN THE RISK-FREE RATE OF RETURN—
3-Month U.S. Treasury Bills, New Issues

| Weekly Volatility | | Monthly Volatility | | Annual Volatility | |
|---|---|---|---|---|---|
| Week Ending (1978) | % Rate | Month (1978) | % Rate | Year | % Rate |
| Dec. 2 | 9.166 | Sept. | 7.836 | 1977 | 5.265 |
| Nov. 25 | 8.696 | Aug. | 7.036 | 1976 | 4.989 |
| Nov. 18 | 8.593 | July | 7.074 | 1975 | 5.838 |
| Nov. 11 | 9.028 | June | 6.707 | 1974 | 7.886 |
| Nov. 4 | 8.454 | May | 6.430 | 1973 | 7.041 |
| | | | | 1972 | 4.071 |

Source: *Federal Reserve Bulletin*, various issues.

The upward shift in the SML is indicated in Figure 4–4 by SML′. Given that the slope of the SML (the risk aversion of the market) remains constant, the required rate of return of the market portfolio will now be 16 percent. Although there are many factors affecting the risk-free rate of return, the most powerful appear to be expectations about inflation and government policies. Individual business firms have no control over the risk-free rate of return.

Equation 4–4 $[k = RFR + (k_m - RFR)\beta]$ and the corresponding security-market line (SML) will be used in our discussion of the determination of prices for common stocks and bonds. We will show how changes in the risk-free rate, the risk aversion of the market $(k_m - RFR)$, or the riskiness of the stock $(\beta)$ will affect the required rate of return of a security, and thus the price of that security.

**FIGURE 4–4**

Security-Market Line— Changes in the Risk-Free Rate of Return

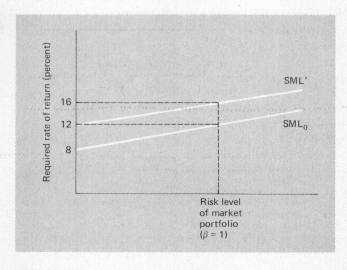

# EFFECT OF CHANGES IN BETA ON THE PRICE OF A PERPETUITY

The previous sections of the chapter discussed the factors affecting the required rate of return of a security. We now must turn our attention to the influence of the required rate of return on the market price of a security. First, we will discuss the effect of the required rate of return of bondholders ($k_d$) on the price of perpetual bonds.

You will recall from Chapter 2 that the equation for computing the present value of a perpetual bond is:

$$PV_{pb} = \frac{I}{k_d}$$

(2-4)

where $I$ is the annual perpetual interest payment, and $k_d$ is the required rate of return of the bondholders. As the riskiness of the bond ($\beta$) changes, the discount rate ($k_d$) will also change. Thus, the present value of the perpetual bond will be affected.

For purposes of illustration, assume we want to determine the present value of perpetual bond A. This bond was sold in 1976, at which time the security market conditions prevailing were as depicted in Figure 4–5. The risk-free rate was 8 percent, and the rate of return of the market portfolio 12 percent. In 1976, this bond was viewed as having a relatively low level of risk ($\beta = 0.5$), and thus the required rate of return of the bondholders was 10 percent.[11] Accordingly, the bond was sold for $1,000 in 1976, and had an annual interest payment of $100 (a perpetuity).[12]

Many factors have changed since the bonds were originally sold. By 1980, the firm that issued the bonds has changed considerably, and the level of the firm's nondiversifiable risk has increased. In fact, the bond's level of risk ($\beta$) has increased from 0.5 to 1.0. As shown in Figure 4–5, the required rate of return of the bonds also increased, to 12 percent.[13] Using the equation for computing the present value of a perpetual bond, the new value of the bond is:

$$PV_{pb}\ (1980) = \frac{I}{k_d} = \frac{\$100}{0.12} = \$833.33$$

Note that as the required rate of return increased, the price of the bond declined.

The price of bond A will not be at equilibrium until the actual rate of return to the bondholder is 12 percent. If the price had remained at $1,000, owners of those bonds would sell them and use the proceeds to purchase

---

[11]$k_d$ = RFR + ($k_m$ − RFR)$\beta$ = 8% + (12% − 8%)0.5 = 10%

[12]$PV_{pb} = \dfrac{I}{k_d} = \dfrac{\$100}{0.10} = \$1,000$

[13]$k_d$ (1980) = RFR + ($k_m$ − RFR)$\beta$ = 8% + (12% − 8%)1.0 = 12%

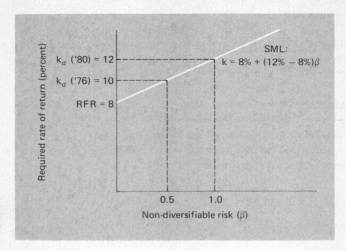

FIGURE 4–5

Security-Market Line

another corporation's bonds with the previous level of risk. They would dispose of bond A because it now has a higher risk level. These actions would reduce the market price of bond A, and thus increase the rate of return to the buyer. The market would continue this adjustment until the price of bond A declines to $833.33. The bondholder paying $833.33 earns an actual rate of return of 12 percent, which is equal to the required rate of return.

Note that if the riskiness of the bond had decreased (β goes down), the bond price would have increased. For example, if beta in 1980 had been 0.25, the required rate of return at that time would have been 9 percent ($k_d = 8\% + (12\% - 8\%)0.25 = 9\%$), and the price of the bond would have been $1,111 ($100/0.09). Thus, the change in price is inversely related to changes in the level of nondiversifiable risk (β).

## EFFECT OF CHANGES IN THE SML ON THE PRICE OF A PERPETUITY

In the preceding example, the security-market line did not change. The only factor that changed was the riskiness of the bond itself. But changes in the security-market line will also lead to changes in the price of perpetual bond A. For example, assume that the risk-free rate of return increases from 8 percent in 1976 to 12 percent in 1980, and thus the SML shifts as shown in Figure 4–6.

Note that we are going back to the original situation. The riskiness of bond A is reflected by a beta of 0.5. Furthermore, we are assuming that the increase in the risk-free rate will not affect the risk premium of the market ($k_m - RFR$). Thus, $k_m$ will increase to 16 percent. The new required rate of return for bond A can be computed as follows:

$$k_d = RFR + (k_m - RFR)\beta = 12\% + (16\% - 12\%)0.5 = 14\%$$

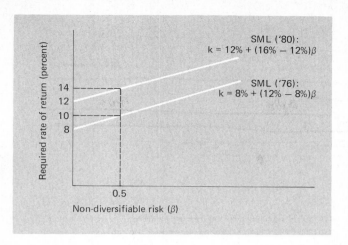

Therefore, the new price of bond A will change from $1,000 to $714.29. The computation would be as follows:

$$PV_{pb} = \frac{I}{k_d} = \frac{\$100}{0.14} = 714.29$$

Note that if the risk-free rate had declined rather than increased, the required rate of return of bond A would have declined and the price of the bond increased. That is, changes in the price of the bond are inversely related to changes in the risk-free rate of return.

Changes in the risk aversion of the market will also lead to changes in security prices. For example, as the market becomes more risk-averse (demands more compensation for taking risk), the risk premium for a given security will increase. This situation is depicted in Figure 4-7. In this example, the required rate of return of the market portfolio increased from 12 percent in 1976 to 24 percent in 1980. Note that the risk-free rate (8 percent) and the riskiness of the bond ($\beta = 0.5$) remain unchanged. Therefore, the required rate of return of bond A will be:

$$k_d = RFR + (k_m - RFR)\beta = 8\% + (24\% - 8\%)0.5 = 16\%$$

Perpetual bond A will fall in price from $1,000 to $625. The new price of bond A is computed as follows:

$$PV_{pb} = \frac{I}{k_d} = \frac{\$100}{0.16} = \$625$$

Note that if the risk aversion of the market had declined rather than increased, the required rate of return of perpetual bond A would have declined, and thus the price of the bond increased. That is, changes in the price of the bond are inversely related to changes in the risk aversion of the market.

Note once again that there has been no change in the riskiness of the

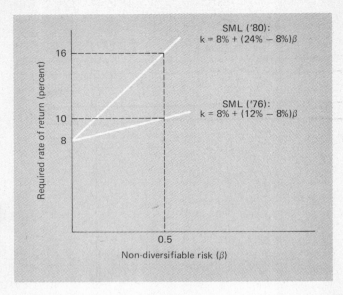

SML ('80):
k = 8% + (24% − 8%)β

SML ('76):
k = 8% + (12% − 8%)β

Required rate of return (percent)

16

10

8

0.5

Non-diversifiable risk (β)

**FIGURE 4-7**

Security-Market
Line—Change in the
Risk Aversion of the
Market

security (β remained constant) in the two previous examples. The price of the security changes because conditions in the security markets have changed. The management of the firm has no control over these market conditions, but it must understand the effect of market changes on the value of the firm's securities.

## REQUIRED RATES OF RETURN AND THE PRICE OF COMMON STOCK

It is now time to discuss the most important topic of the chapter—and perhaps of the entire book!—the effect of risk on the price of common stock. Before we proceed, however, let us review some materials from Chapter 2.

The price of common stock is greatly dependent on the future cash flows (dividends) and their expected growth. Chapter 2 developed formulas to be used to calculate the price of common stock under two different assumptions: (1) no growth, and (2) expected constant growth, in dividends paid on common stock. The formulas derived in that chapter were as follows:

| NO GROWTH | CONSTANT GROWTH |
|---|---|

$$\text{Price} = \frac{D}{k_s} \quad \text{(equation 2-7)} \qquad \text{Price} = \frac{D_1}{k_s - g} \quad \text{(equation 2-9)}$$

where $D_1$ = the expected dividend next year

$k_s$ = the required rate of return of the stockholder (the rate of return that could be earned on securities with the same risk)

$g$ = the expected constant growth rate in dividends

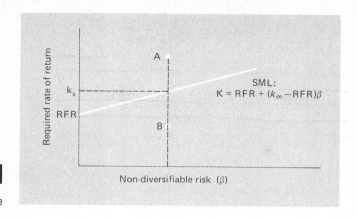

FIGURE 4–8

Security-Market Line

In Chapter 2, we assumed the required rate of return of the stockholders $(k_s)$ as given. At this point we will examine the determination of $k_s$ in detail.[14]

We are not saying that the actual rate of return that is earned on common stock is always equal to the required rate of return of the stockholders. However, there are mechanisms in the competitive market that will not allow these rates to be different for a significant period of time. Let us illustrate this point with an example. Figure 4–8 shows a situation in which two stocks, A and B, of identical levels of nondiversifiable risk have actual rates of return different from the rate of return required by the security market $(k_s)$ at that level of risk.

What will happen if stock A has a rate of return higher than the required rate of return for its risk level? Investors in the market will recognize that stock A has a higher rate of return than all other securities at the same risk level, and they will purchase stock A. With this increase in the demand for stock A, the market price will increase, and the increase in the price of A will reduce the rate of return to the buyer of stock. The upward pressure on the price of A will continue until it ceases to be "superior" to other securities with the same risk level. This will occur when the actual rate of return of stock A is equal to the market's required rate of return $(k_s)$ for the beta of the security.

Stock B has a rate of return that is lower than the required rate of return $(k_s)$ for its risk level. Investors in the market will recognize that stock B has a rate of return lower than all other securities with the same risk level, and they will sell stock B. This reduction in demand will lead to a fall in the market price and an increase in the actual rate of return. The decline in the price of stock B will continue until B has an actual rate of return that is no

---

[14]The valuation formulas above are based upon assumptions discussed in Chapter 2. They are used here to illustrate the effect of certain factors on stock price. As will be discussed in Chapter 14, these valuation formulas are not well suited for actual market computations. They are used here only because they are easy to understand.

longer "inferior" to that of other securities with the same risk level. This will occur when the actual rate of return of stock B is equal to the required rate of return, as specified by the stock's beta. Thus, the competitive market brings actual rates of return into equality with required rates of return for specific risk levels.

The required rate of return of common stock is related to the riskiness of that stock and the security market's reaction to that risk as summarized by the SML. The logical relationship between risk ($\beta$), the security-market line, and the required rate of return of a common stock is illustrated through the following example. We will assume that common stock Z has an expected annual dividend for next year ($D_1$) of $2 per share, and the dividend is expected to increase at a 5 percent constant annual rate. Let us also assume that the initial assessment of the risk of stock Z by market participants is equivalent to a beta of 0.8. The risk-free rate of return is 6 percent, and the rate of return of the market portfolio is 11 percent. Therefore, the required rate of return ($k_s$) for stock Z will be equal to:

$$k = RFR + (k_m - RFR)\beta$$

$$k_s \text{ of } Z = 6\% + (11\% - 6\%)0.8 = 10\%$$

The price of stock Z would be computed, using equation 2–9, as follows:

$$PV_Z = \frac{D_1}{k_s - g} = \frac{\$2.00}{0.10 - 0.05} = \$40$$

Next, assume that changes in business factors (for example, the dropping of a lawsuit against the firm, which would reduce uncertainty) lead to a reduction in the beta of the security from 0.8 to 0.4. With no changes in the SML, the required rate of return declines from 10 to 8 percent.[15] This change in the required rate of return of the stock will cause an increase in market price to $66.67. The computation of the new price would be as follows:

$$PV_Z = \frac{D_1}{k_s - g} = \frac{\$2.00}{0.08 - 0.05} = \$66.67$$

A decline in the nondiversifiable risk *reduces* the required rate of return and *increases* the price of common stock. A decline in the nondiversifiable risk of common stock leads to an increase in stockholder wealth, other things being equal. An increase in the nondiversifiable risk *increases* the required rate of return and *decreases* the price of common stock.

An increase in the risk-free rate leads to a higher required rate of return for stock Z, and thus a lower price. For example, if the risk-free rate changes from 6 to 10 percent, the security-market line shifts from $SML_0$ to $SML_1$. This change is illustrated in Figure 4–9. Note that the risk level of stock Z is a beta

---

[15] $k_s = 6\% + (11\% - 6\%)0.4 = 8\%$

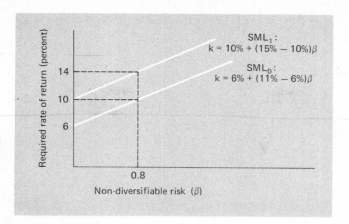

**FIGURE 4–9**

Security-Market
Line—Change in the
Risk-Free Rate of
Return

of 0.8, our original situation. The new equation for the security-market line $(SML_1)$ will be:[16]

$$k = RFR + (k_m - RFR)\beta = 10\% + (15\% - 10\%)\beta$$

Thus, the new required rate of return of stock Z will be equal to:

$$k_s \text{ of } Z = 10\% + (15\% - 10\%)0.8 = 14\%$$

The new market price of stock Z will be $22.22. The price would be computed as follows:

$$PV_Z = \frac{D_1}{k_s - g} = \frac{\$2.00}{0.14 - 0.05} = \$22.22$$

Increases in the risk-free rate of return (for example, during the 1970s), will reduce the price of common stock and stockholder wealth, other things being equal. Reductions in the risk-free rate will have the opposite effect.

Finally, increases in the risk aversion of the market will tend to drive down the price of common stocks. (The opposite is, of course, also true.) In our example, the change in the market risk aversion is illustrated by a shift from $SML_0$ to $SML_2$ in Figure 4–10. In this case, the required rate of return of the market portfolio $(k_m)$ has increased to 16 percent, with no change in the risk-free rate of return of 6 percent. The equation for $SML_2$ is:

$$k = RFR + (k_m - RFR)\beta = 6\% + (16\% - 6\%)\beta$$

With the beta of stock Z remaining at 0.8, the required rate of return of

---

[16]We assume no change in the risk aversion of the market $(k_m - RFR)$. Note that the beta of stock Z has returned to the original situation.

CHAP. 4 Risk and the Value of Common Stock

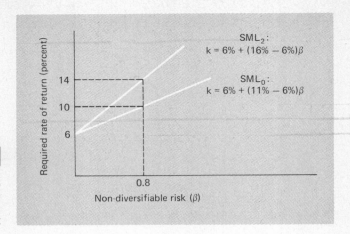

FIGURE 4–10

Security Market
Line—Change in the
Risk Aversion of the
Market

the stockholders will increase to 14 percent.[17] The new price of common stock will be \$22.22, computed as follows:

$$PV_Z = \frac{D_1}{k_s - g} = \frac{\$2.00}{0.14 - 0.05} = \$22.22$$

## RISK AND STOCKHOLDER WEALTH

Stockholder wealth is affected by the amount of nondiversifiable risk associated with a particular common stock and the rate of compensation demanded by the market for taking risks. Increases or decreases in common-stock prices indicate changes in stockholder wealth. At any given time, the level of stockholder wealth (and stock price) will be affected by:

1. The nondiversifiable risk of the stock (β), which is in turn determined by:
   a. The variability of expected cash flows to stockholders relative to the market portfolio, and
   b. The correlation of the particular stock's expected cash flows with the expected cash flows of other securities (market portfolio).
2. The current rate of compensation being demanded by the market for taking risk (SML), which is in turn determined by:
   a. The risk-free rate of return, and
   b. The current level of risk aversion of the market.

Changes in any of these factors will change the discount rate used to compute common-stock prices and thus stockholder wealth. Corporate management, in its quest for stockholder-wealth maximization, must understand the importance of these factors. The quest for stockholder-wealth

---

[17] $k_s$ of Z = 6% + (16% − 6%)0.8 = 14%

maximization implies that management must consider not only the cash-flow implications of various decision alternatives, but also their risk implications. Choosing alternatives that increase the riskiness of the firm, while increasing expected future cash flows, *may lead to a reduction in stockholder wealth*. In general, the profit opportunities must be large enough to offset the increase in risk, if stockholder wealth is to be increased. Restated in terms of equation 2–9, management must evaluate decision alternatives in terms of their effect on *both* expected future cash flows to stockholders ($D_1$ and g) and the required rate of return to stockholders ($k_s$).

$$PV_s = \frac{D_1}{k_s - g}$$

(2-9)

## RISK AND THE VALUE OF SMALL BUSINESSES

The relationship between risk and the value of small businesses is more difficult to analyze. In a general sense, we know that the greater the uncertainty of the future cash flows of the owners of a small business, the lower the value of that business, other things being equal. Thus, for small businesses, just as for large corporations, there should be an inverse relationship between risk and the owner's wealth.

However, there are important differences between the two cases. Most important is the fact that the equity of smaller businesses is not sold in a competitive market. The differences in the markets for these two types of equity are outlined in Table 4–10.

TABLE 4–10

DIFFERENCES IN EQUITY MARKETS

| Characteristic | Competitive Market for Common Stock | Market for Small-Business Equity |
|---|---|---|
| Nature of item sold | Large number of homogeneous units | Differentiated units |
| Number of buyers | Many | Limited |
| Number of sellers | Many | Limited |
| Available information | Large amount | Limited |
| Speed at which new information is disseminated | Rapid | Slow |

In the less competitive market for small businesses, it is possible that buyers of equity will demand compensation for *both* diversifiable and nondiversifiable risks. Market prices may reflect market imperfections and/or information advantages. In addition, the owners of small businesses may be unable to achieve the level of diversification available on the major stock exchanges. That is, owners and potential owners (who are limited in numbers) may be forced to commit a very large portion of their investment capital to a single firm. Since buyers of smaller businesses are forced not to be portfolio holders, they are taking additional risks. Presumably, these buyers will demand compensation for the additional risk. The higher rate of compensation will be reflected in higher required rates of return and relatively low values for owner's equity (other things being equal).

Thus, while it is possible to say that the risk and value of smaller businesses are inversely related, it is not possible to extend the analysis. The amount of diversifiable risk will vary from business to business, and will often require additional compensation. The security-market line, which represents the relationship between nondiversifiable risk and required rates of return, may not be appropriate for establishing the discount rate for small businesses. Given the present state of knowledge, such discount rates must be estimated on an ad hoc basis. This means that there are likely to be substantial differences of opinion about the value of any small business sold in such an imperfect market.

**SUMMARY**    Common-stock prices and stockholder wealth depend not only on expected future cash flows associated with the stock, but also on the riskiness of the stock ($\beta$). Our discussion in this chapter has proceeded along the following lines:

1. The risk of the stock is related to the uncertainty associated with future dividend payments. This uncertainty is introduced by business- and financial-risk factors.

2. Market participants are risk-averse and will acquire risky stocks only if they receive adequate compensation for the additional risk. In our competitive market, portfolio holders will demand compensation only for non-diversifiable risk (measured by $\beta$).

3. The security market's attitude towards risk is summarized by the security-market line. The required rate of return of a security is a function of (1) the risk-free rate of return, (2) the rate of return of the market portfolio, and (3) the level of risk (beta) of the security. The required rate of return can be summarized by the following equation:

$$k = \text{RFR} + (k_m - \text{RFR})\beta$$

4. The price of common stock and stockholder wealth are inversely related to both the required rate of return and the nondiversifiable risk of the stock. Relatively low levels of nondiversifiable risk result in relatively low required rates of return and, other things being equal, a relatively high common-stock price and stockholder wealth.

1. Give some examples of risky everyday activities, and explain why they are risky.

2. Collect information about the "Big 4" auto makers. What are the different sources of risk affecting these corporations? Which of these four corporations do you think has the most risky securities?

3. Can you think of any groups (say, 30-year-old doctors, or senior citizens) that tend to have above- or below-average amounts of risk aversion with respect to financial matters? Explain.

4. Explain how the rate at which compensation is paid for nondiversifiable risk is established.

5. Explain the meaning of diversifiable and nondiversifiable risk. Give some illustrations.

6. Explain how portfolios can minimize the risk taken by an investor.

7. Why does the competitive security market pay compensation only for nondiversifiable risk?

8. What is a competitive market?

9. Explain how the competitive security market establishes the required rate of return for an individual common stock.

10. Using the approach developed in this chapter, explain how a high rate of inflation is apt to affect the required rate of return on common stocks and stockholder wealth.

11. Using the approach developed in this chapter, explain how an increase in the risk aversion of the market will affect the required rate of return on common stocks and stockholder wealth.

12. Explain how the competitive market establishes a price for common stock. Give an illustration.

13. Discuss the relationship between changes in required rates of return and stockholder wealth. Assuming that cash flows are unchanged, what other factors can affect stockholder wealth?

14. Give a verbal explanation of the equation $k = RFR + (k_m - RFR)\beta$. Explain the meaning of each of the terms of the equation.

15. Explain why the term $(k_m - RFR)\beta$ is a measure of the risk premium of an individual security.

16. Why is a stock with a low $r_{s,m}$ likely to have a relatively small amount of nondiversifiable risk?

**PROBLEMS**

1. The returns of the common stock of the Johnston Corporation have a standard deviation $(\sigma_s)$ of 15%. The returns of the market portfolio of risky securities has a standard deviation of 10% $(\sigma_m)$. Calculate the riskiness of the stock if the correlation between the returns of the stock and the market portfolio is:
   a. +0.5
   b. +0.8
   c. +1.0

2. The returns of the market portfolio have a standard deviation of 8%. The correlation between the returns of the stock and the market portfolio is +0.8.

Calculate the riskiness of the stock if the standard deviation of the returns of the stock is:

a. 6%     b. 8%     c. 14%     $.8\left(\frac{.06}{.08}\right)$  $.8\left(\frac{.08}{.08}\right)$  $.8\left(\frac{.14}{.08}\right)$

3. You are planning to invest in common stocks. The following stocks and their potential cash flows are available in the market:

| Economic Conditions | Cash Flows of Stock F | Cash Flows of Stock G |
|---|---|---|
| Boom | $500 | $500 |
| Normal | $300 | $300 |
| Recession | $100 | $100 |

*(handwritten annotations: "1000", "600", "200" beside Stock F; "1000", "600", "200" and "1000", "600", "200" beside Stock G; "NO because they have +1 correlation")*

a. You can purchase any of these three alternatives: (1) two shares of F, or (2) two shares of G, or (3) one share of F and one share of G. What will be the potential outcomes of the portfolios' cash flows under the three possible economic conditions?

b. Have you been able to reduce the risk of the investment through diversification? Explain.

4. You are planning to invest in common stocks. The following stocks and their potential cash flows are available in the market:

| Economic Conditions | Cash Flows of Stock L | Cash Flows of Stock M |
|---|---|---|
| Boom | $500 | $100 |
| Normal | $300 | $300 |
| Recession | $100 | $500 |

Note: The probability of each economic condition's occurring is the same.

a. You can purchase any of these three alternatives: (1) two shares of L, or (2) two shares of M, or (3) one share of L and one share of M. What will be the potential outcomes of the portfolios' cash flows under the three possible economic conditions?

b. Have you been able to reduce the risk of the investment through diversification? Explain.

5. Assume that the American economy at present has the following characteristics: (1) The risk free rate of return is 8%, and (2) the rate of return of the market portfolio is 14%.

a. Show the equation and graphical representation depicting the security-market line.

b. Show the changes (in the equation and the graph) that will take place in the SML if the risk-free rate increases to 10%. Assume no change in the market risk aversion.

c. Using the original information, show the changes (in the equation and the graph) that will take place in the SML if the rate of return of the market portfolio increases to 16%. Is this change an indication of an increase or decrease in the risk aversion of the market?

*(handwritten beside problem 5:*
$k = 8\% + (14\% - 8\%)\beta$
$k = 10\% + (14\% - 10\%)\beta$
$k = 10\% + (16\% - 10\%)\beta$
increase *)*

6. The security-market line is represented by the following equation:

$$k = 6\% + (12\% - 6\%)\beta$$

a. Calculate the required rate of return of a security with a beta of 1.2.
b. Calculate the required rate of return of a security with a beta of 0.4.
c. Calculate the required rate of return of a security with a beta of 1.0.
d. Using your answer to part $a$, calculate the required rate of return of the security if the risk-free rate increases to 8%. Assume that the risk aversion of the market remains unchanged.

7. You own a perpetual bond that is expected to pay annual interest of $80 from now until infinity. The risk-free rate of return is 6%, and the rate of return of the market portfolio is 12%.
   a. Calculate the market price of the perpetuity if the riskiness of the bond is depicted by a beta of 0.5.
   b. Calculate the market price of the perpetuity if the riskiness of the bond is depicted by a beta of 1.2.
   c. What will be the effect on the market price of the bond (parts $a$ and $b$), if the risk-free rate of return increases to 8% and there is no change in the risk aversion of the market?
   d. What will be the effect on the market price of the bond (parts $a$ and $b$, RFR = 6%) if the rate of return of the market portfolio increases to 14%?

   *[handwritten: $\frac{80}{.09} = 888.8\overline{8}$]*
   *[handwritten: $6 + (12 - 6) \cdot 5 = 9\%, 8 + (.04) \cdot 5 = 10\%$]*
   *[handwritten: $\frac{80}{.132} = 606.06$]*
   *[handwritten: $6 + (12 - 6)1.2 = 13.2\%, 8 + (.04)1.2 = 12.8$]*
   *[handwritten: $A\downarrow, B\downarrow$]*
   *[handwritten: decrease $6\% \rightarrow (8\%)$]*

8. There are two perpetual bonds traded in the market. Bond A pays annual interest of $100 and has a beta of 1.2. Bond B pays annual interest of $80 and has a beta of 0.5. The security-market line is represented by the following equation: $k = 6\% + (14\% - 6\%)\beta$.
   a. Calculate the price of both perpetuities.
   b. Which bond, or bonds, would you buy if the market price of A were $600 and the market price of B were $700?

9. The stock of the Allied Corporation is actively traded in a competitive market. The market anticipates that dividends will be $5 per share and will remain constant in the foreseeable future. The current SML can be represented by the following equation:

$$k = 10\% + (14\% - 10\%)\beta$$

Calculate the market price of the stock of the Allied Corporation if beta is equal to:
   a. 1.0    b. 1.5    c. 0.5
Why are the results in parts $a$, $b$, and $c$ different?

10. The stock of the Christine Corporation is actively traded in a competitive market. The market anticipates that the dividend that will be paid next year ($D_1$) will be $5 and that the dividends will grow at a constant annual rate of 5% for the foreseeable future. The SML can be represented by the following equation: $k = 10\% + (14\% - 10\%)\beta$. Calculate the market price of the stock of the Christine Corporation if beta is equal to:
   a. 1.0    b. 1.5    c. 0.5

   *[handwritten: $\frac{5}{.14 - .05} = 55.56$]*
   *[handwritten: $5/.16^{-.05} = 45.45$]*
   *[handwritten: $14\%$]*  *[handwritten: $12\%$]*  *[handwritten: $71.43$]*

11. The American Manufacturing Corporation today paid a dividend of ($D_o$) of $5. The past growth rate has been 5% annually, and such growth is expected to continue in the future. The risk level of the firm is reflected by a beta of 1.5. The SML can be represented by the following equation:

$$k = 8\% + (14\% - 8\%)\beta$$

a. Calculate the market price of the stock of American Manufacturing.
b. Calculate the market price of the stock if the risk-free rate declines to 6% and there is no change in the risk aversion of the market (no change in the slope of the SML).
c. Using the original information (RFR = 8%), calculate the market price of the stock of American Manufacturing if the rate of return of the market portfolio increases to 16%.

12. National Heaters Corporation manufactures gas heaters. The riskiness of the cash flows is such that the corporation's beta is 1.0. The current dividend ($D_o$) of National's common stock is $2 per share. The market anticipates dividends will increase at an annual rate of 6%. The corporation is considering going into solar heaters and anticipates that this action would allow dividends to grow at an annual constant rate of 8%. The risk of the corporation, however, will increase; thus, beta will change to 1.5. Should the corporation, in its quest for stockholder-wealth maximization, enter the solar-heating field? Assume that the SML can be represented by $k = 8\% + (14\% - 8\%)\beta$.

$$\frac{2(1-.06)}{.14-.06} = \$23.50$$

$$\frac{2(1-.08)}{.17-.08} = 20.44$$

*don't change*

# APPENDIX 4A
## STATISTICAL MEASURES OF RISKINESS

As noted in the body of Chapter 4, the riskiness of an individual security ($\beta$) is related to the standard deviation of the expected returns of that security ($\sigma_s$) and the correlation between those returns and the returns of the market portfolio ($r_{s,m}$). This appendix is designed as a brief review of the statistical concepts of standard deviation and correlation.

### STANDARD DEVIATION

The standard deviation ($\sigma$) is a measure of dispersion—a measure of the variability of a population. For example, consider the student populations presented in Table 4A–1. The ages of the students in group A vary much more than the ages of students in group B. In this case, we base our observation about the dispersion of the two groups on the range of the ages observed between them. The standard deviation is a more precise method of measuring the relative variability of different populations. The standard deviation of ages in Group A will be higher than the standard deviation of ages in Group B. That is, the standard deviation indicates relative dispersion.

## TABLE 4A-1

DISTRIBUTION OF STUDENTS BY AGE
(Hypothetical)

| Group A | Group B |
|---------|---------|
| 60 | 24 |
| 55 | 23 |
| 45 | 23 |
| 44 | 22 |
| 30 | 22 |
| 25 | 22 |
| 25 | 21 |
| 22 | 21 |
| 22 | 21 |
| 21 | 20 |

The basic formula for computing standard deviations is presented as equation 4A–1. The steps involved in computing the standard deviation are outlined below it.

$$\sigma = \sqrt{\Sigma \, (x_i - \overline{x})^2 P_i} \qquad (4A-1)$$

where $\sigma$ = standard deviation

$x_i$ = the value of specific observations (age, dividend, etc.)

$\overline{x}$ = the mean value of all observations

$P_i$ = the probability of occurrence of each observation

In order to compute the standard deviation:

1. Compute the mean of the population $(\Sigma x_i P_i)$.
2. Compute the deviation from the mean for each observation $(x_i - \overline{x})$.
3. Square the deviation from the mean $(x_i - \overline{x})^2$.
4. Take a weighted average of the squared deviations from the mean, using the probability of each occurrence as the appropriate weights.
5. Take the square root of the sums of squared deviations.

Table 4A-2 illustrates the procedures for computing the standard deviation. The expected cash flows of two projects, X and Y, are presented in the illustration. A cursory view reveals that the cash flows of project Y are less volatile, and have lower dispersion, than those of project X. This same conclusion is reached by computing the standard deviation of both projects. The standard deviation of X ($\sigma_x = 109.5$) is greater than the standard deviation of Y ($\sigma_y = 44.7$). Therefore, we can conclude that the dispersion, and thus the risk, of the expected cash flows of project X are greater than the dispersion of the expected cash flows of project Y.[18]

### COMPUTATION OF THE STANDARD DEVIATION

#### Project X

| $x_i$ | $P_i$ | Step 1 $x_i P_i$ | Step 2 $(x_i - \bar{x})$ | Step 3 $(x_i - \bar{x})^2$ | Step 4 $(x_i - \bar{x})^2 P_i$ |
|---|---|---|---|---|---|
| 100 | 0.1 | 10 | $-200$ | 40,000 | 4,000 |
| 200 | 0.2 | 40 | $-100$ | 10,000 | 2,000 |
| 300 | 0.4 | 120 | 0 | 0 | 0 |
| 400 | 0.2 | 80 | 100 | 10,000 | 2,000 |
| 500 | 0.1 | 50 | 200 | 40,000 | 4,000 |
| | | $\bar{x} = 300$ | | (Average deviation)$^2$ =12,000 | |

Step 5 $\sigma_z = \sqrt{12,000} = 109.5$

#### Project Y

| $x_i$ | $P_i$ | $x_i P_i$ | $(x_i - \bar{x})$ | $(x_i - \bar{x})^2$ | $(x_i - \bar{x})^2 P_i$ |
|---|---|---|---|---|---|
| 200 | 0.1 | 20 | $-100$ | 10,000 | 1,000 |
| 300 | 0.8 | 240 | 0 | 0 | 0 |
| 400 | 0.1 | 40 | 100 | 10,000 | 1,000 |
| | | $\bar{x} = 400$ | | (Average deviation)$^2$ = 2,000 | |

$\sigma_y = \sqrt{2,000} = 44.7$

## THE CORRELATION COEFFICIENT

The correlation coefficient (r) is a measure of association. That is, it measures *how closely* one variable is associated (correlated) with another. Note that the correlation analysis is multivariate. The behavior of one variable is "explained" in terms of another variable. If changes in one variable "explain" all the variability of another, there is a perfect correlation between the two variables. If changes in one variable "explain" *none* of the variability of another, there is no correlation between the variables.

The correlation coefficient may be thought of as the ratio of the amount of variability in variable y explained by changes in variable x, to the total

---

[18]A larger standard deviation does not necessarily mean a greater amount of relative dispersion. This problem can be solved by the use of the coefficient of variation. This coefficient is equal to the standard deviation divided by the mean: $\dfrac{\sigma_x}{\bar{x}}$

## CORRELATION COEFFICIENT

$$\text{Correlation coefficient} = r_{x,y} = \frac{n\Sigma xy - (\Sigma x)(\Sigma y)}{\sqrt{n(\Sigma x^2) - (\Sigma x)^2}\,\sqrt{n[\Sigma y^2] - (\Sigma y)^2}}$$

Numerical Example:

| Occurrences | x | y | xy | $x^2$ | $y^2$ |
|---|---|---|---|---|---|
| n = 1 | 100 | 50 | 5,000 | 10,000 | 2,500 |
| n = 2 | 120 | 55 | 6,600 | 14,400 | 3,025 |
| n = 3 | 105 | 54 | 5,670 | 11,025 | 2,916 |
| n = 4 | 130 | 60 | 7,800 | 16,900 | 3,600 |
| n = 5 | 140 | 60 | 8,400 | 19,600 | 3,600 |
| Totals | 595 | 279 | 33,470 | 71,925 | 15,641 |

$$\text{Correlation coefficient} = \frac{5 \times 33,470 - 595 \times 279}{\sqrt{5 \times 71,925 - (595)^2}\,\sqrt{5 \times 15,641 - (279)^2}}$$

$$= \frac{167,350 - 166,005}{\sqrt{359,625 - 354,025}\,\sqrt{78,205 - 77,841}}$$

$$= \frac{1,345}{\sqrt{5,600}\,\sqrt{364}} = \frac{1,345}{\sqrt{2,038,400}} = \frac{1,345}{1,427.7}$$

$$= +0.942$$

variability in variable y: (Explained variation in y/Total variation in y). The formula for computing the correlation coefficient and a numerical illustration are presented in Table 4A–3.

Note that in this case, the correlation coefficient is +0.942. That is, almost all the variability in y is explained by the variability of x. This is a very unusual situation. Normally, correlation coefficients fall somewhere between 0 and 1. In other words, usually there is some correlation, but not a perfect correlation between variables.

Also note that the sign of the correlation coefficient may be either positive or negative (in this example, the sign was positive). A positive correlation indicates that as x increases, y increases. A negative correlation indicates that as x increases, y *decreases*. Mathematically, the correlation coefficient can fall between +1 (a perfect positive correlation) and −1 (a perfect negative correlation).

**PROBLEMS**   **1.** Calculate the standard deviation of the following distribution:

| Observation $(x_i)$ | Probability $(P_i)$ |
|---|---|
| 300 | 0.1 |
| 400 | 0.2 |
| 500 | 0.4 |
| 600 | 0.2 |
| 700 | 0.1 |

**2.** Calculate the standard deviation of the following distribution:

| Observation $(x_i)$ | Probability $(P_i)$ |
|---|---|
| $150,000 | 0.2 |
| $200,000 | 0.6 |
| $250,000 | 0.2 |

**3.** Calculate the correlation coefficient between the following cash flows:

| A | B |
|---|---|
| $300 | $200 |
| 400 | 250 |
| 600 | 350 |
| 200 | 200 |
| 400 | 380 |

**BIBLIOGRAPHY**  Since the topics of the first seven chapters are so closely related, one comprehensive bibliography covering all seven chapters is included at the end of Part One.

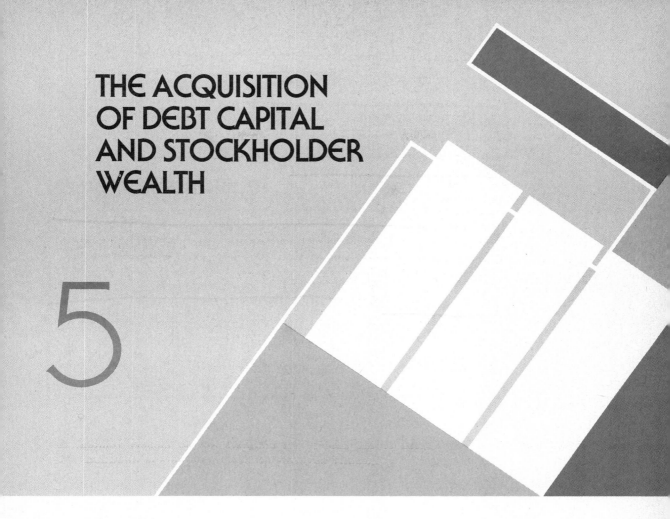

# THE ACQUISITION OF DEBT CAPITAL AND STOCKHOLDER WEALTH

5

## INTRODUCTION

Every asset acquired by a firm must be financed in some manner. Unless the funds are available internally, the choice is between debt and equity capital for such financing.

This chapter will examine the general guidelines that govern the corporation's acquisition of debt capital, and Chapter 6 will address the acquisition of equity capital. To decide between the two methods, we will use the principles developed in earlier chapters, evaluating each alternative in terms of its effect on the present wealth of the existing stockholders.

## TYPES OF CAPITAL

The corporate balance sheet provides a convenient framework for examining the various capital alternatives available to the firm. Table 5-1 is the actual balance sheet for Midland-Ross Corporation as of December 31, 1977. Midland-Ross is a diversified producer of industrial equipment, with sales of almost $500 million in 1977. The left-hand side of the balance sheet lists the assets that have been acquired by Midland-Ross and their current book values. The right-hand side represents claims against such assets. In a sense, the items on the left side are financed by the items shown on the right side of the balance sheet. An increase in total assets (left side) must be financed by

TABLE 5-1

### CONSOLIDATED BALANCE SHEET

Midland-Ross Corporation and Subsidiaries
December 31, 1977
(thousands of dollars)

| Assets | | Liabilities and shareholders' equity | |
|---|---|---|---|
| Cash | 6,510 | Accounts payable | 42,391 |
| Marketable securities | 39,237 | Advance billings on contracts | 17,122 |
| Accounts receivable | 73,135 | Accrued compensation | 16,140 |
| Inventories | 83,710 | Other liabilities | 11,189 |
| Contracts in process | 18,094 | Current portion of long-term liabilities | 2,878 |
| Prepaid expenses | 1,743 | Income taxes | 8,088 |
| Deferred income tax benefits | 2,929 | Total current liabilities | 97,808 |
| Total current assets | 225,358 | | |
| | | 5.75% sinking-fund debentures | 10,678 |
| Investments in associated companies | 10,067 | 8.00% promissory notes | 35,000 |
| Long-term notes receivable | 15,855 | 7.50% and 8.00% notes payable | 7,257 |
| Funds held for capital projects | 2,706 | 5.65% and 6.75% industrial revenue bonds | 7,155 |
| Intangibles and other assets | 11,723 | Other long-term liabilities | 11,857 |
| Total | 40,351 | Deferred income taxes | 6,898 |
| | | Total long-term liabilities | 78,845 |
| Land and improvements | 10,367 | Serial preferred, Series A | 3,805 |
| Buildings | 48,301 | Serial preferred, Series B | 8,419 |
| Machinery and equipment | 149,531 | Common stock | 27,381 |
| | 208,199 | Additional paid-in capital | 21,980 |
| Less: Allowances for depreciation | 95,387 | Retained earnings | 140,283 |
| Net property, plant, and equipment | 112,812 | Shareholders' equity | 201,868 |
| Total assets | 378,521 | Total liabilities and shareholders' equity | 378,521 |

an increase in liabilities or equities (right side). These liability and equity accounts represent the total capital raised by the firm over time.

Table 5-1 suggests that a corporation has a wide choice among capital alternatives. Midland-Ross, for example, has used five different types of long-term debt. In addition, two different preferred-stock issues and six different types of current liabilities are outstanding. All these sources of funds are in addition to stockholders' equity.

The "real world" of capital acquisition at the corporate level is extremely complex. Increases (or decreases) in assets are financed by many different liabilities and equities. Since each item in the balance sheet has peculiarities of its own, it is impossible at this time to discuss each account or each financing possibility in detail. Instead, this chapter attempts to develop a set of guidelines that can be used to evaluate various financing alternatives open to the firm.

| TABLE 5-2 |
|---|

HYPOTHETICAL BALANCE SHEET

| Assets | Liabilities and equity |
|---|---|
| | Current liabilities |
| | + Long-term liabilities |
| Current assets | = Total debt capital[a] (1) |
| | |
| | Common stock |
| | + Retained earnings |
| + Fixed assets | = Total equity capital (2) |
| Total assets | (1) + (2) = Total capital |

[a]In this book, the words *debt* and *liabilities* are used interchangeably. Thus, long-term liabilities are sometimes referred to as long-term debt. Total debt capital is identical to total liabilities.

Table 5-2 is a simplified balance sheet designed to illustrate the focus of our discussion. First, we will develop guidelines for making choices between total debt and total equity. This choice is most frequently encountered when management must choose between stocks and bonds. Table 5-2 shows that the decision is much more complicated than that. In fact, we are developing principles that govern the relationship between total liabilities of a corporation and total equity. A second set of guidelines, to be presented in Chapter 6, is more straightforward, since only two accounts are involved: common stocks (in which we include additional paid-in capital) and retained earnings. These guidelines apply to the situation in which the firm must decide between raising new equity through common-stock sales and raising equity through the retention of earnings.

## REQUIRED RATES OF RETURN ON DIFFERENT TYPES OF CAPITAL

Differences in the required rate of return on specific types of capital raised by the firm will depend on the security market's perception of differences in risks associated with each type of capital. Remember, risk refers to the uncertainty of future cash flows to the suppliers of capital. If, for example, the supplier of debt capital (lender) is relatively uncertain about receiving the interest and principal payments associated with a specific bond issue, that bond issue will be viewed by the market as relatively risky. The security market will require a higher rate of return if there is a greater uncertainty associated with expected future cash flows. As explained in Chapter 4, business factors (business risk) and financial factors (financial risk) are both related to the uncertainty of the expected future cash flows.

A security-market line confronting the hypothetical Bubba Corporation is presented in Figure 5-1. The Bubba Corporation is financed completely by equity (uses no debt). If business conditions change for the worse, there will be an increase in the risk level from $\beta_1$ to $\beta_2$. This increase in risk for Bubba Corporation will result in a higher required rate of return by the stockholders owning its common stock. The corporation's cost of acquiring new equity capital is increased accordingly.

## DEBT RISK COMPARED TO EQUITY RISK

From the point of view of the supplier of capital to a corporation, the purchase of a debt security (bond) is always less risky than the purchase of equity (common stock). There are two reasons for this difference in risk:

1. Before any cash can be distributed to the owners of common stock, all contractual interest and principal payments must be made on debt securities.

**FIGURE 5-1**

Security-Market Line

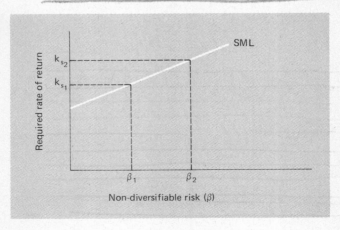

**FIGURE 5-1**

Security-Market Line

Suppliers of debt have first claim on the earnings of the firm. The suppliers of equity capital have a residual claim on such earnings. Furthermore, the dollar amount of interest payment is fixed in the contract.[1] Dividend payments are not fixed by contract.

2. If the corporation is liquidated, all the claims of debtholders must be satisfied before any payment can be made to the stockholders. If the firm should be liquidated, debtholders are much more likely to have their claims against the assets of the corporation satisfied than would equity suppliers.

The fact that debtholders have a "senior" claim against the earnings and assets of the corporation means that the debtholders' expected future cash flows are always more certain, and thus less risky, than those of the stockholders of a given corporation. Since debt is less risky, suppliers of debt have a lower required rate of return ($k_d$) than do suppliers of equity capital ($k_s$). This situation is shown in Figure 5-2.

The required rate of return on debt ($k_d$) is lower than the required rate of return on equity ($k_s$) because the risk taken by debtholders ($\beta_d$) is lower than the risk assumed by the stockholders ($\beta_s$). Therefore, the cost to the firm of obtaining debt capital will be lower than the cost of obtaining equity capital, *all other things being equal*.

$$k_d < k_s$$

## CHANGES IN COSTS AND STOCKHOLDER WEALTH

Before we discuss the relationship between the types of capital used by the firm and the present wealth of existing stockholders, let us review some basic ideas and assumptions about changes in cost and stockholders' present wealth.

Changes in operating expenses will affect the size of expected dividend payments. Assuming that revenues and risk remain constant, a policy

---

[1]There are some rarely used bonds (income bonds) for which this is not true.

**FIGURE 5-2**

Security-Market Line

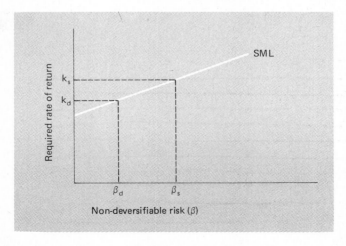

designed to lower expenses will increase profits, thus increasing potential and expected dividends. The increase in expected dividends will drive up the price of common stock and stockholders' present wealth.[2] Increases in expenses will have the opposite effect on the present wealth of existing stockholders.

Policies undertaken by the firm to reduce expenses may also alter the riskiness of the firm. In such cases, the dollar advantage of lower expenses may be offset by increases in the required rate of return of the stockholders caused by the higher risk level. It is possible that the increase in the required rate of return would be so great as to actually reduce the market price of common stock despite higher expected dividends. For example, assume that the Amy Corporation introduces a cost-cutting policy that involves the relocation of production facilities. It is estimated that this change will reduce costs and permit dividends to be increased from $6 to $9 per year. At the same time, the move involves considerable risk, since the necessary pool of skilled labor may not be available at the new location. What happens to the price of common stock will depend on exactly what happens to the required rate of return of the stockholders. The following three consequences are possible:

1. *Stockholder wealth unchanged.* If, under the original conditions, the firm had a dividend payment of $6 per year and a required rate of return of 10 percent, the stock price will be $60:[3]

$$\text{Price} = \frac{D_1}{k_s} = \frac{\$6}{0.10} = \$60 \text{ (assumes no growth)}$$

Now assume that the movement to a new location increases expected dividends to $9 per year. Furthermore, the security market's perception of the risk of the Amy Corporation is such that the required rate of return of the stockholders increases from 10 to 15 percent. The situation is shown in Figure 5-3, where $\beta_0$ is the original risk level, and $\beta_a$ is the risk level of Amy Corporation after the move. This change in the risk level causes the increase in the required rate of return from 10 to 15 percent. Under these conditions, the price of common stock will be unaffected by the move and will remain at $60:

$$\text{Price} = \frac{D_1}{k_s} = \frac{\$9}{0.15} = \$60 \text{ (assumes no growth)}$$

---

[2]There is a difference between profits and cash flows. It is possible for a firm to make a profit and still be unable to generate sufficient cash flows to pay dividends. This situation becomes less likely as the time horizon increases. However, assume in this chapter that profits are identical with cash flows, in order to simplify the presentation. This problem is discussed more fully in Chapter 9.

[3]The assumption of no growth is made in order to simplify computations. Other valuation formulas could be used with the same results.

FIGURE 5-3

Security-Market Line

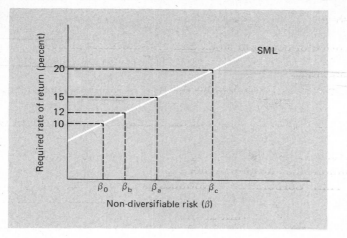

The tendency for the price of common stock to increase owing to the expected increase in dividends is exactly offset by the increase in the risk of Amy Corporation.

2. *Stockholder wealth increased.* If the increase in the required rate of return is smaller ( say, 12 percent) owing to a lower increase in risk (to $\beta_b$), the price of Amy's common stock will increase to $75:

$$\text{Price} = \frac{D_1}{k_s} = \frac{\$9}{0.12} = \$75 \text{ (assumes no growth)}$$

3. *Stockholder wealth decreased.* If the market perception of the risk of Amy Corporation ($\beta_c$) causes an increase in the required rate of return to 20 percent, the price of common stock will fall below the original $60 level, despite the expected increase in dividends. The new market price of the common stock of the Amy Corporation will be $45:

$$\text{Price} = \frac{D_1}{k_s} = \frac{\$9}{0.20} = \$45 \text{ (assumes no growth)}$$

The purpose of these examples has been to demonstrate that programs designed to reduce costs must also be evaluated in terms of their effect on the risk level of the firm. The goal of cost reduction may not always be consistent with the objective of maximizing the present wealth of the stockholders.

## THE DEBT RATIO AND STOCKHOLDER WEALTH

### DISREGARDING TAXATION FACTORS

Thus far we have shown that debt has a lower required rate of return than equity has for a given corporation, because the holder of a debt security has a lower risk level than a stockholder has. Since investors will require a lower rate of return on debt, debt will cost the firm less than equity. Remember, however, we are concerned with the maximization of stockholder wealth and not with cost minimization. There is significant evidence that the use of debt increases the risk level of the stockholder, causing a corresponding increase in required rates of return on equity. Thus, the use of debt has a positive result for stockholders, insofar as it reduces the costs to the firm. However, there is also a negative effect, in that the risk to the stockholders is increased. Remember that reductions in costs may reduce the stockholders' present wealth if risks are increased beyond an acceptable level.

Studies indicate that, *in the absence of corporate income taxation*, the required rate of return of the stockholders increases by an amount just sufficient to offset the cost saving introduced by using lower-cost debt. Under this condition, the present wealth of existing stockholders will be unaffected by increases in the proportion of debt used by the corporation. This situation is illustrated in Table 5-3. Under these hypothetical conditions, as the debt ratio ($\theta$) increases from 0.30 to 0.35, expected dividends increase from $10 to $11, since the use of additional debt reduces the costs of the firm by $1. However, using debt also increases the risk to common stockholders, and thus the required rate of return of common stock. In this case, the required rate of return increased from 20 to 22 percent, which is just enough to keep the price of common stock constant at $50.[4]

### TABLE 5-3

EFFECT OF CHANGES IN THE DEBT RATIO ($\theta$) ON THE PRICE OF COMMON STOCK[a]

| Debt ratio[b] ($\theta$) | Cost saving from use of lower-cost debt | Expected dividends per year | $k_s$ | Price of common stock[c] |
|---|---|---|---|---|
| 0.30 | $0 | $10 | 20% | $50 |
| 0.35 | $1 | $11 | 22% | $50 |

[a]This example is an illustration only. The exact offset of increased risk and cost saving is a matter of considerable controversy.

[b]The debt ratio ($\theta$) is defined as the market value of debt divided by the market value of all capital supplied to the firm (debt plus equity). The use of market instead of book values is discussed in Chapter 13. The debt ratio is computed as follows:

$$\text{Debt ratio } (\theta) = \frac{\text{Market value of debt capital}}{\text{Market value of all capital}}$$

[c]The price of common stock is computed by $D/k_s$ (assumes no growth).

----

[4]The proof of this proposition requires efficient-market assumptions and is beyond the scope of this book. See Kenneth J. Boudreaux and Hugh W. Long, *The Basic Theory of Corporate Finance* (Englewood Cliffs, N.J.: Prentice-Hall, 1977), pp. 181–90. It should be noted that this "exact balancing out" feature is controversial. The beginning finance student should focus on the general tendency.

The central point of this discussion is that increases in the debt ratio both reduce the cost of acquiring capital and increase the financial risk of the firm. *In the absence of corporate income taxation*, there is a tendency for these two factors to offset each other, leaving stockholder wealth substantially unchanged. In the absence of corporate taxation, there would be little pressure on management to use debt financing as a means of increasing stockholder wealth.[5]

## INCLUDING TAXATION FACTORS: AFTER-TAX COST OF DEBT TO THE FIRM

Market forces determine the required rate of return for debt suppliers of the firm $(k_d)$. However, the after-tax cost of debt to the firm is not the same as the required rate of return of the debtholders. Interest payments are tax-deductible to the firm; thus, they reduce the amount of income taxes paid by the firm. This situation is illustrated in Table 5–4, in which it is assumed that the required rate of return of debt is 8 percent, the corporation borrows $1,000, and the corporate income tax rate is 40 percent. As shown in the table, incurring $80 in interest payments reduces earnings after taxes by only $48. By allowing corporations to deduct interest payments, the government assumes part of the payment to the debt supplier.

**TABLE 5–4**

BAD NEWS CORPORATION AFTER-TAX COST OF DEBT

|  | Without debt | With debt | Difference |
|---|---|---|---|
| Earnings before interest and taxes | $1,000 | $1,000 | 0 |
| − Interest | 0 | − 80 | $80 |
| = Earnings before taxes | $1,000 | $920 | $80 |
| − Corporate taxes (40%) | − 400 | − 368 | − 32[a] |
| = Earnings after taxes | $600 | $552 | $48 |

[a]Interest tax subsidy.

In this illustration, the supplier of debt receives $80 from the corporation. Of this amount, $48 comes from the firm's earnings after taxes, and $32 from a reduction in tax payments by the corporation. The $32 may be called an interest tax subsidy (ITS), and the $48 is the after-tax dollar cost to the

---

[5]Corporations requiring very large amounts of capital may find debt financing attractive because the use of various types of financing broadens the base of potential capital suppliers. That is, the firm may be able to offer securities to individuals with different levels of risk aversions. This factor is likely to be of importance only when capital needs are very large.

corporation. As has been shown, the after-tax cost of debt to the corporation $(k_d^*)$ is lower than the required rate of return of the debtholders $(k_d)$. The actual relationship between the cost of debt and the required rate of return of the debtholders is presented in equation 5–1.

$$\begin{array}{c} \text{After-tax} \qquad \text{Required rate of} \\ \text{cost of debt} = \text{return of debtholders} \times (1 - \text{Tax rate}) \end{array}$$

$$k_d^* = k_d(1 - T) \tag{5-1}$$

Using equation 5–1, the firm can determine its after-tax cost of debt. For example, if the required rate of return of debt $(k_d)$ is 8 percent and the tax rate is 40 percent, the after-tax cost of debt $(k_d^*)$ will be equal to 8%(1 - 0.40), or 4.8 percent. It should be noted that payments to the suppliers of equity capital (dividends) are not deductible for income tax purposes. Thus, the required rate of return of the stockholders $(k_s)$ is exactly the same as the cost of equity to the corporation.

The interest tax subsidy (ITS) is that portion of the interest charge that is "paid" by the government. As illustrated in Table 5–4, the payment is not made directly by the government to the suppliers of debt capital. Instead, the firm pays the interest to the suppliers of debt, and the government allows the firm to pay less in income taxes. The net result of this indirect "payment" to debt suppliers is substantially the same as if the government made direct payments to debt suppliers.

The actual interest-tax-subsidy rate can be computed by multiplying the required rate of return on debt by the marginal tax rate. Equation 5–2 illustrates this computation:

$$\text{ITS(rate)} = k_d(T) \tag{5-2}$$

where ITS(rate) = rate of interest tax subsidy

$k_d$ = required rate of return on debt

$T$ = marginal tax rate

Therefore, for the Bad News Corporation, the ITS(rate) would be 3.2 percent (8% x 0.40). Note that as the tax rate increases, so does the ITS rate. If the tax rate were 100 percent, the government would wind up assuming the entire cost of the debt.

The effect of taxes and the ITS can also be illustrated with another numerical example. Table 5–5 shows who actually pays the interest to debt suppliers at various tax rates. As the rate increases, the interest tax subsidy increases, and so does the "cost" to the government. The cost of debt capital to the firm is reduced as the corporate income tax rate increases.

TABLE 5-5

### BAD NEWS CORPORATION

| Amount borrowed | $k_d$ | Required dollar return | Tax rate | After-tax $ paid by the firm[a] | Paid by the government (ITS) $80(T) |
|---|---|---|---|---|---|
| $1,000 | 8% | $80 | 40% | $48 | $32 |
| $1,000 | 8% | $80 | 60% | $32 | $48 |
| $1,000 | 8% | $80 | 80% | $16 | $64 |
| $1,000 | 8% | $80 | 100% | 0 | $80 |

[a]$80(1 − tax rate)

## EFFECT ON STOCKHOLDER WEALTH

So we see that in the real world, stockholders are not indifferent to the amount of debt employed by the firm because their present wealth is affected by the debt ratio of the firm. The present wealth of existing stockholders will be increased by the use of debt, because in the real world, *interest payments are tax-deductible*, and the after-tax cost of debt to the firm ($k_d^*$) is lower than the required rate of return of the debtholders ($k_d$). As the firm increases its use of debt, there are two sources of cost saving:

1. *Cost saving due to a lower required rate of return on debt than on equity.* This cost saving tends to be offset by increases in the required rate of return on equity, owing to the increased risk assumed by stockholders as the use of debt increases. Whether or not the increased risk precisely offsets the cost saving is a matter of controversy. The beginning student should focus on the tendency for increased risk to offset increased return.

2. *Cost saving due to the tax deductibility of interest payments.* This cost saving has no effect on the risk borne by the firm's stockholders, since it does not reflect any change in the firm's debt ratio. Since the tax deductibility of payments on debt reduces cost, it permits the firm to increase dividends. An increase in dividends without a corresponding increase in risk (leaving the required rate of return unchanged) will, by definition, increase stock price and stockholder wealth.

Thus, the use of debt tends to increase stockholder wealth, not because debt has a lower required rate of return than equity but because interest payments on debt are deductible expenses for corporate income tax purposes.

This situation is illustrated in Table 5–6, which is a continuation of Table 5–3. Note, however, that in Table 5–6 the additional cost saving that is due to the deductibility of interest payments is introduced. For purposes of illustration, the benefits to the firm owing to this deductibility have been assumed. It is assumed also that the additional saving will result in an increase in the expected dividends, from $10 in Table 5–3 to $11.50 in Table 5–6 (when $\theta$ equals 0.30). When $\theta$ equals 0.35, expected dividends will increase from $11 in Table 5–3 to $13.50 in Table 5–6. This second cost saving will not affect the risk taken by the suppliers of equity, and thus there is no offsetting change in the required rate of return of the stockholders ($k_s$). Hence, the price of common stock increases from $57.50 to $61.36 as $\theta$ increases, and thus the present wealth of the stockholders is increased. Increasing the debt ratio to 50 or 75 percent, or even higher, may result in greater increases in the value of common stock, because that portion of the cost saving that is due to the deductibility of interest payments will not be offset by increases in the required rate of return of stockholders. Common-stock prices may continue to increase, and thus greater stockholder wealth may be achieved.

## TABLE 5-6

### EFFECT OF CHANGES IN THE DEBT RATIO ON THE PRICE OF COMMON STOCK[a]

| Debt ratio | First cost saving, due to lower cost of debt | Expected dividend per year | $k_s$ | Price of common stock, interest not deductible[b] | Second cost saving, due to interest deductibility | Expected dividends per year | $k_s$ | Price of common stock, interest deductible[b] |
|---|---|---|---|---|---|---|---|---|
| 0.30 | $0 | $10 | 20% | $50 | $1.50 | $11.50 | 20% | $57.50 |
| 0.35 | $1 | $11 | 22% | $50 | $2.50 | $13.00 | 22% | $61.36 |

[a]Numbers selected are arbitrary and have been chosen for purposes of illustration only.

[b]Price $= \dfrac{D_1}{k_s}$ (assumes no growth)

This discussion has important implications for management. To illustrate, assume that the Poten Corporation is planning to acquire $1 million in assets. In raising the funds, the management of Poten must decide on the relative proportions of debt and equity capital. Our discussion thus far suggests the following preliminary guidelines:

1. Ths use of debt will result in cost saving greater than that required to offset increased risk to stockholders.
2. If management uses no debt ($\theta = 0$) it will be ignoring this lower cost of financing. The zero-debt alternative is inconsistent with management's choice to maximize stockholder wealth.
3. As $\theta$ is increased, low-cost debt is substituted for high-cost equity. For example, if $700,000 worth of low-cost debt is used, management will need only $300,000 of high-cost equity.

**4.** This suggests that management should select a very high level of θ or, taken to its extreme, use only debt. True, the risk to the stockholders will be greater at the higher level of θ. This increased risk will, however, be more than offset by cost savings. The net result will be an increase in common-stock price and in stockholder wealth.[6]

At this point in our analysis, we must conclude that the management of Poten, and the management of all other corporations, should be using very high proportions of debt capital in order to maximize stockholder wealth.

## ACTUAL DEBT RATIOS

One of our major objectives thus far has been to show the powerful market and tax-law forces driving the modern corporation toward the use of debt. To the extent that a corporation remains concerned with the present wealth of the stockholders, and that tax laws permitting the deductibility of interest continue, there will be a strong tendency toward the use of debt. The actual extent to which corporations use debt is presented in Table 5–7. These debt ratios are based on book rather than market values, and are thus not precisely comparable to θ as it has been discussed in the previous pages. The surprising feature of Table 5–7 is that the ratios of book debt to total capital are so low. Corporations may be able to lower capital costs by increasing debt. Why don't they?

TABLE 5–7

### TOTAL LIABILITIES AS A PERCENTAGE OF TOTAL CAPITAL, SELECTED INDUSTRIES
(Book Values)

| Industry | Total liabilities as a percentage of total capital |
|---|---|
| Coal mining | 50% |
| General building contractors | 84% |
| Dairy products | 52% |
| Tobacco manufacturers | 52% |
| Furniture and fixtures manufacturing | 50% |
| Newspapers | 41% |
| Ferrous metals industries | 47% |
| Office and computer machines | 50% |
| Electric services | 62% |
| Food stores | 60% |
| Hotels | 78% |

Source: Derived from *Almanac of Business and Industrial Financial Ratios*, 1978 Edition (Englewood Cliffs, N.J.: Prentice-Hall, 1978).

---

[6]As you will see at a later point in this chapter, there are other factors that offset the tax deductibility of interest payments on debt. These factors limit the extent to which firms use debt.

# FACTORS LIMITING THE USE OF DEBT

There are several reasons why firms limit the extent to which they incur debt. One important factor is related to the cost of bankruptcy. As the firm increases its debt ratio, the probability of its being unable to meet interest and principal payments is increased. Thus, the probability of bankruptcy increases, and this in turn offsets the advantages of debt.[7]

The tax-deductibility feature of interest payments is partially offset by the fact that effective personal income tax rates on interest income are higher than those on income from common stock.[8] This difference in personal income tax treatment essentially drives up the before-tax required rate of return on debt and tends to offset the corporate tax deductibility of interest payments. For any firm, the optimal debt ratio will reflect the relative importance of these two tax forces. There is a general feeling among economists (but no conclusive empirical evidence) that the advantages of tax deductibility of interest payments at the corporate level are great enough to overcome the unfavorable personal income tax treatment given to interest income. The beginning student should view the personal income tax treatment of interest income as a mild constraint on the firm's use of debt. Certainly, the tax disadvantage of interest income is not so great as to discourage the use of debt in its entirety.

Another factor that appears to limit the extent to which firms use debt relates to the objective of the firm. You will recall from Chapter 1 that the goal of maximizing the present wealth of existing stockholders is a constrained objective. Management pursues this objective within the bounds of certain social, legal, and organizational constraints. Management's survival in its present positions is probably one such constraint. If a firm goes into bankruptcy, the cost to top-level management will be very high. Managers may lose their positions and may face difficulties in obtaining similar jobs with other firms. These severe consequences to management may result in the development of "safe" policies that fall somewhat short of the maximization of stockholder wealth. The final result may be a lower-than-optimal capital structure.

Security-market imperfections may also contribute to lower-than-expected debt ratios. Such things as interest-rate ceilings and legal restrictions on the type of loans made by financial institutions may result in credit being unavailable to high-debt, high-risk firms. Or, if funds are available, the interest rates may exceed those that would have been

---

[7]See Appendix 5A for a more detailed discussion of bankruptcy cost.

[8]The lower effective rate on income from common stock is due to the fact that a substantial portion of common-stock income is received in the form of appreciation (increase) in stock price. The gain in stock price is considered a capital gain and, if the stock is held for more than one year, taxed at a lower effective tax rate. Appendix 6A presents a more detailed explanation of the personal income tax treatment of income received from common stock and from bonds.

established in a competitive market. This "loan-shark effect" suggests that debt markets for high-debt firms have too few suppliers of funds to be consistent with the competitive-market assumption. The imperfection of the market allows those few participants who do supply debt funds to charge higher-than-competitive rates, thus reducing or eliminating the advantage of debt. The net result may be that management will establish debt ratios below the level that would have been established in the absence of these market imperfections.

The preceding analysis suggests that for each firm there is an optimal debt ratio ($\theta$). The optimal debt ratio is defined as the debt ratio that maximizes stockholder wealth. At debt ratios below the optimal, management is failing to take full advantage of the tax-deductibility feature of debt financing. At debt ratios above the optimal, management has increased debt to such an extent that bankruptcy costs (and perhaps other factors) tend to outweigh the tax-deductibility advantage of debt. Thus, management must attempt to achieve an optimal debt structure in order to maximize stockholder wealth, as illustrated in Figure 5–4.

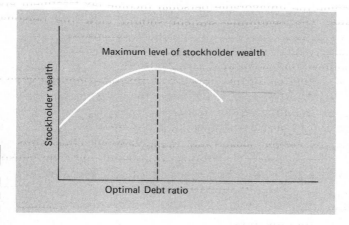

**FIGURE 5–4**

Effect of the Optimal Debt Ratio on Stockholder Wealth

## IMPLICATIONS FOR MANAGEMENT

There are powerful forces that compel the stockholder-wealth-maximizing firm toward the heavy use of debt financing. The first thing corporate management must realize is that it is possible to have too little or too much debt. Management concerned with stockholder wealth would be behaving inconsistently if it opposed the use of *any* debt; it should also recognize that too much debt may be contrary to the interest of the stockholders. Somehow, management must seek the elusive optimal capital structure.[9] This it can do

---

[9]Procedures used for estimating the optimal debt ratio are discussed in Chapters 14 and 18.

by studying the reactions of the security markets to changes in the debt ratio of the firm.

The optimal capital structure will be related to the level of business risk that characterizes the corporation. This business risk, combined with the financial risk induced by increasing the debt ratio, determines the probability of bankruptcy. Corporations with low business risk are likely to have relatively high optimal capital structures (debt ratios). For example, the percentage decline in the cash flows to public utilities during a recession is lower than that to automobile firms. Consumers cannot postpone the purchase of natural gas for home heating as easily as they can postpone the purchase of a new car. Thus, the cash flows of public utilities are usually less volatile than those of automobile manufacturers. This factor results in a relatively low level of business risk for public utilities and permits the public utility industry to have a higher debt ratio than the automotive industry.

Management must also recognize the crucial role played by corporate taxes in the determination of the optimal capital structure. The major advantage of debt is that debt-service charges (interest) are tax-deductible, whereas the service charges on equity (dividends) are not tax-deductible. Consider the implications for the optimal capital structure of any of the following changes in the tax laws:

1. *Elimination of corporate taxes.* Such a development would eliminate the major attraction of debt financing. The expected value of bankruptcy costs and the increase in the required rate of return of the stockholders would outweigh any advantages of debt. The corporation would reduce the use of debt.

2. *Changes in the corporate tax rate.* A reduction in the tax rate would tend to reduce the advantage of debt, and thus reduce the optimal debt ratio. Increasing the corporate tax rate would tend to increase the interest tax subsidy, and thus to raise the optimal debt ratio.

3. *Common-stock dividends becoming tax-deductible.* Tax deductibility for dividends on common stock has been proposed by various tax experts. Such a development would reduce the advantage of debt, and thus reduce the optimal debt ratio.

Management must realize that corporate taxation has a profound effect not only profits directly, but also on the capital structure of the firm. Changes in tax rates, or in the deductibility of interest or dividends, would change the advantages of using debt or equity.

## THE USE OF DEBT IN SMALLER BUSINESSES

The tax deductibility of interest payments, and thus the interest tax subsidy, apply as well to small as to big businesses. The nature of the American tax laws and economic system give added incentive to the wealth-maximizing smaller business to use a large proportion of debt capital. First, the required rate of return of both debt and equity capital tend to be higher for small businesses. This higher cost tends to increase the value of the interest tax subsidy. In addition, new equity capital and long-term debt capital are frequently unavailable to smaller firms. This forces smaller firms into the relatively high use of trade credit (accounts payable) and short-term bank loans. The net result of all these factors is very high debt ratios for small firms in the real world.

It must be noted that smaller businesses also have an optimal debt ratio. Beyond a certain level, increases in the debt ratio will increase the financial risk of the firm to such a point that the value of owners' equity declines. Below that certain level, increases in the debt ratio will result in an increase in the value of owners' equity. Thus, managers of small businesses must also search for the illusive optimal debt ratio.

**SUMMARY**     This chapter has shown that there are powerful forces that encourage the firm to raise capital in the form of debt:

   1. Firms are encouraged to use debt because interest payments are tax-deductible. In effect, the government provides an interest tax subsidy (ITS) to firms using debt capital. This is equivalent to the government's paying part of the interest cost.
   2. The fact that the required rate of return on debt is lower than the required rate of return on equity is not an important incentive to use debt. This follows from the fact that the lower required rate of return on debt is offset by the increased riskiness of common stock, leaving stockholder wealth unchanged. It is the tax deductibility of debt rather than its lower required rate of return that encourages its use.

While the tax deductibility of interest encourages the use of debt, other factors discourage the use of a high proportion of debt capital. The most important of these factors are:

1. The increased expected cost of bankruptcy
2. The fact that the effective personal tax rate on interest income is greater than that on income from common stock
3. Constraints on management
4. Security-market imperfections

As the firm increases the proportion of debt capital, the advantages of debt (tax deductibility of interest) begin to be offset by the disadvantages of debt. At some point, an optimal debt ratio is reached. The optimal debt ratio is defined as the point at which the advantages and disadvantages of debt are combined in such a way as to maximize stockholder wealth. It is management's task to achieve and maintain the optimal debt ratio, thus maximizing stockholder wealth.

1. Discuss the meaning of the words *debt* and *liability* as used in this book. Give several alternative ways of expressing the debt ratio.

2. Why is the required rate of return on debt lower than the required rate of return on equity? Why isn't the cost of debt to the firm equal to the required rate of return on debt?

3. Under what conditions would the reduction of a corporation's costs increase stockholder wealth? Explain.

4. How much debt is actually used by corporations? Would you expect more or less debt to be used? Explain your answer.

5. Why should the firm use debt financing rather than equity financing?

6. Discuss how personal taxes and market imperfections affect the decision to use debt capital.

7. The advantage of debt financing results from two factors: (1) lower debt cost because of the lower required rate of return on debt, and (2) the tax deductibility of interest. True or false? Explain your answer.

8. How and why does the expected cost of bankruptcy increase as the debt ratio increases?

**PROBLEMS**

1. The American Car Corporation wants to compute the required rate of return of its debtholders and its stockholders. The nondiversifiable risk ($\beta$) of the debt of the corporation is 0.8. the nondiversifiable risk ($\beta$) of the stock of the corporation is 1.2. The risk-free rate of return is 8%, and the rate of return of the market portfolio is 12%.
   a. Calculate the required rate of return of the debtholders.
   b. Calculate the required rate of return of the stockholders.
   c. Construct a security-market line showing the required rates of return of the debtholders and stockholders, as well as the nondiversifiable risk.
   d. Calculate the after-tax cost of debt and equity to American Car if the tax rate is 40%.

2. The Acme Manufacturing Corporation is considering moving its production facilities, primarily for the purpose of reducing labor costs. The current riskiness of the stock of the firm is depicted by a $\beta$ of 0.6. This move, however, will increase the riskiness of the firm, and thus $\beta$ will increase to 0.8. The move will also increase the expected dividends from a *constant* $5 per share (no growth) to a new *constant* level of $6 per share. The SML can be represented by the following equation: $k = 6\% + (10\% - 6\%)\beta$. Should Acme move the production facilities?

3. The before-tax interest payment of a corporation is $100,000 annually. Calculate the annual interest tax subsidy (in dollars) and the after-tax cost to the corporation, if the applicable tax rate is:
   a. 0    b. 20%    c. 40%    d. 60%

4. The riskiness of the bonds of the National Steel Corporation is depicted by a beta of 0.6. The SML is represented by the following equation: $k = 8\% + (13\% - 8\%)\beta$.
   a. Calculate the required rate of return of the bondholders.

b. Calculate the interest tax subsidy rate, if the corporation has a tax rate of 40%. (.11 × .40 = 4.4% $K_d^* = K_d(1-T) =$
   c. Calculate the after-tax cost of debt to National Steel. 6.6%

5. The Acme Corporation has the following balance sheet as of December 31, 1979:

| | |
|---|---|
| Current liabilities | $300,000 |
| Long-term liabilities | $800,000 |
| Total equity capital | $2,400,000 |

1,100,000  3,500,000
θ 31.4%

   a. Calculate the firm's debt ratio ( θ ) if the book values shown in the balance sheet are *exactly* the same as their market values.

# APPENDIX 5A
# Bankruptcy Costs and The Debt Ratio

There is much controversy about the issue of why corporations limit the amount of debt incurred. This appendix summarizes and simplifies these issues.

The most widely accepted reason for restricting the debt ratio is related to the costs of bankruptcy. As the firm's debt ratio is increased, the probability of bankruptcy also increases, because the firm must meet interest payments and debt repayments in accordance with contracts made with debtholders. When business conditions deteriorate, the firm may be able to reduce dividend payments, but it can not unilaterally reduce interest payments or debt repayments. This required outflow of cash in periods of deteriorating economic conditions may force the firm into bankruptcy. *All other things being equal*, the higher the debt ratio, the higher the costs associated with debt servicing, and thus the higher the probability of bankruptcy. Indeed, this increased probability of bankruptcy is the reason $k_d$ and $k_s$ increase as $\theta$ increases.

If the firm goes into bankruptcy, certain costs are incurred. These include such items as (1) legal and administrative costs, (2) increased management costs of dealing with high-debt-firm management, (3) the opportunity cost of lost business during bankruptcy, and (4) the opportunity cost of foregone investments. These are dollar costs that are paid out or not received by the firm owing to bankruptcy. As the firm increases its debt ratio, the expected value of these bankruptcy costs is increased. This point is illustrated in Table 5A–1. The expected value increases not because dollar costs increase, but because the probability of bankruptcy increases. The increase in the expected value of bankruptcy cost has the same effect on the present wealth of existing shareholders as has any other cost increase. An increase in expected bankruptcy costs reduces expected dividends and thus reduces the present wealth of existing shareholders.

TABLE 5A–1

THE MONK CORPORATION:
Expected Bankruptcy Costs and the Debt Ratio

| Debt ratio (1) | Probability of bankruptcy (2) | Dollar costs of bankruptcy[a] (3) | Expected value of bankruptcy cost[b] (2) × (3) |
|---|---|---|---|
| 0.25 | 0.10 | $1,000,000 | $100,000 |
| 0.50 | 0.30 | $1,000,000 | $300,000 |
| 0.75 | 0.60 | $1,000,000 | $600,000 |

[a]We have assumed $1,000,000 to be the dollar cost of bankruptcy.

[b]Expected value = Dollar bankruptcy cost × Probability of bankruptcy

An increase in the debt ratio ( $\theta$ ) has two effects on the corporation. On the one hand, costs are reduced owing to the tax deductibility of interest payments. On the other hand, costs are increased owing to the increased expected value of bankruptcy. The net result of these two opposing cost factors will depend on the level of $\theta$. Some economists believe that at low debt ratios, the costs saving due to the deductibility of interest outweighs the cost increases associated with the increased expectancy of bankruptcy. As $\theta$ increases, the expected bankruptcy cost may increase more rapidly than cost saving due to interest deductibility. At some level of $\theta$, these two cost factors will exactly cancel each other. The point at which the change in expected bankruptcy costs exactly equals the change in cost saving due to interest deductibility is known as the optimal value of $\theta$, or the optimal capital structure. Increases in $\theta$ up to the optimal capital structure will result in a net saving to the firm, and thus to the present wealth of the stockholders. Beyond the optimal capital structure, the change in expected bankruptcy costs exceeds the change in cost saving due to interest deductibility. At debt ratios higher than the optimal, the present wealth of existing stockholders is reduced.

This situation is illustrated in Table 5A-2. The Table shows the relationship between these two cost factors. Benefits due to interest deductibility and costs due to higher expected bankruptcy costs increase as $\theta$ increases. The net contribution to stockholders increases until $\theta$ equals 40 percent, which is the optimal capital structure. Below a debt ratio of 40 percent, savings due to the deductibility of interest outweigh higher expected bankruptcy costs. Beyond a debt ratio of 40 percent, the added savings due to the deductibility of interest are not enough to offset higher

THE DEMBO CORPORATION: NET RESULT OF CHANGES IN THE DEBT RATIO
(Hypothetical Data)

| Debt ratio $\theta$ | Cost reduction due to interest deductibility | Probability of bankruptcy | Cost increase due to expected bankruptcy[a] | Contribution to stockholder wealth |
|---|---|---|---|---|
| 0.0 | 0 | 0.0 | 0 | 0 |
| 0.10 | $70,000 | 0.01 | $ 10,000 | + $ 60,000 |
| 0.20 | $140,000 | 0.05 | $ 50,000 | + $ 90,000 |
| 0.30 | $210,000 | 0.10 | $100,000 | + $110,000 |
| 0.40 | $280,000 | 0.14 | $140,000 | + $140,000 |
| 0.50 | $350,000 | 0.24 | $240,000 | + $110,000 |
| 0.60 | $420,000 | 0.40 | $400,000 | + $ 20,000 |
| 0.70 | $490,000 | 0.55 | $550,000 | − $ 60,000 |
| 0.80 | $560,000 | 0.64 | $640,000 | − $ 80,000 |

[a]Dollar bankruptcy costs have been assumed to be $1,000,000.

expected bankruptcy costs. Thus, a 40 percent ratio of total debt to total assets is the optimal capital structure for the Dembo Corporation.

Figure 5A-1 shows the relationship between $\theta$ and the present wealth of existing stockholders. The present wealth of the stockholders is equal to *OA* dollars in the absence of debt. By increasing debt to 40 percent, the corporation can add *AB* dollars ($140,000) to the expected cash flows of the firm. Present wealth is maximized at the optimal capital structure ($\theta = 40\%$). Beyond the optimal capital structure, present wealth decreases and may even fall below the original level of OA dollars. For example, at a debt ratio of 80 percent, the expected cash flows to stockholders would decline by $80,000.

**FIGURE 5A-1**

The Dembo Corporation: Relation Between Debt Ratios and Present Wealth of Stockholders (Hypothetical Data)

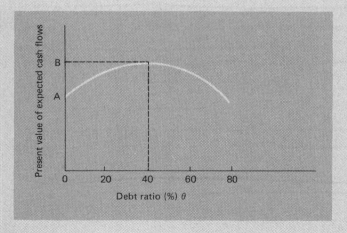

**PROBLEM**

1. Calculate the optimal capital structure of the Alina Corporation, given that the dollar bankruptcy cost is $10,000,000 and given the following information:

| Debt Ratio | Cost Reduction Due to Interest Deductibility | Probability of Bankruptcy |
|---|---|---|
| 0.0 | 0 | 0.01 |
| 0.1 | $1,000,000 | 0.03 |
| 0.2 | $2,000,000 | 0.10 |
| 0.3 | $3,000,000 | 0.25 |
| 0.4 | $4,000,000 | 0.40 |
| 0.5 | $5,000,000 | 0.60 |
| 0.6 | $6,000,000 | 0.80 |

**BIBLIOGRAPHY** Since the topics of the first seven chapters are so closely related, one comprehensive bibliography covering all seven chapters is included at the end of Part One.

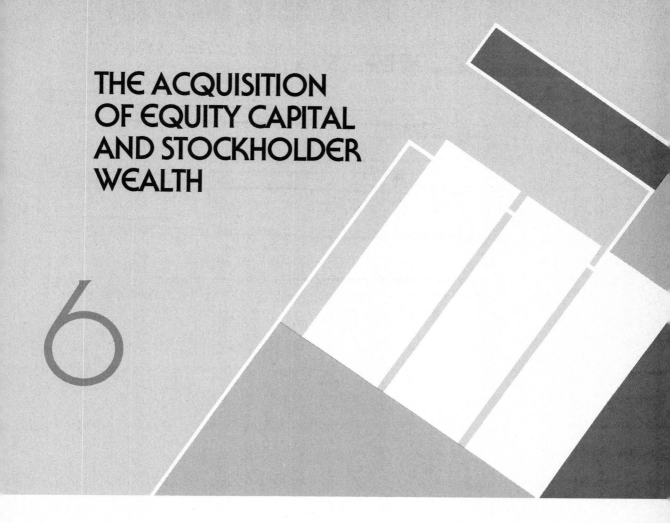

# THE ACQUISITION OF EQUITY CAPITAL AND STOCKHOLDER WEALTH

6

## INTRODUCTION

The corporation can raise additional equity financing in two basic ways.[1] First, additional equity financing can be obtained by selling new shares of common stock to either new or existing stockholders. The purchasers of these new shares forego either current consumption or alternative investment opportunities in order to purchase the new stock. Or the corporation can increase equity capital through the retention of earnings. The equity

---

[1]Preferred stock is an infrequently used type of financing with some of the characteristics of equity. The discussion of preferred stock will be postponed until a later chapter.

acquired through the retention of earnings actually comes from existing shareholders, since, when earnings are retained, they cannot be paid out in dividends to those shareholders. The foregone dividends represent a cost to the stockholder. The stockholders receive additional equity in the firm at the cost of dividends they could have used for consumption or investment.

The wealth of existing stockholders is affected by the method the firm uses to acquire additional equity capital. In the next sections of this chapter, we will show how existing income tax laws and market transaction costs encourage corporations to raise equity capital through the retention of earnings rather than through the sale of new common stock.

TABLE 6–1

THE CHUCKO CORPORATION: FINANCIAL INFORMATION

|  | Initial situation, situation A | Sell new stock, situation B | Retain earnings, situation C |
|---|---|---|---|
| **BALANCE SHEET** | | | |
| Current assets | $500 | $500 | $500 |
| Fixed assets | $500 | $600 | $600 |
| Total assets | $1,000 | $1,100 | $1,100 |
| | | | |
| Debt | $400 | $400 | $400 |
| Common stock | $200 | $300 | $200 |
| Retained earnings | $400 | $400 | $500 |
| | | | |
| Total liabilities & equity | $1,000 | $1,100 | $1,100 |
| **ADDITIONAL INFORMATION ABOUT THE FIRM** | | | |
| Net earnings | $100 | $110 | $110 |
| Number of shares | 10 | 11 | 10 |
| Dividends per share | $10 | $10 | $11 |
| Price per share | $100 | $100 | $110 |

ASSUMPTIONS

1. Net earnings are equal to 10% of total assets.
2. If new common stock is sold, $100 in earnings is paid to the stockholders in the form of dividends. No earnings are retained.
3. If no new common stock is sold, the firm retains $100 and pays no dividends.
4. The required rate of return of the stockholders is 10%. The change in the debt ratio does not affect this required rate of return.
5. No personal income taxes or transaction costs are incurred.
6. Dividends are expected to remain constant after the initial change. Therefore, the price of common stock would be equal to the expected dividend over the required rate of return of the stockholders: $P = D/k_s$.

## STOCKHOLDER WEALTH

We begin our comparison of new-common-stock financing and retained-earnings financing by evaluating each of these alternatives under the unrealistic condition of no personal income taxes and no transaction costs. Under these conditions, the stockholder of the firm should be indifferent as to the financing alternatives. In the following sections, we will show exactly how the personal income tax laws and the security market's transaction costs shift the stockholders from a position of indifference to a position of preference for retained earnings. Historically, the retention of earnings has resulted in a greater increase in stockholder wealth than has the issuance of new common stock.

Table 6–1 provides financial information on the hypothetical Chucko Corporation. In the initial situation (A), the present wealth of existing stockholders is equal to the value of common stock. If, for example, a single stockholder held the entire ten shares, total wealth for that person would be $1,000 (10 x $100). In situation B, new-common-stock financing is used , and a dividend of $10 per share is received by the stockholders. Since the dividend per share remains at $10, there is no increase in the market price of the common stock. The present wealth of the owners of the *original ten shares* of stock is increased only by the $100 received in the firm of dividends. There is no stock price appreciation.

When earnings are retained (situation C), no dividends are received for the one period. This permits the firm to increase assets without increasing the number of shares of stock outstanding. Since the firm now has more assets per share, future dividends per share and the market price of common stock are increased. The present wealth of existing shareholders is increased by $100. As the situation is summarized in Table 6–2, existing stockholder wealth is unaffected by the method of financing used by the corporation. This, of course, assumes that no personal income taxes and transaction costs are incurred.

TABLE 6–2

THE CHUCKO CORPORATION:
PRESENT WEALTH OF EXISTING SHAREHOLDERS

| | | |
|---|---|---|
| Present wealth (initial situation, A) | = 10 shares × $100 per share | = $1,000 |
| Present wealth (stock sale, situation B) | = 10 shares × $100 per share + $100 dividend | = $1,100 |
| Present wealth (retained earnings, situation C) | = 10 shares × $110 per share | = $1,100 |

## THE EFFECT OF PERSONAL INCOME TAXES

Thus far we have assumed that the stockholders do not have to pay any personal income taxes. This assumption is, of course, not realistic. There are potential taxes on the increase in the present wealth of the stockholders, and such taxes have important implications for the method used by the firm to raise equity capital.[2]

An increase in the present wealth of a stockholder represents income to the recipient, and exposes the stockholder to a current or future tax liability. However, the amount and timing of the tax liability will depend on the manner in which present wealth has been increased. When dividends are received, the entire amount is subject to taxation.[3] On the other hand, *only 40 percent of the appreciation in stock prices is subject to taxation.*[4] This exclusion of the part of the increase in wealth that is due to stock-price appreciation reduces the effective tax rate on such gains. In effect, income received in the form of higher stock prices is taxed at a lower rate than income received in the form of dividends. Dividend income is not only subject to relatively high taxes, but those taxes are payable for the year during which the dividends are received. Gains that are due to the appreciation in stock prices, however, are not subject to taxation until the stock is sold, thus reducing the present value of the tax liability. *The combined effect of excluding 60 percent of the stock-price appreciation and permitting the postponement of taxes on income from that appreciation causes a strong preference on the part of stockholders for raising equity through retained earnings.* Management use of retained-earnings financing reduces stockholders' tax liabilities and results in an increase in stockholder wealth.

The effect of this difference on the after-tax present wealth of the stockholder can be illustrated with an extension of our previous example about the Chucko Corporation, described in Table 6–1. We will make the following assumptions: (1) The shareholder is at a 30 percent marginal tax rate, (2) the shareholder sells all his stock after receiving the dividend or upon the increase in market price, and (3) the stockholder paid $100 for each share of common stock. Situation B assumed that the Chucko Corporation sold $100 in new common stock and paid $100 in dividends. Our hypothetical shareholder (owning all ten percent shares) will receive the $100 in dividends. His after-tax wealth will be $1,070, as shown in Table 6–3.

What will be the after-tax wealth of our hypothetical shareholder if the firm retains the entire $100 and pays no dividends (situation C)? The shareholder will receive no dividends and would thus have no tax liability

---

[2]Appendix 6A describes the tax treatment of income from securities in greater detail. However, it may be omitted without loss of continuity.

[3]We will ignore the $100 dividend exclusion in the discussion in this chapter.

[4]Assuming that the stock has been held for more than one year.

TABLE 6-3

CHUCKO CORPORATION:
STOCKHOLDER WEALTH, SITUATION B
(Selling New Common Stock)

| | |
|---|---:|
| Dollars from the sale of the 10 shares of stock | $1,000 |
| Income from the sale of 10 shares of stock | 0 |
| Less: Taxes on the sale of the stock | 0 |
| Plus: Income from dividends | 100 |
| Less: Taxes on dividends (30%)[a] | − 30 |
| Total stockholder wealth | $1,070 |

[a]We are ignoring the $100 dividend exclusion.

on dividends. However, if the shareholder sells the stock for $1,100, he will realize a $100 gain: price realized (10 x $110) less original cost of the stock (10 x $100). Only $40 of the gain will be taxed, and the tax liability will be 30 percent or $40, or $12. The after-tax present wealth of the stockholder will be $1,088, as shown in Table 6–4. Thus, given the simplyfing assumptions outlined above, the wealth of the stockholder is higher if management raises funds through earnings retention rather than through the sale of new stock. This very simple example illustrates the advantage of capital gains when compared to dividend income. The U.S. tax laws encourage corporations to retain earnings rather than sell new stock.

TABLE 6-4

CHUCKO CORPORATION:
STOCKHOLDER WEALTH, SITUATION C
(Earnings Retention)

| | |
|---|---:|
| Dollars from the sale of 10 shares of stock | $1,100 |
| Income from the sale of 10 shares of stock | 100 |
| Less: Taxes on the sale of stock (30% of $40)[a] | − 12 |
| Plus: Income from dividends | 0 |
| Less: Taxes on dividends | 0 |
| Total stockholder wealth ($1,100–$12) | $1,088 |

[a]Assumes that the stock has been held for more than one year.

## THE EFFECT OF TRANSACTION COSTS

The distribution of income to stockholders exposes both the individual and the corporation to various transaction costs. The amount of transaction costs will depend on several factors, including the manner in which income is distributed. There is a tendency for transaction costs to be lower when income is distributed through earnings retention rather than dividends, but as we will see shortly, this advantage of retained earnings may not hold for all stockholders at all times.

A corporation incurs various expenses when it sells new stock to the public. These are usually referred to as *flotation costs*. They are incurred in order to pay for the services of investment bankers, security salespeople, and government agencies. A typical corporation selling a $50 million stock issue will incur marketing and other costs of approximately $1.5 million. The flotation costs associated with new issues of common stocks depend in the size of the issue, the stability of the corporation, the available market for the stock of the firm, and the like. Owing to flotation costs, the corporation will have to sell more shares than it would have issued in the absence of those costs. The "extra" shares that must be issued to cover flotation costs will reduce the expected cash flows per share to the stockholders. This tends to keep the price of common stock below the level at which it would have been in the absence of the flotation costs. As a general rule, the present wealth of the stockholders will be higher if flotation costs are eliminated. The corporation can eliminate these costs by retaining earnings rather than issuing new common stock. Thus, earnings retention reduces cost and increases stockholder wealth.

The stockholder may also incur certain transaction costs, usually called *brokerage costs*, in the sale or purchase of common stocks. The extent to which the stockholder will incur brokerage costs will depend on the method used by the firm to raise equity capital *and* the stockholder's plans for the disposition of his income from common stock. To illustrate this point, assume two hypothetical stockholders:

1. One stockholder desires income for consumption purposes.
   a. If the firm retains income and pays no dividends, the stock price should increase and the stockholder could realize income by selling some shares. However, in this case, brokerage fees are incurred. That is, the stockholder must pay to sell stock in order to receive income.
   b. If the firm sells new common stock and pays dividends to existing stockholders, the stockholder receives income and has no brokerage costs. This is the preferred alternative for the stockholder desiring income.
2. The second stockholder does not desire present consumption but wants to reinvest income in a corporation with similar risk.
   a. If the firm sells new stock and pays dividends, the existing stockholder will receive those dividends. However, when the stockholder reinvests this income, brokerage costs will be incurred, thus reducing the amount that can be reinvested.
   b. If the firm pays no dividends and retains all earnings, the stockholder's equity in the firm will increase without payment of brokerage costs. This is the preferred alternative for the reinvestment-oriented stockholder.

It is clear that the corporation can maximize the present wealth of the stockholders by minimizing their brokerage costs. However, a general policy cannot be prescribed for *all* corporations, since different stockholders have different needs or desires for current consumption and reinvestment of earnings.

## CONSISTENT DIVIDEND POLICIES

Corporations wishing to maximize the present wealth of existing stockholders should pursue a long-term consistent dividend policy, because investors evaluate the dividend policy of a corporation before they buy stocks.

People in high income tax brackets are attracted to stock in corporations that retain a large proportion of their earnings, since this enables wealthy stockholders to minimize tax liabilities and to control the timing of tax payments. A corporation moving from a policy of earnings retention to a policy of high dividends will upset these people's investment plans and encourage them to dispose of their stock. This in turn will create a downward pressure on stock prices and be contrary to the goal of maximizing the present wealth of existing shareholders.

Dividend-seeking investors, on the other hand, will be unhappy with a corporation that moves from a policy of paying dividends to a policy of earnings retention. These people will be forced to incur transaction costs in order to receive current income, and will also be forced to assume unwanted risks. Dividend seekers are apt to dispose of stocks of companies that shift their policy in that direction.

In fact, corporations recognize that investors prefer a consistent dividend policy, and thus they change these policies infrequently and only after much deliberation. Most corporations set dividends by establishing a long-term dividend-payout ratio. Such a policy is illustrated in Table 6–5, which shows an earnings forecast by the Drago Corporation for a five-year period. In this case, the corporation decides to retain 75 percent of the five-year earnings forecast, and pay the remainder, or 25 percent, in dividends. Drago forecasts $6 million in earnings after taxes over the five-year period, thus making $1.5 million available for dividends. The corporation can stablize dividend payments by paying $300,000 in dividends each year. Retained earnings will fluctuate while dividends remain constant over the five-year period.

The illustration above can be varied in many ways. Higher or lower payout ratios can be used. Many corporations pursue a policy of gradually increasing dividends. The Drago Corporation could, for example, pay out less in 1985 and gradually increase the dividends over the five-year period, with the total for the period remaining at $1.5 million. In any case, the corporation should establish a policy, communicate this policy to existing and potential stockholders, and maintain the consistency of the policy, not changing it appreciably unless significant changes take place in the business environment. The consistency of policy will enable stockholders to minimize tax liabilities and brokerage costs and in turn facilitate the maximization of their present wealth.

TABLE 6-5

### DRAGO CORPORATION: DIVIDEND PLAN

| Year | Expected earnings after taxes | Dividend planned | Retained earnings anticipated |
|------|------|------|------|
| 1985 | $1,000,000 | $300,000 | $  700,000 |
| 1986 | 1,300,000 | 300,000 | 1,000,000 |
| 1987 | 1,200,000 | 300,000 | 900,000 |
| 1988 | 900,000 | 300,000 | 600,000 |
| 1989 | 1,600,000 | 300,000 | 1,300,000 |
| Totals | $6,000,000 | $1,500,000[a] | $4,500,000 |

[a]Dividends over five years = 25% of earnings over the five years.

Keep in mind also that prospective dividend changes are monitored closely by the stock market. It is generally believed that dividend decisions have great significance. For example, a reduction in dividends is often regarded by the stock market as a sign of financial weakness in the firm; therefore, dividend reductions are usually followed by a decline in stock price. Management recognizes this market tendency and is therefore very reluctant to reduce dividends. Many managers feel that a gradual growth in dividends has the most favorable effect on stock price. Many firms try very hard to maintain this gradual growth in order to signal the market that the prospects for the firm continue to be excellent.

## WHY PAY DIVIDENDS?

Thus far, we have suggested that the present wealth of stockholders is best served if the firm raises new equity capital through the retention of earnings rather than the sale of new common stock, because of the personal income tax laws and the flotation costs associated with issuing new stock. The effect of brokerage costs on present wealth is less clear. On balance, it appears that the interests of stockholders are best served when corporations raise new equity capital by retaining earnings. Indeed, actual corporate behavior is consistent with this observation. Table 6–6 shows the relative use of retained earnings and the sales of new common stock over the past three decades. For every $1 of equity raised through the sale of new common stock, $4.46 (more than 80 percent of new equity) was raised through earnings retention.

But if earnings retention is so attractive to stockholders, why are any dividends paid? Why doesn't the firm simply retain all earnings and permit stockholders to gain income through their disposal of common stock? Certainly, the tremendous tax advantages would suggest that such a policy would maximize the present wealth of existing stockholders.

First, not all investors are in high income tax brackets. The tax advantage of increasing present wealth through earnings retention may be

TABLE 6–6

EQUITY SOURCES FOR NONFINANCIAL CORPORATE BUSINESS, 1960–75 (In Millions)

| Year | Retained earnings | New equity issues[a] | Total increase in equity | Retained earnings as a % of total equity |
|------|------------------|---------------------|--------------------------|------------------------------------------|
| 1975 | 26,791 | 9,908 | 36,699 | 73 |
| 1974 | 29,476 | 4,097 | 33,573 | 88 |
| 1973 | 28,822 | 7,883 | 36,705 | 79 |
| 1972 | 20,577 | 10,992 | 31,569 | 65 |
| 1971 | 13,404 | 11,435 | 24,839 | 54 |
| 1970 | 8,068 | 5,694 | 13,762 | 59 |
| 1969 | 14,447 | 3,406 | 17,853 | 81 |
| 1968 | 17,551 | (159) | 17,392 | 101 |
| 1967 | 18,806 | 2,397 | 21,203 | 89 |
| 1966 | 21,863 | 1,259 | 23,122 | 95 |
| 1965 | 19,983 | (28) | 19,955 | 100 |
| 1964 | 15,417 | 1,145 | 16,562 | 93 |
| 1963 | 11,588 | (341) | 11,247 | 103 |
| 1962 | 10,367 | 369 | 10,736 | 93 |
| 1961 | 8,071 | 2,121 | 10,192 | 79 |
| 1960 | 8,766 | 1,365 | 10,131 | 87 |
| Total, 1960–75 | 273,997 | 61,473 | 335,470 | 82 |

[a]Negative figures indicate that for particular years, nonfinancial corporations repurchased more stock than they sold.

Source: Board of Governors of the Federal Reserve System, *Flow of Funds*.

offset by the transaction costs involved in the sale of common stock for current income. For example, assume that a person has a relatively low taxable income and is paying taxes at a marginal rate of 20 percent. If the person receives dividends of $1,000, taxes of $200 must be paid, and the after-tax increase in present wealth is $800.[5] If, on the other hand, earnings are retained by the company and present wealth is increased through an increase in stock price, the person desiring current income can sell $1,000 worth of the stock. Assuming the original cost of the shares sold is $500, the tax on the capital gain from the sale of the stock will be $40.[6] The after-tax change in present wealth of the stockholder would be $960 minus any brokerage costs of selling the stock. If these transaction costs exceed $160, the after-tax change in present wealth for dividends ($800) is greater than the after-tax change in present wealth for the sale of the stock. And, most important, the stockholder would have $1,000 less in stock for future

---

[5]We are ignoring the $100 dividend exclusion.

[6]The gain realized would be the selling price less original cost—in this case, $500. Taxes are imposed on only 40% of the gain. Therefore, the tax on this gain would be 20% of $200, or $40.

appreciation than before the sale. Under such circumstances, people would prefer to receive income in the form of dividends.

Of course, the situation outlined above is not likely to occur frequently in the real world. Few stockholders have tax rates as low or incur transaction costs as high as those used in the illustration. There must be other reasons why the firm pays dividends.

Unfortunately, there is no one really convincing factor that explains the payment of dividends. It is possible that the desire for consistent dividend policies outweighs the advantages of retaining earnings within the firm. Perhaps the informational content of dividends encourages their use. Perhaps stockholders misunderstand the implications of the tax laws and the different treatment given the dividend and capital gain income. Perhaps the certainty of dividends makes them attractive to stockholders. In any case, stockholders seem to desire some dividends and firms continue to pay them, despite the fact that personal income tax laws discourage the payment.

The desire to maximize the present wealth of existing stockholders is a very important factor influencing the corporation's dividend decision, but not the only one. Whether the corporation raises equity through the sale of common stock or retention of earnings, additional factors will play a part in the decision process. Present-wealth maximization takes place within additional limitations, established by the following factors:

1. *Legal restrictions.* Laws regulating corporations require that dividends be paid out of current or past earnings. Essentially, when dividends are paid, the earnings item in the balance sheet is reduced. The law prohibits this amount from becoming negative, and it also prohibits the reduction of other capital accounts to facilitate dividend payments.

2. *Contractual restrictions.* Frequently, corporations agree to restrict dividend payments until specified lenders are satisfied that the corporation's debts will be repaid. This provides additional protection to the lender and helps the corporation reduce its cost of debt.

3. *Stability of earnings.* Corporations with stable sales are likely to have a higher dividend payout ratio, since they can better predict future cash flows. This minimizes the risk of being unable to meet promised dividend payments and helps maintain a consistent dividend policy.

4. *Capital-markets access.* Smaller corporations, which have limited and costly access to capital markets in which common stock is sold, are more likely to retain earnings.

5. *Tax laws.* Corporations are not permitted to retain earnings solely to minimize the personal income tax of the stockholders. Basically, the firm can retain earnings only if the funds can be utilized for a business purpose. Retained earnings that do not meet this criterion may be subject to an Improper Accumulation Tax under Section 531 of the Internal Revenue Code. In practice, this provision is rarely employed by the IRS, and almost never against widely held corporations.

## EQUITY FINANCING IN SMALL BUSINESSES

The increase in owner's equity of small firms is also taxed differently from ordinary income received directly by the owner. Just as in the case of common stock, 60 percent of the income due to increases in the value of the firm is excluded from personal income taxation. Owners of smaller firms may also be able to postpone the payment of taxes by reinvesting in their businesses;[7] the tax laws strongly encourage smaller businesses to maximize the value of owner's equity through the retention of earnings.

It is difficult to evaluate the effect of the fact that small corporations attempting to offer a new issue of common stock face extremely high flotation costs. As a result of these costs, such companies either raise equity directly from a few large investors (without incurring flotation costs), or establish a high earnings-retention policy.

To the extent to which the common stock of smaller corporations is traded, brokerage costs are very high. Once again, however, the stockholders of smaller corporations tend to avoid this situation by making direct sales to investors.

When all the factors affecting earnings retention are considered, there is no reason to suspect that the forces generating it in smaller firms are any weaker than similar forces affecting large corporations.

**SUMMARY** A firm with a need of equity capital may raise that equity either by selling new common stock or by retaining earnings (not paying dividends). Personal income tax laws tend to encourage the retention of earnings, since income received in the form of stock-price appreciation is taxed at a lower effective tax rate than income received in the form of dividends. It is clear that personal income taxes of stockholders, as well as the brokerage fees they pay, can be minimized if firms pursue consistent dividend policies. In establishing a dividend/retained-earnings policy for the firm, management must weigh the tax advantage of retained earnings to stockholder wealth against the beneficial result of consistent dividends on stock prices.

Management pursuit of a policy with respect to capital acquisition implies more than the memorization of a set of simple rules. First, management must recognize its objective of stockholder-wealth maximization. Next, the complex tax laws and other factors affecting stockholder wealth must be analyzed carefully with reference to their effect on stockholder wealth. In the final analysis, management must subjectively balance out the advantages and disadvantages of these many factors.

---

[7]A more detailed discussion on this point is presented in Chapter 8.

1. How do personal income tax laws affect the decision regarding earnings retention vs. new common stock?
2. What is a consistent dividend policy?
3. Why is a consistent dividend policy important?
4. Explain why a stockholder desiring income for consumption purposes will tend to prefer a stock that pays dividends.
5. Explain why a stockholder desiring to reinvest his income will tend to prefer stock of a firm that retains a large proportion of its earnings.
6. Explain the meaning of the statement, "Dividend decisions have an informational content." How does the informational aspect of dividends affect dividend policy.
7. What are the implications of Table 6–6? How can the pattern presented in the table be explained?
8. Discuss the factors (other than taxes and transaction costs) that affect the decision whether to retain earnings or issue new common stock.

**PROBLEMS**

1. The Christine Corporation wishes to evaluate its current debt ratio ($\theta$) and to determine if the corporation has the optimal capital structure. The current debt ratio is 0.4. The required rate of return of the stockholders is 12%. The dividend expected next year ($D_1$) is $5, and the constant annual growth rate in dividends is 4%. The firm is considering increasing its debt ratio to 0.5. This increase will change the market's expectations as to future dividends: The expected dividend next year ($D_1$) will increase to $6, and the market will anticipate a growth in dividends of 5%. The stockholders, however, will increase their required rate of return to 15%, owing to the increase in financial risk.
   a. Calculate the market price of the stock of the Christine Corporation with the current debt ratio.
   b. Calculate the market price of the stock of the Christine Corporation with the proposed debt ratio.
   c. Should the Christine Corporation change the debt ratio? Explain.
2. The marginal tax rate of a stockholder is 30%. Calculate the effect on after-tax income of the stockholder of:
   a. Receiving a $1,000 dividend payment (ignore the dividend exclusion)
   b. Receiving a $1,000 long-term capital gain
3. The AnnCa Corporation has 100,000 shares outstanding. Jack Williams owns 1,000 shares in the corporation. The market price of AnnCa's common stock is currently $50 per share. The firm earns $500,000 during 1980, and is considering two alternatives: (1) Pay a $5-per-share dividend, or (2) retain the funds within the firm. If the firm pays the $5 dividend (alternative 1), the market price is expected to remain constant. If the firm retains the $500,000 (alternative 2), the market price of the stock is expected to increase to $55.
   a. Calculate the wealth of Jack Williams for both alternatives in the absence of personal income taxes and transaction costs.
   b. Calculate the wealth of Jack Williams for both alternatives in the absence of only transaction costs. Williams has a 40% marginal tax rate on ordinary income. (Ignore the dividend exclusion and assume that Williams plans to

liquidate his investment in AnnCa.) In addition, Williams bought the stock two years ago for $50 per share.

# APPENDIX 6A
# FEDERAL TAXATION OF PERSONAL INCOME FROM SECURITIES

As you are no doubt aware, the U.S. government imposes a tax on personal income.[8] Since the U.S. tax laws have a profound effect on personal investment decisions, this appendix is included to provide a brief review of the federal personal income tax laws as they apply to income received from securities.

The amount of taxes paid on income during a given year is dependent on three factors: (1) the filing status of the taxpayer, (2) the amount of income, and (3) the type of income received. Table 6A–1 shows the basic 1979 tax rates for taxpayers who are classified as either single or married.[9] A single taxpayer pays 70 percent on all taxable income in excess of $108,300. Married taxpayers must have taxable incomes of $215,400 before the 70 percent marginal tax rate is reached. Thus, the actual taxes paid on income will vary with the filing status of the taxpayer. In the examples that follow, it will be assumed that the taxpayer is married and filing a joint return. Keep in mind that a taxpayer with another filing status would be subject to different tax rates and thus pay a different amount of taxes.

Federal income tax laws differentiate between personal-services income and other forms of income. Personal-services income may be defined as that income received from physical or mental labor without the aid of significant capital equipment or capital funds. The most important types of personal-services income are wages and salaries. The maximum tax rate on personal-services income is 50 percent.

Income derived from financial or economic investments—for example, from dividends, interest, or stock-price appreciation—is not considered personal-services income, and is thus not subject to the 50 percent maximum tax rate. Such income, with some exceptions, would be taxed at the marginal tax rates shown in Table 6A–1. The 70 percent maximum tax rate may apply to this type of income.

Table 6A–2 shows the tax that a married couple, without children, would pay on $300,000 taxable income. Note that when the income is derived solely from wages and salaries rather than solely from interest, the total tax paid is lower, since the maximum tax rate of 50 percent is applied to taxable income in excess of $60,000.

---

[8] Most states and a few local governments also levy a tax on personal income.

[9] A taxpayer may also be classified as a "head of household." The tax rate applicable to these taxpayers is between those of single and married taxpayers.

## INDIVIDUAL TAX-RATE SCHEDULES APPLICABLE TO 1979 INCOME

FOR SINGLE TAXPAYERS, if amount of taxable income is:[a]

| Over: | But not over: | Then tax is: | | Of excess over: |
|---|---|---|---|---|
| $2,300 | $3,400 | $0 plus 14% | | $2,300 |
| $3,400 | $4,400 | $154 | 16% | $3,400 |
| $4,400 | $6,500 | $314 | 18% | $4,400 |
| $6,500 | $8,500 | $692 | 19% | $6,500 |
| $8,500 | $10,800 | $1,072 | 21% | $8,500 |
| $10,800 | $12,900 | $1,555 | 24% | $10,800 |
| $12,900 | $15,000 | $2,059 | 26% | $12,900 |
| $15,000 | $18,200 | $2,605 | 30% | $15,000 |
| $18,200 | $23,500 | $3,565 | 34% | $18,200 |
| $23,500 | $28,800 | $5,367 | 39% | $23,500 |
| $28,800 | $34,100 | $7,434 | 44% | $28,800 |
| $34,100 | $41,500 | $9,766 | 49% | $34,100 |
| $41,500 | $55,300 | $13,392 | 55% | $41,500 |
| $55,300 | $81,800 | $20,982 | 63% | $55,300 |
| $81,800 | $108,300 | $37,677 | 68% | $81,800 |
| $108,300 | | $55,697 | 70% | $108,300 |

FOR MARRIED TAXPAYERS FILING JOINT RETURNS, if amount of taxable income is:[a]

| Over: | But not over: | Then tax is: | | Of excess over: |
|---|---|---|---|---|
| $3,400 | $5,500 | $0 plus 14% | | $3,400 |
| $5,500 | $7,600 | $294 | 16% | $5,500 |
| $7,600 | $11,900 | $630 | 18% | $7,600 |
| $11,900 | $16,000 | $1,404 | 21% | $11,900 |
| $16,000 | $20,200 | $2,265 | 24% | $16,000 |
| $20,200 | $24,600 | $3,273 | 28% | $20,200 |
| $24,600 | $29,900 | $4,505 | 32% | $24,600 |
| $29,900 | $35,200 | $6,201 | 37% | $29,900 |
| $35,200 | $45,800 | $8,162 | 43% | $35,200 |
| $45,800 | $60,000 | $12,720 | 49% | $45,800 |
| $60,000 | $85,600 | $19,678 | 54% | $60,000 |
| $85,600 | $109,400 | $33,502 | 59% | $85,600 |
| $109,400 | $162,400 | $47,544 | 64% | $109,400 |
| $162,400 | $215,400 | $81,464 | 68% | $162,400 |
| $215,400 | | $117,504 | 70% | $215,400 |

[a]Taxable income equals adjusted gross income *minus* personal exemptions and *minus* any itemized deductions that exceed the zero-bracket amount (formerly called the standard deduction). The zero-bracket amount is $2,300 for single taxpayers, and $3,400 for married taxpayers filing jointly.

### TAXES ON $300,000 TAXABLE INCOME: SALARY vs. INTEREST

| $300,000 Income from salary | | $300,000 Income from interest | |
|---|---|---|---|
| Tax on the first $60,000 | = $ 19,678 | Tax on the first $215,400 | = $117,504 |
| Tax on remaining $240,000 (50%) | = 120,000 | Tax on remaining $84,600 (70%) | = 59,220 |
| Total tax | = $139,678 | Total tax | = $176,724 |

As noted earlier, the maximum tax rate applied to dividend income is 70 percent. The taxation of dividend income is complicated by the fact that small amounts of dividend income are excluded from taxation. For an individual, the first $100 in dividend income received from common or preferred stock is excluded from taxation; for married taxpayers, the first $200 if the stock is owned jointly. For example, if a married taxpayer receives exactly $200 in dividends, no taxes need be paid on that amount; if the couple receives $5,000 in dividend income, taxes must be paid on only $4,800 ($5,000 − $200) of it.

The actual tax paid on the dividend income after the exclusion will depend on the total income earned by the taxpayer. The situation presented in Table 6A-3 illustrates a case in which the tax payment on dividend income is increased dramatically owing to higher levels of personal-services income. The point of this example is to show that different taxpayers will pay different amount of taxes on the *same amount of dividend income*. Those with high levels of taxable income pay a large proportion of their taxable dividend income (up to 70 percent) in the form of taxes.

**TABLE 6A-3**

### TAX ON $5,000 DIVIDEND INCOME
(Married Taxpayers, $4,800 Taxable)

| | Personal-services taxable income of $30,000 | Personal-services taxable income of $215,400 |
|---|---|---|
| Taxable dividend income | $4,800 | $4,800 |
| × Marginal tax rate | 37% | 70% |
| = Taxes paid | $1,776 | $3,360 |

Income from securities may also be received in the form of interest payments. However, taxes must be paid on the *entire* amount of interest income. There is no interest exclusion similar to the dividend exclusion. As shown in Table 6A-2, the 50 percent maximum tax rate for personal-services income does not apply to interest income. Thus, it is possible to pay up to 70 percent of the interest received in taxes.

Gains on the sale of securities (stocks, bonds, and so on) are considered capital gains and are subject to a special tax treatment. If a stock or bond has been held for more than one year, gains on the sale are considered *long-term capital gains*. Gains on stocks or bonds held for one year or less are considered *short-term capital gains*. Short-term capital gains are taxed in the same manner as interest income. However, taxpayers are permitted to exclude 60 percent of long-term capital gains from income taxation.[10] For example, assume that a taxpayer purchases stocks for $10,000 and sells them at a later date for $15,000. The amount of capital gains subject to taxation depends on the length of time the taxpayer owned the stock. This is illustrated in Table 6A–4.

**TABLE 6A–4**

INCOME SUBJECT TO TAXATION ON A CAPITAL GAIN OF $5,000

| | Amount subject to taxation |
|---|---|
| Short-term capital gain (1 year or less) | $5,000 |
| Long-term capital gain (more than 1 year) | $2,000[a] |

[a]Gain − 60% Exclusion = $5,000 − 60% of $5,000 = $2,000

The exclusion of 60 percent of long-term capital gains income from taxable income reduces by more than half the effective tax rate paid by the taxpayer. This feature of the tax laws is especially attractive to people in high tax brackets. Table 6A–5 illustrates the computations for the effective tax rates on capital gains income for married taxpayers at two different levels of personal-services income. Remember that a taxpayer with a different filing status or different personal-services income would have a different effective tax rate on long-term capital gains.

**TABLE 6A–5**

EFFECT OF LONG-TERM CAPITAL GAIN EXCLUSION (60%) ON DIFFERENT TAX RATES
($5,000 gain)

| | Income from gain | Taxable income due to the gain | Tax paid on the gain | Effective tax rate (tax paid/gain) |
|---|---|---|---|---|
| For married taxpayers with $30,000 personal-services income | $5,000 | $2,000 | $740 (37%) | 14.8% |
| For married taxpayers with $215,400 personal-services income | $5,000 | $2,000 | $1,400 (70%) | 28% |

---

[10]We will not discuss the tax treatment when the taxpayer has both capital gains and losses.

### CASH FLOWS TO TAXPAYER WITH TAXABLE INCOME OF $30,000

| Type of income | Before-tax cash flows | Taxes | Effective tax rate (tax/income) |
|---|---|---|---|
| Dividends | $5,000 | $1,776 | 35.5% |
| Interest | 5,000 | 1,850 | 37% |
| Short-term capital gains | 5,000 | 1,850 | 37% |
| Long-term capital gains | 5,000 | 740 | 14.8% |

Tables 6A–6 and 6A–7 summarize the different taxes paid on cash flows received from securities. The tax treatment of dividends is slightly more beneficial than that of interest income; however, the difference in taxes paid is very small. There is a significant advantage in the tax treatment of long-term capital gains compared to that of other income from securities. The tax benefit of long-term capital gains applies to all taxpayers, regardless of level of income. However, it is of greater importance to the wealthier taxpayer. A taxpayer with $30,000 in taxable income is able to reduce taxes from $1,776 to $740 (a savings of $1036), when income is received in the form of long-term capital gains rather than dividends. For the taxpayer with $215,400 in taxable income, the tax payment falls from $3,360 to $1,400 (a savings of $1,960).

### CASH FLOWS TO TAXPAYER WITH TAXABLE INCOME OF $215,400

| Type of income | Before-tax cash flows | Taxes | Effective tax rate (tax/income) |
|---|---|---|---|
| Dividends | $5,000 | $3,360 | 67.2% |
| Interest | 5,000 | 3,500 | 70% |
| Short-term capital gains | 5,000 | 3,500 | 70% |
| Long-term capital gains | 5,000 | 1,400 | 28% |

The significant differences between the tax treatments of long-term capital gains and of dividends may result in a built-in preference by stockholders for capital gains as opposed to dividend income. A corporation retaining funds should be able to invest those funds in a manner that will lead to increases in future earnings. This future-earnings information would be received by the market and lead to an increase in the market price of the firm's common stock (other things being equal). Thus, the tax laws encourage corporations to retain earnings rather than to pay dividends to stockholders.

**1.** Mr. and Mrs. Jack have a taxable income of $50,000 from personal services (wages). They file a joint return.
   a. Calculate the amount of taxes they have to pay.
   b. Calculate the *additional tax* if they receive an additional $1,000 dividend payment on stock held jointly.
   c. Calculate the *additional tax* (do not include the information in part *b*) if they receive an additional $1,000 in interest.
   d. Calculate the *additional tax* (do not include the information in parts *b* and *c*) if they realize a $1,000 long-term capital gain.
   e. What would be the effect on the amount of taxes to be paid if Mr. Jack were a single taxpayer? (Do not compute.)

**2.** Mr. and Mrs. Doe have a taxable income of $300,000 from personal services (salary). The Does file a joint return.
   a. Calculate the amount of taxes the Does have to pay.
   b. Calculate the *additional tax* if the Does receive an additional $10,000 dividend payment on stock held jointly.
   c. Calculate the *additional tax* (do not include the information in part *b*) if the Does receive an additional $10,000 in interest.
   d. Calculate the *additional tax* (do not include the information in parts *b* and *c*) if the Does realize a $10,000 long-term capital gain

**BIBLIOGRAPHY**   Since the topics of the first seven chapters are so closely related, one comprehensive bibliography covering all seven chapters is included at the end of Part One.

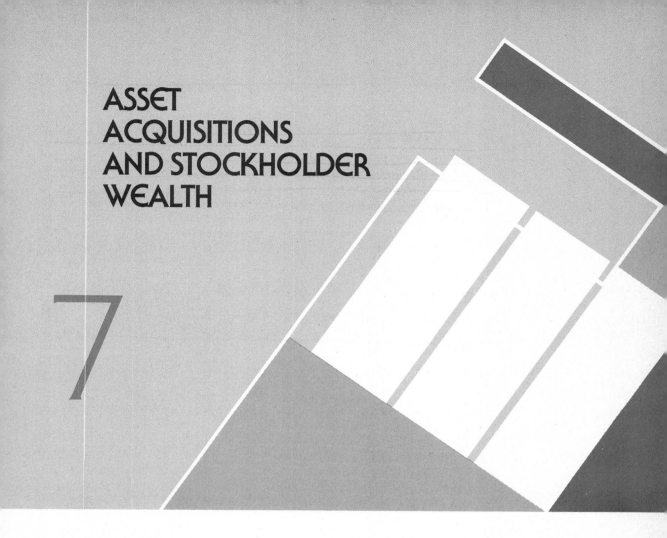

# ASSET ACQUISITIONS AND STOCKHOLDER WEALTH

## 7

## INTRODUCTION

Chapters 5 and 6 were devoted to the theory of capital acquisition. There we outlined a general conceptual framework useful for the evaluation of financial policies related to the size of corporate debt, equity financing, and dividend policy. In this chapter we move on to another part of financial theory, the theory of asset acquisition. We will develop general conceptual guidelines that will be useful for the evaluation of policies related to such phenomena as building a new plant or replacing machinery.[1] Whereas

---

[1]Practical computational procedures for making asset-acquisition decisions are discussed in Chapters 9 through 14.

Chapters 5 and 6 were related to the right-hand side of the balance sheet, Chapter 7 is devoted to an analysis of the decisions related to the left side. As we will see, however, it is impossible to treat these topics completely independently of each other.

Management should recognize that asset acquisition has a direct effect on the present wealth of existing stockholders. Newly acquired assets will be combined with existing assets, thus directly affecting stockholders' expectations of dividends and their perception of the riskiness of the firm's common stock. These two factors affect the price of common stock and, by definition, stockholder wealth. For this reason, stockholders are concerned with the marginal effect of asset acquisitions on the future dividends and riskiness of the firm.

## ASSET ACQUISITION FOR A NO-DEBT CORPORATION

First let us discuss the subject with relation to a no-debt corporation.[2] The attractiveness of an asset-acquisition alternative to the stockholders is dependent upon the expected rate of return on the asset and the rate of return required by the stockholders. For example, assume that the Roan Corporation is considering the acquisition of a piece of raw land, which it plans to hold for one year and then sell. Of course, there are risks involved in such an acquisition, and the stockholders will want to be compensated for these risks. Management can establish a required rate of return for the land acquisition based upon the estimated nondiversifiable risks of the project. In Figure 7–1, the risk of the land acquisition ($\beta_L$) is measured on the horizontal axis. The now familiar security-market line is used to estimate the required rate of return on the asset ($k_a$). The required rate of return on the asset (17 percent) is the rate that management must earn on the asset in order to compensate the stockholders for the risk they are taking in acquiring it.[3]

The expected rate of return can be calculated using the cost (all costs are assumed to be incurred at the present time) and the expected net sales price (to be received one year from now). For a one-year holding period, the expected rate of return can be computed using the following equation:

$$\frac{\text{Expected rate of return}}{\text{(1-year holding period)}} = \frac{\text{Cash inflow at time } t_1}{\text{Cash outflow at time } t_0} - 1 \qquad (7\text{-}1)$$

If the Roan Corporation acquires the land for $100,000 and expects to sell it for $117,000, the expected rate of return is 17 percent: ($117,000/$100,000) - 1.[4]

---

[2] The assumption of no debt simplifies the presentation of the basic ideas associated with the theory of asset acquisition. We will treat debt as a separate factor in a later section of this chapter.

[3] Remember, we are assuming that the firm does not use debt.

[4] We will assume that there are no taxes paid on this transaction.

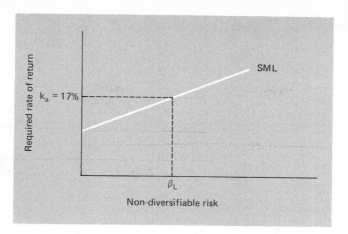

**FIGURE 7-1**

Security-Market Line
and Roan Corporation
Land Acquisition

Management's decision with respect to the acquisition of the land should be based on the acquisition's effect on stockholder wealth. In the Roan case, the expected rate of return is exactly equal to the required rate of return on the asset, just sufficient to compensate the stockholders for the risk they are taking. Note that if the expected rate of return had been 20 percent, the return would have been greater than that required by the stockholders, and the acquisition of the land would increase stockholder wealth. If the expected rate of return had been 15 percent, it would not have been adequate to compensate the stockholders for the risk undertaken. If management acquires an asset with an expected rate of return below the required rate of return, stockholder wealth will be reduced.

Table 7–1 looks at the same land project in dollar terms. With an expected rate of return of 17 percent, stockholders expect a dollar return of $17,000. This is the amount required to compensate them for the risk undertaken. Stockholders are probably indifferent to proposals with expected returns that equal required returns, since the competitive market provides many other opportunities for such investments. If the expected return on the asset is 20 percent, the stockholders will receive $3,000 more than the required amount to compensate them for the risk taken. From the stockholders' point of view, this situation is very desirable, since the competitive market offers no such opportunities. If the expected rate of return is 15 percent, the dollar returns will be $2,000 less than the required amount to compensate the stockholders for the risk taken. The risk of the stock has been increased without adequate compensation. The price of common stock and stockholder wealth should decline.

The observations above can be generalized into guidelines for corporate decision making. The first guideline is that corporations seeking to increase stockholder wealth must select those asset-acquisition alternatives in which the expected rate of return exceeds the required rate of return on the asset. Stated another way, the corporation should select asset-acquisition alternatives that have expected rates of return above the security-market line.

TABLE 7–1 ·

ROAN CORPORATION: EXPECTED CHANGES IN STOCKHOLDER WEALTH FOR DIFFERENT
EXPECTED RATES OF RETURN ON RAW-LAND ACQUISITION
(Outlay = $100,000)

| Expected Rate of return | Expected $ return | Required $ return[a] | Excess contributions to stockholder wealth[b] |
|---|---|---|---|
| 15% | $15,000 | $17,000 | − $2,000 |
| 17% | $17,000 | $17,000 | 0 |
| 20% | $20,000 | $17,000 | + $3,000 |

[a]Required rate of return × $100,000.

[b]Amount contributed to stockholder wealth beyond that required to compensate for risk. This amount is received one year in the future.

Figure 7–2 illustrates a possible asset-acquisition decision alternative. In this situation, the Rach Corporation must choose between two assets, A and B. Asset B has a higher level of nondiversifiable risk ($\beta_b$) and also a higher expected rate of return than that of asset A. Note, however, that the expected rate of return on asset B is 20 percent, just high enough to offset the higher level of risk. The effect of the corporation's acquisition of asset B should be neutral. Higher expected dollar dividends will be offset by higher risk, leaving stock price unchanged. The firm will not increase the present wealth of the stockholders by acquiring asset B.

The acquisition of asset A, on the other hand, will increase the price of common stock, because stockholders' expectations for increased dividends will exceed those required by the risk level of asset A. When the expected rate of return (16 percent) exceeds the required rate of return (13 percent) for the asset, the price of common stock should increase. The opposite is also

FIGURE 7–2

Security-Market Line

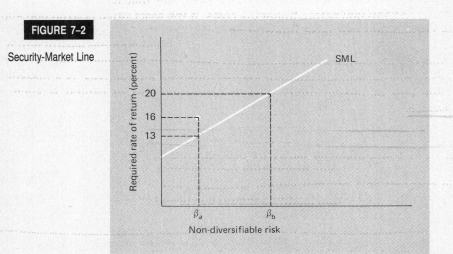

PART ONE: The Theory of Finance

true; if the expected rate of return is below the required rate of return for an asset, risk will be increased more than expected dividends, and the price of common stock will decline if the asset is acquired.

Thus far, our presentation has led to the following observations about the selection of assets by firms wishing to maximize stockholder wealth:

1. Stockholder wealth will be increased if a corporation selects assets with expected rates of return in excess of their required rates of return.
2. A corporation selecting an asset with an expected rate of return below the required rate of return will decrease stockholder wealth.
3. The expected rate of return by itself tells us little about the desirability of selecting an asset. It is possible that alternatives with lower expected rates of return are more attractive than those with higher expected rates of return. The firm must compare the expected rate of return of an asset to the required rate of return for that asset. The required rate of return is determined by the level of nondiversifiable risk of the asset, and can be obtained from the security-market line.

## THE ASSET-SPECIFIC COST OF CAPITAL

Thus far, we have been examining the guidelines for acquisition of assets by a no-debt corporation. This assumption was used in order to simplify the determination of the required rate of return on an asset. In this section, we will examine the asset-acquisition decision process in the context of a firm with debt in its capital structure. We will show that the guidelines developed earlier require only modification for their application to firms with debt.

In order for an asset acquisition to be attractive to a corporation's stockholders, the dollar return must be greater than the dollar cost of obtaining the funds needed to finance the asset. For example, assume a firm is considering the acquisition of a one-year asset that has expected dollar returns of $110,000 before financing costs. If the asset price is $100,000 and the corporation can raise funds at an average cost of 15 percent, the total dollar financing costs will be $15,000. Obviously, stockholder wealth will be reduced if the corporation acquires this asset. What is needed, then, in order to evaluate the attractiveness of asset-acquisition alternatives, is a measure of the cost of raising funds. The asset-specific cost of capital is such a measure.

Throughout the discussion of asset acquisition, we will assume that the corporation is at the optimal capital structure.[5] The corporation views all assets as being financed partly by debt and partly by equity. For example, assume that a firm owns production facilities with a value of $12 million. If the corporation's optimal capital structure calls for a debt ratio ($\theta$) of 25 percent, the production facilities should be viewed as financed by $3 million

---

[5]If the corporation is not at the optimal capital structure, it should attempt to achieve this objective. The concept of the optimal capital structure was introduced in Chapter 5. Techniques for estimating the optimal capital structure are discussed in Chapter 14 and 18.

in debt and $9 million in equity funds. The same applies to all other assets owned by the firm and, most important, all assets that the firm is considering for purchase. If the corporation is considering for purchase a $20 million new facility on the East Coast, it should view the facility as being financed by $5 million in debt capital ( $\theta = 25\%$ ) and $15 million in equity capital. The actual cost of capital needed to acquire the $20-million facility will be a weighted average of the cost of equity and the cost of debt. The procedure for computing the weighted-average cost of capital is outlined in Table 7–2. Owing to the level of risk, the market requires a 16 percent rate of return on equity ($k_s$) and a 10 percent rate of return on debt ($k_d$). The FLO Corporation's tax rate is 20 percent. Thus, the after-tax cost of debt ($k_d^*$) to FLO Corporation is 8 percent. In this example the asset specific cost of capital ($k_f^*$) is 14 percent.

TABLE 7–2

FLO CORPORATION:
NEW FACILITY, ASSET-SPECIFIC AND WEIGHTED-AVERAGE COST OF CAPITAL

| Type of capital | Dollar amount | Percentage | Weight | Component cost | Product |
|---|---|---|---|---|---|
| Debt | $5,000,000 | 25% | 0.25 | $k_d^* = 8\%$ | 2% |
| Equity | $15,000,000 | 75% | 0.75 | $k_s = 16\%$ | 12% |
| Total | $20,000,000 | 100% | 1.00 | | $k_f^* = 14\%$ |

Weighted-average cost of capital = $k_f^*$ = 14% = Asset-specific cost of capital

The asset-specific cost of capital ($k_f^*$) is not constant over time.[6] Shifts in the security-market line will change the after-tax cost of debt ($k_d^*$) and the cost of equity ($k_s$). If, for example, the risk-free rate of return declines from its present level, the required rates of return on both debt and equity will decline. The result will be a lower cost of capital. The firm must continuously evaluate the security markets to ascertain the appropriate costs. These updated costs, multiplied by the weights derived from the optimal capital structure, will yield the appropriate cost of capital. The important points in this section of the chapter can be summarized as follows:

1. The firm uses a weighted average of debt and equity costs in computing the asset-specific cost of capital ($k_f^*$) needed for financing new assets.
2. It is assumed that the firm has an optimal capital structure, and that the market values (not book values) of debt and equity are used to determine the weights for computing the cost of capital.
3. The component costs are related to the required rates of return in the security markets. The required rate of return on debt ($k_d$) must be adjusted, owing to the

---

[6]In order to avoid repetition, we will use the words *cost of capital* to mean the weighted-average cost of capital. Therefore, when the term *cost of capital* appears throughout the book, it means a computation similar to that shown in Table 7–2.

tax deductibility of interest payments. Thus, the after-tax cost of debt $(k_d^*)$ is lower than the required rate of return of the debtholders $(k_d)$. No such adjustment is required for equity. The cost of equity to the corporation is equal to the required rate of return of the stockholders $(k_s)$, because dividend payments are not tax-deductible.

Additional discussion about the cost of capital and practical computational procedures will be presented in greater detail in Chapters 13 and 14.

## ASSET ACQUISITION FOR A CORPORATION WITH AN OPTIMAL CAPITAL STRUCTURE

In the no-debt corporation discussed earlier, we used the required rate of return on equity $(k_s)$ as the required rate of return on the asset $(k_a)$ being considered for acquisition. In this section we will show that for a corporation using debt, the required rate of return on an asset $(k_a)$ is equal to the cost of capital for the asset. If the expected rate of return on an asset exceeds the cost of capital for it, stockholders will receive compensation in excess of what is required to compensate them for the risk undertaken.

A numerical example will illustrate this proposition. Assume that the FLO Corporation is considering the acquisition of an asset costing $100,000 (at $t_o$). The asset has an expected rate of return of 14 percent and an expected life of one year. In other words, the firm will have a net after-tax cash inflow, before financing costs, of $114,000 at $t_1$. The FLO Corporation has an optimal debt ratio of 25 percent, an after-tax cost of debt $(k_d^*)$ of 8 percent, and a cost of equity $(k_s)$ of 16 percent. As shown previously in Table 7–2, the cost of capital for an asset under these conditions is 14 percent. Thus, the FLO Corporation has an expected rate of return of 14 percent and a cost of capital of 14 percent. What happens to stockholder wealth when the expected rate of return equals the asset-specific cost of capital?

The acquisition of the asset will require that $100,000 in capital funds be raised by the firm. Of this amount, debt suppliers will provide $25,000 and equity suppliers $75,000 ($\theta = 25\%$). The return to the suppliers of capital is outlined in Table 7–3. Here we see that with an expected return on the asset of 14 percent, the asset is able to meet the required returns of both debt suppliers and equity suppliers. *The project is able to "support" a required rate of return on equity $(k_s)$ of 16 percent even though the expected return on the project is only 14 percent.* This is possible because high-cost equity is combined with low-cost debt. Note that in this situation, the expected rate of return on the asset is exactly equal to the asset-specific cost of capital of the asset. Under this condition, stockholders receive just enough dollars to compensate them for the risk undertaken. When the expected rate of return equals the cost of capital, there is no "excess" return to the stockholders and no change in stockholder wealth.

TABLE 7–3

FLO CORPORATION:
ASSET ACQUISITION—EXPECTED RATE OF RETURN = 14%

|  | Debt suppliers | Equity suppliers | Total |
|---|---|---|---|
| Amount supplied | $25,000 | $75,000 | $100,000 |
| Required $ return | $2,000 (8% of $25,000)[a] | $12,000 (16% of $75,000) | $14,000 |
| Expected $ return | $2,000 | $12,000 | $14,000 |
| Excess return to equity | 0 | 0 | 0 |

[a]Note: The debt suppliers will actually receive $2,500 (10%). However, the after-tax cash outflows to the FLO Corporation will be only $2,000; the remainder is the interest tax subsidy of $500.

Consider what will happen if the expected rate of return on the asset is 20 percent rather than 14 percent. That is, the firm expects to have a net after-tax cash flow of $120,000 (at $t_1$) before financing costs. In this case, the expected rate of return exceeds the asset-specific cost of capital. This case is shown in Table 7–4. Since the return to the suppliers of debt is fixed, the expected return cannot exceed the required return. When the expected rate of return on the asset is 20 percent, however, there is an excess return of $6,000, and the entire amount goes to the suppliers of equity capital (stockholders), making the expected return to stockholders 24 percent ($18,000/$75,000). This excess return of $6,000, to be received one year in the future, represents an increase in stockholder wealth.

TABLE 7–4

FLO CORPORATION:
ASSET ACQUISITION—EXPECTED RATE OF RETURN = 20%

|  | Debt suppliers | Equity suppliers | Total |
|---|---|---|---|
| Amount supplied | $25,000 | $75,000 | $100,000 |
| Required $ return | $2,000 (8% of $25,000)[a] | $12,000 (16% of $75,000) | $14,000 |
| Expected $ return | $2,000 | $18,000 | $20,000 |
| Excess return to equity | 0 | $6,000[b] | $6,000 |

[a]See footnote to Table 7–3.

[b]The effect or excess return to equity on assets will be discussed in greater detail within the context of the optimal capital structure as discussed in Chapters 14 and 18.

Whenever the expected rate of return exceeds the cost of capital of an asset, there will be an excess return available to the stockholders, representing compensation beyond the amount required to compensate them for the risk undertaken. Thus, for firms using debt, the required rate of return on an asset $(k_a)$ is the cost of capital for that asset $(k_j^*)$. Expected rates of return above this required rate of return, which is the cost of capital, will provide returns in excess of those that could be received in a competitive market. Management wishing to maximize stockholder wealth should undertake such investments.

When the expected rate of return is below the cost of capital, the acquisition of the asset will reduce stockholder wealth. This is illustrated in Table 7–5, in which the expected rate of return on the project is 12 percent. That is, the firm expects to receive a net after-tax cash flow of $112,000 (at $t_1$) before financing costs. Suppliers of debt have first claim on the cash flows and receive their required return of $2,000. Suppliers of equity receive only $10,000, which is not enough to compensate them for the risk undertaken. In such a case, the price of common stock should fall and stockholder wealth will be decreased. Thus, when the firm acquires an asset with an expected rate of return below the cost of capital for that asset, stockholder wealth is decreased.

**TABLE 7–5**

FLO CORPORATION
ASSET ACQUISITION—EXPECTED RATE OF RETURN = 12%

|  | Debt suppliers | Equity suppliers | Total |
|---|---|---|---|
| Amount supplied | $25,000 | $75,000 | $100,000 |
| Required $ return | $2,000 (8% of $25,000)[a] | $12,000 (16% of $75,000) | $14,000 |
| Expected $ return | $2,000 | $10,000 | $12,000 |
| Excess return to equity | 0 | − $2,000 | − $2,000 |

[a]See footnote to Table 7–3.

The discussion above has been designed to illustrate four basic guidelines that can be used for the evaluation of asset-acquisition alternatives by a firm using debt:

1. When a firm invests in an asset with an expected rate of return greater than the asset-specific cost of capital, the present wealth of the stockholders increases.
2. When a firm invests in an asset with an expected rate of return equal to the asset-specific cost of capital, the present wealth of the stockholders remains unchanged.
3. When a firm invests in an asset with an expected rate of return lower than the asset-specific cost of capital, the present wealth of the stockholders declines.
4. The minimal acceptable rate of return on an asset is equal to the asset-specific cost of capital.[7]

---

[7]Remember, the correct definition of the cost of capital is the weighted-average cost of capital, as described in Table 7–2.

# MAXIMUM PERMISSIBLE DOLLAR OUTLAY FOR AN ASSET (M$O)

Once the cost of capital for an asset has been estimated, the maximum permissible dollar outlay (M$O) can be computed. The M$O is the maximum dollar amount that could be paid at the present time in order to acquire that asset. If the actual dollar outlay is less than the M$O, stockholder wealth will be increased.

In a general sense, most of us recognize that the amount we can afford to pay for an asset at the present time will depend on the amount and timing of the cash flows expected from the asset. In order to translate this concept into a specific dollar measurement, management needs the following information:

1. The amount of expected cash inflows.
2. The timing of the expected cash inflows. Cash received today is worth more than cash received in the future.
3. The cost of acquiring the capital required to purchase the asset.

In order to illustrate this concept, let us compute the maximum dollar outlay that the Amy Corporation can spend at the present time for the acquisition of an asset that has expected cash inflows of $120,000. This amount represents all cash receipts less all cash outflows (labor, raw materials, taxes, and so on) other than those involved in financing the asset. For simplicity, we will assume that the entire amount of net cash inflows will be received at the end of one year. In addition, assume that the security-market line depicted in Figure 7–3 prevails, and that security markets assess the risk of the Amy Corporation's stock at level $\beta_s$ and the risk of debt at $\beta_d$. Finally, assume that the Amy Corporation has an optimal debt ratio of $(\theta)$ of 25 percent and a tax rate of 50 percent.

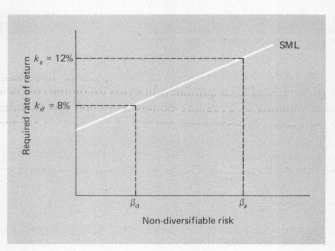

FIGURE 7–3

Security-Market Line

The computation of cost of capital for the Amy Corporation is shown in Table 7–6. From Figure 7–3 we can obtain the required rate of return for debt and equity suppliers. Assume that the required rate of return of debt suppliers is 8 percent and the required rate of return on equity is 12 percent. Thus, the after-tax cost of debt to the Amy Corporation will be 4 percent [8%(1 − .5)]. No tax adjustment is required for $k_s$, since dividends are not tax-deductible. As shown in Table 7–6, the asset-specific cost of capital is 10 percent.

### TABLE 7–6

AMY CORPORATION:
ESTIMATED COST OF CAPITAL FOR ACQUIRING NEW ASSET

| Type of capital | Weight | Component cost | Product |
|---|---|---|---|
| Debt | 0.25 | $k_d^* = 4\%$ | 1.0% |
| Equity | 0.75 | $k_s = 12\%$ | 9.0% |
| Total | 1.00 | | $k_f^* = 10\%$ |

The maximum permissible dollar outlay for the asset is the present value of the expected future net cash inflows for the asset. The cost of capital should be used as the discount rate. The M$O is computed as follows:

$$\text{M\$O} = \text{PV of cash inflows} = \frac{\text{Cash Inflows in Year 1}}{1 + k_f^*} = \frac{\$120,000}{1.10} = \$109,091$$

The maximum dollar outlay that can be expended at the present time for the asset in question will be $109,091. If management disburses this amount for the asset, stockholder wealth will remain unchanged, since the $120,000 expected at the end of the year will be just sufficient to repay the acquisition price of $109,091 and the required dollar return on capital of $10,909. Stated another way, since the corporation has a cost of capital of 10 percent for the asset, $10,909 must be paid to debt and equity capital suppliers for use of their capital. Since this financing cost of $10,909 plus the principal amount of $109,091 equals $120,000, no surplus is available to equity suppliers. Stockholders receive compensation for the risk taken, but no more.

The present value of the cash inflows determines the maximum permissible dollar outlays. The M$O can be used as a standard for evaluating the effect of the actual dollar outlay on stockholder wealth. The decision process would be as follows:

1. If the actual dollar outlay is less than the M$O (PV of cash inflows), stockholder wealth is increased.

2. If the actual dollar outlay is equal to the M$O (PV of cash inflows), stockholder wealth is unchanged.
3. If the actual dollar outlay is greater than the M$O (PV of cash inflows), stockholder wealth is reduced.

We are assuming in this chapter that the outlays are made today $(t_o)$. For example, if an asset acquisition requires an expenditure of $1,000, it is assumed that the actual outlay takes place at the present time rather that at some future date.[8]

## THE NET PRESENT VALUE OF AN ASSET (NPV)

The change in the value of stockholder wealth that results from the acquisition of an asset is called the net present value (NPV) of the asset. The NPV can be computed by subtracting the actual dollar outlay (A$O) from the present value of cash inflows (M$O).

$$\text{Net present value} = \text{Present value of cash inflows} - \text{Actual dollar outlay} \qquad (7\text{--}2)$$

The meaning of net present value should be clearly understood. If an asset-acquisition alternative has a positive net present value, it means that the expected dollar cash inflows are large enough to yield compensation to the stockholders *in excess of* their required rate of return. The net present value is the dollar amount by which stockholder wealth is increased when the asset is acquired by the firm.

For purposes of illustration, let us reexamine the asset being considered for acquisition by the Amy Corporation. If we assume that this asset can be purchased for $100,000, the increase in stockholder wealth (NPV) can be computed as follows:

*Step 1.* Compute the present value of cash inflows:

$$\text{PV of cash inflows} = \frac{\text{Cash inflows}}{1 + k_f^*} = \frac{\$120,000}{1.10} = \$109,091$$

This is the maximum amount that the Amy Corporation can expend today for an asset returning $120,000 one year from now.

*Step 2.* Compute the actual dollar outlay (A$0). The actual dollar outlay is given as $100,000.

*Step 3.* Compute the net present value (change in value of stockholder wealth):

---

[8]More complicated situations are discussed in Appendix 9A.

$$\text{NPV} = \text{PV of cash inflows} - \text{Actual dollar outlay}$$

$$= \$109{,}091 - \$100{,}000 = \$9{,}091$$

In the example above, the Amy Corporation can acquire an asset for $100,000. This asset will return $120,000 one year from now. Table 7–7 shows what happens to the $20,000 difference between cash inflows one year from now $(t_1)$ and the actual cash outflows taking place today $(t_o)$. As indicated in the table, equity suppliers will receive an excess of $10,000, However, this $10,000 will not be received until one year from now $(t_1)$. We know that in present-value terms, a dollar received one year from now is worth less than a dollar received today. Therefore, the net present value of the project (increase in the value of stockholder wealth) is the present value of the excess returns received at a future time:

$$\text{NPV} = \frac{\$10{,}000}{1 + k_f^*} = \frac{\$10{,}000}{1.10} = \$9{,}091$$

---

**TABLE 7–7**

AMY CORPORATION
DISTRIBUTION OF THE DIFFERENCE BETWEEN CASH
OUTFLOWS AND CASH INFLOWS OF $20,000

| | |
|---|---:|
| 1. Required rate to debt suppliers[a] (Supplied $25,000 at a cost to the firm of 4%) | $1,000 |
| 2. Required rate of return to equity suppliers (Supplied $75,000 at a cost to the the firm of 12%) | $9,000 |
| 3. Excess return to equity suppliers one year from today $(t_1)$ | $10,000 |
| 4. Total distributed one year from now | $20,000 |

[a]The firm needs $100,000 to acquire the asset. Since θ is 25%, the firm will use $25,000 in debt and $75,000 in equity. Furthermore, the actual return to debt suppliers will be $2,000. However, only $1,000 represents the after-tax cash outflow to the firm. The remainder is the interest tax subsidy.

---

Thus, the difference ($20,000) is divided into required rate of return of debt suppliers, required rate of return of equity suppliers, and excess return to equity suppliers—the return beyond what is required for the risk undertaken. Net present value represents the present value of the returns received by equity suppliers *in excess of (net of) the return required for the risk undertaken by suppliers of capital.*

In the Amy Corporation example, the project under consideration has a positive net present value. That is, the acquisition of the asset will increase the value of stockholder wealth. Asset-acquisition alternatives frequently have a negative net present value, signifying that the expected dollar cash inflows are inadequate to meet the required rate of return of the stockholders. In such cases, stockholder wealth will be reduced by the amount of the negative net present value.

As will be discussed in greater detail in Chapters 9 and 10, under almost all circumstances management should use net present value as the basis for decisions relating to asset acquisitions, in order for those decisions to be consistent with the goal of stockholder-wealth maximization.

## THE USE OF AN ASSET-SPECIFIC COST OF CAPITAL

Different assets have different risk levels, and the security market evaluates risk and required rates of return for each asset acquisition. It follows, then, that different assets will be associated with different required rates of return for debt and equity, as well as resulting in different costs of capital. For proper evaluation of the effect of an asset-acquisition alternative on stockholder wealth, a discount rate reflecting the risk of that asset must be used in computing net present values. A single firm may have to use multiple discount rates. The net present value will reflect changes in stockholder wealth only when an asset-specific cost of capital is used. Only then can we be sure that the expected future dollar inflows are in excess of returns required by suppliers of capital.

For example, assume that the Amy Corporation had proceeded as many real-world firms are likely to do. Rather than spending the time and effort to compute an asset-specific cost of capital, management decided to use an overall historical cost of capital that reflects the riskiness of the corporation's present assets. Assume for purposes of illustration that the present assets of the corporation are considerably riskier than the asset being considered for acquisition. Management has been using a cost of capital $(k_j^*)$ of 25 percent for its other projects. If this cost of capital is applied to the new asset, the net present value becomes a negative $4,000 and the corporation would refuse to acquire the new asset. The net present value of the asset, using a cost of capital of 25 percent, is computed as follows:

*Step 1.* Compute the present value of cash inflows:

$$\text{PV of cash inflows} = \frac{\text{Cash inflow in year one}}{1 + k_j^*} = \frac{\$120,000}{1.25} = \$96,000$$

*Step 2. Compute the actual dollar outlay (A$0). The actual dollar outlay required remains at $100,000.*

*Step 3.* Compute the net present value (NPV):

$$\text{NPV} = \text{PV of cash inflows} - \text{Actual dollar outlay}$$
$$= \$96{,}000 - \$100{,}000 = -\$4{,}000$$

In this case, management will make an error, by failing to recognize that the security market will have lower required rates of return on less-risky assets. The required dollar returns to capital suppliers are overestimated, and the excess returns to equity suppliers are underestimated.

The specific procedures used to compute the asset-specific cost of capital will be discussed in detail in a later chapter. However, it seems appropriate at this point to discuss the general nature of the problems associated with the estimation of the cost of capital. The central problem facing management is estimating the asset-specific cost of capital to be used in evaluating an asset acquisition is the difficulty of determining the amount of risk and, thus, the required rate of return that the market will assign to a specific asset. In fact, the security markets evaluate the riskiness of *groups of assets* that are combined in the form of a corporation. There is a tremendous amount of information regarding these groups of assets (firms), but almost none for specific assets. This predicament has led management to use the market's evaluation of groups of assets as a proxy for its evaluation of a specific asset. Thus, for example, the management of a corporation may estimate that for the existing group of assets under its control, the required rate of return on debt ($k_d$) is 8 percent, and the required rate of return on equity ($k_s$) is 16 percent. Management can use this information to compute the cost of capital for the firm's existing assets. Such an example is presented for the GNC Corporation in Table 7–8. It is assumed that the optimal capital structure is 20 percent and that the tax rate is 50 percent.

**TABLE 7–8**

GNC CORPORATION:
COST OF CAPITAL FOR THE FIRM'S ASSETS TREATED AS A GROUP

| Type of capital | Weights | Component cost | Product |
|---|---|---|---|
| Debt | 0.20 | $k_d^* = 4\%$[a] | 0.8% |
| Equity | 0.80 | $k_s = 16\%$ | 12.8% |
| Total | 1.00 | | $k_f^* = 13.6\%$ |

[a]$k_d^* = k_d(1 - \text{Tax rate})$

In the case of the GNC Corporation, the security-market estimates of $k_d$ and $k_s$ represent current estimates of the risk of existing assets of the firm taken *as a group*. These estimates can be used to estimate the asset-specific cost of capital by using certain assumptions.

If the asset being evaluated for acquisition by the firm has risk characteristics similar to the other assets owned by the firm, it is generally assumed that the security market will assign the corporation's required rates of return to the specific asset. For example, assume that GNC Corporation's actual assets at the present time consist of a chain of 400 supermarkets in the Midwest. Under consideration is the acquisition of a small chain of ten supermarkets located in the Denver area. The management of GNC is likely to believe that the security market will assign the same cost of capital to the asset acquisition as it does to the firm as a whole. Thus, GNC will use its cost of capital (13.6 percent) as a proxy for the asset-specific cost of capital. This assumption is commonly called *the assumption of constant risk.*

The other procedure that is frequently used is that of risk-adjusted discount rates. Again, management uses the market-determined required rate of return for existing assets of the firm as a starting point for estimating the asset-specific cost of capital. After studying how the security market has reacted to similar situations, management adds or subtracts from the required rate of return of the existing assets of the corporation. For example, the management of GNC may have perceived that the security market will view the Denver acquisition as riskier than the firm's existing assets, owing to the difference in location, since the security market considers supermarkets to be riskier in the Denver area than those in the Midwest. The management of GNC, after a review of the required rates of return established by the security market for retailing firms based in the Denver area, compares them to midwestern firms. This evaluation may cause management to add an extra amount, a risk adjustment, to the GNC overall rate. Thus, the Denver acquisition will be evaluated using an asset-specific cost of capital of 14.6 percent rather than 13.6 percent, the present cost of capital of GNC Corporation's existing assets. The difference will reflect a premium for the additional risk of the Denver assets.

The student should recognize that there is no clear-cut superiority of one assumption over the other. The success of management will depend on how well the assumption reflects reality. If a risk adjustment is employed when none is needed, management may make a serious error. Of course, management could also make a serious error by not using a risk adjustment when one is required by the circumstances.

A word of caution: Management should always use the asset-specific cost of capital. The cost of capital for the existing assets of the firm is used only as starting point for estimating an asset's specific cost of capital.

## ASSET ACQUISITIONS FOR SMALLER BUSINESSES

The general principles outlined in this chapter apply to both large and small businesses. That is, small businesses will maximize owner's equity by choosing assets on the basis of their net present values. Small businesses must also use an asset-specific cost of capital when computing the net present value of an asset acquisition. A specific problem facing smaller businesses relates to the procedures used to compute the asset-specific cost of capital. These difficulties will be discussed in Chapters 13 and 14.

**SUMMARY**

The primary purpose of this chapter was to describe the methodology used for asset acquisitions. The use of the methods described is consistent with the goal of maximizing the wealth of the stockholders. The first step is to determine the required rate of return of an asset considered for acquisition by the firm. The firm obtains this information from the security-market line. Stockholders' wealth will be maximized if the firm acquires assets with an expected rate of return in excess of their asset-specific cost of capital. The specific cost of capital of an asset is the weighted average of the required rates of return by debt and equity suppliers based on the market evaluation of the nondiversifiable risk of the asset.

A very common assumption is the substitution of the firm's cost of capital for the asset-specific cost of capital. This assumption is valid *only* if the optimal capital structure and the risk level of the firm remain unchanged when the asset is acquired. Adjustments must be made to the cost of capital of the firm when the risk of the new asset differs from the risk of existing assets.

Finally, we discussed the concept of net present value (NPV), one of the most important tools available to management to achieve its goal of maximizing the wealth of the stockholders. NPV is equal to the present value of cash inflows less the actual dollar outlays. The acquisition of assets with a positive net present value will increase stockholder wealth. The acquisition of assets with a negative net present value will reduce stockholder wealth.

**QUESTIONS FOR DISCUSSION**

1. Suppose a large corporation acquires a new asset with relatively low expected cash flows and relatively high risk. What will happen to the price of the corporation's common stock? Explain your answer.
2. How is the expected rate of return calculated for an asset being held for a one-year period? Would this procedure provide adequate results for longer periods?
3. What does the word *excess* refer to when we talk about excess returns to stockholders?
4. Why will stockholder wealth be decreased if the expected return is less than the required rate of return of an asset? (Assume a no-debt corporation.)
5. Give a verbal description of the asset-specific cost of capital. Describe the role played by the security market in the determination of the asset-specific cost of capital.
6. What is the relationship among $k_d$, $k_d^*$, $k_s$, and $k_f^*$?

7. Describe how the expected rate of return and the cost of capital can be used to decide among asset-acquisition alternatives. How does this relate to stockholder wealth?

8. Exactly why is the maximum permissible dollar outlay (M$O) for an asset the greatest amount the firm can pay for an asset? How is the M$O computed?

9. Explain the relationship between M$O, A$O, and net present value.

10. How does net present value relate to stockholder wealth?

11. Discuss how an incorrect asset-specific cost of capital can lead to poor management decisions.

12. How and why is a risk-adjusted discount rate used in asset-acquisition decisions? How is the asset-specific cost of capital estimated?

**PROBLEMS**

1. The Lamar Corporation is considering the acquisition of a building. The building will cost $150,000 today ($t_o$), and the expected sales price one year from today ($t_1$) is $180,000. (Assume that there are no corporate income taxes and that the firm is financed 100% by equity.)
   a. Calculate the expected rate of return of the acquisition.
   b. The security-market line is represented by the following equation:

   $$k = 10\% + (15\% - 10\%)\beta.$$

   Should the Lamar Corporation acquire the building if the riskiness of this asset is depicted by:
      i. $\beta = 0.5$?      ii. $\beta = 1.0$?      iii. $\beta = 3.0$?
   c. Calculate the maximum risk ($\beta$) of the building that will still allow its purchase.

2. Calculate the weighted-average cost of capital of the Fancy Corporation, given the following information:
   a. The SML can be represented by $k = 6\% + (10\% - 6\%)\beta$.
   b. The risk level of common stock is depicted by a $\beta$ of 2.0.
   c. The risk level of the bonds is depicted by a $\beta$ of 1.0.
   d. The Fancy Corporation has a tax rate of 40%.
   e. The Fancy Corporation's optimal capital structure ($\theta$) is 30% debt.

3. Calculate the asset-specific cost of capital, given the following information:
   a. The required rate of return of the stockholders is 20%.
   b. The required rate of return of the bondholders is 10%.
   c. The tax rate is 30%.
   d. The optimal debt ratio ($\theta$) is 40%.

4. The Marine Services Corporation is considering the acquisition of an asset that will cost $300,000. The expected rate of return of the asset is 15%. The risk of the asset is such that stockholders have a required rate of return of 16%, and bondholders of 10%. The optimal debt ratio ($\theta$) is 30%. Assume Marine Services pays no income taxes, and use the format presented in Table 7–3.
   a. Calculate the expected dollar return to debt suppliers.
   b. Calculate the expected dollar return to equity suppliers.
   c. Calculate the excess dollar return to debt suppliers.

d. Calculate the excess dollar return to equity suppliers.

e. Should Marine Services acquire the asset? Explain.

5. The William Corporation is contemplating the acquisition of an asset. This asset has expected cash flows of $100,000 one year from now and $80,000 two years from now. These cash flows represent all cash inflows and outflows other than those involved in financing the asset. The cost of capital of the corporation, and also of the asset, is 10%.

a. What is the maximum permissible dollar outlay for the asset?

b. Describe the effect on the wealth of the William Corporation's stockholders if the firm acquires the asset, and:

   i. The actual dollar outlay is $150,000.

   ii. The actual dollar outlay is $160,000.

6. The Miramar Corporation is considering a plant expansion. The expansion will cost $200,000 today ($t_o$). The expected dollar returns are $100,000 one year from now ($t_1$) and $150,000 two years from now ($t_2$). The $\beta$ of the corporation's common stock is 1.0, and the $\beta$ of the bonds is 0.6. The SML can be represented by $k = 7\% + (12\% - 7\%)\beta$. The firm's tax rate is 40%. The firm's optimal debt ratio ($\theta$) is 0.5. The riskiness of the asset is *identical* to the riskiness of the firm.

a. Calculate the asset-specific cost of capital.

b. Calculate the maximum permissible dollar outlay.

c. Calculate the effect on the wealth of Miramar's stockholders (NPV) if the expansion is undertaken.

d. Would the NPV of the proposed expansion be the same if the riskiness of the asset were not identical to the riskiness of the firm? Explain.

*[handwritten margin notes:]*

$k_s = 12$
$k_d = 10$
$k_d^* = 6$
$WAC = 9$
$NPV = 17,995$

*[handwritten notes below problem 6:]*

discount cashflows at same WACC of firm
assume risk asset = risk firm

if asset is riskier or less then it should
be discounted at rate for similar assets
on market. AS Cost of Capital

# APPENDIX 7A
# DIVERSIFICATION OF RISK WITHIN THE FIRM

One of the assumptions that underlies modern financial theory is that people hold their wealth in portfolios composed of many assets. These portfolios are assumed to be of such a nature that the person has been able to diversify all diversifiable risks, and only nondiversifiable risks remain in the portfolio. These assumptions have important implications for the stockholders' evaluation of management with respect to asset-acquisition policy and, in turn, all management practices.

First, the stockholder will place no premium on the common stock of a corporation that combines assets in order to eliminate diversifiable risks. Remember, the stockholder's portfolio already possesses diversification for this purpose. A competitive securities market will not pay a premium for something that market participants already possess. Careful thought must be given to this illusive notion.

Students, and many others, become confused over this issue because they cannot differentiate between diversifiable, nondiversifiable, and total risk. It is true that a corporation can reduce the total riskiness associated with its dividends by selecting assets that are not closely correlated. Thus, for example, a large conglomerate corporation can in all probability eliminate diversifiable risk and minimize total risk (to the level of nondiversifiable risk). The stockholder could accomplish the same objective by purchasing the shares of many smaller corporations. Since stockholders can do for themselves what the conglomerate does, no premium would be paid for the conglomerate's common stock.[9] Thus, if wealth maximization of the stockholders is the objective of management, no premium should be attached to an asset solely because it provides diversification and a stabilization of the corporation's cash flows. The sole criterion should be the relationship between the expected rate of return and the required rate of return of the asset. There is no reason for a firm to choose a project with an expected rate of return lower than the required rate of return obtained from the security-market line, merely because it reduces the uncertainty of corporate cash flows.

The discussion above leads to the conclusion, reflected in Figures 7–1 and 7–2, that stockholders will demand compensation for only the nondiversifiable risk associated with an asset, not the total risk. The meaning of nondiversifiable risk when applied to an asset-acquisition alternative is sometimes difficult to understand. The nondiversifiable risk of the asset will be determined by the same factors that determine the nondiversifiable risk of a security: first, the total uncertainty associated with the expected cash flows from the asset; second, the correlation of the asset's expected cash flows *with those of the total market*. Note that the important correlation is with the total market, not with the expected cash flows of the firm's other assets. Diversification within the firm is unimportant. Diversification within the total market for securities is important, because it determines the nondiversifiable risk and, together with the security-market line, establishes a required rate of return.

Corporations may find it profitable to acquire assets that result in diversification. Whenever a corporation can acquire assets with a rate of return in excess of the asset-specific cost of capital, the asset should be acquired. Diversification is the result of such actions, not the reason for them.

Although modern financial theory suggests that diversification within the firm has no independent value, many observers feel that this statement is too strong. They point to the preference of stockholders for stable dividends as an indication of the pressure on management to diversify. Diversification within the firm is one way of stabilizing dividends. In addition, the

---

[9]Review the discussion of competitive markets in Chapter 4.

probability of bankruptcy and its expected cost should be lower for diversified firms.

The beginning student should avoid this unresolved controversy and focus on the primary reason for asset acquisitions. That is, an asset should be acquired if the acquisition results in an increase in stockholder wealth. Stockholder wealth is increased when the asset acquired has a positive net present value.

**BIBLIOGRAPHY**     Since the topics of the first seven chapters are so closely related, one comprehensive bibliography covering all seven chapters is included at the end of Part One.

## Summary of Part One

The first seven chapters of *Managerial Finance: Theory and Techniques* focus on a general conceptual framework for use in financial decision making. This framework, called the theory of finance, provides management with a convenient context within which a broad range of financial problems can be analyzed and solved. The theory suggests that decision alternatives be evaluated in terms of a simple criterion: their effect on stockholder wealth. Since stockholder wealth is a function of expected future dividends and risk, each decision alternative must be evaluated in terms of these two factors. An outline of Part One is presented below.

### OUTLINE OF PART ONE

A. Two basic assumptions
   1. Management's goal is the maximization of stockholder wealth.
   2. Management's activities are evaluated by a competitive security market.
B. Effect of expected future dividends on stock prices and stockholder wealth
   1. High expected dividends tend to have a positive effect on stockholder wealth.
   2. The earlier the dividends are received, the higher the stockholder wealth.
C. The uncertainty attached to expected future dividends
   1. Since stockholders are risk avoiders, they expect to be compensated for the amount of nondiversifiable risk undertaken. Market participants expect compensation for nondiversifiable risk only.
   2. The security-market line expresses the relationship between nondiversifiable risk and the rate of return required by the competitive security market.

3. The required rate of return for a particular stock will be affected by three factors:
   a. The risk-free rate of interest
   b. The risk aversiveness of the security market
   c. The stock's nondiversifiable risk ($\beta$)
   Changes in any of these factors will change the required rate of return on the stock.
4. There is an inverse relation between the required rate of return on a stock and the price of the stock. A change in stock prices affects stockholder wealth.

D. Decision alternatives relating to the acquisition of capital are evaluated in terms of effect on stockholder wealth.
1. There is an optimal debt ratio at which the benefit of using tax-deductible debt financing begins to be offset by the increased expected cost of bankruptcy, security-market imperfections, and constraints imposed by the special interests of management.
   a. Stockholder wealth is maximized at the optimal debt ratio.
   b. The firm can use too much or too little debt.
2. There are strong economic and legal factors that encourage the use of earnings retention rather than issuance of new common stock. Thus, there is a tendency to raise new equity through earnings retention.
   a. Retained-earnings financing tends to minimize personal income tax liabilities.
   b. Retained-earnings financing tends to reduce the cost to the firm of raising funds.
   c. Consistent, long-term dividend policies reduce stockholders' brokerage costs.

E. Decision alternatives relating to the acquisition of assets are evaluated in terms of effect on stockholder wealth.
1. The asset-specific cost of capital is a weighted average of the costs of equity and debt.
   a. The cost of debt and the cost of equity reflect the riskiness of the specific asset.
   b. This average incorporates the weights derived from the optimal capital structure for the asset.
2. In order to increase stockholder wealth, an asset-acquisition alternative must provide the stockholders with a return beyond that required for the risk undertaken. Returns received by the stockholders are of two types: (a) returns received as compensation for taking risk, and (b) returns in excess (or deficiency) of those required to take the risk.
3. Net present value (NPV) is the measure of the present value of the excess (net) returns.
   a. NPV is computed by discounting the expected future cash flows associated with the asset by the asset-specific cost of capital.
   b. NPV represents the change (positive = increase; negative = decrease) in stockholder wealth.

F. Within the conceptual framework of Part One, all decision alternatives are evaluated in terms of their effect on stockholder wealth.

Parts two, three and four of the book will discuss specific financial decisions confronting management and suggest a number of techniques that can be used to evaluate decision alternatives. Since it is impossible to discuss every potential decision alternative, or every possible technique, we have been forced to make choices. Our choices reflect the following criteria:

1. The importance of the problem
2. The soundness of the technique
3. The level of expertise of the reader

## SUGGESTIONS FOR STUDENT READING, PART ONE

There is an extensive literature concerning the relationship among risk, return, and stockholder wealth. What follows is a brief annotated list of books we believe will be most helpful to the serious undergraduate student of finance.

**Primary Books**

Boudreaux, Kenneth J., and Hugh W. Long, *The Basic Theory of Corporate Finance*. Englewood Cliffs, N.J.: Prentice-Hall, 1977.

> This is a rigorous but readable treatment of the theory of finance. Chapters 1 through 7 deal specifically with the relationship among the value of equity claims, expected cash flows, and risk. This book should be the beginning point of any further study of the theory of finance. An integrated picture of the entire theory is presented.

Copeland, Thomas E., and J. Fred Weston, *Financial Theory and Corporate Policy*. Reading, Mass.: Addison-Wesley, 1979.

> This book should be read after *The Basic Theory of Corporate Finance.* Included in this book are excellent reviews of the controversial points of the theory of finance. In addition, the book ties together the literature of finance. This is a relatively advanced but readable book.

**Other Books**

Haley, Charles W., and Lawrence D. Schall, *Theory of Financial Decision*. New York: McGraw-Hill, 1973.

> Chapter 5 is particularly useful in examining the nature and meaning of risk.

Lorie, James, and Richard Brealy, *Modern Developments in Investment Management*. New York: McGraw-Hill, 1973.

> This book discusses both the theoretical and empirical aspects of capital markets.

Van Horne, James D., *Financial Management and Policy,* 5th ed. Englewood Cliffs, N.J.: Prentice-Hall, 1980.

> A very complete second-level textbook in financial management. There are excellent discussions throughout the book on the critical aspects of the theory of finance.

Weston, J. Fred, and Eugene F. Brighham, *Managerial Finance,* 5th ed. Hillsdale, Ill: Dryden Press, 1975.

The appendixes of this book provide convenient summaries of many important theoretical points.

**Articles**   The literature of the theory of finance is huge and usually inappropriate for the beginning student. Those searching for a bibliography in this area are referred to the Copeland and Weston or Van Horne book.

# THE ACQUISITION
# OF ASSETS

# Introduction to PART TWO

Part One of this book was intended to provide the student with an overall view of the process of financial decision making. In Part Two, Chapter 8 through 14, we will take a closer look at the techniques used to evaluate the effect of asset acquisitions on stockholder wealth. The word *asset* should be emphasized, since this is the primary focus of this section. In a sense, Part II deals with decisions relating to the left-hand side of the balance sheet.

As discussed in Chapter 7, the effect of asset-acquisition decisions on stockholder wealth will depend on the amount, timing, and riskiness of the cash flows associated with various alternatives. In Chapter 8 we will show how tax laws affect the cash flows of an asset, since it is necessary to consider the tax implications of each asset-acquisition alternative in order to make decisions consistent with stockholder-wealth maximization.

Chapters 9 and 10 are devoted to decisions relating to long-term-asset acquisitions (plant, equipment, and so on). This is one of the most difficult topics in finance, but it is also one of the most interesting and important. Chapter 11 deals with the acqui-

sition of current assets (accounts receivable, inventories, cash, and marketable securities). Chapter 12 examines asset acquisitions within an international context.

A fact we discussed in Chapter 7 and will develop in Chapters 9 through 12 is that the asset-specific cost of capital plays a central role in decisions relating to asset acquisitions. Most of the techniques we will deal with in Chapters 9 through 12 require an accurate measure of the asset-specific cost of capital. It is only by the use of that cost (a cost of capital reflecting the riskiness of the asset) that we can obtain a true indication of the effect of asset-acquisition alternatives on stockholder wealth. Since the asset-specific cost of capital is so important, we have devoted two chapters (13 and 14) to a discussion of the procedures in developing reliable estimates of it. These two chapters are of crucial importance, since the financial decision maker must have confidence in the fact that it is possible to make such estimates. This confidence will encourage the use of asset-acquisition techniques consistent with the goal of stockholder-wealth maximization.

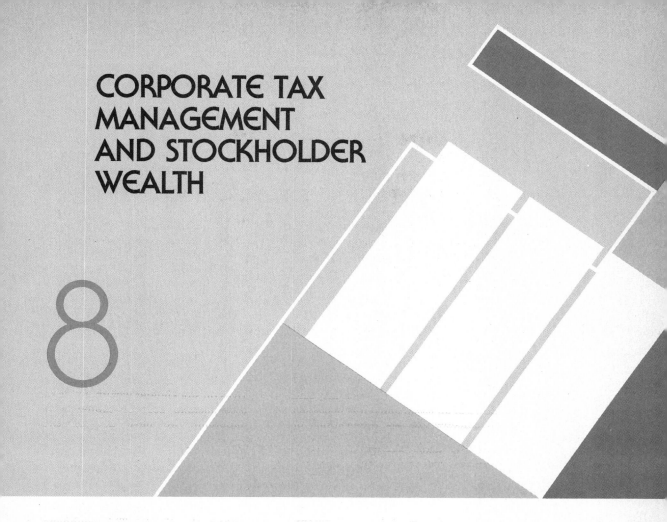

# CORPORATE TAX MANAGEMENT AND STOCKHOLDER WEALTH

8

## INTRODUCTION

Corporate management should approach corporate tax expenses in much the same way that it approaches other expenses incurred by the firm. Other things being equal, the minimization of corporate taxes will maximize the cash available to stockholders and therefore stockholder wealth. But just as in other cases, the benefit of cost saving could be offset by an increase in the riskiness of the firm. Thus, corporate tax-management strategies should be evaluated in terms of their effect on both total taxes paid and the riskiness of the firm. In the interest of stockholder wealth, management should pursue a tax/risk-minimization strategy.

The purposes of this chapter are twofold. First, we provide the reader with an overview of how corporate and personal income taxation works. This information is needed at various points in the chapters that follow. The second objective is to demonstrate how tax management operates at the corporate level. A number of situations are identified in which management must choose among decision alternatives largely on the basis of tax consequences. We highlight some of the factors that will affect the amount and timing of taxes paid, as well as factors that contribute to the riskiness of the firm.

The reader of this chapter will realize that taxation is a very complicated topic. One of our purposes is to demonstrate that tax management is desirable and possible. In practice, management employs tax specialists to execute its tax/risk-minimization program. This chapter is not designed for the tax specialist. It is written to give managers an idea of the kinds of things that can be accomplished by such specialists. In keeping with this objective, we have limited the material in the chapter, excluding many of the exceptions and qualifications found in the tax laws and in court decisions. We must emphasize that the material in this chapter does not provide a sufficient basis for tax planning.

## TAX AVOIDANCE AND TAX EVASION

As noted in Chapter 1, the objective of stockholder-wealth maximization is a constrained objective. In the case of income taxation, most of the constraints are established by law. If management, in its pursuit of stockholder-wealth maximization, exceeds the constraints established by law, it is engaging in *tax evasion.* Tax evasion by definition is against the law. People who evade taxes are subject to fines and imprisonment, and a corporation that does so may have financial penalties assessed against both the firm and the executives involved.

Tax avoidance is another matter. *Tax avoidance* can be defined as the arrangement of financial affairs in such a way as to reduce tax liabilities while *fully complying with the law.* Tax avoidance is not against the law. For example, corporations frequently hold marketable government securities for liquidity purposes. If the securities being held in the portfolio were issued by the U.S. Treasury, the corporation is required to pay federal income taxes on the interest income received. If the securities were issued by a state or local government, the interest is legally exempt from federal income taxes.[1]

In its pursuit of stockholder-wealth maximization, corporate management must exercise, after considering changes in risk, every tax-avoiding opportunity available within the framework of the law. Some stockholders

---

[1]This is not to say that state and local governments' securities are necessarily more rewarding that U.S. government securities. U.S. government securities usually offer a higher before-tax rate of return and a lower risk level than those of local governments. Corporations may prefer to purchase U.S. securities in spite of the tax advantages of state and local governments' securities.

expect management to pursue a tax/risk-minimization strategy, and its failure to do so will reflect unfavorably on management. The words *tax avoidance* may seem to carry a negative overtone, but in reality, there is nothing bad about such a policy. As the famous American jurist, Learned Hand, once stated, "Over and over again courts have said that there is nothing sinister in so arranging one's affairs as to keep taxes as low as possible."[2]

The American tax system is neither the best nor the worst in the world. We ourselves believe that many aspects of that system are unfair or unwise. We feel that true tax reform is of the highest priority and should be addressed by all citizens. However, corporate management is bound by the current tax laws—and just as it must not evade those taxes required by law, it need not voluntarily make payments to the government in excess of those required. Management's task is to serve the stockholders within the constraints established by the law.

## A SIMPLIFIED FORMAT FOR PERSONAL INCOME TAXATION

Table 8–1 shows the major items to be considered in the determination of personal income taxes. The taxpayer must declare all income, unless a specific provision of the tax law excludes such income from taxation. For just a few examples, the following types of income are excluded: (1) interest received on state and local government obligations, (2) scholarships, (3) health insurance contributions made by the employer, and (4) Social Security benefits. Taxpayers can arrange their financial affairs in such a way as to maximize excluded income, thus reducing gross income.

The tax laws permit no deductions unless a specific provision of the law indicates an item to be deductible. Deductions of interest payments, state and local taxes paid, and some medical expenses are all permitted by law. The law also permits deductions for any "ordinary and necessary business expense incurred during the taxable year from carrying on any trade or business,"[3] as long as such expenses are "reasonable." Finally, taxpayers are permitted to take personal exemptions for each dependent ($1,000 as of 1980).[4]

The tax liability of the individual is computed from a set of tax-rate schedules provided by the Internal Revenue Service. The IRS tax rates incorporate the idea of progressive taxation—that is, the higher the taxable income, the higher the applicable marginal tax rate. The schedules for single and married taxpayers for 1979 income are given in Table 8–2. The fourth column in these tables, which gives the marginal percentage tax rates, is the

---

[2] *Commission v. Newman*, 35 AFTR 859 (2nd. Cir., 1947).
[3] Section 162(a), Internal Revenue Code.
[4] There are specific rules that determine if a taxpayer can claim a dependent. Furthermore, additional personal exemptions can be claimed by the blind and those over 65 years of age.

TABLE 8–1

PERSONAL INCOME TAXATION: AN OVERVIEW

---

Income, broadly defined
Less: Exclusions from income
Equals: Gross income
Less: Deductions
Equals: Adjusted gross income
Less: Personal exemptions
Equals: Taxable income
Times: Applicable tax rate
Equals: Tax liability
Less: Tax credits and prepayments (withholdings)
Equals: Tax or refund due

---

most interesting. It shows that higher taxable incomes are subjected to higher personal tax rates.

Using Table 8–2, you can compute not only the tax liability, but also the marginal tax rate. Let us illustrate the difference between these two concepts. Assuming a married couple files a joint return, has a taxable income of $25,000, and does not itemize deductions, their tax is computed as follows:

$$\text{Tax} = \$4,505 + 32\% \times (\$25,000 - \$24,600) = \$4,633$$

Their average tax rate is 18.5 percent ($4,633/$25,000). The marginal tax rate, the rate of the additional tax that must be paid for every additional dollar of income, in this example is 32 percent. If our hypothetical taxpayers increase their taxable income by $100, their taxes increase by $32. The 32 percent marginal tax rate will continue until their taxable income reaches $29,900, after which every additional dollar of income will increase taxes by 37 cents. Thus, the new marginal tax rate is 37 percent, showing that the higher the taxable income, the higher the marginal tax rate.

A number of tax credits are available to individual taxpayers. For example, people purchasing new rental properties may be entitled to a tax credit, and tax credits may be taken for political contributions and the purchase of residential energy-saving devices. The total of tax credits and prepayments made to the federal government are subtracted from the tax liabilities to determine the total tax due.

## A SIMPLIFIED FORMAT FOR CORPORATE INCOME TAXATION

Corporations are treated as separate legal entities by the tax laws. Income, expenses, depreciation, and the like are reported in the corporate tax return and not in that of the stockholders of the corporation. The corporation pays

TABLE 8-2

## TAX RATE SCHEDULES APPLICABLE TO 1979 INCOME

FOR SINGLE TAXPAYERS, if amount of taxable income is:[a]

| Over | But not over | Then tax is | | Of excess over |
|---|---|---|---|---|
| $2,300 | $3,400 | $0 plus 14% | | $2,300 |
| $3,400 | $4,400 | $154 | 16% | $3,400 |
| $4,400 | $6,500 | $314 | 18% | $4,400 |
| $6,500 | $8,500 | $692 | 19% | $6,500 |
| $8,500 | $10,800 | $1,072 | 21% | $8,500 |
| $10,800 | $12,900 | $1,555 | 24% | $10,800 |
| $12,900 | $15,000 | $2,059 | 26% | $12,900 |
| $15,000 | $18,200 | $2,605 | 30% | $15,000 |
| $18,200 | $23,500 | $3,565 | 34% | $18,200 |
| $23,500 | $28,800 | $5,367 | 39% | $23,500 |
| $28,800 | $34,100 | $7,434 | 44% | $28,800 |
| $34,100 | $41,500 | $9,766 | 49% | $34,100 |
| $41,500 | $55,300 | $13,392 | 55% | $41,500 |
| $55,300 | $81,800 | $20,982 | 63% | $55,300 |
| $81,800 | $108,300 | $37,677 | 68% | $81,800 |
| $108,300 | | $55,697 | 70% | $108,300 |

FOR MARRIED TAXPAYERS FILING JOINT RETURNS, if amount of taxable income is:[a]

| Over | But not over | Then tax is | | Of excess over |
|---|---|---|---|---|
| $3,400 | $5,500 | $0 plus 14% | | $3,400 |
| $5,500 | $7,600 | $294 | 16% | $5,500 |
| $7,600 | $11,900 | $630 | 18% | $7,600 |
| $11,900 | $16,000 | $1,404 | 21% | $11,900 |
| $16,000 | $20,200 | $2,265 | 24% | $16,000 |
| $20,200 | $24,600 | $3,273 | 28% | $20,200 |
| $24,600 | $29,900 | $4,505 | 32% | $24,600 |
| $29,900 | $35,200 | $6,201 | 37% | $29,900 |
| $35,200 | $45,800 | $8,162 | 43% | $35,200 |
| $45,800 | $60,000 | $12,720 | 49% | $45,800 |
| $60,000 | $85,600 | $19,678 | 54% | $60,000 |
| $85,600 | $109,400 | $33,502 | 59% | $85,600 |
| $109,400 | $162,400 | $47,544 | 64% | $109,400 |
| $162,400 | $215,400 | $81,464 | 68% | $162,400 |
| $215,400 | | $117,504 | 70% | $215,400 |

[a]Taxable income is equal adjusted gross income *minus* personal exemptions and *minus* any itemized deductions that exceed the zero-bracket amount (formerly called the standard deduction). The zero-bracket amount is $2,300 for single taxpayers, and $3,400 for married taxpayers filing jointly.

taxes on its taxable income at a specified rate, and the stockholders are not subject to taxation unless they receive a taxable distribution, usually in the form of dividends.[5]

The general tax format for individuals, as presented in Table 8–1, is also applicable to corporations. However, the tax laws contain a separate set of regulations covering corporate-income exclusions, deductions, and tax credits. As with personal income, the rate at which corporate income is taxed increases as the amount of taxable income increases. As shown in Table 8–3, however, the maximum tax rate is reached at a relatively low level

TABLE 8–3

CORPORATE TAX RATES APPLICABLE TO 1979 INCOME

If amount of taxable income is:

| Over: | But not over: | Then tax is: | | Of excess over: |
|-------|---------------|--------------|------|-----------------|
| $0 | $25,000 | $0 plus 17% | | $0 |
| $25,000 | $50,000 | $4,250 | 20% | $25,000 |
| $50,000 | $75,000 | $9,250 | 30% | $50,000 |
| $75,000 | $100,000 | $16,750 | 40% | $75,000 |
| $100,000 | | $26,750 | 46% | $100,000 |

of taxable income. Also, the highest marginal tax rate for corporations is only 46 percent, compared to a maximum of 70 percent applicable to individuals. As a result, all but the smallest corporations find themselves in the highest marginal tax rate of 46 percent.

For example, a corporation with a taxable income of $1 million computes its corporate income tax as follows:

| | | |
|---|---|---|
| 17% of $25,000 (1st $25,000) | = | $4,250 |
| 20% of $25,000 (2nd $25,000) | = | $5,000 |
| 30% of $25,000 (3rd $25,000) | = | $7,500 |
| 40% of $25,000 (4th $25,000) | = | $10,000 |
| Tax on first $100,000 of taxable income | = | $26,750 |
| 46% of $900,000 | = | $414,000 |
| Tax on $1,000,000 of taxable income | = | $440,750 |

The implications for larger corporations of the graduated corporate income tax are interesting. First, note that for large corporations with millions of dollars in taxable income, two tax rates apply, since the first $100,000 of taxable income for all corporations carries an effective average

---

[5]There are some exceptions to this rule. The corporation, if it meets all requirements, may elect under Subchapter S to be taxed in a similar manner to a partnership. Furthermore, the courts have pierced the corporate structure if the intent is tax evasion.

tax rate of only 26.75 percent ($26,750/$100,000). The second point, however, is that for very large corporations, the average tax rate approaches the maximum marginal tax rate of 46 percent, since the lower tax rate on the first $100,000 has only a minor overall effect on the average tax rate. As demonstrated in Table 8–4, it is possible to think of large corporations as

TABLE 8–4

AVERAGE TAX RATES AND TAXABLE INCOME

| Taxable income | Tax on first $100,000 | Tax on remainder | Total tax | Average tax rate[a] |
|---|---|---|---|---|
| $1,000,000 | $26,750 | $414,000 | $440,750 | 44.1% |
| $5,000,000 | $26,750 | $2,254,000 | $2,280,750 | 45.6% |
| $10,000,000 | $26,750 | $4,554,000 | $4,580,750 | 45.8% |
| $25,000,000 | $26,750 | $11,454,000 | $11,480,750 | 45.9% |
| $50,000,000 | $26,750 | $22,954,000 | $22,980,750 | 46.0% |

[a]Average tax rate is equal to the total tax divided by the taxable income and rounded to the nearest one decimal place.

having an overall 46 percent tax rate on all their taxable incomes. The table shows that corporations with a taxable income of $5 million have an effective average tax rate of 45.6 percent, and corporations with $50 million in taxable income have an effective average tax rate of 46 percent.

## CORPORATE TAXATION ON SALES OF ASSETS

Not all corporate income is taxed at the rates presented in Table 8–3. Income resulting from the sale of certain types of assets, held for more than one year, is taxed at a rate of 28 percent. For large corporations, this represents a significant tax reduction. For purposes of corporate tax planning, there are basically two types of assets qualifying for this favorable treatment:

1. Section 1231 of the Internal Revenue Code classifies certain fixed assets (plant, equipment, etc.) as "tax depreciable" assets. Income resulting from the sale of these assets may be taxed at the 28% rate if the asset has been held for more than one year.
2. Capital assets are those assets not usually bought and sold by the firm in its ordinary line of business. For example, a manufacturing corporation's marketable securities constitute capital assets. Income resulting from the sale of capital assets held for more than one year is taxed at the 28% rate.

The sale of tax-depreciable assets and capital assets does not automatically result in the generation of income to the corporation. In the case of capital assets (marketable securities and the like), the corporation may incur either a loss or a gain when the asset is sold. For example, a corporation may purchase marketable securities at a cost of $100,000 and sell them at a later date for only $90,000. Although the corporation receives $90,000 in cash for the securities, it receives no income; it actually has a negative income, or loss. The firm's income will be increased only if the securities are sold for more than $100,000. If the corporation sells the securities for $110,000, it has a gain of $10,000, and that gain is subject to taxation.

Two important points follow from this example:

1. When a corporation sells a capital asset (such as marketable securities) at a price in excess of cost, income is generated. The income generated from the sale of capital assets is known as "capital gains income."
2. When capital gains income results from the sale of assets held for more than one year, it is called long-term capital gains income, and it is subject to a maximum tax rate of 28%.[6]

The tax implications of the sale of depreciable assets (Internal Revenue Code, Section 1231) are somewhat different from those stated above. The firm must first determine the gain or loss on the sale of the asset. The gain on the sale of a depreciable asset is equal to the sales price less the book value (original cost less accumulated depreciation) of the asset. There are three possible outcomes to this calculation: (1) The gain exceeds the accumulated depreciation of the asset (in other words, the sales price is higher than the original cost); (2) the gain is less than the accumulated depreciation (the sales price is less than the original cost, but greater than the book value of the asset); and (3) the firm experiences a loss on the sale of the asset (the sales price is less than the book value). These three possible outcomes will have different tax implications.

First, let us illustrate case 1, in which the sales price is greater than the original cost. A corporation purchased a machine four years ago for $100,000, and has taken $60,000 in depreciation on the machine (accumulated depreciation) over the period. Therefore, the book value of the machine is $40,000. The machine is sold today for $130,000. Ordinary income of the corporation is currently over $1 million, so its marginal tax rate is 46 percent. What is the tax consequence of the sale of the machine? The gain on the sale is $90,000 (sales price of $130,000 less the book value of $40,000). The tax law requires this gain to be divided into two categories: (1) the accumulated depreciation taken on the asset, and (2) the excess of the sales price over the original cost of the machine. In this case, the accumulated depreciation taken on the asset has been $60,000, and the excess over the original cost is $30,000. The tax rate applicable to the accumulated depreciation is equal to the ordinary income tax rate of the corporation—in this case, 46 percent. The tax rate applicable to the excess over the original

---

[6]The corporation is not obligated to use this alternative 28% rate. Corporations earning less than $50,000 have a marginal tax rate on taxable income of only 20%. Therefore, they will pay taxes on the gain at the 20% and not the 28% rate.

cost is equal to the long-term capital gains rate of 28 percent. Thus, the total tax on the sale of the machine will be:

| | | |
|---|---|---|
| Tax on "recapture" of depreciation | 46% of $60,000 = | $27,600 |
| Plus: Tax on excess over original cost | 28% of $30,000 = | $ 8,400 |
| Total tax on the sale of the machine | = | $36,000 |

Using the same example, what is the tax consequence in case 2, if the machine is sold for, say, $70,000? The gain on the sale is $30,000 (sales price of $70,000 less book value of $40,000). The entire gain is subject to the "recapture" provision, since the gain is less than the accumulated depreciation taken over the life of the asset. Thus, the tax on the sale of the asset will be $13,800 (46 percent of $30,000). In this case, the firm depreciated an amount in excess of the actual realized depreciation on the asset.

In case 3, what is the tax consequence if the machine is sold for $30,000? The loss on the sale is $10,000 (sales price of $30,000 less book value of $40,000). In this case, an insufficient amount of depreciation was claimed in previous years. At the time of the sale, this "unclaimed" depreciation can be recognized as an expense. This recognition of the previously unclaimed depreciation is known as a book loss and results in a reduced tax liability for the firm.[7] The reduction in taxes owing to a book loss can be computed as follows:

$$\text{Tax reduction owing to a book loss} = \text{Amount of the loss} \times \text{Ordinary income tax rate applicable}$$
$$= \$10,000 \times 0.46 = \$4,600$$

The previous discussion is summarized in Figure 8–1. The original cost of the machine was 0–A dollars. The book value of the machine at the time of the sale is 0–B dollars. Given that a firm has a gain on the sale, it must first "recapture" all accumulated depreciation (and pay taxes at the ordinary corporate tax rate) before it can use the long-term capital gains rate of 28 percent. Losses on the sale of this type of asset can be offset against ordinary income.

This section has been designed to show that income received from the sale of depreciable or capital assets is taxed differently from ordinary corporate income. In addition, we have shown that there are several complicating factors relating to the taxation of depreciable assets (Section 1231).[8] The discussion of depreciable assets serves as important background information for our presentation of asset acquisition, the subject of Chapters 8 and 9 of this book.

---

[7]We are assuming that this is the only depreciable asset sold by the firm during the taxable year.

[8]These rules apply to depreciable equipment. Different tax rules apply to buildings.

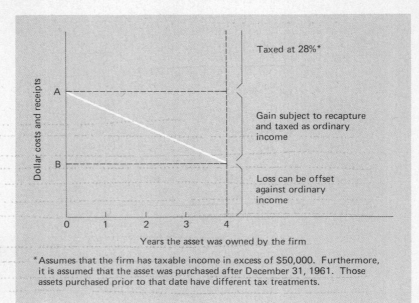

FIGURE 8-1

Taxation of
Depreciable Assets
Under Section 1231

*Assumes that the firm has taxable income in excess of $50,000. Furthermore, it is assumed that the asset was purchased after December 31, 1961. Those assets purchased prior to that date have different tax treatments.

## AVERAGING OF LOSSES

Business firms do suffer losses owing to declines in sales, changes in consumer tastes, sudden increases in costs, and innumerable other factors. The effect on the firm of such losses is ameliorated by the carryback-carryforward provisions of the tax laws. When a firm experiences a loss in one year, it can offset that loss against either past or future profits. For purposes of taxation, losses fall into two categories:

1. *Capital losses,* defined as losses associated with the disposal of capital assets (securities, etc.).
2. *Ordinary losses,* defined as losses associated with the regular activities of the firm. Cost increases in raw materials, for example, may generate ordinary losses. In addition, losses associated with the sale of depreciable assets are included as ordinary losses.

Note that depreciable assets are treated in an unusual manner. When a depreciable asset is sold at a gain, part of the gain may be taxed at the lower, long-term capital gains rate of 28 percent. However, when the sale of a depreciable asset results in a loss (sales price is less than book value), the loss is treated as an ordinary loss.[9]

---

[9]We are assuming that the aggregate result of all Section 1231 transactions made during the year is a loss.

Capital losses can be offset *only* against past or future capital gains. The general rule of capital losses is that the corporation can offset such losses against capital gains realized during the last three years. If it does not have sufficient capital gains during the last three years to entirely offset the capital losses incurred during this year, it is permitted to offset the remainder against any capital gains it realizes during the next five years.[10]

Ordinary-income losses can be offset *only* against past or future ordinary income. Special attention must be paid to the carryback-carryforward provisions of ordinary losses. The general rule is to carry ordinary losses back three years and then forward for seven years. If a corporation experiences a loss during 1980, it must first offset that loss against its 1977 ordinary income. The corporation would file an "amended return" for 1977, by "merging" the 1980 loss with the 1977 income, and would receive a tax refund. Given that 1980 losses are larger than the income in 1977, the firm can offset the "unused" loss against 1978 income, and receive another tax refund. If the 1980 losses are greater than the combined 1977 and 1978 income, it can then offset the "unused" loss against 1979 income, and receive a tax refund for that year. If the losses incurred during 1980 exceed the combined income for the last three years, the "unused" loss can be offset against future ordinary income of the corporation during the next seven years. There is no flexibility in this carryback provision.[11] A corporation experiencing a loss in 1980 *cannot choose* among the last three years; it *must* go back to 1977, then 1978, and finally 1979. The following numerical example may help illustrate how the carryback-carryforward provisions of the tax laws are enforced.

Table 8–5 shows the taxable income and taxes paid by the Christine Corporation during the period from 1977 through 1979. The corporation made a profit during these three years. During 1980, it experienced a loss of $900,000. The firm was able to go back to 1977, bring the adjusted taxable income to zero, and thus receive a refund of $118,750. Then, because Christine Corporation still had an "unused" loss of $600,000, it was able to do the same for 1978. The firm still had an "unused" loss of $300,000, which enabled it to reduce the taxable income for 1979 to $700,000, and thus receive a total refund of $375,500. The corporation would have preferred to offset the entire loss against its 1979 income, thus reducing taxable income for 1979 to only $100,000, and receive a tax refund of $414,000. However, this is not allowed under the present tax rules. Note that the $900,000 loss incurred during 1980 had an economic value. Christine Corporation was able to ameliorate the effect of the $900,000 loss by receiving a $375,500 tax refund.

---

[10]We are not going to expand this general description of capital losses. Although the carryback-carryforward provisions of capital losses are of significant importance to the corporation, we are more interested in discussing the treatment of ordinary losses in this chapter.

[11]The firm can elect not to carry back losses, but to carry them forward.

**TABLE 8–5**

## CHRISTINE CORPORATION
### EFFECT OF ORDINARY LOSSES ON TAXES
(\$900,000 loss in 1980)

| Year | Actual taxable income | Taxes paid[a] | Adjusted taxable income | Adjusted taxes due | Tax refund |
|------|------------------------|----------------|--------------------------|---------------------|-------------|
| 1977 | \$300,000 | \$118,750 | 0 | 0 | \$118,750 |
| 1978 | \$300,000 | \$118,750 | 0 | 0 | \$118,750 |
| 1979 | \$1,000,000 | \$440,750 | \$700,000 | \$302,750 | \$138,000 |
| 1980 | − \$900,000 | 0 | 0 | 0 | 0 |

Total tax refund = \$375,500

[a]Assumes that the existing tax rates have been in effect throughout the period.

The same numerical example can be adjusted to illustrate the effect of the carryforward provision of the tax laws. If the 1980 loss had been \$2 million, the corporation would be able to offset all income during the 1977–1979 period. It would receive a tax refund equal to all taxes paid during the period, or \$678,250. Furthermore, the firm has utilized only \$1.6 million of its 1980 loss. The "unused" loss can be used to reduce taxable income in 1981, or if that is not possible, in any of the succeeding years until 1987. If the firm fails to have total taxable income of \$400,000 from 1981 to 1987, the "unused" loss *cannot* be used to reduce 1988 income taxes.

This provision of the tax laws reduces the effect of losses on the cash flows of corporations, since current losses can be offset against past or future profits. But keep in mind that capital losses *cannot* be offset against ordinary income, nor can ordinary losses be offset against capital gains.[12] Ordinary losses can be offset *only* against ordinary income, and capital losses can be offset *only* against capital gains. The resulting tax refunds from unexpected losses, or future tax reductions, improve the cash flows of the corporation during a period of possible financial difficulties.

## TAXES AND THE FORM OF BUSINESS ORGANIZATION

The form of the business organization is substantially related to its total tax liabilities. There are basically three forms of business organizations: sole proprietorships, partnerships, and corporations. The sole proprietorship is the most widely used way of organizing a business enterprise. The main advantage of the sole proprietorship is its simplicity: There are no extraordi-

---

[12]The firm can offset ordinary losses against capital gains *only* if it has not elected to use the alternate long-term capital gains rate of 28%.

nary legal ramifications in starting it, and the tax laws do not differentiate between business income and any other income of its owner. The owner is permitted to declare in his or her tax return all income, expenses, depreciation, and so on, from the business. The tax rates applicable are the individual personal income tax rates.

Partnerships are taxed in a similar manner. The partners declare a pro rata distribution, based on the proportion of ownership, of income, deductions, depreciation, and the like in their respective tax returns.

For both the sole proprietorship and the partnership, personal taxes are paid at the time income is earned by the firm. But in the case of a corporation, the individual stockholder is not liable for personal taxes until income is received from the corporation, usually in the form of dividends.

To a large extent, the selection of the optimal business form for tax purposes will depend on the owner's need for current income.[13] Two very general statements can be made: First, if the owners plan to reinvest earnings in the firm, the corporate form should be selected. Second, if current income is desired, taxes will be minimized when the sole proprietorship or partnership form is selected.

The effect on taxes and income of the business form of organization is illustrated in the following example. Mr. and Mrs. Jeffrey own the William Manufacturing Company, which is managed by Mr. Jeffrey. The firm has good possibilities for growth, and the Jeffreys plan to reinvest a substantial portion of the profits in the business in order to increase its future earnings and market value. They intend to either sell the firm or maintain ownership but hire a professional manager ten years from now, and then to pursue leisure-time activities. In short, the Jeffreys are willing to forego current consumption in order to secure a higher income in ten years.

Table 8–6 shows the after-tax income available to the Jeffreys if they choose to organize the firm as a sole proprietorship. The net income from the business is assumed to be $200,000. After paying personal income taxes (computed using the data in Table 8–2), the Jeffreys wind up with $94,328. They can use this amount for consumption and/or reinvestment in the business.

Now assume that the Jeffreys decide to incorporate. They become stockholders in the corporation, owning 100 percent of its stock. Once they have established the corporation, they may choose to be taxed as a corporation or a partnership (under Subchapter S). If the corporate form is chosen for tax purposes, taxes will be paid at two levels: First, the corporation will have to pay corporate income taxes. Second, the Jeffreys will have to pay personal income taxes on the income they receive from the corporation (both salaries and dividends).

Table 8–7 shows the taxes paid by the William Manufacturing Corporation. In this example, we assume that Mr. Jeffrey receives a salary of $30,000

---

[13]See footnote 5 above, on Subchapter S corporations.

TABLE 8-6

AFTER-TAX INCOME OF MR. AND MRS. JEFFREY,
OWNERS OF WILLIAM MANUFACTURING COMPANY
(A sole proprietorship)

| | |
|---|---|
| Taxable income: | |
| Gross income from the business | $200,000 |
| *Less:* Personal exemptions | − $2,000 |
| Taxable income | $198,000 |
| Tax computation:[a] | |
| Tax on the first $162,400 | $81,464 |
| Tax on the remaining $35,600 | |
| ($35,600 × 0.68) | $24,208 |
| Total tax | $105,672 |

After-tax income = $200,000 − $105,672 = $94,328

[a]Married taxpayers filing a joint return, without itemizing deductions. The Jeffreys have no other dependents.

from the corporation, which is sufficient for current consumption and is "reasonable" in the light of the contribution he makes to the management of the firm. The corporation pays $58,950 in income taxes. The Jeffreys, however, have additional tax liabilities. First, personal income taxes must be paid on the $30,000 salary. Second, if the $111,050 corporate income after taxes is paid to the Jeffreys in the form of dividends, personal income taxes will also have to be paid on this amount. The tax situation in which dividends are paid is illustrated in Table 8–8. After paying corporate taxes and personal income taxes on both salary and dividends, the Jeffreys are left with only $74,658. This is less than the $94,328 they have if they organize the firm as a sole proprietorship. Under the assumptions used in this example thus far, the corporate form reduces the after-tax income of the Jeffreys because it subjects income to two levels of taxation. This situation is commonly referred to as "double taxation."

TABLE 8-7

AFTER-TAX INCOME OF THE WILLIAM MANUFACTURING CORPORATION

| | |
|---|---|
| Corporate taxable income: | |
| Gross income before Mr. Jeffrey's salary | $200,000 |
| *Less:* Mr. Jeffrey's salary | − $30,000 |
| Taxable income | $170,000 |

Corporate taxes[a] = $26,750 + [46% × ($170,000 − $100,000)] = $58,950
Corporate earnings after taxes = $170,000 − $58,950 = $111,050

[a]Using Table 8–3.

TABLE 8-8

## AFTER-TAX INCOME OF MR. AND MRS. JEFFREY

| | |
|---|---|
| Taxable income | |
| Gross income (salary + dividends)[a] | $141,050 |
| *Less:* Personal exemptions | − $2,000 |
| *Less:* Dividend exclusion[b] | − $200 |
| Taxable income | $138,850 |

Tax computation (Table 8–2):

$$\$47,544 + [64\% \times (\$138,850 − \$109,400)] = \$66,392$$

After-tax income = $138,850 − $66,392 = $74,658

[a]The William Corporation pays out all its earnings in dividends.

[b]Married taxpayers holding stocks jointly are permitted to exclude from income the first $200 in dividends.

The Jeffreys can minimize this "double taxation" by retaining the earnings within the corporation rather than paying dividends to themselves. This situation is depicted in Table 8–9. The retention of earnings in the corporation shields them from personal income taxes (not corporate income taxes).[14] In this case, the Jeffreys could reinvest $111,050 in the corporation and will have to pay only $5,593 in personal income taxes. They will have $24,407 for current consumption. The total tax paid by the Jeffreys and the William Corporation is only $64,543 ($5,593 + $58,950). The after-tax income of the Jeffreys and the corporation is $135,457 ($24,407 + $111,050).

TABLE 8-9

## AFTER-TAX INCOME OF MR. AND MRS. JEFFREY
### (if the corporation pays no dividends)

| | |
|---|---|
| Taxable income | |
| Gross income (salary) | $30,000 |
| *Less:* Personal exemptions | − $2,000 |
| Taxable income | $28,000 |

Tax computation (Table 8–2):

$$\$4,505 + [32\% \times (\$28,000 − \$24,600)] = \$5,593$$

After-tax income of the Jeffreys = $30,000 − $5,593 = $24,407

Earnings after taxes of the William Corporation (from Table 8–7) = $111,050

---

[14]We assume that the retention of $111,050 has a valid business purpose other than tax avoidance. If the Jeffreys are unable to demonstrate such a purpose, the corporation may be subject to an accumulated-earnings tax.

The Jeffreys cannot use the after-tax earnings of the William Corporation for their own personal consumption. However, in terms of their goal of retiring ten years from now, the election of the corporate form of organization and the retention of earnings by the corporation are most appropriate. The Jeffreys have less available for current consumption but are maximizing the amount that can be reinvested in the firm. Their total "income" (if we include reinvested funds in the William Corporation) is highest under this alternative. If the goal of the Jeffreys had been current consumption rather than retirement in ten years, the sole proprietorship would have best served their purpose.

Of course, taxes are not the sole factor in determining the optimal form of business organization. Owners should also consider such things as the costs incurred in forming a corporation, liability exposure, and access to capital markets. Good tax planning, however, can result in increasing cash flows and present wealth of the owners.

## TAX IMPLICATIONS OF VARIOUS DEPRECIATION ALTERNATIVES

When a firm acquires a fixed asset (plant, equipment, or the like), a cash payment is usually made to the seller. In most cases, the buying firm would prefer to recognize the entire cash payment as a deductible expense for the year in which the outlay took place. For example, a firm purchasing a $100,000 machine for cash would ordinarily prefer to claim the entire amount as a current expense and thus reduce taxable income for the year by $100,000. It would reduce taxes by $46,000 (assuming a marginal tax rate of 46 percent), and reduce the net cost of the machine to $54,000 ($100,000 cash outlay minus $46,000 tax reduction).

However, the Internal Revenue Service will not permit a firm to recognize the cash outflow as an expense immediately. The IRS requires that the expense be recognized over the entire expected life of the machine. As one alternative, the firm is permitted to spread the cost of the machine evenly over the life of the asset. For the $100,000 machine with an expected life of five years (after which the machine is expected to be worthless), the firm is permitted to recognize, and deduct for tax purposes, an expense of $20,000 each year for the next five years, instead of $100,000 during the first year. In most cases, this IRS restriction results in higher present value of taxes paid by the firm, and thus lower stockholder wealth.

The process of spreading the cost of the fixed asset over the expected life of the asset is called *depreciating the asset*. The firm is usually permitted the choice of several depreciation methods. The straight-line depreciation method spreads the original costs evenly over the expected life of the asset. Accelerated depreciation methods allocate relatively high amounts of depreciation to the early years of the life of the asset, which reduces taxes in the early years and is more beneficial to the corporation and its stock-holders.[15]

Let us illustrate the effects of different methods of depreciation on the taxes paid by the firm, using our $100,000 machine. The machine has an expected life of five years and no salvage value in five years. It generates an annual depreciation of $20,000 for five years, if the straight-line method of depreciation is used. This deduction will allow the firm to reduce taxes by $9,200 (46 percent of $20,000) every year for the next five years.[16] The present value of the tax reduction, using Table 2–4, and assuming a discount rate of 10 percent, will be:

$$\text{Present value of tax reduction} = \frac{\$9,200}{1.100} + \frac{\$9,200}{1.210} + \frac{\$9,200}{1.331} + \frac{\$9,200}{1.464} + \frac{\$9,200}{1.611}$$
$$= \$34,874$$

Table 8–10 illustrates the effect of a change in the method of depreciation on the present value of the tax reduction. The firm uses the sum-of-years'-digits rather than the straight-line method of depreciation. Note that the present value of the tax reduction increases to $37,082 with sum-of-years-digits from $34,874 under the straight-line method of depreciation.

---

**TABLE 8–10**

PRESENT VALUE OF TAX REDUCTION WITH SUM-OF-YEARS'-DIGITS DEPRECIATION

|  | Year 1 | Year 2 | Year 3 | Year 4 | Year 5 |
|---|---|---|---|---|---|
| Depreciation expense[a] | $33,333 | $26,667 | $20,000 | $13,333 | $6,667 |
| Tax reduction (46%) | $15,333 | $12,267 | $9,000 | $6,133 | $3,067 |
| Present value of tax reduction = | $\dfrac{\$15,333}{1.100}$ + | $\dfrac{\$12,267}{1.210}$ + | $\dfrac{\$9,200}{1.331}$ + | $\dfrac{\$6,133}{1.464}$ + | $\dfrac{\$3,067}{1.611}$ = $37,082 |

[a]See Appendix 8A for the techniques to determine the amount of depreciation.

---

Thus, the present value of the tax reduction is higher under an accelerated method of depreciation. The reason for this is not that the firm is allowed to deduct a greater dollar amount of depreciation; the total amount of depreciation taken over the five-year period is the same ($100,000) under either method. It is not that the firm pays less taxes; the total tax reduction of the firm will be the same ($46,000) under either method. The present value of the tax reduction increases because the accelerated method of depreciation allows the firm to take a greater dollar amount of depreciation in the earlier years and a lower amount in the later years of the life of the asset, so that it receives the tax reduction at an earlier date.

---

[15]See Appendix 8A for a review of the most frequently used depreciation methods.
[16]We assume the corporation is at the 46% marginal tax rate.

The IRS has restrictions on the rate at which other expenses can be recognized. For example, the flotation costs associated with a new bond issue must be recognized over the life of the bond issue. This process is known as *amortizing the flotation costs.* As a general rule, firms would prefer to accelerate the process. Another example is the treatment of depletable assets (oil, gas, minerals). The rate at which charges can be made against income for using up these assets, known as *depletion allowances,* has created a considerable controversy. Firms would prefer to accelerate these depletion charges, but in recent years, Congress has limited the rate at which such allowances can be taken, in the belief that the depletion allowances had been so high as to represent a virtual subsidy to the firm. Amortization and depletion rates as well as depreciation rates should be analyzed closely by the firm, because of their effect on taxes and stockholder wealth.

## INVESTMENT TAX CREDIT

The investment tax credit is a provision of the law that enables the firm to reduce tax liabilities during the year in which "qualified" investments are undertaken. The purpose of the law is to encourage new capital investments, thus leading to greater productivity of the U.S. economy.

"Qualified"

The tax laws define "qualified investments" as new depreciable tangible personal property held in the conduct of a trade or business. This definition includes depreciable plant and equipment purchased by a firm, but it does not include real estate, stocks, bonds, and the like. Furthermore, the property must be acquired for business rather than personal purposes.[17]

The firm is permitted to take as a tax credit a certain percentage of the cost of the qualified investment, subject to some limitations. Congress intended to encourage those investments that lead to greater productivity in the American economy. Because long-term investments enhance productivity for a longer period of time than short-term investments, the percentage of the cost that can be taken as a tax credit is a factor of the expected life of the qualified asset. Table 8–11 gives the investment tax credit rates for assets with different expected lives.

Tax credits are generally more advantageous to a taxpayer than are tax deductions. Table 8–12 illustrates the differences between tax credits and deductions. Firm B has a $100,000 deduction, firm C has a $100,000 tax credit (the asset has an expected life of seven years or more), and firm A has neither. Tax deductions reduce taxable income, thus reducing taxes by the amount of the deduction times the tax rate. Using the example shown in Table 8–12, a $100,000 deduction reduces the taxes of firm B by $46,000

---

[17]We are not going to enter into a detailed explanation of qualified investments. For specific cases, the reader is encouraged to review tax services, such as Prentice-Hall or Commerce Clearing House.

TABLE 8–11

COMPUTATION OF THE TAX CREDIT FOR AN INVESTMENT

| Expected life of qualified investment | Investment tax credit rate as a percentage of total cost |
|---|---|
| Less than 3 years | 0 |
| 3 to 5 years | 3⅓% |
| 5 to 7 years | 6⅔% |
| 7 or more years | 10% |

(when compared to firm A). Tax credits directly reduce tax liabilities dollar for dollar. Thus, the $100,000 tax credit available to firm C reduces the tax liability by the full $100,000 (when compared to firm A).

TABLE 8–12

EFFECT OF TAX CREDITS AND TAX DEDUCTIONS

|  | Firm A | Firm B | Firm C |
|---|---|---|---|
| Gross receipts | $1,000,000 | $1,000,000 | $1,000,000 |
| *Less:* Deductions | − $600,000 | − $700,000 | − $600,000 |
| Taxable income | $400,000 | $300,000 | $400,000 |
| *Times:* Tax rate | a | a | a |
| Taxes | $164,750 | $118,750 | $164,750 |
| *Less:* Tax credits | 0 | 0 | $100,000 |
| Taxes due | $164,750 | $118,750 | $64,750 |

[a]Corporate taxes were computed in accordance with the rates shown in Table 8–3.

   The Revenue Act of 1978 further complicated the determination of the maximum amount of investment tax credits that can be claimed by a firm during a given taxable year. The maximum investment tax credit is equal to the first $25,000 in taxes, plus:

| Year in which the investment is made | |
|---|---|
| 1979 | 60% of taxes payable over $25,000 |
| 1980 | 70% of taxes payable over $25,000 |
| 1981 | 80% of taxes payable over $25,000 |
| 1982 and thereafter | 90% of taxes payable over $25,000 |

   Therefore, the firm cannot reduce tax liabilities to zero using the investment tax credit unless total taxes due are less than $25,000. The maximum amount that could have been claimed by firm C (Table 8–12) during 1979 would have been $25,000 plus 60 percent of ($164,750 − $25,000), or $108,850. Since the investment tax credit was only $100,000, the entire credit can be claimed by the firm during 1979. Given that the firm has tax credits in excess of the maximum allowed, the tax credit can be carried back three years and forward seven years.

*tax credit back 3 for 7*

From the firm's point of view, careful consideration must be paid to the timing of asset acquisition, and hence tax credits. This has been complicated by the fact that Congress has varied the tax-credit rate in accordance with its perceptions of the needs of the American economy. Firms may accelerate or slow down asset-acquisition plans depending on present and anticipated changes in the investment-tax-credit rates and regulations.

## TAXES OTHER THAN FEDERAL

Federal income taxes are applicable to all business firms operating within the United States. The effect of such taxes on the cash flows of the firm will be the same whether the firm conducts operations in California or in New York. However, state and local government bodies impose taxes that do vary from state to state, or even between localities within a state. A variety of these local taxes affect the cash flows of the firm—for example, state and local income taxes, property taxes, fees, and taxes on inventories.

The decision of the firm to conduct operations in a given area is influenced by many factors, such as labor costs and availability and costs of energy. State and local taxes are also important. For example, many firms consider the establishment of West Coast warehousing facilities in Nevada instead of California, because of tax advantages, as well as lower wage rates and other factors. Possible disadvantages of being located away from the large population centers in California are outweighed by such advantages in Nevada.

Generally speaking, the lower the level of local taxation, the more advantageous it is to locate in such areas. But remember, there are other factors to consider. For example, New Hampshire is considered one of the lowest tax jurisdictions in the United States. A firm manufacturing surfboards may consider this to be an advantage. However, the greatest market for surfboards is located on the West Coast, and the advantages of lower local taxes may be offset by the disadvantage of being located so far from the principal market.

It is beyond the scope of this book to analyze the specific tax laws of various states, counties, and municipalities. However, the firm must evaluate the effect of local taxes on the future cash flows associated with any investment decision.

**SUMMARY** All decisions made by the financial manager impinge on the cash flows of the firm. Taxes have a significant effect on those cash flows. Thus, financial managers must have a basic understanding of tax laws. They need not be experts on taxation, but they must be aware of possible tax opportunities, as well as potential tax traps that will affect the cash flows of the firm. They must be able to recognize their own limitations and consult expert tax advisors within or outside the firm if circumstances require them to do so.

There is nothing sinister in attempting to minimize taxes by following the tax laws. This is the definition of tax avoidance. This chapter has described some of the areas that may permit a reduction in the tax liabilities of the firm. The determination of the form of business organization, the correct recognition and timing of depreciation, special tax treatment of depreciable assets, the uses of the investment tax credit, the carryback-carryforward provisions, and taxes other than federal are just some of the tax considerations that affect the cash flows of the firm. Proper tax planning can minimize taxes, maximize after-tax cash flows, and thus lead to increases in stockholder wealth.

**QUESTIONS FOR DISCUSSION**

1. Discuss the differences between tax evasion and tax avoidance. Include some examples of each.
2. What are the factors that should be considered in determining if an expense incurred by a corporation is deductible for tax purposes?
3. What are the tax advantages and disadvantages of the corporate form of organization when compared to a sole proprietorship?
4. What are the tax implications on the sale of a depreciable asset—for example, a machine? Discuss the tax effect of a loss or gain on the sale of the machine.
5. What are the tax implications to the firm of the carryback-carryforward provisions of the tax law?
6. "Federal income taxes are the only tax consideration that must be considered by the firm." Comment on the validity of this statement.
7. Why is it important that management be aware of tax policies and procedures?
8. Discuss several ways in which management can contribute to stockholder wealth through proper tax planning.
9. After reading this chapter, you are an expert on federal taxation of corporations. True or false? Comment.

**PROBLEMS** *Use Tables 8–2 and 8–3 to answer the following problems.*

1. What will be the level of gross income in which the corporate tax would exactly equal the personal income tax? Assume a married taxpayer filing a joint return, with no children, and without itemized deductions. *Hint:* You may want to use the following equation:

$$\$4,505 + 0.32(X - 24,600 - 2,000) = (0.17 \times 25,000) + 0.20(X - 25,000)$$

where $X$ = gross income.

2. Calculate the corporate income tax on the following levels of taxable income:
   a. $50,000    b. $100,000    c. $200,000    d. $10,000,000

3. Given a married taxpayer filing jointly, with no children and no itemized deductions, calculate the personal income tax on the following levels of adjusted gross income. (Each personal exemption is $1,000.)
   a. $10,000    b. $20,000    c. $40,000    d. $60,000

4. A corporation has ordinary income of $500,000 during 1980. In the same year, it sells for $50,000 a machine purchased five years before. The original cost of the machine was $60,000, and the book value is currently $40,000.

   a. What will be the *total* taxes paid by the corporation?
   b. What would be the *total* taxes paid by the corporation if the machine was sold for $70,000?

5. Calculate the after-tax cash flow for a corporation, given the following information:

| | |
|---|---|
| Sales | $800,000 |
| Deductible cash expenses | $400,000 |
| Depreciation | $100,000 |

6. Calculate the tax paid by a corporation if its taxable income during the last three years has been as follows. (Assume that the present tax rules and rates have been and will be in effect for all years.)

| Year | Taxable Income |
|---|---|
| 1977 | $500,000 |
| 1978 | 500,000 |
| 1979 | 500,000 |

   a. What would be the tax refund (and from which years) if the corporation had a loss of $600,000 in 1980.
   b. What would be the tax refund (and from which year) if the corporation had a loss of $3,000,000 in 1980?
   c. Using the information in part b, what will be the taxes paid in each year by the corporation if it has the following performance in the future:

| Year | Taxable Income |
|---|---|
| 1981 | $500,000 |
| 1982 | 500,000 |
| 1983 | 500,000 |
| 1984 | 500,000 |
| 1985 | 500,000 |
| 1986 | 500,000 |
| 1987 | 500,000 |

186    PART TWO: The Acquisition of Assets

7. A corporation purchases a $3-million machine that qualifies for the investment tax credit. The machine has an expected life of eight years.
   a. What will be the investment tax credit?
   b. What will be the amount of credit that can be taken in 1980 if the taxes paid by the corporation during 1980, before the tax credit was claimed, were $400,000?
   c. What would be the investment tax credit if this machine had an expected life of only six years?

8. The Allied Manufacturing Corporation has ordinary income of $1 million during 1980. In the same year, the company sells a machine for $100,000. This machine was purchased in 1975 for $300,000, and the current book value is $200,000. What will be the *total* taxes paid by the corporation in 1980?

9. Calculate the after-tax cash flows of a corporation, given the following information:

| | |
|---|---|
| Sales | $5 million |
| Deductible cash expenses | $3 million |
| Depreciation | $1 million |

10. Mr. and Mrs. Johnson own and operate a duplication-service business as a sole proprietorship. The business generates a taxable income of $100,000. The Johnsons keep $22,095 for their own personal consumption. The remainder (after-tax income minus $22,095) is used for the expansion of the business. (*Note:* The 50% maximum tax rate does not apply in this case.)
    a. Assuming that the Johnsons have no children and no other income, and do not itemize deductions, calculate the amount currently available for business expansion.
    b. Would the amount available for business expansion increase if the Johnsons incorporated the business? In order to simplify the problem, assume *no* dividends are paid, and that the new corporation can pay the Johnsons (and deduct) a salary large enough to provide them with an after-tax income of $22,095. (*Hint:* Try $26,600.)
    c. Would you recommend the corporate form of organization to the Johnsons, given the previously made assumptions?
    d. Assuming that the Johnsons use *all* the business after-tax income for consumption purposes, would your answer change? (Do not compute.)

# APPENDIX 8A
## Depreciation Methods

The amount of depreciation taken by the firm has a significant effect on taxes paid by the firm, and thus its cash flows. The amount of depreciation is affected by three variables: (1) the estimated life of the asset, (2) the expected salvage value at the end of the life of the asset, and (3) the method of depreciation used by the firm.

The first step in computing the depreciation allowance is to determine the economic life of the asset. The IRS has guidelines for the expected life of various assets. The firm can use these guidelines, or may assume a different expected life for the asset based on its own experience. If the guidelines are not used, however, the firm should be prepared to justify its assumptions to the IRS. Generally, a shorter expected life will increase the depreciation expense and thus increase the present value of cash flows. The economic life of an asset is not the same as its operating life. An automobile, for example, may last eight to ten years with proper care and maintenance. Many firms, however, have a policy of replacing their automobile fleet every three years. Such firms would use three years as the economic life of the automobiles.

The second step in computing depreciation is to determine the expected salvage value of the asset at the end of its economic life. The IRS requires an estimation of the salvage value when it is expected to be greater than 10 percent of the original cost. An estimate of the expected salvage value of an automobile after three years and, say, 50,000 miles of operation can be made from figures provided by the market for used cars. Other, more specialized assets may not have such a market, and the determination of expected salvage value can be relatively difficult, but somehow the firm must provide a reasonable estimate.

The third step in computing depreciation is to choose among the depreciation methods acceptable to the IRS. These methods are (1) straight line, (2) sum-of-years' digits, (3) double declining balance, and (4) any other consistent method.[18]

The straight-line method of depreciation has one main virtue, its simplicity. The amount of depreciation claimed each year of the economic life of the asset is the same. It is computed as follows:

$$\text{Depreciation to be taken each year} = \frac{\text{Original cost} - \text{Expected salvage}}{\text{Number of years of economic life}}$$

We will illustrate depreciation methods by using the same numerical example for all three methods of depreciation discussed in this appendix, so that you can compare the three.

A firm purchases a depreciable asset for $120,000. The firm estimates the economic life of the asset to be ten years and its expected salvage value at the end of ten years to be $20,000. Using this example, the amount of depreciation that can be claimed using the straight-line method will be as follows:

$$\text{Depreciation} = \frac{\$120,000 - \$20,000}{10} = \$10,000 \text{ per year}$$

---

[18]For certain property, the IRS allows only 1½ rather than double declining balance—a matter that is beyond the scope of this book. The firm can use any other consistent method, if that method reflects its operation. For example, the firm could use the units-of-production method, the operating-day method, or the income-forecast method. However, these methods will not be discussed here.

Table 8A–1 shows the amount of depreciation taken each year, as well as the book value of the asset at the end of each year, if the straight-line method is used. Note that the total depreciation claimed is equal to the original cost less the expected salvage value ($100,000), and that the book value declines at a constant rate until it reaches the expected salvage value of $20,000 at the end of its economic life.

**TABLE 8A–1**

STRAIGHT-LINE METHOD OF DEPRECIATION

| Year | Depreciation claimed | Book value at the end of the year |
|------|---------------------|-----------------------------------|
| 1 | $10,000 | $110,000 |
| 2 | 10,000 | 100,000 |
| 3 | 10,000 | 90,000 |
| 4 | 10,000 | 80,000 |
| 5 | 10,000 | 70,000 |
| 6 | 10,000 | 60,000 |
| 7 | 10,000 | 50,000 |
| 8 | 10,000 | 40,000 |
| 9 | 10,000 | 30,000 |
| 10 | 10,000 | 20,000 |
| | $100,000 | |

Since 1953, the IRS has allowed various methods that accelerate the depreciation claimed. The rationale for such accelerated depreciation is that the economic value may be higher for a new than an older asset. A new car, for example, should have fewer mechanical failures than an older one, so greater economic value may be derived from the first year than the third year of the life of an automobile.

The sum-of-years' digits is a method that allows the firm to increase depreciation during the earlier years of an asset while decreasing it for its later years.[19] The equation used to determine the depreciation is:

$$\frac{\text{Depreciation}}{\text{for year x}} = \frac{\text{Number of years remaining in the life of the asset}}{\text{Arithmetic sum of all the years in the economic life of the asset}} \times (\text{Original cost} - \text{Expected salvage})$$

The denominator of the fraction seems a very complex computation, but it is really very simple. For our example (ten years), it is simply the addition of all

---

[19]For accelerated methods of depreciation—sum-of-years' digits or double declining—the economic life of the asset must be greater than three years.

the years, or $1 + 2 + 3 + 4 + 5 + 6 + 7 + 8 + 9 + 10 = 55$. There is an equation that will simplify this computation, using N for the number of years in the life of the asset:

$$\text{Arithmetic sum} = N \left( \frac{N + 1}{2} \right)$$

$$= 10 \left( \frac{10 + 1}{2} \right) = 55$$

The computation of the allowable depreciation, using the sum-of-years' digits method, is shown in Table 8A–2. Notice two important points in this table: (1) The total amount of depreciation over the ten years ($100,000) is identical to that claimed when the straight-line method was used, and (2) the firm is permitted to claim the depreciation at an earlier date than with the straight-line method.

TABLE 8A–2

SUM-OF-YEARS'-DIGITS METHOD

| Year | Depreciation claimed | | Book value at the end of the year |
|------|---------------------|---------|--------------------|
| 1  | 10/55($100,000) = | $18,182 | $101,818 |
| 2  | 9/55($100,000) =  | 16,364  | 85,454   |
| 3  | 8/55($100,000) =  | 14,545  | 70,909   |
| 4  | 7/55($100,000) =  | 12,727  | 58,182   |
| 5  | 6/55($100,000) =  | 10,909  | 47,273   |
| 6  | 5/55($100,000) =  | 9,091   | 38,182   |
| 7  | 4/55($100,000) =  | 7,273   | 30,909   |
| 8  | 3/55($100,000) =  | 5,455   | 25,454   |
| 9  | 2/55($100,000) =  | 3,636   | 21,818   |
| 10 | 1/55($100,000) =  | 1,818   | 20,000   |
|    | Total             | $100,000 |         |

The double-declining-balance method of depreciation allows the firm to claim as depreciation a percentage of the book value of the asset at the end of the preceding year. The first step is to determine the percentage rate of annual depreciation under straight line; in our example, it is 10 percent. The second step is to double that amount, or $2 \times 10\% = 20\%$. This is the percentage that can be applied to the book value at the end of the preceding year in order to determine the annual depreciation expense. Table 8A–3 shows the allowable depreciation under the double-declining-balance method. Note that the depreciation claimed each year is 20 percent of the book value of the asset at *the end of the preceding year*, not cost minus salvage, as under the previous methods.

DOUBLE-DECLINING-BALANCE METHOD

| Year | Depreciation claimed | Book value at the end of the year |
|------|----------------------|-----------------------------------|
| 1  | 20% of 120,000 = $ 24,000 | $96,000 |
| 2  | 20% of  96,000 =   19,200 | 76,800 |
| 3  | 20% of  76,800 =   15,360 | 61,440 |
| 4  | 20% of  61,440 =   12,288 | 49,152 |
| 5  | 20% of  49,152 =    9,830 | 39,322 |
| 6  | 20% of  39,322 =    7,864 | 31,458 |
| 7  | 20% of  31,458 =    6,292 | 25,166 |
| 8  | 20% of  25,166 =    5,033 | 20,133 |
| 9  | a                         133 | 20,000 |
| 10 | a                           0 | 20,000 |
|    |            $100,000 |  |

aThe firm cannot depreciate an asset below its book value. Thus, the firm claims in year 9 $133 in depreciation instead of 20% of $20,133. In other cases (for example, if this asset had no expected salvage value), the firm would be unable to fully depreciate the asset. The IRS allows the firm the option to change to the straight-line method. In this case, the change would be made in year 7.

Many students confuse book value with the market value of an asset. Book value is the original cost less the accumulated depreciation taken. Our example illustrated three different methods of depreciation that can be used on an asset. The method chosen by the firm will not affect the market value of the asset during the next ten years. It will, however, affect its book value, as shown in Figure 8A–1. This figure shows that the book value of the asset will differ if a different method of depreciation is used by the firm. After five years, the book value will be $70,000, $47,273, or $39,322. Obviously, the market value of the asset in five years cannot equal all three possible book values. The book value is only an artificial value that does not necessarily equal the market value.

## THE EFFECT OF THE METHOD OF DEPRECIATION ON THE PRESENT VALUE OF CASH FLOWS

Now that we have discussed the various alternative methods of depreciation, let us illustrate the effect of these depreciation methods on the cash flows of the firm. We will use the same numerical example but will add some additional assumptions: First, this asset will generate $80,000 in annual

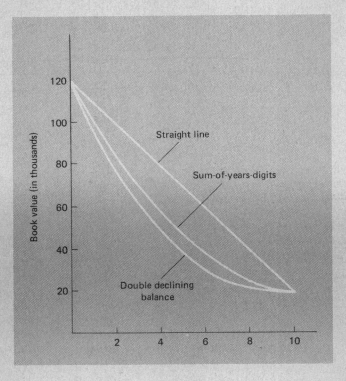

Book Value of an
Asset under Various
Methods of
Depreciation

sales every year for the next ten years, and the cash expenses (other than taxes and financing costs) associated with the sales will be $50,000 every year for the next ten years. Finally, we will assume that the firm's marginal tax rate is 46 percent. Table 8A–4 shows the incremental cash flows of the firm when the straight-line method of depreciation is used. Note that depreciation has been added back to earnings after taxes in order to determine the cash flows. This is done because depreciation is a noncash expense and does not leave the firm.

To state the table another way, the actual cash inflows are $80,000 in sales, and the actual cash outflows are $59,200 ($50,000 in cash expenses plus $9,200 in taxes). Thus, the net cash flows are the differences between inflows and outflows, or $20,800. The present value of the cash flows generated by the asset is $135,536.

Table 8A–5 shows the cash flows of the firm if the sum-of-years'-digits method of depreciation is used. The significant difference between this table and Table 8A–4 is in the timing of cash flows, and thus in the present values of such flows. Notice that the actual cash flows, without taking into consideration present values, are identical under both methods of depreciation.[20] However, owing to the difference in timing, the present value of cash

---

[20]The actual cash flows under both methods are $208,000 for operations plus $20,000 in expected salvage.

### PRESENT VALUE OF INCREMENTAL CASH FLOWS
(Straight Line)

|  | Years 1–10 |
|---|---|
| Sales | $80,000 |
| − Cash expenses | − 50,000 |
| − Depreciation | − 10,000 |
| Earnings before taxes | 20,000 |
| − Taxes (46%) | − 9,200 |
| Earnings after taxes | 10,800 |
| + Depreciation | 10,000 |
| Cash flows | $20,800 |

Present value of cash flows discounted at 10%[a] = $135,536

[a]Present value of $20,800 received every year for ten years *plus* the present value of the expected salvage of $20,000 in year 10.

flows when using the sum-of-years'-digits method of depreciation ($139,491) is greater than with the straight-line ($135,536). This difference is due to the fact that cash flows under sum-of-years' digits are received earlier than under straight line.

Finally, Table 8A–6 shows the cash flows of the firm if the double-declining method of depreciation is used. The results, in comparison to those of the straight-line method, are similar to those obtained with the

### PRESENT VALUE OF INCREMENTAL CASH FLOWS
(Sum-of-Years' Digits)

|  | 1 | 2 | 3 | 4 | 5 | 6 | 7 | 8 | 9 | 10 |
|---|---|---|---|---|---|---|---|---|---|---|
| Sales | 80,000 | 80,000 | 80,000 | 80,000 | 80,000 | 80,000 | 80,000 | 80,000 | 80,000 | 80,000 |
| − Cash expenses | 50,000 | 50,000 | 50,000 | 50,000 | 50,000 | 50,000 | 50,000 | 50,000 | 50,000 | 50,000 |
| − Depreciation | 18,182 | 16,364 | 14,545 | 12,727 | 10,909 | 9,091 | 7,273 | 5,455 | 3,636 | 1,818 |
| Earnings before taxes | 11,818 | 13,636 | 15,455 | 17,273 | 19,091 | 20,909 | 22,727 | 24,545 | 26,364 | 28,182 |
| − Taxes (46%) | 5,436 | 6,273 | 7,109 | 7,946 | 8,782 | 9,618 | 10,454 | 11,291 | 12,127 | 12,964 |
| Earnings after taxes | 6,382 | 7,363 | 8,346 | 9,327 | 10,309 | 11,291 | 12,273 | 13,254 | 14,237 | 15,218 |
| + Depreciation | 18,182 | 16,364 | 14,545 | 12,727 | 10,909 | 9,091 | 7,273 | 5,455 | 3,636 | 1,818 |
| Cash flows | 24,564 | 23,727 | 22,891 | 22,054 | 21,218 | 20,382 | 19,546 | 18,709 | 17,873 | 17,036 |

Present value of cash flows discounted at 10%[a] = $139,491

[a]Present value of annual cash flows plus the present value of the expected salvage in year 10.

## PRESENT VALUE OF INCREMENTAL CASH FLOWS
### (Double Declining Balance)

|  | 1 | 2 | 3 | 4 | 5 | 6 | 7 | 8 | 9 | 10 |
|---|---|---|---|---|---|---|---|---|---|---|
| Sales | 80,000 | 80,000 | 80,000 | 80,000 | 80,000 | 80,000 | 80,000 | 80,000 | 80,000 | 80,000 |
| − Cash expenses | 50,000 | 50,000 | 50,000 | 50,000 | 50,000 | 50,000 | 50,000 | 50,000 | 50,000 | 50,000 |
| − Depreciation | 24,000 | 19,200 | 15,360 | 12,288 | 9,830 | 7,864 | 6,292 | 5,033 | 133 | 0 |
| Earnings before taxes | 6,000 | 10,800 | 14,640 | 17,712 | 20,170 | 22,136 | 23,708 | 24,967 | 29,867 | 30,000 |
| − Taxes (46%) | 2,760 | 4,968 | 6,734 | 8,148 | 9,278 | 10,183 | 10,906 | 11,485 | 13,739 | 13,800 |
| Earnings after taxes | 3,240 | 5,832 | 7,906 | 9,564 | 10,892 | 11,953 | 12,802 | 13,482 | 16,128 | 16,200 |
| + Depreciation | 24,000 | 19,200 | 15,360 | 12,288 | 9,830 | 7,864 | 6,292 | 5,033 | 133 | 0 |
| Cash flows | 27,240 | 25,032 | 23,266 | 21,852 | 20,722 | 19,817 | 19,094 | 18,515 | 16,261 | 16,200 |

Present value of cash flows at 10%[a] = $141,190

[a]Present value of annual cash flows plus the present value of the expected salvage in year 10.

sum-of-years' digits. The present value of the cash flows when using the double-declining method of depreciation ($141,190) is greater than with straight line ($135,536). The difference is due to the fact that cash flows under double declining are received earlier than under straight line.

**PROBLEMS**

1. A corporation purchases a machine for $100,000. The equipment has an expected salvage value of zero in five years. The expected life of the machine is five years.
   a. Calculate the depreciation expense for each year, assuming the straight-line method of depreciation is used.
   b. Calculate the depreciation expense for each year, assuming the sum-of-years'-digits method of depreciation is used.
   c. Calculate the depreciation expense for each year, assuming the double-declining-balance method of depreciation is used.

2. The American Trucking Company is planning to purchase a new diesel truck. Revenues from the truck are expected to be $100,000 per year for four years. Cash expenses (wages, fuel, etc.) are expected to be $50,000 per year for four years. The cost of the truck is $40,000. The truck has an expected salvage value of $10,000 in four years. Assume that the marginal tax rate of the firm is 40%.
   a. Calculate the after-tax cash flows of the truck if the firm uses the straight-line method of depreciation.
   b. Calculate the after-tax cash flows of the truck if the firm uses the sum-of-years'-digits method of depreciation.

**SELECTED BIBLIOGRAPHY**

It is very difficult to prepare a bibliography on taxation, since such books are usually out of date by the time of their publication. The tax environment changes from day to day. Congress can change the tax law, courts can give a different interpretation of existing sections of the Internal Revenue Code, and the IRS can make new regulations.

The first step in searching for a solution to a tax problem should be to consult the IRS publication on the specific topic. For example:

Publication 17. *Your Federal Income Tax.*
Publication 334. *Tax Guide for Small Business.*

If you are not able to find an answer to your tax problem in IRS publications, the second step should be to consult the latest edition of the textbooks used in basic tax courses in American universities. Two of the most widely used textbooks are:

*Federal Tax Course.* Englewood Cliffs, N.J.: Prentice-Hall, latest edition.
PHILLIPS, LAWRENCE C., and WILLIAM H. HOFFMAN, *West's Federal Taxation.* St Paul, Minn.: West Publishing Company, latest edition.

Finally, some intricate tax questions may not be sufficiently covered in the aforementioned textbooks. The most current materials on taxation are presented by tax services. They are continuously updated in order to keep abreast of current developments. Two of the most widely used tax services are published by:

Prentice-Hall, Inc.
Commerce Clearing House.

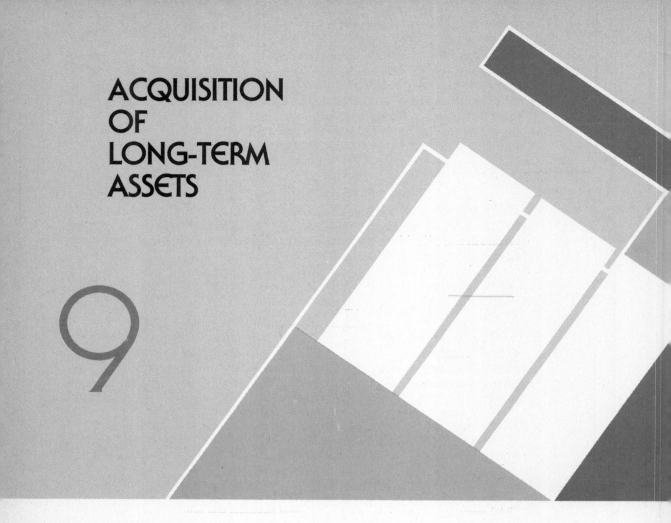

# ACQUISITION
# OF
# LONG-TERM
# ASSETS

9

## INTRODUCTION

Chapter 9 is devoted to an examination of the conceptual framework and specific techniques that should be employed by the firm considering the acquisition of long-term assets.[1] We begin with a review of the types of assets likely to be owned by a corporation. This is followed by a more detailed examination of the meaning of long-term assets and the crucial significance of decisions regarding their acquisition. Before proceeding to the computa-

---

[1]Students may find it useful to review Chapter 7 at this point.

tional procedures recommended for use, we show that long-term-asset decisions involve a broad range of inputs from all levels of management. Indeed, in order to understand the strategy of long-term-asset acquisition, the student must have some understanding of the behavioral dynamics of the organization in which the decision is made.

## LONG-TERM ASSETS

A simplified balance sheet for the LIZ Corporation is presented in Table 9–1. On the left-side of the balance sheet, you will see the category of assets identified as "long-term assets," which we deal with in this chapter. Techniques applicable to current assets will be discussed at a later point in this book.

**TABLE 9–1**

LIZ CORPORATION:
Simplified Balance Sheet

| Assets | Liabilities and equities |
|---|---|
| Current assets: | Current liabilities: |
|   Cash | |
|   Marketable securities | |
|   Accounts receivable | |
|   Inventories | |
| Long-term assets: | Long-term debt: |
|   Investments | |
|   Fixed assets | |
| | Equity |
| Total assets | Total liabilities and equity |

The category of long-term assets is not as straightforward as it sometimes seems. Its most important subcategory, called *fixed assets*, includes property, plant, and equipment. Another important subcategory of long-term assets is called *investments*. Investments usually represent ownership positions taken in other firms. For example, Chrysler Corporation has hundreds of millions of dollars invested in associated companies and unconsolidated subsidiaries. These investments represent long-term commitments and differ significantly from securities held for limited periods to meet known needs (marketable securities).

The key characteristic common to all long-term assets is that such assets are expected to provide benefits to the firm over a long period of time. In addition, outlays for long-term assets are likely to be of substantial size. Building a new factory or acquiring an investment position in an associated firm usually involves large cash outlays. Once management has committed itself to these large expenditures that are expected to yield benefits over a considerable period of time, the firm's flexibility is reduced. For example, when a firm spends $20 million to build a plant in a new market area, a commitment to a strategy of market development is made. The abandonment of that strategy usually involves a large cost, so the options open to the firm are considerably reduced once the expenditure for the plant is made.

It should be noted that there are other decisions made by the firm that, while not affecting long-term assets in an accounting sense, are closely related to the concept of long-term-asset acquisitions. For example, expenditures for research and development reduce the firm's flexibility, involve large outlays, and are expected to yield benefits over a period of many years. Therefore, the research and development effort can be viewed as creating an intangible long-term asset—even though not recognized as such by accountants—that generates long-term cash flows.[2]

A large, long-term advertising campaign can be viewed in a similar light. We can view the advertising effort as establishing a conceptual long-term asset—again, not recognized as such by accountants. The advertising may result in such things as brand recognition, favorable attitude toward the company, and increased sales over a long period of time. Note that the advertising-expenditure decision is similar to the decision involving the acquisition of a plant, in that both involve large outlays, reduce the firm's flexibility, and generate long-term benefits.

So we can see that, at least for decision-making purposes, the category of long-term assets is more extensive than it first appears. In the following sections, we will develop techniques for making decisions relating to long-term-asset acquisitions. Although we use fixed assets to illustrate the application of our recommended techniques, keep in mind that the techniques have broader applicability. They should be applied not only to acquisition situations involving other long-term assets appearing on the balance sheet, but also to what might be called "conceptual" long-term assets. The techniques presented in this chapter are appropriate to any decision-making situation that (1) calls for a large outlay, and (2) yields benefits to the firm over a long period of time.

## ORGANIZATION OF THE DECISION PROCESS

Corporations typically apply elaborate procedures in situations involving the acquisition of long-term assets. There are several reasons why management gives special attention to these situations. First, because long-term assets tend to require large outlays, mistakes are very costly and difficult to rectify. Decisions relating to current assets, such as the extension of trade credit to a customer, require a lower outlay and can be reversed relatively

---

[2]At one time, R&D expenditures were treated as assets, but as a result of abuses and other problems, the accounting profession abandoned this practice.

easily. For this reason, firms tend to review each long-term-asset acquisition at several different management levels and devote considerable effort to it.

The second characteristic of long-term-asset acquisitions that calls for elaborate review procedures relates to the difficulty of the decision itself. The firm makes large long-term-asset acquisitions relatively infrequently. It is not every day that the firm builds a new factory, acquires another firm, or embarks upon an expensive research and development effort or a large advertising campaign. Current-asset acquisition decisions, on the other hand, are made virtually every day. For example, trade credit is frequently extended to many customers, and the firm is able to accumulate substantial experience with respect to this decision. Management can, in many cases, learn how to estimate the costs and benefits of trade credit by trial and error. But a trial-and-error procedure is not appropriate in cases involving the acquisition of long-term assets.

Long-term-asset acquisition decisions are also difficult because they typically involve estimating both cash inflows and cash outflows in the distant future. For example, consider the information required for a decision relating to the construction of a steel mill that will take five years to plan and build and, once built, will have a useful life of 30 years. First of all, there is the problem of estimating planning and construction costs over the initial five-year period. This is especially difficult during periods of inflation. Next, net cash inflows (profits) for a 30-year period must be estimated. This requires estimates of market potential, prices, labor costs, raw-materials costs, and technological change. It is not difficult to see why decisions relating to such projects are scrutinized carefully.

One final difficulty associated with long-term-asset acquisitions relates to the time factor. The costs and benefits associated with current-asset acquisitions both take place near the present. This is not the case for long-term-asset acquisitions; timing of both cash inflows and outflows is crucial in these acquisitions.

Although many other decisions are delegated to lower-level management personnel, decisions having long-term consequences are reserved by top management. Therefore, the final decision-making authority for significant expenditures on long-term assets usually rests with a corporation's board of directors or a committee composed of high-ranking executives.[3] Production, marketing, and financial personnel serve as sources of information, collecting and processing data and perhaps making recommendations, but in the final analysis it is the upper echelons of management that make the decisions regarding long-term-asset acquisitions.

The role played by staff personnel in the decision-making process, however, is not insignificant. On the contrary, if sound asset-acquisition decisions are to be made and stockholder wealth is to be maximized, it is

---

[3]Fixed-asset acquisition decisions requiring small outlays may be delegated to lower-level management. In any case, the principles being developed in Chapter 9 and 10 should be used.

important that the entire management group understand both the overall process and the unique roles the various parties play in this decision making. Marketing and production personnel must understand the financial decision-making process in order to provide the required information inputs. Financial management personnel must understand marketing and production processes in order to organize and interpret data received from these sources. Top management must understand how all the different pieces of a complex business organization fit together. Sound acquisition decisions can be made only if the people involved have an understanding of the goal of stockholder-wealth maximization and of how various alternative courses of action will affect the achievement of that goal.

## STAGES IN THE LONG-TERM-ASSET ACQUISITION PROCESS

For purposes of explanation and discussion, it is convenient to look at the long-term-asset acquisition process as a series of stages. Although this sequence represents an ideal situation that is to some extent unrealistic, this technique does permit us to focus on certain crucial aspects of the decision-making process. A brief outline of the stages in long-term-asset acquisition is presented in Table 9–2.

**TABLE 9–2**

STAGES IN LONG-TERM-ASSET ACQUISITION PROCESSES

| Stage | Description |
| --- | --- |
| I | Review the goal of the firm and perceived constraints on the achievement of this goal. |
| II | Search for alternative asset acquisitions. |
| III | Estimate the size of cash flows, the timing of cash flows, and the uncertainty attached to the cash flows. |
| IV | Rank all projects in terms of contribution to stockholder wealth. |
| V | Choose among alternatives. |
| VI | Conduct regular post-audits of all decisions in order to assess the strengths and weaknesses of the procedures employed. |

Stage I is largely the province of top-level management. The board of directors should periodically review the extent to which it wishes to pursue stockholder-wealth maximization. For example, the acquisition of a competitor may increase stockholder wealth if the acquisition is unchallenged by the Anti-Trust Division of the U.S. Department of Justice; here, the possibility of legal entanglements and potential penalties acts as a constraint. In other situations, factors such as product liability and truth and fairness in advertising constrain management actions. Only the highest level of corporate management is in a position to evaluate these situations. Another constraint facing management relates to the availability of capital to be used in expansion. For instance, the corporation may have more attractive opportunities than it can accept, owing to the lack of funds. There are dozens of other legal, social, and organizational constraints on the corporation.

Stage I, the attempt by top management to maximize stockholder wealth within perceived constraints, is not merely a mechanical or computational process. The strategies adopted for the firm reflect business judgments. The final strategies adopted in this stage reflect a broad range of considerations. In a sound long-term-asset acquisition process it is most important that (1) a well-planned strategy, consistent with stockholder-wealth maximization, be adopted; and (2) both the strategy and its rationale be disseminated to the next level of management. It is unreasonable to expect lower-level management to make sound recommendations for asset acquisitions when top management fails to come to grips with the issue of constraints on stockholder-wealth maximization, or fails to convey agreed-upon strategies to the staff responsible for the development and evaluation of long-term-asset acquisition.

Stage II is largely the domain of production and marketing management personnel. Ideas relating to new markets, new products, and new production methods come largely from these two groups. The most serious error that can be made in this stage is the failure to consider a substantial range of alternatives. For purposes of illustration, assume that the top management of a firm currently serving customers in New York and New Jersey has decided that in the interest of stockholder-wealth maximization, it should expand the firm's production and sales into the New England area. Management personnel responsible for new plant development identify several possible locations in the target market area, prepare a detailed financial evaluation for each location, and present these recommendations to top management. Have all alternatives been considered? Was it possible to purchase an existing facility from a competitor? Should the firm close its current factory located in New Jersey and build a new, large, centrally located factory, perhaps in upstate New York? The questions can continue indefinitely. They show that there are many more alternatives than may appear at first glance.

And of course, there are many more alternatives available than can be examined in detail. For example, it would be very expensive for management to evaluate every possible building site in the New England region. Thus, the search for alternatives must be a limited search. Business judgments, based upon marketing and production experiences, must be employed. Poor judgments will lead to poor decisions. No amount of sophisticated analysis is going to result in a sound decision if it is applied to the wrong alternative.

Stage III calls for a unified effort by management personnel from the areas of production, marketing, and finance. At this stage, the amount, timing, and certainty of cash flows must be estimated. Forecasts of unit sales and prices for a number of years are required. Estimates of production and construction costs must be obtained. Financial managers must collect this information and prepare a detailed statement of periodic cash flows. This procedure will be discussed in greater detail later in this chapter; at this point, we must only emphasize the broad range of inputs required for the development of the cash-flow analysis, and the fact that cash flows cannot be estimated with certainty. Fortunately, methods for dealing with uncertain cash flows have been developed and will be presented in Chapter 10.

Stage III differs from the first two stages in being more "technical" and less "judgmental" in nature. As you will find out, the techniques of Stage III are discussed at length in this book, whereas little more will be written about Stages I and II. Do not conclude, however, that Stage III is more important than the other stages. In fact, sound application of techniques is dependent on the foundation laid in the first two stages. Always remember that there is more to asset-acquisition decisions than a technique for data manipulation. On the other hand, when based on reliable infrastructure, the proper handling and interpretation of data can minimize the possibility of costly errors.

Stage IV involves the ranking of the various projects available to the firm. Both this chapter and the next will examine specific ranking techniques in considerable detail. Although financial management personnel are usually responsible for the execution of these ranking techniques, it is important to remember that this is only another small step in a complex process. Also keep in mind that the reliability of the final rankings depends on the recognition by financial management personnel that the goal of the firm, even though subject to various constraints, is stockholder-wealth maximization. The techniques used in ranking alternative investment opportunities must be consistent with this goal.

In Stage V, the rankings prepared by financial personnel and supported by production and marketing data are presented to top management. At this stage, the whole process is once more reviewed and a decision is made. On the basis of additional information, or a refocusing of the goals of the firm, rankings may be altered. In the final analysis, it is the responsibility of top management to adopt those investment alternatives consistent with the maximization of stockholder wealth.

Stage VI takes place months and years after decisions have been made. Nevertheless, it is an important part of the decision-making process, because it calls for a detailed post-audit of the investment. The financial management personnel involved in the post-audit process are interested in evaluating assumptions, data, and techniques used by the firm in making past fixed-asset decisions, in the hope that such an examination will lead to the establishment of improved procedures in the future.

The combination of Stages I through VI constitutes a complex set of activities extending over a long period of time, requiring talented and competent managerial personnel, and involving substantial cost. The stage process implies that long-term-asset acquisitions are evaluated in groups rather than case by case. If stockholder wealth is to be maximized, the capital funds available to the firm must be allocated to the best alternatives.[4] In fact, many large firms develop formal long-term-asset acquisition plans, and constantly update and reevaluate them. The intent of the planning process is to avoid mistakes and maximize the returns of the stockholders.

## PATTERN OF CASH FLOWS—A NEW FIXED ASSET

During Stage III of the long-term-asset acquisition process, management must evaluate the size, timing, and uncertainty associated with the asset acquisition. Typically, marketing and production personnel provide data on revenues and costs of the proposal to the finance staff. The finance people then adjust the data and develop an overall picture of the amount and timing of cash flows. Since this book is primarily concerned with financial management, its focus is on finance rather than marketing and production. The procedures used to forecast revenues and costs are included in many books on marketing, production, and engineering. In this section, we use the acquisition of fixed assets to illustrate the appropriate financial techniques.

The cash-flow pattern associated with fixed-asset acquisitions is predictable. Initially there will be large cash outflows, expenditures made to purchase and install the fixed asset and make it operable. Cash outflows exceed cash inflows during this initial period (net cash outflow). This is followed by a second period, in which cash inflows exceed cash outflows (net cash inflow). The second-period cash inflows come from payments received from sales, and the cash outflows result from payments made for materials and labor used in the production process. The period of net cash inflows usually lasts for a number of years, much longer than the initial period of net cash outflows. The third period takes place at the end of the asset's useful life, when the asset is sold or salvaged. Depending on the salvage value, the cash inflows at this time may be large or small. The total pattern of cash flows is summarized in Table 9–3.

TABLE 9–3

TYPICAL CASH-FLOW PATTERN FOR A FIXED-ASSET ACQUISITION

| Period | Cash flow situation | Description |
|--------|--------------------|-------------|
| 1 | Net cash outflows | Firm acquires the assets. |
| 2 | Net cash inflows | Firm uses the asset to generate sales. |
| 3 | Net cash inflows | Firm disposes of the asset. |

For purposes of illustration, consider the cash flows associated with some industrial welding equipment being evaluated by the financial

---

[4]A popular term for this entire process is *capital budgeting*.

management group of the California Welding Corporation. The cash-flow data are summarized in Table 9–4. Note that in year 0, there is a net cash outflow.[5] This is followed by a period of net cash inflows over the next eight years.

TABLE 9–4

CALIFORNIA WELDING CORPORATION:
CASH FLOWS ASSOCIATED WITH ACQUISITION OF WELDER

| Year | Type of net cash flow | Amount | Purpose or source |
|------|-----------------------|--------|-------------------|
| 0 | Out | ($5,000,000) | Payment for welder |
| 1 | In | $1,400,000 | Receipts from sales − payments |
| 2 | In | $1,400,000 | " |
| 3 | In | $1,400,000 | " |
| 4 | In | $1,400,000 | " |
| 5 | In | $1,400,000 | " |
| 6 | In | $1,400,000 | " |
| 7 | In | $1,400,000 | " |
| 8 | In | $1,400,000 | " |
| 8 | In | $1,000,000 | Receipts from salvage value of the welder[a] |

[a]In some unusual circumstances, the cash flows associated with the salvage of an asset may result in a net cash outflow.

## CASH FLOW, REVENUE, AND EXPENSES

Before going further, let us define the term *cash flow* and explain how it differs from the more commonly used revenue and cost concepts. Cash flows are defined as actual money payments or receipts. The terms revenue and costs, as commonly used, refer to accounting transactions made on an accrual basis. For example, California Welding will be required to make a cash outlay of $5 million at time 0 if it purchases the industrial welding equipment under consideration. Neither generally accepted accounting principles nor the IRS permit California Welding to recognize this $5 million as an expense occurring at time 0. Instead, the cost or expense must be spread over the life of the asset. As we saw in Chapter 8, the process of spreading the cost over the life of the asset is called *depreciating the asset*. This process, as applied to California Welding, is illustrated in Table 9–5.

[5]We are assuming, for simplicity, that all cash outflows take place at the same instant. Appendix 9A illustrates the methodology used when cash outflows take place over several years.

In this example, we assume that the total outlay for the equipment is $5 million, that the equipment will have a useful life of eight years, that at the end of eight years the equipment will have a salvage value of $1 million, and that the straight-line method of depreciation is used. Based on these assumptions, the annual depreciation expense will be $500,000.[6] You can see that over the life of the asset, the total cash outflows required for the acquisition equal the total depreciation expense over the life of the asset *plus* the salvage value at year 8. Note, however, that cash flows and depreciation expense recognition differ significantly in their time patterns.[7]

ANNUAL CASH OUTFLOWS AND DEPRECIATION EXPENSE
ASSOCIATED WITH THE WELDER[a]

| Year | Cash outflow | Depreciation expense |
|------|------|------|
| 0 | $5,000,000 | 0 |
| 1 | 0 | $500,000 |
| 2 | 0 | $500,000 |
| 3 | 0 | $500,000 |
| 4 | 0 | $500,000 |
| 5 | 0 | $500,000 |
| 6 | 0 | $500,000 |
| 7 | 0 | $500,000 |
| 8 | ($1,000,000)[b] | $500,000 |

[a]Ignores the costs and revenues associated with sales during years 1 through 8.

[b]A negative cash outflow is the same as a cash inflow resulting from salvage.

The evaluation of fixed-assets acquisition alternatives requires information about both the amount and timing of cash flows *and* the amount and timing of expenses associated with the cash flows. Cash-flow information is important to management and stockholders because it indicates how much and when cash must be accumulated to pay for the asset. The expense information is important because such expenses reduce the corporate income tax liability, and this reduction has a positive effect on the periodic net cash inflows received by the firm.

---

[6]Depreciation $= \dfrac{\text{Cost} - \text{Salvage}}{\text{Useful life}} = \dfrac{\$5,000,000 - \$1,000,000}{8} = \$500,000$

[7]In order to simplify calculations, we will assume that the equipment purchased by California Welding does not qualify for the investment tax credit.

# COMPUTING THE PERIODIC CASH INFLOW

Let us continue with the California Welding illustration, so that we can actually compute the periodic cash inflow for the welder. We will assume that the welder will generate sales of $5 million a year. These sales will be partially offset by expenses of $3 million (in addition to depreciation and taxes).[8] California Welding is required to pay a 40 percent tax on its income. Table 9–6 is a combined annual income statement and annual cash-inflow statement for California Welding for years 1 through 8. Note that the earnings-after-taxes figure is not indicative of cash receipts. The discrepancy is attributable to the fact that depreciation is a noncash expense; thus, there is no cash outflow as a result of depreciation. As shown in Chapter 8, depreciation represents the recognition of an expense associated with a cash outlay made in an earlier period. Net cash income per year is always equal to earnings after taxes plus noncash expenses. Since depreciation is a noncash expense for the period in which it is recognized, earnings after taxes plus depreciation equals net cash flows.

**TABLE 9–6**

CALIFORNIA WELDING CORPORATION:
INCOME AND CASH-INFLOW STATEMENTS, YEARS 1 THROUGH 8[a]

|  | Income (expense) | Cash inflow (cash outflow) |
|---|---|---|
| Sales | $5,000,000 | $5,000,000 |
| − Expenses (other than depreciation & taxes) | (3,000,000) | (3,000,000) |
| − Depreciation | (500,000) | |
| Earnings before taxes | $1,500,000 | |
| − Taxes (40%) | (600,000) | (600,000) |
| Earnings after taxes | $900,000 | |
| + Depreciation | 500,000 | |
| = Cash inflows (per year) | $1,400,000 | $1,400,000 |

[a]These statements exclude activities of the firm unrelated to the welder acquisition. They reflect this project only.

We are now in a position to take another look at Table 9–4. When all factors are considered (initial cost, sales, operating expenses, depreciation, taxes, and salvage), the cash flows are as they appear in Table 9–4. Management and stockholders are interested in the cash flows because cash

---

[8]We assume that sales and expenses will be constant over the eight-year period.

is needed to pay for the equipment and cash expenses as well as to make payments to stockholders and suppliers of debt capital.

The work required to construct a cash-flow statement is less complicated than it first appears. The process can be visualized as composed of three steps: *First,* the cash outlay for the purchase of the fixed asset should be estimated. *Second,* the periodic cash inflows are estimated by adding depreciation to the earnings after taxes of the project. The *third step involves* the estimation of salvage value. Note that the receipts from salvage value constitute a nontaxable cash inflow. Cash, but no income, is generated by such a transaction. The firm disposes of one asset (machinery) and acquires another asset (cash).

The initial cash outlay includes not only the cost of the fixed asset, but also many related expenses. For example, the initial outlay of the California Welding Corporation should also include related installation costs. The firm actually paid $4.5 million for the machinery, but it paid $500,000 to have the machine installed. This $500,000 is viewed as part of the total cash outflows. Note that installation expenses are depreciated over the life of the asset. We could also have introduced additional complications, such as training costs and tax credits, but these would have made the analysis more difficult. These additional factors will be introduced later in the chapter. Furthermore, the actual cash outflows of many fixed assets occur over a number of periods rather than at time 0, as assumed for California Welding. This problem is discussed in Appendix 9A.

## EVALUATING CASH FLOWS

The cash-flow data, although important, are not alone sufficient to make a determination of an asset's contribution to stockholder wealth. For one thing, the cash inflows and outflows take place at different times. For another, these data make no allowance for the costs associated with financing the asset. These two problems have already been discussed in Chapter 7. Now let us briefly review the earlier discussion and develop specific techniques that can be applied in realistic asset-acquisition situations.

The asset-specific cost of capital plays a central role in the process of evaluating the cash flows associated with asset-acquisition alternatives. As we said in Chapter 7, if the expected rate of return of an asset exceeds the asset-specific cost of capital, then the asset is generating a sufficient amount of cash to compensate the suppliers of capital for the risk undertaken, *and add an additional "surplus" to stockholder wealth* (Table 7-4). The net present value (NPV) represents the dollar value of this "surplus" that is added to stockholder wealth when the cash flows are discounted by the asset-specific cost of capital. Thus, both the rate-of-return and net-present-value techniques permit us to evaluate the effect of an asset's expected cash flows on stockholder wealth. Net present value and rate of return are consistent decision-making techniques when *single assets are being considered for acquisition.*[9] The decision rules are as follows:

1. *Acquire the asset* (stockholder wealth is increased) if:
   a. Net present value is greater than zero, or
   b. Rate of return exceeds the asset-specific cost of capital.
2. *Do not acquire the asset* (stockholder wealth is reduced) if:
   a. Net present value is less than zero, or
   b. Rate of return is less than the asset-specific cost of capital.
3. *Be indifferent to asset acquisition* (stockholder wealth is unchanged) if:
   a. Net present value equals zero, or
   b. Rate of return is equal to the asset-specific cost of capital.

## COMPUTING NET PRESENT VALUE

As discussed in Chapter 7, the net present value of an asset-acquisition alternative is equal to the present value of the cash inflows *minus* the present value of the cash outflows associated with the asset, discounted at the asset-specific cost of capital.

$$\text{Net present value} = \frac{\text{Present value of inflows}}{\text{(Maximum dollar outlay)}} - \frac{\text{Present value of outflows}}{\text{(Actual dollar outlay)}}$$

Remember that the discount rate *must* be equal to the asset-specific cost of capital. With this knowledge and a set of present-value tables, it is possible to compute net present values with little difficulty.

For purposes of illustration, let us return to the welding-equipment acquisition being considered by California Welding (Table 9–4 provides the cash flows expected from the asset). We will also assume that the asset-specific cost of capital for this welder is 28 percent ($k_f^*$). The cash flows and present values are shown in Table 9–7. Note that the present value of the inflows is less than the present value of the outflows—hence, a negative net present value. This means that the cash inflows are not sufficient to compensate the stockholders for the risk undertaken. If the California Welding Corporation acquires the asset, stockholder wealth will be *decreased* by $554,600. Of course, the firm should not acquire the asset.

## AN ASSET ACQUISITION WITH MORE COMPLICATED CASH FLOWS

The cash flows in the California Welding example represent a simple fixed-asset-acquisition evaluation. In actual business situations, there are additional complications. Although it is impossible to discuss every possible complication, we will demonstrate the general nature of the problems.

[9]Two other methods, payback and average rate of return, used for evaluating asset-acquisition alternatives are presented in Appendix 9B.

TABLE 9-7

CALIFORNIA WELDING CORPORATION:
Net Present Value of the Welder

| Year | Cash flow & type | | Present value |
|------|------------------|--------|---------------|
| 1–8 | $1,400,000 | Inflow | $PVA_{1-8}^{28\%} = \$1,400,000(3.076)^a = \$4,306,400$ |
| 8 | $1,000,000 | Inflow | $PV_8^{28\%} = \$1,000,000(0.139)^b = \underline{\$\ \ 139,000}$ |
| | | | Present value of inflows = $4,445,400 |
| 0 | ($5,000,000) | Outflow | $PV_0 = (\$5,000,000)(1) = \underline{(\$5,000,000)}$ |
| | | | Net present value = ($554,600) |

$^a3\ \text{Coef}_8^{28\%}$

$^b2\ \text{Coef}_8^{28\%}$

For purposes of illustration, assume that the J-Net Corporation is considering the purchase of new weaving equipment. J-Net is an old firm currently paying taxes at the 40 percent marginal tax rate, and its current tax payments are over $2 million. The machine under consideration can be purchased for $400,000. If it is purchased, an additional $60,000 will be required for installation. In addition, the firm expects that $40,000 will be required to train personnel to operate the equipment. Finally, the new equipment fully qualifies for the investment tax credit.

TABLE 9-8

J-NET CORPORATION:
Cash Outflows Associated with New Weaving Equipment

| Year | Cash outflow | Purpose |
|------|--------------|---------|
| 0 | $400,000 | Payment for the equipment |
| 0 | $60,000 | Payment for installation |
| 0 | $24,000 | After-tax cost of training expenses |
| 0 | ($46,000) | Investment tax credit (reduces taxes of the firm) |
| 0 | $438,000 | Total outflows in year 0 |

The actual cash outflows associated with the acquisition are presented in Table 9–8. The treatment of installation costs is the same as in the previous example. These expenses must be depreciated over the life of the asset. The treatment of training expenses and the investment tax credit is less obvious. For purposes of the tax-credit computation, installation costs are viewed as part of the purchase price of the machinery. Thus, the firm can claim a tax credit on the total cost of $460,000 (price + installation). With a current tax credit rate of 10 percent, the taxes of the firm will be reduced by $46,000 (10 percent of $460,000) in the year of the purchase. The investment tax credit in effect reduces the required cash outflows.

The tax law also affects cash outflows for training costs. The law permits such costs to be treated as expenses in the year in which they take place. This reduces taxable income and taxes payable. The tax saving owing to training costs is equal to the training costs times the tax rate of the firm. The after-tax cash outflow associated with training costs is equal to the before-tax costs less the tax saving. The following illustration shows the determination of the after-tax cash outflows:

$$\text{Tax saving} = \text{Before-tax cost} \times \text{Tax rate}$$
$$\$16,000 = \$40,000 \times 0.40$$
$$\text{After-tax cash flows} = \text{Before-tax cost} - \text{Tax savings}$$
$$\$24,000 = \$40,000 - \$16,000$$

Or:

$$\text{After-tax cash flows} = \text{Before-tax cost}(1 - \text{Tax rate})$$
$$\$24,000 = \$40,000(1 - 0.40)$$

The procedures applied to training costs highlight the fact that tax consequences must always be considered. Note that training costs are treated differently from installation costs. The tax laws are full of such apparent inconsistencies, and tax experts can play an important role in the determination of the actual cash outlays associated with the acquisition of a fixed asset.

TABLE 9–9

J-NET CORPORATION:
Cash Inflows Associated with the Acquisition
of New Weaving Equipment (years 1 through 10)

|  | Cash inflows (cash outflows) |
|---|---|
| Sales | $200,000 |
| − Expenses (other than depreciation and taxes) | (100,000) |
| − Depreciation (straight-line) | (46,000) |
| Earnings before taxes | $54,000 |
| − Taxes (40%) | (21,600) |
| Earnings after taxes | $32,400 |
| + Depreciation | 46,000 |
| Net cash inflow every year | $78,400 |

The weaving equipment has an economic life of ten years. J-Net does not expect any salvage value on the equipment ten years from now. The firm uses the straight-line method of depreciation. The purchase of the equipment will allow J-Net to generate sales of $200,000 every year for the next ten years. The cash expenses associated with manufacturing (labor, raw materials, and so on) are expected to be $100,000 every year for the next ten years. The asset-specific cost of capital is 10 percent. The determination of the annual cash inflows is shown in Table 9–9.

We are now in a position to compute the net present value for the weaving equipment. The overall cash flows and the net-present-value computations for the decision are summarized in Table 9–10.

The net present value of the project is equal to the present value of the cash inflows less the present value of the cash outflows, discounted at the asset-specific cost of capital. For this illustration, the NPV of the asset is $43,768. Since J-Net will increase stockholder wealth through the purchase of the equipment, if should proceed with the acquisition.

TABLE 9–10

J-NET CORPORATION:
Cash Flows and Net Present Values Associated with New Weaving Equipment

| Year | Description | Cash flows |
|------|-------------|------------|
| 0 | Initial cash outflows | ($438,000) |
| 1–10 | Periodic cash inflows | $78,400 |
| 10 | Change in cash flows due to salvage | 0 |

|  | Net present value | |
|------|-------------|------------|
| Year | Cash flows | Present value |
| 1–10 | $78,400 | PV $\frac{10\%}{1-10}$ = $78,400(6.145)[a] = $481,768 |
| 0 | ($438,000) | PV$_0$ = ($438,000)(1) = ($438,000) |
|  |  | Net present value = $43,768 |

[a]3 Coef.$\frac{10\%}{10}$.

# CASH FLOWS FOR REPLACEMENT DECISIONS

In any firm, the replacement of fixed assets is an ongoing process that presents several conceptual and computational problems. In a conceptual sense, the decision to replace an existing fixed asset is only indirectly related to its condition or age. Fixed assets should be replaced whenever such a replacement will increase stockholder wealth. For example, assume that in 1972 a firm purchased an expensive computer system. At the time of purchase, the system had an expected useful life of ten years. In 1974, however, a big breakthrough in computer technology took place. Even though the firm had a relatively new and dependable computer system, management determined that the new generation of computers would increase profits and stockholder wealth. The firm disposed of what some people might consider a perfectly good system and acquired a new one. Again, the decision was based on stockholder-wealth considerations.

Technological change is only one factor contributing to the need for continuous review of fixed assets. As fixed assets age and wear out, maintenance and repair costs are likely to increase. As the product mix of the firm changes, existing fixed assets may fit into the production process less well then they did in the past. Changes in the cost of raw materials may also force the firm to reevaluate fixed assets. For example, rapid increases in petroleum prices may force firms to abandon processes that require large amounts of petroleum derivatives. Such change agents force firms to consider the replacement of existing fixed assets.

The pattern of cash flows associated with replacements is similar to that of cash flows in new-asset acquisitions. Initially, there will be a large net cash outflow. This will be followed by a relatively long period of net cash inflows. Finally, at the end of the asset's life, there may be an extra cash inflow due to salvage. But although the general pattern of cash flows is the same in new acquisitions and replacements, there are differences in the cash-flow estimating procedures.

The initial cash outlay for a replacement is affected by the cash inflow received from the sale of the old fixed asset and by certain tax consequences that may result from the sale of the old equipment. The tax consequences of the sale of the old asset are particularly troublesome. Figure 8–1 is reproduced here as Figure 9–1, in order to facilitate the discussion at this point. As suggested by Figure 9–1, there are three possible tax consequences with the sale of a fixed asset:[10]

1. If the sales price of the asset is the same as the book value of the asset, there will be no tax consequence associated with the sale. In this case, accumulated depreciation is equal to the actual decline in the market value of the asset.
2. If the sales price of the asset is less than the book value, the firm has underdepreciated the asset. The additional decline in market value can be recognized at the time the asset is sold. This recognition increases the expenses, and thus reduces taxes and results in a net cash inflow.
3. If the firm disposes of the asset at a price in excess of book value, the firm must pay additional taxes. The appropriate tax rate and amount of the tax liability will depend on the sales price and the length of time the asset was owned by the firm. In any case, the firm has a tax liability and a net cash outflow.

Review Chapter 8 for a more complete discussion about these possibilities.

---

[10]We will assume throughout this chapter that the old equipment is sold to a party not related to the firm selling the new equipment. The rules for trade-ins are different and will not be discussed in this book.

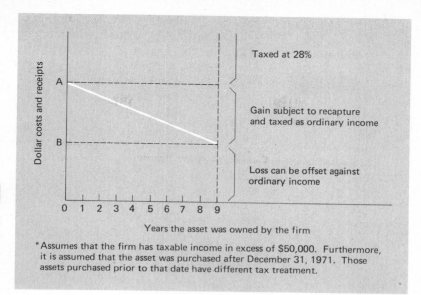

*Assumes that the firm has taxable income in excess of $50,000. Furthermore, it is assumed that the asset was purchased after December 31, 1971. Those assets purchased prior to that date have different tax treatment.

**FIGURE 9–1**

Taxation of Depreciable Assets Under Section 1231 (OA = Original cost; OB = Book value at time of sale)

In order to illustrate the procedures used to compute the initial cash outlay in a replacement decision, consider the problem faced by the Replace Corporation, a manufacturer of home air-conditioning equipment. The firm is considering the replacement of a piece of equipment used to manufacture air-conditioning units. Information on both the old and the new equipment is provided below:

- *Old Fixed Asset.* The old fixed asset was purchased five years ago for $4 million. At the time of the purchase, it had an estimated useful life of 15 years and an estimated salvage value of $1 million in 15 years. This asset can be sold today for $2 million. The expected salvage value in ten years remains at $1 million. This equipment permits the firm to generate annual sales of $5 million with annual expenses of $3 million. The firm expects these sales and expense figures to remain constant for the next ten years. The firm uses the straight-line method of depreciation.
- *New Fixed Asset.* The new equipment will cost $10 million and have a useful life of ten years. At the end of ten years, it is expected to have a salvage value of $2 million. If the equipment is acquired, the Replace Corporation expects sales to be increased by $1 million above present levels and expenses to be reduced $500,000 below current levels. Replace pays taxes at a 40% rate, and the new fixed asset will fully qualify for the investment tax credit.

The cash flows associated with the acquisition of the new fixed asset are presented in Table 9–11. All the transactions are planned to take place at the present time. Note that the net cash outflow is the result of several factors, and is well below the actual price of the new equipment. The four factors that must be considered in every replacement decision are (1) the payment for the new fixed asset, (2) the receipts from the sale of the old fixed asset, (3) the receipts associated with the investment tax credit on the new fixed asset, and (4) the additional *tax payment* or *tax reduction* resulting from the disposal of the old fixed asset.

TABLE 9-11

REPLACE CORPORATION:
Net Cash Outflows Associated with the Replacement of Manufacturing Equipment

| | After-tax cash outflows |
|---|---|
| Payment for new equipment | $10,000,000 |
| Less: Receipts from the sale of the old equipment | ($2,000,000) |
| Less: Receipts associated with the investment tax credit[a] | ($1,000,000) |
| Less: Additional tax benefit from the sale of the old equipment[b] | ($400,000) |
| Net cash outflow | $6,600,000 |

[a]Investment tax credit is equal to 10% of the $10,000,000 cost.

[b]The determination of the tax consequence on the sale of the old equipment would be as follows:

Book Value = Original Cost − Accumulated depreciation = $4,000,000 − 5 × $200,000 = $3,000,000

Gain (Loss) = Sales price − Book value = $2,000,000 − $3,000,000 = ($1,000,000)

The firm has a $1 million loss on the sale of the old equipment. Thus, Replace Corporation will be able to reduce tax payments by $1 million times the tax rate of 40%, or $400,000. Since the reduction of tax payments will reduce the cash outflows of the firm, it is entered as a negative amount. If the sale of the old equipment had resulted in a gain to Replace, the firm would have been forced to pay additional taxes; thus, it would have resulted in a cash outflow.

The periodic cash inflows for the new asset in the replacement decision can be determined by constructing cash-inflow statements for the Replace Corporation under two alternatives. The first statement indicates the periodic cash inflows if the old machine is kept in operation. The second indicates the cash inflows if the new machine replaces the old equipment. The difference between the two cash inflows is the appropriate figure to use in evaluating the contribution of the replacement equipment to stockholder wealth. In the Replace Corporation illustration, the firm will have a net cash inflow of $1,280,000 if the old machine is retained, as shown in Table 9-12. If the old machine is replaced with the new, the net cash inflow will be $2,420,000, as shown in the same table. The difference, $1,140,000, is the periodic net cash inflow and represents the benefit that accrues to the firm if it undertakes the replacement proposal.

In practice, it is easier to work with the *changes* in cash flows, by constructing a statement of periodic net cash inflows *if the new equipment is purchased*. Such a statement is provided in Table 9-13, which contains the same information as that in Table 9-12. In computing the net cash inflows, special attention must be given to the signs associated with the changes in

TABLE 9-12

## REPLACE CORPORATION:
### Periodic Cash-Inflow Statements (years 1 through 10)

|  | Cash inflows if present equipment is kept | Cash inflows if new equipment is acquired |
|---|---|---|
| Sales | $5,000,000 | $6,000,000 |
| − Expenses (other than taxes and depreciation) | (3,000,000) | (2,500,000) |
| − Depreciation[a] | (200,000) | (800,000) |
| Earnings before taxes | $1,800,000 | $2,700,000 |
| − Taxes (40%) | (720,000) | (1,080,000) |
| Earnings after taxes | $1,080,000 | $1,620,000 |
| + Depreciation | 200,000 | 800,000 |
| Net cash inflow every year | $1,280,000 | $2,420,000 |

[a]The firm uses the straight-line method of depreciation on both the old and the new asset.

cash flows. The cash flow associated with the old machine is subtracted from the cash flows resulting from the acquisition of the new. Note that the change in depreciation so computed is + $600,000, which is then subtracted from sales receipts. The change in cash expenses is − $500,000. When this amount is subtracted from sales receipts, it becomes a positive number.

TABLE 9-13

## REPLACE CORPORATION:
### Change in Periodic Net Cash-Inflow Statements (years 1 through 10)

|  | Change in cash flows (new − old) |
|---|---|
| ΔSales | $1,000,000 |
| − ΔExpenses (other than depreciation and taxes) | 500,000 |
| − ΔDepreciation | (600,000) |
| ΔEarnings before-taxes | $900,000 |
| − ΔTaxes (40%) | (360,000) |
| ΔEarnings after taxes | $540,000 |
| + ΔDepreciation | 600,000 |
| ΔNet cash inflow every year | $1,140,000 |

Infrequent users of these statements will have fewer difficulties if they use the more cumbersome format shown in Table 9–12. However both alternatives, if used correctly, will yield the same results.

One more important item must be mentioned in the computation of the Replace Corporation's cash flows: salvage value. If the firm does not make the replacement, it will receive $1 million in 1990 as salvage of the existing equipment. If the replacement is made, the firm foregoes this $1 million in 1990 and receives $2 million today (1980). The change in 1990 cash flows due to salvage is equal to the expected salvage value of the new air-conditioning manufacturing equipment less the expected salvage value on the old. Thus, the change in 1990 salvage cash flows is $1 million ($2 million on the new machinery less $1 million on the old).

Table 9–14 summarizes the discussion of cash flows in replacement decisions by giving the complete cash-flow picture for Replace Corporation if it replaces the existing equipment. Note that there are three cash flows of interest to the firm. These are the data required to make the replacement decision in a fashion consistent with the objective of stockholder-wealth maximization.

**TABLE 9–14**

REPLACE CORPORATION:
Net Cash Flows Associated with the Replacement of Manufacturing Equipment

| Year | Description | Cash inflow (cash outflow) |
|------|-------------|----------------------------|
| 0 | Initial cash outlay | ($6,600,000) |
| 1–10 | Periodic net cash inflows | $1,140,000 |
| 10 | Change in cash inflow due to salvage | $1,000,000 |

What is the effect on stockholder wealth if the Replace Corporation accepts the replacement alternative? Assume that the replacement asset has an asset-specific cost of capital of 9 percent. The net-present-value computations are shown in Table 9–15. In this illustration, net present value is positive. The cash inflows more than compensate for the risk undertaken. Should the firm acquire the fixed asset if a "surplus" of $1,138,520 will be added to stockholder wealth? Of course, the firm should acquire the new asset.

**TABLE 9–15**

REPLACE CORPORATION:
Net Present Value of Manufacturing Equipment

| Year | Cash flows | Present value |
|------|-----------|---------------|
| 1–10 | $1,140,000 inflow | $PVA_{1-10}^{9\%} = \$1,140,000(6.418)^a = \$7,316,520$ |
| 10 | $1,000,000 inflow | $PV_{10}^{9\%} = \$1,000,000(0.422)^b = \$\ \ 422,000$ |
| | | Present value of inflows = $7,738,520 |
| 0 | ($6,600,000) outflow | $PV_0 = (\$6,600,000)(1) = \underline{(\$6,600,000)}$ |
| | | Net present value = $1,138,520 |

$^a$3 Coef.$_{10}^{9\%}$

$^b$2 Coef.$_{10}^{9\%}$

# THE INTERNAL RATE OF RETURN

We have discussed the rate of return previously at various places in the book. The procedures used to compute annual rates of return for single amounts and annuities were described in Chapter 3. In Chapter 7, the relationships among stockholder wealth, rate of return, and the asset-specific cost of capital was discussed. Now it is time to bring these two parts together, apply them to relatively realistic cash-flow data, and show how the firm can use rate-of-return techniques to make decisions consistent with stockholder-wealth maximization. When rates of return are computed for specific fixed-asset alternatives, the resulting figure is called the *internal rate of return (IRR)*. This is the same rate-of-return idea discussed earlier, but we are applying it in the context of fixed-asset acquisitions.

First of all, it must be acknowledged that in realistic situations, the computations of IRR can be both time-consuming and frustrating. As you will see, the nature of the real-world problem is such that a technique much like trial and error must be employed. On occasion, many errors are made and many trials are needed. This is a fact of life that must be faced by professors, students, and managers. The annoyance is present for all of us. Understand that it should not be difficult to comprehend the meaning of the IRR; the difficulties lie in its computation.

The internal rate of return may be defined as the discount rate that equates the present value of cash inflows to the present value of cash outflows. For example, we can compute the IRR for an investment with a cash outflow of $6,418 today and annual cash inflows of $1,000 every year for ten years. The formula for computing the present value of an annuity is appropriate. We solve for the rate:

$$PVA_{10}^? = A(3 \text{ Coef}_{10}^?)$$

$$\$6{,}418 = \$1{,}000(3 \text{ Coef}_{10}^?)$$

Essentially, we are looking for a discount rate, indicated by the question mark. This discount rate will provide a 3 Coef. of exactly the right size (6.418) to establish the equality. In this case, the discount rate is 9 percent. As demonstrated in Chapter 3, it is not hard to find.

If we are dealing with a single sum, a similar procedure is employed. For purposes of illustration, assume that we wish to compute the IRR of an asset-acquisition alternative with a cash outflow of $120,000 at time 0 and a single cash inflow of $465,116 to be received 20 years from now. Again we must search for the discount rate that will establish the equality. In this case, the appropriate discount rate is easily computed to be 7 percent.

$$PV = FV_{20}^{?}(2 \text{ Coef.}_{20}^{?})$$

$$\$120{,}000 = \$465{,}116(2 \text{ Coef.}_{20}^{?})$$

$$2 \text{ Coef.}_{20}^{?} = \frac{\$120{,}000}{\$465{,}116} = 0.258$$

Unfortunately, fixed-asset acquisition problems do not typically fit into either of the situations covered above. The typical fixed-asset acquisition has a cash outflow at time 0, followed by a series of cash inflows, and followed finally by a single salvage cash inflow. To illustrate, assume that a firm is considering the acquisition of a fixed asset that will require a cash outflow of $84,990 at time 0. The asset is expected to have an annual net cash inflow of $15,000 every year for the next ten years and a salvage value of $25,000 at the end of year 10. In our notation system, the problem can be described as follows:

$$PV = FVA_{10}^{?}(3 \text{ Coef.}_{10}^{?}) + FV_{10}^{?}(2 \text{ Coef.}_{10}^{?})$$

$$\$84{,}990 = \$15{,}000(3 \text{ Coef.}_{10}^{?}) + \$25{,}000(2 \text{ Coef.}_{10}^{?})$$

Note that the solution for this equation requires two different coefficients to arrive at a single amount.[11] The mathematical properties of this situation are such that no general solution is available (except in the simplest cases) to find the IRR. Hence, we must proceed on a trial-and-error basis.

Let us apply a trial-and-error technique to this problem. Remember that we want the present value of the inflows to equal the present value of the outflows ($84,990). First, let us try a 12 percent discount rate and observe the results:

$$PV_{\text{inflows}}^{12\%} = \$15{,}000(3 \text{ Coef.}_{10}^{12\%}) + \$25{,}000(2 \text{ Coef.}_{10}^{12\%})$$

$$= \$15{,}000(5.650) + \$25{,}000(0.322) = \$84{,}750 + \$8{,}050$$

$$= \$92{,}800$$

Note that the present value of the inflows is greater than the present value of the outflows ($84,990) when a discount rate of 12 percent is used. This means that the present value of the inflows must be reduced by *raising* the discount rate used. Let us try a 16 percent discount rate.

$$PV_{\text{inflows}}^{16\%} = \$15.000(3 \text{ Coef.}_{10}^{16\%}) + \$25{,}000(2 \text{ Coef.}_{10}^{16\%})$$

$$= \$15{,}000(4.833) + \$25{,}000(0.227) = \$72{,}495 + \$5{,}675$$

$$= \$78{,}170$$

Now we have gone too far. This discount rate is too high, and the present value of the inflows is well below the present value of the outflows ($84,990). But we have learned something. The IRR must be somewhere between 12 and 16 percent. Let us try 14 percent.

---

[11]In some special and unusual circumstances; there may be more than one discount rate that will equate the present value of cash inflows and outflows. For a more detailed explanation of this problem, see James C. Van Horne, *Financial Management and Policy*, 4th ed. (Englewood Cliffs, N.J.: Prentice-Hall, 1977), pp. 104–6.

$$PV_{\text{inflows}}^{14\%} = \$15,000(3 \text{ Coef.}_{10}^{14\%}) + \$25,000(2 \text{ Coef.}_{10}^{14\%})$$

$$= \$15,000(5.216) + \$25,000(0.270) = \$78,240 + \$6,750$$

$$= \$84,990$$

At a 14 percent discount rate, the present value of the cash inflows is *exactly equal* to the present value of the cash outflows. Therefore; the IRR of this project is 14 percent, representing the annual rate of return on the investment.[12] If this rate of return (IRR) is greater than the true annual cost of acquiring funds (the asset-specific cost of capital), then the acquisition of the asset will yield a "surplus" return to stockholders and thus contribute to stockholder wealth.

You may have identified one potential source of trouble in the IRR computational procedures. Which discount rate should be tried first? And how much should the discount rate be increased or decreased when the first attempt was unsuccessful? People who work with rates of return have developed short-cut approximation techniques. Computers and programmed calculators are able to speed through the process outlined above. For the student, however, there is only trial and error. The best advice we can give the student is this: Remember what you are trying to do. *Search for a discount rate that will equate the present value of cash inflows with the present value of cash outflows (NPV = 0).*


## PRACTICAL APPLICATIONS OF THE INTERNAL RATE OF RETURN

We have presented three asset-acquisition decisions in this chapter: those of the California Welding Corporation, J-Net Corporation, and Replace Corporation. Let us now compute the internal rate of return of each of these alternatives, starting with California Welding. The cash flows of the project were presented in Table 9–4. Remember that the cost of capital for the welder being considered for acquisition by the corporation is 28 percent. The computations for the IRR are presented in Table 9–16. Note that when the discount rate of 20 percent is used, the present value of the inflows is greater than the $5 million outflow. When a discount rate of 24 percent is used, the present value of the inflows is slightly below the $5 million cash outflow. This means that the discount rate that will equate the present values of cash inflows and outflows lies somewhere between 20 and 24 percent. In the case of the welding equipment, the IRR of 23.8 percent is below the cost of capital of 28 percent.[13] This indicates that the returns associated with the welder are

---

[12]In some circumstances, this 14% may not be the true annual rate of return, because the IRR assumes all cash flows received from the investment are reinvested at the IRR. This may or may not be possible.

[13]See Appendix 9C for the interpolation of the IRR.

insufficient to cover costs associated with the equipment *and* meet the required return of capital suppliers. If the California Welding Corporation undertakes the project, equity suppliers will suffer. We know from our previous calculations of NPV that stockholder wealth will *decrease* by $554,600. Once again, in this single-asset-acquisition situation, both IRR and NPV give the same indication of the attractiveness of the project. The NPV, however, has the advantage of providing the dollar value of the decrease in stockholder wealth.

### TABLE 9–16

#### CALIFORNIA WELDING:
#### IRR COMPUTATIONS FOR WELDER ACQUISITION

Present value of cash outflows = $5,000,000
Cash inflows: Years 1–8 = $1,400,000
           Year 8 = $1,000,000

Present value of inflows = $1,400,000(3 Coef.$_8^?$) + $1,000,000(2 Coef.$_8^?$)

At 24%, PV$_{inflows}$ = $1,400,000(3.421) + $1,000,000(0.179) = $4,968,400
At 20%, PV$_{inflows}$ = $1,400,000(3.837) + $1,000,000(0.233) = $5,604,800

Interpolated IRR[a] = 20% + $\dfrac{\$604,800}{\$636,400}$ × 4% = 23.8%

[a]The techniques that can be used for the interpolation of the IRR are shown in Appendix 9C.

Let us compute the IRR of the weaving equipment being considered for acquisition by the J-Net Corporation. The asset-specific cost of capital is 10 percent, and the cash flows were summarized in Table 9–10. The computations of the IRR for this project are presented in Table 9–17. Note that when the discount rate is 12 percent, the present value of the inflows is greater than the $438,000 cash outflows. When a discount rate of 14 percent is used, the present value of the inflows is below the $438,000 cash outflows. This means that the discount rate that will equate the present values of cash inflows and outflows lies somewhere between 12 and 14 percent (in fact, slightly above 12 percent). Since the IRR of the project exceeds the asset-specific cost of capital, the purchase of the equipment will increase stockholder wealth.

Let us now compute the IRR for the air-conditioning manufacturing equipment being considered by the Replace Corporation. The asset-specific cost of capital is 9 percent, and the cash flows were summarized in Table 9–15. The computations for the IRR of this project are presented in Table 9–18. Remember that to determine the IRR, we must find a discount rate that will equate the present value of cash inflows and outflows. As you can see in Table 9–18, a discount rate of 12 percent yields a present value of cash inflows in excess of $6.6 million, and a discount rate of 14 percent yields a

TABLE 9-17

## J-NET CORPORATION:
## IRR COMPUTATIONS FOR WEAVING EQUIPMENT

Present value of cash outflows = $438,000
Cash inflows: Years 1–10     =   $78,400

Present value of inflows      =   $78,400(3 Coef.$_{10}$)

At 12%, $PV_{inflows} = \$78,400(5.650) = \$442,960$
At 14%, $PV_{inflows} = \$78,400(5.216) = \$408,934$

Interpolated IRR[a] $= 12\% + \dfrac{\$\ 4,960}{\$34,026} \times 2\% = 12.3\%$

[a]See Appendix 9C.

present value of cash inflows below $6.6 million. This means that the actual IRR lies somewhere between 12 and 14 percent. Through interpolation, the IRR can be estimated at 12.6 percent.

TABLE 9–18

## REPLACE CORPORATION:
## IRR COMPUTATION FOR MANUFACTURING EQUIPMENT

Present value of cash outflows = $6,600,000
Cash inflows: Years 1–10     = $1,140,000
            Year 10     = $1,000,000

Present value of inflows      = $1,140,000(3 Coef.$_{10}$) + $1,000,000(2 Coef.$_{10}$)

At 12%, $PV_{inflows} = \$1,140,000(5.650) + \$1,000,000(0.322) = \$6,763,000$
At 14%, $PV_{inflows} = \$1,140,000(5.216) + \$1,000,000(0.270) = \$6,216,240$

Interpolated IRR[a] $= 12\% + \dfrac{\$163,000}{\$546,760} \times 2\% = 12.6\%$

[a]See Appendix 9C.

Since the air-conditioning manufacturing equipment has an IRR of 12.6 percent and a cost of capital of 9 percent, the acquisition of the equipment will increase stockholder wealth. If the equipment is acquired, all costs and the required return of the suppliers of capital are met. In addition, there will be a "surplus" available to stockholders. The IRR does not tell us the dollar amount of the surplus, only the fact that a surplus exists. On the other hand, NPV procedures yield a specific dollar figure for the surplus to stockholders. Note that in cases when single assets are being considered for acquisition, IRR and NPV techniques both indicate the same, and correct, decision. In single-asset acquisitions, it makes no difference whether NPV or IRR is used as the method for evaluating cash flows.

## NPV COMPARED TO IRR

The fact that net present value and internal rate of return yield consistent results in cases where single assets are being considered for acquisition can be seen in the three numerical examples presented in this chapter. The results from these three illustrations are presented in Table 9–19.

TABLE 9–19

COMPARISON BETWEEN THE NPV AND IRR OF THREE INVESTMENT PROPOSALS

| Proposal | NPV | Decision | IRR | Decision |
|---|---|---|---|---|
| California Welding ($k_f^* = 28\%$) | ($554,600) | No | 23.8% | No |
| J-Net ($k_f^* = 10\%$) | + $43,768 | Yes | 12.3% | Yes |
| Replace ($k_f^* = 9\%$) | + $1,138,520 | Yes | 12.6% | Yes |

The relationship between NPV and IRR can also be examined using the appropriate mathematical expressions. Net present value has been defined as the present value of the future cash inflows discounted at the asset-specific cost of capital, less the present value of the cash outflows. NPV can be expressed mathematically by the following equation:

$$\text{NPV} = \sum_{t=1}^{n} \frac{\text{Cash inflows}_t}{(1 + k_f^*)^t} - \text{Cash outflows}$$

(9-1)

Thus, if NPV is positive, the present value of the cash inflows discounted at the asset-specific cost of capital is greater than the cash outflows.

The IRR is defined as the discount rate that discounts future cash inflows back to the original cash outflows. The IRR can be expressed mathematically as follows:

$$\text{IRR:} \sum_{t=1}^{n} \frac{\text{Cash outflows}_t}{(1 + i)^t} = \text{Cash outflows}$$

(9-2)

Therefore, the present value of the future cash inflows discounted at the IRR is equal to the original cash outflows. If a project has a positive NPV, the present value of the cash inflows discounted at the asset-specific cost of capital is greater than the present value of the same cash inflows discounted at the IRR. This statement can be expressed mathematically as follows:

$$\sum_{t=1}^{n} \frac{\text{Cash inflows}_t}{(1 + k_j^*)^t} > \sum_{t=1}^{n} \frac{\text{Cash inflows}_t}{(1 + i)^t}$$

The reader must realize that a comparison is being made of the same investment proposal using both NPV and IRR. Thus, the future cash inflows of the project will be the same regardless of the method being used. Therefore, the only difference between the two terms of the previous mathematical expression is the discount rate used. If the numerator of a fraction is the same, a larger denominator is required in order to obtain a smaller answer. Thus, the asset-specific cost of capital must be smaller than the internal rate of return if NPV is positive.

**SUMMARY**

Since long-term assets typically (1) require large outlays, (2) reduce the flexibility of the firm, and (3) yield benefits over a long period of time, firms analyze the acquisition of such assets very carefully. The final decision relating to the acquisition of large-scale long-term assets is usually reserved for top management. However, lower levels of production, marketing, and finance personnel all play a crucial role in the decision-making process, so it is important that all management personnel understand the purpose and process associated with long-term-asset acquisitions. We have summarized this process in the form of a series of six stages.

One important step in the long-term-asset acquisition process involves the estimation of the cash flows associated with the asset. The typical asset acquisition will require a cash outflow at a time near the present. This will be followed by periodic cash inflows, usually covering a number of years. Finally, the typical asset has an additional cash inflow at the time it is salvaged. Cash-flow information is central to decision making.

In single-asset-acquisition situations, cash flows can be evaluated using either net present value (NPV) or internal rate of return (IRR). When the IRR is greater than the asset-specific cost of capital, the acquisition of the asset results in a "surplus" contribution to stockholder wealth. The NPV is the dollar value of that "surplus" contribution. The computation of IRR and NPV should be viewed within the entire process of long-term-asset acquisitions. To be sure, poor computational procedures will lead to poor decisions. However, even the soundest computational procedures, if used with incorrect data, cannot be expected to result in good decisions.

**QUESTIONS DISCUSSION**

1. Discuss the nature of "conceptual" long-term assets. How do they compare to more conventional long-term assets? How do they compare to short-term assets?

2. Explain why the firm pays special attention to decisions relating to long-term-asset acquisitions.

3. What role is played by the following groups in the large-scale long-term-asset acquisition decision?
   a. Top management
   b. Production management personnel
   c. Marketing management personnel
   d. Financial management personnel

4. Prepare a short outline of each stage in the long-term-asset acquisition process.

5. Give some examples of how deficiencies in Stages I and II can lead to poor long-term-asset acquisition decisions.

6. Explain how cash-flow estimations for new-asset acquisition situations differ from replacement decisions.

7. Explain the difference between the income statement and cash-inflow statements used in long-term-asset acquisitions.

8. Explain why the firm should reject a long-term-asset acquisition if the IRR is lower than the asset-specific cost of capital.

9. Explain why a firm should accept a long-term-asset acquisition alternative with a positive NPV.

10. Give a verbal description of the processes used to compute the NPV and IRR. Why is it difficult to compute the IRR?

11. Explain the points at which the tax laws influence the long-term-asset acquisition decision.

12. Explain why NPV and IRR are consistent methods of evaluation when one asset is being considered for acquisition.

**PROBLEMS**

1. The Acme Tubing Corporation is considering the acquisition of a bending machine. The cash outflow at time 0 is $20,000, and the firm expects net cash inflows of $5,000 every year for eight years. The asset-specific cost of capital is 10%. Compute both the NPV and the IRR, and indicate whether or not the firm should acquire the asset.

2. The Ritch Corporation is considering the acquistion of a new piece of fabricating equipment. The cash outflow in year 0 is $100,000. Future net cash inflows are estimated to be $40,000 in year 1, $50,000 in year 2, and $30,000 in year 3. The asset-specific cost of capital is 15%. Compute both the NPV and IRR, and indicate whether or not the firm should acquire the asset. (Use the present-value formula rather than the tables.)

3. Ace Trucking Corporation is considering the purchase of some equipment that will be used to expand current operations. The equipment will cost $100,000 and has an expected life of ten years. Ace uses the straight-line method of depreciation and expects the salvage value of the equipment to be $10,000 ten years from now. This equipment fully qualifies for the investment tax credit. The acquisition of this equipment will allow Ace to expand revenues by $40,000 every year for the next ten years. Cash expenses (other than taxes) will increase by $20,000 every year for the next ten years. The asset-specific cost of capital is 10%, and the firm's tax rate is 40%.

a. What are the cash outflows in year 0 if Ace purchases this equipment?
b. What are the expected cash flows for years 1 through 10 (do not forget salvage) if Ace purchases the equipment?
c. Should Ace acquire the equipment? (Show NPV and IRR.)
d. What would be the effect (do not calculate) on NPV and IRR of the asset if Ace switches to the sum-of-years'-digits method of depreciation?

4. Beta Corporation is considering the replacement of its present manufacturing equipment. Technological changes have developed new equipment that will increase output and reduce operating expenses. Beta's present equipment was purchased five years ago for $80,000. When the equipment was originally purchased, it had an expected life of fifteen years, and an expected salvage value of $5,000 at the end of that time. These expectations have not changed. However, Beta has the opportunity of selling the equipment today for $40,000. Current annual sales are $50,000, and current annual expenses are $40,000. Sales and expenses are expected to remain constant for the ten-year period if the old equipment is kept by the firm.

The new equipment will cost $150,000; it has an expected life of ten years and an expected salvage value of $20,000 in ten years. The purchase of the new equipment will result in an increase in annual sales of $10,000, while annually reducing cash expenses by $20,000 every year for ten years. The new equipment fully qualifies for the investment tax credit. The asset-specific cost of capital is 10%.

Should Beta purchase the new equipment? Assume that the firm uses the straight-line method of depreciation and has a marginal tax rate of 40%. (You can use the format shown in Table 9–12 or Table 9–13.)

5. The Sigma Corporation is considering the replacement of some old equipment that was purchased ten years ago for $35 million. At the time of the purchase, it had an estimated useful life of 30 years and an estimated salvage value of $5 million in 30 years. This equipment can be sold today for $27 million. The expected salvage value at the end of its useful life (20 years from today) remains at $5 million. This equipment allows the firm to generate annual sales of $10 million, with corresponding annual expenses of $8 million. The firm expects sales and expenses to remain constant over the next 20 years if the old equipment is kept.

The new equipment will cost $55 million and have a useful life of 20 years, at the end of which it is expected to have a salvage value of $10 million. If the equipment is acquired, the Sigma Corporation expects annual sales to be increased by $2 million and annual expenses to be reduced by $0.5 million. These changes in sales and expenses are expected to remain the same for the entire 20-year period. The Sigma Corporation uses the straight-line method of depreciation on all equipment. In addition, the firm's tax rate is 40%, and the new equipment fully qualifies for the investment tax credit.
a. Calculate the net cash outflows if the Sigma Corporation replaces the equipment. (You can use the format shown in Table 9–12 or Table 9–13.)
b. Calculate the periodic cash inflows if the Sigma Corporation replaces the equipment.
c. Should the Sigma Corporation acquire the new equipment if its asset-specific cost of capital is 8%?

6. The high cost of fuel has created a problem for Reliable Trucking, whose trucks

have a very high fuel consumption. These trucks were purchased two years ago for $100,000. At the time of the purchase, the trucks had an expected life of eight years and an expected salvage value of $20,000 at the end of year 8. Reliable can sell the trucks today for $30,000. Current revenues for the trucks are $80,000 per year. Cash expenses (including fuel) are $60,000 per year. Revenues and expenses are expected to remain constant for the entire six-year period if the old trucks are kept.

Reliable can purchase new trucks from Energy Savers for $150,000. These new trucks have an expected life of six years and can be sold for $30,000 six years from now. They will allow Reliable to reduce fuel expenses by $30,000 every year for the next six years. The investment tax credit can be used if the trucks are purchased. Reliable uses the straight-line method of depreciation, and its tax rate is 40%. The asset-specific cost of capital is 10%.

Calculate the NPV and IRR of the purchase of Energy Savers' trucks. Should Reliable acquire the new trucks? (You can use the format shown in Table 9–12 or 9–13.)

7. Allied Corporation is planning to replace an old machine, purchased five years ago for $30,000. When it was purchased, the machine had an expected life of fifteen years and no expected salvage value at the end of its life. (Note: The machine has ten years of life at the present time, and no expected salvage ten years from now.) The old machine can be sold today for $18,000. The new machine will cost $60,000 and fully qualifies for the investment tax credit. The expected useful life of the new machine is ten years, and it has an expected salvage value of $10,000 in ten years. The purchase of the machine will cause an annual increase in sales of $3,000 and an annual reduction in costs of $4,000 for the life of the machine.

Allied Corporation uses the straight-line method of depreciation and has a marginal tax rate of 40%. Allied's firmwide cost of capital is 12 percent. However, the riskiness of the new machine is such that its asset-specific cost of capital is only 10%. Should the Allied Corporation purchase the new equipment? (Note: You must use the format shown in Table 9–13.)

8. Ann Carol Boutiques is considering the acquisition of sewing machines. The machines will cost $60,000, they will have an expected useful life of four years, and salvage in year 4 is expected to be $20,000. These machines qualify for the investment tax credit. The company uses the sum-of-years'-digits method of depreciation. The purchase of the sewing machines will allow the firm to increase sales by $100,000 every year for the next four years. Cash expenses (other than income taxes) will be $70,000 every year for the next four years. The asset-specific cost of capital is 16%, and the firm's tax rate is 40%.
   a. Calculate the cash outflows in year 0 if Ann Carol Boutiques purchases the sewing machines.
   b. What are the expected cash flows of the firm for years 1 through 4 if the sewing machines are purchased? (Hint: Cash flows will not be the same for every year.)
   c. Should Ann Carol purchase the sewing machines?

9. California Airlines is considering the replacement of the computer used to keep track of reservations. The old computer has a book value of $8 million, an expected useful life of eight years, and no expected salvage value in eight years. It can be sold today for $1 million. A new computer, costing $6 million, can be

purchased today. This computer has an expected salvage value of $2 million at the end of its useful life of eight years. The acquisition of the new computer will reduce costs by $600,000 every year for eight years, and it fully qualifies for the investment tax credit. The firm uses the straight-line method of depreciation. California Airline's tax rate is 40%, and its asset-specific cost of capital is 14%.

   a. Calculate the cash outflows if California Airlines purchases the new computer.
   b. Calculate the expected cash inflows for years 1 through 8 if the computer is purchased. (*Note:* Be very careful about the change in depreciation, and use the format shown in Table 9–13.)
   c. Should California Airlines purchase the new computer?

# APPENDIX 9A
## The Present Value of Cash Outflows

Throughout this chapter, one unrealistic assumption was made: that all cash outflows took place at time 0. We made this assumption in order to simplify the numerical computations. In the real world, however, the acquisition of long-term assets may require cash outflows over a long period of time. For example, a decision by Consolidated Edison to build a power generating plant may require cash outflows spread over a very long period. The firm will disburse funds for the evaluation of the project; permits must be obtained, and plans submitted for approval; then land must be acquired and construction begun. The construction of the power plant may take several years. Thus, Consolidated Edison will disburse funds over a long period of time, *before any cash inflows are generated from the project.*

The net present value of a project with cash outflows occurring over a certain period will be equal to the present value of the expected cash inflows less the present value of cash outflows, discounted at the asset-specific cost of capital. NPV can be expressed mathematically by the following equation:

$$\text{NPV} = \sum_{t=0}^{n} \frac{\text{Cash inflows}_t}{(1 + k_f^*)^t} - \sum_{t=x}^{n} \frac{\text{Cash outflows}_t}{(1 + k_f^*)^t} \qquad (9A\text{-}1)$$

Let us illustrate the application of equation 9A–1 with a numerical example. The Wilson Manufacturing Corporation is considering an expansion of its production facilities. The expansion will require the purchase of land, construction of a building, and installation of machinery. The land costs $500,000 and must be paid at time 0; the building will cost $2 million. The building contract calls for the payment of $500,000 at time 0, a $1 million construction progress payment exactly one year from now ($t = 1$), and a final payment of $500,000 two years from now ($t = 2$). Equipment will be installed at a cost of $2 million, to be paid two years from now ($t = 2$), when the installation is completed. This equipment will fully qualify for a 10 percent investment tax credit.[14] Table 9A–1 shows the net cash outflows of Wilson Manufacturing if the expansion is undertaken.

WILSON MANUFACTURING CORPORATION:
Cash Outflows

| Item | Year | Amount | Total cash outflow |
|------|------|--------|--------------------|
| Land purchase | 0 | $ 500,000 | |
| Building | 0 | 500,000 | |
| Total in year 0 | | | $1,000,000 |
| Building | 1 | $1,000,000 | |
| Total in year 1 | | | $1,000,000 |
| Building | 2 | $ 500,000 | |
| Equipment | 2 | 2,000,000 | |
| Investment tax credit | 2 | (200,000) | |
| Total in year 2 | | | $2,300,000 |

The firm expects the expansion to allow an annual sales increase of $4.1 million from year 3 through year 12. Annual expenses (except for depreciation and taxes) are expected to be $3 million in those years. The expected salvage value of the building and equipment is expected to be zero twelve years from now. The firm anticipates that the land can be sold twelve years from now for $500,000. Wilson Manufacturing uses the straight-line method of depreciation.[15] The firm's marginal tax rate is 40 percent, and the asset-specific cost of capital is 12 percent. Should the firm undertake the expansion?

Table 9A–2 shows the expected periodic cash inflows of the project. The firm expects to receive $820,000 every year in years 3 through 12. In addition, the land will be sold twelve years from now for $500,000. The total cash flows associated with the expansion are shown in Table 9A–3.

The final step in this procedure is to compute the net present value of the proposal. NPV is equal to the present value of all cash inflows less the present value of all cash outflows, discounted at the asset-specific cost of capital. Thus, the NPV would be:

---

[14]This ignores changes in depreciation schedules and assumes that the firm can fully use the investment tax credit.

[15]Note that the firm can depreciate only the building and equipment. Land cannot be depreciated.

### WILSON MANUFACTURING CORPORATION:
### PERIOD CASH INFLOWS

|  | Year 3–12 |
|---|---|
| Sales | $4,100,000 |
| − Cash expenses | (3,000,000) |
| − Depreciation[a] | (400,000) |
| Earnings before taxes | $ 700,000 |
| − Taxes (40%) | (280,000) |
| Earnings after taxes | $ 420,000 |
| + Depreciation | 400,000 |
| Net cash inflows every year | $ 820,000 |

[a]Depreciation $= \dfrac{\$4,000,000 - 0}{10} = \$400,000$ per year

$$NPV = \$820,000(3 \text{ Coef.}^{12}_{12\%} - 3 \text{ Coef.}^{2}_{12\%}) + \$500,000(2 \text{ Coef.}^{12}_{12\%})$$
$$- [\$1,000,000(2 \text{ Coef.}^{0}_{12\%}) + \$1,000,000(2 \text{ Coef.}^{1}_{12\%}) + \$2,300,000(2 \text{ Coef.}^{2}_{12\%})]$$

$$= \$820,000(6.194 - 1.690) + \$500,000(0.257)$$
$$- [\$1,000,000(1) + \$1,000,000(0.893) + \$2,300,000(0.797)]$$

$$= + \$95,680$$

The project should be accepted, because it will increase stockholder wealth by $95,680. Note that if all cash outflows took place at time 0, the project would have been rejected.[16] The cost to the firm, however, is lower if cash outflows take place in the future rather than at the present time.

### WILSON MANUFACTURING CORPORATION:
### Cash Flows Associated with Expansion

| Year | Description | Cash flow |
|---|---|---|
| 0 | Cash outflow | ($1,000,000) |
| 1 | Cash outflow | ($1,000,000) |
| 2 | Cash outflow | ($2,300,000) |
| 3–12 | Periodic cash inflows | $ 820,000 |
| 12 | Salvage value of land | $ 500,000 |

[16]NPV (if all cash outflows took place at year 0) = $PV_{inflows} - PV_{outflows}$ = $3,821,780 − $4,300,000 = ($478,220)

1. The Williams Manufacturing Corporation plans to expand its production facilities. The facilities required for the expansion will take one year to complete. The firm will pay today ($t_0$) $300,000 for land acquisition. The cost of the construction of the building ($800,000) will be paid exactly one year from now ($t_1$). The equipment will cost $600,000, to be paid exactly one year from now ($t_1$). The equipment (but not the building or the land) fully qualifies for the investment tax credit.

   The expansion of production capacity will allow the firm to increase sales by $1 million every year for 15 years ($t = 2$ through $t = 16$). Cash expenses (other than taxes) are estimated to be $600,000 every year for 15 years ($t = 2$ through $t = 16$). The expected value of the land 16 years from now is $300,000, that of the building is zero, and that of the equipment is $200,000. The firm uses the straight-line method of depreciation on the building and the equipment. The asset-specific cost of capital is 12%, and the marginal tax rate is 40%.

   a. Calculate the present value of the cash outflows if the production expansion is undertaken.
   b. Calculate the present value of the cash inflows if the production expansion is undertaken.
   c. Should Williams Manufacturing expand production facilities?

# APPENDIX 9B
## Evaluation of Long-Term-Asset Acquisition: Alternative Techniques

In Chapter 9 we discussed two techniques for the evaluation of long-term-asset acquisition alternatives: (1) net present value, and (2) internal rate of return. The use of these two techniques is consistent with the goal of stockholder-wealth maximization. There are, however, two other techniques used by business firms. They are known as "payback period" and the "average rate of return." The use of these techniques may or may not give results consistent with the stockholder-wealth-maximization goal. They are presented in this appendix, not because of their correctness, but because of their extensive use in the real world. We will discuss the techniques and point out their potential pitfalls. It should be noted that neither of these techniques can be linked directly to stockholder wealth, and for this reason, they are not recommended for use.

## PAYBACK PERIOD

The payback period is defined as the number of years it will take the firm to recover its original investments. The welder-acquisition example shown in Table 9–4 can be used to illustrate the computations of the payback period. The firm invests $5 million today and realizes cash inflows of $1.4 million per year in years 1 through 8, plus an additional $1 million in year 8. Since the cash inflows are constant, it will take 3.57 years ($5,000,000/$1,400,000) before the original investment is recovered by the firm.[17] Thus, the payback period is 3.57 years.

The basic advantage of payback is its simplicity. It is very easy to compute the payback period, and the significance of the result can be understood by the layman. There are two other potential advantages to payback. First, the method may be used as an unsophisticated risk adjustment. For example, a capital investment in an unstable foreign country may present high risks of expropriation. Management may impose an arbitrary payback period of two years in order to adjust to the expropriation risk.[18] The second possible advantage of payback is that firms facing a significant liquidity problem may be interested in projects with a fast recuperation of the original investment.

Payback, however, has two basic disadvantages: (1) It does not consider the time value of money, and (2) it pays no attention to the cash flows of the project *after* the payback period. Table 9B–1 shows two projects, A and B. The payback of both projects is identical, two years. If we assume the same level of risk for both projects, however, project B is clearly superior to A. The firm recovers the original investment faster with project B ($900 is received earlier). Furthermore, the cash flows after the payback period are greater for project B.

### TABLE 9B–1

|  |  | A | B |
|---|---|---|---|
| Cash outflow |  | ($1,000) | ($1,000) |
| Cash inflow in year | 1 | $ 100 | $ 900 |
|  | 2 | $ 900 | $ 100 |
|  | 3 | $ 100 | $ 300 |
|  | 4 | $ 100 | $ 300 |
|  | 5 | $ 100 | $ 300 |
|  | 6 | $ 100 | $ 300 |
| Payback period |  | 2 years | 2 years |

It is our opinion that payback should never be used as the *only* criterion in the asset-acquisition process. It may be used as a complement to more rigorous techniques, such as net present value.

---

[17]We assume the cash inflows are received evenly throughout the year.

[18]There are, however, better forms of risk adjustments. The use of NPV implies discounting the future cash flows at the asset-specific cost of capital, which reflects the risk of the cash flows from the asset.

# AVERAGE RATE OF RETURN

The average rate of return is defined as follows:[19]

$$\text{Average rate of return} = \frac{\text{Average profit during the period}}{\text{Average investment during the period}} \quad \text{(9B-1)}$$

It is convenient to illustrate the average rate of return with a numerical example. Table 9B–2 shows an income statement for an asset-acquisition alternative. The average profit during the period is the average of the earnings after taxes of the firm for the four-year period, or $67,500. We assume that the firm invested $400,000 and the asset we depreciated at a rate of $100,000 per year for four years. Thus, the investment to the firm was $400,000 for the first year, $300,000 for the second year, $200,000 for the third year, and $100,000 for the fourth year—making the average investment for the period $250,000.[20]

### TABLE 9B–2

INCOME STATEMENTS FOR ASSET-ACQUISITION ALTERNATIVE (thousands)

|  | Year 1 | Year 2 | Year 3 | Year 4 |
|---|---|---|---|---|
| Sales | $500 | $600 | $700 | $800 |
| — Cash expenses | (400) | (400) | (450) | (500) |
| — Depreciation | (100) | (100) | (100) | (100) |
| E.B.T. | 0 | $100 | $150 | $200 |
| — Tax (40%) | 0 | 40 | 60 | 80 |
| E.A.T. | 0 | $60 | $90 | $120 |

$$\text{Average profit during the period} = \frac{0 + 60 + 90 + 120}{4} = \$67,500$$

$$\text{Average investment during the period} = \frac{400 + 300 + 200 + 100}{4} = \$250,000$$

$$\text{Average rate of return} = \frac{\$67,500}{\$250,000} = 27\%$$

---

[19]There are other variations of the average rate of return. For example, see Erich A. Helfert, *Techniques of Financial Analysis*, 4th ed. (Homewood, Ill.: Richard D. Irwin, 1977), pp. 129–31.

[20]Given that the firm uses the straight-line method of depreciation, the average investment may be approximated as follows:

$$\text{Average investment during the period} = \frac{Investment}{2}$$

There are several serious problems associated with average-rate-of-return techniques. First, the technique uses accounting profits rather than cash flows as the basic input. Second, the timing problem is ignored; that is, no consideration is given to the fact that the flows are spread unevenly over the interval. Third, the meaning of the accounting rate of return (27 percent in our example) is not clear. How high must the accounting rate of return be before a project is accepted? There is no general answer to this question.

## OVERVIEW OF APPENDIX 9B

This book is designed to show that NPV is the "best" technique for the evaluation of asset-acquisition alternatives. This is because, when used properly, it gives an unambiguous dollar indication of the change in stockholder wealth. In single-asset situations, the IRR is also acceptable, because it indicates the direction of change (but not the amount) in stockholder wealth. Payback period, average rate of return, and other methods are not related directly to stockholder wealth and may lead to poor decisions. Of course, in many asset-acquisition situations, the decision will be the same regardless of the technique employed. For example, projects that have positive NPVs may also tend to have short payback periods, so in most cases, the use of either technique will result in the same decision. However, there are situations in which the techniques will yield different decisions, and a mistake can result in large losses to the firm.

The only real advantage of payback is its simplicity. Admittedly, it is easier to compute than NPV is. Today, however, the new generation of business decision makers is better prepared to understand the NPV concept. Remember, NPV is the correct indicator of change in stockholder wealth. The use of payback period and average rate of return will lead to acceptance of some investment alternatives that are inconsistent with stockholder-wealth maximization.

PROBLEM    1. The National Trucking Corporation is considering the acquisition of a truck that costs $50,000, has an expected life of five years, and has an expected salvage value of $20,000 in five years. The truck does not qualify for the investment tax credit. The firm expects revenue to be $40,000 and operating expenses to be $25,000 every year for five years. National uses the straight-line method of depreciation and has a marginal tax rate of 40%.
a. Calculate the payback period for the truck.
b. Calculate the average rate of return of the truck.

# APPENDIX 9C
## Interpolation of the Internal Rate of Return

In the body of Chapter 9, internal rates of return were presented in the form of ranges. That is, the IRR for the equipment being considered for acquisition by the California Welding Corporation was computed as falling between 20 and 24 percent. Note that an interpolated IRR of 23.8 percent was also included in Table 9–16. This interpolated value is an estimate of the actual IRR. It represents an attempt to narrow down the 20 to 24 percent range and provide a single point estimate of the IRR. The interpolation technique employed is a basic algebraic operation that many students learned in their high school mathematics courses. We will review the technique in this appendix and apply it to the IRR estimation problem.

Remember that the true IRR is the discount rate that results in the present value of the inflows equaling the present value of outflows. In order to interpolate the IRR, the following steps are required:

- Step 1. Find a discount rate that results in the present value of the inflows being slightly greater than the present value of outflows.
- Step 2. Find a discount rate that results in the present value of inflows being slightly lower than the present value of outflows.

The true IRR must rest somewhere between these two discount rates, and it can be estimated by using an interpolation technique. The formula for the interpolated IRR is presented in equation 9C–1.

$$\text{Interpolated IRR} = \begin{matrix} \text{lower} \\ \text{discount} \\ \text{rate} \end{matrix} + \left[ \left( \frac{\underset{\text{(lower DR)}}{PV_{\text{inflows}}} - \underset{}{PV_{\text{outflows}}}}{\underset{\text{(lower DR)}}{PV_{\text{inflows}}} - \underset{\text{(higher DR)}}{PV_{\text{inflows}}}} \right) \times \left( \begin{matrix} \text{Higher} \\ \text{discount} \\ \text{rate} \end{matrix} - \begin{matrix} \text{Lower} \\ \text{discount} \\ \text{rate} \end{matrix} \right) \right] \qquad (9C\text{-}1)$$

For purposes of illustration, let us compute the interpolated IRR for a fixed asset being considered for acquisition by the AnnCa Corporation. The cash flows associated with the asset are:

| Year | Description | Cash Flows |
|------|-------------|------------|
| 0 | Initial cash outlay | ($3,890) |
| 1–5 | Periodic net cash inflows | $1,000 |

In this example, the present value of the cash outflow is $3,890. The next step is to find a discount rate that results in a present value of inflows slightly greater than $3,890. Using an 8 percent discount rate, the present value of inflows will be equal to $3,993:

---

Note: We would like to express our thanks to Professor Cherukuri U. Rao, California State College, Stanislaus, for providing the material on which this appendix is based.

$$PV^{8\%}_{\text{inflows}} = \$1,000(3 \text{ Coef.}^{8\%}_5) = \$1,000(3.993) = \$3,993$$

When a 10 percent discount rate is used, the present value of the cash inflows will be slightly lower than $3,890:

$$PV^{10\%}_{\text{inflows}} = \$1,000(3 \text{ Coef.}^{10\%}_5) = \$1,000(3.791) = \$3,791$$

Thus far we have found discount rates that "bracket" the true IRR; that is, the true IRR lies somewhere between 8 and 10 percent. We can estimate, using equation 9C–1, the true IRR by interpolation.

$$\text{Interpolated IRR}^{21} = 8\% + \left[\left(\frac{103}{3,993 - 3,791}\right) \times (10\% - 8\%)\right] = 9.02\%$$

Note that the interpolated IRR is an estimate of the true IRR. *It is not exactly equal to the true IRR.* In this case, the true IRR is 9 percent. That is, when a discount rate of 9 percent is used, the present value of the cash inflows will exactly equal the net present value of the outflows. This can be estimated by looking up 3 Coef.$^{9\%}_5$, which is 3.890.

$$PV^{9\%}_{\text{outflows}} = \$3,890$$

$$PV^{9\%}_{\text{inflows}} = \$1,000(3.890) = \$3,890$$

$$PV^{9\%}_{\text{inflows}} = PV^{9\%}_{\text{outflows}}$$

Figure 9C–1 is a graphical representation of the IRR. As can be seen, the interpolated IRR (9.02 percent) is greater than the true IRR (9.0 percent). The error is introduced by the fact that the true *curvilinear* relationship is being estimated by a *linear* relationship. This approximation technique is quite acceptable as long as the range in discount rates is small (2 to 4 percent). The technique will yield poor estimates when wider ranges are used. For example, if we had interpolated between 16 percent ($PV^{16\%}_{\text{inflows}} = \$3,274$) and 2 percent ($PV^{2\%}_{\text{inflows}} = \$4,713$), the interpolated IRR would have been 10 percent.[22] This is a long way from the true 9 percent rate. You can apply your imagination to Figure 9C–1 and visualize how increasing the range of estimates drives the broken line to the right, resulting in less-accurate estimates of the true IRR.

Interpolation is a useful technique because it allows us to narrow down our range and develop a point estimate. For example, our tables do not provide discount values for 21, 22, and 23 percent. Thus, in the California Welding example, the most we could say was that the true IRR lies somewhere between 20 and 24 percent. With interpolation, it is possible to compute a more specific estimate (23.8 percent).

---

[21]At 8%, PV of inflows($3,993) − PV of outflows($3,890) = $103

[22]Interpolated IRR = $2\% + \left[\dfrac{823}{1,439} \times 14\%\right] = 10\%$

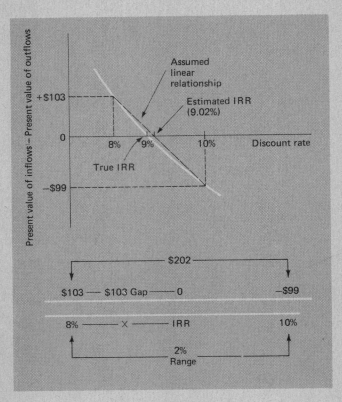

**FIGURE 9C–1**

Interpolation of the
Internal Rate of Return

**PROBLEMS**

**1.** Calculate the interpolated IRR of the following investment proposal:
Cash outflows (time 0) = $100,000
Periodic cash inflows (years 1 through 10) = $20,000

**2.** Calculate the interpolated IRR of the following investment proposal:
Cash outflows (t = 0) = $110,000
Cash inflows (t = 1) = $80,000
Cash inflows (t = 2) = $60,000

**SELECTED BIBLIOGRAPHY**

BIERMAN, H., JR., and SEYMOUR SMIDT, *The Capital Budgeting Decision,* 4th ed. New York: McMillan, 1975.

BODENHORN, D., "A Cash-Flow Concept of Profit," *The Journal of Finance,* March 1964, 16–31.

COPELAND, THOMAS E., and J. FRED WESTON, *Financial Theory and Corporate Policy.* Reading, Mass.: Addison-Wesley, 1979.

HASTIE, LARRY K., "One Businessman's View of Capital Budgeting," *Financial Management,* 3 (Winter 1974), 36–44.

HELFERT, ERICH A., *Techniques of Financial Analysis.* Homewood, Ill.: Richard D. Irwin, 1977.

HIRSCHLEIFER, J., *Investment, Interest and Capital.* Englewood Cliffs, N.J.: Prentice-Hall, 1970.

JEAN, WILLIAM H., *Capital Budgeting.* Scranton, Pa.: International Textbook Company, 1969.

LEVY, HAIM, and MARSHALL SARNAT, *Capital Investment and Financial Decisions*. Englewood Cliffs, N.J.: Prentice-Hall, 1978.

MAO, JAMES C., "The Internal Rate of Return as a Ranking Criterion," *Engineering Economist*, XI (Winter 1966), 1–13.

MERVILLE, L.J., and L.A. TAVIS, "A Generalized Model for Capital Investment," *Journal of Finance*, 28 (March 1973), 109–18.

NELSON, CHARLES R., "Inflation and Capital Budgeting," *Journal of Finance*, 31 (June 1976), 923–31.

PETRY, GLENN H., "Effective Use of Capital Budgeting Tools," *Business Horizons*, 19 (October 1975), 57–65.

PETTY, J. WILLIAM, and OSWALD D. BOWLIN, "The Financial Manager and Quantitative Decision Models," *Financial Management*, 4 (Winter 1976), 32–44.

TATOM, JOHN A., and JAMES E. TURLEY, "Inflation and Taxes: Disincentives for Capital Formation," *Review of the Federal Reserve Bank of St. Louis*, 60 (January 1978), 2–8.

VAN HORNE, JAMES C., *Financial Management and Policy*, 5th ed. Englewood Cliffs, N.J.: Prentice-Hall, 1980.

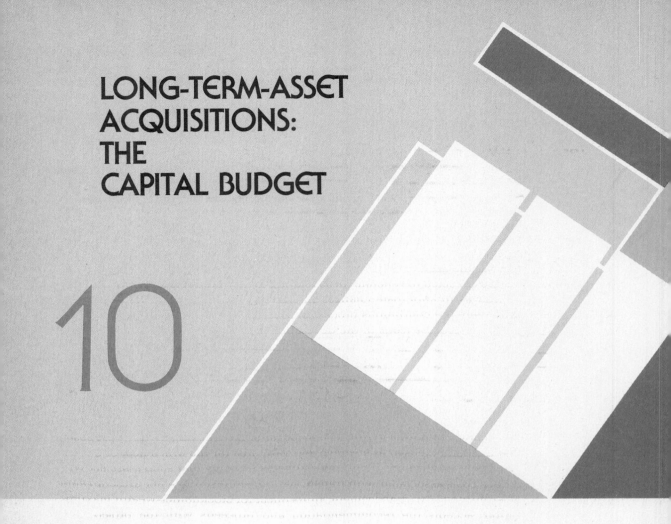

# LONG-TERM-ASSET ACQUISITIONS: THE CAPITAL BUDGET

# 10

## INTRODUCTION

This chapter builds upon the concepts developed in Chapter 9. Here, long-term-asset acquisitions will be examined within the context of a plan developed by the firm. We will show that the firm typically has many potential acquisition alternatives and that it is necessary to examine certain characteristics of each. Once this is done, the firm sifts through the alternatives and evaluates possible "packages" of long-term-asset acquisitions using net-present-value techniques. So the focus in this chapter, rather than being on the relationship between individual asset-acquisition alternatives and stockholder wealth, is on the effect on stockholder wealth of acquiring "packages of assets." The decision criterion to be developed specifies that the firm should choose that "package" of long-term-asset acquisitions that maximizes the wealth of stockholders.

## THE NEED FOR A CAPITAL BUDGET

As discussed in Chapter 9, the firm wishing to maximize stockholder wealth must involve production and marketing management personnel in the long-term-asset acquisition decision process. These groups, along with top management, play a critical role in the development of asset-acquisition alternatives (Stage II). For example, production-engineering personnel are expected to monitor current technology and make recommendations concerning the acquisition of new cost-reducing technology. Marketing personnel are expected to generate ideas relating to new products and new markets, as well as to anticipate changes in existing markets. In the well-managed firm, there is a continuous process of search and reevaluation. In the typical case, this process leads to the development of a large number of long-term-asset acquisition alternatives.

When firms are faced with multiple opportunities, special problems arise. One of the most crucial can be called the "timing problem." That is, the attractiveness of various asset-acquisition alternatives may depend on the order in which they are considered. As an illustration, assume that a manufacturing corporation owns a parcel of undeveloped land adjacent to its major production facility. The manager of the trucking division proposes that this land be used as a garage and yard area for the firm's fleet of trucks. The manager develops cash-flow estimates showing that such a project will reduce costs associated with transportation and result in a net present value of $1 million. Top management, in its quest for stockholder-wealth maximization, accepts the recommendation and proceeds with the project. Six months later, the production management group recognizes that additional plant capacity is needed to meet increasing demand for the firm's products. Had the land in question not been used for the trucking division, it could have been used for such expansion, and the resulting increase in stockholder wealth (net present value) would have been $5 million. If both alternatives had been considered at the same time, the plant expansion would have been chosen because of its greater contribution to stockholder wealth. The fact is that when projects are considered on a piecemeal basis, the order in which they are considered becomes a key factor.

In order to minimize the influence of proposal timing and certain other factors, most corporations develop formal capital budgets that are long-term-asset acquisition plans. Most large firms today have one-year plans, and many also have five- or ten-year capital budgets. The essence of the capital budget is to force consideration of all alternatives at the same time, and to choose that "package" of alternatives that maximizes stockholder wealth.

## THE RELATIONSHIPS AMONG ALTERNATIVES

The evaluation of many alternatives poses special problems to the firm, since there are sometimes complex interrelationships among alternatives. For purposes of constructing a long-term-asset acquisition plan (capital budget), it is convenient to identify two or more acquisition alternatives as being (1) independent of each other, (2) interrelated, or (3) mutually exclusive.

Alternatives are considered *mutually exclusive* if the acceptance of one must lead to the rejection of the others. For example, consider the case of a firm that is reviewing the possibility of replacing a piece of packaging equipment. Assume that the firm has three alternatives: First, it can keep the old equipment. Second, the old equipment can be replaced by Type X equipment. Third, the firm can acquire Type Y equipment. In this case, the alternatives are mutually exclusive. The acceptance of one must lead to the rejection of the others. It is not possible to accept more than one of a set of mutually exclusive alternatives.

Alternatives are *interrelated* when the cash flows of one are affected by the acceptance or rejection of another.[1] In some cases, asset acquisitions, when evaluated singly, may result in expected decreases in stockholder wealth; but when they are considered as a package, stockholder wealth is expected to increase. That is, the acceptance of one alternative enhances the attractiveness of the other.

For purposes of illustration, consider the case of an automobile manufacturer that has an opportunity to acquire a new, faster unitized welder that will weld 40 percent more automobile bodies in a given period. The auto manufacturer can also acquire a new high-speed conveyor system that will speed up the movement of parts to the welder and completed car bodies away from the welder. Individually, these alternatives may not be attractive to the firm. What is the advantage of acquiring a faster welder if parts cannot be delivered fast enough to keep the welder running at the higher rate? Why acquire a faster conveyor system when the old welder is incapable of keeping up with the faster pace? In this case, each project considered individually will have a negative effect on stockholder wealth (negative net present value); but when the two assets are considered as a "package," they may have a positive net present value. One project enhances the other.

The fact that projects are interrelated does not always imply enhancement of cash flows. It is possible that investment alternatives considered independently may have a positive effect on stockholder wealth but, when considered as a package, will make net present value negative. For example, assume that a downtown department store is considering an expansion into the suburbs, and that management has located two suitable sites approxi-

---

[1]Mutually exclusive alternatives have a special type of interrelatedness.

mately five miles from each other. Management proceeds to compute the net present value (the addition to stockholder wealth) of each project independently, and concludes that each project will lead to an increase in stockholder wealth. However, when the projects are considered as a package, it becomes apparent that the building of two stores will reduce the sales of each, because the stores will compete for the same customers. In such a case, two alternatives that are attractive when considered separately make up a package that is unattractive, owing to the fact that the acceptance of one project reduces the expected cash flows of the other. That is, the cash flows of these two projects are interrelated.

Asset-acquisition alternatives may also be *independent* of each other. Two alternatives are independent of each other when the acceptance of one does not affect the cash flows of the other. Most asset-acquisition alternatives fall into this category.[2] For example, the alternative of replacing an old piece of production equipment and the alternative of replacing an old truck may be viewed as independent alternatives. The cash flow associated with the one project is not likely to be dependent on the acceptance or rejection of the other.

## AN INTEGRATED EXAMPLE

In this chapter, we will construct a series of long-term-asset acquisition plans (capital budgets) for a hypothetical firm called the United States Petroleum Corporation (USPC). This firm is assumed to be a large, integrated oil company-similar to Texaco, Shell, or Mobil. USPC is involved in oil exploration, production, transportation, refining, and distribution. Its annual sales are in excess of $5 billion.

At the present time, the board of directors is working on the capital budget for the coming year. The marketing, production, and financial staffs have developed ten projects for consideration as potential acquisitions. Descriptions of these proposals are presented in Table 10–1. A summary of pertinent financial facts for each alternative—including cash flows, asset-specific cost of capital, net present values, and internal rates of return for each—is shown in Table 10–2.

Note that the initial outlay ranges from $10 million to $100 million. Note also the fact that the security-market line has been used by financial managers to evaluate the riskiness of these asset acquisitions and establish rates of return for debt and equity suppliers. The security-market line confronting USPC is presented in Figure 10–1 (p. 245). Financial managers have estimated the risks of debt and equity *for each asset separately*. Financial staff personnel have then used these risk estimates and the SML to estimate the cost of debt ($k_d$), the cost of equity ($k_s$) and an asset-specific cost

---

[2]Although it may be argued that all activities of the firm are interrelated, in many cases these interrelationships are small. For practical purposes, such activities can be evaluated as independent alternatives.

TABLE 10-1

### UNITED STATES PETROLEUM CORPORATION (USPC):
Description of Asset-Acquisition Alternatives

*Independent alternatives*

| | |
|---|---|
| Project A | *Midwestern Pipeline.* This project is designed to facilitate the shipment of refined petroleum products from the company's Gulf Coast refineries to important market areas in the Midwest. The pipeline will also be used to transport products of other oil companies. Although the project is expensive, it will reduce current transportation costs and provide additional revenues in the form of fees charged to other users. This is a low-risk project, with a $k_j^*$ of 10%. |
| Project B | *Less Cost Service Stations.* This project represents an opportunity to acquire an independent chain of service stations located in a market area not served by USPC at this time. This is a moderate-risk project, with a $k_j^*$ of 14%. |
| Project C | *Los Angeles Refinery.* This project represents an opportunity to construct a new refinery in the Los Angeles area. The plan calls for the refinery to process oil from the Alaska oil fields. This is a higher-risk project, with a $k_j^*$ of 16%. |
| Project D | *Super Tanker Acquisition.* This project represents an opportunity of transporting crude oil from Iran and the Arabian Peninsula to refineries in New England. It is planned that the tankers will be used to transport USPC crude oil and the petroleum of other firms. Owing to unstable political conditions in the producing areas, the project has a high risk ($k_j^* = 20\%$). |
| Project E | *Continental-Shelf Drilling Consortium.* This project represents an opportunity to buy into a new consortium of oil companies being formed to explore the continental shelf off the east coast of the United States. Although there are some good indications that oil will be found in the area, considerable uncertainty remains as to the amount of and access to the oil. This project has a very high risk, with a $k_j^*$ of 24%. |

*Mutually exclusive projects*

| | |
|---|---|
| Project F | *Fuel-Oil Capacity Expansion.* USPC recognizes that it has the potential to increase the output of its major refinery in Texas. One alternative is to increase the capacity for fuel-oil production. This alternative is relatively inexpensive and has a relatively low risk ($k_j^* = 12\%$). |
| Project G | *Gasoline Capacity Expansion.* As a mutually exclusive alternative to the fuel-oil capacity expansion, USPC can increase its Texas refinery's capacity to produce gasoline. This project is relatively expensive, because of the additional refining steps required and new legislation concerning gasoline additives. This project is of higher risk, since changes in |

*Table 10-1 continued*

automotive engine technology may permit the use of alternative automobile fuels ($k_f^*$ = 16%).

### Interrelated alternatives

| | |
|---|---|
| Project H | *Computer Refinery Control System.* This project represents an opportunity to acquire for the main USPC refinery a new control system incorporating the latest technology. The new control system will minimize changeover time and closely regulate types of input and the output of various refined products. This system is expected to increase refinery output and reduce costs. Owing to the new technology employed in the system, it has a relatively high risk ($k_f^*$ = 16%). |
| Project I | *Additional Storage Capacity.* USPC has the opportunity to add to the storage capacity of the Texas refinery. This project is a low-risk project ($k_f^*$ = 10%), since there is a nationwide shortage of storage capacity. |
| Project J | *Computer and Storage.* Projects H and I are interrelated. Although each could be adopted by itself, there are tremendous advantages associated with acquiring both assets at the same time. If the computer control system is to be used at peak efficiency and thus refinery output increased, additional storage capacity will be needed. The additional capacity will permit more efficient refinery production. The risk of this combination of projects is relatively low ($k_f^*$ = 12%), since the storage facility would have other uses should the expected benefits of computerization fail to materialize. |

of capital ($k_f^*$) *for each asset.* As suggested by the nature of the security-market line, projects with high risks have higher asset-specific costs of capital. Stated another way, the asset-specific cost of capital is an indicator of the relative riskiness of the various assets under consideration.[3]

The projects being considered by USPC are divided into three categories. There are five independent asset-acquisition alternatives, of which the board of directors can choose none, one, two, three, four, or all. There are two mutually exclusive alternatives, of which the firm can choose only one. Finally, there are two interrelated alternatives, of which the firm can choose either or both. Note that the two interrelated alternatives "enhance" each other; the cash inflows resulting from accepting both alternatives are substantially larger than those from either alone. As you can see from Table 10–2, the useful life for the mutually exclusive alternatives is the same (20

---

[3]The actual procedures employed in the estimation of risk, required rates of return, and the asset-specific cost of capital will be discussed in Chapters 13 and 14.

TABLE 10-2

UNITED STATES PETROLEUM CORPORATION:
Financial Information for Asset-Acquisition Alternatives

### INDEPENDENT ALTERNATIVES

|  | Pipeline | Stations | Refining | Tanker | Drilling |
|---|---|---|---|---|---|
| Asset-specific cost of capital ($k_j^*$) | 10% | 14% | 16% | 20% | 24% |
| Initial outlay at time $t_0$ ($) | $100,000,000 | $30,000,000 | $70,000,000 | $20,000,000 | $40,000,000 |
| Periodic cash inflows ($) [a] | $12,414,649 | $5,059,875 | $14,147,130 | $4,998,750 | $8,033,742 |
| Useful life (years) | 30 years | 20 years | 25 years | 15 years | 30 years |
| Net present value ($) | $17,032,896 | $3,511,552 | $16,255,053 | $3,369,157 | ($6,579,634) |
| IRR (%) | 12% | 16% | 20% | 24% | 20% |
| Present-value index [b] | 0.170 | 0.117 | 0.232 | 0.168 | (0.164) |

### MUTUALLY EXCLUSIVE ALTERNATIVES

|  | Fuel oil | Gasoline | Computer | Storage | Both |
|---|---|---|---|---|---|
| Asset-specific cost of capital ($k_j^*$) | 12% | 16% | 16% | 10% | 12%[c] |
| Initial outlay at time $t_0$ ($) | $10,000,000 | $50,000,000 | $20,000,000 | $40,000,000 | $60,000,000 |
| Periodic cash inflows ($) [a] | $2,053,388 | $9,340,557 | $3,927,729 | $6,512,536 | $14,996,251 |
| Useful life (years) | 20 years | 20 years | 15 years | 15 years | 15 years |
| Net present value ($) | $5,336,755 | $5,380,162 | $1,897,089 | $9,534,349 | $42,139,465 |
| IRR (%) | 20% | 18% | 18% | 14% | 24% |
| Present-value index [b] | 0.534 | 0.108 | 0.095 | 0.238 | 0.702 |

[a] The periodic cash inflows are assumed to be the same for each year during the projects' useful life. In order to simplify computations, we have assumed that there will be no salvage value.

[b] Present-value index = $\dfrac{\text{Net present value}}{\text{Initial outlay}}$

[c] A weighted average of the two components' $k_j^*$.

years), and the useful life of the interrelated alternatives is also identical (15 years). This was done in order to simplify the analysis.

## CAPITAL BUDGETING, INDEPENDENT ALTERNATIVES

Let us first discuss the planning for long-term-asset acquisitions (capital budget) under the simplest conditions. In order to simplify the discussion, two assumptions will be made. First, only the independent asset-acquisition

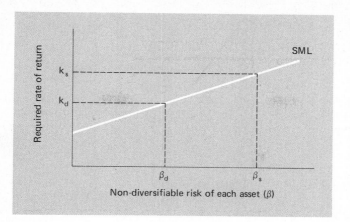

**FIGURE 10–1**

Security-Market Line
Faced By United
States Petroleum
Corporation

alternatives (A, B, C, D, and E) will be considered. We will proceed as if the mutually exclusive (F and G) and interrelated (H, I, and J) did not exist. The second assumption is that the firm has an unlimited amount of capital available. Both these assumptions will be modified as we proceed through the remainder of the chapter.

When alternatives are independent and the firm is unrestricted in the amount of capital it can use to acquire long-term assets, the capital budget is relatively straightforward. The process involved can be visualized as a series of steps:

- *Step 1.* Identify possible alternatives.
- *Step 2.* Estimate the asset-specific cost of capital for each alternative.
- *Step 3.* Estimate the cash outflows.
- *Step 4.* Estimate the periodic cash inflows.
- *Step 5.* Compute the net present value of each project.
- *Step 6.* Plan to acquire those assets with a positive net present value.

You are already familiar with the procedures required to complete the capital budget. Chapter 9 covered steps 1, 3, 4, and 5, and computation of the asset-specific cost of capital was discussed in general terms in Chapters 5, 6, and 7. The asset-specific cost of capital will be discussed in greater detail in Chapters 13 and 14. In this simplest case, the firm will accept all those projects with a positive net present value.

The summary of the capital budget is presented in Table 10–3, with the projects ranked in order of their contribution to stockholder wealth (net present value). Note that the total increase in stockholder wealth will reach a maximum ($40,168,658) if the first four assets are acquired. The addition of the drilling consortium to the assets to be acquired will reduce stockholder wealth below the maximum potential amount.

The decision rule in constructing a long-term-asset acquisition plan (capital budget) is this:

**TABLE 10–3**

UNITED STATES PETROLEUM CORPORATION:
SUMMARY OF CAPITAL BUDGET
(Independent Alternatives Only; No Limitations on Available Capital)

| Asset | Outlay | Net present value | Accumulated increase in stockholder wealth | Decision |
|---|---|---|---|---|
| Pipeline | $100,000,000 | $17,032,896 | $17,032,896 | Acquire |
| Refinery | $70,000,000 | $16,255,053 | $33,287,949 | Acquire |
| Stations | $30,000,000 | $3,511,552 | $36,799,501 | Acquire |
| Tanker | $20,000,000 | $3,369,157 | $40,168,658 (Max.) | Acquire |
| Drilling | $40,000,000 | ($6,579,634) | $33,589,024 | Do not acquire |

*Decision Rule #1. Independent alternatives and unrestricted capital:*
Acquire each and every asset with a positive net present value.

As demonstrated in Table 10–3, this decision rule is consistent with the stockholder-wealth maximization of the firm. The wealth of the stockholders will increase by $40,168,658 if the first four projects are accepted by the firm.

The IRR could have also been used as the basis of a decision rule for constructing this particular capital budget. The IRR method will result in accepting all assets for which the IRR is greater than the asset-specific cost of capital. USPC would have obtained the same results using NPV or IRR under our present assumptions. Remember that the decision rule discussed thus far applies *only* to the case in which all assets are independent and the availability of capital is not restricted.

## CAPITAL RATIONING, INDEPENDENT ALTERNATIVES

Quite frequently, firms have many more asset-acquisition alternatives with a positive net present value than they have capital available. This may be caused by the inability of management to obtain funds from external sources. Perhaps the security markets are unreasonably pessimistic, or the total funds available in those markets are limited. In such cases, management must select the "package" of alternatives that yields the greatest contribution to stockholder wealth. The selection of the best package appears to be a simple matter, but as always, appearances can be deceiving.[4]

The procedure of rationing a limited amount of funds among a number

---

[4]We will assume throughout this chapter that this limitation on the available capital is only for the current period. When capital limitations occur over multiple periods, the analysis follows the same conceptual approach as the one-year case but is more complex. See Edwin Elton, "Capital Rationing and External Discount Rates," *Journal of Finance*, June 1970, pp. 573–84.

of asset-acquisition alternatives is called *capital rationing*.[5] The procedures used in a capital-rationing situation for which all asset-acquisition alternatives are independent are illustrated in the following example. Assume that the Bridge Corporation has eight asset-acquisition alternatives, all of which are independent of each other. For the firm to acquire all the assets that have positive net present values, $375,000 would be required. Unfortunately, the Bridge Corporation has only $175,000 capital available, and these funds must be allocated in a fashion consistent with the maximization of stockholder wealth. The information on the eight alternatives is presented in Table 10–4. How should the Bridge Corporation ration its $175,000 capital?

## TABLE 10–4

BRIDGE CORPORATION:
ASSET-ACQUISITION ALTERNATIVES RANKED
BY NPV (Alternatives Are Independent)

| Asset | Initial Outlay | Net Present Value | Present-Value Index[a] |
|-------|----------------|-------------------|------------------------|
| A | $100,000 | $200,000 | 2.0 |
| B | $60,000 | $36,000 | 0.6 |
| C | $150,000 | $30,000 | 0.2 |
| D | $25,000 | $27,500 | 1.1 |
| E | $30,000 | $24,000 | 0.8 |
| F | $10,000 | $15,000 | 1.5 |
| G | $90,000 | ($2,000) | (0.02) |
| H | $25,000 | ($6,000) | (0.24) |

[a]Present-value index $= \dfrac{\text{Net present value}}{\text{Initial outlay}}$

This is a measure of the amount of net present value generated by each dollar of initial outlay.

Two possible packages of assets falling within the $175,000 restriction in available capital are presented in Table 10–5. Package I was selected on the positive amount of net present values and contains the two assets with the highest NPVs. Note, however, that the firm should reject package I and choose package II, which contributes more to stockholder wealth. Package II is superior even though it includes assets D, E, and F that have relatively low net present values.

The exclusion of assets B and C from package II takes place because of the relatively large initial outlay required to generate the net present value.

---

[5]Some financial theorists argue that capital rationing is inconsistent with stockholder-wealth maximization, since the firm should choose *all* projects that add to stockholder wealth. These theorists view the capital-rationing constraint as being irrational. We discuss capital rationing here because real firms frequently operate under such constraints. Students and managers are advised, however, to recognize that setting the capital ration at an unrealistically low level would itself be contrary to stockholder-wealth maximization.

TABLE 10-5

## BRIDGE CORPORATION:
## POSSIBLE PACKAGES OF ASSETS

*Package I: Selected on the basis of NPV per asset*

| Asset | Initial outlay | Net present value | Present-value index |
|-------|---------------|-------------------|---------------------|
| A | $100,000 | $200,000 | 2.0 |
| B | 60,000 | 36,000 | 0.6 |
| Total | $160,000 | $236,000 | |

*Package II: Selected on the basis of NPV per dollar of initial outlay*

| Asset | Initial outlay | Net present value | Present-value index |
|-------|---------------|-------------------|---------------------|
| A | $100,000 | $200,000 | 2.0 |
| F | 10,000 | 15,000 | 1.5 |
| D | 25,000 | 27,500 | 1.1 |
| E | 30,000 | 24,000 | 0.8 |
| Total | $165,000 | $266,500 | |

Asset D, for example, has almost the same net present value as assets B and C, but a much lower initial outlay. When funds are unlimited, the initial cash outlay is irrelevant. As long as the firm can compensate suppliers of capital for supplying funds and have an "excess" for equity suppliers, the firm should acquire the asset. When funds are limited, however, the firm should choose those projects that will maximize the net present value (equivalent to the increase in stockholder wealth) for the capital available.

The present-value index is an indicator of the net present value per dollar of initial outlay.[6] It is computed by dividing net present value by the initial cash outlay for the asset acquisition. Notice that package II includes those alternatives with the highest present-value indexes. This is consistent with the objective of stockholder-wealth maximization. Thus, we now have a second capital-budgeting decision rule:

> *Decision Rule #2. Independent alternatives and capital rationing:* In capital-rationing situations with independent alternatives, select the package of assets with the highest *total* net present value.

Although the present-value index is a good indicator of contribution to stockholder wealth in capital-rationing situations, it cannot be used mechanically. For example, let us consider once more the capital budget of the United States Petroleum Corporation. This time, it will be assumed that

---

[6]In a sense, the IRR is also a measure of the amount of net present value generated by a given initial outlay. Thus, the IRR can also be used to screen projects in capital-rationing situations. The present-value index is preferred because it is (1) easier to understand and (2) easier to compute.

USPC has only $100 million available for the acquisition of long-term assets.[7] As shown in Table 10–6, under such conditions the best package comprises the refinery and gas stations (the total NPV for this combination of assets is $19,766,605). Even though the pipeline has the second highest present-value index, it cannot be included if the firm is to stay within the capital-rationing constraint. Both the tanker and the stations alternatives are feasible within the $100 million constraint. Stations, while having a lower present-value index, has a higher NPV and should thus be selected. The difference in the indications results from the differences in the size of the initial cash outlay.

**TABLE 10–6**

UNITED STATES PETROLEUM CORPORATION:
SUMMARY OF CAPITAL BUDGET
(Independent Alternatives Only; Capital Available Limited to $100 million)

| Asset | Initial outlay | Net present value | Present-value index |
|-------|----------------|-------------------|---------------------|
| Refinery | $70,000,000 | $16,255,053 | 0.232 |
| Pipeline | $100,000,000 | $17,032,896 | 0.170 |
| Tanker | $20,000,000 | $3,369,157 | 0.168 |
| Stations | $30,000,000 | $3,511,552 | 0.117 |

| Package I | Package II | Package III[a] |
|-----------|------------|----------------|
| Refinery & stations | Refinery & tanker | Pipeline |
| Total NPV = $19,766,605 | Total NPV = $19,624,210 | Total NPV = $17,032,896 |

[a]Other possible packages exist, but they are obviously inferior.

The point of this discussion is to illustrate that the present-value index is useful but cannot be used in a mechanical fashion. Capital-rationing situations usually require that management use good common sense as well as proper techniques.

## CAPITAL BUDGETING, MUTUALLY EXCLUSIVE ALTERNATIVES

Thus far, the discussion of the capital budget has been confined to budgets with independent alternatives. In this section, we will show how mutually exclusive alternatives can be analyzed and included in the capital budget. Just as before, we will begin by assuming that there is no restriction on the capital available to the firm. The following section will discuss mutually exclusive alternatives under capital-rationing constraints.

In the absence of capital rationing, the procedures for including

---

[7]We are still assuming that all projects are independent. Thus, USPC can only select from projects A, B, C, D, and E. We are assuming that the other projects do not exist.

mutually exclusive alternatives in the capital budget are reasonably straight-forward. First, the "best" mutually exclusive alternative is chosen—the one with the highest NPV. This choice will provide the highest contribution to stockholder wealth. At this point, the "best" alternative is included in the capital budget if it has a positive net present value. All other mutually exclusive alternatives are dropped from consideration, regardless of their respective NPVs, because they are, by definition, mutually exclusive with the "best" alternative.

The USPC capital budget can be used to illustrate these procedures. The firm can acquire the first seven alternatives. However, a choice must be made between the fuel-oil capacity expansion (project F) and the gasoline capacity expansion (project G). The firm cannot accept both because they are mutually exclusive. Going back to Table 10-2, we can see that the net present value for the fuel-oil alternative is $5,336,755, and the net present value for the gasoline alternative is $5,380,162. The gasoline project is the "best" alternative even though it has a lower present-value index than the fuel-oil project. Remember that NPV is equal to the contribution of an asset to the wealth of the stockholders. Thus, *in the absence of capital rationing*, the gasoline alternative should be included in the capital budget. The revised plan for asset acquisitions (capital budget) is presented in Table 10–7.

TABLE 10–7

UNITED STATES PETROLEUM CORPORATION:
SUMMARY OF CAPITAL BUDGET
(Independent and Mutually Exclusive Alternatives Only; No Limitation on Capital)

| Asset[a] | Initial outlay | Net present value | Accumulated increase in stockholder wealth | Decision |
|---|---|---|---|---|
| Pipeline | $100,000,000 | $17,032,896 | $17,032,896 | Acquire |
| Refinery | $70,000,000 | $16,255,053 | $33,287,949 | Acquire |
| Gasoline[a] | $50,000,000 | $5,380,162 | $38,668,111 | Acquire |
| Stations | $30,000,000 | $3,511,552 | $42,179,663 | Acquire |
| Tanker | $20,000,000 | $3,369,157 | $45,548,820 (Max.) | Acquire |
| Drilling | $40,000,000 | ($6,579,634) | $38,969,186 | Do not acquire |

[a]The fuel-oil alternative is not included because it is mutually exclusive with the gasoline alternative. The gasoline alternative is better because it has a higher net present value.

The gasoline alternative was selected for inclusion in the capital budget on the basis of its higher net present value. The internal rate of return *should not be used as the basis* for selecting from a group of mutually exclusive alternatives. If the IRR had been used in the USPC situation, the fuel-oil instead of the gasoline project would have been included in the capital budget, resulting in a lower total stockholder wealth. We are now in a position to state the third capital-budgeting decision rule:

*Decision Rule #3. Mutually exclusive alternatives and no capital rationing:* When the firm has unlimited available capital, the mutually exclusive alternative with the highest positive net present value should be included in the capital budget. This alternative and all other independent alternatives with positive net present value should be accepted by the firm.

Many students have difficulty recognizing that a firm can maximize stockholder wealth by choosing a project with a lower IRR but a higher NPV—that the asset with the lower rate of return can produce the maximization of stockholder wealth. The difficulty in this concept lies in the lack of clear understanding of net present value. Remember that NPV is the "excess" return to the stockholders of the firm, *after the suppliers of both debt and equity capital have been compensated* for the risk undertaken. Remember also, we are assuming in this section that there is no capital rationing. The firm does not have to reject any project with a positive NPV because of the unavailability of funds.

Let us illustrate this concept with a numerical example. The William Manufacturing Corporation has two mutually exclusive asset-acquisition alternatives. These projects (A and B) are shown in Table 10–8. Each project has a positive NPV (NPV$_A$ = $22,900; NPV$_B$ = $25,133). The firm, however, can choose only one of the alternatives. In order to be consistent with stockholder-wealth maximization, the firm should choose alternative B, even though B has a lower IRR than A.[8]

**TABLE 10–8**

WILLIAM MANUFACTURING CORPORATION:
FINANCIAL INFORMATION FOR ASSET-ACQUISITION ALTERNATIVES

|  | MUTUALLY EXCLUSIVE | | Hypothetical asset B − A |
|---|---|---|---|
|  | Project A | Project B |  |
| Asset-specific cost of capital ($k_j^*$) | 10% | 10% | 10% |
| Initial outlay at time $t_0$ | $100,000 | $150,000 | $50,000 |
| Periodic cash inflows | $ 20,000 | $ 28,500 | $ 8,500 |
| Useful life | 10 years | 10 years | 10 years |
| Net present value | $ 22,900 | $ 25,133 | $ 2,233 |
| IRR (%) | 15.1% | 13.8% | 11.1% |
| Present-value index | 0.229 | 0.168 | 0.045 |

---

[8] We are assuming two projects with the same asset-specific cost of capital in order to simplify the discussion of the topic. Although the two mutually exclusive projects for USPC (fuel oil and gasoline) did not have the same asset-specific cost of capital, the same conceptual framework applies.

The advantage of alternative B can be illustrated by examining the return on the additional $50,000 initial outlay associated with it. Should the firm undertake this additional outlay? It will result in a periodic cash inflow to the firm of $8,500 for ten years. Since the asset-specific cost of capital for this "hypothetical asset" costing $50,000 is 10 percent, the net present value is a positive $2,233. Note that the IRR on this "hypothetical asset" is 11.1 percent, which is greater than the asset specific cost of capital.

This "hypothetical asset" is nothing more than the differences in cash flows between alternatives B and A. Thus, the present value of the additional periodic cash inflow of B ($28,500 − $20,000) is greater than the additional cash outlays ($150,000 − $100,000). Therefore, the *additional value* of project B when compared to project A is profitable to the firm. This statement is true *only* if we maintain the assumption of no capital rationing.

## CAPITAL RATIONING, MUTUALLY EXCLUSIVE ALTERNATIVES

The decision process relating to long-term-asset acquisitions becomes more complicated when the firm is limited by the amount of capital available. Whenever capital rationing exists, management must consider the amount of capital required to acquire the asset as well as the net present value of the asset. Stockholder wealth tends to be increased if those assets with higher present-value index numbers (PVI) are included in the final package accepted by management.[9] For purposes of illustration, consider the five "best" packages available to the management of USPC, given a capital limitation of $100 million. The information about the packages is presented in Table 10–9.

The selection of package IV increases stockholder wealth by the largest amount ($24,960,965). Included in package IV is the mutually exclusive alternative of fuel oil. Note that when the amount of capital was unrestricted, the fuel-oil alternative was rejected because gasoline had a higher net present value. Under conditions of capital rationing, however, the fuel-oil alternative is accepted and the gasoline alternative rejected. This change takes place because of the differences between the projects' initial cash outlays. When capital is in short supply (capital rationing), both the net present value and the initial cash outlays (present-value index) of the projects must be considered. When capital is unlimited, the initial outlay is unimportant. Therefore:

> *Decision Rule #4. Mutually exclusive alternatives and capital rationing:* In capital-rationing situations with independent and mutually exclusive alternatives, all mutually exclusive alternatives with positive net present values must be considered for inclusion in the capital budget. The package of assets with the highest *total* net present value is then selected.

---

[9]The limitations of the PVI were discussed earlier, and they also apply in this case, as well as in the following interrelated-alternatives case.

TABLE 10–9

## UNITED STATES PETROLEUM CORPORATION:
## FIVE PACKAGES OF ASSETS
### (Independent and Mutually Exclusive Alternatives Only)

| Package | Assets included | PVI | Initial outlay | Net present value |
|---------|----------------|------|----------------|-------------------|
| I | Refinery | 0.232 | $70,000,000 | $16,255,053 |
|   | Stations | 0.117 | 30,000,000 | 3,511,552 |
|   |          |       | $100,000,000 | $19,766,605 = Total NPV |
| II | Refinery | 0.232 | $70,000,000 | $16,255,053 |
|    | Tanker | 0.168 | 20,000,000 | 3,369,157 |
|    |        |       | $90,000,000 | $19,624,210 = Total NPV |
| III | Pipeline | 0.170 | $100,000,000 | $17,032,896 = Total NPV |
| IV | Refinery | 0.232 | $70,000,000 | $16,255,053 |
|    | Tanker | 0.168 | 20,000,000 | 3,369,157 |
|    | Fuel oil | 0.534 | 10,000,000 | 5,336,755 |
|    |          |       | $100,000,000 | $24,960,965 = Total NPV |
| V | Gasoline | 0.108 | $50,000,000 | $ 5,380,162 |
|   | Stations | 0.117 | 30,000,000 | 3,511,552 |
|   | Tanker | 0.168 | 20,000,000 | 3,369,157 |
|   |        |       | $100,000,000 | $12,260,871 = Total NPV |

## CAPITAL BUDGETING, INTERRELATED ALTERNATIVES

The procedures used to evaluate interrelated alternatives are similar to those employed in the evaluation of mutually exclusive alternatives. The first step in the process of evaluating a group of interrelated alternatives is the development of an exhaustive set of mutually exclusive alternatives from the set of interrelated alternatives. Then, net present value and the present-value index must be computed for each mutually exclusive–interrelated alternative. The basis for inclusion of the alternatives in the capital budget is the same as that discussed in the sections devoted to the analysis of mutually exclusive alternatives.

The development of an exhaustive set of mutually exclusive alternatives requires the application of common sense. For example, assume that three interrelated asset-acquisition alternatives—X, Y, and Z—are under consideration by the ANU Corporation. Remember, the fact that these three alternatives are interrelated means that the acceptance of one has an effect on the expected cash flows of the others. Thus, the expected cash flows associated with combinations of these assets differs from the sum of the cash flows derived from each individually.

A list of mutually exclusive alternatives derived from the three interrelated assets is presented in Table 10–10. This table shows that seven mutually exclusive alternatives can be developed from the three interrelated assets. These are mutually exclusive because the acceptance of one implies the rejection of the others, and the set is exhaustive because no other combinations are possible.

TABLE 10–10

ANU CORPORATION:
MUTUALLY EXCLUSIVE LONG-TERM-ASSET
ACQUISITION ALTERNATIVES DEVELOPED
FROM INTERRELATED ASSETS X, Y, AND Z

| Single-asset alternatives | Two-asset alternatives | Three-asset alternatives |
|---|---|---|
| X | X & Y | X, Y, & Z |
| Y | X & Z | |
| Z | Y & Z | |

In the United States Petroleum Corporation case, there are two interrelated alternatives: the computer control system and the increased storage capacity. Looking back at Tables 10–1 and 10–2, you will see that by consideration of the simultaneous acquisition of the two interrelated alternatives, a third alternative (with different cash flows) is created. For including the interrelated alternatives in the USPC capital budget, the procedures are identical to those employed in the mutually exclusive situation. In the absence of capital rationing, that mutually exclusive–interrelated alternative with the highest net present value is included in the capital budget. By definition, the other alternatives cannot be included.

A capital budget for USPC that includes the interrelated alternatives is presented in Table 10–11. Note that only the alternative labeled "Both" is included. This is because the net present value is greater when both the computer and the storage facilities are acquired. Stockholder wealth will be maximized if all alternatives with positive net present values are acquired. The drilling alternative is rejected because it would reduce stockholder wealth below the maximum amount.[10]

Thus we have:

*Decision Rule #5. Interrelated alternatives and no capital rationing:* Interrelated alternatives should always be evaluated as mutually exclusive–interrelated alternatives. When the firm is unrestricted by the availability of capital, that mutually exclusive–interrelated alternative

---

[10]Independent alternatives could also be combined. There is no point in making such combinations because the cash flows of the combinations will not differ from the sum of the cash flows of the individual assets.

TABLE 10–11

UNITED STATES PETROLEUM CORPORATION:
OPTIMAL CAPITAL BUDGET
(No Limitations on Capital Available for Investment)

| Asset[a] | Initial outlay | Net present value | Accumulated increase in stockholder wealth | Decision |
|---|---|---|---|---|
| Both | $ 60,000,000 | $42,139,465 | $42,139,465 | Acquire |
| Pipeline | 100,000,000 | 17,032,896 | 59,172,36i | Acquire |
| Refinery | 70,000,000 | 16,255,053 | 75,427,414 | Acquire |
| Gasoline | 50,000,000 | 5,380,162 | 80,807,576 | Acquire |
| Stations | 30,000,000 | 3,511,552 | 84,319,128 | Acquire |
| Tanker | 20,000,000 | 3,369,157 | 87,688,285 | Acquire |
| Drilling | 40,000,000 | (6,579,634) | 81,108,651 | Do not acquire |

[a]The fuel-oil alternative is not included because it is mutually exclusive with the gasoline alternative. In the absence of capital rationing, the mutually exclusive alternative with the highest positive NPV is included in the capital budget.

with the highest positive net present value should be included in the capital budget.

## CAPITAL RATIONING, INTERRELATED ALTERNATIVES

When capital rationing is in effect, the firm proceeds as it did with mutually exclusive alternatives. As shown previously in Table 10–9, packages of assets are constructed using the present-value index as a general guide. All these packages must keep the initial outlays within the boundaries established by the capital restriction.

The final capital budget for USPC is presented in Table 10–12. This is the package that maximizes stockholder wealth. Note that several investments with very high net present values are omitted from the final package. Once again, this is because when capital is limited, the size of the initial cash outlay is of crucial significance. Primarily, it is net present value per dollar of initial outlay that determines inclusion in the optimal package. The stations alternative was included even though it had a relatively low present-value index, because it is the best choice for the last $30 million available to the firm. The tanker alternative had a higher present-value index, but its selection would have meant that $10 million of available capital would not have been used by the firm. The stations alternative has the advantage of using all the remaining capital.

*Decision Rule #6. Interrelated alternatives and capital rationing:* In capital-rationing situations with independent, mutually exclusive, and interrelated alternatives, all alternatives with a positive net present value must be considered for inclusion in the capital budget. The package of assets with the highest total NPV is then selected.

**TABLE 10–12**

UNITED STATES PETROLEUM CORPORATION:
OPTIMAL CAPITAL BUDGET
(New Capital Limited to $100 Million)

| Assets included | PVI | Initial outlay | Net present value |
|---|---|---|---|
| Both computer & storage | 0.702 | $60,000,000 | $42,139,465 |
| Fuel oil | 0.534 | 10,000,000 | 5,336,755 |
| Stations | 0.117 | 30,000,000 | 3,511,552 |
| | | $100,000,000 | $50,987,772 = Total NPV |

**SUMMARY**  The objective of this chapter, building on the material presented in earlier chapters, is to show how management should make choices from the many long-term-asset acquisitions likely to be available. A capital budget reflecting the effect of various alternatives on stockholder wealth must be constructed. The procedures used to construct it will depend on two factors: (1) the types of alternatives available to the firm, and (2) whether or not the firm must operate under conditions of capital rationing. As a guide for decision making, six decision rules were developed:

- *Rule #1. Independent alternatives and no limitation on capital.* The firm should acquire each and every asset with a positive net present value.
- *Rule #2. Independent alternatives and capital rationing.* The firm should select the package of assets with the highest total net present value.
- *Rule #3. Mutually exclusive and no limitations on capital.* The mutually exclusive alternative with the highest positive net present value should be included in the capital budget.
- *Rule #4. Mutually exclusive alternatives and capital rationing.* All mutually exclusive alternatives must be considered for inclusion in the capital budget. The package of assets with the highest total net present value is then selected.
- *Rule #5. Interrelated alternatives and no limitations on capital.* Interrelated alternatives should be evaluated as mutually exclusive–interrelated alternatives. That mutually exclusive–interrelated alternative with the highest positive net present value should be included in the capital budget.
- *Rule #6. Interrelated alternatives and capital rationing.* All mutually exclusive–interrelated alternatives with positive net present values must be considered for inclusion in the capital budget. The package of assets with the highest total net present value is then selected.

We have stressed the need for using both net present value and the present-value index in making capital-budgeting decisions. The primary focus has been on the net present value per package of assets, and the present-value index is a convenient device for selecting assets for inclusion in the optimal package.

Once again, this chapter demonstrates that the decision-making process is not mechanical. Sound business judgments are required for stockholder-wealth-maximization decisions.

**QUESTIONS FOR DISCUSSION**

1. Discuss and give examples of the differences between independent, mutually exclusive, and interrelated asset-acquisition alternatives.
2. Outline the asset-acquisition procedure that should be used when acquisition alternatives are independent, and explain. Why is this procedure consistent with stockholder-wealth maximization? How does capital rationing affect this procedure?
3. Explain how the firm should proceed in the capital-budgeting situation in which mutually exclusive proposals are present. How will capital rationing affect the procedure? How are the recommended procedures related to stockholder wealth?
4. Explain how the firm should proceed in capital-budgeting situations in which interrelated alternatives are present. How are the procedures related to stockholder-wealth maximization?
5. What is a capital budget, and why is it needed?
6. Discuss the relationship between IRR and NPV. Under which conditions will a firm maximize stockholder wealth by choosing alternatives with relatively low NPVs? Explain your answer.
7. Discuss the limitations of the present-value index as a tool for making asset-acquisition decisions under conditions of capital rationing.
8. Under conditions of capital rationing, it is possible that alternatives with the highest net present value are excluded from the final capital budget. Explain why this is possible.
9. Under capital rationing, the firm may accept mutually exclusive alternatives that would have been rejected if capital had been unrestricted. Explain.

**PROBLEMS**

1. The Lancer Corporation is currently preparing its 1981 capital budget. The firm has two asset-acquisition alternatives that are independent.

- *First Alternative:* The firm can purchase new manufacturing equipment. This equipment has an initial cash outlay of $15 million. Periodic cash inflows are $2.5 million for 15 years. The asset-specific cost of capital is 12%.
- *Second Alternative:* The firm can purchase another firm. The initial cash outlay is $20 million. The expected periodic cash inflows are $4 million for 20 years. The asset-specific cost of capital is 18%.

   a. Which alternative should be accepted by the Lancer Corporation in the absence of capital rationing? Show the increase in stockholder wealth.
   b. Which alternative should be accepted if Lancer has only $20 million available for investments? Show the increase in stockholder wealth.

2. The American Rail Corporation is preparing its capital budget. The finance staff

has prepared the following financial information on the available asset-acquisition alternatives:

| Project[a] | Cost | Net present value | PVI |
|------|------|------------------|------|
| A | $40 million | $20 million | 0.50 |
| B | $40 million | $10 million | 0.25 |
| C | $20 million | $6 million | 0.30 |

[a]Projects B and C are mutually exclusive. The cash flows of project A are independent from those of B and C.

a. Which projects should be selected by American Rail if there is no capital rationing? Show the increase in stockholder wealth.
b. Which projects should be selected if American Rail has only $60 million available for investments? Show the increase in stockholder wealth.

3. Payless Discount Stores is considering expansion in Austin, Texas. The firm can open one store or two stores. Given that two stores are opened, their cash flows are interrelated. The financial staff has prepared the following analysis (in millions of dollars):

| Store | Initial cash outlay | Periodic cash inflows | Life | $k_j^*$ |
|-------|--------------------|-----------------------|------|--------|
| South Austin | $30 | $5 | 20 years | 12% |
| North Austin | $40 | $6 | 20 years | 12% |
| Both stores | $70 | $10 | 20 years | 12% |

a. What should be the capital-budgeting decision if the firm has no capital rationing? Show the increase in stockholder wealth.
b. What should be the capital-budgeting decision if the firm has only $40 million available for the Austin investment? Show the increase in stockholder wealth.

4. The American Pipe Corporation is planning its 1981 capital budget. The following four proposals have been presented by marketing and production personnel. It is the responsibility of the finance staff to evaluate the effect of these proposals on stockholder wealth.

- *Proposal A:* The production personnel recommend the installation of a new control system. This alternative will involve an initial cash outlay of $10 million. The periodic cash inflows are expected to be $1.8 million for ten years. There is no expected salvage value on this asset. The asset-specific cost of capital is 10%.
- *Proposal B:* The marketing department recommends an expansion of existing facilities. The initial cash outlay is $30 million. The periodic cash inflows are expected to be $5 million for 15 years. There is no expected salvage value. The asset-specific cost of capital is 14%.
- *Proposal C:* The marketing department recommends an expansion of the warehouse facilities of the firm in order to improve service to customers in California. The initial cash outlay is $20 million. The periodic cash inflows are

expected to be $3 million for 30 years. There is no expected salvage value. The asset-specific cost of capital is 16%.

- *Proposal D:* The trucking department recommends the purchase of a new fleet of trucks. The initial cash outlay is $20 million. The periodic cash flows are expected to be $6 million for five years. There is no expected salvage value for the trucks. The asset-specific cost of capital is 9%.

These four projects are independent. The acquisition of any one of the alternatives will not influence the cash flows of the other three.

   a. Prepare a table (similar to Table 10-2) with the financial information for these four proposals. Show the NPV, IRR, and PVI of each of the four alternatives.

   b. Which projects should be undertaken by the firm in the absence of capital rationing?

   c. Which projects should be undertaken by the firm if American Pipe has only $30 million available for investments?

5. Before American Pipe makes its final capital-budgeting decisions, the trucking department presents an additional proposal. Proposal E is to purchase Super-Trucks. These trucks are more efficient than those mentioned in proposal D. The trucks will cost $30 million. The periodic cash flows are expected to be $8.6 million for five years. There is no expected salvage value for Super-Trucks. The asset-specific cost of capital is 9%. You must recognize that Super-Trucks (proposal E) and Trucks (proposal D) are mutually exclusive.

   a. Prepare the capital budget of American Pipe (consider projects A, B, C, D, and E) in the absence of capital rationing.

   b. Which projects (A, B, C, D, or E) should be undertaken if American Pipe has only $30 million available for investments?

6. The board of directors of the American Canning Corporation (ACC) is evaluating possible asset acquisitions by the firm. The financial staff of ACC has prepared the following summary of available alternatives to ACC (in millions of dollars). The first five alternatives (A, B, C, D, and E) are independent; the next two (F and G) are mutually exclusive; H and I are interrelated. If ACC chooses only H, the NPV is $15 million. If ACC chooses only I, the NPV is $10 million. However, if *both* projects are accepted, the NPV would be $30 million.

| Project | Initial outlay | Net present value | Present-value index |
|---------|----------------|-------------------|---------------------|
| A | $50 | $10 | 0.20 |
| B | $100 | $15 | 0.15 |
| C | $30 | $10 | 0.33 |
| D | $10 | $8 | 0.8 |
| E | $10 | $8 | 0.8 |
| F | $50 | $20 | 0.4 |
| G | $10 | $10 | 1.0 |
| H | $20 | $15 | 0.75 |
| I | $20 | $10 | 0.5 |
| Both H & I | $40 | $30 | 0.75 |

   a. Which projects should be accepted by ACC if there is no capital rationing? Indicate the increase in stockholder wealth.

b. Which projects should be accepted if ACC has only $100 million available for investments? Indicate the increase in stockholder wealth.

**SELECTED BIBLIOGRAPHY**

BAUMOL, W. S., and R. E. QUANDT, "Investment and Discount Rates under Capital Rationing," *The Economic Journal,* 75 (June 1965), 317–29.

BIERMAN, H., JR., and SEYMOUR SMIDT, *The Capital Budgeting Decision,* 4th ed. New York: McMillan, 1975.

BOUDREAUX, KENNETH J., and HUGH W. LONG, *The Basic Theory of Corporate Finance.* Englewood Cliffs, N.J.: Prentice-Hall, 1977.

BRIGHAM, EUGENE F., "Hurdle Rates for Screening Capital Expenditure Proposals," *Financial Management,* 4 (Autumn 1975), 17–26.

BUSSEY, LYNN E., and G. T. STEVENS, JR., "Formulating Correlated Cash Flow Streams," *Engineering Economist,* 18 (Fall 1972), 1–30.

COPELAND, THOMAS E., and J. FRED WESTON, *Financial Theory and Corporate Policy.* Reading, Mass.: Addison Wesley, 1979.

ELTON, EDWIN J., "Capital Rationing and External Discount Rates," *Journal of Finance,* XXV (June 1970), 573–84.

HILLER, FREDERICK S., "A Basic Model for Capital Budgeting for Risky Interrelated Projects," *Engineering Economist,* 20 (Fall 1974), 37–49.

HIRSHLEIFER, J., *Investment, Interest and Capital.* Englewood Cliffs, N.J.: Prentice-Hall, 1970.

LEVY, HAIM, and MARSHALL SARNAT, *Capital Investment and Financial Decisions.* Englewood Cliffs, N.J.: Prentice-Hall, 1978.

LORIE, JAMES H., and LEONARD J. SAVAGE, "Three Problems in Rationing Capital," *Journal of Business* XXVIII (October 1955), 227–39.

NELSON, CHARLES R., "Inflation and Capital Budgeting," *Journal of Finance,* 31 (June 1976), 923–31.

VAN HORNE, JAMES C., "Capital Budgeting under Conditions of Uncertainty as to Project Life," *Engineering Economist,* 17 (Spring 1972), 189–99.

———, *Financial Management and Policy,* 5th ed. Englewood Cliffs, N.J.: Prentice-Hall, 1980.

———, "A Note on Biases on Capital Budgeting Introduced by Inflation," *Journal of Finance and Quantitative Analysis,* VI (January 1971), 653–58.

WEINGARTNER, H. MARTIN, "Capital Budgeting of Interrelated Projects: Survey and Synthesis," *Management Science,* XII (March 1966), 485–516.

# THE ACQUISITION OF CURRENT ASSETS

## 11

## INTRODUCTION

In its quest for stockholder-wealth maximization, management must consider the effect of each decision on the level of the firm's expected cash flows and on the riskiness of those cash flows. Decisions related to current assets are no exception. What will possible changes in current assets do to the expected cash flows of the firm? What will they do to the riskiness of the firm's cash flows? These are the questions management must ask. These are the questions that will be addressed in this chapter.

Although there are several types of current assets, what they have in common is significantly more liquidity than the other assets owned by the firm; that is, current assets can be converted into cash with relative ease. For example, it is much less difficult to liquidate inventories than fixed plant and equipment. In order to facilitate our analysis, liquid current assets will be divided into three categories: (1) liquid funds (including cash and marketable securities), (2) accounts receivable, and (3) inventories. For each category, guidelines for making asset acquisition/disbursement decisions will be developed.

At the outset it should be recognized that decisions relating to the size of the firm's investment in particular current assets involve optimization rather than minimization. Firms seek to achieve the *right* amount rather than the *minimum* amount of a current asset. For example, a firm can eliminate accounts receivable (minimization) by insisting on cash payments. This action may minimize accounts receivable but, in most cases, stockholder wealth will suffer because sales and profits will be lost. On the other hand, allowing current assets to increase beyond the point necessary for the conduct of the firm's ordinary activities results in the need for additional capital. Remember, an increase in assets must be financed, and capital is not free. Increased financing costs, without additional benefits to the firm, will tend to reduce stockholder wealth. Thus, stockholder wealth may suffer because the firm has too small or too large an investment in the individual current-asset categories. Management's job is to find the elusive optimal amount that lies between these two extremes.

The asset reservoir model, illustrated in Figure 11–1, can be used as a conceptual framework for decisions relating to current-asset acquisition/disbursements. It is convenient to think of each asset—liquid funds, accounts receivable, and inventories—as having its own reservoir. The assets flow into their respective reservoirs on a more or less continuous basis. That is, cash is received, accounts receivable extended, and inventories purchased. These inflows tend to raise the level of the reservoir. Offsetting this increase of current assets in the reservoir are regular outflows. Accounts receivable are reduced as customers pay bills; cash and inventories are also reduced in the firm's ordinary course of business.

The problem in current-asset management arises from the fact that

**FIGURE 11–1°**

Asset Reservoir Model

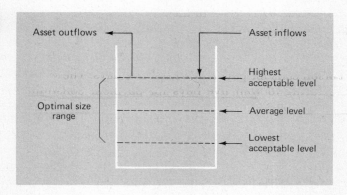

PART TWO: The Acquisition of Assets

periodic inflows of each asset are not likely to exactly coincide with the periodic outflows. In some periods, more is added to the inventory reservoir than is taken out, resulting in an increase in the inventory level. In other periods, more inventories are taken out of the reservoir than added to it. Thus, the amount of the reservoir will vary from period to period. As suggested by Figure 11–1, it is best to view the reservoirs of current assets as having a highest and a lowest acceptable level. Management's task is to manage the inflows and outflows of current assets so that the amounts are maintained within these levels, or within the "optimal size range."

This chapter develops overall guidelines and specific techniques useful in maintaining current assets within the optimal size ranges. The techniques currently employed in current-asset management call for an estimation of differences in profits associated with alternative current-assets levels. The emphasis is on revenue, costs, and profits, as distinct from cash flows. Underlying the analysis of current-asset decisions is the reasonable assumption that those alternatives with higher expected profits will also have higher expected cash flows to stockholders. In addition, risk is usually incorporated into the analysis on a subjective level. The current-asset management techniques used today do not attempt to develop a direct measure of the effect on stockholder wealth. Instead, alternative profit information is subjected to an intuitive adjustment for risk. The final result of such procedures is that the relationship between the current-asset management techniques and stockholder wealth are not as clear as that between techniques for fixed-asset decision making and stockholder wealth. However, the current-asset management techniques presented in this chapter can be interpreted in the context of stockholder wealth.

## ACCOUNTS RECEIVABLE

Accounts receivable arise from the extension by the firm of what is called "trade credit." Trade credit is extended when the firm sells to a customer and permits the customer to postpone payment for a short period of time.

Assume that the Charlotta Fashion Manufacturing Corporation sells $50,000 in ladies garments to the Larson Stores Corporation. The goods are shipped to Larson Stores and are recorded on Charlotta Manufacturing's books as a sale (revenue of $50,000). Larson Stores, however, is not required to pay cash upon receipt of the merchandise. Instead, Charlotta's agreement with Larson calls for payment within five days. The willingness of Charlotta Manufacturing to wait five days for payment constitutes an extension of trade credit and gives rise to the balance-sheet entry called "accounts receivable." The account receivable represents a promise by the buyer to pay the seller for the goods received. When the $50,000 payment is received from Larson Stores, the account receivable is eliminated.

Trade credit is an integral part of almost all interfirm transactions in the American economy. Almost every firm is extended credit by its suppliers, and in turn extends credit to its customers.[1] One reason for the use of trade credit is that it is simply more convenient than selling on a cash basis. Trade credit permits specialization of functions within the firm, since the people responsible for the movement of goods are not the same ones involved in the movement of funds. Today, trade-credit extensions are an ordinary part of doing business. Buyers expect trade credit to be extended to them and would in most cases be reluctant to buy from a firm that demanded cash on delivery. The firm selling to other firms in the United States has virtually no choice; trade credit must be extended. Thus, almost all American firms selling to other firms have accounts receivable.

The extension of trade credit may have a significant effect on the firm's profitability and stockholder wealth. Failure to extend trade credit will tend to restrict sales and may impair profits of the firm. On the other hand, the extension of credit is costly. First, there is the cost of raising capital to finance accounts receivable. Second, there is the possibility of losses due to nonpayment by customers (bad-debt cost).[2] The benefits of increased sales must be weighed against these two costs.

Table 11-1 provides a simplified illustration of the possible relationships among trade credit, accounts receivable, profits, and stockholder wealth. If the Radelli Corporation insists on cash on delivery, profit after credit-policy costs will be $365,000. Note that under these conditions, the firm has no accounts-receivable financing costs and no bad-debt losses. The next column shows what happens under a credit policy of "net 10 days."[3] Under these hypothetical conditions, sales are dramatically higher, as is profit before credit-policy costs. The increased sales, however, are partially offset by the fact that accounts receivable must be financed and bad-debt losses will be incurred.[4] Under the hypothetical conditions associated with the net-10-day policy, the benefits of increased sales outweigh the costs of financing accounts receivable and bad-debt losses. Thus, profit after credit-policy costs is higher than it would have been under the COD terms. This, of course, need not have been the case. The credit-policy costs could have been greater than the benefits of increased sales. Such a situation is illustrated under the net-30-day policy. Note that credit-policy costs have increased to such a high level that profit after those costs is lower than in either of the other two cases.

You are now in a position to appreciate the complexity of what might be called "management of accounts receivable." For one thing, it *may be*

---

[1]High-risk firms may not receive trade credit. And in a few industries, such as aircraft sales, it is customary to make payments before delivery. These are exceptions to the general situation.

[2]There are other costs, such as credit checking and administrative costs, but these tend to be relatively small for most firms.

[3]The buyer is expected to pay the net amount due in ten days.

[4]The increased investment in accounts receivable is equal to the costs expended in order to generate the accounts. In our example, costs are equal to 90% of sales. That is, in order to increase accounts receivable by $100, the firm must spend $90 for materials, labor, and so on.

TABLE 11-1

## RADELLI CORPORATION:
### Profit After Credit-Policy Costs, Selected Credit Policies[a]

| | Cash on delivery | Net 10 days | Net 30 days |
|---|---|---|---|
| Daily sales | $10,000 | $15,000 | $16,000 |
| Annual sales (365 × daily sales) | $3,650,000 | $5,400,000 | $5,840,000 |
| Annual profit before credit-policy costs (10% of sales) | $365,000 | $540,000 | $584,000 |
| Accounts receivable (daily sales × average collection period)[b] | 0 | $150,000 | $480,000 |
| Investment in accounts receivable[c] | 0 | $135,000 | $432,000 |
| Cost of financing accounts receivable[d] | 0 | $27,000 | $108,000 |
| Bad-debt losses[e] | 0 | $54,000 | $116,000 |
| Credit-policy cost (total) | 0 | $81,000 | $224,000 |
| Profit after credit-policy costs (before taxes) | $365,000 | $459,000 | $360,000 |

[a]These are hypothetical situations, designed only to illustrate certain relationships among sales, accounts receivable, and profit after credit costs.

[b]It is assumed that all customers pay on the last day of the "grace" period. Thus, the average collection period under net 10 days is ten days, and under net 30 days is 30 days.

[c]Although the firm carries receivables at invoice prices, its investment is only 90% (costs) of the face value of receivables.

[d]The asset-specific cost of capital for accounts receivable increases as credit policy is liberalized, because the risk of nonpayment also increases. We have assumed an asset-specific cost of capital of 20% for accounts receivable with net-10-day terms and 25% with net-30-day terms. This asset-specific cost of capital applies to the firm's investment in accounts receivable.

[e]Bad-debt losses are assumed to increase as the average collection period increases. This reflects the possibility that the increase in sales may involve the extension of credit to customers with lower creditworthiness. We have assumed bad-debt losses as a percentage of sales to be 1% under the net-10-day terms, and 2% under the net-30-day terms.

profitable (or it may not) for the firm to maintain accounts receivable even though such receivables require financing. Second, it *may be* profitable (or it may not) for the firm to extend credit and increase accounts receivable even though some bad-debt losses might be incurred. The management of trade credit and accounts-receivable financing should be evaluated in terms of profits rather than the maintenance of zero bad-debt losses. In effect, the management of accounts receivable involves the establishment of credit standards and credit terms that maximize profit after credit-policy costs and thus maximize stockholder wealth.

## CREDIT TERMS AND STOCKHOLDER WEALTH

The credit terms offered to the customers of the firm indicate the agreed-upon conditions for payment. The terms may call for cash on delivery (COD), in which case no credit is extended. The terms may require full payment on a specific date (n/30), in which case payment is expected 30 days after the products are received by the customer.[5] Finally, the firm may offer a discount for early payment. This is usually expressed as, for example, 2/10,n/30. In such a case, the customer can take a 2 percent discount from the face value of the invoice if payment is made within the first ten days. Payment after this ten-day "discount period" must be at the full face value of the invoice and is expected 30 days after the customer has received the products. The example given of 2/10,n/30 is only one of a common set of credit terms. Others, such as 1/10,n/30 or 3/15,n/60, may be offered by the firm.

Three factors determine the effect of credit terms on profits: (1) the discount period, (2) the amount of the discount offered, and (3) the number of days by which final payment must be made. These variables determine the cost to the customer of missing the discount and the "interest-free" credit extended by the firm during the discount period. The cost to the buyer of not taking the discount can be computed, on an annualized basis, by the following equation:[6]

$$\begin{matrix} \text{Annualized} \\ \text{cost} \\ \text{of missing} \\ \text{the discount} \end{matrix} = \frac{\text{Dollar value of}}{\begin{matrix}\text{the discount}\\\hline \text{Face value} \_ \text{Dollar value}\\ \text{of invoice} \quad \text{of discount}\end{matrix}} \times \frac{360 \text{ days}}{\begin{matrix}\text{Number of days} \_ \text{Discount}\\ \text{to final payment} \quad \text{period}\end{matrix}} \quad (11\text{-}1)$$

A numerical example will illustrate the use of the equation. If the credit terms are 2/10,n/30, and the face value of the invoice is $1,000:

$$\begin{matrix}\text{Cost of missing}\\ \text{the discount}\end{matrix} = \frac{2\% \text{ of } \$1,000}{\$1,000 - 2\% \text{ of } \$1,000} \times \frac{360}{30 - 10} = \frac{20}{1,000 - 20} \times \frac{360}{20}$$

$$= 0.3673 = 36.73\%$$

If the discount is missed, the customer has to pay the full face value of the invoice ($1,000) 30 days after the products are received. If the customer pays for the products within the ten-day discount period, the payment will be only $980 [$1,000 − (2% × $1,000)]. Thus, the cost of missing the discount is $20. The alternatives open to the firm are to pay $980 on the tenth day (there is no advantage in paying on the first day) or to pay $1,000 on the thirtieth day. Given that the firm misses the discount period, it would be able to use the $980 for an additional 20 days. The percentage cost of using this money would be 2.04 percent ($20/$980), but only for a 20-day period. In order to determine the *annual rate*, we must multiply this amount by the number of 20-day periods in one year (360 days/20 days).

From the seller's point of view, there are two advantages of offering discounts. First, sales may be increased, since the discount is similar to a

---

[5]This 30-day period may begin with the date specified in the invoice, rather than the date the products are received.

[6]We are following a common industry practice of using a 360-day year in order to simplify computations.

price reduction. For example, assume that a buyer has been purchasing materials on a 2/10,n/30 basis and has been regularly taking the discount (paying $980 on the tenth day for each $1,000 purchase). If the seller offers credit terms of 3/10,n/30, it is essentially offering a lower price, since only $970 needs to be paid on the tenth day. The profitability of such a strategy (from the seller's point of view) will depend on the effect of the new discount policy on the sales of the firm. Sales and profits before discounts must increase sufficiently to offset the lost revenue from the higher discount offered.

The second advantage to the seller of offering discounts is a reduction in accounts-receivable financing cost. Collections will be speeded up as buyers take advantage of the discounts. Cash is received by the seller at an earlier date, thus reducing the amount of capital required to finance accounts receivable. In a general sense, the higher the cost to the buyer of not taking discounts, the more likely it is that the discount offered will increase the seller's sales and reduce the seller's accounts receivable. Table 11–2 shows the cost of not taking discounts for selected credit terms. Once again, the advantages of the higher discount percentage (greater sales, lower accounts receivable) may be offset by the lost revenue associated with the discounts taken by customers.

TABLE 11–2

### ANNUAL COST TO BUYER OF NOT TAKING DISCOUNT,[a]
#### Selected Credit Terms

| Credit term | Cost | Credit term | Cost | Credit term | Cost |
|---|---|---|---|---|---|
| 1/10,n/20 | 36% | 1/10,n/30 | 18% | 1/10,n/60 | 7% |
| 2/10,n/20 | 74% | 2/10,n/30 | 37% | 2/10,n/60 | 15% |
| 3/10,n/20 | 111% | 3/10,n/30 | 56% | 3/10,n/60 | 22% |

[a]Using equation 11–1, and assuming a $1,000 sale. The percentage cost would be identical if sales of $100 or $1,000,000 had been assumed.

Table 11–2 also suggests that the firm may be able to increase sales by extending the maturity of accounts receivable. In a sense, the seller may be providing an important financing component to its customers. For example, the credit terms 1/10,n/60 represent a cost of funds of only 7 percent to buyers. In order for accounts-receivable financing to be attractive to the buyer, the discount percentage has to be small and the maturity date far in the future. Otherwise, buyers will usually find less expensive forms of short-term financing. Note that the policy of increasing the maturity date may increase sales, but it will also increase accounts receivable and their financing cost. The benefits of increased sales must be weighed against the increased cost of accounts-receivable financing.

# CREDIT STANDARDS

By extending trade credit to a larger or smaller number of buyers, the firm has some control over its level of sales. Of course, extending trade credit is one thing and collecting on accounts receivable another. Extension of trade credit to customers who fail to pay increases the level of bad-debt losses to the firm. Thus, the profitability of the firm and stockholder wealth will reflect the benefit of increased sales weighed against increased bad-debt losses.

The process of weighing the benefits of increased sales against increased bad-debt losses takes place when management establishes credit standards. Typically, management proceeds by establishing risk classes for potential buyers. For each class, management estimates bad-debt-loss ratios and average collection periods. The riskier classes will have higher bad-debt-loss ratios and higher accounts receivable owing to a higher average collection period (thus, a higher dollar cost of financing accounts receivable). Management must then decide which classes of customers provide opportunities for profitable sales. Finally, as customers apply for trade credit, management reviews their creditworthiness and places them in one of the predetermined classes. Trade credit is extended only if the buyer is included in a class of customers that provides a profit opportunity to the firm.

As an illustration, consider the hypothetical credit classes developed by the Pfunder Corporation, presented in Table 11–3. Once the classes have been established, management must evaluate the profitability of each class of customer. Such an analysis for the Pfunder Corporation is shown in Table 11–4. The cost of financing receivables reflects the riskiness of the various risk classes and is derived from the security-market line. Since Class 1 customers' receivables have virtually no risk, their asset-specific cost of capital is lower than that of the receivables of Class 5 customers.

Finally, management estimates the increase in profits due to the increase in sales resulting from the extension of credit. For Class 3 customers, this is equal to 16 percent of $100 million, or $16 million. However, the firm experiences $1 million (1 percent of $100 million) in bad-debt losses. This will reduce profits to only $15 million. Since the firm's investment in accounts receivable will increase by $8.4 million [ AR = (ACP × S)/360 = (36 × $100,000,000)/360] owing to the extension of trade credit, the cost of financing receivables will increase. The dollar financing cost of $8.4 million in investment in receivables for this risk class is $840,000 (10 percent of $8,400,000). Thus, the net result for the firm of extending credit to Class 3 customers is a net increase in profits of $14,160,000. As shown in Table 11–4, the firm should extend credit to customers in the first four classes, and reject credit to customers in Class 5. For Class 5 customers, credit-policy costs outweigh the benefits of increased sales.

TABLE 11-3

## PFUNDER CORPORATION:
### Credit Classes

Class 1: Firms with *perfect* credit rating. There is no possibility of bad-debt losses. For example, the U.S. government, American Telephone & Telegraph, etc.

Class 2: Firms with an *almost perfect* credit rating. The probability of bad debts is so small as to be virtually zero. For example, General Motors, Southern California Edison, etc.

Class 3: Firms with a *good* credit rating. There is some probability of bad debts; however, it is small. For example, a large corporation experiencing temporary financial difficulties, or a small firm with an excellent history of payments.

Class 4: Firms with *substandard* credit rating. There is a significant probability of bad debts. For example, a large corporation experiencing fundamental financial difficulties, or a small firm having some temporary financial difficulties.

Class 5: Firms with a *poor* credit rating. There is a very high probability of bad debts. For example, a large corporation in bankruptcy proceedings, or a new small firm in financial diflculties.

## CLASSIFICATION OF CUSTOMERS

Credit managers must evaluate each customer and place each in the risk class that accurately reflects the customer's individual risk level. Relatively sophisticated statistical techniques may be employed, but the classification is based on the experience and judgment of the credit manager.[7] Credit judgments must be based on information, and such information is available from a number of sources.

The financial statements of the customer firm can be examined to determine the extent of the firm's profitability, liquidity, prior indebtedness, and management efficiency.[8] Financial statements give an overall view of the firm that should be supplemented by additional information. There are a number of companies that provide credit reports on the payment experience of almost all firms of moderate size or larger.[9] They furnish information on (1) the firm's banking activities, (2) the current suppliers of the firm, (3) payment experience of current suppliers, (4) the extent to which the firm

---

[7] An excellent discussion of the use of discriminate analysis to determine credit extension is included in James C. Van Horne, *Financial Management and Policy,* 4th ed. (Englewood Cliffs, N.J.: Prentice-Hall, 1977), pp. 402–10.

[8] Procedures for financial-statement analysis will be discussed in Chapter 19.

[9] Two of the best known credit-reporting agencies are Dun & Bradstreet and TRW.

TABLE 11–4

## PFUNDER CORPORATION:
## PROFITABILITY OF CREDIT CLASSES

|  | Class 1 | Class 2 | Class 3 | Class 4 | Class 5 |
|---|---|---|---|---|---|
| Potential sales | $20,000,000 | $40,000,000 | $100,000,000 | $300,000,000 | $500,000,000 |
| Bad debts as a percentage of sales | 0% | 0.1% | 1% | 5% | 15% |
| Average collection period (days)[a] | 30 | 32 | 36 | 40 | 90 |
| Asset-specific cost of capital of receivables | 8% | 9% | 10% | 12% | 20% |
| Increase in profits before credit-policy cost due to increased sales (16% of sales) (1) | $3,200,000 | $6,400,000 | $16,000,000 | $48,000,000 | $80,000,000 |
| Minus: Bad-debt losses (2) | 0 | −$40,000 | −$1,000,000 | −15,000,000 | −$75,000,000 |
| Level of accounts receivable | $1,666,667 | $3,555,555 | $10,000,000 | $33,333,333 | $125,000,000 |
| Investment in receivables[b] (84%) | $1,400,000 | $2,986,667 | $8,400,000 | $28,000,000 | $105,000,000 |
| Minus: Cost of financing investment in receivables[c] (3) | $112,000 | $268,800 | $840,000 | $3,360,000 | $21,000,000 |
| Net effect on profits = (1) − (2) − (3) | $3,088,000 | $6,091,200 | $14,160,000 | $29,640,000 | ($16,000,000) |

[a]The average collection period measures the number of days between the time sales are made and the time payments are collected. The average collection period can be obtained using the following equation:

$$\text{Average collection period (ACP)} = \frac{\text{Accounts receivable (AR)}}{\text{Sales per day}} = \frac{360 \times \text{AR}}{\text{Sales}}$$

[b]It is assumed that costs are 84% of sales. Thus, the investment in receivables is 84% of the increase in accounts receivable.

[c]The firm must obtain the expected cost of the accounts receivable for each class of customers and multiply this amount by the asset-specific cost of capital for the accounts receivable at each level of risk.

takes discounts, and (5) many other aspects of the firm relevant to the trade-credit-extension decision. They will also provide upon request a more detailed credit investigation of potential customers.

Of course, the more thorough the investigation of the potential customer, the greater the cost incurred by the firm. Each of the information-gathering strategies above involves the expenditure of time and money. The benefits of these expenditures (avoidance of bad-debt losses) must be weighed against the cost of gathering the information. Small dollar amounts of trade-credit extension do not warrant large outlays to gather the necessary information. Large trade-credit extensions, however, should be based upon substantial information in order to avoid large losses to the firm.

It should be noted that the procedures used in the management of credit policy and accounts receivable fail to explicitly consider the amount, timing, and riskiness of cash flows; the focus is on annual revenues and costs. Thus, the relationship between various credit-policy alternatives and stockholder wealth must be dealt with on a judgmental basis. Recently, economists have begun a reformulation of this topic, and the prospects for a direct linkup between credit policy and stockholder wealth appear to be promising.[10] For the present, however, managers must use change in profits as an indicator of changes in stockholder wealth.

## INVESTMENT IN INVENTORIES

Inventories constitute another type of current asset. As with other current assets, the size of inventories may be too large or too small. For stockholder-wealth maximization, management must keep inventories within an optimal size range.

The firm maintains different types of inventories for different purposes. Since different factors affect the optimal size range for each type of inventory, it is best to view the inventory problem as finding optimal size ranges for each type.

There are three major types of inventories: (1) raw materials, (2) work in progress, and (3) finished goods. Raw-materials inventory is maintained in order to ensure the continuity of the production process. When the production process is complex, outages of even one type of production input may bring the entire process to a halt and result in substantial losses to the firm. The physical nature of the raw-materials inventory varies from industry to industry and from firm to firm. In the steel manufacturing industry, coal is a major component of raw-materials inventory. In the automotive industry, preassembled components from suppliers constitute an important type of raw-materials inventory. Cloth for the garment industry, sugar for soft-drinks bottlers, and chemicals for drug manufacturers are other examples. Note that the existence of raw-materials inventory implies production. Firms primarily engaged in the wholesale or retail trade or a service industry do not typically hold raw-materials inventory.

Work-in-progress inventories comprise partially completed goods being produced by the firm. An unfinished automobile is part of the work-in-progress inventory, as are partially completed garments, furniture, and the likes. Work-in-progress inventories are also a characteristic of firms involved in the production of goods; firms involved solely in trade or services do not have them. Work-in-progress inventories are required because the production process takes time. The length of the production cycle (a technological factor) and the total volume of production determine the size of the work-in-progress inventory. For example, manufacturers of complex computer equipment are likely to have substantial work-in-

---

[10]A particularly useful series of articles on this topic appeared in the Winter 1977 edition of *Financial Management*.

progress inventories, since the length of the production cycle is very long. On the other hand, the manufacturer of a plastic novelty, such as identification badges, will have little work-in-progress inventory, since the production cycle has only a few short steps. Since these inventories are determined by technical factors, the control of management over them is based upon its control of the production process itself. Work-in-progress inventory can be reduced by shortening the production cycle or increasing the efficiency of the existing process.

Inventories of finished goods are maintained by almost all firms (manufacturers, wholesalers, or retailers) engaged in the sale of a product as distinct from a service. The products in a department store are a part of finished-goods inventory. Automobiles are part of finished-goods inventory for both automobile manufacturers and dealers. Coal, a part of raw-materials inventory for the steel industry, is part of the finished-goods inventory for a firm in the coal-mining industry.

The general relationship among the three types of inventories is summarized in Figure 11–2. It is convenient to think of the production process as being smooth or even over time, and to look at the reservoir of work-in-progress inventory as being fixed by technological factors.[11] The level of finished-goods inventory varies considerably as sales vary. When sales decline, finished-goods inventory increases; in order to slow down the growth of finished-goods inventory, the firm must slow down the production process. But orders of raw materials usually cannot be turned off as quickly as the production process, and the result is increased raw-materials inventory. An increase in sales reverses the process: Finished-goods inventory declines, production is increased, but raw-materials purchases are likely to lag behind the increased production pace, thus reducing the raw-materials inventory. For some firms, this causal chain operates one or more times every year; for others, only once during a business cycle. In any case, almost all firms experience unanticipated changes in both finished-goods and raw-materials inventories, owing to unanticipated changes in sales.

Anticipated changes in sales can also lead to changes in the size of the finished-goods inventory. Producers of goods that sell on a seasonal basis (for example, toys) may find it profitable to maintain the level of production at a relatively steady pace all year, as opposed to changing production to meet seasonal demands. Producing for finished-goods inventory and then selling from that inventory may permit the firm to minimize the size of its production facilities, maintain a skilled labor force, and reduce overtime labor costs. Thus, it may be profitable for the firm to vary the size of finished-goods inventory over the year.

---

[11]In reality, the firm's ability to alter the production process gives it some control over work-in-progress inventory.

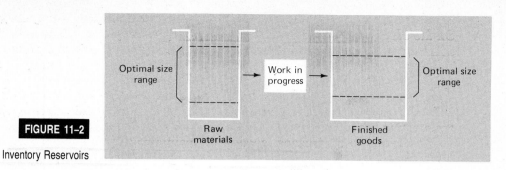

**FIGURE 11-2**

Inventory Reservoirs

Fluctuations in raw-materials inventory can be attributed to another factor. The economics of buying raw materials is such that their unit cost is often lower when large quantities are purchased. For one thing, buyers can often purchase at a discount when they place large orders. In addition, the administrative and handling costs of placing one large order may be lower than the cost of continuous ordering. Large infrequent orders, of course, imply fluctuating levels of raw-materials inventory.

So there are many economic factors that contribute to fluctuations in both finished-goods and raw-materials inventories—part of them attributable to unanticipated changes in the level of sales, part to management's desire to maximize profits and stockholder wealth by minimizing costs.

The process of cost minimization is more complicated than it first appears, owing to the fact that different costs are related to inventory size in different ways. Some costs will decrease as inventory size increases (declining inventory costs) and other costs will increase (rising inventory costs).

*Declining inventory costs* are made up of (1) stockout costs, (2) unit ordering costs, and (3) if quantity discounts are available, unit purchase price (loss of discounts). The existence of stockout costs has been implied but not specified in the previous paragraphs. Stockout costs represent the profits lost when inadequate finished-goods inventory restricts sales (cost of sales foregone). The desire to keep stockout costs at an acceptable level is one of the prime motivations for holding inventories. Frequent stockouts are incompatible with the sales strategy of having goods immediately available for customer use. The more frequently stockouts take place, the more nearly a sales strategy is one of custom production. Firms desiring a rapid-delivery sales strategy maintain finished-goods inventory in order to promote customer loyalty and reduce the possibility that customers will buy from competitors with immediately available goods. Declining inventory costs are another way of looking at the benefits associated with holding inventories.

*Rising inventory costs* are those costs that increase as the level of inventories increases. Included in this category are (1) the cost of raising capital to finance the investment in inventories (financing costs), (2) storage costs, (3) costs of servicing and maintaining inventories if applicable, (4) losses due to physical deterioration of inventories, (5) losses due to obsolescence of inventories, and (6) theft, pilferage, and other losses. These rising costs work to offset the advantages of declining costs.

The relationship among declining, rising, and total inventory costs is summarized in Figure 11–3. Note that initially, total inventory costs decrease. This is due to the relatively rapid decline in stockout costs. As inventories increase, the reduction in stockout costs changes more slowly. At level I, total cost of inventories reaches its minimum. At inventory levels greater than I, rising costs outweigh the benefits of holding inventories (declining costs). The level I is the optimal level of inventories. For given expectations with respect to sales and costs, this is the level of inventories that will maximize stockholder wealth.

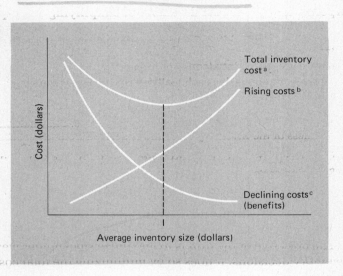

**FIGURE 11–3**

Inventory Costs and Inventory Size

## INVENTORY MANAGEMENT MODELS

The preceding discussion was a simplification designed to illustrate the fundamental economic relationships underlying inventories. The inventory management problem has been studied extensively, and a number of useful mathematical models for inventory management, based upon the observed relationships among the many variables, have been developed. These models attempt to answer three questions:

1. How much should be ordered each time?
2. At what point should the firm acquire inventories?
3. How large a stock should be maintained to compensate for unanticipated changes in sales (safety stock)?

Once these three questions have been answered, it is a relatively simple matter to compute the optimal average level of inventories.

The model for inventory decision making is easiest to understand if it is presented in the form of an illustration. Assume that the California Bedding Company, a wholesale mattress supply company, is attempting to determine an optimal strategy for inventory decisions. The company serves as the western distributor for one of the largest latex-mattress manufacturers in the United States. Management is trying to decide how often orders for mattresses should be placed with the manufacturer and how large such orders should be. Should large orders be placed every few months, or should many small orders be placed every week or so? How many mattresses should be ordered each time?

In order to illuminate the basic underlying relationships, we will incorporate into the model a number of simplifying assumptions:[12]

1. The California Bedding Company sells mattresses at a rate of 1,200 per week (60,000 per year). This rate remains constant throughout the year and is known with perfect certainty (constant usage).
2. The cost of purchasing each mattress is $100 and is the same regardless of order size (constant purchase price).
3. The firm has only two rising costs: (1) annual storage costs of $7 per mattress, and (2) annual financing costs of $5 per mattress. The financing cost reflects the riskiness of the inventory asset and is derived from the security-market line. In percentage terms, it may be viewed as the asset-specific cost of capital for inventories. Inventories with different levels of risk will have different financing costs.
4. The firm has only one declining cost: order costs of $576 per order. This includes the cost of placing and processing the order.
5. Delivery time is constant and known with perfect certainty.

The objective of the firm is to maximize stockholder wealth. In the case of inventory decisions, it does so by minimizing the total costs of inventory. That is, those inventory costs that rise with inventory size are weighed against those that decline with inventory size. Using this approach and the previously made assumptions, it is possible to compute the optimal order size:[13]

$$EOQ = \sqrt{\frac{2FS}{C}}$$

(11-2)

Where EOQ = economic order quantity (optimal order size)

$S$ = annual sales (60,000 per year)

$F$ = cost per order placed (declining costs)

$C$ = storage and financing cost per unit (rising costs)

For the California Bedding Company, the economic order quantity will be:

---

[12]Other inventory models, using less restrictive assumptions, are available for "real-world" use.

[13]See Appendix 11B for the derivation of this equation.

$$EOQ = \sqrt{\frac{2 \times 60{,}000 \times 576}{12}} = 2{,}400 \text{ mattresses}$$

Thus, the optimal strategy for the firm calls for placing orders for 2,400 mattresses at a time. Assuming a constant usage rate, the average inventory will be 1,200 units (Average inventory = EOQ/2 = 2,400/2 ). Thus, California Bedding will place 25 orders (60,000/2,400) during the year.

The point at which the firm reorders (reorder point) is crucial. The firm must reorder in such a fashion that inventories reach zero at exactly the same time the new shipment arrives. In general terms, the reorder point (the level of inventories at which the order is placed) is a function of delivery time. Mathematically, it can be expressed as follows:

$$\text{Reorder point} = \left( \begin{array}{c} \text{Number of units used during} \\ \text{the delivery period} \end{array} \right) + \text{Safety stock} \quad \text{(11-3)}$$

For example, if the delivery time for mattresses to California Bedding is one week, the reorder point is 1,200 mattresses. The basic relationship is summarized in Table 11–5. Note that if the delivery time had been two weeks, the new order would have to be placed at the same time the old order was received.

TABLE 11–5

CALIFORNIA BEDDING COMPANY:
Re-order Point

| Week | Activity | | Inventory level |
|------|----------|---|-----------------|
| 0 | Receive shipment | | 2,400 |
| 1 | Re-order 2,400 mattresses ⎫ | Delivery | 1,200 |
| 2 | Old inventory exhausted ⎭ | Time | 0 |
| 2 | New shipment arrives | | 2,400 |

## SAFETY STOCKS

In the California Bedding Company example, we have assumed constant usage and constant delivery time. In addition, we have assumed that these constants are known with perfect certainty. These assumptions are not realistic, since the possibility of the firm's running short of inventory has been eliminated, so there can be no stockout costs. However, stockouts are the most difficult problem facing the management of the firm. Stockout costs are due to lost sales and profits and the erosion of customer loyalty that takes place when the firm is unable to satisfy orders.

To minimize the possibility of stockouts that are due to fluctuating demand or variable delivery times, the firm usually maintains safety stocks. That is, rather than timing deliveries so that they arrive at the same time existing inventories reach zero (as shown in Table 11–5), the firm plans for the arrival of the new shipment somewhat before this point. Thus, if all goes the way the firm expects, there should be a positive level of inventories at the shipment's arrival time. This is what is called the "safety stock." It represents a hedge against unforeseen sales or shipment delays.

There are mathematical techniques that permit us to compute the optimal safety stock. Let us illustrate the logical nature of the process of computing it without going through all the details.[14] First, the firm must compute expected stockout costs for various levels of inventory. This expected value reflects foregone profits (present and future) and the joint probabilities of demand and delivery times. Table 11–6 shows the expected stockout costs at different levels of safety stock. Notice that high safety stocks can reduce the expected stockout costs to zero, and that when no safety stocks are maintained, the expected stockout costs increase. These costs must be weighed against the holding and financing costs of the safety stocks (rising costs). Notice that in the California Bedding example, the safety stock that minimizes the total cost (stockout + holding) is 200 mattresses.

**TABLE 11–6**

CALIFORNIA BEDDING COMPANY:
Optimal Safety Stock

| Safety stocks of mattresses | Expected stockout costs | Holding & financing costs | Total cost |
|---|---|---|---|
| 600 | 0 | $7,200 | $7,200 |
| 400 | $ 500 | 4,800 | 5,300 |
| 200 | 1,800 | 2,400 | 4,200 |
| 0 | 4,800 | 0 | 4,800 |

If the economic-order-quantity model is combined with the safety-stock procedures, a new expected average level of inventories can be computed as follows:

$$\text{Expected average inventories} = \frac{\text{EOQ}}{2} + \text{Safety stock} \tag{11-4}$$

The first term in equation 11–4 represents the average inventory with constant usage and delivery under perfect certainty. The second term represents the addition to the expected average inventory that is due to variable sales and delivery times.

This expected average inventory is the level of inventory investment that will maximize stockholder wealth. At this average level, the benefits of

---

[14]A more comprehensive review of this problem is included in Richard I. Levin and Charles A. Kirkpatrick, *Quantitative Approaches to Management*, 3rd ed. (New York: McGraw-Hill, 1975), Chap. 7.

increased sales due to the maintenance of safety stocks (the reciprocal of stockout costs) are weighed against certain costs involved in holding inventories. Note that one of the costs included in the analysis is financing cost. This financing cost is based upon the asset-specific cost of capital for the particular inventory and reflects its riskiness—the fact that stockholders will expect a higher return on relatively risky inventories.

It should be noted that a direct link between inventory management models and stockholder-wealth maximization would require information on the amount, timing, and riskiness of the cash flows associated with inventories. The implied assumption underlying current practices is that cash flows and expenses are identical. In addition, it is assumed that all cash flows take place at the same time and have the same degree of risk. For this reason, the inventory models discussed above should be viewed as generating results that are *usually* consistent with stockholder-wealth maximization. It is hoped that new techniques more specifically related to stockholder wealth will be developed in the future.

## LIQUID FUNDS

Liquid funds are defined as the two balance-sheet entries of (1) cash, and (2) marketable securities. Liquid funds are of such a nature that they can be used without great difficulty to make payments, so they are held by the firm in anticipation of future required payments.[15] That is, the firm accumulates liquid funds in order to make future payments for such things as wages, taxes, materials, and equipment. Obviously, it is very important that the firm make such payments, since failure to do so is likely to result in legal action against the firm. As the firm reduces its level of liquid funds, it increases the possibility of being unable to meet unanticipated payments (other things being equal), thus increasing the prospects of legal action. Therefore, relatively low levels of liquid funds imply a relatively high level of risk.

Not only is maintaining an adequate supply of liquid funds less risky, but such a policy may also result in increased net profits. These increased potential profits can come from several sources:

1. Since adequate liquid funds reduce the risk of legal actions against the firm, both debt and equity suppliers will have a positive view of adequate cash balances and are likely to require lower rates of return for firms with such balances. Stated another way, adequate balances of liquid funds are likely to be associated with lower betas and a lower cost of financing.
2. Adequate liquid funds can enable the firm to take discounts when offered, resulting in a substantial decline in the costs of materials.

---

[15]For most businesses, cash comprises primarily checking-account deposits at a commercial bank, plus a relatively small amount of currency on hand (petty cash).

3. Adequate liquid funds can enable the firm to take advantage of unforeseen business opportunities. For example, a firm with adequate liquid funds may be able to take advantage of a special low price on the purchase of equipment.
4. Finally, adequate liquid funds may reduce the need for panic borrowing when unforeseen business emergencies arise.

So we can see that there is a considerable incentive—minimization of risk and possibility of increased profits—for the firm to hold liquid funds. These benefits are, however, at least partly offset by the cost of holding liquid funds. Current assets such as cash and marketable securities must be "financed" in the same manner as long-term assets. That is, capital is supplied to the firm in anticipation that the capital suppliers will receive compensation for both the postponement of consumption and the risk undertaken. It is convenient to visualize liquid funds as having an asset-specific cost of capital similar to the asset-specific cost of capital associated with long-term assets. The dollar returns on liquid funds must be great enough to compensate the suppliers of debt and equity for postponement of consumption and the risk. If the dollar returns are above those returns required by the suppliers of capital, stockholder wealth will be increased. Increasing liquid funds when there is little possibility of increasing profits (when previous levels of liquid funds were adequate) or of little reduction in the riskiness of the firm will be detrimental to stockholder wealth.

In practice, the financial manager should estimate the optimal level of liquid funds using procedures similar to those involved in inventory decisions. Rather than attempting to capture the benefits of holding liquid funds, management attempts to reduce the costs of running out of liquid funds (stockout costs). This is the same phenomenon looked at from a different point of view. Within the context of stockout costs, the benefits to the firm are the reductions in:

1. Expected firmwide cost of capital to the firm
2. Expected cost of discounts foregone
3. Expected cost of business opportunities foregone
4. Expected cost of panic borrowing

Note that these costs are declining liquid-funds costs. That is, they are reduced as the level of liquid funds is increased.

Offsetting the declining liquid-funds costs is the increased cost of financing liquid-funds balances. The higher the level of such balances, the greater the amount of capital that must be raised by the firm and the greater the dollar cost of financing. Note that the firmwide rate of cost of capital is a declining cost, but the dollar cost of raising funds to finance liquid funds is an increasing cost. Looked at from another angle, the firm can reduce the overall cost rate at which it can acquire funds by maintaining adequate liquid balances. Of course, once an adequate level of liquid funds has been

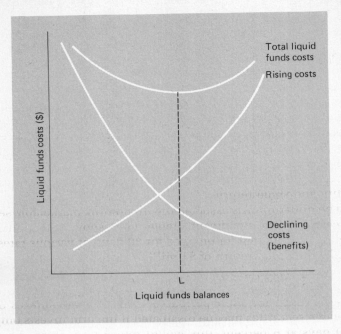

**FIGURE 11–4**

Liquid-Funds Costs
and the Size of
Liquid-Funds Balances

achieved, there will be no further reductions in the firmwide cost of acquiring funds.

The firm must balance the rising cost of increased financing against the declining costs. This relationship is summarized in Figure 11–4. Note that at a certain level of liquid-funds balances (L), the total cost of liquid funds is minimized. This is the point at which the net benefits to the firm are maximized. The firm should increase liquid funds to that point and maintain balances at that level. There are a number of models, similar to inventory models, that are helpful in analyzing particular situations for individual firms. The exact model selected for use will depend on the firm's pattern of liquid-funds inflows and outflows.[16]

As in the case of inventory models, cash management models provide only a general indication of the change in stockholder wealth. A model that emphasizes stockholder wealth would require explicit consideration of the amount, timing, and riskiness of all cash flows. Until such models are developed, the material provided in this chapter will provide at least a rough estimation of which policies are most likely to benefit the stockholders of the corporation.

––––––––––
[16]A variety of cash models have been developed in financial theory. For example, see William J. Baumol, "The Transactions Demand for Cash—An Inventory-Theoretic Approach," *Quarterly Journal of Economics*, 65 (November 1952), 545–56; Merton H. Miller and Daniel Orr, "A Model of the Demand for Money by Firms," *Quarterly Journal of Economics*, 80 (August 1966), 413–35; William Beranek, *Analysis of Financial Decisions* (Homewood, Ill.: Richard D. Irwin, 1963), pp. 345–87.

## MARKETABLE SECURITIES

Cash is, by definition, perfectly liquid and always available for payment of the firm's obligations. But its disadvantage is that currency and checking-account balances earn no return. As an alternative to cash, the firm can hold marketable securities, which are instruments (usually debt) that can be converted into cash *easily and without loss*. The major advantage of holding marketable securities as distinct from cash is that they earn interest, thus contributing to the firm's profits. Thus marketable securities provide *both* liquidity and some return.

The dollar returns associated with holding marketable securities rather than cash can be significant. Table 11–7 shows the dollar return on a $1-million investment for one and for 30 days, at various rates of return. For example, the dollar return of $1 million invested for 30 days, given a rate of return of 8 percent, is $6,575. This return is large enough to permit the firm to hire and pay specialists to keep track of cash flows, and to invest such unneeded funds for short periods of time. The advantages of investing in marketable securities may be dissipated if the firm invests only, say, $1,000. For 30 days at 8 percent, this would return only $6.58. So for very small firms, the purchase of marketable securities may not be economical; they may find depositing excess funds in savings accounts at commercial banks to be their best alternative.

### TABLE 11–7

#### DOLLAR RETURNS OF INVESTING $1 MILLION IN MARKETABLE SECURITIES

| Rate of Return | 1-Day Period[a] | 30-Day Period[a] |
|:---:|:---:|:---:|
| 6% | $164 | $4,932 |
| 8% | $219 | $6,575 |
| 10% | $274 | $8,219 |

[a]Dollar return $= \dfrac{\text{Dollar return on \$1 million}}{365 \text{ days}} \times \text{Number of days held}$

There are many different situations in which the firm can earn an extra margin of return by investing liquid funds in marketable securities. For purposes of illustration, assume that a large corporation must make a $5 million tax payment in 30 days, pay a dividend of $25 million to the stockholders in 15 days, and make a progress payment of $10 million on a construction project in 60 days. Assume further that the necessary liquid funds of $40 million are available to the firm at the present time, but cannot be invested in plant and equipment or other long-term-return projects because the funds will be needed in the near future. In reality, the firm has two alternatives: (1) Keep the $40 million in a checking account, or (2) invest the $40 million in marketable securities. The increase in the before-tax revenues associated with the marketable-security alternative is almost one quarter of a million dollars. In order to simplify the computations, we have assumed that the 8 percent return is net of any transaction cost. The computations are outlined in Table 11-8.

**TABLE 11-8**

### BEFORE-TAX REVENUES ASSOCIATED WITH HOLDING MARKETABLE SECURITIES

| Amount of Liquid Funds | Date Needed | Before-Tax Revenues | |
|---|---|---|---|
| | | Firm Holds Cash | Firm Holds Marketable Securities Yielding 8%[a] |
| $5 million | 30 days | 0 | $32,877 |
| $25 million | 15 days | 0 | $82,192 |
| $10 million | 60 days | 0 | $131,507 |
| Total before-tax revenue = | | 0 | $246,576 |

[a]Before-tax Revenue $= \dfrac{8\% \times \text{Amount of liquid funds}}{365 \text{ days}} \times \text{Days funds are invested}$

The increased before-tax revenue associated with the marketable-security alternative also involves some risks to the firm. In practice, firms can minimize this risk by purchasing securities with (1) low default risk, (2) low marketability risk, and (3) low interest-rate risk.[17] The following paragraphs explain these different dimensions of the risk of holding marketable securities and indicate the means open to the firm to reduce such risks.

The default risk associated with a security reflects the probability that the issuer of the security will be unable to fulfill the cash-flow expectations of the purchasers. For example, preferred stock has a greater default risk than bonds of the same firm, because bonds have a senior claim on the earnings and assets of the firm. Debt securities of a small, volatile corporation are likely to have higher default risk than the debt securities of a large established firm such as General Motors. This lower default risk reflects the high degree of certainty associated with General Motors' interest and principal payments on their bonds. A firm wishing to minimize default risk can do so by purchasing *debt securities of low-risk firms and governments*.

Interest-rate risk refers to the fluctuations in the market price of securities owing to shifts in the security-market line. As the risk-free rate of return changes, the required rate of return of a security will also change.

---

[17]Holding liquid funds also involves the risk of losing purchasing power due to inflation. This risk, however, is the same for both the cash and the marketable-securities alternatives.

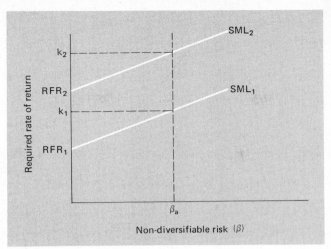

**FIGURE 11-5**

Change in the
Security-Market Line
and Change in the
Required Rate
of Return

Figure 11–5 shows that as the risk-free rate increases from $RFR_1$ to $RFR_2$, the required rate of return of a security with a risk level of $\beta_a$ will increase from $k_1$ to $k_2$. As noted in earlier chapters, the higher required rate of return implies a higher market discount rate for the cash flows associated with the security, and a lower current market price for the security.

Consider a situation in which a firm has $1 million to invest for 30 days, and two possible investment opportunities: (1) Invest the $1 million in a U.S. government security maturing in 30 days and paying an annual 8 percent return, or (2) invest the $1 million in a U.S. government 20-year bond paying an annual 9 percent rate of return.[18] The dollar interest earned on the 30-day security will be $6,575. The dollar return on the 20-year bond (interest earned for 30 days at a 9 percent annual rate) will be $7,397. At first glance it appears that the 20-year bond is a better investment, but this will be true only if the price remains constant during the 30-day holding period. If the security-market line shifts upward and increases the required rate of return of the 20-year bond to 10 percent, the market price will fall.[19] The new market price will be:

$$\text{Price of the bond} = \$90,000(3 \text{ Coef.}_{20}^{10\%}) + \$1,000,000(2 \text{ Coef.}_{20}^{10\%})$$

$$= \$90,000(8.514) + \$1,000,000(0.149) = \$915,260$$

This decline in the market price of the 20-year bond would result in a loss to the firm. At the beginning of the period, the firm had $1 million in cash. At the end of the 30 days, the firm receives $7,937 in interest plus $915,260 from the sale of the bond, for a total of $922,657—a loss of $77,343.

Of course, the required rate of return of the long-term bond could have

---

[18]Note that the long-term rate (9%) is higher than the short-term rate (8%). This is true most of the time (but not all the time). This topic will be discussed more fully in Chapter 15.

[19]If we want to be absolutely precise, the holding period would be 19 years and 11 months. The difference in price, however, will be insignificant.

decreased (the SML shifts downward).[20] In this case, the price of the 20-year bond would increase, resulting in an unanticipated profit to the firm.

This inability to predict with perfect certainty the value of the 20-year bond in 30 days is the meaning of interest-rate risk. Remember, the firm holds liquid funds in order to meet known disbursement needs. The firm would like to earn a measure of return while maintaining the ability to meet its cash needs, but it does not want to jeopardize its ability to make required future payments.

The firm can virtually eliminate the interest-rate risk by purchasing short-term securities. In our example, as an alternative to purchasing a 20-year government bond, the firm can purchase a 30-day government security. The maturity value of the 30-day security is known with perfect certainty (this maturity value is stated on the security). The firm is assured of receiving both the interest and principal payment in 30 days, thus minimizing the interest-rate risk. Note, however, that the interest return (8 percent) on the 30-day security is lower than the interest rate (9 percent) on the 20-year security. This difference is due to the lower risk involved in the ownership of the 30-day security. Thus, the strategy of a firm wishing to minimize interest-rate risk is quite clear: *Buy only short-term securities.*

Marketability risk is the risk of being unable to dispose of a security at a date prior to its maturity. It is the risk that there will be no buyers if the funds are needed earlier than expected. Assume, for example, that a firm has a surplus of $5 million in its checking account and that it anticipates using this $5 million to make a tax payment in 30 days. The firm could purchase a 30-day (minimizes interest-rate risk) high-quality debt security (minimizes risk of default). Further assume that after ten days, an unforeseen event takes place and the $5 million is needed immediately. If the security purchased by the firm has a good secondary market, the firm can simply sell the security, thus receiving cash. But if the security has a poor secondary market, the firm may have to wait for the funds or make some other arrangements for raising funds. Thus, the firm can minimize the risk of being unable to reconvert marketable securities to cash (marketability risk) by *purchasing only those securities that are actively traded on a day-to-day basis* (have a good secondary market).

There is an additional dimension to marketability risk. The marketability risk of a security reflects the possibility of quickly selling the security without making a significant change in its market price. There are many securities that can be sold without affecting market price when the amount involved is relatively small ($1 million). Some firms, however (for example, Exxon Corporation), may have to invest $100 million in idle cash. Exxon's financial manager must choose securities with a market breadth so large that the sale of $100 million would not adversely affect the market price.

---

[20]Changes in the slope of the SML (risk aversion) will have similar effects on the price of long-term bonds.

To summarize, the maintenance of balances of liquid funds reduces the riskiness of the firm and may also create profit-making opportunities. The disadvantage of holding liquid funds lies in the fact that they must be "financed," since capital suppliers expect to be compensated for advancing funds. The firm can minimize the cost of holding liquid funds by investing a portion of the funds in marketable securities. The firm invests in marketable securities in order to maintain a high degree of liquidity; the rate of return earned is of secondary importance. The firm maintains the liquidity of marketable securities by minimizing risk. The types of risk and the appropriate risk-minimization strategy for the firm are summarized in Table 11–9.

**TABLE 11–9**

MARKETABLE SECURITIES—
Types of Risk and Risk-Minimization Strategies

| Type of risk | Risk-minimization strategy |
|---|---|
| Default risk | Buy *debt* securities of *high quality*. |
| Interest-rate risk | Buy *short-term* securities. |
| Marketability risk | Buy securities that are *actively traded* on a day-to-day basis, and consider the breadth of the market. |

Marketable securities should be short-term, highly marketable, high-quality debt instruments. There are a number of securities possessing these characteristics; the most frequently used are:

1. U.S. Treasury bills
2. Negotiable certificates of deposit of large commercial banks
3. Bankers' acceptances
4. Prime commercial paper

The detailed characteristics of these different marketable securities are discussed in the next section.

**Instruments Used As Marketable Securities**

*Treasury Bills.* The U.S. Treasury bill (T bill) is the most widely used marketable security. T bills are short-term (91 days, 182 days, 26 weeks, or 52 weeks) debt obligations of the U.S. government. They are purchased at a discount (you pay less than par value). The return to the purchaser is the difference between the price paid at the time of the purchase and the par value of the bill upon maturity. Treasury bills can be purchased directly from the Federal Reserve System at weekly auctions. A corporation can enter a bid in these auctions without utilizing a dealer in securities. However, most corporations have found it advantageous to purchase T bills from dealers who make a market in them and are willing to purchase and sell them at quoted prices.

Treasury bills meet all the requirements for marketable securities. Since they are short-term, the interest-rate risk is minimized. Furthermore, T bills can be purchased in the secondary market with maturities to meet any requirements of the firm, up to one year. Treasury bills are also highly marketable; they can be sold easily, and the proceeds can be available to the firm within hours. Furthermore, even large sales—for example, $100 million—of Treasury bills will have little or no effect on the market price. There were approximately $176 billion in Treasury bills outstanding in 1980, and the sale of $100 million in Treasury bills would have no appreciable effect in such a broad market. Since T bills are debt instruments, the purchaser knows with perfect certainty exactly how many dollars will be available upon maturity. And since they are issued by the U.S. government, there is no risk of default for these instruments. The Federal Reserve can always "create" the money required for repayment of such securities upon maturity.

***Negotiable Certificates of Deposit (CDs).*** CDs are large-denomination (over $100,000) time deposits issued by large commercial banks. They have short maturity dates—usually less than six months—and active secondary markets.[21] CDs meet almost all the requirements of the marketable-security portfolio. They are short-term debt instruments (low interest-rate risk) of large commercial banks (low default risk). CDs also have little marketability risk. In 1980, outstanding negotiable CDs issued by large commercial banks amounted to approximately $222 billion. This is a large market, and it would appear that large sales would have little or no effect on market price.

Whereas Treasury bills are a homogeneous security, CDs are issued by many large banks, and are thus differentiated. The marketability of the Bank of America's CDs may be different from that of those issued by Chase Manhattan. Sales of $20 million in the Bank of America's CDs can be made in the market without a significant effect on the market price. The marketability of negotiable CDs is excellent, unless an extremely large amount of them issued by a single bank are sold, or the CDs have been issued by a relatively smaller bank. To all intents and purposes, however, this problem is hypothetical. Firms with large amounts of idle cash can purchase CDs of different banks and thus ameliorate this problem.

It should be noted that the default risk of CDs, although minimal, is higher than that of Treasury bills. Some banks have experienced financial difficulties in recent times, and holders of the negotiable CDs issued by these banks have had to wait until the maturity of the instruments in order to

---

[21]Do not confuse negotiable CDs with those CDs sold by commercial banks to small depositors (under $100,000). The small CDs are not negotiable, and they are usually purchased by individuals for income rather than liquidity purposes.

recoup the full investment, because of the turmoil in the secondary market.[22] Occasionally, the news of a bank's financial difficulties may cause a decline in the value of its CDs in the secondary market. However, since their appearance in 1961, the financial record of negotiable CDs has been excellent. We must conclude that, with some very minor reservations, negotiable CDs of "safe" banks meet all the requirements of the marketable-securities portfolio.

***Bankers' acceptances (BAs).*** Bankers' acceptances are financial instruments that allow the borrower to obtain short-term credit by getting his or her bank to "accept" a time draft. Once the time draft is "accepted," the commercial bank is obligated to pay the owner of the bankers' acceptance the face value of the instrument upon maturity.[23] Bankers' acceptances are short-term debt instruments (usually less than six months) of banks, with a reasonably efficient secondary market ($48 billion outstanding in 1980). Thus, the default risk taken by the purchaser of a bankers' acceptance is similar to that of purchasing negotiable CDs of the "accepting" bank. As in the case of negotiable CDs, management should consider the stability and safety of the bank "accepting" the time draft. Bankers' acceptances meet all the requirements, with very minor exceptions, of the marketable-securities portfolio because they have low default risk, low interest-rate risk, and low marketability risk.

***Commercial Paper.*** Commercial paper is defined as unsecured, short-term (less than 270 days) promissory notes of large, financially sound corporations. Since commercial paper is a short-term, high-quality debt instrument, it has little interest-rate risk. Although the total volume outstanding is large ($117 billion in 1980), the secondary market (sales of commercial paper before maturity) is not as developed as that of Treasury bills, negotiable CDs, or bankers' acceptances. Most commercial paper is purchased by corporations with the intention of holding it until maturity. Thus, its degree of marketability is not as good as that of the other, previously discussed instruments, and some marketability risk is present.

---

[22]For example, the Franklin National Bank experienced extreme financial difficulties in 1974. The Federal Reserve System and FDIC intervened to prevent the failure of the bank. Eventually, Franklin was acquired by another bank. Although holders of negotiable CDs did not lose any funds, the market value of their CDs in the secondary market declined during the period.

[23]Bankers' acceptances are usually the result of international transactions. For example, an American firm wants to purchase some products from a Japanese firm. The Japanese firm may require a letter of credit from the buyer. The buyer obtains the letter of credit from its commercial bank. Once the Japanese firm has fulfilled all the stated requirements of the letter of credit and provided proper documentation, the bank is obligated to pay the seller in accordance with the terms of payment. If the agreement calls for payment in 90 days, the bank will "accept" a draft for payment 90 days from such date. At that time, the bank's credit backs up the bankers' acceptance. Thus, the owner of the bankers' acceptance can easily sell it in the secondary market.

There is also some risk of default. Dealers in commercial paper attempt to maintain their reputation by thoroughly analyzing the financial conditions of corporations whose commercial paper they are marketing. However, there have been cases where commercial paper was sold by corporations that later encountered severe financial difficulties. For instance, purchasers of the commercial paper issued by the Penn Central Railroad suffered financial losses on their investment. Thus, we can conclude that commercial paper issued by "safe" corporations meets most (but not all) of the requirements of the marketable-securities portfolio. Commercial paper is, however, somewhat more risky than T bills, negotiable CDs, and bankers' acceptances.

Why should the manager of the marketable-securities portfolio purchase any securities other than Treasury bills? Treasury bills have virtually no risk of any type, whereas the other three instruments discussed have at least small amounts of risk. The basic reason marketable securities other than Treasury bills are purchased is that their return is higher. Table 11–10 shows the rates of return for the various financial instruments discussed in this chapter. The financial manager may be willing to take the increased risk in order to gain increased return.

### TABLE 11–10

YIELDS ON VARIOUS SECURITIES
(For the Week Ending July 29, 1978)

| Security | Annualized yield |
| --- | --- |
| 3-month Treasury bills | 6.83% |
| Negotiable certificates of deposit (3 months) | 8.17% |
| Prime bankers' acceptances (90 days) | 7.97% |
| Prime commercial paper (90 to 119 days) | 7.86% |

Source: *Federal Reserve Bulletin*, August 1978.

Table 11–11 provides a convenient summary of the four major types of marketable securities and of other instruments available to the firm. Note that the table lists three different types of commercial paper (indicated by the letters CP in the first column) and two different types of tax-exempt securities. The last column indicates the basis on which these securities are sold. Some are sold at a discount, in which case the interest earned represents the difference between the discounted price and the maturity value. For example, assume that the Treasury sells a $1-million Treasury bill due to mature in one year. This represents a promise by the Treasury to pay $1 million in one year. The Treasury actually receives less than $1 million today. If the discounted price is $917,431, the buyer of the T bill would be earning $82,569 in interest, which is an annual 9 percent rate ($82,569/ $917,431).

Note that CDs and tax-exempts are sold on a yield basis. This means

TABLE 11–11

MARKETABLE SECURITIES

| Obligation | Denominations | Maturities | Marketability | Basis |
|---|---|---|---|---|
| United States Treasury bills | U.S. government obligation. U.S. Treasury auctions 3- and 6-month bills weekly, and 1-year bills monthly. (TB and OT) | $10,000 to $1 million | Up to 1 year. | Excellent secondary market. | Discounted. Actual days on a 360-day year. |
| Prime sales finance paper | Promissory notes of finance companies placed directly with the investor. (CP) | $1,000 to $5 million ($25,000 minimum order) | Issued to mature on any day from 3 to 270 days. | No secondary market. Under certain conditions, companies will buy back paper prior to maturity. Most companies will adjust rate. | Discounted or interest-bearing. Actual days on a 360-day year. |
| Dealer paper    I. Finance | Promissory notes of finance companies sold through commercial-paper dealers. (CP) | $100,000 to $5 million | Issued to mature on any day from 15 to 270 days. | Good secondary market. Buyback arrangement usually can be negotiated through the dealer. | Discounted or interest-bearing. Actual days on a 360-day year. |
| Dealer paper    II. Industrial | Promissory notes of leading industrial firms sold through commercial-paper dealers. (CP) | $500,000 to $5 million | Usually available on certain dates between 30 and 180 days. | Good secondary market. | Discounted. Actual days on a 360-day year. |
| Prime bankers' acceptances | Time drafts drawn on and accepted by a banking institution, which in effect substitutes its credit for that of the importer or holder of merchandise. (BA) | $25,000 to $1 million | Up to 6 months. | Good secondary market. | Discounted. Actual days on a 360-day year. |
| Negotiable time certificates deposit | Certificates of time deposit at a commercial bank. (CD) | $500,000 to $1 million | Unlimited. | Good secondary market. | Yield basis. Actual days on a 360-day year. Interest at maturity. |
| Short-term tax-exempts    I. Project notes of local public agencies. | Notes of local agencies secured by a contract with federal agencies and by pledge of "full faith and credit" of U.S. | $1,000 to $1 million | Up to 1 year. | Good secondary market. | Yield basis. 30-day month on a 360-day year. Interest at maturity. |
| Short-term tax-exempts    II. Tax and bond anticipation notes. (TE) | Notes of states, municipalities, or political subdivisions. | $1,000 to $1 million | Various, usually 3 months to 1 year from issue. | Good secondary market. | Yield basis. Usually 30 days on a 360-day year. Interest at maturity. |

Source: Morgan Guaranty Trust Co. of New York, June, 1980.

that the purchaser of a $1 million negotiable CD would pay $1 million (no discount). Upon maturity, the purchaser would receive the $1 million plus the stated interest rate. If, for example, the rate of interest is 9 percent annually and the CD has a maturity of one year, the buyer receives $1,090,000 at maturity.

## CASH BALANCES

Liquid funds may be held in the form of cash balances rather than of marketable securities. Actually, all inflows to and outflows from the reservoir of liquid funds involve cash balances. Receipts are initially credited to cash balances, and payments are made from cash balances. This situation is illustrated in Figure 11–6. Note that the reservoir of liquid funds is partitioned into two sections. Inflows and outflows of the reservoir *as a whole* involve only the cash section. The purchase and sale of marketable securities involve only the movement of funds from one part of the liquid-funds reservoir to another. From the firm's point of view, it is desirable to minimize the size of the reservoir of liquid assets devoted to cash balances and to maximize the size of the marketable-securities section, the portion of liquid funds earning interest. There is little or no increase in risk associated with holding marketable securities (when they have the characteristics discussed in the previous section), and the marketable securities can be converted into cash in a matter of hours, should the need arise.

The optimal size of cash balances held by the firm is determined by several factors:

1. The required pattern of cash outflows from the reservoir of liquid funds
2. The pattern of cash inflows into the reservoir of liquid funds

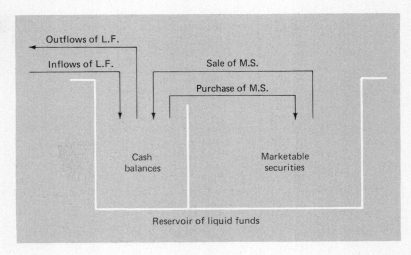

**FIGURE 11–6**

Reservoir of Liquid Funds: Cash Flows

Outflows of L.F.

Inflows of L.F.

Sale of M.S.

Purchase of M.S.

Cash balances

Marketable securities

Reservoir of liquid funds

3. The transaction costs involved in transferring funds between the two parts of the liquid-funds reservoir (cash and marketable securities)
4. The rate of return that could be earned on marketable securities

There are many possible combinations of inflows and outflows for the liquid-funds reservoir as a whole. A number of extreme situations are discussed below in order to illustrate the range of possibilities facing the firm.[24]

1. *Regular daily cash inflows equal daily cash outflows* (perfect certainty). In this situation, the firm can conduct its day-to-day operations by making daily cash disbursements from daily cash receipts. No other regular cash balances are needed. Funds being held for longer-term needs (taxes, etc.) can be held in the form of marketable securities.

2. *Cash inflows occur at the beginning of the month and payments are spread evenly over the entire month* (perfect certainty).[25] In this case, the firm has more cash on hand than necessary early in the month. The firm should invest the idle cash balances in marketable securities and sell off the securities during the month. Funds being held for longer-term known needs should also be invested in marketable securities.

3. *Regular cash inflows are received daily during the month and all outflows take place at the end of the month* (perfect certainty).[26] In this case, the firm should use daily cash receipts to immediately purchase marketable securities. The securities should be sold at the end of the month. Other balances of marketable securities should be maintained to meet longer-term needs.

4. *The pattern of cash inflows and cash outflows is erratic* (uncertain). In this case, firms should maintain cash balances within an optimal range. When cash flows decline to the lowest acceptable level, marketable securities should be sold. They should be purchased when the highest acceptable cash level is reached. There is a general technique (the inventory model) that may be useful to the firm in establishing the lowest and highest acceptable levels, as well as the optimal size of the marketable-securities sales.

The situations above are designed to illustrate the range of possibilities that face the firm. Different firms find themselves in different situations, and probably none corresponds precisely to the four illustrations. Note that all but the first situation call for frequent purchases and sales of marketable securities. The optimal size of such purchases will depend on the transaction costs associated with the purchase and sale and the rate of return that can be earned on the securities. Obviously, it does not pay to purchase

---

[24]The determination of the optimal level of cash balances is further complicated by the fact that most American banks require business borrowers to maintain a certain amount of funds—"compensating balances"—in a checking account as a condition of the loan. Because these compensating balances cannot be used for day-to-day transactions, they increase the amount of cash that the firm must maintain. The effect of compensating balances on the net cost of borrowing will be discussed in Chapter 16.

[25]This situation is known as the Baumol model. For a more complete discussion, see William J. Baumol, "The Transactions Demand for Cash—An Inventory-Theoretic Approach," *Quarterly Journal of Economics*, 65 (November 1952), pp. 545–56.

[26]For a more complete description of this situation, see William Benarek, *Analysis of Financial Decisions* (Homewood, Ill.: Richard D. Irwin, 1963), pp. 345–87.

securities when the transaction costs exceed the interest received during the holding period.

More insight into the problem can be gained by examining the situation in which cash inflows are received at the beginning of the period and outflows are spread evenly over the entire period (situation 2). The exercise is designed to show that the size of marketable securities sales may be either too large or too small, and to illuminate the factors affecting the optimal size of marketable-securities sales. The equation for computing the optimal size of these sales is presented as equation 11–5 (known as the Baumol model). Remember that inflows occur at the beginning of the period and outflows are spread evenly throughout the period.

$$\text{Optimal size of marketable-security sales} = MS_0 = \sqrt{\frac{2Afn}{r}} \tag{11-5}$$

where: $MS_0$ = optimum dollar size of marketable securities to be sold at regular intervals

$A$ = dollar cash inflows at the beginning of the period

$f$ = dollar transaction costs (both purchase and sale)

$n$ = number of time periods that occur within one year

$r$ = annual rate of return on marketable securities

Let us illustrate the use of this equation with a numerical example. A corporation receives cash inflows of $30 million at the beginning of each month (assume a month has 30 days). It costs $1,000 every time marketable securities are purchased or sold, and the annual rate of return on marketable securities is 8 percent. The optimum size of each security sale can be computed as follows:

$$MS_0 = \sqrt{\frac{2 \times 30,000,000 \times 1,000 \times 12}{0.08}} = \$3,000,000$$

The results show that when the firm receives the $30 million at the beginning of the month, it should immediately purchase $27 million in marketable securities and keep only $3 million in cash balances. During the rest of the month, the firm would have to sell $3 million in marketable securities every three days in order to meet cash outflows (a total of nine sales during the month). In this manner, the net return on marketable securities will be maximized, there is little additional risk, and stockholder wealth is maximized.

Some readers may find the strategy dictated by the Baumol model unreasonable. It seems ridiculous to sell $3 million in marketable securities every three days instead of making larger, less frequent sales. Table 11–12 shows that sales can be too large or too small. Note that the average amount invested in marketable securities is inversely related to the size of the sale of securities. If, for example, the firm receives $30 million at the beginning of the month, it can invest $27 million if the optimal sale size is $3 million. With a $10-million optimal sale size, only $20 million will be invested at the beginning of the month. That is, the smaller the sale size, the greater the amount of funds available for investment in marketable securities. The average amount of funds invested for the period can be computed by dividing the initial purchase of securities ($30 million – Size of sale) by 2. The interest return on the marketable securities is directly related to the average amount invested. Thus, an order size of $1 million has a higher average investment and a higher interest return than the $3-million sale size. *If there were no transaction costs*, the firm would always choose the lowest possible sale size.

**TABLE 11–12**

NET RETURN OF INVESTING IDLE CASH IN MARKETABLE SECURITIES
(Baumol Conditions)

| Dollar Size of the Sale (S) | Average Amount Invested[a] | Return for the Period[b] | Transaction Costs[c] | Net Return |
|---|---|---|---|---|
| $3,000,000 | $13,500,000 | $90,000 | $9,000 | $81,000 |
| $1,000,000 | $14,500,000 | $96,667 | $29,000 | $67,667 |
| $10,000,000 | $10,000,000 | $66,667 | $2,000 | $64,667 |

[a]Average amount invested $= \dfrac{A}{2} - \dfrac{S}{2}$

[b]Return for the period = Average amount invested $\left( \dfrac{\text{Annual rate of return on marketable securities}}{\text{Number of periods in one year}} \right)$

[c]Transaction costs = $1,000 × Number of transactions during the period

Note, however, that frequent small sales have high transaction costs. In our example, a strategy employing a sales size of $1 million will require 29 different sales, and at $1,000 each, the total cost will be $29,000. Higher transaction costs offset the higher interest return associated with the $1-million-sale-size strategy. The best of the alternatives presented in Table 11–12 is that calling for periodic $3-million sales every three days. The relatively high average investment more than compensates for the $9,000 in transaction costs.

Equation 11–5 is applicable only under the Baumol conditions. Other equations, however, can be developed for other situations. In any case, the optimal sale size will be a function of both the rate of return on marketable securities and the transaction costs.

**Cash Management Policies**

A sound cash management program implies more than buying and selling marketable securities. For one thing, it is most important that the firm implement an accurate cash forecasting program. This will permit the development of its marketable-securities strategy as well as other financial policies. The techniques used in cash forecasting are most often presented in accounting courses and are reviewed in Appendix 11A.

The firm should also pursue a policy of speeding up cash collections. Many steps can be taken to achieve this objective. For example, checks received by the firm should be deposited as soon as possible. Applications for tax refunds should be made as soon as the information is available. Other techniques are not as obvious or as simple. For example, the state of Alaska chartered a jet plane to fly to New York the checks it received from the sale of oil leases. This seems irrational, since the checks could have been deposited in Alaskan banks and the proceeds eventually credited to the state's checking accounts. State authorities, however, recognized that they could save two or three days in collection time by depositing the checks in New York banks. The income received from investing in T bills for an additional two or three days more than paid for the cost of chartering the plane. Since the amount realized on the oil-leases sale was almost $1 billion, even a few days extra of interest income amounted to a large sum of money. The same principles apply if the amount realized is smaller. If the expected returns of having the funds available at an earlier date exceeds the costs of earlier collection of the funds, the firm should take the steps necessary to collect the funds at the earlier date.

One common method of speeding up cash collections is to create a lockbox system. To illustrate such a system, a large oil company has customers in Southern California who make payments on gasoline credit-card balances that amount to $1 million a day. If customers mail their checks to the company's New York headquarters, it may take over a week from the time a check is mailed until the company has the funds available for investment. The mail could take three or four days to reach New York, a day may be lost processing the checks at the company's headquarters, and two days may be used for collection of the checks by the New York bank. The firm could significantly reduce this time by having the customers mail the checks to a post office box in, for example, Pasadena. It will probably take only one or two days for the mail to arrive in Pasadena; a local commercial bank will pick up the checks at the post office and deposit them in the company's checking account with the local bank; the time required to clear the checks will be shorter because most of the checks will be drawn on Southern California banks; and the Pasadena bank will wire-transfer the funds daily to the corporation's New York bank. Thus, the total time span between the moment the customer mails the check and the time the firm has the funds available may be cut to only three days, releasing large amounts of funds for investment in marketable securities. Of course, the return on the marketable securities must be compared to the costs associated with the lockbox system, since the Pasadena bank will impose service charges and may require deposits in order to provide the service. The firm should be willing to undertake any system to speed up cash collections if the marginal return on the funds released exceed the marginal cost of the system.

In addition to speeding up cash collections, the firm should attempt to slow down cash payments in order to increase liquid-funds balances. Some of the possible techniques should be obvious. When property tax payments must be postmarked on December 10, the firm should not mail the check on December 1. If the property tax payment is, for example, $1 million, the firm could invest this amount for ten days in marketable securities. When suppliers give the firm 30 days for payments, there is no need to pay before the due date. Thus, we may generalize by saying that the firm need not make payments before the due date of such payments.

Other "slowdown" techniques may be more costly or difficult to implement. The use of the "float" is one example of the slowdown technique.[27] Let us assume that the firm pays its employees with $10 million in checks every Friday, and that past experience indicates that only $6 million will be presented for payment at the company's bank on Monday, another $3 million will be presented on Tuesday, and the remaining $1 million on Wednesday. The firm does not need to have the entire $10 million in its account on Friday. It could invest the entire $10 million in Treasury bills on Friday, sell $6 million on Monday and deposit the proceeds in the bank, sell $3 million on Tuesday and deposit the proceeds, and sell the final $1 million and deposit it on Wednesday. Thus the firm will be able to earn a return on the $10 million *without undertaking any additional risks.* As long as the returns outweigh the cost, the risk is unaffected, stockholder wealth will be increased.

SUMMARY   There are three major classes of current assets: (1) liquid funds, (2) accounts receivable, and (3) inventories. In order to maximize stockholder wealth, the firm must maintain each type of current asset within the appropriate optimal size range. The techniques used to evaluate the optimality of different current-asset reservoirs varies depending on the asset. That is, the techniques used in establishing accounts-receivable size differ from those employed in establishing inventory size. All the different techniques in the chapter do, however, have something in common: They all attempt to weigh the benefits of different current-asset reservoir sizes against the cost and the risks associated with the current assets. The optimal size of the current-asset reservoir reflects the risk–return tradeoff and its effect on stockholder wealth.

---

[27]There is a fine line separating legal and illegal uses of the float. In February 1976, the TI Corporation, a subsidiary of Transamerica, pleaded no contest to a federal check-kiting charge and paid a $10,000 fine. The alleged scheme involved depositing insufficiently funded checks for large amounts, which were later covered by other insufficiently funded checks from other banks. It was alleged that TI was in this way able to inflate its checking account by over $100 million.

The benefits of accounts-receivable balances are the higher profits associated with higher sales. Offsetting these benefits are bad-debt losses and financing costs. The benefits associated with inventories are the reductions in declining costs (especially stockout costs). Rising costs (especially financing and holding costs) tend to offset the declining costs. The benefits and costs associated with liquid funds are similar to those of inventories. The increased financing costs must be weighed against the benefit of declining liquid-funds costs.

Note that in the case of each current asset, the logical process is identical. Benefits are weighed against increasing costs. Remember that financing cost (an increasing cost) is a function of risk. Higher levels of risk are reflected in greater financing costs.

**QUESTIONS FOR DISCUSSION**

1. Why do firms invest idle cash on an overnight or daily basis? What factors are important in deciding whether or not it is profitable to make such investments?
2. Discuss some of the techniques management can employ to slow down cash payments and expedite the receipt of cash. Why are such techniques profitable to the firm?
3. Evaluate the following statement: "Our credit manager is the best in the industry. We have had zero bad-debt losses for over ten years."
4. How do credit terms affect stockholder wealth?
5. Evaluate the following statement: "Inventory safety stocks should be established at such a level that the firm never runs out of inventories."
6. The current-asset problem is a minimization rather than an optimization problem. True or false? Explain your answer.
7. Define *liquid funds* and outline the conceptual framework used to establish their optimal level.
8. What are the risks associated with holding marketable securities (as distinct from holding cash)? Explain how the firm can minimize such risks.
9. Which securities are most frequently held as marketable securities? Why are these and not other marketable securities held by the firm?
10. If there were no transaction costs, the firm would always choose to sell the smallest possible amount of marketable securities at one time. True or false? Explain why firms make large sales of marketable securities each time.
11. Outline the benefits and costs of extending trade credit, and explain the conceptual framework that can be used to establish the optimal level of accounts receivable.
12 Explain how a trade-credit classification procedure can be used to make trade-credit decisions.
13. Discuss the major types of inventories and the factors contributing to fluctuations in the level of each type.
14. Describe the conceptual framework employed to make inventory decisions. What are the benefits and costs of holding different levels of inventory?
15. What questions do inventory models attempt to answer? What are the important variables affecting the solutions generated by these models?

16. All the techniques used for establishing the level of particular current assets have something in common. What is it? Why is it important?

**PROBLEMS** *Use a 360-day year in your computations.*

1. What is the dollar return the firm will receive if it invests $20 million for 90 days, at an annual rate of:
   a. 6%?    b. 8%?    c. 10%?

2. The Premier Corporation received $50 million in cash at the beginning of each month. This cash is disbursed evenly throughout the month. Treasury bills are currently paying 6% per annum. The transaction cost of selling Treasury bills is $5,000 per sale. (Assume the purchase cost is zero.)
   a. What will be the optimal dollar size of Treasury bills to be sold at regular intervals?
   b. Calculate the net return to the firm.
   c. Has the risk of the firm changed by investing in Treasury bills instead of keeping the funds in a checking account? Explain.
   d. Will the firm's risk change if the $50 million investment is made in 20-year U.S. government bonds?

3. The Jackson Corporation is a major New York wholesaler of canned goods. The firm has a long-term contract with Maria's, a supermarket chain in Puerto Rico. The contract requires Jackson to deliver a specified number of cases of canned goods weekly. Maria's is required to make a $1 million payment every Friday morning. The Jackson Corporation has two choices: first, to deposit the check in a Puerto Rican bank, in which case the funds will not be available for investment until four days later; second, to send an employee to pick up the check on Friday morning and return the same day to New York, in which case, the funds will be available for investment the same day. The cost of transportation and the employee's time is $400.
   a. Should the Jackson Corporation pick up the check in Puerto Rico, if the rate of return on Treasury bills is 8%? Explain.
   b. Should the Jackson Corporation pick up the check in Puerto Rico, if the rate of return on Treasury bills is 6%? Explain.

4. The Williams Corporation has $5 million available for investment. The funds will be needed in 30 days for a property tax payment. The firm has the following two alternative investment opportunities: (1) a 30-day Treasury bill paying an annual return of 6%, or (2) a 20-year U.S. government bond paying an annual return of 8%.
   a. Calculate the dollar return of investing the funds in either alternative, assuming the SML remains unchanged.
   b. Calculate the dollar return of investing in the 20-year U.S. government bond, if the SML changes in such a way that the required rate of return of 20-year government bonds changes to 10% during the 30-day period.
   c. Which alternative would you recommend to the Williams Corporation? Explain.

5. The Ohio Paper Corporation is considering extending credit to some customers with higher risk levels (lower credit rating). The firm's annual profit before credit-policy costs is 15%. These customers can be separated into the following classes:

|                     | Class A       | Class B       |
| ------------------- | ------------- | ------------- |
| Potential sales     | $10 million   | $30 million   |
| Bad debts as a percentage of sales | 5% | 12% |
| Asset-specific cost of capital of receivables | 12% | 20% |
| Average collection period | 36 days | 90 days |

a. What will be the cash flows to the firm if credit is extended to Class A customers?
b. What will be the cash flows to the firm if credit is extended to Class B customers?

6. The AnnCa Corporation is planning to change its credit terms from 3/10,n/30 to 3/10,n/60. Management wants to evaluate the effect of such a change on stockholder wealth. The credit manager has prepared the following estimates of the effect of the change on the firm:

|                     | Present (3/10,n/30) | Proposed (3/10,n/60) |
| ------------------- | ------------------- | -------------------- |
| Expected sales      | $10 million         | $12 million          |
| Percentage of customers taking the discount | 90% | 40% |
| Average collection period | 12 days | 40 days |
| Asset-specific cost of capital of receivables | 10% | 10% |

Should the AnnCa Corporation change its credit terms, if its annual profit before credit-policy costs is 15%?

7. The Fullerton Manufacturing Corporation wants to determine the economic order quantity for a product used in the manufacturing process. The firm uses 300,000 units during the year. The annual holding and financing cost is $10 per unit. The cost of preparing and forwarding each purchase order is $6.
   a. What is the economic order quantity?
   b. How many orders would the firm have to place each year?

8. The American Chemical Corporation desires to manage inventories of oil products in a manner consistent with maximization of stockholder wealth. The firm has prepared the following information on its inventories of petroleum products (use a 50-week year):

- Weekly usage rate = 20,000 units
- Delivery period = 2 weeks
- Annual financing and holding costs of 1 unit of petroleum = $0.20
- Cost of preparing one purchase order = $1,000
- Desired level of safety stocks = 50,000 units

   a. Determine the economic order quantity.
   b. Determine the reorder point.

c. Based upon the previous results, calculate the expected average level of inventory.

9. The Alliance Television Wholesalers Company has prepared the following analysis of the expected stockout costs at various levels of safety stocks:

| Safety Stocks (television sets) | Expected Dollar Stockout Costs |
|:---:|:---:|
| 0 | $10,000 |
| 100 | $5,000 |
| 150 | $3,000 |
| 200 | $1,000 |
| 250 | $500 |
| 300 | 0 |

Calculate the safety stock that should be maintained by Alliance, if the cost of financing and holding each television set is $20 per year.

# APPENDIX 11A
## The Cash Budget

Good cash management requires an adequate forecast of the cash needs of the firm. Such a forecast is provided by the cash budget, which incorporates all the expected cash inflows and outflows of the firm over the forecast period. Management can then predict periods of excess cash (when investments in marketable securities may be advisable), as well as periods in which additional funds may be necessary.

Before a cash budget is constructed, two factors should be taken in consideration: (1) the time span it is to cover, and (2) the nature of the transactions to be included. The period of time to be covered by the cash budget (six months, one year, or two years) will depend on the ability of the firm to make accurate cash forecasts. Since periodic cash flows in the distant future are difficult to predict, cash budgets are usually restricted to periods of two years or less. Management must also decide whether the budget will be constructed on a daily, weekly, biweekly, or monthly basis. The shorter the time period, the more information will be gained by management about the cash position of the firm, but the higher will be the costs of obtaining such information.

Beginning students in finance commonly confuse cash budgets with income statements. Income statements are constructed on an accrual basis and measure the profits of the firm over a certain period of time. Cash budgets, on the other hand, measure the actual cash flows of the firm, which are not the same as profits. All transactions that give rise to an inflow or outflow of cash during a given period should be included in the cash budget.

Thus, sales are not entered into the cash budget until they are collected; expenses are not entered until they cause an actual cash outflow from the firm. Furthermore, certain transactions (sales of stock, purchases of assets, and the like), which are not included in the income statement, must be included in the cash budget because they affect the cash position of the firm. Noncash expenses (depreciation, amortization, and so on) are included as expenses in the income statement but are *not* included in the cash budget because they do not constitute actual cash outflows for the firm.

Let us illustrate the cash budget with an example. The National Toy Corporation wants to prepare a monthly cash budget for the last six months of the year. National Toy manufactures and sells toys to department stores. Toy sales are highly seasonal in nature, increasing significantly during the last three months of the year, owing to the Christmas season. Department stores build up their toy inventories during this period. National Toy must increase its inventories during the summer in order to be able to satisfy toy demand during the fall. Thus, the firm must spend funds (in labor and raw materials) before making collections.

Table 11A-1 shows the sales and the expenses for labor and raw materials for National Toy in the months in which they are accrued. The collection history of the firm indicates that 20 percent of the sales are collected in the same month sales are made, and the remainder (80 percent) in the month following the sale. Expenses of labor and raw materials are paid in the month *after* they are incurred. In addition, the firm has the following transactions that may or may not affect its cash position:

**TABLE 11A-1**

NATIONAL TOY CORPORATION:
SALES AND EXPENSES IN THE MONTH
THEY ARE ACCRUED
(Not Cash Flows)

| Month | Sales | Expenses |
|---|---|---|
| June | $10,000 | $18,000 |
| July | $20,000 | $30,000 |
| August | $30,000 | $70,000 |
| September | $40,000 | $80,000 |
| October | $100,000 | $100,000 |
| November | $200,000 | $80,000 |
| December | $100,000 | $30,000 |
| January | $20,000 | $12,000 |

1. The firm's selling and administrative expenses are $10,000 per month. These expenses are paid in the same month they are incurred.
2. The firm makes a $5,000 lease payment every month for its warehouse facilities.

3. The depreciation expense for the fixed assets of the firm is $6,000 per month.
4. Tax payments of $20,000 and $40,000 are made in the months of September and December respectively.
5. National Toy must make a payment of $50,000 to the bank in October, as the repayment for a term loan.
6. The firm plans to make a $60,000 dividend distribution to its stockholders in November.
7. The firm plans to issue long-term bonds. These bonds will net National Toy $200,000, which will be received by the firm during November.

National Toy has, as of July 1, $200,000 in cash balances. The firm's policy is to maintain a minimum balance of $100,000 at all times.[28] Table 11A–2 shows a worksheet that can be used to show the effect of these transactions on the cash position of the firm. Note that collections during the month of July include $4,000 on the July sales (20 percent of July sales); plus $8,000 from sales made in June (80 percent of June sales). Furthermore, the

TABLE 11A–2

**NATIONAL TOY:**
**CASH-BUDGET WORKSHEET**
**(Thousands Omitted)**

|  | June | July | August | Sept. | Oct. | Nov. | Dec. | Jan. |
|---|---|---|---|---|---|---|---|---|
| Sales | $10 | $20 | $30 | $40 | $100 | $200 | $100 | $20 |
| Collections (20%) |  | $4 | $6 | $8 | $20 | $40 | $20 |  |
| Collections (80%), prior month |  | $8 | $16 | $24 | $32 | $80 | $160 |  |
| Bond issue |  | — | — | — | — | $200 | — |  |
| Total cash inflows |  | $12 | $22 | $32 | $52 | $320 | $180 |  |
| Purchases | $18 | $30 | $70 | $80 | $100 | $80 | $30 | $12 |
| Payments |  | $18 | $30 | $70 | $80 | $100 | $80 |  |
| Selling & administrative |  | $10 | $10 | $10 | $10 | $10 | $10 |  |
| Lease payment |  | $5 | $5 | $5 | $5 | $5 | $5 |  |
| Taxes |  |  |  | $20 |  |  | $40 |  |
| Term-loan repayment |  |  |  |  | $50 |  |  |  |
| Dividend payment |  | — | — | — | — | $60 | — |  |
| Total cash outflows |  | $33 | $45 | $165 | $145 | $115 | $135 |  |
| Change in cash during the month |  | ($21) | ($23) | ($133) | ($93) | + $205 | + $45 |  |

[28]The policy may be due to the desire of National Toy to maintain some precautionary balances, or to compensating-balance requirements imposed by its banks. Compensating balances are discussed in greater detail in Chapter 16.

$200,000 received by National Toy from the bond issue is included in the cash budget as an inflow in the month of November, although it is not included in the income statement of the firm.

Cash outflows are treated in a similar manner. Payments for labor and raw materials of $18,000 were made in the month of July, even though the expenses were incurred during June. The term-loan payment ($50,000 in October) and the dividend payment ($60,000 in November) are included in the cash budget even though they are not expenses. Note that depreciation is not included in the cash budget, since it is not associated with a cash outflow from the firm.

The change in cash (total inflows minus total outflows) for each month indicates a net cash outflow to the firm for each month from July to October. The firm has a monthly net cash inflow for November and December. Table 11A–3 shows a summary of the cash position of the firm. For each month, cash at the beginning of the month ($200,000 on July 1) plus the change in cash during the month ($21,000 during July) equals the cash at the end of the month without borrowing ($179,000 at the end of July). When the firm borrows or repays any amount during the month, such an amount should be added or subtracted in order to obtain the actual cash at the end of the month.

Table 11A–3 reveals a potential problem for the months of September and October. The firm will have to borrow $77,000 in September and an additional $93,000 in October. These borrowings can be repaid during the month of November.

What actions can National Toy take to reduce this problem? First, the firm may be able to obtain a short-term loan from a commercial bank or some other financial institution.[29] If it is impossible to do so, the firm can try other

TABLE 11A–3

NATIONAL TOY:
CASH BUDGET
(Thousands Omitted)

|  | July | Aug. | Sept. | Oct. | Nov. | Dec. |
|---|---|---|---|---|---|---|
| Cash at the beginning of the month | $200 | $179 | $156 | $100 | $100 | $135 |
| + Change in cash | ($21) | ($23) | ($133) | ($93) | $205 | $45 |
| = Cash at the end of the month (without borrowing) | $179 | $156 | $23 | $7 | $305 | $180 |
| + Borrowings (repayments) | 0 | 0 | $77 | $93 | ($170) | 0 |
| = Actual cash at the end of the month | $179 | $156 | $100 | $100 | $135 | $180 |

---

[29]Short-term loans are discussed in Chapter 16.

alternatives—for example, try to issue the long-term bonds in September rather than November, postpone the $60,000 dividend payment until December, or attempt to postpone payments on raw materials or to induce their customers (by giving discounts) to pay for the toys at an earlier date. The information revealed in the cash budget gives National Toy an important advantage: It recognizes the cash problem *before it takes place*, thus giving the firm the opportunity to seek alternative solutions some time before the problem is actually faced.

**PROBLEMS**

1. Prepare a three-month (January, February, and March) cash budget for the National Supplies Corporation. The firm has $5,000 in cash on January 1. National Supplies desires to maintain a minimum of $3,000 in cash at all times. The firm collects 75% of sales in the same month that sales are made, and the remainder (25%) in the month following the sale. Purchases are equal to 80% of the current month's sales. Payments are made in the month following the purchase. Other cash payments are $1,000 per month. The depreciation expense is $1,000 per month. The actual and expected sales are as follows:

| Month | Sales | |
|---|---|---|
| December | $5,000 | Actual |
| January | $4,000 | Forecast |
| February | $3,000 | Forecast |
| March | $2,000 | Forecast |

2. The Gerhard Corporation has to prepare a cash budget for the last six months of the calendar year. The firm has $100,000 as of July 1, and desires to maintain a minimum cash balance of $50,000 at all times. The actual and forecast monthly sales and purchases of the firm are as follows:

| Month | Sales | Purchases | |
|---|---|---|---|
| June | $500,000 | $300,000 | Actual |
| July | $600,000 | $360,000 | Forecast |
| August | $800,000 | $480,000 | " |
| September | $900,000 | $540,000 | " |
| October | $1,000,000 | $600,000 | " |
| November | $800,000 | $480,000 | " |
| December | $600,000 | $360,000 | " |
| January | $400,000 | $240,000 | " |

Gerhard collects 20% of its sales in the month sales are made, and the remainder (80%) in the month following the sale. Purchases are paid for in the month *after* they are incurred. Furthermore, Gerhard plans to sell some assets in November. The firm will realize $200,000 from the sale, and will collect these funds in November. Gerhard pays $200,000 in salaries every month. The firm's other cash expenses, equal to 10% of sales, are paid in the same month they are incurred. The depreciation expense of the firm is $50,000 per month. Gerhard must pay in taxes $50,000 in September and $60,000 in December. The firm plans to pay a dividend of $100,000 in August.

  a. Prepare a cash budget for the last six months of the calendar year. Indicate the amount and timing of borrowings, and the month in which repayment may be possible.

  b. Assume that Gerhard needs to borrow, and that, owing to conditions beyond its control, the firm is unable to do so. What actions can be taken by management to reduce the effect of this problem?

## APPENDIX 11B
## Derivation of the Economic-Order-Quantity Formula

In Chapter 11, economic order quantity was defined as:

$$EOQ = \sqrt{\frac{2FS}{C}}$$

(11B-1)

In this appendix, we will discuss both the principles and the methodology used in obtaining the EOQ formula.

There are two costs of inventory: (1) declining inventory costs, and (2) rising inventory costs. Thus, the total cost of inventories is:

$$\text{Total cost} = \text{Declining costs} + \text{Rising costs}$$

(11B–2)

The declining costs are a function of the total number of orders placed each year. Thus, the declining inventory costs would be equal to the number of orders placed, times the cost of placing each order. Mathematically, the declining inventory cost is equal to: $[(S/Q)F]$.[30] The rising inventory costs are a function of the *average level of inventory* and the cost of each unit of inventory. Mathematically, the increasing cost is equal to $(Q/2 + SS)C$.[31]

We can substitute these expressions into equation 11B–1. The new equation will be:

$$\text{Total cost} = \left(\frac{S}{Q}\right)F + \left(\frac{Q}{2} + SS\right)C$$

(11B-3)

By obtaining the partial derivative of the total cost with respect to quantity of units ordered and equating it to zero, we can determine the minimum total cost. Thus, equation 11B–3 would be modified as follows:

---

[30] $S$ = annual sales; $Q$ = order quantity; $F$ = ordering cost.

[31] $SS$ = safety stock: $C$ = financing and holding cost per unit of inventory.

$$\frac{\partial TC}{\partial Q} = 0$$

$$-\frac{SF}{Q^2} + \frac{C}{2} = 0$$

$$\frac{C}{2} = \frac{SF}{Q^2}$$

$$Q^2 = \frac{2SF}{C}$$

$$Q = EOQ = \sqrt{\frac{2SF}{C}} \qquad \text{(11B-4)}$$

Note that if $Q$ units (the economic order quantity, EOQ) are ordered each time, the total cost of inventories will be minimized.

**SELECTED BIBLIOGRAPHY**

ATKINS, JOSEPH C., and YONG H. KIM, "Comment and Correction: Opportunity Cost in the Evaluation of Investment in Accounts Receivable," *Financial Management,* 6 (Winter 1977), 71–74.

BAUMOL, WILLIAM J., "The Transactions Demand for Cash—An Inventory-Theoretic Approach," *Quarterly Journal of Economics,* 65 (November 1952), 545–56.

BAXTER, NEVINS D., "Marketability, Default Risk and Yields on Money-Market Instruments," *Journal of Financial and Quantitative Analysis,* 3 (March 1968), 75–85.

BERANEK, WILLIAM, *Analysis of Financial Decisions.* Homewood, Ill.: Richard D. Irwin, 1963.

BIERMAN, HAROLD JR., CHARLES P. BONINI, and WARREN H. HAUSMAN, *Quantitative Analysis for Business Decisions,* 5th ed. Homewood, Ill.: Richard D. Irwin, 1977.

DYL, EDWARD A., "Another Look at the Evaluation of Investment in Accounts Receivable," *Financial Management,* 6 (Winter 1977), 67–70.

HALEY, CHARLES W., and ROBERT C. HIGGINS, "Inventory Control Theory and Trade Credit Financing," *Management Science,* 20 (December 1973), 464–71.

LEVIN, RICHARD I., and CHARLES A KIRKPATRICK, *Quantitative Approaches to Management,* 3rd ed. New York: McGraw-Hill, 1975.

MEHTA, DILLEP R., *Working Capital Management.* Englewood Cliffs, N.J.: Prentice-Hall, 1974.

SCHIFF, MICHAEL, and ZVI LUBER, "A Model for the Integration of Credit and Inventory Management," *Journal of Finance,* 29 (March 1974), 133–40.

SMITH, KEITH V., *Management of Working Capital.* New York: West Publishing Company, 1974.

VAN HORNE, JAMES C., *Financial Management and Policy,* 5th ed. Englewood Cliffs, N.J.: Prentice-Hall, 1980.

WALIA, TIRLOCHAN S., "Explicit and Implicit Cost of Changes in the Level of Accounts Receivable and the Credit Policy Decision of the Firm," *Financial Management,* 6 (Winter 1977), 75–78.

# ASSET MANAGEMENT IN AN INTERNATIONAL CONTEXT

## 12

## INTRODUCTION

Since the end of World War II, American firms have become heavily involved in international business. Although American exports constituted only 7 percent of the U.S. gross national product in 1979, this low percentage figure is somewhat misleading. In dollar terms, $182 billion in goods and services were exported and $206 billion imported. This makes the United States the world's largest importer and exporter.

U.S. firms have been dealing with both industrialized and developing nations. For example, approximately 60 percent of American exports go to other developed nations, and the remaining 40 percent to developing nations. In addition, American business firms have billions of dollars invested in foreign countries. International transactions have become a significant aspect of almost every large corporation and of many smaller firms. The business manager of today and tomorrow must learn how to deal with this very important new dimension of American business.

The internationalization of American business presents special opportunities for both American firms and the other nations of the world. American firms can use their advanced technology to earn substantial profits in foreign countries. At the same time, foreign clients may be provided with goods and services at prices below those that would be available in the absence of international trade and investment. In addition, foreign firms are frequently able to supply goods and services to American firms and consumers at prices below those that would prevail in the absence of world trade. Thus, international trade and investment can be profitable for both American and foreign firms *and* can benefit both U.S. citizens and those of the rest of the world.[1]

For the American firm, international economic activity presents not only possibilities for profit but also some special problems and risks. These transactions are usually more risky for an American firm than are dealings that take place within the United States. A whole host of international political factors make the cash flows associated with an international transaction less certain, and this uncertainty implies additional risk. Wars, revolutions, nationalization of industry, currency restrictions, and many other political factors can change what appeared to be a profitable business opportunity into a staggering loss. International economic developments and frequent shortages of business information create other risks for American companies engaged in international business. As in the other situations presented in this book, these special international risks must be weighed against the substantial possibilities of high benefits. This weighing of benefits and risk is the topic of this chapter.

Before proceeding with a discussion of international dimensions of asset management, it is necessary to say something about stockholder-wealth maximization in an international context. As we saw in Chapter 1, the goal of stockholder-wealth maximization (a constrained objective) seems to be a reasonable description of how American firms behave. It was also argued that stockholder-wealth maximization contributes to the well-being of American society as a whole. Competitive forces in the American economy are sufficiently strong to ensure that the public welfare is not jeopardized by wealth-seeking activity. The efficiency and productivity of the American economy bears witness to the economic consequence of individual wealth-seeking in a competitive environment.

---

[1]The inherent advantages of foreign trade and investments to the participating countries are discussed in all international-economics textbooks. For example, see Charles P. Kindleberger, *International Economics*, 4th ed. (Homewood, Ill.: Richard D. Irwin, 1968); or Delbert A. Snider, *Introduction to International Economics*, 6th ed. (Homewood, Ill.: Richard D. Irwin, 1975).

Stockholder-wealth maximization in an international context is much more difficult to analyze. In some foreign places, the forces of competition are not present. It is at least conceivable that American stockholder-wealth-maximization behaviors are incompatible with the interest of foreign citizens. Thus, the role of American business firms in foreign countries, especially in those countries with developing economies, has serious political and even moral overtones. Foreigners, after all, are interested in their own well-being. American businesses' growing awareness of the hopes, aspirations, and goals of these foreign economic partners has emerged in recent years as a new and not fully understood constraint on the stockholder-wealth-maximizing activities of the firm. This additional constraint, imposed by foreigners on American firms (and the firms of other industrialized nations), introduces new problems and uncertainty in the international financial decision-making process.

## INTERNATIONAL TRADE-CREDIT RISK

Just as it may be profitable for the firm to extend trade credit to domestic customers, it may also be profitable to make similar extensions to foreign buyers. The general principles of evaluation of international trade-credit extensions are the same as those for domestic trade credit. Basically, the firm must weigh the benefits of increased international sales against the expected bad-debt losses and the cost of financing accounts receivable. Credit standards and credit terms must be established in the special context in which international transactions take place.

There are broad classes of factors that affect the riskiness of international trade-credit extensions. One class relates to the possibility of nonpayment by the buyer. Included in this class are business and political risk. For one thing, it may be difficult to obtain the information necessary for classification of individual firms into the appropriate trade-credit risk categories. This is especially true for American sellers just entering the international trade arena, or in dealing with firms in developing nations that have poor business-information systems. The absence (or extreme costliness) of information may result in misclassification, poor estimates of bad-debt losses, and greater uncertainty with respect to the cash flows associated with a sale. Note that there are two possible undesirable consequences of this situation. The most obvious result of poor information is that on occasion, the firm will incur increased bad-debt losses. However, the tendency of American firms to withdraw from relatively uncertain transactions with foreign firms may result in even greater foregone profits. American firms selling to foreign firms must develop a risk classification system similar to that presented in Table 11–3, so that the uncertainty can be balanced against potential profits of trade-credit extension.

Differences in national legal systems also create an element of risk in international trade-credit extensions. Most business transactions among

American firms are subject to the provisions of the Uniform Commercial Code. A California firm selling to a firm in New York knows exactly the legal recourse available should the buyer fail to meet the terms of the sales agreement. Foreign sales may be subject to different legal rules from those applying to domestic transactions. In complicated transactions, it may be necessary to employ foreign legal counsel. This may be expensive and may reduce the expected profits associated with the transaction.

Political actions in foreign countries also create an element of uncertainty. If a country that has long been a political ally of the United States undergoes a revolution, the new government may be hostile to both the government and American business, and may block payments to American firms. There are also less dramatic political developments that could cause substantial slowdown in such payments. A nation experiencing severe economic difficulties may place a moratorium on international payments. Or prolonged revolutionary fighting in a country may result in the inability of firms to pay for goods received. These are among the many international political factors that affect the riskiness of trade-credit extensions.

An American firm can take several measures to reduce the risk of nonpayment by foreign customers. For example, the U.S. Export-Import Bank (Eximbank), a government agency, lends money to foreign purchasers of certain U.S. goods in order that direct payments can be made to American suppliers. Eximbank also guarantees U.S. bank loans made to foreign purchasers of U.S. goods, usually capital equipment. These government programs can be used by some firms to reduce the risk of international trade credit. Also, the Foreign Credit Insurance Association, a private association of 60 U.S. insurance firms, provides insurance to firms extending international trade credit; but there is a fee charged for this insurance, and of course, this reduces both the risk and the profitability of international trade-credit extensions.

In order to reduce the risk of nonpayment of international trade credit, an American seller may require the use of a letter of credit, which can protect both the buyer and the seller. For example, assume that an American company sells some products to a Japanese firm and requires a letter of credit as means of payment. The American company specifies the terms of the sale. If these terms are acceptable, the Japanese firm would go to a Japanese bank and apply for a letter of credit. The Japanese bank, if it so desires, issues such a letter of credit, which specifies *in detail* all the steps that must be completed by the American seller before payment is to be made. If the American firm complies with all the specifications in the letter of credit and submits to the Japanese bank the proper documentation to prove it has done so, the Japanese bank guarantees the payment on the due date. On that date, the American firm is paid *by the Japanese bank, not by the buyer of the products*. Therefore, the credit standing of the Japanese bank stands behind the payment. The benefits to the seller are self-evident; but there are benefits to the buyer also. The buyer is not obligated to pay for the products until all the specifications of the letter of credit have been met. The cost of the letter of credit is the fee charged by the Japanese bank. These fees result in reduced risk and reduced profitability.

## REDUCING EXCHANGE-RATE RISK FOR INTERNATIONAL TRADE CREDIT

Financial decisions made in the domestic operations of U.S. firms are simplified by a common currency, dollars. When a firm based in California does business in Texas, the costs, revenues, and taxes are all denominated in the same unit of account, the U.S. dollar. However, the same circumstances do not apply when the U.S. firm undertakes business operations in, say, the United Kingdom. The basic unit of account in the United Kingdom is the pound (£). Thus, costs, revenues, and taxes are incurred partly in U.S. dollars and partly in British pounds. In cases in which payment is specified in foreign currency units, the American seller extending trade credit to a foreign firm faces the risk that the foreign currency will decline in value relative to the dollar. This "two-currency" situation generates exchange-rate risks. Essentially, this is the risk that the seller will be paid in currency of diminished value.

The exchange rate is the price of one currency in terms of another. If, for example, $2.26 is required to acquire one British pound, the exchange rate is £1 = $2.26. Before 1971, the foreign exchange rate was fixed by international agreement. The individual country had the responsibility of preventing the fluctuation (±1 percent was allowed) of the foreign exchange rate of its currency. This system, at least for the U.S. dollar, ended in 1971.[2] Since then, the exchange rates between the dollar and foreign currencies have fluctuated in response to economic conditions.

The present international monetary system may best be defined as an imperfect, freely fluctuating exchange rate. The exchange rate between two currencies is determined by free market forces, subject to some intervention by government agencies. The classic supply-demand schedule shown in Figure 12–1 may help illustrate the forces that currently determine the exchange rate between two currencies. Those factors that tend to increase the supply or decrease the demand schedules for a given currency would cause a decrease of the value of this currency in foreign exchange markets. Factors that decrease the supply or increase the demand schedule would cause an increase in the value of the currency.

Downward pressures, other things being equal, on the value of a currency would take place given the following conditions:

1. Continuous deficits in balance of payments. A simple example of a balance-of-payments deficit would be a situation in which total payments to foreigners exceed total receipts from foreigners. Such deficits would increase

---

[2]Recently, some members of the Common Market have attempted to reduce the volatility of the exchange rates between their currencies by developing the European Currency Unit (ECU). It is still too early to evaluate the success of this agreement.

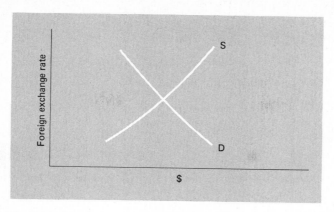

**FIGURE 12–1**

Supply and Demand
for a Currency

the supply of a currency in forward markets, placing a downward pressure on the value of the currency.

2. High rates of inflation play a significant role in the decline in value of a currency. Inflation makes a country's products less attractive to foreigners and foreign products more attractive to the country. Therefore, deficits in balance of payments will increase, worsening the situation described above.

3. Declining interest rates make investments by foreigners in the country less attractive, therefore reducing the demand for the country's currency.

4. The government may artificially increase the demand for its currency by purchasing it in foreign markets. It would have to pay for such purchases with other currencies acceptable to the sellers. International reserves comprise convertible currencies and gold. A decline in the level of a country's international reserves diminishes the ability of that country's government to buy its currency in foreign markets.

5. Uncertainty about the political stability of a country may introduce a downward pressure on the value of its currency. Recent events in Italy serve to illustrate the effect of this variable. Fears of Communist party gains in recent elections prompted sales of liras in foreign markets. This increase in the supply of liras had an adverse effect on their price.

It should be noted that the factors listed above are not related to the exchange rate in any mechanical fashion. It is best to look at the exchange rate between the dollar and other currencies as being established in a relatively competitive foreign exchange market. The participants in this market commit themselves to deliver, or take delivery of, certain amounts of currencies at specific dates. The rates that these foreign exchange market participants are willing to accept will depend upon their anticipations with respect to future exchange rates and the transaction costs. This process is summarized in Figure 12–2.

Here is an example of the nature of exchange-rate risk. Assume that the American Furniture Corporation, a furniture manufacturer, is negotiating a

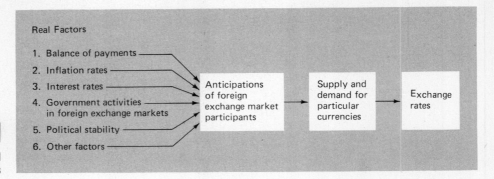

**FIGURE 12–2**

Anticipations and Exchange Rates

Real Factors

1. Balance of payments
2. Inflation rates
3. Interest rates
4. Government activities in foreign exchange markets
5. Political stability
6. Other factors

Anticipations of foreign exchange market participants

Supply and demand for particular currencies

Exchange rates

sale to British Stores, a chain of retail stores located in the London area. The sale will be made on May 2, 1980. American Furniture is interested in receiving dollars for its products, since American workers, suppliers, and bankers all insist on payment in dollars. British Stores wants to pay in pounds, since its customers pay for purchases in pounds. American Furniture wants $225,900 for the merchandise it plans to ship. Since the current exchange rate is £1 = $2.2590 on May 2, 1980, American is willing to accept £100,000. Both parties agree that shipment will take place immediately and British Stores will pay £100,000 90 days after May 2. When the £100,000 payment is received, American plans to exchange the pounds for dollars and use the dollars to meet its financial obligations.

Given that the exchange rate remains constant, the American firm will receive £100,000 in 90 days and will exchange it for $225,900, thus receiving the amount desired for the products. However, the actual exchange rate 90 days after May 2 may be higher or lower than £1 = $2.2590. If the foreign exchange rate is £1 = $2.1590, the U.S. firm would receive only $215,900 for the £100,000. This decline in the value of the British pound relative to the dollar may cause a loss on the transaction. Of course, if the exchange rate 90 days after May 2 had been £1 = $2.3000, the U.S. firm would have an "unanticipated" profit of $4,100. American Furniture does not know on May 2 what the exchange rate will be 90 days in the future. Therefore, unexpected losses or profits may take place due to foreign exchange fluctuations.

The American firm can reduce the risks caused by exchange-rate fluctuations by entering into a forward exchange transaction. The spot rate is the current value of a unit of foreign currency in terms of U.S. dollars. *The forward rate is the value of a unit of foreign currency to be delivered some time in the future* in terms of dollars. Table 12–1 shows the number of dollars recently required to obtain British pounds, Japanese yen, or German marks to be delivered at various maturities.

Future markets for currencies can be used to minimize the risk of exchange-rate fluctuations. For example, American Furniture may agree to accept £100,000 in 90 days from British Stores. Simultaneously, American Furniture can enter into a contract to sell £100,000 for $224,350 in 90 days. American Furniture will receive fewer dollars than would have been

TABLE 12-1

**U.S. DOLLARS REQUIRED TO PURCHASE ONE UNIT
OF FOREIGN CURRENCY, AS OF MAY 2, 1980**

| Time of purchase | British pound | Japanese yen | West German mark |
|---|---|---|---|
| Spot | $2.2590 | $0.004179 | $0.5490 |
| 30 days | $2.2510 | $0.004187 | $0.5510 |
| 90 days | $2.2435 | $0.004191 | $0.5546 |
| 180 days | $2.2365 | $0.004214 | $0.5591 |

justified by the exchange rate in the spot market at the time the sale is made ($225,900). However, American knows exactly how many dollars it will receive in 90 days: It will take the £100,000 received from British Stores and exchange it for $224,350. In effect, American Furniture has accepted a lower price but has eliminated the foreign exchange risk. That is, although American Furniture does not know what the exchange rate will be 90 days after May 2, the firm is guaranteed $224,350 no matter what the rate turns out to be. It will receive £100,000 from the British buyer and use these funds to pay for the forward contract.

The same logic would apply if an American firm has a contractual obligation to pay £100,000 to a British firm in 90 days. The U.S. firm would have to pay $225,900 for £100,000 if it purchases the required pounds at the spot rate. Because it does not have to pay until 90 days from now, the firm may prefer to wait 90 days before obtaining the £100,000. However, if it does not want to take the risks inherent in fluctuations in the exchange rate, the American firm may purchase a contract for £100,000 to be delivered in 90 days for $224,350, thus removing the uncertainties caused by possible fluctuations in the exchange rate.

The foreign exchange market is dominated by large commercial banks, which buy and sell foreign exchange on behalf of their customers. They quote their customers a certain bid and ask price; for example, a bank might be willing to pay $2.25 for a British pound to be delivered in 90 days, or to sell one pound that will be delivered in 90 days for $2.255. The foreign exchange market is of such a size that it is able to accommodate almost all hedging transactions desired by U.S. firms. Spot and forward contracts may be purchased and sold in all major trading currencies. However, a firm may encounter some difficulties in hedging transactions that are denominated in currencies not actively traded in this market.

The advantage of the forward exchange market is the reduction in the risk taken by a firm in foreign transactions. That is, the intent of a firm entering into a forward exchange contract is *not* to make a profit out of changes in the exchange rate, but to prevent fluctuations in profits caused by such changes.

## FOREIGN LONG-TERM-ASSET ACQUISITION

The framework for evaluation of foreign long-term-asset acquisitions is similar to that for asset acquisitions in a domestic context. Management must evaluate the effect on the wealth of the corporation's stockholders of the amount, timing, and riskiness of the cash flows associated with the foreign long-term asset. As in the case of domestic acquisitions, management must compute the amount and timing of after-tax cash outflows and inflows to the American corporation (Chapter 9). These cash flows must be discounted using the asset-specific cost of capital that reflects the riskiness of the particular asset. Finally, the asset must be evaluated in the context of the capital budget (Chapter 10).

But although the framework used to evaluate foreign and domestic long-term-asset acquisitions is the same, there are a number of complicating factors. The complications are illustrated by the model in Figure 12–3. This model, while only one of several possible situations, provides a useful context for evaluating foreign long-term-asset acquisitions. First and most important, note the cash flows to and from the American parent firm. The amount, timing, and riskiness of these dollar cash flows will be evaluated by the competitive stock market and will determine the effect of the foreign investment on stockholder wealth. Management must focus on these dollar cash flows in evaluating the attractiveness of the asset acquisition.

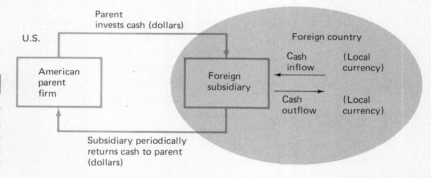

**FIGURE 12-3**

Typical Model of an American Firm's Acquisition of a Long-term Asset in a Foreign Country

The dollar cash flows to and from the parent are typically funneled through a foreign operating subsidiary.[3] The foreign subsidiary conducts business with the foreign economies, so it receives revenue in the form of foreign currency and must make payments in foreign currency. Since the foreign subsidiary is subject to the laws of the nation in which it operates, taxes must be paid to the foreign government, and laws regulating the inflow and outflow of dollars and other currency to or from the foreign country must be adhered to.

---

[3]In this section, the word *subsidiary* is used in a general sense; it may refer to either a foreign branch operation or a foreign corporation owned by the parent. The distinction between the two forms will be discussed later in this chapter.

This foreign subsidiary faces not only the usual business and financial risk but also a number of other risks. In many cases, the assets of a foreign subsidiary face the possibility of nationalization. This may not be accompanied by fair compensation to the parent, and the parent may lose all or part of the dollars that have been invested in the subsidiary. For example, substantial losses were incurred by firms that had invested in Cuban subsidiaries before the Castro government came into power and nationalized American firms.

In addition, firms acquiring assets through a foreign subsidiary face a foreign exchange risk. The subsidiary's cash inflows and outflows are typically in the form of local currency. As discussed previously, the exchange rate between a foreign currency and the dollar is not stable. Should economic conditions in the foreign country deteriorate, the value of its currency relative to the dollar may decline. Thus, even though cash flows to the foreign subsidiary materialize at the forecast level, the foreign currency may buy fewer dollars, substantially reducing the cash inflows to the American parent firm.

At the present time, there is no method of substantially reducing the *long-term* exchange-rate risks inherent in long-term-asset acquisitions.[4] Generally speaking, the forward market for foreign exchange does not offer protection beyond one year. This means that should the foreign currency decline relative to the dollar, the dollar cash flows to the parent will decline, and there is little the firm can do about it. Of course, the exchange-rate risk works two ways. If the dollar declines relative to the foreign currency, unexpected profits can be made. For example, in the 1970s, those firms that had invested in Germany and Japan at earlier dates captured substantial gains as the dollar declined relative to the deutsche mark and Japanese yen.

The preceding paragraphs have shown that although foreign asset acquisitions should be evaluated in terms of their effect on stockholder wealth, the estimation of the amount, timing, and riskiness of cash flows could be considerably more difficult than in domestic asset acquisitions. The following sections will describe in greater detail how several of these factors affect cash flows to the parent firm. Finally, an integrated example of a foreign asset-acquisition situation will be presented.

## MANAGING POLITICAL RISKS IN FOREIGN ASSET ACQUISITION

Management must recognize and deal with the substantial political risk involved in foreign investment. There are a number of things that the firm can do to reduce these ever-present risks.

---

[4]The firm may be able to arrange a "swap" of currencies. This transaction involves buying and selling the currency at different dates. Foreign central banks, in some rare instances, offer long-term swap agreements. However, the exchange rate offered is well below spot market conditions prevailing at the time of the agreement.

First, management must explicitly consider the political tradition and stability of the nation in which investments are being planned.[5] Some nations, such as the United Kingdom and Switzerland, have strong legal traditions that tend to protect the property of foreign investors. Investments in nations with legal traditions not so strongly oriented toward protection of property rights, or nations with less political stability, may still present favorable investment opportunities. However, stockholders will demand higher rates of return as compensation for higher risks.

Management can also reduce the probability of unfavorable actions by foreign governments by recognizing that those governments, just like ours, act to protect the interests of their own society. Management's prior recognition of this constraint can head off many unpleasant consequences. In today's world, payoffs to government officials, the undermining of government authority, poor working conditions, and the like are not apt to be tolerated for long periods of time. Cooperation with the aspirations of foreign nations and good corporate citizenship may sound trite, but they are very important and can avert many unfavorable actions. It is important that management keep in mind that the constraints on stockholder-wealth maximization vary from country to country.

Parent firms can also protect foreign investments by insuring them. The United States has a quasi-public insurance corporation called the Overseas Private Investment Corporation (OPIC).[6] For a relatively small fee, OPIC will insure new investments in many developing nations against most political risks. This insurance scheme can go a long way to alleviate such risk.

## TAXES AND FOREIGN ASSET ACQUISITIONS

In evaluating long-term-asset acquisitions, cash flows must be evaluated on an after-tax basis. In foreign asset acquisitions, both U.S. and foreign taxes must be considered when estimating after-tax cash flows. This process is further complicated by the fact that in some cases, foreign income taxes paid may be used to offset U.S. income taxes.

An American firm can conduct foreign operations through either of two types of business organizations. On the one hand, foreign operations can be conducted through a foreign *corporate subsidiary*. In this case, a separate foreign corporation, owned entirely or in part by the parent firm, is established in the foreign country. The foreign corporate subsidiary becomes a legal entity separate from that of the parent firm. On the other hand, the American parent firm can simply establish a *branch subsidiary* in the foreign country. The branch subsidiary is legally a part of the parent firm.

---

[5]Good business decisions require that management understand a broad range of subject matter not usually associated with business decision making (i.e., history, political science, anthropology, etc.).

[6]Several other industrialized nations have similar organizations.

These two different forms of subsidiary organizations can have very important implications for the cash flows associated with the acquisition of a foreign asset. Since it is a separate legal entity, the foreign corporate subsidiary is classified as a foreign citizen for purposes of U.S. corporate income taxation. Income earned by any foreign citizen is not subject to U.S. income taxes unless it is earned within the United States or the foreign citizen resides in the United States. Foreign corporate subsidiaries are treated the same as any other foreign citizen, and thus do not have to pay U.S. income taxes. The American parent pays U.S. income taxes only on the dividend income it receives from the foreign corporate subsidiary. That is, dividends paid by the corporate subsidiary to the parent are viewed as income earned in the United States. But depending on the situation, the foreign corporate subsidiary may choose not to pay dividends for a considerable period of time, in which case the American parent can effectively postpone the payment of U.S. taxes on income earned by the subsidiary. Of course, at some time the parent will want to recoup its investment, so it will have to pay taxes eventually. But the present value of postponed tax payments is lower than that of taxes paid at the time income is earned by the subsidiary.[7]

If the American parent establishes a branch subsidiary as distinct from a corporate subsidiary, U.S. income taxes must be paid as income is earned by the subsidiary. Since there is no opportunity to postpone U.S. taxes, their present value may be higher for the branch-subsidiary than for the corporate-subsidiary form of business organization. Note that it makes no difference if earnings are repatriated.

There are other considerations involved in selecting the business form of the foreign operations. If the parent firm is expecting losses in foreign operations, it may consider the branch form of organization, which will permit the parent firm to use such losses to offset income earned by the parent in the United States. In addition, firms that plan to repatriate all their foreign income may be indifferent as to the form of subsidiary organization. Finally, if a parent firm plans to reinvest the earnings of the foreign subsidiary rather than repatriate them, organizing the subsidiary in the form of a corporation may result in reduced U.S. taxes. There are, of course, reasons other than taxation that influence the form of business organization selected by parent firms for foreign subsidiaries. Taxes are, however, one of the most important factors affecting the cash flows associated with a foreign long-term-asset acquisition.

Whether the subsidiary is organized in the corporate or the branch form, it must pay foreign taxes. Some of the foreign countries may impose an income tax. However, in order to minimize the double taxation of income earned by foreign subsidiaries, the U.S. tax laws permit the parent firm to

---

[7]There are exceptions to this general rule. Some American firms have formed foreign corporations for the purpose of tax avoidance. Congress has changed specific provisions of the tax laws to prevent such abuses.

TABLE 12–2

INCOME STATEMENT OF THE FOREIGN SUBSIDIARY

| | |
|---|---:|
| Taxable income | $1,000,000 |
| Foreign income taxes paid (30%) | $300,000 |
| After-tax income | $700,000 |
| – Dividend to the parent | – $700,000 |
| Retained earnings of the subsidiary | 0 |

### U.S. TAXATION OF DIVIDENDS RECEIVED BY THE PARENT CORPORATIONS

| | |
|---|---:|
| Dividends received | $700,000 |
| + Foreign income taxes paid by the subsidiary on dividends | + 300,000 |
| = U.S. taxable income | $1,000,000 |
| U.S. taxes (40% of taxable income) | $400,000 |
| – Foreign tax credit | – 300,000 |
| U.S. taxes payable | $100,000 |

Total taxes paid (foreign + U.S.) = $300,000
+ $100,000 = $400,000

offset against its U.S. income taxes any foreign income taxes it has paid (subject to certain restrictions).

To illustrate the offset, called the "foreign tax credit," Table 12–2 outlines a hypothetical situation in which a foreign subsidiary has a taxable income of $1 million.[8] All after-tax income is forwarded to the U.S. parent firm (repatriated) at the time it is earned. Note that in Table 12–2, the foreign income tax rate (30 percent) is lower than the U.S. income tax rate (40 percent). The first section of the table shows that the foreign subsidiary must pay a tax of $300,000 to the foreign government. The second section shows that an additional tax of $100,000 must be paid by the parent firm to the U.S. government. The U.S. government imposes taxes on the before-tax income of the firm. Thus, the parent corporation must reconstruct its taxable income. The parent corporation has received $700,000 in dividend income; therefore, its total taxable income will be equal to the dividend received ($700,000) plus any foreign income taxes paid by the subsidiary on such income ($300,000), or a total of $1 million. The U.S. tax on $1 million of taxable income is $400,000. However, the parent corporation can take as a tax credit an amount equal to the foreign income taxes paid on the dividends, or $300,000. Thus, the U.S. taxes payable by the parent corpora-

---

[8]The foreign subsidiary, of course, will have earnings, taxes, and so on in foreign currency. In order to simplify the computations, however, we are providing the equivalent dollar value of each of these items.

tion would be $100,000. Note that the total taxes paid by the parent *and* the subsidiary ($400,000) are exactly equal to the taxes that would have been paid had the income been earned within the United States. The U.S. corporate income tax laws are constructed in such a fashion that no penalty is attached to earning income in foreign countries.

The situation outlined in Table 12–3 is slightly different. In this case, the foreign tax rate is *higher* than the U.S. tax rate. The foreign subsidiary pays $500,000 in taxes to the foreign government, so no additional taxes are paid to the U.S. government by the parent corporation. Note, however, that the parent does not receive a "refund" for the "extra" taxes that were paid because the income was earned abroad. Foreign income taxes can be used as a credit against U.S. taxes only to the extent that would have been paid had the income been earned within the United States. When the foreign tax rate is *lower* than the U.S. tax rate, the U.S. tax laws raise the overall tax to the level paid on income earned within the United States. When the foreign tax rate is *higher* than the U.S. tax rate, there is no attempt to reduce total taxes paid by the parent and subsidiary to a level comparable to that paid on an equal amount of domestic income.[9]

TABLE 12–3

INCOME STATEMENT OF THE FOREIGN SUBSIDIARY

| | |
|---|---:|
| Taxable income | $1,000,000 |
| Foreign income taxes paid (50%) | $500,000 |
| After-tax income | $500,000 |
| − Dividend to the parent | − $500,000 |
| Retained earnings of the subsidiary | 0 |

U.S. TAXATION OF DIVIDENDS RECEIVED BY THE
PARENT CORPORATION

| | |
|---|---:|
| Dividends received | $500,000 |
| + Foreign income taxes paid by the subsidiary on the dividends | + $500,000 |
| = U.S. taxable income | $1,000,000 |
| U.S. taxes (40% of taxable income) | $400,000 |
| − Foreign tax credit | − $400,000[a] |
| = U.S. taxes payable | 0 |

Total taxes paid (foreign + U.S.) = $500,000
+ 0 = $500,000

[a]Note that although foreign income taxes paid were $500,000, the foreign tax credit cannot exceed the U.S. taxes.

---

[9]A firm conducting operations in a number of foreign countries may elect to consolidate all its foreign operations for the purpose of the foreign tax credit. In this case, it may be able to use the "excess" foreign taxes paid by merging it with foreign taxes lower than the U.S. rate.

When the foreign subsidiary is organized in the form of a corporation, the repatriation of income to the parent may be postponed. According to the U.S. tax laws, the postponement of income repatriation must be accompanied by a postponement of claiming the foreign tax credit. If, for example, the corporate subsidiary in the previous examples decided to reinvest all the after-tax profits in the foreign country (pay no dividends to the parent), none of the foreign taxes paid could be used as a foreign tax credit for U.S. income tax purposes. The parent firm includes no part of the income of the foreign subsidiary and no foreign tax credit in its U.S. tax return. Upon the eventual repatriation of the earnings of the subsidiary, of course, the foreign tax credit can be used. If, on the other hand, the subsidiary repatriates 75 percent of its after-tax income to the parent, 75 percent of the income taxes paid to the foreign government can be claimed as a foreign tax credit. The other portion of the foreign income taxes paid (25 percent) can be claimed as a foreign tax credit when the remaining income is repatriated.[10]

Another important feature of the U.S. tax laws is worth noting. The foreign tax credit provision applies to foreign *income taxes only*. Foreign subsidiaries also pay property taxes, sales taxes, value-added taxes, royalties on minerals extracted, and many other taxes. In many cases, only a small portion of the total taxes paid by the foreign subsidiary can be used as a tax credit against U.S. income taxes, because such taxes are not considered *income taxes*.

Thus, we can see that U.S. tax laws have an important effect on the cash flows associated with the acquisition of a long-term asset in a foreign country. The type of subsidiary organization, the type of taxes paid to the foreign government, the foreign income tax rate, the U.S. income tax rate, and the rate at which income is repatriated to the parent will all affect the net present value of a foreign long-term-asset acquisition.

## CASH FLOWS TO A SUBSIDIARY AND CASH FLOWS TO THE PARENT

As shown in Figure 12–3, there are two cash flows involved in international long-term-asset acquisitions. We have shown that the relevant cash flow for measuring the acquisition's effect on stockholder wealth is the cash flow to the parent firm. It is the stockholders of the parent firm whose wealth is to be maximized.

In practice, the asset acquisition must be evaluated at two levels. First, the cash flows between the subsidiary and the foreign economy must be evaluated. If these cash flows yield a positive net present value, using the

---

[10]Thus, in the example in Table 12–2, the dividend received by the parent would be equal to $525,000 (75% of $700,000). The U.S. taxable income would be $750,000 (75% of $700,000 plus 75% of $300,000). The U.S. taxes would be $300,000 (40% of $750,000). The firm, however, can take as a foreign tax credit 75% of the foreign income taxes paid, or $225,000. Thus, total U.S. taxes payable would be $75,000.

methodology discussed in Chapters 9 and 10, then the acquisition is desirable from the subsidiary's point of view. However, an asset acquisition that is attractive from the subsidiary's point of view may not be attractive to the parent. Such situations arise when the U.S. parent must pay additional U.S. income taxes, or when there are foreign government restrictions on the amount of income that is permitted to be repatriated. For example, Chile imposed a number of restrictions on cash outflows of subsidiaries in December 1974. Prior approval had to be obtained from Chile's Foreign Investment Committee for dividend repatriation. The committee required that dividends be paid out of verified net profits, and they were limited annually to 14 percent of invested funds. Other forms of repatriation, such as capital distributions, debt repayments, royalties, or fees, were also subject to restrictions.

Restrictions such as these exist also in many other developing nations. They are designed to force foreign investors to reinvest earnings in the nation in which they were earned. These restrictions probably do encourage reinvestments; however, they also tend to discourage new investments, by restricting the cash flows to the parent, thus limiting possible increases in stockholder wealth. Today, American businesses and the governments of developing nations conduct lengthy negotiations and arrive at mutually agreeable repatriation rates before an investment is made. This effort reflects the goal of having both parties, the developing nation and the American firm, share in the benefits of doing business there.

## NPV OF A FOREIGN INVESTMENT: AN EXAMPLE

Let us illustrate the evaluation of long-term-asset acquisitions with an example. The National Refrigeration Corporation is considering the establishment of manufacturing facilities in Parana. The firm plans to establish a foreign corporate subsidiary to manufacture and sell refrigerators in Parana. An investment of 100 million pesos (the local currency of Parana) will be required. The project is expected to generate sales by the subsidiary of 50 million pesos every year for ten years; cash expenses are expected to be 25 million pesos every year for ten years. The equipment will be depreciated using the straight-line method, and no salvage is expected at the end of ten years. At that time, the assets of the subsidiary will be owned by the government of Parana. The corporate income tax rate in Parana is 20 percent. The asset-specific cost of capital that reflects the riskiness of the cash flows is 16 percent.

From the subsidiary's point of view, there is absolutely no difference between this problem and the problems discussed in Chapters 9 and 10, except that the cash flows are stated in pesos rather than dollars. As shown in Table 12–4, the NPV of this project to the subsidiary is a positive 6,326,000 pesos. There is, however, one important difference. We are concerned with the maximization of the wealth of National Refrigeration's stockholders, and this is affected by the cash flows of National Refrigeration and *not* the cash flows of the foreign subsidiary. Thus, we must analyze the effect of the foreign investment on the cash flows of the parent corporation.

### TABLE 12–4

NATIONAL REFRIGERATION CORPORATION:
NET PRESENT VALUE TO THE FOREIGN SUBSIDIARY
(In Paranian Pesos)

|  | Years 1–10 |
|---|---|
| Sales | 50,000,000 |
| − Cash expenses | − 25,000,000 |
| − Depreciation | − 10,000,000 |
| = Earnings before taxes | 15,000,000 |
| − Foreign income taxes (20%) | − 3,000,000 |
| = Earnings after taxes | 12,000,000 |
| + Depreciation | 10,000,000 |
| = Annual cash flows | 22,000,000 |

NPV = 22,000,000(3 Coef.$_{10}^{16\%}$) − 100,000,000

= 22,000,000(4.833) − 100,000,000 = 6,326,000

In many instances, this is a very complex computational procedure. Certain simplifying assumptions, however, will be made in order to reduce the computations and illustrate the major relationships. These assumptions are:

1. The exchange rate is 2 pesos = $1. This exchange rate will remain constant *for the entire 10-year period* (no exchange-rate risk).
2. The parent corporation provides all the funds required for the investment at time 0 (100 million pesos = $50 million).
3. The foreign subsidiary will repatriate to the parent *all earnings after taxes*. Thus, the parent corporation receives an annual dividend of $6 million (12 million pesos/2).
4. The government of Parana requires all foreign investors to deposit in a government checking account (earning no interest) all depreciation cash flows. Thus, at the end of 10 years, the foreign subsidiary will have accumulated 100 million pesos in a checking account. National Refrigeration has an agreement with the Paranian government to repatriate such funds at the end of 10 years. Thus, 10 years from now, the parent corporation will receive $50 million (100 million pesos/2).
5. The U.S. tax rate is 40%, and the foreign tax credit is applicable in this situation.[11]

---

[11]The investment tax credit does not apply to investments made by American firms in foreign countries.

## TABLE 12–5

NATIONAL REFRIGERATION CORPORATION:
PERIODIC CASH FLOWS TO AND FROM SUBSIDIARY
(In Dollars)

|  | Years 1–10 |
|---|---|
| Dividend received | $6,000,000 |
| + Foreign income taxes paid | + $1,500,000 |
| = U.S. taxable income | $7,500,000 |
| U.S. taxes (40% of taxable income) | $3,000,000 |
| − Foreign tax credit | − $1,500,000 |
| U.S. taxes payable | $1,500,000 |

Periodic cash flows to the parent[a] = Dividends
− U.S. taxes payable
= $6,000,000 − $1,500,000 = $4,500,000

[a]Note that the subsidiary's depreciation charges are not included in the periodic cash flows, since, by assumption, they remain in the foreign country. In this simplified example, they will flow back to the parent in year 10 rather than on a periodic basis (see assumption #4).

Table 12–5 shows the cash flows to National Refrigeration. Note that the cash outflows in year 0 equal $50 million. Periodic cash inflows are equal to the annual dividend received ($6 million) less the U.S. taxes payable each year ($1.5 million), or $4.5 million. Finally, there is the repatriation of $50 million from the depreciation cash flows. As shown in Table 12–6, if the investment is undertaken, stockholder wealth will decline by $16,901,500. Thus, the project should not be accepted by National Refrigeration.

## TABLE 12–6

NATIONAL REFRIGERATION CORPORATION:
Net Present Value to the Parent

| Year | Description | Cash flows |
|---|---|---|
| 0 | Initial cash outflows | $50,000,000 |
| 1–10 | Periodic cash flows | $4,500,000 |
| 10 | Depreciation cash flows | $50,000,000 |

$$\text{NPV} = \$4,500,000(3 \text{ Coef.}_{10}^{16\%}) + \$50,000,000(2 \text{ Coef.}_{10}^{16\%})$$
$$- \$50,000,000$$
$$= \$4,500,000(4.833) + \$50,000,000(0.227)$$
$$- \$50,000,000$$
$$= (\$16,901,500)$$

This problem illustrates a situation in which the project has a positive net present value for the subsidiary but a negative NPV for the parent. This difference between the two NPVs is due to the following factors:

1. The U.S. income tax rate (40%) is higher than the Paranian income tax rate (20%).

2. We have assumed that the depreciation cash flows will be maintained in a checking account earning no interest, and will not be returned to the parent until the end of the project's life.

Note that we could have made different assumptions, and thus obtained different results. For example, we could have returned the depreciation cash flows to the parent periodically, or allowed them to earn interest. In addition, the foreign exchange rate may not (in most cases will not) remain constant over the entire ten-year period as assumed. If the value of the Paranian peso declines (for example, to 3 pesos = $1), the cash flows to the parent will be lower in dollar terms, thus affecting NPV and stockholder wealth. Finally, the subsidiary might repatriate only a certain percentage of earnings before taxes in the form of dividends. This change would affect the dividends received and the U.S. taxes payable by the parent corporation, thus affecting NPV and stockholder wealth.

SUMMARY   Since international business is increasingly important to American firms, managers must learn how to analyze the financial aspects of international transactions. The profitability of these transactions must be weighed against their riskiness. American firms should establish a classification system for accounts receivable that will permit the evaluation of the risk-adjusted profitability of international trade credit. The risk of nonpayment of international trade credit may be reduced by utilizing letters of credit, the Export-Import Bank, and the Foreign Credit Insurance Corporation. The exchange-rate risk involved in international trade credit may be minimized by entering the forward market for foreign exchange.

The conceptual framework for international long-term-asset acquisitions is similar to that employed for the evaluation of domestic long-term assets. The analyst must focus primary attention on the cash flows of the parent firm. These cash flows should be discounted at a rate that reflects the relative riskiness of the international investment. Net present value to the parent, incorporated into a capital-budgeting framework (Chapter 10), should be the final basis for making decisions of this type. It should be remembered that political factors, possible exchange-rate fluctuations, and both U.S. and foreign tax laws have important implications for the decision process. Even though it may be possible to use the insurance program of the Overseas Private Investment Corporation (OPIC) to minimize certain political risks, the opportunities to minimize exchange-rate risks are limited. Before long-term assets are acquired, detailed analysis of political, social, and tax factors is required.

This chapter's emphasis on risk should not mislead the reader into thinking that international transactions are so risky that they should be avoided. In the authors' opinion, nothing could be less desirable to the firm. International business can provide advantages to both American firms and the citizens of foreign countries. In most cases, withdrawing from international operations would be bad for the stockholders of American corporations and bad for foreign citizens, especially those residing in less-developed nations.

This chapter focused on risk, and was designed to highlight the special risk factors of international operations. Once the special risk factors are understood, the decision-making process for international operations is strikingly similar to that employed in domestic situations.

**QUESTIONS FOR DISCUSSION**

1. American investments in foreign countries that have a positive net present value will also benefit the citizens of the nation in which the investment is made. Discuss.

2. Why is the extension of international trade credit more risky than the extension of domestic trade credit?

3. How can an American firm minimize the risk of nonpayment of international trade credit?

4. How does a letter of credit protect both the buyer and the seller in international trade-credit situations?

5. Discuss the nature of exchange-rate risk and how forward exchange transactions can be used to minimize such risk.

6. How can the trade-credit customer categories developed in Chapter 11 be adapted to international trade-credit situations?

7. Discuss the relationship between the two different cash flows involved in international investment.

8. Discuss the nature of the political risks involved in international long-term-asset acquisitions, and explain how these risks can be minimized.

9. Within the context developed in Chapters 9 and 10, explain how international long-term-asset acquisition alternatives should be evaluated.

10. Explain how the type of organization used by the parent in setting up a foreign subsidiary will affect foreign and U.S. income taxes.

11. Total income taxes paid by the parent and the subsidiary on income earned in the foreign country will always be equal to the total income taxes paid by the parent on the same amount of income earned within the United States. True or false? Explain.

12. All taxes paid by subsidiaries may be used as a tax credit to offset U.S. income taxes. True or false? Explain your answer and discuss the implications for American businesses.

13. How do fluctuating exchange rates affect decisions related to international acquisitions of long-term assets? How will expected cash flows be affected?

**1.** The foreign exchange rate between the U.S. dollar and the West German mark is as follows:

| Spot | $0.50 = 1 DM |
|---|---|
| 30 days | $0.51 = 1 DM |
| 90 days | $0.52 = 1 DM |
| 180 days | $0.53 = 1 DM |

a. How many dollars will be needed to purchase 1 million West German marks for delivery today?

b. How many dollars will be needed to purchase 1 million West German marks for delivery in 90 days?

c. Assume that the firm will receive 1 million West German marks in 30 days. If the firm sells the marks in the forward market, how many dollars will it receive in 30 days?

d. Assume that a firm will receive 1 million West German marks in 180 days. If the firm sells the marks in the forward market, how many dollars will it receive in 180 days?

**2.** The AnnCa Corporation owns 100% of the stock of a foreign corporate subsidiary. The subsidiary earns $5 million before taxes in the foreign country. The foreign subsidiary repatriates, in the form of dividends, all earnings after taxes. The U.S. corporate tax rate is 40%.

a. Calculate the dividend received, the U.S. taxes payable, and the cash flows to the parent, if the foreign income tax rate is 30%.

b. Calculate the dividend received, the U.S. taxes payable, and the cash flows to the parent, if the foreign income tax rate is 50%.

**3.** The Christine Corporation owns two foreign corporate subsidiaries. These subsidiaries are located in different countries—subsidiary A in a country with an income tax rate of 50%, and subsidiary B in a country with an income tax rate of 20%. The earnings before taxes are $1 million for subsidiary A and $2 million for subsidiary B. Both subsidiaries repatriate all their earnings after taxes in the form of dividends to the Christine Corporation. The U.S. tax rate is 40%.

a. Calculate the total dividends received, U.S. taxes payable, and net benefits received by the Christine Corporation if the corporation *does not* consolidate foreign earnings.

b. Calculate the total dividends received, U.S. taxes payable, and net benefits received by the firm if the corporation *does* consolidate foreign earnings. (See footnote 9 above)

c. Which method should be used by the Christine Corporation?

**4.** The William Manufacturing Corporation conducts operations in a foreign country. The foreign operations generate $5 million annually in earnings before taxes. The foreign income tax rate is 20%. Only 60% of earnings after taxes are repatriated to William Manufacturing. The U.S. tax rate is 40%. (See footnote 10 above.)

a. Calculate the annual cash flows received, U.S. taxes payable, and the net benefit to William Manufacturing, if the foreign operations are conducted as a *branch subsidiary*.

b. Calculate the annual cash flows received, the U.S. taxes payable, and the net benefits to William Manufacturing, if the foreign operations are conducted through a *foreign corporate subsidiary*.

c. Which method of organization would you recommend to the William Manufacturing Corporation?

5. Gerhard Industries is considering the establishment of manufacturing operations in a foreign country. Gerhard will have to invest $20 million in a foreign corporate subsidiary. The foreign exchange rate is 3LC = $1. The foreign subsidiary will use the 60 million in local currency to purchase equipment. This equipment has an expected useful life of six years and no salvage value at the end of six years. The foreign subsidiary uses the straight-line method of depreciation. Sales are expected to be LC40 million, and cash expenses LC18 million every year for six years. The foreign income tax rate is 20%. The foreign subsidiary will repatriate all earnings after taxes to Gerhard Industries in the form of dividends. The foreign government requires all depreciation cash flows to be deposited in a checking account earning no return. These funds can be repatriated at the end of six years. The foreign exchange rate is expected to remain constant during the entire period. The asset-specific cost of capital that reflects the riskiness of the asset is 14%. The U.S. tax rate is 40%.

a. Calculate the change in the wealth of Gerhard's stockholders (NPV) if the project is undertaken.

b. What will be the effect on NPV (do not calculate) if the exchange rate declines over the 6-year period (i.e., to 3.5LC = $1)?

c. What will be the effect on NPV (do not calculate) if the exchange rate increases over the 6-year period (i.e., to 2.5LC = $1)?

6. The Champion Corporation is considering a foreign investment. The initial cash outlay will be $10 million. The current foreign exchange rate is 2LC = $1. Thus, the investment in foreign currency will be LC20 million. The assets acquired have a useful life of four years and no expected salvage value. The firm uses the straight-line method of depreciation. Sales are expected to be LC20 million and cash expenses LC10 million every year for four years. The foreign income tax rate is 30%. The foreign subsidiary will repatriate all earnings after taxes to Champion in the form of dividends. Furthermore, the depreciation cash flows will be repatriated during the *same year* they accrue to the foreign subsidiary. The asset-specific cost of capital that reflects the riskiness of the cash flows is 12%. The U.S. tax rate is 40%.

a. Should the Champion Corporation undertake the investment, if the foreign exchange rate is expected to remain constant during the 4-year period?

b. Should the Champion Corporation undertake the investment, if the foreign exchange rate is expected to be as follows:

| Year 0 | LC2.0 = $1 |
| Year 1 | LC2.2 = $1 |
| Year 2 | LC2.4 = $1 |
| Year 3 | LC2.6 = $1 |
| Year 4 | LC2.8 = $1 |

**SELECTED BIBLIOGRAPHY**

BAYALIS, ARTHUR E., "The Documentation Dilemma in International Trade," *Columbia Journal of World Business,* Spring 1976, 15–22.

CORNELL, BRADFORD, "Spot Rates, Forward Rates, and Exchange Market Efficiency," *Journal of Financial Economics*, August 1977, 55–66.

EITEMAN, DAVID K., and ARTHUR I. STONEHILL, *Multinational Business Finance*, 2nd ed. Reading, Mass.: Addison-Wesley, 1979.

HACKETT, JOHN T., "The Multinational Corporation and World Wide Inflation," *Financial Executive*, February 1975, 64–73.

HOWARD, FRED, "Overview of International Taxation," *Columbia Journal of World Business*, Summer 1975, 5–11.

KINDLEBERGER, CHARLES P. *International Economics*, 4th ed. Homewood Ill.: Richard D. Irwin, 1968.

MURENBEELD, MARTIN, "Economic Factors for Forecasting Foreign Exchange Rate Changes," *Columbia Journal of World Business*, Summer 1975, 81–95.

Overseas Private Investment Corporation, *An Introduction to OPIC*. Washington, D.C., 1973.

RIEHL, HEINZ, and RITA M. RODRIGUEZ, *Foreign Exchange Markets: A Guide to Foreign Currency Operations*. New York: McGraw-Hill, 1977.

RODRIGUEZ, RITA M., and E. EUGENE CARTER, *International Financial Management*, 2nd ed. Englewood Cliffs, N.J.: Prenitce-Hall, 1979.

SNIDER, DELBERT A., *Introduction to International Economics*, 6th ed. Homewood, Ill.: Richard D. Irwin, 1975.

SOLOMON, R., *The International Monetary System, 1945–1976; An Insider's View*. New York: Harper & Row, 1977.

WESTERFELD, JANICE M., "An Examination of Foreign Exchange Risk under Fixed and Floating Regimes," *Journal of International Economics*, May 1977, 181–200.

WESTON, J. FRED, and BART W. SORGE, *Guide to International Financial Management*. New York: McGraw-Hill, 1977.

————, *International Managerial Finance*. Homewood, Ill.: Richard D. Irwin, 1972.

ZENOFF, DAVID B., and JACK ZWICK, *International Financial Management*. Englewood Cliffs, N.J.: Prentice-Hall, 1969.

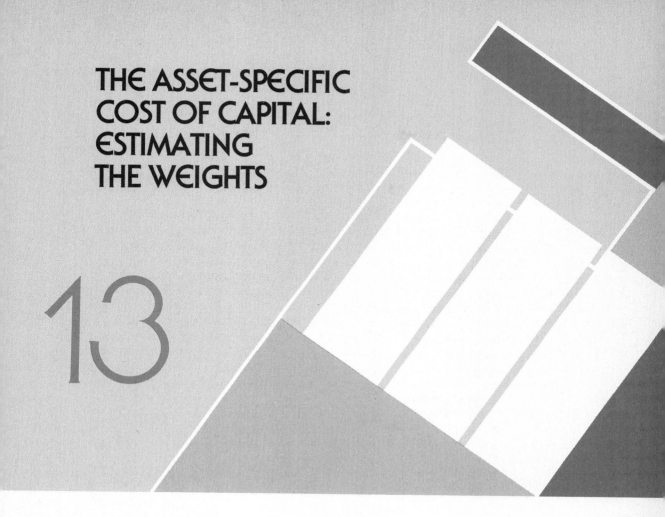

# THE ASSET-SPECIFIC COST OF CAPITAL: ESTIMATING THE WEIGHTS

## 13

## INTRODUCTION

The concept of an asset-specific cost of capital was introduced in Chapter 7 and has been integrated into many of the other chapters of the book. We have shown thus far, for example, how the cost of capital is an important consideration in evaluating the stockholder-wealth implications of the acquisition of both long- and short-term assets. Different assets are apt to have different levels of nondiversifiable risk, resulting in the establishment of different required rates of return. The fact that capital suppliers have different required rates of return for different assets tends to lead toward the establishment of a unique cost of capital for each asset, called the asset-specific cost of capital. This chapter and the next are devoted to the development of procedures for making numerical estimates of the asset-specific cost of capital.

*The asset-specific cost of capital is one of the most important concepts presented in this book.* Stockholder-wealth-maximizing decisions are dependent upon the firm's use of the asset-specific cost of capital ($k_f^*$). Unfortunately, there is a tendency to avoid its use, because it is relatively difficult to estimate. We will show in Chapters 13 and 14 that the difficulties involved in estimating $k_f^*$ are overstated. Anyone possessing a sound conceptual framework and willing to apply only a moderate amount of effort can easily estimate the asset-specific cost of capital. The reward to those that persevere in this task is the knowledge that they are using a cost of capital that truly reflects the riskiness of the assets being considered for acquisition, and armed with this knowledge, they can pursue stockholder-wealth-maximizing strategies. No other cost-of-capital concept can provide this advantage.

The asset-specific cost of capital has been defined as a weighted average of the costs associated with the different types of financing. Before we proceed with a more detailed examination of this concept, a brief review is necessary. Let us consider again the asset-specific cost of capital for the new facility being considered for acquisition by the FLO Corporation. This information was presented originally in Table 7–2, and it is duplicated here in Table 13–1.

**TABLE 13–1**

FLO CORPORATION:
Weighted-Average Cost of Capital

| Type of capital | Dollar amount | Percentage | Weight | Component cost | Product |
|---|---|---|---|---|---|
| Debt | $5,000,000 | 25% | 0.25 | $k_d^* = 8\%$ | 2% |
| Equity | $15,000,000 | 75% | 0.75 | $k_s = 16\%$ | 12% |
| Total | $20,000,000 | 100% | 1.00 | | $k_f^* = 14\%$ |
| Weighted-average cost of capital = $k_f^* = 14\%$ | | | | | |

Note that the asset-specific cost of capital ($k_f^*$) is the weighted average of the cost of debt and the cost of equity, adjusted for the tax deductibility of interest payments. It was possible to compute the asset-specific cost of capital in Chapter 7 *only because crucial information was provided in the text.* Most important, the textual material included (1) the required rate of return on equity, (2) the required rate of return on debt, (3) the corporation's marginal tax rate, and (4) information on the optimal capital structure (used to compute the weights). Of course, in the real world, such information is not readily available from textbooks. On the contrary, the estimates of the variables needed to compute the asset-specific cost of capital must be derived from the real-world financial markets. It is our purpose in this chapter to present a conceptual framework that will enable the financial manager to determine the weights used in computing the asset-specific cost of capital.

## COSTS OF CAPITAL: ASSET-SPECIFIC AND FIRMWIDE

It is usually impossible to directly compute the asset-specific cost of capital. Seldom do suppliers of capital advance funds for the purchase of specific assets. Instead, they demand required rates of return that compensate for the level of nondiversifiable risk inherent in the cash flows of the *combined assets* of the firm, rather than the risk of any single asset owned by the firm.

It is convenient to visualize the *firmwide cost of capital* as a weighted average of the asset-specific costs of capital of *all the assets owned by the firm*. For purposes of illustration, assume that a new firm, the Matto Corporation, is considering the acquisition of two assets. The first is a small, well-established supermarket chain in Texas; the other is an established national toy-manufacturing company. Matto has no existing operations at present and may acquire either, neither, or both the alternatives.

Financial information relating to the two possible asset-acquisition alternatives is presented in Table 13–2. Note that the supermarkets are considerably less risky than the toy acquisition. The lower risk is reflected in the lower required rates of return on debt and equity, as well as a lower asset-specific cost of capital. Of these two alternatives, only the acquisition of the supermarkets will increase stockholder wealth. This is reflected in the fact that the internal rate of return (IRR) of the supermarkets is greater than its asset-specific cost of capital. As discussed in Chapters 7 and 9, the acquisition of this asset would result in returns that are large enough to compensate suppliers of capital for the risk undertaken *and* provide a "surplus" to the equity suppliers. The opposite is true for the toy-acquisition

### TABLE 13–2

**MATTO CORPORATION:**
Asset-Acquisition Alternatives

|  | Supermarkets | Toy manufacturing |
|---|---|---|
| $k_s$ (cost of equity) | 16% | 21% |
| $k_d$ (required rate of return on debt) | 10% | 15% |
| $k_d^*$ (after-tax cost of debt)[a] | 6% | 9% |
| $\theta$ (optimal capital structure) | 40% | 25% |
| $k_f^*$ (asset-specific cost of capital)[b] | 12% | 18% |
| IRR (internal rate of return) | 14% | 16% |

[a]Assumes a tax rate of 40%. $k_d^* = k_d(1 - \text{Tax rate})$

[b]$k_f^* = \theta k_d^* + (1 - \theta)k_s$

alternative. The cash flows are not large enough to compensate for the risk undertaken by the suppliers of capital. This is indicated by the fact that the internal rate of return of the asset is below the asset-specific cost of capital.

The firmwide cost of capital for the Matto Corporation will depend on the particular assets that are acquired. If Matto operates as a single-asset corporation, the firmwide cost of capital ($k_w^*$) is equal to the asset-specific cost of capital ($k_f^*$), since the nondiversifiable risk of the firm is equal to the nondiversifiable risk of the single asset. If Matto operates as a multiple-asset corporation (acquires both the supermarkets and the toy company), the firmwide cost of capital ($k_w^*$) is a weighted average of the asset-specific costs of capital ($k_f^*$). The formula for computing the firmwide cost of capital is presented as equation 13–1:

$$\text{Firmwide cost of capital} = k_w^* = \frac{\Sigma \; k_{f_i}^* \times L_i}{\Sigma \; L_i} \tag{13-1}$$

where $L_i$ = the weight assigned to asset $i$

This equation indicates that $k_w^*$ is a weighted average of the asset-specific costs of capital, with the weights ($L_i$) reflecting the relative size of the asset involved.[1] In order to simplify the computations for the Matto Corporation example, we have assumed that the two assets are of equal size. As shown by the use of equation 13–1, the firmwide cost of capital ($k_w^*$) for the Matto Corporation is 15 percent if both assets are acquired. Note that this is a weighted average and does not have to equal either of the asset-specific costs of capital. This $k_w^*$ is the actual cost at which funds can be raised by the firm when both assets are acquired. Using equation 13–1:[2]

$$\text{Matto Corporation } k_w^* = \frac{12(1) + 18(1)}{1 + 1} = 15\%$$

The asset-specific ($k_f^*$), not the firmwide ($k_w^*$), is appropriate for the computation of the increase in stockholder wealth associated with the acquisition of an individual asset. For example, if the $k_w^*$ is used as the basis for evaluating the supermarket acquisition, Matto Corporation would reject this alternative (the internal rate of return for supermarkets is lower than the firmwide cost of capital) and accept the toy alternative (IRR > $k_w^*$). These are poor decisions. As we know already, the acquisition of the supermarkets would increase stockholder wealth (IRR > $k_f^*$), and the acquisition of the toy company reduce stockholder wealth (IRR < $k_f^*$).

This example allows us to visualize exactly what happens when the firmwide rather than the asset-specific cost of capital is used as the basis for making asset-acquisition decisions:

---

[1]Although the fact is not crucial for the development of the ideas included in this chapter, the student may be interested in knowing that the present values of the cash inflows should be used as the basis of determining weights.

[2]Equal weights of 1 have been assigned to each asset.

1. The cost of obtaining funds for high-risk investments ($k_f^*$) is *understated* by using the firmwide cost of capital ($k_w^*$).
2. The cost of obtaining funds to acquire low-risk investments ($k_f^*$) is *overstated* by using the firmwide cost of capital ($k_w^*$).

This discussion was designed to illustrate a very important point: that the appropriate discount rate to be used in asset-acquisition situations may be quite different from the actual cost of funds to the firm. For example, a firm acquiring new trucks may find that the market will provide funds at a rate of 12 percent. This 12 percent rate, however, reflects the riskiness of the firm's assets *in total*, not the riskiness of the specific asset (trucks). If decisions are going to be consistent with stockholder-wealth maximization, a measure of the asset-specific cost of capital ($k_f^*$) rather than of the firmwide cost of capital ($k_w^*$) is needed.

## A MATCHED-PAIR PROCEDURE FOR ESTIMATING $k_f^*$

It is one thing to state that the asset-specific cost of capital is the "correct" cost of capital to use in asset-acquisition situations, and another to estimate the value of $k_f^*$. This follows from the fact that information about capital costs is available for firms but not for specific assets. What does a business decision maker do in such circumstances? Real-world managers confront this problem all the time. Since there is no escape, they must develop substitute methodologies. If the asset-specific cost of capital cannot be measured directly, indirect measures must be developed. An indirect measurement of the asset-specific cost of capital is, after all, better than no estimate at all.

As an alternative to the direct approach, a "matched-pair" approach can be employed. This involves the identification of market-tested single assets or groups of assets with risk levels approximately equal to the risk level of the asset in question. For example, assume that the Hender Corporation is considering the acquisition of assest L and needs an estimate of the cost of capital of this specific asset. After considerable investigation, the Hender management concludes that the nondiversifiable risk of asset L is approximately equal to the nondiversifiable risk of the Tilo Corporation as a whole. That is, management perceives that the uncertainty of the cash flows associated with asset L is similar to the uncertainty of the cash flows of the Tilo Corporation. In this sense, the Hender Corporation's asset L and the Tilo Corporation become a "matched pair."

Since the Tilo Corporation is an operating business firm with capital claims currently outstanding, a market test is available. Because asset L has the same nondiversifiable risk as the Tilo Corporation, the firmwide cost of capital established by the capital market for the Tilo Corporation can be used as "equivalent" to the asset-specific cost of capital of asset L. Notice that the market-test procedure involves the estimation of a firmwide cost of capital asset-specific cost of capital ($k_j^*$). This is an indirect measurement of the asset-specific cost of capital. In each case, a specific asset is matched with an entire firm. The result is a "matched pair." Computing the cost of capital for one item in the pair provides an estimate for the other item.

The next step in estimating the asset-specific cost of capital is developing techniques for computing the firmwide cost of capital ($k_w^*$). Remember, do not confuse our interest in computing $k_w^*$ with the idea that this value is the "correct" discount rate to be used in asset-acquisition situations. Clearly, using the firmwide cost of capital as a discount rate is incorrect from a conceptual point of view. It is used only as an indirect measure of the asset-specific cost of capital. Only the use of the asset-specific cost of capital will generate decisions consistent with the objective of stockholder-wealth maximization.

Note that the emphasis is on the cost of *additional* capital raised to finance a specific asset. When a firm is used as part of a matched pair, there is some danger that the historical costs paid by such firm will be confused with the cost of new capital. Stockholder-wealth-maximization techniques as applied to asset acquisitions require that we have a measure of the current costs of capital, those being demanded by the capital market at the present time. If an asset going to increase stockholder wealth, current standards for required rates of return must be met. Our focus in this book is on the cost of capital raised at the present time; thus, both the firmwide and asset-specific cost-of-capital concepts as employed in this book are marginal-cost concepts. As used here, the asset-specific cost of capital could also have been called the marginal asset-specific cost of capital. The firmwide cost of capital could have been called the marginal firmwide cost of capital.

## ESTIMATING THE WEIGHTS FOR THE FIRMWIDE COST OF CAPITAL

In order to estimate the firmwide cost of capital ($k_w^*$), we must weight the cost of each component in accordance with its relative importance in the capital structure. The resulting firmwide cost of capital is a weighted average of the various component costs. This section will discuss the general problems and procedures involved in estimating the weights for the cost-of-capital computation.

The weights that should be used in computing the asset-specific cost of capital are those that reflect the relative use of the different types of capital in the firm's optimal capital structure. In effect, the firm is viewed as choosing the capital structure that maximizes stockholder wealth. In this way, the firm establishes "target" ratios for the use of each type of capital. For example, a firm estimates that stockholder wealth will be maximized by maintaining a debt ratio of 40 percent. This 40 percent becomes a target for the firm. Although the cash for a particular asset acquisition may be raised in any number of ways, over the long run the firm will maintain the 40 percent debt ratio. This optimal or target use of debt becomes the weight incorporated in the computation of the cost of capital.[3]

The present capital structure of a corporation is reflected in the existing relative uses of capital. In the examples used in this chapter, there are four components in the capital structure of the corporation: (1) current liabilities, (2) long-term debt, (3) preferred stock, and (4) common equity. Table 13–3 illustrates a hypothetical corporation's capital structure.

**TABLE 13–3**

### CAPITAL STRUCTURE—AN ILLUSTRATION

| Types of capital | Market value, Existing dollar amount | Capital structure (%) |
|---|---|---|
| Current liabilities | $2,000,000 | 20% |
| Long-term debt | $3,000,000 | 30% |
| Preferred stock | $1,000,000 | 10% |
| Common equity | $4,000,000 | 40% |
| Total | $10,000,000 | 100% |

The firmwide cost of capital is a measure of the firm's cost of raising capital. The actual dollar returns required by the capital suppliers will depend on two factors: (1) the planned relative use of different types of capital, and (2) the particular cost of each type of capital to be used by the firm.

An illustration will clarify this proposition. Consider the case of the Vicki Corporation. Vicki's management has decided that it will attempt to maintain an optimal balance among the various types of capital it uses. The corporation's plan is presented in Table 13–4. The relative-use data pre-

**TABLE 13–4**

### VICKI CORPORATION: PLANNED SOURCES OF NEW CAPITAL

| Type of capital | Percentage use |
|---|---|
| Current liabilities | 20% |
| Long-term debt | 40% |
| Preferred stock | 10% |
| Common equity | 30% |
| Total | 100% |

[3]See Thomas E. Copeland and J. Fred Weston, *Financial Theory and Corporate Policy* (Reading, Mass.: Addison-Wesley, 1979). pp. 279–81.

sented in this table can then be combined with the current cost data for each type of capital in order to arrive at the firmwide cost of capital. Such a computation is presented in Table 13–5.

TABLE 13–5

VICKI CORPORATION:
FIRMWIDE COST OF CAPITAL

| Type of capital (1) | Weight (%) (2) | After-tax cost[a] (3) | Weighted product (2) × (3) |
|---|---|---|---|
| Current liabilities | 0.20 | 0% | 0 |
| Long-term debt | 0.40 | 6% | 2.4% |
| Preferred stock | 0.10 | 13% | 1.3% |
| Common equity | 0.30 | 18% | 5.4% |

Weighted-average firmwide cost of capital = $k_w^* = 9.1\%$

[a]The determination of the after-tax costs for each type of capital will be discussed in Chapter 14.

Note that the firmwide cost of capital for the Vicki Corporation is 9.1 percent. This $k_w^*$ reflects current percentage uses rather than historical uses of various types of capital. For example, it is assumed that should management raise $1 million in new capital, $200,000 would be in the form of current liabilities, $400,000 in long-term debt, $100,000 in preferred stock, and $300,000 in common equity. These are actual dollar amounts and reflect current market values.

In the real world, management is faced with a very large number of possible structures of planned sources of funds. Five such possibilities are presented in Table 13–6, along with hypothetical firmwide costs of capital. Structure A illustrates a situation in which management raises all its funds in the form of common equity. Equity is relatively expensive because stockholders have no "guaranteed" return and, most important, because returns to stockholders are not deductible to the firm. Structure C represents the optimal capital structure for the firm, since the firmwide cost of capital of the Vicki Corporation is minimized at this capital structure. The lower $k_w^*$ reflects the fact that the costs of preferred stock, long-term debt, and current liabilities are lower than the cost of equity, since there is a higher "guarantee" of return on these types of funds. In addition, debt-service charges are tax-deductible to the firm. The advantage of structure C lies in the fact that it brings lower-cost sources of funds into the firm's capital structure, *without being offset by increases in the required rate of return on equity.* Structures D and E represent the situation in which "too much of a good thing is bad." In these cases, so much debt and so little equity are used that the probability of bankruptcy is increased. As the probability of bankruptcy increases, the cost of all sources of funds increases. Thus, alternatives D and E result in a higher firmwide cost of capital.

TABLE 13-6

## VICKI CORPORATION:
## FIVE POSSIBLE CAPITAL STRUCTURES

| Component | STRUCTURES | | | | |
|---|---|---|---|---|---|
| | A | B | C | D | E |
| Current liabilities | 0% | 5% | 20% | 25% | 30% |
| Long-term debt | 0% | 10% | 40% | 50% | 55% |
| Preferred stock | 0% | 10% | 10% | 10% | 10% |
| Common equity | 100% | 75% | 30% | 15% | 5% |
| Total | 100% | 100% | 100% | 100% | 100% |
| Firmwide cost of capital (assumed) | 20% | 15% | 11% | 15% | 18% |

The relationship between the capital structure of the firm and the firmwide cost of capital is summarized in Figure 13–1. This curve emphasizes three important points:

1. The firmwide cost of capital $(k_w^*)$ will be above the minimum if too high a percentage of capital is in the form of common equity (structure A).
2. The firmwide cost of capital will be above the minimum if too large a percentage of capital is obtained in the form of debt (structure E).
3. There is (somewhere) an optimal capital structure for the firm (structure C). This capital structure incorporates the various sources of funds in just the right proportion. At such a point, the firmwide cost of capital is minimized.

It should be noted that this optimal capital structure is optimal in terms of its effect on stockholder wealth. This situation is illustrated in Figure 13–2. The movement from capital structure A to C will increase stockholder

FIGURE 13-1

Vicki Corporation:
Firmwide-Cost-of-
Capital Curve

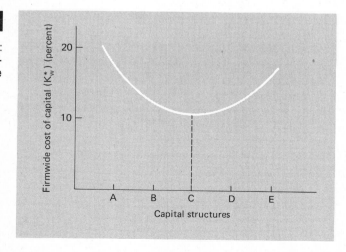

wealth because lower-cost types of financing are used in increasing amounts. As the firm moves from structure C to structure E, the advantages of lower-cost types of financing are more than offset by increased bankruptcy costs and market imperfections.[4] In this case, cost minimization *leads to* stockholder-wealth maximization, because the lower costs involved already reflect the greater financial risks to the firm and its stockholders. Note that the optimal capital structure is defined in terms of both the minimization of the firmwide cost of capital *and* the maximization of stockholder wealth.

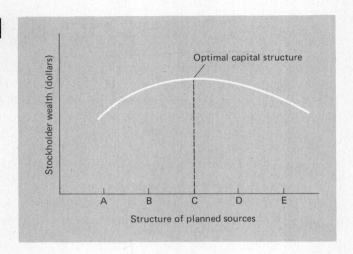

**FIGURE 13–2**

Vicki Corporation: Structure of Planned Sources of Funds and Stockholder Wealth

The firm must continuously monitor its cost of capital. Changes in component costs may lead to changes in the optimal capital structure as riskiness is altered. In addition, changing component costs will be reflected in the actual costs assigned to each component in the cost-of-capital computations. Neither financial practice nor financial theory has advanced to the point at which it is possible to specify the precise proportions to be included in the optimal capital structure. At the present time, firms are using considerable business judgment to establish the capital-structure proportions. The risk–return characteristics of alternative strategies are evaluated as to their effect on stockholder wealth. In practice, most management groups attempt to maintain a capital structure within an optimal range. That is, after reviewing its own experience and that of other firms, management attempts to maintain its capital structure within certain boundaries, as shown in Figure 13–3. The optimal range is the range of capital structures that enable the firm to capture most of the advantages of the tax deductibility of debt-service charges. Maintaining the capital structure within this optimal range will approximately maximize stockholder wealth.

When computing the cost of capital, the firm should use those weights

---

[4]See Chapters 5 and 6 for a more complete discussion of this topic.

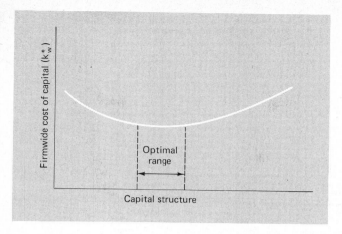

**FIGURE 13–3**

Optimal Range
of Capital Structures
for the Firm

that reflect the relative use of the different sources of capital *in the firm's optimal capital structure.* Thus, the very first thing that management must do when computing the firmwide cost of capital is to estimate the optimal capital structure for the firm under investigation.

## OPTIMAL CAPITAL STRUCTURE

### EXISTING CAPITAL STRUCTURE AS AN INDICATOR OF OPTIMAL CAPITAL STRUCTURE

In computing the firmwide cost of capital, it is often assumed that the actual current market values of the capital components represent the optimal capital structure of the firm. That is, it is assumed that the firm has already positioned itself within the optimal range. Since the firm desires to maintain this "optimality," new capital will be raised in the same proportions as current market values. Thus, quite frequently, the percentage of market value for each capital component in the existing capital structure is used as the basis for the weights in cost-of-capital computations.

The assumption of optimality of the existing capital structure must be used with caution. There is no doubt that an optimal capital structure, or an optimal range, must exist. All firms should, and well-managed firms do, attempt to achieve this optimality. These "truths" do not imply, however, that the firm's balance sheet always represents the optimal situation. Three of the more important situations in which the current market values may not indicate the optimal capital structure are outlined below:

1. *Poor management.* Management may simply be making mistakes. The stockholder-wealth implications of capital structure may be misunderstood.
2. *Changing capital-market conditions.* Capital-market conditions may have changed recently, and the firm may be currently reevaluating the relative use of various sources of capital. A rapid increase in stock price, for example, may

drive up the value of equity to a level above optimality. It may take some time for management to adjust to such a change.

3. *Changes in the risk of the firm.* New projects under consideration may alter the riskiness of the firm. Current market values will reflect the risk of the present assets of the firm. The firm should consider the capital structure as it will be *after* investments under consideration have been completed.

In summary, the estimation of the weights to be used in the cost-of-capital computations, like almost every other business decision, requires substantial judgment. The existing relative market values of capital can be used as a first estimate. However, caution is advised. The analyst should keep in mind that the weights should reflect the optimal capital structure of the firm.

Before proceeding with our discussion of the procedures to be used to compute the firmwide cost of capital, let us review:

1. The firmwide cost of capital is a weighted average of the asset-specific costs of capital of *all* the assets owned by the firm.
2. The firmwide-cost-of-capital curve is saucer-shaped, thus suggesting that there is an optimal range of capital structures that maximize stockholder wealth.[5]
3. In computing the firmwide cost of capital, it is often assumed that the firm has achieved an optimal capital structure. In such a case, the actual market weights of the capital components can be used in the computation. This procedure, however, must be used with caution.

## BOOK VALUES AND MARKET VALUES OF CAPITAL

In estimating the optimal capital structure of the firm, it is important to note that market values rather than book values of the various capital components are used. These market values give a truer picture of the amount of each component outstanding, *and a better idea of the riskiness of the firm.*

For purposes of illustration, assume that the Levatino Corporation issued bonds for $10 million one year ago. At that time, the firm agreed to pay 8 percent interest ($800,000) each year for 20 years and to repay the principal amount ($10 million) after 20 years. At the present time, interest rates are considerably higher than 8 percent. This higher interest rate reflects rapid economic growth and high levels of inflation. If the Levatino Corporation had to borrow the $10 million today instead of one year ago, the interest rate would be 12 percent per year ($1.2 million) even though the risk of the firm remained the same.

In a situation like this, the actual indebtedness of the firm is reduced. That is, there is a reduction in the number of dollars the firm would have to pay at this moment in order to discharge its debt obligation. Increased interest rates have driven down the present value of its debt. This point is

---

[5]There is some controversy surrounding this assertion. Actual empirical evidence, however, supports it. See Copeland and Weston, *Financial Theory and Corporate Policy*, p. 322.

illustrated in Table 13–7. As shown, the increasing discount rate (from 8 to 12 percent) and constant payments have resulted in a lower present value of debt. This lower present value of debt results in a lower market value of that debt.

TABLE 13–7

LEVATINO CORPORATION:
MARKET VALUE OF BONDS

A. At time of issue (prevailing rate of interest 8%):
Present value of debt = \$ Interest payment (3 Coef.$_{1-19}^{8\%}$) + (Interest + Payment of principal) (2 Coef.$_{20}^{8\%}$)
= \$800,000(9.604) + \$10,800,000(0.215) = \$10,000,000

B. One year later (prevailing rate of interest 12%):
Present value of debt = Interest (3 Coef.$_{1-18}^{12\%}$) + (Interest + Principal) (2 Coef.$_{19}^{12\%}$)
= \$800,000(7.250) + \$10,800,000(0.116) = \$7,052,800

The present market value rather than the book value of debt indicates the extent to which the firm is actually in debt, and the extent to which suppliers of capital are subject to risk. This is because the amount of a debt obligation reflects the amount that the firm must pay in order to get itself out of debt. The firm could enter the market and buy back the debt at a lower cost (\$7,052,800).[6] If, for some reason, the Levatino Corporation's debtholders refused to sell at the market price, management could simply buy an equivalent debt issue of another firm (with equivalent risk and maturity). These newly purchased bonds would become an asset that essentially offset the Levatino debt and would thus result in a net debt position of zero. Levatino could use the cash flows from such acquired bonds to pay principal and interest on their own outstanding debt.

## COMPUTING WEIGHTS—AN ILLUSTRATION

Once convinced that the firm has achieved an optimal capital structure, the analyst can compute the weights in a relatively direct manner. For example, consider the case of the Rocho Corporation, a large firm with publicly traded bonds and both preferred and common stock. The balance sheet for the Rocho Corporation is presented in Table 13–8.

The values of the capital components shown in the balance sheet are historical and in most cases do not reflect the current capital structure of the firm. The firm's optimal capital structure (which is used for determining the weights) should reflect the current rather than historical relative uses of

---

[6]This procedure assumes that there are no market imperfections, and that the purchase would not affect the market price.

TABLE 13-8

ROCHO CORPORATION:
BALANCE SHEET
(December 31, 1979)

| Assets | | Liabilities and equity | |
|---|---|---|---|
| Current assets | $5,000,000 | Current liabilities | $2,000,000 |
| Fixed assets | 6,000,000 | Bonds (8% due in 1996)[a] | 5,000,000 |
| | | Preferred stock ($100 par)[b] | 2,000,000 |
| | | Common Equity: | |
| | | Common stock ($1 par)[c] | 100,000 |
| | | Paid-in surplus | 900,000 |
| | | Retained earnings | 1,000,000 |
| Total assets | $11,000,000 | Total liabilities and equity | $11,000,000 |

[a]Current market price of each $1,000 bond = $800

[b]Current market price of preferred stock = $50 per share

[c]Current market price of common stock = $60 per share

capital. The current relative use is multiplied by the current cost of each capital component to arrive at the current firmwide cost of capital. Thus, the historical values included in the balance sheet must be adjusted to current market values.

In the Rocho Corporation example, the presence of current market-price information (footnotes in the balance sheet) permits the computation of market values:

1. The price of bonds has declined 20%. Thus, the new market value of bonds is $4 million.
2. There are 20,000 shares of preferred stock outstanding (total book value over par value). Since each share has a current market price of $50, the total market value of preferred is $1 million.
3. There are 100,000 shares of common stock outstanding (total book value over par value). Since each share is currently selling for $60, the total market value of common equity is $6 million.
4. Book values and market values for liabilities maturing in less than one year are not likely to differ significantly. Thus, the market value of current liabilities is estimated as $2 million (book value).

A summary of both the book- and market-value information for the Rocho Corporation is presented in Table 13–9. There are two very important points illustrated by the table. First, note that the market value of *total* liabilities and equity is different from the *total* book value. Book values represent historical and not current market values. As capital-market conditions change, so does the value of the liability and equity accounts. The second important point relates to the percentages of the various sources of capital. In the Rocho Corporation example, equity has a much greater weight when measured in terms of market rather than book values. In computing the firmwide cost of capital for Rocho, the percentages of total market values would be used as the basis for establishing the weight of each capital component. This procedure is based on the assumption that Rocho is in an optimal capital structure. If the firm has not achieved an optimal capital structure, adjustments must be made.

**TABLE 13–9**

ROCHO CORPORATION:
BOOK AND MARKET VALUES OF LIABILITIES AND EQUITIES

| Item | Book value | % | Market value | % |
|------|-----------|------|-------------|------|
| Current liabilities | $2,000,000 | 18.2% | $2,000,000 | 15.4% |
| Bonds | $5,000,000 | 45.5% | $4,000,000 | 30.8% |
| Preferred stock | $2,000,000 | 18.2% | $1,000,000 | 7.7% |
| Common equity | $2,000,000 | 18.2% | $6,000,000 | 46.2% |
| Total | $11,000,000 | 100.1%[a] | $13,000,000 | 100.1%[a] |

[a]Rounding error.

**SUMMARY**   The general procedure used in estimating the asset-specific cost of capital involves matching the specific asset in question with an existing firm having the same amount of nondiversifiable risk. The next step is to compute the cost of capital for the firm $(k_w^*)$ and use this firmwide cost of capital as an estimate of the asset-specific cost of capital.

The weights used in the cost-of-capital computation should reflect the relative uses of the different types of capital in the firm's optimal capital structure. In computing the weights, book values of capital are converted to market values, since the market values give a better indication of the true amounts of the various types of capital currently employed by the firm. In effect, the weights used in computing the firmwide cost of capital are the proportions of the market values of the various types of capital.

It is most important to recognize that although the firmwide cost of capital $(k_w^*)$ is computed, our real interest is in developing an asset-specific cost of capital $(k_f^*)$. The firmwide cost of capital is computed only if it is considered as the other half of a "matched pair" with the asset-specific cost of capital. The firmwide cost of capital is used as an estimator of the asset-specific cost of capital. To be consistent with stockholder-wealth maximization, asset-acquisition decisions must employ the asset-specific cost of capital.

**QUESTIONS FOR DISCUSSION**

1. How does the asset-specific cost of capital $(k_f^*)$ differ from the firmwide cost of capital $(k_w^*)$?
2. Why is the firm apt to make poor decisions if the firmwide cost of capital is

used as the discount rate when computing the net present value for a specific asset?

3. Why is it difficult to make direct estimates of the asset-specific cost of capital? What alternatives are open to the firm?

4. Why is the optimal capital structure used as the basis for establishing weights when computing the firmwide cost of capital?

5. What is meant by a firm's optimal capital structure, and how does it relate to stockholder wealth?

6. Is the firm always within the optimal range of capital structures? Why, or why not?

7. What business judgments are involved in computing the weights used in estimating the firmwide cost of capital?

8. What is the appropriate procedure to be used in the risk-pairing technique for estimating the asset-specific cost of capital?

9. Describe the "matched-pair procedure" for estimating the asset-specific cost of capital.

10. Why is the market value of debt superior to the book value of debt in indicating the extent to which a firm has debt outstanding?

**PROBLEMS**

1. The Gerhard Manufacturing Corporation wants to compute its firmwide cost of capital. The firm's optimal debt ratio ($\theta$) is 0.3. The required rate of return of the bondholders is 8%. The required rate of return of the stockholders is 15%. Gerhard's marginal tax rate is 40%. Calculate the firmwide cost of capital of Gerhard Manufacturing.

2. The AnnCa Corporation wants to estimate its firmwide cost of capital. The optimal debt ratio ($\theta$) of the AnnCa Corporation is 0.6. The required rate of return of the bondholders is 10%. The required rate of return of the stockholders is 16%. The marginal tax rate applicable to the AnnCa Corporation is 40%. Compute AnnCa's firmwide cost of capital.

3. The Gerhard Manufacturing Corporation is planning an asset acquisition. After extensive evaluation, management concludes that the riskiness of the asset is similar to that of the AnnCa Corporation. The pertinent information for the Gerhard Corporation is presented in problem 1, and for the AnnCa Corporation in problem 2. Determine the asset-specific cost of capital that should be used to evaluate the proposed asset acquisition.

4. The current capital structure of the Zanadu Supplies Corporation is as follows:

| | |
|---|---|
| Current liabilities[a] | $50 million |
| Long-term debt (8% due in 1996)[b] | $100 million |
| Preferred stock (par value = $100)[c] | $50 million |
| Common stock (par value = $10)[d] | $300 million |
| Retained earnings | $100 million |

[a]The current market value of current liabilities is $50 million.
[b]Long-term bonds have a par value of $1,000. The current market value of long-term bonds is $800.
[c]The current market price of preferred stock is $80 per share.
[d]The current market price of common stock is $12 per share.

a. Calculate the weights of the various components of the capital structure of Zanadu Supplies if book values are used.

b. Calculate the weights of the various components of the capital structure of Zanadu Supplies if market values are used.

c. Which of these measures of capital structure should be used to compute the firmwide cost of capital of Zanadu? Explain.

5. The current capital structure of the Denbo Corporation is as follows:

| | |
|---|---|
| Current liabilities[a] | $100,000 |
| Long-term debt (10% due in 1990)[b] | $900,000 |
| Preferred stock (par value = $100)[c] | $500,000 |
| Common stock (par value = $10)[d] | $300,000 |
| Retained earnings | $500,000 |
| | $2,300,000 |

[a]The market value of current liabilities is $100,000.

[b]Each long-term bond has a par value of $1,000 and a current market price of $851.

[c]The current market price of preferred stock is $80 per share.

[d]The current market price of common stock is $50 per share. There are 30,000 shares outstanding at the present time.

a. Calculate the weights of the various components of the capital structure of the Denbo Corporation.

b. Calculate the firmwide cost of capital of the Denbo Corporation, given:

| | |
|---|---|
| Before-tax cost of current liabilities | 8% |
| Before-tax cost of long-term debt | 12% |
| Cost of preferred stock | 13% |
| Cost of equity | 15% |
| Marginal tax rate | 40% |

6. Christie's Pet Stores has five possible capital-structure alternatives. The firm's marginal tax rate is 40%. The required rates of return of debt and equity at various debt ratios are as follows:

| Capital Structure | Debt Ratio | $k_d$ | $k_s$ |
|---|---|---|---|
| A | 0.0 | 10% | 14% |
| B | 0.2 | 12% | 15% |
| C | 0.4 | 14% | 19% |
| D | 0.6 | 18% | 26% |
| E | 0.8 | 24% | 30% |

Calculate the firmwide cost of capital for Christie's Pet Stores for each of the possible capital structures.

**SELECTED BIBLIOGRAPHY**

ARDITTI, FRED D., and HAIM LEVY, "The Weighted Average Cost of Capital as a Cutoff Rate: A Critical Analysis of the Classical Textbook Weighted Average," *Financial Management*, 6 (Fall 1977), 24–34.

BERANEK, WILLIAM, "Some New Capital Budgeting Theorems," *Journal of Financial and Quantitative Analysis*, 13 (December 1978), 809–24.

BOUDREAUX, KENNETH J., and HUGH W. LONG, *The Basic Theory of Corporate Finance.* Englewood Cliffs, N.J.: Prentice-Hall, 1977.

COPELAND, THOMAS E., and J. FRED WESTON, *Financial Theory and Corporate Policy*, Reading, Mass.: Addison-Wesley, 1979.

DONALDSON, GORDON, *Corporate Debt Capacity*. Boston: Division of Research, Harvard Business School, 1961.

———, "New Framework for Corporate Debt Capacity," *Harvard Business Review*, 40 (March–April 1962), 117–31.

HAUGEN, ROBERT A., and LEMMA W. SENBERT, "The Irrelevance of Bankruptcy Costs to the Theory of Optimal Capital Structure," *Journal of Finance*, 33 (June 1978), 383–94.

SCHALL, LAWRENCE D., "Firm Financial Structure and Investment," *Journal of Financial and Quantitative Analysis*, 6 (June 1971), 925–42.

SCOTT, JAMES H., JR., "Bankruptcy, Secured Debt, and Optimal Capital Structure," *Journal of Finance*, 32 (March 1977), 1–20.

SHARPE, WILLIAM F., "Capital Asset Prices: A Theory of Market Equilibrium," *Journal of Finance*, 19 (September 1964), 425–42.

VAN HORNE, JAMES C., *Financial Management and Policy*, 5th ed. Englewood Cliffs, N.J.: Prentice-Hall, 1980.

WESTON, J. FRED, "Investment Decisions Using the Capital Asset Pricing Model," *Financial Management*, 1 (Spring 1973), 25–33.

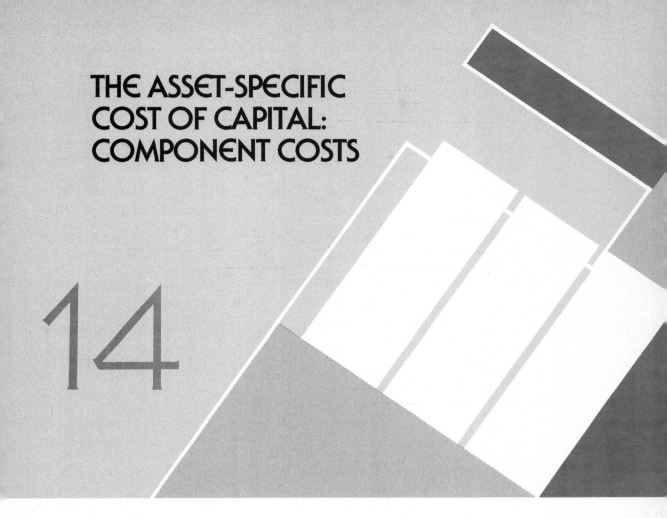

# THE ASSET-SPECIFIC COST OF CAPITAL: COMPONENT COSTS

## 14

## INTRODUCTION

In order to estimate the firmwide cost of capital, it is necessary to estimate the cost of each component in the capital structure. These components are (1) current liabilities, (2) long-term debt, (3) preferred stock, and (4) common equity. The procedures used are different for each capital component, and they require judgment by the analyst.

The cost of common equity is by far the most difficult of the components to estimate. The final estimate of the cost of equity should be based upon more than one estimating procedure; therefore, the procedure recommended involves the use of four different methodologies.

The next sections of the chapter describe various techniques for the estimation of the various sources of capital. These costs will be multiplied by the weights in the optimal capital structure. The final result will be a weighted-average firmwide cost of capital $(k_w^*)$, which is then used as an estimator of the asset-specific cost of capital $(k_j^*)$.

## COST OF CURRENT LIABILITIES

Under certain conditions, a large portion of the current liabilities of the firm can be considered "free." Accounts payable, for example, usually represent "free" capital to the firm as long as the firm takes all available discounts.[1] Other "free" sources of short-term capital to the firm are accrued wages, accrued taxes, advance billings, and the like. Under usual conditions, the firm has no interest payments associated with these types of financing. Current liabilities such as bank loans or the current portion of long-term debt do have interest charges and thus cannot be considered "free" to the firm. But usually, the "nonfree" portion of current liabilities constitutes only a small proportion of the total, unless interest-bearing current liabilities are very important, or the firm is failing to take discounts on accounts payable or is paying penalties on accruals. In such cases, an estimate of the costs of current liabilities must be made.

*After-tax basis*

*

It is important to remember that the cost-of-capital computations include costs after taxes. Thus, if the interest rate on bank loans is 10 percent and the firm is paying taxes at a marginal tax rate of 46 percent, the after-tax cost of interest to the firm is only 5.4 percent.[2] Similarly, when the firm fails to take discounts, it is in effect borrowing at a positive rate. This rate, which is usually expressed in before-tax terms, must be converted to an after-tax basis. Thus, if the before-tax cost of not taking the discount is 20 percent, the after-tax cost to the firm is 10.8 percent, assuming a marginal tax rate of 46 percent. The cost-of-capital computations always consider financing costs on an after-tax basis.

## COST OF LONG-TERM DEBT

Information about the current cost of long-term debt to individual firms is available from several sources. If the corporation already has publicly traded debt outstanding, the capital market itself will provide the required rate of return of the debtholders. These data can be adjusted for taxes and other

---

[1]Current liabilities are discussed in greater detail in Chapter 16.
[2]After-tax cost = Before-tax cost × (1 − Tax rate). See Chapter 5 for a more detailed explanation.

YTM

factors in order to estimate the cost of long-term debt to the firm. The yield to maturity on outstanding bonds is commonly used as an estimate of the market's current required rate of return on the corporation's bonds.[3]

For example, assume that the New Paltz Corporation issued a series of bonds four years ago. At that time, the bonds had a maturity of 14 years and carried a coupon interest rate of 8 percent. Each bond was originally sold at a price of $1,000 and had a promised interest payment of $80 annually, but increases in the overall level of interest rates has led to a decline in the price of the bond. At the present time, each bond has a market price of $774. This means that the buyer of the bond is entitled to receive $80 a year for ten more years and, at the end of ten years, the $1,000 face value of the bond (representing a $226 appreciation in value). The yield to maturity of this bond is 12 percent.[4] This yield to maturity indicates the required rate of return by the capital market for the existing bonds of the New Paltz Corporation. If the corporation plans to sell new bonds, those bonds would have substantially the same risk as the old ones. Thus, the yield to maturity of existing bonds is an excellent indicator of the required rate of return on new bonds.[5] The cost of long-term debt for the New Paltz Corporation, assuming a tax rate of 46 percent, is 6.48 percent. This amount is equal to the required rate of return on the bonds, times 1 minus the marginal tax rate of the firm [12% × (1 − 0.46)].

The use of the existing-bond methodology to establish the cost to the firm of issuing new long-term debt is limited by the fact that relatively few firms have publicly traded bonds.[6] The estimation of the cost of long-term debt when bonds are not publicly traded can be done in one of two ways. First, it may be possible to identify publicly traded bonds of other firms that have similar risk characteristics to those of the firm. Second, management can consult capital-market specialists (investment bankers, commercial bankers, and so on) who can give an estimate of the rate of return that will probably be demanded by the market for the long-term debt of the firm. In all cases, however, the required rate of return must be converted to an after-tax cost of debt to the firm.

---

[3]The computational procedure used to determine the yield to maturity of long-term bonds is discussed in Chapter 3.

[4]Present value = Annual interest(3 Coef.$_{10}^?$) + Maturity value(2 Coef.$_{10}^?$)

$$\$774 = \$80(3\ Coef._{10}^?) + \$1,000(2\ Coef._{10}^?)$$

Using Tables 3-2 and 3-3, you will find that the coefficients at 12% will generate the desired equality:

$$\$774 = \$80\ (5.650) + \$1,000(0.322) = \$774$$

Thus, the yield to maturity of the existing bonds is 12%.

[5]The fact that the appreciation in the bond price is taxed differently from interest payments tends to make the yield-to-maturity method less than a perfect estimate of the required rate of return on new bonds. Furthermore, additional factors such as call provisions will affect the yield to maturity. These factors will be discussed in Chapter 17.

[6]A more detailed explanation of the bond market is provided in Chapter 17.

## COST OF PREFERRED STOCK

The procedures used to estimate the cost of preferred stock are similar to those used to estimate the cost of debt. If the firm has preferred stock outstanding, the yield on that stock may be used as an estimate of the yield on new preferred stock. Consider the case of the Warwick Corporation, which issued preferred stock 20 years ago at a price of $100 (equal to the par value). At the time it was issued, the stock paid a constant annual dividend of $6 per share. Owing to general increases in interest rates, the stock has become unattractive at a price of $100 per share, and the price has declined to $60 per share. Since this preferred stock has no maturity (is a perpetuity), it is a relatively simple task to compute the current required rate of return of preferred stockholders as 10 percent ($6/$60).[7] This in effect says that under present market conditions, a preferred stock with an annual dividend of $6 will bring a price of only $60. Thus, if the firm wished to sell new preferred stock at a price of $100 (par value), the capital market would require an annual dividend of $10 (10 percent) to compensate the preferred stockholders for the risk undertaken. In the case of preferred stock, the required rate of return is equal to the cost to the firm. No tax adjustment is required, since dividends paid on preferred stock are not a tax-deductible expense to the firm. Preferred dividends are paid out of the after-tax earnings.

The use of the existing-preferred-stock methodology is limited, in that relatively few firms use this mean of long-term financing, and many issues of preferred stock are not publicly traded.[8] Just as in the case of bonds, the alternatives open to management wishing to estimate the cost of preferred stock under such conditions revolve around the identification of comparable firms or consultation with capital-market specialists.

## COST OF COMMON EQUITY

### FORECAST OF DIVIDENDS (PROCEDURE I)

The cost of common equity is relatively difficult to estimate. The difficulty stems from the fact that stockholders' expectations of dollar returns are unknown. For example, the buyer of a bond has expectations of receiving contractually specified interest and principal payments. These expected dollar returns to bondholders can be compared to the current market price of the bonds, and a yield to maturity estimated. This procedure is not applicable to common equity because, although the price of the common stock is known, dividends expected by the stockholders are unknown.

Of course, it is possible to make a forecast of future dividends of

---

[7]See equation 2–5, in Chapter 2.
[8]See Chapter 18 for a more detailed discussion of preferred stock.

common stock. This forecast-of-dividends approach utilizes the concepts associated with the determination of the price of common stock, discussed in Chapter 2. As noted, the price of common stock can be thought of as equal to the present value of the expected future dividends discounted at the required rate of return of the stockholders. Thus, the price of common stock can be expressed mathematically as follows:[9]

$$\text{Price of common stock} = \sum_{i=1}^{\infty} \frac{D_i}{(1 + k_s)^i}$$

(14-1)

If dividends are expected to remain constant, equation 14-1 can be simplified to:

$$\text{Price of common stock} = \frac{D}{k_s}$$

(14-2)

Equation 14-2 can be changed to:

$$k_s = \frac{D}{P}$$

(14-3)

Equation 14-3 can be used for estimating the required rate of return of common stocks, *if dividends are expected to remain constant.*

The forecast-of-dividends approach for estimating the required rate of return of the stockholders is to estimate the expected constant dividend and incorporate it, along with the known stock price, into equation 14-3. For example, the expected annual dividend of the common stock of the Roscoe Corporation is $6 per share. This dividend is expected to remain constant into the distant future. If Roscoe's common stock is currently selling for $30 per share, the required rate of return on the common stock can be estimated as follows:

$$k_s = \frac{D}{P} = \frac{\$6}{\$30} = 0.2 \text{ or } 20\%$$

In cases where dividends will not remain constant, it is possible to incorporate the probability of growth in dividends into the conceptual framework. If future dividends are expected to grow at a constant annual rate of g, the market price of common stock can be estimated by equation 2-9.

$$P = \frac{D_1}{k_s - g}$$

(2-9)

which can be modified as follows:

$$k_s = \frac{D_1}{P} + g$$

(14-4)

---

[9]This equation is identical to equation 2-6.

In equation 14–4, $D_1$ is the dividend expected one year from now, and g represents the expected growth rate of the dividends of the firm. For instance, assume that the dividend expected next year for the Lewisburg Corporation is $2.40, and that this dividend is expected to increase at a constant growth rate of 2 percent per year. If the price of common stock is $20, the required rate of return of the stockholders can be computed as follows:[10]

$$k_s = \frac{D_1}{P} + g = \frac{\$2.40}{\$20.00} + 0.02 = 0.14 \text{ or } 14\%$$

The key to the use of equations 14–3 and 14–4 for making realistic estimates of $k_s$ lies in management's ability to estimate capital-market expectations of the future dividends of the firm. The records of past dividends provide limited assistance in predicting either future dividends or their expected growth rate. The future is not simply an extension of the past. As illustrated in Table 14–1, dividend patterns can be quite erratic. Some corporations have stable dividends, some have increasing or decreasing dividends, and some do not pay dividends at all.

TABLE 14–1

FIVE-YEAR DIVIDEND RECORDS OF ACTUAL CORPORATIONS

| Year | Uniroyal | Westinghouse | Oscar Meyer | Texas Intl. Airlines | Crane Co. |
|------|----------|--------------|-------------|----------------------|-----------|
| 1973 | $0.70 | $0.972 | $0.43 | 0 | $0.44 |
| 1974 | $0.70 | $0.972 | $0.51 | 0 | $0.66 |
| 1975 | $0.65 | $0.972 | $0.63 | 0 | $0.96 |
| 1976 | $0.50 | $0.972 | $0.67 | 0 | $1.18 |
| 1977 | $0.50 | $0.972 | $0.825 | 0 | $1.30 |

Source: Corporate annual reports.

The proper use of the forecast-of-dividends approach requires that we keep in mind *exactly* what is being estimated. We are trying to duplicate the logic applied by the capital market in establishing the required rate of return on common equity. As you can see, this is a difficult task requiring considerable business experience and judgment. The forecast-of-dividends approach does provide some important insights into the required rate of return of common equity. But this procedure should be augmented and revised with alternative methods of estimating the required rate of return of the stockholders.

---

[10]The limitations of the equation are discussed in greater detail in Chapter 2.

# HISTORICAL RATES OF RETURN (PROCEDURE II)

Another procedure used to estimate the required rate of return on common equity is known as the historical-rate-of-return approach. It involves the computation of the actual rates of return on common stock of the firm during the recent past. It then assumes that the required rate of return of common equity will be equal to the historical average. For purposes of illustration, consider the returns to the stockholders of the Theummes Corporation, shown in Table 14–2. Note that this approach incorporates price changes as well as dividends received into the rate of return of the stockholders. Computed on an annual basis, the rate of return associated with the stock over the five-year period ranged from a negative 10 percent to a positive 30 percent. The average rate of return over the five years is 10 percent. The historical rate of return may be used as a guide for estimating the capital market's expected rate of return for stocks of similar risk.

## TABLE 14–2

THEUMMES CORPORATION:
ANNUAL RATES OF RETURN OF COMMON STOCK

| Year | Price at beginning of the year | Price at end of the year | Change in price | Annual dividend | Total dollar return[a] | Annual rate of return[b] |
|------|------|------|------|------|------|------|
| 1973 | $26 | $30 | $4 | $1 | $5 | 19% |
| 1974 | $30 | $31 | $1 | $1 | $2 | 7% |
| 1975 | $31 | $27 | ($4) | $1 | ($3) | (10%) |
| 1976 | $27 | $27 | 0 | $1 | $1 | 4% |
| 1977 | $27 | $34 | $7 | $1 | $8 | 30% |

[a]The total dollar return equals the change in market price during the year *plus* dividends received during the year.

[b]Annual rate of return equals the total dollar return dividend by the price at the beginning of the year.

Just as in the case of every procedure we have discussed and will discuss in the following pages, the historical-rate-of-return approach must be accompanied by sound business judgment; it cannot be applied automatically. The past performance of the firm may not reflect the future of the firm. Business conditions may change, and thus expectations based upon historical data may be incorrect.[11] The analyst must adjust historical data in order to accommodate potential future changes and their effect on the future returns to the stockholders of the firm.

---

[11]There is an additional problem associated with measuring the historical rate of return. The computed historical rate of return will vary with the time period employed.

# SECURITY-MARKET LINE (PROCEDURE III)

A third procedure used for estimating the required rate of return of common equity ($k_s$) involves the application of our knowledge of the security-market line. This approach has the advantage of incorporating current market perceptions of the riskiness of the firm into the estimate of the required rate of return of equity. In order to understand this approach, a review of several principles is needed.

A security-market line is presented in Figure 14–1. The nondiversifiable risk of both debt and equity are indicated as $\beta_d$ and $\beta_s$. As discussed in an earlier chapter, the nondiversifiable risk of debt is always lower than that of equity. As the riskiness of the firm increases, both $\beta_d$ and $\beta_s$ increase. The difference (risk premium) between the required rates of return for different levels of nondiversifiable risk of debt and equity will remain relatively constant.[12]

To illustrate, consider the information on the Ritat Corporation presented in Table 14–3. Using this information plus an estimate of the required rate of return of debt ($k_d$), it is possible to estimate the required rate of return of common stock. These estimates are based upon the historical observation that the risk premium (extra return required by the stockholder when compared to the bondholder of the same firm) ranges between four and

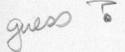

**TABLE 14–3**

RITAT CORPORATION:
CHANGES IN NONDIVERSIFIABLE RISK AND CHANGES IN THE REQUIRED RATE OF RETURN

| Nondiversifiable-risk situation | Required rate of return of stockholder $k_s$ | Required rate of return of bond $k_d$ | Risk premium $k_s - k_d$ |
|---|---|---|---|
| Original level of risk | 16% ($\beta_s$) | 11% ($\beta_d$) | 5% |
| New level of Risk | 18% ($\beta_s'$) | 13% ($\beta_d'$) | 5% |

---

[12]For example, the difference between the required rate of return of equity and the required rate of return of debt can be expressed as follows:

$$\text{Risk premium} = k_s - k_d$$
$$= RFR + (k_m - RFR)\beta_s - [RFR + (k_m - RFR)\beta_d]$$
$$= (k_m - RFR)\beta_s - (k_m - RFR)\beta_d = (k_m - RFR)(\beta_s - \beta_d)$$

If the level of nondiversifiable risk changes, the mathematical expression of the risk premium will change to:

$$\text{Risk premium} = (k_m - RFR)(\beta_s' - \beta_d')$$

Thus, we assume that $(\beta_s - \beta_d) = (\beta_s' - \beta_d')$.

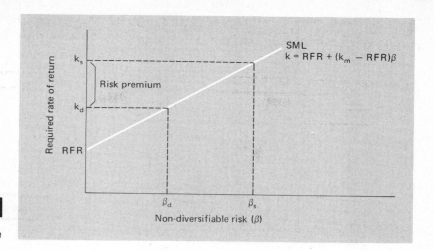

FIGURE 14–1

Security-Market Line

six percentage points.[13] A range of estimates of actual companies is shown in Table 14–4.

Note that this procedure provides a range of estimates rather than a point estimate. This is due to the fact that each of these bonds has unique characteristics that affect their respective yields to maturity. The major attractiveness of this approach is that current market information is incorporated into the procedure. That is, the market has established required rates of return for bonds that incorporate all currently available information to the market about the firm's level of nondiversifiable risk, the risk-free rate

TABLE 14–4

ESTIMATES OF REQUIRED RATES OF RETURN ON COMMON STOCK:
AN SML APPROACH FOR SELECTED CORPORATIONS

| Corporation | Current market interest on long-term debt $(k_d)^a$ | Risk premium $(k_s - k_d)$ | Range of Estimates of $k_s$ |
|---|---|---|---|
| American Telephone & Telegraph | 9.2% | 4 to 6% | 13.2–15.2% |
| Westinghouse | 9.6% | 4 to 6% | 13.6–15.6% |
| Crane Company | 10.8% | 4 to 6% | 14.8–16.8% |
| Texas Intl. Airlines | 11.8% | 4 to 6% | 15.8–17.8% |
| Fedders Corporation | 12.8% | 4 to 6% | 16.8–18.8% |
| Food Fair Stores | 15.4% | 4 to 6% | 19.4–21.4% |

[a]Data reflect market conditions as of December 1978 on outstanding bonds due to mature in 1992 or later.

---

[13]See Lawrence D. Schall and Charles W. Haley, *Introduction to Financial Management* (New York: McGraw-Hill, 1979), p. 191. It should also be noted that the variability within this 4%-to-6% range is probably related to the firm's nondiversifiable risk and the amount of debt employed by the particular firm.

of return, and so on. This current market informations on bonds, combined with the historical risk premium of common stocks, will help us arrive at an estimate of the market's required rate of return of common stock. Neither the forecast-of-dividends nor the historical-rate-of-return approach includes information about the capital market's current perceptions of the firm's level of risk.

## A STATISTICAL APPROACH (PROCEDURE IV)

It is possible to use a more direct procedure for estimating the required rate of return of common equity. Such an approach involves the use of statistical techniques to estimate the intercept and the slope of the security-market line. These estimates provide information on the risk-free rate of return and the price of additional increments of risk demanded by the market. In addition, an estimate of the level of nondiversifiable risk ($\beta$) of the common stock is made. With this information, the required rate of return of a specific common stock can be estimated.

A simplified procedure for making such estimates is presented in Appendix 14A. Note, however, that the estimates of the SML and the nondiversifiable risk of the stock made in the appendix are based on historical data. The application of this procedure to current market conditions must be based on good business judgment. That is, even though the procedures are statistical in nature, there is a substantial amount of judgment underlying the selection of the statistics.

## RECOMMENDATIONS FOR ESTIMATING THE COST OF COMMON EQUITY

Estimates of the cost of equity should begin with the security-market-line approach (procedure III). This will narrow the range of estimates. Adjustments within this range should be made using the forecast-of-earnings and historical-rates-of-return approaches. If possible, the statistical approach outlined in Appendix 14A should also be used to estimate the cost of common equity. The use of the security-market-line approach as the starting point for the final estimate places the *current* market perceptions of the riskiness of the firm at the forefront of the analysis. Since no one method is completely satisfactory, however, several estimating procedures should be used. We will illustrate in a later section of this chapter.

## EFFECT OF FLOTATION COSTS

When the firm issues bonds, preferred stock, or common stock to the public, it normally incurs flotation costs. For example, if General Motors plans to issue a $100-million bond issue to the public, it would enter into a contract with an investment banker in order to facilitate the sale of the bonds. The investment banker (or group of investment bankers) typically acquires the bonds from General Motors and proceeds to sell them to the general public.[14] This procedure involves considerable expense, which must be born by General Motors, and thus increases the cost of capital to the firm.

Here is an example. Assume that the required rate of return of the long-term bonds issued by the Anton Corporation is 8.4 percent, and that the flotation costs paid to the investment banker on each of the $1,000 bonds sold to the public is 9.8 percent. The interest will be paid annually and the bonds will mature in ten years. Under these conditions, the actual cost to the firm is 10 percent, even though the required rate of return of the bondholders is only 8.4 percent. This discrepancy results from the fact that the suppliers of debt capital advance $1,000 to the firm and expect to be compensated on the entire amount, but the firm receives only $902 (even though it must pay interest on the entire $1,000). The difference of $98 is the cost of flotation and covers the cost and profit of the investment banker. This situation is summarized in Table 14–5.

TABLE 14–5

ANTON CORPORATION:
COST OF HYPOTHETICAL LONG-TERM DEBT ISSUE TO THE PUBLIC

| | |
|---|---|
| Price of the bond | $1,000 |
| Required rate of return of the bondholders ($k_d$) | 8.4% |
| Required annual $ return of bondholders (Price $\times k_d$) | $84 |
| Dollar flotation cost (Price $\times$ Flotation cost) | $98 |
| Net proceeds of each bond to the firm (Price $-$ Flotation cost) | $902 |
| Before-tax cost to the firm of debt capital | 10%[a] |

[a]This percentage cost is arrived at by a procedure similar to that used to estimate the yield to maturity of bonds. We know that the present value of the bonds to the firm is $902. The firm must make annual interest payments of $84 for 10 years plus repayment of the principal of $1,000 in year 10. The true cost to the firm is obtained by estimating the discount rate that equates the present value of the outflows with the $902 cash inflow. This is accomplished on a trial-and-error basis similar to the computation of the IRR. For this example, the percentage cost is 10%.
$902 = $84(3 \text{ Coef.}_{.10}^{?}) + $1,000(2 \text{ Coef.}_{.10}^{?})$
For 10%: $84(6.145) + $1,000(0.386) = $902

Thus, when the firm sells bonds to the public and incurs flotation costs, the cost of debt to the firm increases. This is also true when the firm issues new common or preferred stock, but in these cases, it is easier to adjust for flotation costs, because the capital claims have no maturity date. For example, assume that the Anton Corporation can sell new common stock at $100 per share with a flotation cost of $10 (10 percent) per share. Also assume that the required rate of return on Anton's equity is 15 percent. In this case, the percentage cost to the firm is 16.7 percent. The computational

[14]See Chapter 15 for a more detailed discussion of flotation costs and the role of the investment banker.

procedures used to arrive at that cost to the firm are shown in Table 14–6. The same procedure can be used to estimate the flotation costs to the firm of new issues of preferred stock.

**TABLE 14–6**

ANTON CORPORATION:
COST OF HYPOTHETICAL COMMON-STOCK ISSUE TO THE PUBLIC

| | |
|---|---|
| Price of common stock | $100 |
| Required rate of return of the stockholders ($k_S$) | 15% |
| Required annual $ return of stockholders (Price $\times$ $k_S$) | $15 |
| Dollar flotation costs | $10 |
| Net proceeds per share to the firm (Price − Flotation costs) | $90 |
| Percentage cost to the firm of funds raised by the sale of common stock to the public[a] | 16.7% |

$$^a\text{Cost} = \frac{\text{Expected dollar cost}}{\text{Net proceeds}} = \frac{\$15}{\$90} = 0.167 = 16.7\%$$

$$\text{or Cost} = \frac{\text{Required rate of return}}{1 - \text{Flotation cost}} = \frac{0.15}{1 - 0.10} = 0.167 = 16.7\%$$

In many cases, the firm need not incur flotation costs. Many bond issues are direct placements. Direct placement is the sale of the entire issue directly to one buyer—say, a large insurance company, or a pension fund. In such cases, flotation costs are zero or extremely small. New common stock may also be sold with little or no flotation costs. Many firms, for example, give existing stockholders the right to purchase additional common stock directly from the firm at prevailing market prices. This procedure minimizes the stockholders' brokerage fees as well as reducing the flotation costs to the firm.

American corporations raise most of their new equity by retaining earnings rather than through the sale of new common stock. One advantage of retained earnings is that the firm eliminates flotation costs. Thus, the cost of retained earnings is equal to the required rate of return of the stockholders ($k_s$). The cost of selling new equity is equal to $k_s$ adjusted for flotation costs.

$$\text{Cost of retained earnings} = k_s$$

$$\text{Cost of new equity to the firm} = \frac{k_s}{1 - \text{Flotation costs}} \qquad (14\text{-}5)$$

There is an important implication of having two different costs for equity funds, which can best be understood through an example. Assume that the Anton Corporation plans to raise $10 million in equity funds. If the entire increase in equity comes from retained earnings, the cost to the firm will be 15 percent ($k_s$). If the entire increase in equity comes from the sale of new common stock and the flotation cost is 10 percent, the cost will be 16.7 percent, as illustrated in Table 14–6. If the increase in equity comes from both sources, the cost will be equal to a weighted average of the two costs.

# ESTIMATING THE ASSET-SPECIFIC COST OF CAPITAL

The entire procedure for estimating the asset-specific cost of capital is based upon the assumption that we have a clear understanding of risk and can measure the *relative* riskiness of assets and firms. First, let us review the meaning of risk. As noted in Chapter 4, risk refers to the uncertainty associated with expected future cash flows. Assets or groups of assets (firms) with substantial variability in expected future cash flows are more risky than those with relatively little expected variability. As also noted in Chapter 4, riskiness is also affected by the correlation of the specific asset's cash flows with the cash flows of the market in general. The effect of diversification on the riskiness of portfolios will depend on how closely the cash flows of a particular asset are correlated with the market's cash flows. Highly correlated cash flows mean that the effect of diversification on the portfolio will be small (nondiversifiable risk is high). Low or negative correlation means that the nondiversifiable risk will be relatively low.

In practice, it is very difficult to directly measure the riskiness of the expected cash flows of a particular asset. For example, a firm planning the construction of a new factory may have no direct historical experience that will yield estimates of either the expected future variability of cash flows or the correlation of the cash flows with those of the market. The inability to directly measure the riskiness of specific assets has led to the adoption of the technique called "matched pairing," which was discussed briefly in Chapter 13.

The "matched-pair technique," to reiterate, involves the identification of a firm with risk characteristics similar to those of the asset in question. The procedure can be described as follows:

1. Gather information about the cash flows of the specific asset and the market portfolio.
2. Gather information about the cash flows of a number of different corporations with publicly traded securities.
3. Have a management group (or a group of investors) identify that firm whose riskiness is closest to the riskiness of the asset under consideration. This firm then becomes the other half of the "matched pair."
4. The firmwide cost of capital ($k_w^*$) for the publicly traded firm is computed and is then used as a measure of the asset-specific cost of capital ($k_f^*$).

The "matched-pair technique" duplicates the logic of the market, as long as management or the panel of investors has evaluated risk in a fashion similar to that of the market as a whole. An absolute measure of the risk is not required. Thus, the firmwide cost of capital of the publicly traded firm can then be used as a proxy for the asset-specific cost of capital. The difficulty lies in choosing a publicly traded firm with similar risk characteristics to those of the asset.

## AN INTEGRATED EXAMPLE

The Marlboro Corporation manufactures electronic equipment. The firm, founded in 1949, now has a diversified product line that includes electronic components, measuring devices, television and radio transmission equipment, and other electronic equipment used by the armed forces. Marlboro is currently considering entry into the subscription television field. The company has the patents and technical competence to build TV descramblers that can be rented to those consumers wishing to subscribe to the Marlboro service and installed in their television sets.

One alternative open to Marlboro's management is to construct a new factory that will be used to assemble descramblers.[15] The financial data for this alternative are presented in Table 14–7. Note that the construction of the factory will require a cash outlay today. There will be cash inflows over a 20-year period. For simplification, we have assumed that the factory will be worthless at the end of 20 years.

### TABLE 14–7

MARLBORO DESCRAMBLER FACTORY:
AFTER-TAX FINANCIAL DATA

| Year | After-tax cash flows | |
| --- | --- | --- |
| 0 | ($20 million) | Outflow |
| 1–20 | $ 3 million | Annual inflows |

Management recognizes that the expected cash flows are not known with certainty. The subscription television industry has some risks that may be different from those of the Marlboro Corporation. Management does not, however, know exactly the level of risk of the proposed project. Accordingly, the appropriate rate at which to discount the expected future cash flows for this particular asset is unknown.

The financial management personnel at Marlboro decide to "pair" the riskiness of the descrambler factory with the riskiness of one of five firms for which a firmwide cost of capital can be computed. The five firms selected are these:

1. The Highland Mills Corporation. This company manufactures woven fabrics used in the fashion trade.
2. The Milton Radio Corporation. This company manufactures citizens'-band radios for the wholesale market.

---

[15]The firm may have, of course, other alternatives to building a new factory. These other alternatives should also be considered, as described in Chapter 10. We will discuss only one potential alternative here.

3. **The Hudson Markets Corporation.** This company owns over 800 supermarkets located throughout the United States.
4. **The Great Eastern Utility Corporation.** This company supplies gas and electric services in the northeastern United States.
5. **The Marlboro Corporation.** Management has decided to evaluate the riskiness of the project relative to the existing risk of the firm itself.

Management proceeds to collect financial and operating data about each of these possible "pair" firms—such information as expected sales, costs, income, competition, technological change, and the like.

Management must now decide which of these five corporations has risks similar to those involved in the descrambler-factory project. A panel of investors or others may assist in this task. There is no fixed format to follow. Management is trying to estimate how the market as a whole would evaluate the riskiness of the proposed project.

Let us assume that those consulted arrive at a rough consensus that the risks of the descrambler factory are comparable to those of the Milton Radio Corporation. Note that this panel has rejected the notion that the riskiness of the project is similar to that of the Marlboro Corporation. Thus, in this case, the Marlboro Corporation is not used as the basis for estimating the asset-specific cost of capital ($k_f^*$) for the descrambler factory. For other potential asset acquisitions, the situation may differ. Other assets may have risk levels similar to that of Marlboro, or any of the other three firms.

The next step involves the computation of the firmwide cost of capital for the Milton Radio Corporation, whose current balance sheet is presented in Table 14–8. After a thorough analysis of the financial situation of Milton Radio, Marlboro's management concludes that current market values of

**TABLE 14–8**

### THE MILTON RADIO CORPORATION: BALANCE SHEET, December 31, 1979

| Assets | | Liabilities and equity | |
|---|---|---|---|
| Current assets | $4,000,000 | Accounts payable | $1,000,000 |
| | | Bank loans (10%) | 1,000,000 |
| | | Current liabilities | $2,000,000 |
| Net fixed assets | 6,000,000 | Long-term debt (8%) | |
| | | (maturing in 1989) | 4,000,000 |
| | | Preferred stock (issued in 1951; 10,000 shares) | 1,000,000 |
| | | Common stock (100,000 shares) | 1,000,000 |
| | | Retained earnings | 2,000,000 |
| | | Total equity | $3,000,000 |
| Total assets | $10,000,000 | Total liabilities and equities | $10,000,000 |

liabilities and equity are approximately optimal for an investment of such a risk level. Thus, Marlboro's management decides to use the existing market values of capital as the basis for computing the weights to be used in cost-of-capital conputations. The current market values and relative weights are presented in Table 14–9.

TABLE 14–9

THE MILTON RADIO CORPORATION:
MARKET VALUES AND COST OF CAPITAL WEIGHTS,
December 31

| Capital type | Book value | Market value | Weights |
|---|---|---|---|
| Accounts payable | $1,000,000 | $1,000,000 | 9% |
| Bank loans | $1,000,000 | $1,000,000 | 9% |
| Long-term debt[a] | $4,000,000 | $3,096,000 | 29% |
| Preferred stock[b] | $1,000,000 | $ 500,000 | 5% |
| Common stock[c] | $3,000,000 | $5,000,000 | 47% |
| Total | $10,000,000 | $10,596,000 | 99% (rounding error) |

[a]Bonds originally issued at $1,000 par value are now selling for $774. Market value = Book value × 0.774 = $3,096,000.

[b]Preferred stock is currently selling for $50 per share. Market value = $50 × 10,000 shares = $500,000.

[c]Common stock is currently selling for $50 per share. Market value = $50 × 100,000 shares = $5,000,000.

Thus, we have obtained the relative weights of the various types of capital used by the Milton Radio Corporation. In order to determine the firmwide cost of capital of Milton, we must obtain the after-tax cost of each of the various types of capital. Such a determination would be as follows:

**Cost of Accounts Payable**  It is assumed that the Milton Radio Corporation is taking all discounts on accounts payable. Thus, the cost of accounts payable is zero.

**Cost of Bank Loans**  The interest rate paid on bank loans is 10 percent. The after-tax cost of bank loans equals 10%(1 − Tax rate) = 5.4% (assuming that the Milton Radio Corporation is paying taxes at a marginal tax rate of 46 percent).

**Cost of Long-Term Debt**  The yield to maturity on existing long-term debt can be used as a measure of the current required rate of return on long-term debt. In this case, the yield to maturity is equal to 12 percent.

$$\$774 = \$80 \ (3 \ \text{Coef.}_{.10}^{?}) + \$1,000 \ (2 \ \text{Coef.}_{.10}^{?})$$

$$= \$80(5.650) + \$1,000(0.322) = \$774$$

The cost of debt to the firm equals the required rate of return of the debtholders, multiplied by (1 − Tax rate), or 12%(1 − 0.46) = 6.48%.

The dividend paid on preferred stock is $7 per share. Given a current market price of $50, the required rate of return of preferred stockholders would be 14 percent ($7/$50). The cost to the firm is exactly the same as the required rate of return, because preferred dividends are not tax-deductible.

**Cost of Equity**  The cost of equity will be estimated in three ways. We will assume that there are no flotation costs. Basic data for computing the cost of equity using the forecast-dividends and the average-rate-of-return approaches are presented in Table 14–10. Note that each of the three methods used suggests a cost of debt around 17 to 18 percent (a consistency that is not always present). We will make a business judgment and estimate the cost of equity at 18 percent.

TABLE 14–10

THE MILTON RADIO CORPORATION:
STOCK-PRICE AND DIVIDEND INFORMATION

| Year | Beginning price ($) | Closing price ($) | Change in price ($) | Dividend ($) | Total return ($) | Annual rate of return |
|------|---------|---------|---------|---------|---------|---------|
| 1976 | 29 | 32 | 3 | 1 | 4 | 14% |
| 1977 | 32 | 41 | 9 | 2 | 11 | 34% |
| 1978 | 41 | 43 | 2 | 3 | 5 | 12% |
| 1979 | 43 | 47 | 4 | 3 | 7 | 16% |
| 1980 | 47 | 50 | 3 | 1 | 4 | 9% |

1. *Security-Market Line.* The cost of equity can be computed by adding 4 to 6 percentage points to the required rate of return on debt. The required rate of return on debt has already been computed at 12 percent. Thus, using this approach, the cost of equity should be between 16 and 18 percent.

2. *Historical Rate of Return.* The average rate of return over the five-year period was 17 percent.

3. *Forecast Dividend.* Dividends have been growing at a phenomenal rate over the five-year period. However, that growth has slowed down in recent years. We will assume that the annual dividend in 1981 will be $4 per share and that the dividends will grow at a rate of 10 percent thereafter. This is a business judgment that must be made by the financial personnel in the Marlboro Corporation. The cost of equity using this approach is computed as follows:

$$k_s = \frac{D_1}{P} + g = \frac{4}{50} + .10 = 0.18 = 18\%$$

4. *Final Estimate.* We will make our final estimate of the cost of equity at 18 percent. This is at the high end of the range suggested by the security-market-line approach and is consistent with the high cost figures suggested by the forecast-of-dividends and historical-rates-of-return approaches.

The computation of the $k_w^*$ for the Milton Radio Corporation is presented in Table 14–11. This estimate is based upon weights derived from Milton's current capital structure and is based upon the assumption that Milton has an optimal capital structure.

TABLE 14–11

THE MILTON RADIO CORPORATION:
FIRMWIDE COST OF CAPITAL

| Capital source | After-tax cost | Weight | Product |
|---|---|---|---|
| Accounts payable | 0 | .09 | 0 |
| Bank loans | 5.4% | .09 | 0.49% |
| Long-term debt | 6.48% | .29 | 1.88% |
| Preferred stock | 14.0% | .05 | 0.7% |
| Common stock | 18.0% | .47 | 8.46% |
| | | | $k_w^* = 11.53\%$ |

The management of the Marlboro Corporation is now in a position to evaluate the effect of the descrambler factory on stockholder wealth. Using the estimate of Milton Radio's firmwide cost of capital, Marlboro management estimates the asset-specific cost of capital for the descrambler factory at 12 percent.[16] This indirect estimate of $k_f^*$ reflects the fact that the descrambler factory and Milton Radio are believed to possess approximately the same amount of nondiversifiable risk. With this newly estimated $k_f^*$, we can now compute the net present value for the project. As is shown, the factory has a positive effect on stockholder wealth.

$$\text{Net present value} = \text{PV inflows} - \text{PV outflows}$$

$$= 3,000,000(3 \text{ Coef.}_{20}^{12\%}) - \$20,000,000$$

$$= \$5,542,000$$

That is, after all required payments are made to capital supplies (based on the asset's risk), there will be a "surplus" available to the equity suppliers. The present value of this surplus (NPV) is equal to $5,542,000. Thus, management should proceed with the descrambler factory.

## ASSET-SPECIFIC COST OF CAPITAL IN SMALLER BUSINESSES

The procedures used to estimate the asset-specific cost of capital in smaller businesses are essentially the same as those for larger businesses. Management should use a match-pairing technique. That is, the specific asset must

---

[16]The 11.53% was rounded to 12%.

be paired with a firm for which a firmwide cost of capital can be estimated. The matching of the pair is a business judgment and is based upon the expected uncertainty in cash flows. It is not necessary for the firm used in the pairing to be small. All that is required is that the nondiversifiable risk be equal.[17]

## A RISK-GROUP-SPECIFIC COST OF CAPITAL

In actual corporate practice, it may be too time-consuming to compute a new asset-specific cost of capital for each possible asset acquisition. In order to simplify asset-acquisition decisions, management frequently classifies possible asset acquisitions by the amount of risk inherent in each asset. For example, a corporation may classify possible asset acquisitions in the following manner:

1. *Low Risk*: New assets replacing existing assets
2. *Intermediate Risk*: New assets needed to expand existing lines of business
3. *High Risk*: New assets needed to enter new lines of business

Management then proceeds to compute a risk-group-specific cost of capital for each risk category using the same "matched-pair" technique discussed earlier. That is, management will identify a firm with the same nondiversifiable risk as a particular group of assets. A firmwide cost of capital will be computed for each "matched-pair" firm. The risk-group-specific cost of capital will be estimated on the basis of the firmwide cost of capital of the matched pair. Finally, the risk-group-specific cost of capital will be used as an estimator of the asset-specific cost of capital for all assets falling within the risk group. The relationship among the various cost-of-capital concepts is summarized in Figure 14–2. Note that all assets within each class are assumed to have the same nondiversifiable risk and the same asset-specific cost of capital.

**FIGURE 14–2**

Costs of Capital:
Asset-Specific,
Group-Specific, and
Firmwide

One frequently used system for classifying assets is based upon a firm's divisions. That is, a firm may assume that all the assets within a division have the same risk and thus use the division risk group as an estimator of the asset-specific cost of capital for all assets acquired by that division. For example, assume that the Logan Corporation has three divisions: (1) lumber production, (2) trucking, and (3) paper production. The firm would compute

---

[17]There is no need for the small firm acquiring the asset to compute its own cost of capital.

a group-specific cost of capital for each division, using a matched-pair technique. This group-specific cost of capital would then be used to evaluate all asset acquisitions of the particular division. That is, it is assumed that all assets within the division have the same risk and asset-specific cost of capital.

The appropriateness and correctness of group-specific cost of capital would depend on the homogeneity of assets within each risk group. Group-specific costs of capital will not yield reliable estimates of changes in stockholder wealth when there are substantial differences in the nondiversifiable risk among the assets in each class. Although decisions relative to the appropriateness of group-specific cost of capital must be made on a case-by-case basis, there is a general intuitive feeling that the larger the group or division, the less appropriate it is to use it as a basis for a risk class. Risk classes should include a relatively narrow range of risk and relatively few assets.

**SUMMARY**  It is extremely important to remember that the asset-specific cost of capital must be used when evaluating the attractiveness of asset-acquisition alternatives. Only when this figure is used will the effect of the acquisition on stockholder wealth be properly estimated.

Since it is difficult to make direct estimates of $k_j^*$, an indirect method is employed. This method involves pairing a specific asset with a firm having the same risk and computing a firmwide cost of capital ($k_w^*$), which is then used as an indirect measure of $k_j^*$. Weights derived from the optimal capital structure of the risk-paired firm are used in computing the firmwide cost of capital. The cost of the capital components should reflect current market rather than historical costs.

The cost of equity is particularly difficult to estimate. The recommended method involves the use of several different procedures: (1) forecast of dividends, (2) historical rates of return, (3) the security-market line, and (4) statistical.

The estimating procedure for the asset-specific cost of capital is not mechanical; the final estimate reflects a number of necessary business judgments. But whatever the problems involved, a good estimate of $k_j^*$ is needed for good business decision making.

**QUESTIONS FOR DISCUSSION**

1. What business judgments are involved in the procedures used to compute the cost of (a) current liabilities, (b) long-term debt, and (c) preferred stock?
2. What is the major problem associated with the computation of the cost of common equity?
3. Why are several different procedures used to compute the cost of common equity?
4. Why is the yield to maturity of existing bonds of a corporation less than a

perfect estimate of the required rate of return on new bonds for the same corporation?

5. How can management estimate the cost of long-term debt when the matched-pair firm has no publicly traded debt outstanding?

6. Explain the shortcomings of the forecast-of-dividends approach (procedure I) for estimating the cost of equity.

7. Why is it important that the historical-rate-of-return approach to estimating the cost of common equity (procedure II) be used within the context of sound business judgment?

8. The security-market-line approach to estimating the cost of equity (procedure III) is the only approach that includes information about the capital market's *current* perceptions of the firm's current level of risk. Explain.

9. How do flotation costs affect the cost of capital?

10. Explain how the "matched-pairs" technique for estimating the asset-specific cost of capital operates. What are the advantages and difficulties of this approach?

11. Explain how a risk-group-specific cost of capital is employed. Describe the advantages and disadvantages of this approach.

**PROBLEMS**

1. The Americal Corporation obtains short-term financing from two sources: (1) a $5-million commercial bank loan with an annual interest cost of 10%, and (2) $10 million in "free" trade credit. The firm's marginal tax rate is 40%.
   a. Calculate the after-tax cost of the bank loan to Americal.
   b. Calculate the after-tax cost of the trade credit to Americal.
   c. Calculate the weighted-average after-tax cost of short-term debt financing to Americal.

2. The Los Angeles Daily News has $10 million in long-term debt outstanding. Each of these bonds has a par value of $1,000, a coupon interest rate of 6% paid annually, and a maturity of 20 years. Each bond has a current market price of $725.68. The firm's marginal tax rate is 40%.
   a. Calculate the required rate of return of the bondholders.
   b. Calculate the after-tax cost of long-term debt for the Daily News.

3. The MMB Corporation has $50 million in long-term debt outstanding. Each of these bonds has a par value of $1,000, a coupon interest rate of 12% paid annually, and a maturity of ten years. Each has a current market price of $1,123.40. The firm's marginal tax rate is 40%.
   a. Calculate the required rate of return of the bondholders.
   b. Calculate the after-tax cost of long-term debt for the MMB Corporation.

4. National Motors Corporation has preferred stock outstanding. The par value of the preferred stock is $100, and the annual dividend paid is $8 per share. The current market price of the preferred stock is $80 per share. The firm's marginal tax rate is 40%.
   a. Calculate the required rate of return of the preferred stockholders.
   b. Calculate the after-tax cost of preferred stock to National Motors.

5. The current dividend ($D_o$) on the common stock of the Christine Corporation is $5 per share. The current market price is $50.

a. Calculate the cost of retained earnings to Christine Corporation if dividends are expected to remain constant in the foreseeable future.

b. Calculate the cost of retained earnings to Christine Corporation if dividends are expected to grow at a 5% annual rate for the foreseeable future.

c. Calculate the cost of *new* equity in parts *a* and *b*, if the flotation costs are 10% of the market price of each share of common stock.

6. The William Corporation's price and dividend history are shown below:

| Year | Price at beginning of the year | Price at end of the year | Annual dividend |
|------|------|------|------|
| 1976 | $50 | $55 | $7 |
| 1977 | $55 | $68 | $10 |
| 1978 | $68 | $60 | $6 |
| 1979 | $60 | $70 | $8 |
| 1980 | $70 | $80 | $10 |

Calculate the historical rate of return of equity for the William Corporation.

7. With the information provided in problem 2, calculate the cost of common equity for the Los Angeles Daily News, using the security-market-line approach.

8. With the information provided in problem 3, calculate the cost of common equity for the MMB Corporation, using the security-market-line approach.

9. The Jackson Corporation wants to compute its firmwide cost of capital. The present capital structure (assumed optimal) of the corporation is as follows:

Book values

| | | |
|---|---|---|
| Current liabilities[a] | $5 million | 5,000 000 |
| Long-term bonds ($1,000 par value)[b] | $10 million | 8,776,000 |
| Common equity ($5 par value)[c] | $15 million | 30,000,000 |
| Retained earnings | $10 million | |
| | | 43,776,000 |

[a]The cost of current liabilities is zero, and the market value is $5 million.

[b]The long-term bonds have a current market value of $877.60, a coupon interest rate of 8%, and a maturity of 10 years.

[c]The current market price of common stock is $10 per share.

The Jackson Corporation has a marginal tax rate of 40%. The expected dividend on common stock next year ($D_1$) is $1 per share. Dividends are expected to grow at a constant annual rate of 5% for the foreseeable future. There is no flotation cost for either bonds or equity.

a. Calculate the after-tax cost of debt of the Jackson Corporation.

b. Calculate the cost of equity to the Jackson Corporation, using:

    i. The forecast-of-dividends approach

risk premium—ii. The security-market-line approach

c. Calculate the firmwide cost of capital of the Jackson Corporation. Use the forecast-of-dividends approach in your estimate of the cost of equity.

10. The Norman Corporation wants to compute its firmwide cost of capital. The present capital structure (assumed optimal) of the firm is as follows:

|                                          | Book values    |
|------------------------------------------|----------------|
| Current liabilities[a]                   | $10 million    |
| Long-term bonds ($1,000 par value)[b]    | $10 million    |
| Common equity ($10 par value)[c]         | $20 million    |
| Retained earnings                        | $10 million    |

[a]The cost of current liabilities is 8% before taxes, and the market value is $10 million.

[b]The long-term bonds have a current market value of $935.44, a coupon interest rate of 8%, and a maturity of 10 years.

[c]The current market price of common stock is $12 per share.

The Norman Corporation has a marginal tax rate of 40%. The expected dividend on common stock next year ($D_1$) is $1.20 per share. Dividends are expected to grow at a constant annual rate of 4% for the foreseeable future. There is no flotation cost for either bonds or equity.

a. Calculate the after-tax cost of debt to the Norman Corporation.
b. Calculate the cost of equity to the Norman Corporation, using:
   i. The forecast-of-dividends approach
   ii. The security-market-line approach
c. Calculate the firmwide cost of capital of the Norman Corporation. Use the forecast-of-dividends approach in your estimate of the cost of equity.

11. The Norman Corporation is considering the acquisition of a printing press. The correlation coefficient between the expected cash flows of the printing press and the cash flows of the Jackson Corporation (problem 9) is +0.97. The correlation coefficient between the expected cash flows of the printing press and the Norman Corporation (problem 10) is +0.46. The acquisition of the printing press will result in a cash outflow ($t = 0$) of $1 million. The periodic expected cash inflows are $200,000 for years 1 to 10.

   Should the Norman Corporation acquire the printing press? Show the increase in the wealth of Norman's stockholders if the asset is acquired. (*Note:* You may want to round the asset-specific cost of capital to the nearest percentage in the table.)

12. The Dallas Corporation issues a new 10-year bond. The bonds have a par value of $1,000 and pay an annual interest rate of 10%. The flotation cost is 11.3%. Thus, the firm receives for each bond sold only $887. Calculate the before-tax cost to the Dallas Corporation of issuing these bonds.

# APPENDIX 14A
## Using the SML to Estimate Common-stock Rate of Return

The security-market line can be used to estimate the required rate of return of common stock. Remember that the SML is a summary view of the capital market's attitude toward risk.[18] An SML is presented in Figure 14A–1.

---

[18]A review of Chapter 4 may be helpful at this point.

The intercept of the vertical axis represents the risk-free rate of return (RFR). The horizontal axis represents the level of nondiversifiable risk ($\beta$). The beta of the returns for the portfolio composed of all risky securities in the market is 1.0. The general equation representing the SML was expressed as follows:

$$k = RFR + (k_m - RFR)\beta \qquad (4\text{-}4)$$

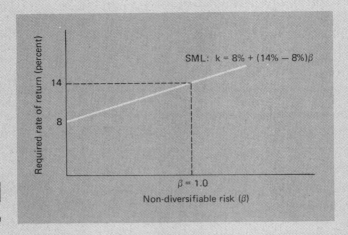

Security-Market Line

Equation 4–4 can be expressed in a different manner, as equation 14A–1. The risk premium will vary among common stocks depending upon the amount of nondiversifiable risk ($\beta$) associated with each.

$$\text{Required rate of return} = k = RFR + \text{Risk premium} \qquad (14A\text{-}1)$$

Stocks with a high level of nondiversifiable risk will have a high risk premium, and vice versa. The risk premium is computed by multiplying the risk premium of the market portfolio ($k_m - RFR$) by the level of nondiversifiable risk of a particular stock. Thus, the risk premium (RP) can be expressed as follows:

$$RP = (k_m - RFR)\beta \qquad (14A\text{-}2)$$

In order to compute the slope of the SML, two points are needed. The two points used most often are, first, the point representing the relationship between zero nondiversifiable risk ($\beta = 0$) and the corresponding rate of return. This is the vertical axis intercept and is called the risk-free rate of return (RFR). Since the rate on U.S. Treasury bills is used as equivalent to the RFR, it is quite easy to obtain. For example, it is reported daily in *The Wall Street Journal*.

The second point is more difficult to estimate. What we need is a security or group of securities for which the level of nondiversifiable risk and the rate of return are both known. It is possible to obtain measures of the rates of return for individual securities, but it is impossible to measure *directly* the amount of nondiversifiable risk. Thus, in deriving a "real-world" SML, a portfolio consisting of all risky securities in the market (market portfolio) is used. Since the market portfolio is, by definition, completely diversified, only nondiversifiable risk remains. In deriving the second point needed to estimate the slope of the SML, an estimate of the rate of return of the market portfolio is used. A beta of 1.0 is assigned as the level of nondiversifiable risk of the market portfolio.

Thus, the information needed to estimate the slope of the SML is (1) the risk-free rate of return (RFR), and (2) the rate of return of the market portfolio ($k_m$). Since the level of nondiversifiable risk is defined as follows:

$$\beta = r_{s,m} \frac{\sigma_s}{\sigma_m}$$

(4-5)

the correlation between the market portfolio and itself is +1.0 (perfect correlation). Thus, the $\beta$ for the market portfolio would be 1.0.

Table 14A–1 shows the hypothetical returns of a portfolio composed of *all* risky securities in the market. This return is equal to 14.5 percent. Let us assume that the risk-free rate is 8 percent. With this information, the SML can be obtained, as illustrated in Figure 14A–2. Note that there have been two points plotted in the graph: First, the RFR is 8 percent, and the $\beta$ of this return is 0; second, the required rate of return of the market portfolio ($k_m$) is 14.5 percent, and the $\beta$ of this return is 1.0. The final step is to draw a straight line between these two points, thus obtaining the SML.

Now all that is required in order to use the SML to estimate the required rate of return of a particular common stock is the level of nondiversifiable risk ($\beta$) of the stock. As discussed in Chapter 4, the appropriate measure of the nondiversifiable risk of an individual security is beta. $\beta$ is computed as follows:

**FIGURE 14A–2**

Security-Market Line

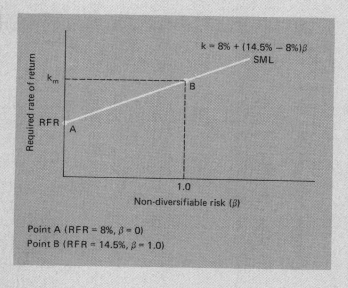

Point A (RFR = 8%, $\beta$ = 0)
Point B (RFR = 14.5%, $\beta$ = 1.0)

CHAP. 14 The Asset-Specific Cost of Capital: Component Costs

## RETURN AND STANDARD DEVIATION OF THE MARKET PORTFOLIO

| Quarter | | Annualized Rate of Return of the Market Portfolio $(k_m)^a$ | $(k_m)^2$ |
|---|---|---|---|
| 1976 | 1st | 14% | 196 |
| | 2nd | 10% | 100 |
| | 3rd | 16% | 256 |
| | 4th | 17% | 289 |
| 1977 | 1st | 12% | 144 |
| | 2nd | 15% | 225 |
| | 3rd | 14% | 196 |
| | 4th | 18% | 324 |
| Totals | | 116 | 1,730 |

Average return during the two-year period $= \dfrac{116}{8} = 14.5\%$

Standard deviation of the Returns of the market portfolio $= \sigma_s = \sqrt{\dfrac{\Sigma(k_m)^2 - \dfrac{(\Sigma k_m)^2}{n}}{n-1}}$

$= \sqrt{\dfrac{1,730 - \dfrac{(116)^2}{8}}{7}} = 2.62\%$

[a]The annualized return of the market portfolio would be equal to:

$$4 \times \frac{\left(\begin{array}{l}\text{Price of the market} \\ \text{portfolio at the end} \\ \text{of the quarter}\end{array} - \begin{array}{l}\text{Price of the market} \\ \text{portfolio at the beginning} \\ \text{of the quarter}\end{array}\right) + \begin{array}{l}\text{Dividends} \\ \text{received during} \\ \text{the quarter}\end{array}}{\begin{array}{l}\text{Price of the market portfolio} \\ \text{at the beginning of the quarter}\end{array}}$$

We have used simple numbers in order to ease calculations. The annual return of the market portfolio can, of course, be negative in any given quarter. The methodology, however, will not be affected by the complexity of the numbers used. Most practitioners use the Standard & Poor's Index as a proxy for the market portfolio.

$$\beta = r_{s,m} \frac{\sigma_s}{\sigma_m}$$

Thus, we must compute three values: (1) the correlation between the returns of the security and the returns of the market portfolio $(r_{s,m})$, (2) the standard deviation of the returns of the security $(\sigma_s)$, and (3) the standard deviation of the returns of the market portfolio $(\sigma_m)$.

Table 14A–2 shows the percentage returns realized on a hypothetical common stock. Using a similar mathematical methodology to that discussed in Appendix 4A, we compute the standard deviation of the returns of this hypothetical common stock ($\sigma_s$) 3.82 percent. The information on the returns of the market portfolio was presented in Table 14A–1. By means of the same statistical techniques, we found the standard deviation of the returns of the market portfolio to be 2.62 percent, as shown in Table 14A–1.

RETURN AND STANDARD DEVIATION
OF HYPOTHETICAL COMMON STOCK

| Quarter | | Annualized Rate of Return of the Common Stock ($k_s$) | $(k_s)^2$ |
|---|---|---|---|
| 1976 | 1st | 15.2% | 231 |
| | 2nd | 12.1% | 146 |
| | 3rd | 18.4% | 339 |
| | 4th | 20.1% | 404 |
| 1977 | 1st | 10.4% | 108 |
| | 2nd | 17.8% | 317 |
| | 3rd | 12.2% | 149 |
| | 4th | 19.9% | 396 |
| Totals | | 126.1 | 2,090 |

Standard deviation of the returns of the common stock $= \sigma_s =$

$$\sqrt{\dfrac{\Sigma(k_s)^2 - \dfrac{(\Sigma k_s)^2}{n}}{n-1}}$$

$$= \sqrt{\dfrac{2{,}090 - \dfrac{(126.1)^2}{8}}{7}} = 3.82\%$$

The next step is to compute the correlation coefficient between the returns of the stock and the market portfolio. The computation of the correlation coefficient is shown in Table 14A–3.[19] The correlation coefficient of the return is equal to +0.89. Thus we have all the necessary information needed to compute the $\beta$ of the stock. Using equation 4–5, the $\beta$ of our hypothetical stock would be:

$$\beta = r_{s,m} \frac{\sigma_s}{\sigma_m} = 0.89 \times \frac{3.82}{2.62} = 1.3$$

The required rate of return of stockholders can be estimated in one of two ways. First, using Figure 14A–2, we can observe that a security with a beta of 1.3 will have a required rate of return of approximately 16.5 percent.

[19]The statistical technique used to compute the correlation coefficient was discussed in Appendix 4A.

### CORRELATION COEFFICIENT BETWEEN THE RETURNS
### OF THE MARKET PORTFOLIO
### AND THE HYPOTHETICAL COMMON STOCK

| Observation | | $k_s$ | $k_m$ | $(k_s)^2$ | $(k_m)^2$ | $(k_s)(k_m)$ |
|---|---|---|---|---|---|---|
| 1976 | 1st | 15.2 | 14 | 231 | 196 | 213 |
| | 2nd | 12.1 | 10 | 146 | 100 | 121 |
| | 3rd | 18.4 | 16 | 339 | 256 | 294 |
| | 4th | 20.1 | 17 | 404 | 289 | 342 |
| 1977 | 1st | 10.4 | 12 | 108 | 144 | 125 |
| | 2nd | 17.8 | 15 | 317 | 225 | 267 |
| | 3rd | 12.2 | 14 | 149 | 196 | 171 |
| | 4th | 19.9 | 18 | 396 | 324 | 358 |
| Totals | | 126.1 | 116 | 2,090 | 1,730 | 1,891 |

$$\text{Correlation coefficient} = r_{s,m} = \frac{n\Sigma k_s k_m - (\Sigma k_s)(\Sigma k_m)}{\sqrt{n(\Sigma k_s^2) - (\Sigma k_s)^2}\ \sqrt{n(\Sigma k_m^2) - (\Sigma k_m)^2}}$$

$$= \frac{(8 \times 1,891) - (126.1 \times 116)}{\sqrt{(8 \times 2,090) - (126.1)^2}\ \sqrt{(8 \times 1,730) - (116)^2}}$$

$$= \frac{15,128 - 14,628}{\sqrt{16,720 - 15,901}\ \sqrt{13,840 - 13,456}} = \frac{500}{\sqrt{314,496}}$$

$$= \frac{500}{560.8} = +0.89$$

Second, we can use equation 4–4 to compute the value of $k_s$ mathematically, as follows:

$$k = RFR + (k_m - RFR)\beta$$

$$k_s = 8\% + (14.5\% - 8\%)1.3$$

$$= 8\% + 8.45 = 16.45$$

The entire computational procedure can be summarized as follows:

- *Step I.* Estimate the risk-free rate of return (RFR) using information readily available in the financial news.
- *Step II.* Estimate the average rate of return of the market portfolio ($k_m$). Standard and Poor's indexes of common stocks may be used as a proxy for the market portfolio. The computational procedures are outlined in Table 14A–1.

- *Step III.* Develop a security-market line. Two points can be used to draw the graph. One point will be the RFR with a β of 0, and the other point the $k_m$ and a β of 1.0. Mathematically, the equation would be:

$$k = RFR + (k_m - RFR)\beta$$

- *Step IV.* Estimate the level of nondiversifiable risk (β) for the stock in question. You must obtain three variables: (1) the standard deviation of the returns of the stock ($\sigma_s$), as shown in Table 14A–2; (2) the standard deviation of the returns of the market portfolio ($\sigma_m$), as shown in Table 14A–1; and (3) the correlation between the return of the stock and the market portfolio ($r_{s,m}$), as shown in Table 14A–3. Once you have obtained these three variables, the β of the stock can be computed as follows:

$$\beta = r_{s,m} \frac{\sigma_s}{\sigma_m}$$

- *Step V.* Using the graph or the equation developed in Step III and the β obtained in Step IV, calculate the required rate of return of the stockholders.

## SOME CONCEPTUAL PROBLEMS

The procedures outlined in this appendix constitute a useful and convenient method for estimating the required rate of return for stocks. But the emphasis here is on the word *estimating*. The procedure does not represent a direct measure of the capital market's required rate of return. An understanding of the difference between the true and estimated required rates of return is essential for the proper application of the technique.

The true required rate of return will reflect the capital market's estimated current risk-free rate, current slope of the SML, expected future variability of returns on stocks, and expected future correlations between individual stocks and the market portfolio. In our computational procedure, we use historical rather than current and future data. This situation is summarized in Table 14A–4.

---

TABLE 14A–4

DATA DIFFERENCES IN COMPUTING TRUE AND ESTIMATED REQUIRED RATES OF RETURN

| Data required for measurement of true rate of return | Data included in computation of estimated rate of return |
|---|---|
| 1a. Current risk-free rate | 1b. Current risk-free rate |
| 2a. Current slope of SML | 2b. Slope based upon historical data |
| 3a. Future $\sigma_s$ and $\sigma_m$ | 3b. Historical $\sigma_s$ and $\sigma_m$ |
| 4a. Future $r_{s,m}$ | 4b. Historical $r_{s,m}$ |

If historical experience is significantly different from current and future conditions, the computed estimate of $k_s$ is going to be a poor measure of the true $k_s$. The following factors should be watched closely:

1. If there have been recent changes in the slope of the SML, the numerical estimates must be adjusted. Changes in the slope of the SML indicate changes in market risk aversiveness.
2. If future volatility in the returns on the stock ($\sigma_s$) or the market portfolio ($\sigma_m$) are expected to differ from past volatility, adjustments must be made in the standard deviations. New-product development or changes in competitive conditions, for example, may result in future volatility being different from past volatility.
3. If the future relationship between returns on the individual stock and the market portfolio are expected to differ from the historical relationship ($r_{s,m}$), the computed value may be a poor estimate of the future relationship. Changing market conditions may, for example, expose the firm to a different amount of earnings fluctuation and increased volatility in returns.

As the remarks above suggest, the computational procedures presented in this appendix are general guidelines. They must be used within the context of sound business judgment—that is, as a guide for making judgments rather than a substitute for judgment. There is nothing mechanical about the final estimate of the required rate of return. Different people making different judgments as to the stability of the estimates could arrive at different estimates of $k_s$. Fortunately, the relationships appear to be sufficiently stable to make the procedures useful.[20]

**PROBLEMS**

1. The risk-free rate of return is 10%. A portfolio including all risky securities in the market has a rate of return of 16%. The standard deviation of the returns of the market portfolio is 6%. The return of a security has a standard deviation of 10%. The correlation coefficient between the returns of the security and the market portfolio is +0.8.
   a. Write the equation, and show the graph depicting the security-market line.
   b. Calculate the level of nondiversifiable risk ($\beta$) of the security.
   c. Calculate the required rate of return of the security.

---

[20]There is also the problem of determining the number of quarters to be used in computing r and $\sigma$. Once again, good business judgment is called for. There is no easy way to say whether the use of eight quarters yields better or worse estimates than the use of 20 quarters.

**2.** The actual returns realized over the last two years on the common stock of the Christine Corporation and those of the market portfolio are presented below. The current rate on Treasury bills is 8%.

| Period | | Annualized Return of the Market Portfolio | Annualized Return of the Christine Corporation |
|---|---|---|---|
| 1978 | 1st | 18% | 22% |
| | 2nd | 15% | 14% |
| | 3rd | 20% | 23% |
| | 4th | 5% | 3% |
| 1979 | 1st | 3% | 1% |
| | 2nd | 12% | 18% |
| | 3rd | 15% | 22% |
| | 4th | 16% | 26% |

a. Prepare the equation, and show the graph representing the security-market line.
b. Calculate the level of nondiversifiable risk of the common stock of the Christine Corporation.
c. Calculate the required rate of return of Christine Corporation's stockholders.

**SELECTED BIBLIOGRAPHY**

ARDITTI, FRED D., "Risk and the Required Return on Equity," *Journal of Finance*, 22 (March 1967), 19–36.

BOUDREAUX, KENNETH J., and HUGH W. LONG, *The Basic Theory of Corporate Finance.* Englewood Cliffs, N.J.: Prentice-Hall, 1977.

BOWER, RICHARD S., and JEFFREY M. JENKS, "Divisional Screening Rates," *Financial Management*, 4 (Autumn 1975), 42–49.

COPELAND, THOMAS E., and J. FRED WESTON, *Financial Theory and Corporate Policy*. Reading, Mass.: Addison-Wesley, 1979.

EZZELL, JOHN R., and R. BURR PORTER, "Flotation Costs and the Weighted Average Cost of Capital," *Journal of Financial and Quantitative Analysis,* 11 (September 1976), 403–14.

GORDON, MYRON J., and LAWRENCE D. SCHALL, "Problems with the Concept of the Cost of Capital," *Journal of Finance*, 29 (September 1974), 1153–63.

HAMADA, R.S., "The Effect of the Firm's Capital Structure on the Systematic Risk of Common Stock," *Journal of Finance*, May 1972, 435–42.

McDONALD, JOHN G., "Market Measures of Capital Cost," *Journal of Business Finance*, Autumn 1970, 27–36.

MODIGLIANI, FRANCO, and H.M. MILLLER, "The Cost of Capital, Corporate Finance and the Theory of Investment," *American Economic Review*, 48 (June 1958), 261–97.

PETRY, GLENN H., "Empirical Evidence on Cost of Capital Weights," *Financial Management*, 4 (Winter 1975), 58–65.

SCHALL, LAWRENCE D., and CHARLES W. HALEY, *Introduction to Financial Management*. New York: McGraw-Hill, 1979.

VAN HORNE, JAMES C., *Financial Management and Policy*, 5th ed. Englewood Cliffs, N.J.: Prentice-Hall, 1980.

# THE ACQUISITION
# OF CAPITAL

# Introduction to PART THREE

Part Three is devoted to an examination of issues relating to the acquisition of capital. The overall objective of the chapters that make up this section is to develop an understanding of the many different types of capital available to the firm, and how the use of these types of capital can be related to stockholder wealth.

Chapter 15, which presents an overview of capital markets, provides a context for understanding the process of acquiring capital. As you will see, the market for capital is multifaceted and dynamic. It is a market that comprises many unique actors, tied together by competitive market forces.

The chapters that follow in Part Three look at each type of capital raised by firms in detail—short-, medium-, and long-term debt capital, as well as equity capital. In addition to providing descriptive and institutional information about each type of capital, we discuss the advantages and disadvantages of using each type, and the effect of this use on stockholder wealth. The student who has completed Part Three should have an understanding of the use of different types of capital within the context of dynamic capital markets and stockholder-wealth maximization.

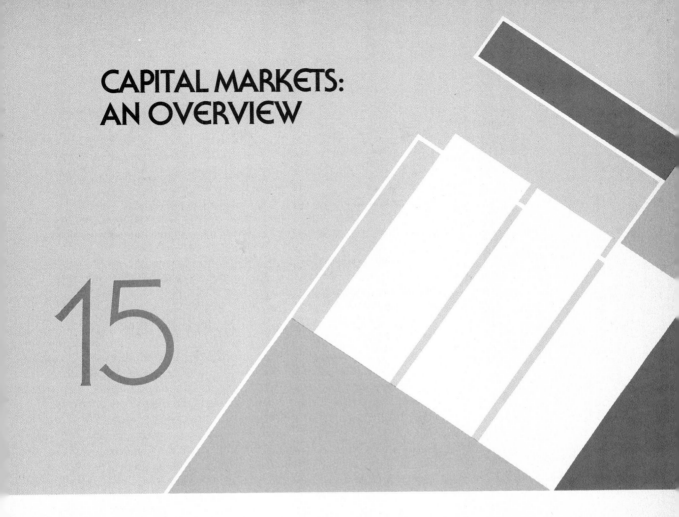

# CAPITAL MARKETS: AN OVERVIEW

## 15

## INTRODUCTION

As you know, the "capital" on the right-hand side of the balance sheet is used to finance the assets on the left side. A substantial portion of the capital raised by American corporations is acquired in what is known as the American capital market, which is the most advanced and sophisticated capital market in the world.[1] Transactions of almost unimaginable size take

---

[1]The capital market is often called the money and capital market, indicating the markets for short-term and long-term capital respectively. We will use the term *capital market* here to refer to the entire market.

place alongside millions of smaller transactions, with capital being moved from those willing to supply it to those demanding it. All this is accomplished with an amazing degree of speed and efficiency.

The capital market is not a place, but a network of participants spread over the entire nation—and to a lesser extent, the whole world—and bound together by a modern information and communication system. This highly efficient capital transfer system is dependent upon a host of specialized capital-market organizations and services that facilitate the movement of capital from suppliers to demanders. For example, a resident of a small town in Texas may provide capital to a large Delaware corporation by using a banking connection in his town that in turn uses the services of a large New York bank. Such transactions, and others many times more complicated, can be completed in a matter of minutes. This is the remarkable nature of the American capital market.

Don't despair if after this brief introduction you are still unable to understand the nature of this market and the process through which capital is moved from suppliers to demanders. It happens that many people, even those that participate in the market, fail to understand its operations. But even though ignorance of capital-market institutions and operations is common, it is not an ideal state of affairs. It is important that corporate management have a basic understanding of this vital part of the American economic system. An understanding of capital markets will help management achieve an optimal mix of the various types of capital available, and thus minimize asset-specific and firmwide costs of capital. This is a basic requirement for making sound decisions relative to the acquisition of assets. After all, if the firm is paying too much to acquire capital or is incurring unnecessary risk when capital is acquired, asset-specific costs of capital will be higher than necessary. This could result in the abandonment of what could otherwise be favorable asset-acquisition opportunities.

This chapter is designed to provide the potential business manager with an overall view of how the capital market operates.[2] The material selected for inclusion is that which is most important for sound business decision making. This chapter is conceptual and descriptive in nature. Specific techniques used in the evaluation of financing alternatives are discussed in the chapters that follow. These techniques, however, cannot be applied effectively unless the capital market as a whole is understood.

---

[2]Owing to space limitations inherent in an introductory text, this overall view is brief. It should, however, be sufficient in terms of general required information, and it provides an introduction to courses and texts devoted exclusively to capital markets. For example, see Roland I. Robinson and Dwayne Wrightsman, *Financial Markets: The Accumulation and Allocation of Wealth* (New York: McGraw-Hill, 1974); or Charles N. Henning, William Pigott, and Robert H. Scott, *Financial Markets and the Economy,* 2nd ed. (Englewood Cliffs, N.J.: Prentice-Hall, 1978).

## A CONCEPTUAL FRAMEWORK

A simplified view of the flow of capital from capital suppliers to capital demanders is presented in Figure 15–1. Note that the flow of capital can follow either of two paths. Capital may flow directly from the supplier to the user. When a firm sells common stock directly to an individual, the capital is flowing directly from the supplier to the user. But much of the capital raised by firms does not come directly from capital suppliers. Typically, firms raise a large portion of their capital through financial intermediaries, who in turn raise the capital from suppliers. For example, individuals place deposits in banks. The banks accumulate many small deposits and then make loans to firms. The firm has raised capital, and capital suppliers have made that capital available; however, the transaction was facilitated by a financial intermediary—in this case, a bank.

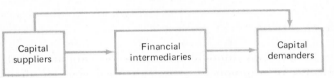

**FIGURE 15–1**

Overview of The
Market for Capital

Before we look more closely at the role of financial intermediaries, a review of the types of capital raised by firms is in order. Basic statistical information on the capital raised by American nonfinancial corporate business for the five-year period 1974–78 is presented in Table 15–1.[3] This table can be viewed as the right-hand side of a combined balance sheet for all American nonfinancial corporate business. To make this presentation clearer, the items appear in a different order than is usually found in the balance sheet, but all the important balance-sheet items are included in the table.

Note also that the capital raised by corporations has been grouped into two major categories: capital raised in capital markets, and capital raised outside capital markets. For the period 1974–78, each of these categories accounted for about 50 percent of the new capital raised by the corporations. It is particularly important to recognize that retained earnings and trade credit, which are important sources of capital to the American corporation, are not raised in the capital market.

New debt constituted the major portion of new capital raised in the capital market, whereas sales of new common stock constituted only a small portion.[4] Corporate bonds, mortgages, and bank loans are the major types of

---

[3]The category of nonfinancial corporate business includes most corporations. Only financial institutions are excluded.

[4]The sale of new common stock should not be confused with sales of existing outstanding shares. Stock-market activity as reported in the press primarily involves sales of stock by one stockholder to another. Such sales among stockholders do not change the amount of capital advanced to business firms.

TABLE 15–1

PERCENTAGE DISTRIBUTION OF CAPITAL RAISED BY NONFINANCIAL CORPORATE BUSINESS
(5-Year Period 1974–78)

| | Total dollars raised (in billions) | % of total capital raised |
|---|---|---|
| *Capital raised in capital markets:* | | |
| Sales of new issues of stock | $ 29.8 | 4.3% |
| New debt (total) | 315.2 | 46.0% |
|    Tax-exempt bonds | 13.4 | 2.0% |
|    Corporate bonds | 110.8 | 16.2% |
|    Mortgages | 78.3 | 11.4% |
|    Bank loans | 66.1 | 9.6% |
|    Commercial paper | 6.6 | 1.0% |
|    Acceptances | 4.6 | .7% |
|    Finance-company loans | 31.8 | 4.6% |
|    U.S. government loans | 3.6 | .5% |
|    Total capital raised in markets | $345.0 | 50.3% |
| *Capital raised outside capital markets:* | | |
| Taxes payable | $ 6.7 | 1.0% |
| Trade debt | 112.4 | 16.4% |
| Miscellaneous liabilities | 13.4 | 2.0% |
| Retained earnings | 208.2 | 30.4% |
|    Total capital raised outside markets | $340.7 | 49.7% |
| Total capital raised | $685.7 | 100.0% |

Source: Board of Governors of the Federal Reserve Board, *Flow of Funds Accounts of the United States,* February 1979.

capital raised through the capital market. As we will discuss later, a portion of this market-raised debt is acquired directly from capital suppliers and another portion through financial intermediaries.

## FINANCIAL INTERMEDIARIES AND CORPORATE CAPITAL

Financial intermediation is the process by which capital suppliers provide funds to financial institutions (banks, savings and loan associations, and so on) and the financial institutions in turn "invest" these funds. What follows is a brief description of the role various financial institutions play in this intermediation process. Emphasis is placed on the nature of the capital flowing into the financial institution and the manner in which the financial institution "repackages" this capital and passes it along to nonfinancial corporate business. It should be noted that nonfinancial corporate business constitutes only one type of financial-institution customer. Financial institutions also provide funds to consumers, noncorporate business, the U.S. government, state and local governments, and foreigners. Thus, financial institutions service a broad range of customers, and nonfinancial corporate customers must compete with these other customers for funds.

Tables 15–2 and 15–3 (see pages 386 and 387) provide information on the outflows of capital from financial institutions. Note that these institutions have been divided into two classes: Nonbank finance includes financial institutions such as savings and loan associations, mutual savings banks, life insurance companies, pension funds, and mutual funds. Commercial banks are treated as a separate category because of the unique role they play in the capital market. However, both nonbank finance and commercial banking provide funds to a broad range of customers. Only a portion of these funds go to corporate businesses.

The statements of sources and uses of funds presented in Tables 15–2 and 15–3 illustrate one of the central features of financial intermediation. Financial institutions receive funds in the form of "deposits" of various types.[5] These funds are provided to capital demanders in a completely different form. Thus, capital suppliers are able to maintain the convenience of a relatively simple structure of deposits, and the financial intermediaries are able to provide funds in a wide variety of forms. The "uses" portion of the tables reinforces the idea that financial institutions deal with many different types of capital demanders, of which corporations constitute only one. Financial institutions, within certain limits, tend to move funds to those uses that offer the highest returns.[6] The movement of funds from one use to another implies that the rates paid by businesses to acquire funds from financial intermediaries will be influenced by the rates other demanders of capital (consumers, governments, and so on) are willing to pay. Business firms must compete for the capital supplied by financial institutions.

The next few sections of this chapter will discuss the role played by several of the more important financial institutions in the United States. The discussion is designed to highlight the potential sources of capital for business and the nature of the competition business faces in acquiring these funds.

## CAPITAL-MARKET PARTICIPANTS

### COMMERCIAL BANKS

The American commercial banking system plays a pivotal role in the provision of capital to business. Let us examine the way banks raise funds and the types of capital supplied by banks to business firms.

---

[5]The word *deposit* as used in this chapter is a general term referring to *all* inflows into *all* financial institutions. For example, an individual's contribution to a retirement plan is officially called a pension-plan reserve. In a real sense, however, it represents a deposit. In a similar sense, life insurance reserves, mutual-fund-shares acquisitions, etc., can be called "deposits."

[6]Financial institutions are often limited by law as to the types of uses they may make of funds. The role of government regulation is discussed in greater detail in Appendix 15A.

TABLE 15–2

## SOURCES AND USES OF FUNDS OF THE COMMERCIAL BANKING SYSTEM FROM 1974 TO 1978[a]
(in billions)

| SOURCES OF FUNDS | Amount | Percentage |
|---|---|---|
| Demand deposits | 61.2 | 13.4 |
| Time deposits | 248.1 | 54.4 |
| Other sources[b] | 25.7 | 5.6 |
| Equity issues | 4.4 | 1.0 |
| Credit-market debt | 17.7 | 3.9 |
| Miscellaneous liabilities | 83.3 | 18.3 |
| Total outside sources | 440.4 | 96.6 |
| + Surplus (retained earnings) | 16.0 | 3.5 |
| Total sources of funds | 456.4 | 100.1 |
| USES OF FUNDS | Amount | Percentage |
| U.S. government securities | 51.5 | 10.8 |
| State and local obligations | 27.8 | 5.8 |
| Corporate bonds | 1.9 | 0.4 |
| Mortgages | 92.7 | 19.4 |
| Consumer credit | 61.8 | 12.9 |
| Bank loans to business | 113.2 | 23.6 |
| Open-market paper | 6.0 | 1.3 |
| Other assets[c] | 101.7 | 21.2 |
| Total financial uses | 456.6 | 95.4 |
| + Plant and equipment | 22.3 | 4.7 |
| Total uses of funds | 478.9[d] | 100.1 |

[a]The banking system includes chartered commercial banks, their domestic affiliates, Edge Act corporations, agencies of foreign banks, and banks in U.S. possessions.

[b]Other sources include float, borrowings from the Federal Reserve Banks, and other interbank claims.

[c]Other assets include corporate equities, security credit, vault cash and member-bank reserves, and other interbank claims.

[d]Note: Total sources, should, by definition, equal total uses. The difference is due to a discrepancy in data collection.

Source: Federal Reserve System, *Flow of Funds Accounts*, 4th Quarter 1978.

As shown in Table 15–4, demand deposits (checking-account balances) constitute approximately 37 percent of total bank deposits. These funds can be withdrawn from banks simply by the writing of checks, and this fact encourages banks to maintain a liquid position, which they can do by extending short-term credit of high quality. By this emphasis on short-term lending, they can use the continuous inflow of cash from the repayment of loans to meet depositor demands, should they reach unexpectedly high levels. The facts that banks have such a large portion of their liabilities in

TABLE 15–3

### SOURCES AND USES OF FUNDS OF PRIVATE NONBANK FINANCIAL INSTITUTIONS FROM 1974 TO 1978
(In Billions)

| SOURCES OF FUNDS | Amount | Percentage |
|---|---|---|
| Time and savings accounts | 280.0 | 38.0 |
| Insurance and pension reserves | 240.4 | 32.7 |
| Corporate bonds | 27.0 | 3.7 |
| Mortgages | 7.2 | 1.0 |
| Open-market paper | 22.7 | 3.1 |
| Money-market-funds shares | 10.8 | 1.5 |
| Federal Home Loan Bank loans | 17.5 | 2.4 |
| Security repurchase agreements | 4.4 | 0.6 |
| Other sources[a] | 92.8 | 12.6 |
| Total outside sources | 702.8 | 95.6 |
| + Current surplus | 33.3 | 4.5 |
| Total sources of funds | 736.1 | 100.1 |

| USES OF FUNDS | Amount | Percentage |
|---|---|---|
| Demand deposits and currency | 5.2 | 0.7 |
| Time and savings accounts | 17.9 | 2.4 |
| Corporate equities | 38.7 | 5.2 |
| U.S. government securities | 83.8 | 11.3 |
| State and local government obligations | 39.6 | 5.3 |
| Corporate and foreign bonds | 141.7 | 19.1 |
| Mortgages | 238.4 | 32.1 |
| Consumer credit | 55.1 | 7.4 |
| Other loans | 63.0 | 8.5 |
| Other financial assets[b] | 43.5 | 5.9 |
| Total financial uses | 726.9 | 97.9 |
| + Physical investment | 15.6 | 2.1 |
| Total uses of funds | 742.5[c] | 100.0 |

[a]Other sources include equity issues, bank loans, security credit, profit taxes payable, and miscellaneous liabilities.

[b]Other financial assets include security credit, trade credit, and miscellaneous assets.

[c]Note: Total sources should, by definition, equal total uses. The difference is due to a discrepancy in data collection.

Source: Federal Reserve System, *Flow of Funds Accounts*, 4th Quarter 1978.

demand deposits, and that these deposits are characterized by potential volatility, have created bank investment portfolios dominated by four important characteristics:

1. Banks generally make short-term loans, as distinct from long-term loans.
2. These loans tend to go to customers with a low risk of default. This is, banks

tend to lend only to the best possible customers, and at rates that are usually lower than those available elsewhere.

3. Banks frequently make loans secured by accounts receivable or inventories, thus further reducing the risk of default.

4. Banks are prohibited by law from purchasing common stock.

TABLE 15–4

### COMMERCIAL-BANK DEPOSITS
(December 31, 1979)

|  | Billions of dollars | % of total |
|---|---|---|
| Demand | $377.6 | 36.6% |
| Time | $203.4 | 19.7% |
| Savings | $449.7 | 43.7% |
|  | $1,030.7 | 100.0% |

Source: *Federal Reserve Bulletin*

The potential volatility of demand deposits is to some extent offset by the commercial banking system's holdings of time and savings deposits. The primary type of time deposit is the negotiable certificate of deposit. These are short-term certificates sold by banks (in denominations of $100,000 or greater) primarily to large businesses. The primary type of savings deposit is the traditional passbook savings account. It is important to note that both time and savings deposits have less potential volatility than demand deposits have. This lower probability of unforeseen withdrawal permits banks to extend longer-term loans than would be possible if only demand deposits were accepted.

Table 15–5 provides information on the assets of insured commercial banks. There are several points worth noting in this table. First, note that banks do not supply equity capital to business firms. Second, banks are important purchasers of securities. However, 52 percent of the securities purchased by banks are U.S.-government-issued, and an additional 46 percent are issued by state and local governments. Only a very small percentage of assets are held in the form of corporate bonds. Thus, we can conclude that banks tend to be relatively inactive in providing long-term debt to corporations and heavily involved in shorter-term lending. This preference of banks for shorter maturities reflects the potential volatility of bank deposits.

The distribution of loans made by banks is presented in Table 15–6. Note that of loans made by commercial banks, 24.5 percent are made to individuals and 17.8 percent involve residential mortgages. Most of the remaining 57.7 percent goes to business in one form or another. Of the real estate loans, only construction loans are short-term, with maturities of approximately six to nine months. Loans to individuals tend to have maturities in the one-to-three-year range. The other loans made by banks

**TABLE 15-5**

### COMMERCIAL-BANK ASSETS
(December 31, 1979)

|  | Dollars in billions | % of total |
|---|---|---|
| Cash balances | $ 146.4 | 10.8 |
| Debt securities | 283.2 | 21.0 |
| Loans—net | 860.1 | 63.7 |
| Other assets | 61.2 | 4.5 |
| Total | $1,350.9 | 100% |

Source: *Federal Reserve Bulletin*

tend to be short-term. In early 1979, more than 85 percent of the commercial and industrial loans were short-term. This pattern should provide potential managers with a general idea of the type of capital that can be raised through the commercial banking system.

**TABLE 15-6**

### COMMERCIAL-BANK LOANS
(September 30, 1978)

|  | Billions of dollars | % of total |
|---|---|---|
| Real estate loans: |  |  |
| Construction | $ 25.6 | 3.9 |
| Secured by farmland | 8.4 | 1.3 |
| Residential | 117.2 | 17.8 |
| Secured by other properties | 52.2 | 7.9 |
| Loans to financial institutions | 37.1 | 5.6 |
| Loans for purchase of securities | 15.3 | 2.3 |
| Loans to farmers | 28.1 | 4.3 |
| Commercial and industrial loans | 213.1 | 32.4 |
| Loans to individuals | 161.6 | 24.5 |
| Total | $658.6[a] | 100.0% |

[a]This total is the gross value of loans. A reserve of $7.4 billion must be subtracted from this amount to arrive at the net value of loans.

Source: *Federal Reserve Bulletin.*

## LIFE INSURANCE COMPANIES

Life insurance companies accumulate capital that can be advanced to capital demanders in a number of ways. In recent years, payments into pension funds operated by life insurance companies have constituted the most important source of funds ($21.1 billion in 1979). In addition, life insurance companies receive premiums and accumulate reserves for life insurance policies ($11.7 billion in 1979). Note that these cash inflows to life insurance companies are held in anticipation of future payments, and these future payments are relatively easy to forecast. This ability to forecast future required payments reduces the volatility of life insurance company reserves ("deposits") and permits the companies to advance funds to capital demanders on a relatively long-term basis. The life insurance industry does not have to worry too much about a sudden withdrawal of funds.

The stability of life insurance company reserves has important implications for the form in which capital is supplied to capital demanders. In general, life insurance companies provide long-term funds to both business and governments. Table 15–7 shows the importance of different types of capital extensions made by life insurance companies and gives significant information about potential sources of funds for business:

1. Life insurance companies represent an important source through which corporate management can acquire long-term debt capital. In recent years, life insurance companies have moved very heavily into this area.
2. Even though the life insurance industry holds less than 10% of its assets in the form of common stock, this amounts to billions of dollars. This industry is therefore a potential source of new equity for corporate business.
3. Management may find insurance companies an important source of mortgage funds. Although the life insurance industry contributed only $16.1 billion to the $159.5 billion in mortgage funds advanced in 1979, it provided most of its funds to commercial and industrial borrowers. Approximately 20% of the funds advanced to commercial and industrial mortgage borrowers came from life insurance companies.

TABLE 15–7

DISTRIBUTION OF ASSETS OF U.S. LIFE INSURANCE COMPANIES,
December 31, 1979

|  | Billions of dollars | % of total |
|---|---|---|
| Government securities | $ 20.0 | 4.8 |
| Corporate bonds | 173.1 | 41.1 |
| Corporate stocks | 40.1 | 9.5 |
| Mortgages | 119.2 | 28.3 |
| Policy loans | 34.4 | 8.2 |
| Miscellaneous assets | 33.9 | 8.1 |
| Total assets | $420.7 | 100.0% |

Source: Federal Reserve System, *Flow of Funds Accounts, Assets and Liabilities Outstanding, 1969–79.*

# PENSION FUNDS

Pension funds have a risk exposure similar to that of life insurance companies. That is, future payments to retirees can be forecast with relatively high accuracy. The small likelihood of unexpected withdrawals of pension reserves ("deposits") permits pension funds to provide long-term loans to business. Table 15–8 shows how important these pension funds are in the provision of both long-term debt capital and equity capital to business. Approximately 80 percent of all pension funds are invested in corporate businesses.[7]

### TABLE 15–8

PENSION-FUNDS' ASSET STRUCTURE,
December 31, 1979

|  | Billions of dollars | % of total |
|---|---|---|
| Demand deposits and currency | $ 5.6 | 1.3 |
| Time deposits | 8.7 | 2.1 |
| Corporate equities | 180.0 | 43.3 |
| U.S. Treasury issues | 33.4 | 8.0 |
| U.S. agencies sources | 24.1 | 5.8 |
| State and local obligations | 4.0 | 1.0 |
| Corporate bonds | 141.4 | 34.0 |
| Mortgages | 12.9 | 3.1 |
| Miscellaneous assets | 5.8 | 1.4 |
| Total[a] | $415.9 | 100.0% |

[a]Total of private pension funds plus state and local government employee retirement funds.

Source: Federal Reserve System, *Flow of Funds Accounts; Assets and Liabilities Outstanding, 1969–79.*

The acquisition of corporate bonds by insurance companies and pension funds can be executed in either of two ways. In one case, they can purchase bonds that have been sold to the public and for which a secondary (resale) market exists. In the other case, corporations negotiate directly with the insurance company or pension fund and place the issue directly with it. These private placements of corporate bonds have increased in importance in recent years. In essence, they represent long-term loans made by lenders to corporations.

---

[7]An interesting sidelight of this table is that it shows how the interest of the American worker and the interest of business converge. The widespread collapse of corporate business would play havoc with the pensions of both government and private workers.

# FINANCE COMPANIES

Finance companies constitute another important source of funds for business corporations. Finance companies acquire funds from capital suppliers by selling commercial paper, long-term debt, and common stock. Approximately 50 percent of the funds raised by finance companies are loaned to consumers. Finance companies also provide loans to businesses for the purpose of financing inventories (especially automobiles), equipment, and accounts receivable.

Note in Table 15–9 that the total dollars provided by finance companies are only a small fraction of the amounts provided by insurance companies and pension funds, but finance companies are important because they provide a different type of financing from that provided by these other institutions. The type of credit extended by a finance company corresponds more closely with that provided by commercial banks, but finance companies frequently make loans that banks are unwilling to make because of their high risk. Finance companies make relatively high-risk, high-cost loans to business.

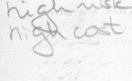

TABLE 15–9

### DOMESTIC FINANCE COMPANIES, BUSINESS CREDIT
### December 31, 1979

| Type of credit | Billions of dollars | % distribution |
|---|---|---|
| Retail automotive (commercial autos) | 15.3 | 21.7 |
| Wholesale automotive | 13.8 | 19.6 |
| Other equipment | 18.9 | 26.9 |
| Accounts receivable | 7.1 | 10.1 |
| All other business credit | 15.3 | 21.7 |
| Total | $70.4 | 100.0% |

Source: Federal Reserve Bulletin

# OTHER NONBANK FINANCIAL INSTITUTIONS

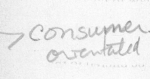

There are a host of other nonbank financial institutions that are active in channeling the flow of capital from suppliers to demanders. Savings institutions, credit unions, and casualty insurance companies are among the more important. This group of financial institutions is not greatly involved in providing funds to business. Savings institutions concentrate heavily in the area of home mortgage lending. Credit unions are primarily involved in consumer lending.

Mutual funds are organizations that sell shares to the public and in turn use the cash that has been raised to buy bonds, stocks, and other securities. The major activity of mutual funds has been in the secondary market for corporate stocks and bonds. That is, mutual funds tend to buy and sell outstanding issues of stocks and bonds rather than providing funds directly to corporate business. However, these institutions are important because they compete with other financial intermediaries for funds from capital suppliers. Thus, they are an integral part of the competitive environment in which business acquires funds.

## CAPITAL-MARKET FACILITATORS

Aside from the financial institutions we have discussed above, there is another group of important capital-market participants. They are called capital-market facilitators, and they include investment bankers, security dealers, and commission brokerage firms. These facilitators differ from financial intermediaries in that they themselves do not accept "deposits" from the public; rather, they serve as a marketing link between the suppliers and demanders of capital.

**Investment Bankers**   One of the most important facilitators of capital flows to corporations is the investment banker. Today, investment bankers have little in common with commercial bankers. They neither accept deposits nor permanently invest their own funds. The investment bankers help corporations market new issues of stocks and bonds. In the usual case, they do this by (1) providing advice as to the timing and pricing of new issues, (2) assisting in completing the legal requirements for new issues, (3) forming a syndicate of commission brokerage firms in order to sell the securities to the public, and (4) accepting some or all of the risk involved in potential price declines in the security during the period when it is being sold to the public.

*advice*
*legal*
*syndicate*
*risk*

To illustrate the general nature of the role played by the investment banker, assume that a leading industrial corporation plans to raise $200 million by selling bonds to the public. The following steps would typically be involved in the issuance of the bonds:

*select*

1. First, the corporation selects an investment banker to manage the new issue of bonds. This selection will be based on a number of factors, including costs and the reputation of the investment banker. Some industries—for example, public utilities—are required by law to choose an investment banker on the basis of competitive bidding.

*forms*
*terms*

2. Next, the managing investment banker assists the firm in filing the appropriate registration forms with the Securities and Exchange Commission and in determining the terms on which the bonds will be offered to the public.

*underwriting*

3. The managing investment banker then sets up an underwriting

syndicate. The underwriting syndicate will purchase the bonds from the corporate issuer at a price below par and sell them to the public at a higher price. The difference between the price the syndicate pays and the price at which it sells the bonds to the public represents the gross margin for the investment banker. The banker's profit is derived by subtracting the expenses associated with advice, counsel, and selling of the bonds from the gross margin. Note that the issuing corporation receives less than the par value of the bond. This represents the cost of issuing the bonds to the public.

4. The investment banker will next form a selling group composed of commission brokers. In many cases, investment bankers themselves are divisions of commission brokerage houses. For example, Merrill Lynch, Pierce, Fenner & Smith, Inc., is both an investment banker and a commission broker. Independent investment bankers frequently have long-standing relationships with many commission brokerage firms. A large number of brokerage firms (300–400) may take part in the process of selling a large issue of securities.

5. Finally, the bonds are purchased by the underwriters and sold to the public. There are thousands of sales personnel ready to facilitate the flow of funds from the capital suppliers to the corporate issuer. The underwriters usually have their funds back in a matter of days.

The scenario above is only one of a number of possible variations, but it shows the important role played by investment bankers in the market for corporate bonds. Investment bankers perform a similar role in the process through which common stock is sold to the public.

**Commission Brokerage Firms**

Brokerage firms, as already noted, play an important role in the issuance of new stocks and bonds. They also have a second vital function in the capital market: They are basically responsible for maintaining secondary markets in stocks and bonds. Many potential buyers of corporate stocks and bonds would be unwilling to execute purchases if they were unable to resell the security should the need arise. The market in which stocks and bonds are resold is by definition a secondary (as distinct from a new-issue, or primary) market. The existence of this secondary (resale) market increases the liquidity of stocks and bonds, thus reducing the riskiness to buyers and, in turn, leading to lower required rates of return by capital suppliers and lower costs of capital to the firm.

The commission brokerage firms are the heart and muscle of the secondary market for stocks and bonds. The stock exchanges in the United States are owned and controlled by their broker members.[8] These exchanges are places where brokers can conveniently match buy and sell orders placed

---

[8]The largest stock exchanges are the New York Stock Exchange and the American Stock Exchange. In addition, there are a number of smaller regional exchanges.

by customers. When organized exchanges are used to execute transactions, the broker never owns the stock but instead, brings buyers together with sellers.

The over-the-counter market is also part of the secondary market, but it operates differently from the organized stock exchanges. The over-the-counter market is generally used to execute sales and purchases of less-active stocks. In this situation, commission brokerage firms actually maintain inventories of selected common stocks. Customer sales and purchases are executed through this inventory. Each stock will have one or more brokers maintaining an inventory of it (known as making the market in the stock). The National Association of Security Dealers has an elaborate computerized information system (called NASDAQ) that provides virtually any sales representative information on buy and sell prices offered by various market makers on different stocks. This over-the-counter market, a secondary market for stock, improves the liquidity of the stock and reduces its riskiness.

The commission brokerage firms also have a third important role in the capital market. These firms usually offer customers margin accounts. This means that customers can purchase securities and borrow part of the purchase price. The commission brokerage firms use bank loans to finance these loans to customers.

**Other Facilitators**  Other important market facilitators include commercial-paper dealers and dealers in bankers' acceptances. These dealers are often departments of the large investment banking establishments. Commercial-paper dealers assist in the marketing of new commercial paper and usually maintain a secondary market for the paper.[9] Dealers in bankers' acceptances maintain a secondary market for the acceptances. This key secondary-market role of the dealers improves liquidity and reduces required rates of return. This in turn reduces the cost to the firms using these types of financing.

## CAPITAL-MARKET RATES

Pick up a copy of *The Wall Street Journal,* or any other newspaper with a good financial section, and look at the diversity of returns being offered and received in the capital market. You will find, for example, that different securities issued by the U.S. government and having the same maturity value sell at different prices. You will find bonds issued by the same large corporation and having the same maturity value and the same maturity date selling at different prices. You will find that preferred stock of one corporation has a lower rate of return than the bonds of another corporation. You will find that interest rates on home mortgages in one region of the

---

[9]Commercial paper is also sold directly by the issuing corporation, without the aid of dealers.

country are higher than those on similar mortgages in other parts of the country. These are only a few examples of the tremendous diversity of rates of return found in the capital market.

At first glance, it may appear that the market is irrational, that the multiple rates of return it offers are part of an incomprehensible mess. Nothing could be further from the truth. The differences in return can be easily explained in terms of different risk structures that exist in the market, and a few capital-market imperfections.

The rate of return to capital suppliers is a function not only of the level of overall rates of return but also of the risk premium associated with a particular capital transfer. As previously discussed in Chapter 11, a capital supplier faces three risks when making capital available to others: (1) default risk, (2) marketability risk, and (3) interest-rate risk.

Default risk refers to the possibility that the capital demander will be unable to meet anticipated payments to the capital supplier. To supply funds to firms with high levels of nondiversifiable risk (β) is to assume relatively high levels of default risk. In addition, factors such as the capital demander's balance of liquid funds and past history of meeting obligations to capital suppliers reflect the degree of default risk incurred by the supplier.

Interest-rate risk refers to the possibility that the market value of the capital supplier's claim against the capital demander will fall, owing to increases in the general level of required rates of return(upward shifts in the SML). As shown in Chapter 11, an upward shift in the SML will increase the required rate of return and discount rate on all outstanding securities. This will reduce the present value of outstanding securities. The possibility of decline in the present value of an outstanding claim is indicative of the interest risk borne by the capital supplier. Such risk can be minimized by supplying capital on a short-term basis.

Marketability risk is the risk that the capital supplier will be unable to sell a capital claim before maturity without having to significantly discount the claim. Marketability risk can be minimized by acquiring capital-market instruments for which a good secondary market exists.

## DEFAULT-RISK STRUCTURE

Part of the observed diversity in market rates of return can be attributed to differences in default risk. U.S. government bonds are less risky than corporate bonds and have relatively low market rates of return. For example, in August 1979, the average market rate of return on corporate bonds was 9.74 percent, while the average rate on long-term U.S. Treasury bonds was 8.90 percent.[10]

Different corporate bonds with different levels of default risk also have

---

[10]*Moody's Bond Survey,* August 27, 1979, p. 892.

different market rates of return. For example, Moody's Investors Services and Standard and Poor's regularly evaluate the default risk associated with corporate bonds and preferred-stock issues. Based upon this evaluation, Moody's places bonds in one of nine default-risk categories.[11] These categories are described in Table 15–10. Note that the default risk is lower for Aaa- and highest for C-rated bonds.

The bond ratings of both Moody's and Standard and Poor's are subjective, in the sense that they are based upon the judgment and experience of the bond-rating personnel. The arbitrariness of the classification process is highlighted by the fact that on occasion, the two rating services give the same corporate bond issue a different default-risk rating. However, the rating procedures are accurate and consistent enough to illustrate the fundamental relationship between default risk and market rates of return. As shown in Table 15–11, those bonds with lower default risk always have lower market rates of return. Note that the risk premiums associated with higher levels of risk are not constant on a year-to-year basis. The differences in yields between a 1964 Baa industrial bond and a 1964 Aaa industrial bond was 55 points (4.87% − 4.32%). This risk premium increased to 79 points by 1973 (8.07% − 7.28%). It is difficult to say whether such changes indicate shifts in the risk aversiveness of the capital market (steeper SML) or changes in the rating system. In any case, it is believed that the risk premiums associated with bonds of different risk (the default-risk structure) change over time.

Bonds issues by the same corporation may have different levels of default risk. Mortgage bonds are bonds secured by specific real property and tend to be less risky than debenture bonds, which are secured by the general assets of the firm. In addition, some debentures are "subordinated" to others. This means that should the corporation go into default, the subordinated debentures have a lower claim on the firm's assets and earnings. At the time subordinated debentures are sold, a document called an indenture spells out precisely the nature of the subordination and thus the risk taken by the buyer of the bond. Bonds with different types of subordination should have different market rates of return.

## INTEREST-RATE-RISK STRUCTURE

As discussed earlier, the interest-rate risk associated with a security is directly related to the time to maturity for that particular security. That is, *other things being equal*, long-term bonds are riskier than short-term bonds. The relationship between time to maturity and the market rate of return can be illustrated by observing the yields to maturity (market rates of return) of U.S. government securities with different maturities. An actual yield curve, as it existed in June 1976, is presented in Figure 15–2. Note that the yield

---

[11]Moody's preferred-stock categories are slightly different and only seven in number.

TABLE 15–10

## KEY TO MOODY'S BOND RATINGS BY DEFAULT RISK

Aaa — Bonds which are rated Aaa are judged to be of the best quality. They carry the smallest degree of investment risk and are generally referred to as "gilt edge." Interest payments are protected by a large or by an exceptionally stable margin, and principal is secure. While the various protective elements are likely to change, such changes as can be visualized are most unlikely to impair the fundamentally strong position of such issues.

Aa — Bonds which are rated Aa are judged to be of high quality by all standards. Together with the Aaa group they comprise what are generally known as high-grade bonds. They are rated lower than the best bonds because margins of protection may not be as large as in Aaa securities or fluctuation of protective elements may be of greater amplitude or there may be other elements present which make the long-term risks appear somewhat larger than in Aaa securities.

A — Bonds which are rated A possess many favorable investment attributes and are to be considered as upper medium grade obligations. Factors giving security to principal and interest are considered adequate but elements may be present which suggest a susceptibility to impairment sometime in the future.

Baa — Bonds which are rated Baa are considered as medium grade obligations i.e., they are neither highly protected nor poorly secured. Interest payments and principal security appear adequate for the present but certain protective elements may be lacking or may be characteristically unreliable over any great length of time. Such bonds lack outstanding investment characteristics and in fact have speculative characteristics as well.

Ba — Bonds which are rated Ba are judged to have speculative elements; their future cannot be considered as well assured. Often the protection of interest and principal payments may be very moderate and thereby not well safeguarded during both good and bad times over the future. Uncertainty of position characterizes bonds in this class.

B — Bonds which are rated B generally lack characteristics of the desirable investment. Assurance of interest and principal payments or of maintenance of other terms of the contract over any long period of time may be small.

Caa — Bonds which are rated Caa are of poor standing. Such issues may be in default or there may be present elements of danger with respect to principal or interest.

Ca — Bonds which are rated Ca represent obligations which are speculative in a high degree. Such issues are often in default or have other marked shortcomings.

C — Bonds which are rated C are the lowest-rated class of bonds and issues so rated can be regarded as having extremely poor prospects of ever attaining any real investment standing.

Source: *Moody's Investors Services, Inc.*

## TABLE 15–11

### MOODY'S CORPORATE-BOND YIELD AVERAGES BY RATING, BASED ON DEFAULT RISK

| Industrials | Aaa | Aa | A | Baa |
|---|---|---|---|---|
| 1964 | 4.32 | 4.41 | 4.47 | 4.87 |
| 1965 | 4.45 | 4.50 | 4.55 | 4.92 |
| 1966 | 5.12 | 5.15 | 5.26 | 5.68 |
| 1967 | 5.49 | 5.55 | 5.72 | 6.21 |
| 1968 | 6.12 | 6.24 | 6.39 | 6.90 |
| 1969 | 6.93 | 7.05 | 7.26 | 7.76 |
| 1970 | 7.77 | 7.94 | 8.33 | 9.00 |
| 1971 | 7.05 | 7.23 | 7.61 | 8.37 |
| 1972 | 6.97 | 7.11 | 7.36 | 7.99 |
| 1973 | 7.28 | 7.40 | 7.63 | 8.07 |
| Aug. 1979 | 9.01 | 9.33 | 9.56 | 10.20 |
| Public Utilities | Aaa | Aa | A | Baa |
| 1964 | 4.42 | 4.44 | 4.52 | 4.74 |
| 1965 | 4.50 | 4.52 | 4.58 | 4.78 |
| 1966 | 5.19 | 5.25 | 5.39 | 5.60 |
| 1967 | 5.58 | 5.66 | 5.87 | 6.15 |
| 1968 | 6.22 | 6.35 | 6.51 | 6.87 |
| 1969 | 7.12 | 7.34 | 7.54 | 7.93 |
| 1970 | 8.31 | 8.52 | 8.69 | 9.18 |
| 1971 | 7.72 | 8.00 | 8.16 | 8.63 |
| 1972 | 7.46 | 7.60 | 7.72 | 8.17 |
| 1973 | 7.60 | 7.72 | 7.84 | 8.17 |
| Aug. 23, 1979 | 9.46 | 9.74 | 10.12 | 10.50 |

Source: Moody's Investors Service, Inc.

curve slopes upward to the right. This tells us that Treasury securities maturing in a short time have lower market rates of return than securities with distant maturity dates.

The reason U.S. Treasury securities are used to illustrate the relationship between rates of return and maturity is that they possess the same zero level of default risk that characterizes all U.S. securities. Remember, the U.S. government can simply create money or use tax receipts to pay the maturity value of the bonds.

On occasion, the yield curve has slopes other than that shown in Figure 15–2. For example, Figure 15–3 shows how the yield curve changed in shape over the period from December 1977 to January 1979. Note that as the yields on Treasury securities rose in general, the yield curve developed a "hump." The "humped yield curve" (January 2, 1979) should not be interpreted as a refutation of the fundamental relationship between maturity and market

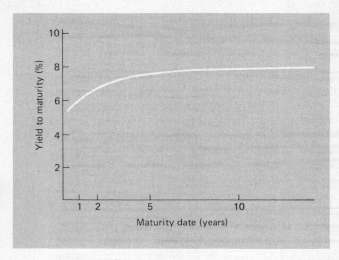

**FIGURE 15–2**

Yield Curve, U.S.
Government Securities
as of June 1, 1976

rates of return (interest-rate risk). There is considerable controversy over the reasons for the unusual shape of the yield curve. One school of thought maintains that capital supplies are not completely able to move from one maturity to another. Banks, for example, usually purchase shorter term securities, and as funds available from these restricted supplies are exhausted, the rate is driven upward. In effect, this theory asserts that the capital market is not a perfect market and that the rates of return may reflect deficiencies in the supply of funds as well as the risk of the security. Another school of thought places primary emphasis on expectations as to future rates. One version claims that when overall rates are expected to increase, capital demanders postpone long-term funds acquisitions in anticipation of a future decrease in rates. This results in a substantial surge in the demand of short-term funds, driving short-term rates to higher levels.[12] At any rate, the "humped" or downward-sloping yield curves are usually viewed as temporary aberrations from the "normal" state of affairs. Under normal conditions, longer maturities involve greater risk, and thus require a higher rate of return.

## A COMPETITIVE MARKET FOR COMMON STOCK

From the discussion in this chapter, we can see that market rates of return on capital and, by implication, the price of securities are the result of a complex set of market activities. In general, it can be said that the forces of supply and demand establish both the general level of required rates of return and the risk premiums assigned to particular securities. The market rate of return and the price of common stock are established in the same fashion as those

---

[12]For a more detailed explanation of the "humped" yield curve, see Henning, Pigott, and Scott, *Financial Markets and the Economy*, Chap. 13.

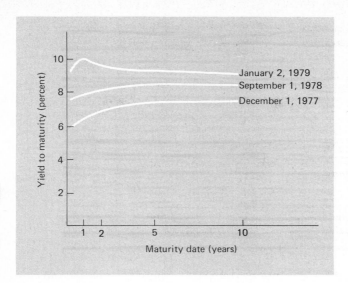

**FIGURE 15–3**

Changes in the Yield Curve, U.S. Government Securities from December 1977 to January 1979

for other securities. Management's pursuit of the goal of stockholder-wealth maximization takes place within the context of the market for capital as it has been discussed in this chapter. It is important to recognize that the market price of common stock is a *market-determined* price as distinct from an *administered* price.

The price of a corporation's common stock is determined in a relatively competitive market. In the United States, almost every corporation with publicly held common stock is scrutinized by hundreds of organizations specializing in the evaluation of stock prices. For example, most of the larger stock brokerage companies, such as E.F. Hutton and Merrill Lynch, provide extensive information about price-change expectations for common stocks. Smaller brokerage firms also provide market participants with information, but on a more limited basis. Major newspapers devote considerable space to the publication of information related to potential stock-price movements. There are hundreds of specialized publications for people interested in the stock market. These publications range from those available to all market participants at a modest cost (*The Wall Street Journal, Barron's,* and so on) to newsletters with subscription rates in the hundreds or thousands of dollars per year and distributed to a select clientele.

The securities industry has developed a system that permits almost instantaneous distribution of information relating to stock-market transactions taking place at the New York and other stock exchanges. This is the modern-day equivalent to the ticker tape. Many brokerage houses have waiting rooms in which the latest transactions as reported by the "tape" are magnified on a display for customer convenience—the electronic scoreboard of the market. In addition, the National Association of Security Dealers has a computer system that gives every member stock brokerage office in the

CHAP. 15 Capital Markets: An Overview

nation instant information on current offer and sale prices of less actively traded common stocks. Thus, information on stock performance is generally available and widely disseminated to the investing public.

The market for common stock is characterized by a large number of participants. It is estimated that over 25 million people are direct owners of common stock.[13] Most of these are potential sellers or buyers of common stocks and, as such, direct participants in the market for common stock.

In addition to individual market participants, there are institutional participants. Mutual funds, pension funds, trust departments of financial institutions, and insurance companies fall into this category. These institutions represent millions of individuals who are unable or unwilling to *directly* participate in the stock market. Naturally, the typical institutional participant buys and sells common stock in larger blocks than individual participants do. As a matter of fact, 54.7 percent of the dollar value of all common-stock transactions is transacted by institutions, as shown in Table 15–12. In addition, the total dollar holdings of institutional participants has been increasing over the years, as indicated in Table 15–13, resulting in a knowledgeable and informed group of market participants that in turn represent millions of individual market participants.

### TABLE 15-12

**STOCK-MARKET TRANSACTIONS BY TYPE OF PARTICIPANTS IN THE NEW YORK STOCK EXCHANGE**
(Value of Shares Traded)

| Participant | 1974 | 1976 |
|---|---|---|
| Financial institutions/intermediaries | 51.4% | 54.7% |
| Individuals | 23.1% | 23.1% |
| NYSE members | 25.5% | 22.2% |

Source: The New York Stock Exchange, *1978 Fact Book.*

The ability of large institutional investors to use their size to generate monopoly profits appears to be minimal. The institutional investors are large enough in numbers and small enough in individual size (relative to the market) to maintain the competitive nature of the market. The most telling proof of the lack of monopoly power by individual institutional participants is their inability to outperform the market. The record clearly indicates that mutual funds, for example, have not been able to earn monopoly profits. For the ten-year period ending in 1979, 59.3 percent of the "growth" mutual

---

[13]Many more are indirect owners of common stock, through pension funds, mutual funds, insurance company holdings, trusts, etc. These individuals do not participate directly in the market for common stock.

TABLE 15-13

ESTIMATED HOLDINGS OF NYSE-LISTED STOCKS BY SELECTED INSTITUTIONAL INVESTORS
(In Billions)

| Type of institution: | 1949 | 1965 | 1973 | 1974 | 1975 |
|---|---|---|---|---|---|
| Insurance companies | 2.8 | 16.4 | 36.4 | 26.7 | 33.2 |
| Investment companies | 3.0 | 34.7 | 46.4 | 31.1 | 40.6 |
| Pension funds (noninsured) | 0.5 | 37.3 | 101.7 | 74.1 | 105.0 |
| Nonprofit institutions | 4.6 | 30.0 | 38.7 | 29.0 | 38.0 |
| Other institutions | 0.2 | 3.7 | 7.9 | 6.4 | 8.4 |
| Subtotal | 11.1 | 122.1 | 229.7 | 167.7 | 225.4 |
| Foreign institutions | 0 | 0 | 0 | 3.3 | 5.1 |
| Total institutional holdings | 11.1 | 122.1 | 229.7 | 171.0 | 230.5 |
| Total market value of all NYSE-listed stock | 76.3 | 537.5 | 721.0 | 511.1 | 685.1 |
| Estimated percentage of the total held by institutions | 14.5% | 22.7% | 31.8% | 33.4% | 33.6% |

Source: The New York Stock Exchange (NYSE), 1978 Fact Book.

funds underperformed Standard & Poor's index of 500 stocks (a market average).

Government regulation of the securities industry also serves to foster the competitive nature of the market for common stock. Although these regulations do have their pitfalls, limitations, and even absurdities, they have tended to strengthen competitive market forces. Government insistence on full and timely disclosure of financial information has made more information available to both present and potential stockholders. Accounting reforms required by various government agencies make this information more usable than ever before. Government prosecution of corporate executives using insider information or engaging in stock-market manipulation has curtailed certain practices inherently unfair to other market participants.

The large number of market participants, the ready availability of financial information, and effective government regulation have created a market for common stock that is certainly competitive. In such a competitive market, the price of common stock is determined by relatively unencumbered supply and demand forces. Contrary to popular belief, even the largest single participant finds it extremely difficult and very risky to attempt to "rig" the market for widely traded stocks. Certain participants may attempt to gain an unfair advantage, but the success rate for such attempts is low both in absolute terms and in terms of effect on overall market activities.

**SUMMARY**  The American capital market is a highly competitive market. Capital is supplied to capital demanders by millions of individuals, frequently through financial intermediaries and/or financial-market facilitators. Different capital suppliers have different risk preferences and supply capital to those demanders with compatible risk characteristics. The market rates of return for different securities reflect these differences in risk and risk preferences. This market segmentation tends to be reinforced by market imperfections, especially those introduced by government regulation of financial institutions.

It is important that the manager of the modern firm understand the dynamics of this capital market, because this is the market in which capital funds for new asset acquisitions are raised. The price and availability of capital will have an important effect on the desirability of various asset-acquisition alternatives. In addition, corporate management should understand the general framework within which stock-price change and stockholder-wealth maximization take place. A quick look at the market for capital may suggest that the market lacks rationality. This conclusion is erroneous. At least in a general sense, it is quite easy to interpret market developments.

**QUESTIONS FOR DISCUSSION**

1. In a quantitative sense, how important are capital markets in providing funds to business? What types of funds are raised both outside and inside the capital markets?

2. Explain the role played by financial intermediaries. Explain how a local savings institution serves as a financial intermediary.

3. Using Table 15–2, summarize the major sources and uses of funds for the commercial banking system during the period 1974–78.

4. Using Tables 15–2 and 15–3, summarize the differences in sources and uses of funds between banking and nonbank financial institutions.

5. What kinds of capital are provided by banks to business? Explain why banks provide capital in such a fashion.

6. Describe the types of capital provided by life insurance companies, and explain why life insurance companies select the forms of capital transfers that they do. What types of funds are made available to business? What types of funds are not made available to business?

7. Describe the types of capital provided by pension funds, and explain why pension funds select the forms of capital transfers that they do. What types of funds are made available to business? What types of funds are not made available to business?

8. Describe the role finance companies play in providing funds to business.

9. Describe the role played by the investment banker in the capital market. Why isn't the investment banker a financial intermediary?

10. Describe the role played by commission brokerage firms in the capital market.

11. Explain the importance of the secondary markets for stocks and bonds. What role is played by commission brokerage firms in this market?

12. Describe the general nature of Moody's bond-rating system and how it is reflected in actual rates of return in the market.

13. Why is the typical yield curve upward-sloping?

14. Summarize the evidence that the market for common stocks is competitive. What are the implications of the competitiveness of the market for making monopoly profits in the market?

# APPENDIX 15A
## Government Regulation Of Financial Markets

Government, both federal and state, plays a pervasive role in financial-market activities. This appendix is divided into two parts. The first part will deal with government regulation of the securities market; the second will touch upon some of the regulations applicable to financial institutions. Regardless of management's opinions as to the desirability of such regulation, it should be aware of the most important government regulations applicable in financial markets and their effect on funds flows.

## GOVERNMENT REGULATION OF SECURITIES MARKETS

The federal government has enacted a series of laws applicable to securities traded in financial markets. These laws were the result of certain abuses that took place during the 1920s. The collapse of the stock market in 1929, of course, provided an impetus for the regulation of securities trading. Government and business both agreed at that time that regulation of the securities markets was necessary in order to restore public confidence in the markets and ensure a continued flow of capital to American businesses.

The basic laws under which the sale of stocks and bonds are regulated are the Securities Exchange Acts of 1933 and 1934. The intent of these laws was to protect the suppliers of capital from fraud and to ensure that information received by investors is truthful, accurate, and complete.[14] The laws attempt to achieve these goals in three ways:

1. *They require full disclosure* of all information affecting the price of a security. Corporations are permitted to hide neither favorable nor unfavorable information from the public. Thus, an oil company must disclose a possible new oil discovery; an electronics manufacturer must disclose that a lawsuit has been filed against the firm. The actual implementation of full

---

[14]Even with complete information, investors may make poor decisions, but the securities laws strive to give the capital suppliers a fair chance. The laws do not and cannot protect the investor from losses.

disclosure sometimes presents problems, which must be turned over to corporate counsel.

2. *Control of insider activities* is also governed by the securities laws. That is, corporate officials and major stockholders are not permitted to profit from insider information (information not available to all investors). Transactions by insiders must be reported to the Securities and Exchange Commission (SEC). The SEC regularly publishes reports of insider trading, using the names of insiders involved in trades. Corporate insiders are permitted to trade in the stock of their corporation if they comply with the reporting requirements. However, they are not permitted to make short-term gains on the stock or sell the stock short.[15]

3. *Controls on the issuing of new stocks* and the trade of outstanding stock is enforced by the SEC. The SEC tries to ensure that information provided to investors in prospectuses for new stocks and annual reports is accurate and complete. Rules have been established to achieve this objective. For example, the SEC has forced firms to modify accounting procedures related to leases, research and development, and foreign exchange. In addition, the SEC is attempting to develop a national market for securities that will give investors better price information.

It should be noted that many of the SEC regulations meet with considerable hostility in the business sector. Management often views the cost of compliance to be greater than any potential benefits to the investing public.

However, the overall result of securities-markets regulation appears to be beneficial to investors. Improved information increases the competitiveness and efficiency of the market. Investor protection broadens market participation, thus contributing to market efficiency. These benefits are partially offset by high compliance cost for business, and the costs associated with delaying new issues of securities in order to comply with administrative procedures established by the SEC.

## GOVERNMENT REGULATION OF FINANCIAL INSTITUTIONS

Financial institutions are subject to numerous regulations, imposed by both federal and state governments, that affect the sources and uses of their funds. In presenting an overview of such regulations and an evaluation of their effect on the assets and liabilities of financial institutions, we will concentrate on federal regulations. Rules imposed by state authorities will be mentioned only if they have wide application.

---

[15]Short sales involve selling a security you *do not own*. The short seller anticipates buying the security at a later date. When stock prices are expected to fall, selling short at a high price and buying later at a lower price to cover the sale can be very profitable. A short sale is a bet that the stock price will decline.

# COMMERCIAL BANKS

The actions of commercial banks are greatly restricted by various regulations. Among them are the following:

1. The ownership of common stocks by banks is severely restricted by law. Banks that are members of the Federal Reserve System are permitted to hold only (1) stock in a Federal Reserve District Bank, (2) stock in a foreign bank or an Edge Act Corporation, and (3) stock acquired when the loan using the stock as collateral goes into default. In this last case, the bank must divest itself of the stock within a reasonable period of time. The combined effect of these regulations is to prevent American banks from serving as a source of equity funds for firms. In many other countries—West Germany, for example—banks are permitted to provide equity funds to business firms.

2. The amount loaned to a single customer is limited by regulations to 10 percent of a bank's capital and surplus. This includes all loans, regardless of maturity; commercial paper; and bonds or any other type of security. This limitation does not apply to securities of the U.S. government or state and local governments. However, it does apply to foreign government securities.

3. The total dollar value of real estate loans is restricted to 70 percent of the time deposits of the commercial bank. This regulation effectively limits the role played by commercial banks in this important market.

4. The interest rate that banks are permitted to pay on savings and time deposits is also limited by regulation. Banks do not have the authority to pay interest rates higher than a specified amount in order to attract new deposits. Negotiable certificates of deposit (over $100,000) are exempt from these regulations.

The regulations above are presented to illustrate the range of restrictions placed on commercial banks. There are many other regulations (dealing with reserve requirements, capital adequacy, loans on securities, and the like) applicable to the commercial banking system. Banks, like other financial institutions, are severely restricted in what they can and cannot do by regulations designed to foster the safety and viability of the commercial banking system.

# SAVINGS AND LOAN ASSOCIATIONS

These financial institutions are required to invest the largest percentage of their funds in real estate mortgages. Savings and loan associations are largely restricted from making business loans or actively entering into the consumer credit area. S&Ls compete with commercial banks for savings and time deposits. Regulations, however, allow S&Ls to pay ¼ of 1 percent more on such deposits, thus giving them a competitive advantage over commercial banks in attracting them.

## LIFE INSURANCE COMPANIES

Life insurance companies are regulated primarily by state governments. Although each state has its own regulations, some of them are common to all states. For example, insurance companies are limited as to the amount of funds they are permitted to invest in common stock. This regulation has been relaxed in recent years, so that the importance of common stocks in the asset portfolios of life insurance companies is increasing (see Table 15–7), but they are still a small percentage of those portfolios.

## PENSION FUNDS

Pension funds are regulated by both government and court decisions. Recent legislation has increased the reporting requirements, funding, and investment limitations of pension funds. Pension funds are also governed by what is known as the "prudent-man rule." This rule requires that they invest their funds much as a prudent man would. Thus, a pension fund is not permitted to invest all its funds in the stock of any one corporation, since a prudent man would not do so.

This appendix has been only an overview of the regulatory environment facing some financial institutions. Our purpose was to illustrate that regulations affect the sources and uses of funds of financial institutions, as well as restricting the types of activities pursued by various market participants.

**SELECTED BIBLIOGRAPHY**

CROSSE, HOWARD D., and GEORGE H. HEMPEL, *Management Policies for Commercial Banks,* 3rd ed. Englewood Cliffs, N.J.: Prentice-Hall, 1980.

Federal Reserve Bank of Cleveland, *Money Market Instruments,* 3rd ed. 1970.

FRIEND, IRWIN, "The Economic Consequences of the Stock Market," *American Economic Review,* Papers and Proceedings, May 1972, 212–19.

————, "Economic Foundations of Stock Market Regulations," *Journal of Contemporary Business,* Summer 1976, 1–27.

HENNING, CHARLES N., WILLIAM PIGOTT, and ROBERT H. SCOTT, *Financial Markets and the Economy,* 2nd ed. Englewood Cliffs, N.J.: Prentice-Hall, 1978.

MICHAELSEN, JACOB B., *The Term Structure of Interest Rates: Financial Intermediaries and Debt Management.* New York: Intex Educational Publishers, 1973.

REED, EDWARD W., RICHARD V. COTTER, EDWARD K. GILL, and RICHARD K. SMITH, *Commercial Banking,* 3rd ed. Englewood Cliffs, N.J.: Prentice-Hall, 1980.

ROBINSON, ROLAND I., and DWAYNE WRIGHTSMAN, *Financial Markets: The Accumulation and Allocation of Wealth,* 2nd ed. New York: McGraw-Hill, 1979.

WOODWORTH, WALTER G., *The Money Market and Monetary Management,* 2nd ed. New York: Harper & Row, 1972.

Statistical information concerning financial markets can be obtained from the following publications:

*Fact Book.* The New York Stock Exchange (annual).

*Federal Reserve Bulletin.* Board of Governors of the Federal Reserve System (monthly).

*Flow of Funds Accounts.* Board of Governors of the Federal Reserve System (quarterly).

*Life Insurance Fact Book.* American Council of Life Insurance (annual).

*Savings and Loan Fact Book.* United States League of Savings Associations (annual).

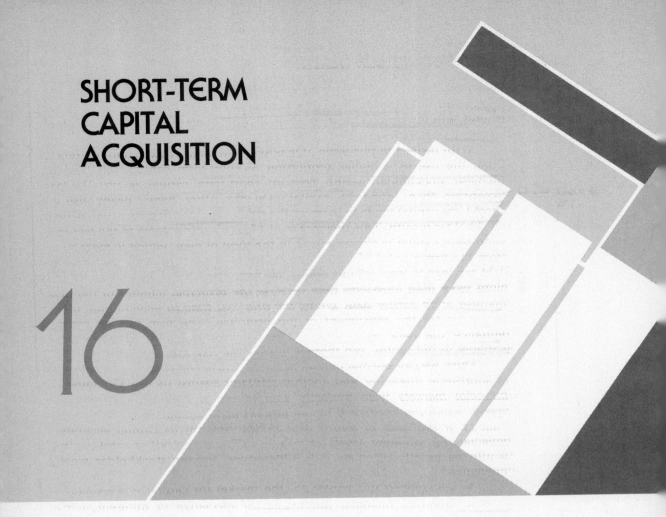

# SHORT-TERM CAPITAL ACQUISITION

# 16

## INTRODUCTION

Up to this point, we have treated debt as a homogeneous entity. But management has a wide range of options as to the type of debt capital to be acquired. Although there are many possible ways to classify alternative capital sources, this book will follow the balance-sheet classification and use two major categories: short-term and long-term. This chapter deals with the acquisition of short-term capital (capital that matures within one year). Chapters 17 and 18 deal with types of capital that have maturities extending beyond one year. In each chapter, we will examine the cost-risk implications of selected types of capital and the effect of various capital-acquisition strategies on stockholder wealth.

# MATURITY AND STOCKHOLDER WEALTH

Before we examine specific types of capital, it is necessary to evaluate the relation between the length of time to maturity and stockholder wealth. That is, how will the proportion of total capital that is short-term affect the price of common stock?

With respect to this issue, it is possible to identify two contrary forces. First, the use of a higher proportion of short-term capital will tend to increase stockholder wealth because short-term capital is usually less expensive than long-term capital.[1] On the other hand, heavy use of short-term capital tends to increase the riskiness of the firm and thus reduce stockholder wealth. This increase in riskiness is attributable to the fact that short-term capital is always raised in the form of debt, which is more risky from the firm's point of view, since failure to make required payments on debt can lead to legal actions against the firm. In addition, short-term debt is more risky than long-term debt because the principal amount of the debt matures at an earlier date, giving the firm less time to generate the funds necessary for the repayment of the principal. The firm can, of course, refinance the debt. Refinancing, however, assumes that funds will be available in the future, and there is always the risk that they will not.

Thus, we can see that one set of forces (lower costs) encourages the use of short-term financing, and another militates against its use. Of course, if financial markets were perfectly competitive and efficient, stockholder wealth would be unaffected by the proportion of capital that is short-term. That is, if the rates of return paid by the firm on its capital accurately reflected the different levels of risk in different maturities, cost savings would be exactly offset by risk differentials, leaving stockholder wealth unchanged.

As we showed in Chapter 15, the market for capital is a segmented market. Different financial intermediaries specialize in different market segments. Thus, for example, even though banks in a sense compete with pension funds, the competition is indirect. Legal and institutional factors hinder the flow of funds from one market to another. Under such conditions, it is quite possible that shortages of funds in certain segments of the market could drive up the costs of some types of capital to a higher point than what is required by their levels of risk.

Although the literature on this point is not clear, there is a general feeling that the proportion of short-term capital can be so high as to reduce stockholder wealth. Presumably, this general feeling reflects the fact that the cost saving associated with the use of short-term capital is insufficient to offset the increased riskiness of the firm.[2] At any rate, management tends to

---

[1]See the discussion in Chapter 15, under "Interest-Rate-Risk Structure."

[2]Limitations on short-term capital may also be explained in terms of bankruptcy costs. Increased proportions of short-term capital lead to increased risk, which leads to increased expectation of bankruptcy (see Appendix 5A).

keep short-term capital within certain limits, and both management and financial analysts view firms with "excessive" short-term debt in an unfavorable light. In practical terms, the only option open to management is to make the decision regarding the optimal proportion of short-term capital on a subjective basis. Independent advice and the experience of other firms may be helpful in this regard.

## SHORT-TERM LOANS
### TYPES OF LOANS

Short-term loans appear in the balance sheet under a variety of titles: short-term borrowings, short-term loans, loans payable, notes payable, and so on. These headings all indicate borrowings that are due for repayment within one year. Commercial banks are by far the most important source of short-term loans to business firms.

These short-term loans can take a number of different forms. The simplest type is what is called a *one-payment loan*, on which the entire principal and interest are due for payment on a specified date in the future. For example, assume that a construction firm borrows $1 million for six months at an annual interest rate of 10 percent. If this is a one-payment loan, both the principal of $1 million and the interest of $50,000 are due to the bank in six months. No periodic payments are made on a one-payment loan.

A *line of credit* represents a more complicated type of loan arrangement with a commercial bank. It is an agreement (often informal) between a bank and its customer by which the bank agrees to allow the customer to borrow up to a maximum specified amount at any time during a specified period. The line of credit may be used all or in part by the borrower. For purposes of illustration, a bank agrees to grant a line of credit of $500,000 to a customer. The customer may utilize the line of credit in several ways. For example, the customer may borrow in small amounts until total borrowings reach the line-of-credit maximum ($500,000). No further borrowing will be permitted until part of the loan is repaid; the amount of debt outstanding must never exceed $500,000. In another situation, the customer may borrow the entire $500,000 immediately, repay it all one month later, and borrow all or part of the $500,000 six months later. A third possibility is that the firm will never use the line of credit.

From the firm's point of view, the line of credit is very attractive, because it permits greater flexibility in the amount and maturity of short-term borrowing. Management can borrow only as much as needed and only when the funds are actually needed. This tends to reduce the dollar interest costs of loans and also reduce the red tape associated with borrowing.

The line-of-credit agreement specifies the cost to and other restrictions placed on the borrower. Included in this agreement will be the interest rate that will be paid by the borrower on actual loans made by the bank. The interest rate may be fixed (for example, 12 percent) or variable (for example, the bank prime rate plus 2 percent). In the usual case, banks also require that customers pay a commitment fee. This relatively small fee (usually ¼ of 1 percent per annum) is paid on the unused portion of the line of credit. Thus, for example, if a customer has borrowed 60 percent of its allocated line of credit, it pays the specified interest rate on that amount and the commitment fee on the unused portion (40 percent) of the line of credit. If the firm is utilizing none of its allocated line of credit, it must still pay the commitment fee on the entire amount.

The line-of-credit agreement may also specify the level of checking-account balances (usually called compensating balances) the borrower is expected to maintain in the bank during the period the line of credit is in effect. Finally, the agreement typically includes a provision specifying that the borrower must reduce its total outstanding debt to zero at some time during the year. This provision is included to keep lines of credit from being used as permanent sources of financing. As noted in Chapter 15, banks prefer to make short- rather than long-term loans.

## ANNUAL EFFECTIVE INTEREST RATES

Computing the effective annual interest rate on loans is more complicated than it first appears. The difficulty stems from the fact that there are several different interest-rate concepts, so that, in many cases, the interest rate stated by the lender is not equal to the annual effective rate of interest. For example, assume that a firm is granted a one-payment loan of $200,000 for exactly one year, at a stated interest rate of 10 percent. At the end of the year, the firm repays the $200,000 loan plus $20,000 in interest. In this case, the stated interest rate *is* equal to the annual effective rate of interest, because the amount available to the firm for the entire year is equal to the amount borrowed. The effective rate is equal to the dollar interest cost divided by the funds available during the year ($20,000/$200,000 = 10%). The annual effective rate for a loan can be computed as follows:

$$\text{Annual effective rate of interest} = \frac{\text{Dollar interest cost}}{\text{Amount available to the firm}} \quad (16\text{-}1)$$

But in some types of loans, the amount actually available to the firm is less than the amount borrowed. For example, assume that the firm borrowed $200,000 on a discounted basis with a stated rate of 10 percent. When a loan is issued on a discounted basis, the interest is deducted from the amount given to the borrower at the time of issuance of the loan. In this case, the borrower received only $180,000 ($200,000 borrowed − $20,000 interest) and, at the end of one year, repays $200,000. In this case, the amount available to the firm is not equal to the stated amount of the loan, and thus the annual effective interest rate is not equal to the stated interest rate. Using equation 16–1, the annual effective interest rate will be 11.1 percent ($20,000/$180,000).

When loans are repaid in installments, it is quite common for the stated rate to be lower than the annual effective rate of interest. For example, assume that a firm borrows $10,000 for one year at a stated interest rate of 5 percent and is expected to repay the loan plus $500 in interest (5% × $10,000) in twelve equal monthly payments. In this case, the $10,000 is not available to the firm for the entire year, since the firm is repaying the loan on a monthly basis. When loans are repaid in equal installments, the average amount of the loan outstanding is *approximately* equal to 50 percent of the stated amount. Thus, the annual effective interest rate on installment loans can be approximated using equation 16–2:

$$\text{Approximate annual effective interest rate, installment loan} = \frac{\text{Dollar interest cost}}{\text{Average amount available to the firm (50\% of stated amount)}} \quad (16\text{-}2)$$

In our illustration, only 50 percent of the stated $10,000, or $5,000, is available to the firm. The annual effective rate of interest is approximately 10 percent ($500/$5,000). As a general rule, the annual effective interest rate on one-year installment loans is approximately double the stated rate.[3]

It should be noted that all the rates discussed thus far are before taxes. Thus, the annual effective interest rate does not represent the actual cost of borrowing to the firm. The after-tax cost to the firm is computed by multiplying the before-tax cost by 1 minus the tax rate:

$$\text{After-tax cost of loans} = \text{Before-tax cost}(1 - \text{Tax rate}) \quad (16\text{–}3)$$

## EFFECT OF COMPENSATING BALANCES

In order to qualify for a loan from a commercial bank, a firm may be required to maintain a specified amount of money in its checking account. Such a required balance is called a "compensating balance" and may be greater than the balance ordinarily maintained by the firm. In fact, firms frequently have to increase their borrowings in order to maintain the specified compensating balances. The increased borrowings result in increased interest payments and increased after-tax cost of short-term debt.

For purposes of illustration, assume that the American Canning Corporation (ACC) needs $1 million for exactly one year. The firm is able to obtain from the Farm State National Bank a single-payment loan (not discounted) calling for a 10 percent rate of interest and a 20 percent

---

[3]Truth-in-lending laws require lenders to provide annual effective interest rates to consumers but not to businesses. These laws do not prohibit the use of any other interest-rate concept. In the typical consumer automobile purchase, for example, both annual effective and installment (lower than the annual) rates will be given to the consumer.

compensating-balance requirement. Assume further that ACC maintains a normal balance of $50,000, which it considers sufficient for meeting regular and emergency payments. Let us now work through the example to determine how much ACC would have to borrow and estimate the annual effective rate of interest.

1. *Amount Borrowed:* The amount borrowed can be computed using the following equation:

Amount borrowed = Amount available
$$+ (CB\% \times \text{Amount borrowed}) - \text{Normal balance}$$

where CB% = the percentage of the amount borrowed required as compensating balance

Amount available = the amount actually needed by the firm          (16-4)

For the ACC example, the amount borrowed is $1,187,500, which is computed as follows:

$$\text{Amount borrowed} = \$1,000,000 + (20\% \times \text{Amount borrowed}) - \$50,000$$

$$80\% \times \text{Amount borrowed} = \$1,000,000 - \$50,000 = \$950,000$$

$$\text{Amount borrowed} = \frac{\$950,000}{0.8} = \$1,187,500$$

In effect, ACC borrows $1,187,500 in order to raise the $1 million needed. The additional $187,500 (Amount borrowed − Amount available) is maintained in the firm's checking account at the Farm State National Bank. The $187,500 plus the firm's normal $50,000 balance (a total of $237,500) equals 20 percent of the loan balance outstanding ($237,500/$1,187,500 = 20%) and satisfies the compensating-balance requirement for the loan.

2. *Dollar Interest Paid:* When compensating balances are required, interest is paid on the entire amount of the loan, even though part of the loan is redeposited and maintained in the bank issuing the loan. In the ACC example, the dollar interest cost is 10 percent of the amount borrowed, or $118,750.

3. *Annual Effective Interest Rate:* As noted in equation 16–1, the annual effective interest rate is equal to the dollar interest cost divided by the amount available to the firm. When compensating balances are required, the amount available to the firm may be less than the amount borrowed. However, interest is paid on the entire amount borrowed. For ACC, the annual interest rate would be computed as follows:

$$\frac{\text{Annual effective}}{\text{interest rate}} = \frac{\text{Dollar interest cost}}{\text{Amount available}} = \frac{\$118,750}{\$1,000,000} = 11.875\%$$

You can see the effect of compensating balances on the effective rate of interest. Unless the firm usually maintains very large balances, the effective rate would be higher than the stated rate. In effect, the borrower pays interest on funds not available to the firm. By changing compensating-balance requirements, banks are able to alter the annual effective rate of interest without changing the stated interest rate.

Compensating-balance requirements fluctuate in much the same fashion as interest rates in general. During periods of weak loan demand, banks do not stress compensating balances, but during periods of strong loan demand, they use the compensating-balance requirements to raise the annual effective rate of interest to the firm. This will, of course, raise the firm's after-tax cost of short-term debt.

## COST OF LINES OF CREDIT

The annual effective interest rate on loans drawn on a line of credit is also greater than the stated interest rate, owing to the commitment fee. The effect of loan commitment fees on the annual effective interest rate can best be explained through the use of an example.

Nu-Toys Corporation is a manufacturer and distributor of toys. Since the toy business is seasonal, the firm increases production during August, September, and October in order to build up inventories for the Christmas season. Shipments are made to department stores in November and early December; collections on sales are concentrated in the months of January, February, and March. Nu-Toys has established a line of credit with the Wheastone National Bank. The maximum amount that the firm can draw on the line of credit is $1 million. The firm needs these funds during the months from August to December in order to finance the increase in inventories. Loans are repaid during the first part of the following year. The expected monthly borrowings and repayments of Nu-Toys are summarized in Table 16–1.

The terms of the Nu-Toy line of credit with the Wheastone Bank call for an annual interest payment of 12 percent (1 percent per month) on the funds that are actually borrowed. In addition, a commitment fee of ¼ of 1 percent per annum is charged on the unused portion of the line of credit. There are no compensating-balance requirements on the line of credit. Monthly balances outstanding, dollar interest costs, and monthly commitment fees are summarized in Table 16–2. From the information provided in the table, the annual effective rate of interest on Nu-Toys borrowings (before taxes) can be estimated as follows:

$$\text{Annual effective interest rate} = \frac{\text{Dollar interest cost}}{\text{Average amount available}}$$

$$= \frac{\$51,458.33}{\$416,666.67} = 12.35\%$$

TABLE 16-1

### THE NU-TOYS CORPORATION:
### FINANCING REQUIREMENTS

| Month | Borrowings (repayments) during the month | Total debt outstanding at the end of the month |
|---|---|---|
| July | 0 | 0 |
| August | $300,000 | $300,000 |
| September | $300,000 | $600,000 |
| October | $300,000 | $900,000 |
| November | $100,000 | $1,000,000 |
| December | 0 | $1,000,000 |
| January | ($100,000) | $900,000 |
| February | ($600,000) | $300,000 |
| March | ($300,000) | 0 |
| April | 0 | 0 |
| May | 0 | 0 |
| June | 0 | 0 |

That is, on an annual basis, Nu-Toys has an average outstanding loan balance of $416,666.67 ($5,000,000/12). The total charge by the bank for the loans extended was $51,458.33 ($50,000 in interest plus $1,458.33 in commitment fees).

Notice that the annual effective interest rate on the line of credit is slightly higher than the stated rate. The commitment fee itself, while resulting in a slight increase in the effective rate, may actually save the firm some money by increasing financing flexibility and convenience. Real-world situations must be evaluated on a case-by-case basis. For example, Nu-Toys may have been forced to borrow the entire $1 million for the seven months the funds were needed. The dollar interest cost on a $1 million, seven-month loan issued at 12 percent is $70,000 (1 percent per month on $1 million for seven months).[4] Nu-Toys would have had idle balances in some months, but it is doubtful that investing the idle balances in marketable securities would compensate for the additional interest expense in having a larger loan. As you can see, the line of credit allows the firm to tailor borrowings to short-term financing needs and thus minimize the cost.

## SECURED LOANS

Most short-term loans are provided by commercial banks and commercial finance companies. Almost all such loans granted by commercial finance companies are secured by some form of collateral, and a high proportion of bank loans are similarly secured. The nature of the security is such that,

---

[4] 1% per month does not *exactly* equal an annual percentage rate of 12%. However, in order to simplify computations, we will use this procedure throughout the chapter.

TABLE 16-2

## THE NU-TOYS CORPORATION: COST OF THE LINE OF CREDIT

| Month | Short-term Debt Outstanding | Unused Portion of Line of Credit | Dollar Interest Cost[a] | Cost of Commitment Fee[b] |
|---|---|---|---|---|
| July | 0 | $1,000,000 | 0 | $208.33 |
| August | $300,000 | $700,000 | $3,000 | $145.83 |
| September | $600,000 | $400,000 | $6,000 | $83.33 |
| October | $900,000 | $100,000 | $9,000 | $20.83 |
| November | $1,000,000 | 0 | $10,000 | 0 |
| December | $1,000,000 | 0 | $10,000 | 0 |
| January | $900,000 | $100,000 | $9,000 | $20.83 |
| February | $300,000 | $700,000 | $3,000 | $145.83 |
| March | 0 | $1,000,000 | 0 | $208.33 |
| April | 0 | $1,000,000 | 0 | $208.33 |
| May | 0 | $1,000,000 | 0 | $208.33 |
| June | 0 | $1,000,000 | 0 | $208.33 |
| Totals | $5,000,000 | $7,000,000 | $50,000 | $1,458.33 |

Average monthly borrowing $= \dfrac{\$5,000,000}{12} = \$416,666.67$

Total borrowing dollar costs $= \$50,000 + \$1,458.33 = \$51,458.33$

[a]The annual interest rate of 12% can be converted to a monthly rate by dividing by 12. Thus, the monthly interest rate is 1%.

[b]The annual rate of the commitment fee is ¼ of 1%, and it can be converted to a monthly rate by dividing it by 12. Thus, the commitment fee expressed on a monthly basis is ¹⁄₄₈ of 1% per month.

should the borrower fail in meeting contractual obligations to the lender, the collateral can be seized by the lender. The lender can then sell the collateral to a third party and recover all or part of the payments owed by the borrower. The use of collateral in the loan-granting process, by reducing the riskiness to the lender, is particularly attractive to banks, since banks seek to make low-risk loans.

Firms prefer to borrow on an unsecured basis, other things being equal. Secured loans tend to be used because they are substantially less expensive or because funds are simply not available otherwise. Firms in very strong financial positions are usually able to raise their short-term funds on an unsecured basis.

As a general rule, current assets serve as collateral for short-term loans. Although long-term assets could be used, these are usually offered as collateral on long-term loans. Marketable securities, even though they are current assets, are usually not used as collateral, since it is probably less expensive to sell the low-yielding marketable securities than to borrow at relatively higher rates. Thus, most short-term secured loans are collateralized by either accounts receivable or inventories.

**Cost of Secured vs. Unsecured Loans**

The analysis of unsecured financing is confused by two seemingly contradictory facts:

1. The cost of the average unsecured loan is less than that of the average secured loan.
2. Some firms can reduce loan costs by borrowing on a secured basis even though the average cost of secured loans is greater than the average cost of unsecured loans.

How is it possible for management to reduce costs by using a relatively expensive type of financing? The answer revolves around the word *average*. The average unsecured loan is made only to firms that have superior creditworthiness. Many firms with an acceptable level of creditworthiness may not qualify for this "average" rate and would be forced to borrow at higher rates. It is possible for the firm to pay less than the unsecured rate of interest appropriate for its particular risk level by borrowing and using certain assets as collateral.

An illustration will help clarify this point. The Teaneck Corporation is applying for a loan. Mr. Barks, the financial manager of the firm, goes to his bank and receives the following information:

1. The bank's annual effective rate for unsecured loans to customers with a superior credit rating is 9%.
2. The bank, however, does not rate the Teaneck Corporation in the superior class, so it is not willing to make an unsecured loan. But Ms. Sid, the loan officer, suggests that such a loan could be obtained from a nonbank source. Ms. Sid estimates that the cost of such an unsecured loan would be 14%.
3. The loan officer advises the financial manager that the bank would be willing to make a loan secured by inventories. The annual effective cost of such a secured loan would be 12%.

From this illustration, we can see how a firm can reduce costs and still pay a rate higher than the average unsecured-loan rate. The saving is attributable to the fact that the firm does not qualify for the "average" unsecured loan. In evaluating financing alternatives, the firm must compare the unsecured loan rate applicable to *that individual firm* (rather than the average rate) to the effective rate associated with secured financing.

**Using Accounts Receivable as Security**

In practice, there is a wide variety of options open to firms wishing to use accounts receivable as collateral for secured loans. Both banks and finance companies offer a range of services that both assist firms in the management of accounts receivable and facilitate the use of accounts receivable as collateral for short-term loans. Firms can choose from among the following services offered by financial institutions:

1. *Credit Checking.* Financial institutions review the payment record and credit standing of potential customers. The extent to which the institution can perform this function better than the firm will be reflected in

a superior classification of customers and lower bad-debt losses.[5] Small firms may find it especially useful to employ the more specialized expertise available to some financial institutions.

2. *Collections.* Financial institutions can handle the actual collections of accounts receivable. Employing their specialized services may increase total collections and, equally important, speed up the collection process. Both these factors will reduce the need for additional financing.

3. *Loans.* In addition to the services above, financial institutions make loans using accounts receivable as collateral.

4. *Assumption of the Risk of Nonpayment.* Under certain circumstances, the financial institution will assume the risk involved in the extension of trade credit. This situation will be discussed more fully when we review factoring of accounts receivable in a later section of this chapter.

These four accounts-receivable services are available to firms individually or as a package. Obviously, it costs the financial institution money to provide such services, and it expects to be compensated by the firm.

Thus, financial institutions do more than just make loans to business firms. They provide a range of services that are often combined with the loan. The combination of borrowing with other services makes it more difficult to estimate the cost of the loan by itself. Thus, the effective annual interest rate of a short-term loan secured by accounts receivable may be difficult to compute. Two common types of arrangements (pledging of accounts receivable and factoring of accounts receivable) are presented below in order to highlight the range of options open to the firm and to establish a conceptual framework for the evaluation of costs and risk implications.

**Pledging Accounts Receivable.** Pledging accounts receivable is the simplest form of short-term borrowing using accounts receivable as collateral. In many cases, the financial institution provides no services other than that of lending the funds. In the typical case, the firm itself will check the credit standing of customers and extend trade credit without prior approval from the financial institution. The institution will review the accounts in order to ensure that the risk of nonpayment is not so high as to make the accounts useless as collateral. Once the creditworthiness of the buyer is established, the financial institution will make a loan to the firm and hold the accounts receivable as security. The firm itself collects from the customer and repays the financial institution. The only fees paid in this simplest case are interest fees, which represent the before-tax cost of short-term loans.[6]

The financial institution will attempt to minimize its risk in two ways. First, only accounts receivable based upon trade-credit extension to reliable customers will be accepted as collateral. Frequently, financial institutions

trade credit

---

[5]See Chapter 11 for a discussion of accounts-receivable management.

[6]Cost-computation procedures were discussed earlier in this chapter.

will require a minimum credit rating provided by an independent credit reporting agency, such as Dun & Bradstreet. The institution also minimizes its risk by restricting loans to less than 100 percent of the face value of the accounts receivable. The percentage of the face value that will be loaned reflects the creditworthiness of the buyers. For example, if the borrower's customers are the U.S. government, AT&T, or General Motors, the lender may be willing to lend up to 90 percent of the value of the receivables. The percentage will be lower if the customers are "mom-and-pop" grocery stores.

As a final protection, financial institutions are sure to insist that the borrower's liability is not limited to the collectibility of the accounts receivable. Should the borrower be unable to collect on an account receivable pledged as security for a loan, the borrower must still repay the loan. This is known as lending *with recourse.* In a sense, all the other assets of the firm serve as a generalized form of security for the loan. The financial institution assumes none of the risk of bad-debt losses.

Firms pledging accounts receivable can use other services provided by financial institutions. Credit checking and collection services are frequently employed by smaller firms in conjunction with pledging. The payment of fees for such services does not represent payment for the acquisition of capital (interest). They are administrative costs paid to outside contractors and resulting in reductions of internal administrative expenses. For example, hiring a bank to collect accounts receivable will result in an increased payment to the bank; however, the outside purchase of this service will reduce the need for an in-house collections department, and thus reduce administrative expenses.

The point is that not all payments made to financial institutions reflect the cost of borrowing funds. Some types of payments (for collections and credit checking) may (or may not) actually lead to an internal cost reduction. The costs of outside services cannot simply be added to the interest rate in order to arrive at the cost of short-term loans in pledging situations.

***Factoring Accounts Receivable.*** Factoring of accounts receivable refers to the "sale" of accounts receivable to a financial institution. In a typical case, a manufacturer will enter into an agreement with a bank or finance company that calls for the financial institution to perform each of the four services associated with accounts-receivable-secured loans. As the manufacturer receives orders from its customers, they are forwarded to the financial institution (called the "factor" when performing this service). The factor checks the credit rating of the customer. Upon approval by the factor, the manufacturer ships the goods to the customer and assigns the invoice to the factor. In the usual case, a large portion of the funds is advanced immediately to the manufacturer. The remaining funds are held as a reserve against disputes between the manufacturer and its customer. This last portion is forwarded to the manufacturer as it is collected by the factor from the customers.

An important characteristic of factoring is that the "sale" of the previously approved accounts receivable is made on *without recourse*. That is, should the accounts receivable be uncollectible because of the customer's inability to pay, it is the factor rather than the manufacturer that suffers the loss. But not all the risks of nonpayment are passed along to the factor. When disputes arise as to quality, merchandise ordered, price, or the like, the manufacturer rather than the factor assumes the liability.

Additional insight into factoring may be gained by looking at it in two slightly different ways:

1. *Factoring as a "Credit Card."* Factoring is to a manufacturer much what a MasterCharge agreement is to a retailer. Sales can be made to customers that have received prior credit approval from the financial institution, and the firm receives immediate payment from the institution. The financial institution rather than the firm assumes the risk of nonpayment by the customer. Just as smaller retailers tend to use MasterCharge, smaller manufacturers tend to use factoring. Both eliminate the need for credit checking and collections, reduce the risk of nonpayment, and speed up the receipt of funds.

2. *Factoring as Two Separate Services.* It is also convenient to look at factoring and its cost as two distinct groups of services. The first group includes credit checking, collections, and risk assumption. The second involves advancing funds to the manufacturer before they are received by the factor. This second service is similar to a loan, although it is not recorded on the manufacturer's books in this fashion.

This "two separate services" framework is actually employed in pricing the services provided by the factor. The first package (credit checking, collections, and risk assumption) costs between 1 and 3 percent of the face value of the invoices. In 1979, the cost of this package in most cases tended to be slightly more than 1 percent. For the service of providing cash to the manufacturer before it is actually collected from the customer, the factor makes an anticipation charge, which is the same idea as an interest charge. This charge tends to be 2 to 3 percent above the bank prime rate. Considering that those firms utilizing the services of factors tend to be relatively weak, and that no compensating balances are required, the rates are not far from those that could be obtained from other short-term lenders.

Let us illustrate a complete factoring arrangement with a numerical example. The Oregon Lumber Corporation, which sells wood products on a net-90-days basis, has entered into a factoring agreement with the Financial Factors Corporation. The agreement specifies that the factor will charge a 2 percent commission and withhold a reserve of 8 percent to cover disputes between the buyers and Oregon Lumber. The factor also makes an annual anticipation charge of 12 percent on the *face value* of the invoice. The charges are computed on a discounted basis. For a sale of $100,000, Oregon Lumber receives $87,000 on the date of the sale and an additional $8,000 upon collection by the factor 90 days later. The methodology used to calculate these numbers is shown in Table 16–3.

**TABLE 16–3**

OREGON LUMBER CORPORATION:
NET FUNDS RECEIVED UNDER THE FACTORING AGREEMENT

| | |
|---|---:|
| Face value of the invoice | $100,000 |
| *Less:* Reserve[a] | (8,000) |
| *Less:* Discounted anticipation charge (interest)[b] | (3,000) |
| *Less:* Factoring commission | (2,000) |
| *Equals:* Funds received on the date of the sale | $87,000 |

[a]The $8,000 will be forwarded to Oregon Lumber upon collection.

[b]The "interest" is 1% per month (12% per year) on the face value of the invoice. Since the firm sells on a net-90-days basis, the interest will be 3% of the face value of the invoice.

The actual "interest" rate is greater than 12 percent a year (1 percent a month) for two reasons. First, the interest charge is subtracted from the funds available to Oregon Lumber (interest is discounted). Second, Oregon Lumber pays "interest" on $100,000 even though $8,000 is held back as a reserve. The actual annual effective rate of "interest" on factored accounts can be computed using equation 16–5:[7]

$$\begin{aligned} \text{Annual effective rate} &= \frac{\text{Dollar cost}}{\text{Dollars available to borrower}} \times \text{Number of periods in a year} \\[2mm] &= \frac{\text{Dollar cost}}{\begin{array}{c}(\text{Face value of invoice} \\ - \text{ Reserve} - \text{Prepaid interest} \\ - \text{ Factoring commission})\end{array}} \times \text{Number of periods in a year} \end{aligned}$$

(16-5)

For the Oregon Lumber Corporation, the true annual effective cost of funds is 13.8 percent:

$$\text{Annual effective rate} = \frac{\$3,000}{\$100,000 - \$8,000 - \$3,000 - \$2,000} \times 4 = 13.8\%$$

Note that the number 4 represents the number of 90-day periods in a year. In effect, multiplying by the number of periods in a year creates an annual rate out of a rate for a shorter period. Also note that the factoring commission of $2,000 is not included in the cost of funds. The factoring commission is a charge for services performed rather than a cost of funds.

---

[7]This formula is an approximation. Interest payments of 1% per month or 3% per three months result in an annual effective rate slightly higher than 12%.

Although factoring and pledging accounts receivable as security for loans are similar in many ways, the accounting treatments are quite different, a fact that highlights the crucial differences between them. Under pledging, when a firm sells to a customer, finished-goods inventories decline and accounts receivable increase. The firm then uses such receivables as collateral for a loan, so cash and loans payable increase. Under factoring, when a firm sells to a customer, inventories decrease and the firm receives cash directly from the factor. No increase in liabilities is involved.

The accounting transactions for each type of arrangement are summarized in Table 16–4. As the table shows, in a technical sense, only pledging results in an increase in capital. In a real sense, however, both factoring and pledging result in the receipt of cash by the firm—which is, of course, the whole purpose of raising capital.

#### TABLE 16–4

ACCOUNTING TRANSACTIONS, PLEDGING
AND FACTORING ACCOUNTS RECEIVABLE

| Pledging | | Factoring | |
|---|---|---|---|
| Assets | Liabilities | Assets | Liabilities & Equity |
| + Cash | + Loans payable | + Cash | |
| + Accounts | | − Inventories | |
| Receivable | | | |
| − Inventories | | | |

In addition to cost, there are several reasons why firms may be reluctant to use factoring. First, it somewhat limits control over accounts-receivable management alternatives. As discussed in Chapter Eleven, the firm should establish credit terms with an eye toward the effect of incremental amounts of accounts receivable on stockholder wealth. For example, the factor's desire for minimizing credit losses may be incompatible with the firm's value-maximization objective. In addition, many firms are reluctant to assign collections to factors because the collection process is often perceived as an integral part of a customer-relations program. To some extent, the personal relationship between buyer and seller is lost when a third party—an impersonal "collector"—gets involved in the collection process. A final fact often considered is that, traditionally, the users of factors have been relatively weak firms. Firms are anxious to avoid the outward appearance of financial fragility. This matter, however, has become less important in recent times; business today often perceives factoring as just another alternative in short-term financing.

**Using Inventories As Security For Loans**    Certain types of raw-materials and finished-goods inventories are frequently used as collateral for secured short-term loans. Inventories of items that can easily be resold without great price reductions are generally preferred by lenders. Perishables (such as tomatoes) or specialized products (such as hula hoops) are not usually regarded as good collateral for loans. Finished-goods inventories of canned goods, automobiles, and appliances are generally accepted as collateral, as are raw-materials inventories such as lumber, coal, and steel. Those items acceptable as collateral are of such a nature that they can be sold in their present physical form with minimum risk of obsolescence or perishability.

There are a number of different arrangements through which inventories can be used to secure loans. The most commonly used procedures are (1) blanket liens, (2) trust receipts, and (3) warehousing. We will describe the mechanics involved in each of these situations and analyze the cost and risk implications of each.

*Blanket Liens.* A blanket lien on inventories gives the lender a priority claim on all the inventories of the borrower. Should the borrower fail to repay the loan, the lender can seize a sufficient part of the borrower's inventories, dispose of them, and use the proceeds to repay the loan. A blanket lien on inventories permits the lender to move quickly to recover funds. It also provides a senior claim on the inventory assets; that is, in case of business liquidation, the proceeds from the disposal of inventories go to the holder of the blanket lien. Only the amount available after blanket-lien claims have been satisfied is available to the firm's other creditors.

The security offered by a blanket lien is limited by practical considerations. Most important, when a blanket lien is used, it is the borrower rather than the lender who maintains control over the inventories. The lender has no real protection against poor management performance or dishonesty on the part of the borrower. It is quite easy for the borrower to reduce inventories below agreed-upon levels without the lender's knowledge. In such cases, the unsuspecting lender may find itself with zero or partial collateral. This shortcoming has led to the development of more precise methods of protecting the value of the inventory collateral. Trust receipts and warehousing are two such methods.

*Trust Receipts.* In order to protect the collateral of a loan, the lender may insist upon the use of trust receipts. When a trust receipt is employed, the loan is backed by a *specific asset,* such as a particular automobile. As soon as the borrower sells the specific asset, the loan must be repaid.

Let us illustrate the use of trust receipts with an example. Automobile dealers are the most frequent users of trust-receipts financing. A dealer with an inventory of 50 cars may need to finance its inventory with a loan from a financial institution. The institution will make a separate loan on *each* of the 50 cars in the inventory. These cars can be readily identified by their respective serial numbers. The car dealer maintains physical possession of the cars in trust for the lender. When a car is sold, the dealer is obligated by the agreement to repay the loan made on that *specific* car, thus reducing the firm's balance by that amount. The dealer, of course, can borrow again on another car when a new car is received from the manufacturer.

From the standpoint of the lender, this procedure is less convenient and more costly than the blanket lien on inventories. There is more paperwork, since, as the loan on each specific asset is repaid, a new loan is prepared for the new asset purchased by the firm to replenish its inventory. But even though the borrower maintains physical possession of the assets, the lender has greater protection under this form of inventory financing than under the blanket lien.[8] In the event of default, the bank has ownership of the assets and can easily sell them to other parties. The lending institution can, and does, check at various times to ensure that the borrower actually has physical possession of the assets.

Trust receipts tend to be used to finance inventories of automobiles, mobile-home trailers, and other high-priced items that can be identified easily by serial numbers. In the past, trust receipts were used to finance inventories of coffee and lawn fertilizer, but the tremendous number of assets involved, coupled with difficulties in identifying specific assets, militates against such uses. The procedure works best when it can be applied to easily identified inventory items, and since the cost of preparing the documentation necessary for a trust receipt is expensive, the procedure is preferred for high-priced items. It should be noted that firms prefer to use unsecured loans rather than trust receipts (when possible) because the cost of preparing and supervising trust deed transactions is passed along to the borrower in the form of higher interest rates.

*Warehousing.* Warehousing of inventories provides an important alternative to the use of trust receipts. In such cases, the inventories used as collateral for a loan are placed in a warehouse supervised by an independent third party.

As an example, the New Paltz Canning Corporation purchases peaches in the late summer and early fall. The peaches are canned and placed in a warehouse. Sales are made throughout the year from the inventory. Early in the fall, the firm has a huge investment in inventories. The firm borrows to finance the inventories and reduces the value of the loan as inventories are sold.

The Station National Bank provides short-term loans to canning companies only if the loans are secured by inventories. The bank requires New Paltz Canning to place the inventories in an independently supervised warehouse and lends only a percentage of the inventories' estimated value. The warehouse supervisor will not permit New Paltz to withdraw inventories from the warehouse unless such withdrawals are approved by the bank. The bank permits withdrawals of inventory from the warehouse only as the loan balance is reduced. By following this procedure, the bank is able to protect the value of the collateral offered by the borrower.

---

[8]We assume, of course, no dishonesty on the part of the borrower.

Depending on the situation, a public or a field warehouse may be used. Public warehouses are run by firms specializing in the storage of inventories and the protection of their collateral value. By definition, a public warehouse is a disinterested third party, capable of providing the supervision of inventories desired by lenders. The major disadvantage of public warehousing is that such warehouses may be located considerable distances from the borrower's premises. This may result in a substantial increase in transportation costs, which may make public warehousing prohibitively expensive.

In order to eliminate transportation cost as a factor in warehousing, the concept of field warehousing has been developed. With field warehousing, the inventory collateral remains on the premises of the borrower, which eliminates transportation costs, but the borrower loses control over the inventories, which eliminates abuses associated with blanket liens. A field warehouse is established by turning over a portion of the borrower's facility to an independent supervisor and notifying the public that the inventories in that section are being used as collateral for a loan. That portion of the facility used as a field warehouse must be secure and available only through the independent supervisor, and the supervisor permits withdrawals of inventory only with the approval of the lender.

The cost of short-term loans secured by inventories can be relatively high. Depending upon the situation, the firm's transportation cost and storage cost may be increased. The extent of the increase will depend on how well the warehousing operation can be integrated with the firm's regular activities. It is reasonable to assume that in most cases, there will be at least some increase in these costs. In addition, the warehouse supervision and administration costs will add to the cost of raising funds using inventory-secured loans. Remember, these costs must be added to the regular interest rate charged by the lender.

Let us illustrate field warehousing. The American Canning Corporation needs $1 million for three months (90 days)—July, August, and September. The firm can obtain a 90-day loan from the Third National Bank if a field warehouse is established to protect the lender. This arrangement includes (1) a 10 percent cost of money to the Third National Bank, (2) no compensating-balance requirements, and (3) warehousing costs of a flat fee of $500 plus 1 percent of the maximum amount of the loan. Therefore, borrowing from the Third National Bank has two costs: the interest cost of the funds borrowed, and the warehousing costs of the inventories used as collateral. The interest cost will be:

$$\text{Interest cost} = 10\%(\$1,000,000)\left(\frac{90 \text{ days}}{360 \text{ days}}\right) = \$25,000$$

Warehousing costs will include a fixed fee of $500 plus 1 percent of the total borrowed, or $10,000. Thus, the total cost (financing and warehousing) of borrowing from the Third National Bank will be:

$$\text{Total cost} = \$25,000 + \$500 + \$10,000 = \$35,500$$

The use of accounts receivable and inventories as security for loans tends to increase the cost of raising funds. Managers know this, and would prefer to use unsecured loans whenever they are available at comparable rates. In some situations, the cost of unsecured loans would be so high that collateral is used to reduce the risk to the lender and bring down the cost. But a well-managed firm uses secured financing only if costs are reduced below those of unsecured loans.[9]

The use of secured (as distinct from unsecured) short-term financing tends to influence asset-specific and firmwide costs of capital in two ways. First, and most obviously, secured financing tends to reduce the cost of short-term financing below that of unsecured financing by the same firm. Second, the use of secured financing tends to increase the risk borne by other debt suppliers and equity suppliers. The increased risk can be attributed to the fact that pledging assets as collateral makes those assets unavailable to other suppliers of capital in case of reorganization or liquidation of the firm. In addition, the possibility of a seizure of assets (especially inventories) may increase the probability of business failure. Thus, the use of secured loans has a mixed effect on stockholder wealth. By offering collateral for loans, management may be able to reduce the costs of borrowing, thus increasing profits and cash flows to stockholders. This tends to increase stockholder wealth. Offsetting this tendency is the increase in the risk borne by stockholders when the firm uses assets as collateral for loans. If management can obtain unsecured short-term financing at or near market rates, it should accept this alternative over the use of relatively expensive secured short-term financing.

At this point, it is necessary to reintroduce an idea presented in several earlier sections. That is, management should view *all* the assets of the firm as being financed by *all* the liabilities and equities. If, for example, a firm desires to borrow funds to increase inventories, it may seek a short-term loan and view the cost of the loan as the appropriate "asset-specific cost of capital" for use in evaluating the asset-acquisition alternative. This is the wrong way to proceed. It turns out that one of the greatest hazards associated with the use of secured financing is that the nature of the security tends to encourage the firm to use component costs rather than asset-specific costs of capital in the decision-making process.

In summary, there is absolutely no reason why secured short-term financing should not be used if (and only if) it is part of the firm's optimal capital structure. Secured financing should not be viewed as "roughly the same" as unsecured short-term financing. In addition, the firm must be careful to avoid the use of the cost of a single type of financing as the appropriate cost to use in asset-acquisition situations.

---

[9]In some cases, firms may view the situation as one in which unsecured loans are simply not available. This should usually be interpreted as, "not available *near current rates*."

# COMMERCIAL PAPER

A firm can also borrow money by issuing commercial paper. Commercial paper consists of short-term unsecured promissory notes issued by large corporations. Basically, large corporations use commercial paper as a substitute for short-term unsecured bank loans. The maturity of commercial paper is always less than 270 days and usually between two and four months.[10] Commercial paper is attractive to firms because its cost is usually lower than the cost of bank loans. Table 16–5 illustrates the relationship between commercial-paper rates and the rate on short-term bank loans. The requirement of compensating balances on bank loans results in even greater differentials than are shown in the table.

### TABLE 16–5

COMPARISON OF INTEREST RATES, PRIME BANK LOANS AND PRIME
COMMERCIAL PAPER
(1972–1979)

| Date | Prime commercial paper (90–119 days) | Commercial-bank prime rate |
|---|---|---|
| July 1979 | 9.87% | 11.54% |
| September 1978 | 8.39% | 9.41% |
| September 1977 | 6.09% | 7.13% |
| September 1976 | 5.33% | 7.00% |
| September 1975 | 6.79% | 8.00% |
| September 1974 | 11.36% | 11.38%[a] |
| September 1973 | 10.31% | 9.88%[a] |
| September 1972 | 5.07% | 5.50%[a] |

[a]For purposes of consistency, these rates have been presented as single amounts. The actual ranges shown in the *Federal Reserve Bulletin* are:

| Sept. 1974 | 10.75% to 12.00% |
| Sept. 1973 | 9.75% to 10.00% |
| Sept. 1972 | 5.25% to 5.75% |

Source: *Federal Reserve Bulletin*, various issues.

The use of commercial paper is limited. Only very large firms with excellent credit standing can raise capital in this fashion. Even some of the best-known firms in the United States do not or cannot sell commercial paper.

The primary purchasers of commercial paper are nonfinancial corporations with temporary surpluses of cash (see Chapter 11). These firms buy commercial paper and hold it as part of a portfolio of marketable securities. Thus, the market for commercial paper is very dependent upon the existence

[10]If maturity exceeds 270 days, the commercial paper must be registered with the U.S. Securities and Exchange Commission. This involves extra cost and reduces the attractiveness of commercial paper with longer maturities.

of short-term excess liquidity in the nonfinancial corporate sector. During peak levels of economic activity, the liquidity of nonfinancial corporations (commercial-paper buyers) is reduced as internal needs for cash increase. Thus, during periods of high economic activity, a seller of commercial paper may be unable to find a buyer. In such times, the rate on commercial paper may actually exceed the rate charged by banks (as in September 1973).

It should also be noted that the commercial-paper market is subject to "panics." During such periods, even large, financially sound corporations may be unable to sell commercial paper. For example, in 1970, the Penn Central Railroad, a large user of commercial paper, entered bankruptcy. Corporate treasurers became reluctant to purchase commercial paper of almost all firms immediately after this failure. Many firms with outstanding commercial paper were temporarily in a very difficult position, as they were forced to seek new sources of short-term financing. The commercial-paper market recovered a short time later, but the episode illustrates the vulnerability of those firms relying too heavily on this source of funds.

The possibility that short-term funds will be unavailable in commercial-paper markets tends to make commercial paper more risky than unsecured bank loans. Commercial-paper users, however, have found a simple way of ensuring against unavailability of funds in the commercial-paper market. Today, firms using commercial paper frequently enter into a simultaneous line-of-credit agreement with a bank. The intent is to use the line of credit only if funds are unavailable from other sources. As discussed earlier, the usual fee for the line of credit is ¼ of 1 percent per year. In effect, the bank receives payments from the commercial-paper user even when no loans are made. The practice of using backup lines of credit and commercial paper simultaneously increases the cost of commercial paper slightly, but the cost remains substantially lower than that of bank loans. In addition, the use of lines of credit brings the risk of commercial paper into equality with the risk of bank loans. Lower cost and identical risk mean increases in stockholder wealth.

## ACCOUNTS PAYABLE

Trade credit constitutes an important source of short-term financing to the firm. Through the process of trade credit, a firm is able to obtain goods and services from a supplier and postpone payment for them. This postponement of payment is an extension of credit by the seller to the buyer. A firm that is using trade credit as a means of financing will have a balance-sheet liability item called "accounts payable." In this section, guidelines relating to the use and misuse of accounts payable will be discussed.[11]

---

[11]Here, we will be looking at trade credit from the point of view of the buyer of goods and services. In Chapter 11, the same topic was viewed from the point of view of the seller. Naturally, these two topics are closely related.

The fact that trade credit is a type of capital is sometimes obscured by the fact that, although other types of capital (bank loans, bonds, and so on) result in cash inflows, there is no movement of cash associated with trade credit. But note that in the absence of the availability of trade credit, the use of other types of capital would be increased. The use of trade credit, even though it does not result in a direct cash flow, reduces the need for cash. In effect, trade credit is a cashless type of capital used to acquire assets.

Trade credit represents a spontaneous and sometimes free source of capital to the firm. It is spontaneous in the sense that it is granted to almost all buyers on a regular basis. It is the type of capital that is relatively easy to obtain. The no-cost attribute of trade credit reflects the fact that in the typical case, buyers are permitted to postpone payment for a number of days without incurring a charge for the postponement.

Accounts payable represent an unsecured type of financing. In the typical case, no specific assets are pledged as collateral. To the buyer of goods and services (firms with the accounts payable), the riskiness of acquiring funds in this fashion is similar to the risk involved in a short-term unsecured bank loan. Accounts payable are less risky than secured loans because there is less possibility of having receivables and/or inventories tied up. Accounts payable are less risky than commercial paper because of the personal relationship between buyer and seller and the possibility of postponement of payment in times of temporary financial difficulty.

An illustration of a typical trade-credit transaction is presented in Figure 16–1. In this transaction, the buyer has a $100,000 account payable at the time of purchase and is permitted 30 days to retire the account. However, if the account is paid within ten days, a discount of 2 percent is applied to the account, and only $98,000 need be paid.

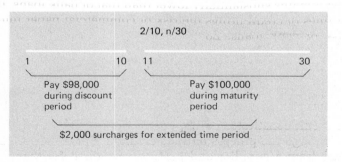

**FIGURE 16–1**

Trade-Credit Payments (2/10, n/30)

Part of the confusion surrounding the analysis of accounts-payable policy is the result of the manner in which the transaction is recorded in the buyer's accounting records. In practice, accounts payable are recorded at face value ($100,000 in Figure 16–1). In an economic sense, however, at the time of purchase, the buyer's liability is only the face value less the discount ($98,000 in Figure 16–1) and not the full face amount. Only the act of postponing payment until a date beyond the discount period increases the liability to the face amount. In other words, it is the act of postponed payment rather than purchase that leads to the additional increase in liabilities. This surcharge for postponement of payment is, in reality, a dollar outflow for the use of capital. It is a capital cost.

Using this context as a frame of reference, it is possible to develop two accounts-payable decision rules:

*Accounts Payable Rule #1:* Always take advantage of the *full discount period.*

Paying prior to the expiration of the discount period will result in stockholder-wealth reductions. The use of free capital reduces the need for expensive capital (such as loans) and reduces dollar outflows for capital with no increase in risk. This results in stockholder-wealth increases.

*Accounts Payable Rule #2:* Postpone payment beyond the end of the discount period only if the surcharge for postponement represents an annual effective interest rate lower than would be paid if the funds were acquired from other sources, such as loans.

This rule can be illustrated by referring back to Figure 16–1. In this example, postponement of payment beyond the discount period resulted in a surcharge of $2,000. Thus, when postponing, the firm pays $2,000 for the use of $98,000 for an additional 20 days. This is equivalent to an annual rate of interest of 36.7 percent. If the firm could negotiate an unsecured bank loan at any rate below 36.7 percent, dollar capital costs would be reduced and stockholder wealth increased.[12]

Only in unusual circumstances is it in the interest of stockholder wealth for the firm to pay the surcharge for postponement. Such situations can arise if the discount offered by the seller is very small, resulting in a low surcharge for postponement. For example, in Figure 16–1, a discount of ½ of 1 percent rather than 2 percent would have resulted in a required payment of $99,500 within the discount period. Postponement of payment beyond the discount period would have resulted in a surcharge of $500 for a total payment of $100,000. The payment of $500 for the use of $99,500 for 20 days represents a annual effective rate of interest of 9 percent.[13] The firm may find it in the interest of stockholder-wealth maximization to pay the 9 percent if funds available from other sources are more expensive.

Another factor that affects the firm's decision to pay the surcharge for

---

[12]The equation for computing the annual effective cost of not taking a discount is given in Chapter 11, as equation 11-1. It is presented here for the reader's convenience:

$$\text{Annual effective cost of missing the discount} = \left( \frac{\text{Dollar value of the discount}}{\text{Face value of invoice} - \text{Dollar value of discount}} \right) + \left( \frac{360 \text{ days}}{\text{Number of days to final payment} - \text{Discount period}} \right)$$

[13]$\text{Annual effective rate} = \dfrac{500}{100,000 - 500} \times \dfrac{360}{30 - 10} = 9\%$

postponement of payment is the length of the maturity period. For example, if the terms in our example had been 2/10,n/70 rather than n/30, the equivalent annual effective rate of interest would have been 12.3 percent.[14] At times, it may be impossible for the firm to acquire short-term loans at a lower rate, and in such cases, postponement of payment is desirable.

The previous discussion suggests that the firm should pay attention to the discounts and maturities offered by suppliers on trade credit. Low discount rates and long maturities may present a favorable financing opportunity. Of course, situations such as these occur infrequently in actual business practice. In most cases, it is in the interest of stockholder-wealth maximization to take the discount and pay on the last day of the discount period.

## LONG-TERM STRATEGIES FOR SHORT-TERM CAPITAL

Thus far, this chapter has given a slightly misleading impression of how the firm should proceed in matters related to short-term capital acquisition. Emphasis has been placed on mechanics and techniques. In actuality, the process of raising short-term capital is highly personalized. Since short-term capital extensions are arranged frequently, there tends to be continuous contact between the capital supplier and the capital demander. Accommodations and adjustments based upon mutual trust are frequent. Reputation and competence are important ingredients in these short-term capital transactions. Management must look at cost over a period of time rather than on a loan-by-loan basis. Cost and risk minimization over a period of time is in the best interest of stockholder wealth.

## SELECTION OF A BANK

Banks play a key role in the short-term financing strategy of the firm. It is very important that firms maintain a permanent banking connection. Banks represent not only an important source of funds but also a valuable resource from which services and advice are available, and they are often willing and able to assist firms through temporary difficulties.

In choosing a bank, management should consider the following factors:

1. *Bank Loyalty*. The bank's loyalty to its customers is an important factor to consider. Ideally, a firm wants a bank that will provide funds at reasonable rates when money-market conditions are tight. It needs a bank that will be accommodating during the inevitable temporary financial difficulties that characterize most firms. For example, one of the big

---

[14]Annual effective rate $= \dfrac{2,000}{100,000 - 2,000} \times \dfrac{360}{70 - 10} = 12.27\%$

**TABLE 16–6**

### SHORT-TERM FINANCING:
### Summary of Possible Cost Savings and Additional Risk

| Type of short-term financing | Cost implications | Risk implications | Comments |
|---|---|---|---|
| **Unsecured financing:** | Usually less costly than secured financing if the firm qualifies. | Less risky than secured loans. | Not available at reasonable rates to many firms. |
| 1. Regular loans | No commitment fee is required | | |
| 2. Line of credit | More flexible than regular loans. Flexibility may reduce dollar financing cost. | | |
| 3. Commercial paper | Tends to be less costly than bank loans. | Risk equal to that of bank loans when backup line of credit is used. | A preferred alternative for firms that qualify. |
| 4. Trade credit | Free capital during the discount period. Tends to be very expensive if the discounts are not taken. | Risk comparable to bank loans. | Always take advantage of the "free" discount period. |
| **Secured financing by accounts receivable:** | Rates are higher than unsecured rates, but reduces financing costs for firms unable to obtain secured loans at favorable rates. | Increases the risk borne by stockholders and other debt suppliers by subordinating their claims. | Used only after careful evaluation of alternatives |
| 1. Pledging | Cost is relatively easy to compute. No hidden charges. Low administrative costs. | Risk of nonpayment is borne by the firm. | |
| 2. Factoring | Costs are higher than pledging, but more "services" are received. | Risk of nonpayment is transferred to factor. Reduces the firm's riskiness. | Savings and risk reductions must be compared to high costs. |

disadvantages of using commercial paper rather than bank loans is that the commercial-paper market is impersonal. Banks, on the other hand, are often willing to refund a loan or permit delayed payment.

2. *Services and Counseling.* Many banks have a formal policy of trying to help their customers grow and prosper. These banks have business-

| Type of short-term financing | Cost implications | Risk implications | Comment |
|---|---|---|---|
| **Secured financing by inventories:** | Same as in accounts receivable. | Same as in accounts receivable. | Used only after careful evaluation of alternatives. |
| 1. Blanket lien | Low administrative cost. Costs are relatively easy to compute. | Permits the firm considerable flexibility. | Provides minimum security to the lender. |
| 2. Trust receipts | High administrative costs. | | Used when inventories can be identified. |
| 3. Public warehouse | Administrative and transportation costs may be very high. | Limited access to inventories increases the firm's riskiness. | Only inventories that can be easily resold are acceptable. |
| 4. Field warehouse | For large inventories, administrative and transportation costs may be lower. | Limited access to inventories increases the firm's riskiness. | Only inventories that can be easily resold are acceptable. |

development specialists on their staffs who can give general advice as well as recommending one or more of a wide range of financial services available in-house or from other financial service institutions. The bank's objective is to have financially sound, loyal customers.

3. *Loan Policy.* Banks differ in size, types of risks they are willing to take, and loan specialization. Each of these factors affects the types of loans banks are likely to make. For example, a textile firm may find it desirable to develop a relationship with a bank that is connected with other firms in the textile industry. Under such circumstances, the bank will recognize unique factors affecting textile firms and can deal with the risk of such firms. Bank size is also important, because the amount that can be lent to any customer is a function of bank size. As a general rule, large firms need large banks.

**SUMMARY**   Short-term capital can be obtained in many different forms. In order to make decisions consistent with stockholder-wealth maximization, management must be able to identify the effect of each alternative on expected cash flows to stockholders and the risk borne by stockholders. Certain cost-saving and risk implications are highlighted in Table 16–6.

The decision with respect to the types of short-term financing to be employed should be made with the knowledge that the firm needs to raise short-term capital on a continuing basis. It is necessary for management to maintain long-lasting relationships in order to ensure the flow of capital at reasonable cost, and to look at the cost and risk implications of various alternatives over a period of time rather than on a loan-by-loan basis.

**QUESTIONS
FOR
DISCUSSION**

1. Explain why stockholder wealth would be unaffected by the proportion of short-term debt used by the firm if capital markets were perfectly competitive and efficient. Why does the firm limit the use of short-term debt?

2. Describe the provisions usually included in a line-of-credit agreement. What is the advantage of a line of credit over a regular short-term loan?

3. Explain why stated interest rates may be different from the annual effective rates of interest.

4. Explain how a firm can reduce financing costs by borrowing on a secured basis even though the average cost of secured loans is higher than the average cost of unsecured loans.

5. Describe the different accounts-receivable services provided by financial institutions and explain how they can be integrated into pledging and factoring agreements.

6. Not all payments made to financial institutions in connection with accounts-receivable-secured financing represent a payment for the use of capital. True or false? Explain your answer.

7. Compare the advantages and disadvantages of the pledging and factoring of accounts receivable.

8. Give some examples of types of inventories that *do not* offer good collateral for a loan. Give the reasons for your selections.

9. Describe the advantages and disadvantages of the following types of inventory-secured financing:
   a. Blanket liens
   b. Trust receipts
   c. Public warehousing
   d. Field warehousing

10. What are the characteristics of commercial-paper issuers, and why do such firms employ a backup line of credit?

11. Describe the "accounts-payable decision rules" and explain why they should be followed by the firm.

12. Why is the firm's selection of a commercial bank important? What factors should enter the selection process?

13. How does a firm go about deciding which type of short-term financing is best for its particular needs?

**PROBLEMS**

1. The AnnCa Corporation desires to borrow $1 million for one year. The First National Bank is willing to lend the funds to AnnCa. The bank offers a one-payment loan with a stated annual interest rate of 12%.
   a. Calculate the annual effective rate of interest if the interest is *not* discounted.

b. Calculate the annual effective rate of interest if the interest is discounted.

c. Calculate the after-tax cost of the loan for both alternatives if AnnCa's marginal tax rate is 30%.

2. The American Trade Corporation needs $1 million in short-term financing. These funds will be needed for one year. The firm can obtain financing from the First National Bank under the following conditions: (1) 12% annual interest rate (not discounted), and (2) a 15% compensating-balance requirement. American Trade normally maintains $50,000 in deposits with First National.

   a. Calculate the amount that must be borrowed by American Trade.

   b. Calculate the actual dollar interest cost of borrowing.

   c. Calculate the effective annual interest rate of the loan.

3. The Burns Mills Corporation sells finished cloth to various clothing manufacturers throughout the United States. The products are sold on a net-60-days basis. Burns Mills enters into a factoring agreement with American Factors. The conditions of the factoring agreement are as follows: (1) a 2% factoring commission, (2) ¾ of 1% per month interest on the face value of the invoice, and (3) a 10% reserve to cover disputes. Burns Mills makes a sale of $500,000 on March 1 (each month has 30 days).

   a. How many dollars will the firm receive on March 1?

   b. What is the annual effective interest rate of the loan?

   c. Would the firm receive any additional funds upon collection of the receivable by American Factors?

   d. Are there any additional costs incurred by the firm, and if so, should these costs be included in the determination of the annual effective interest rate? Explain your answer.

4. California Canning is a packing firm located in the Imperial Valley. The firm cans tomatoes for nationwide distribution. California Canning has a seasonal need for short-term financing. Their borrowing requirements are as follows:

| Month | Borrowings (Repayments) during the month | Total debt outstanding at the end of the month |
|---|---|---|
| January through May | 0 | 0 |
| June | $200,000 | $200,000 |
| July | $300,000 | $500,000 |
| August | $200,000 | $700,000 |
| September | $200,000 | $900,000 |
| October | $100,000 | $1,000,000 |
| November | ($500,000) | $500,000 |
| December | ($500,000) | 0 |

California Canning can obtain a line of credit from the Imperial National Bank for a one-year period (January to December), for up to $1 million. The line of credit has the following conditions: (1) 1¼% per month on the amount borrowed, (2) ¼ of 1% per annum on the unused portion of the line of credit as a commitment fee, (3) no compensating-balance requirements, and (4) a provision that no funds are to be borrowed for at least one month during the calendar year.

   a. Calculate the dollar cost of financing to California Canning.

b. Calculate the annual effective interest rate of the loan.

c. Would the cost of financing change (do not calculate) if the Imperial Bank imposed a 15% compensating-balance requirement on any amount borrowed? California Canning does not maintain any deposits at Imperial Bank at the present time.

5. Calculate the cost of missing the discount of the following credit terms (use a 360-day year). *Hint:* you may want to use a hypothetical purchase—for example, $100.

   a. 2/10,n/60          b. 3/15,n/45          c. 1/10,n/30          d. 4/10,n/90

6. Napa Valley Wineries desires some short-term financing. A commercial bank is willing to extend financing if a field warehouse is established, thus using the inventories as collateral for the loan. Napa Valley needs $1 million for six months. The bank is willing to extend a loan at an annual interest rate of 10% (not discounted). The field-warehousing costs will be $1,000 plus 1% of the maximum amount loaned to the firm. Calculate the dollar financing costs to Napa Valley.

7. The William Corporation desires to borrow funds for a three-month period. The First National Bank is willing to extend credit but requires that accounts receivable be pledged as collateral for the loan. The bank is willing to lend only 90% of the face value of the invoices. The annual stated interest rate is 12%. William Corporation has $1 million in receivables that the bank is willing to accept.

   a. How much can the William Corporation borrow?

   b. Calculate the dollar interest cost of borrowing and the annual affective interest rate.

8. National Farm Machinery Corporation, a large manufacturing company, wants to borrow $20 million for one year, using commercial paper. A commercial-paper dealer reports to National that its commercial paper can be easily refinanced throughout the year. The dealer anticipates the annual cost of commercial paper will be 8%. In addition, the dealer expects that the firm will obtain a backup line of credit from a commercial bank. The First State Bank is willing to extend a $20-million line of credit to National. The cost of this backup line of credit to National would be (1) 12% interest per annum on the amount borrowed, (2) a ½ of 1% commitment fee, and (3) no compensating-balance requirements.

   a. Calculate the annual effective interest rate if National Farm issues commercial paper, *and it can be easily refinanced throughout the year.*

   b. What would be the effect on the annual effective interest rate (do not calculate), if National Farm *cannot* refinance the commercial paper and thus must borrow from the First State Bank.

**SELECTED BIBLIOGRAPHY**

ABRAHAM, ALFRED B., "Factoring—The New Frontier for Commercial Banks," *Journal of Commercial Bank Lending,* 53 (April 1971), 32–43.

BAXTER, NEVINS D., *The Commercial Paper Market.* Princeton, N.J.: Princeton University Press, 1964.

BURNS, JOSEPH E., "Compensating Balance Requirements Integral to Bank Lending," *Business Review,* Federal Reserve Bank of Dallas, February 1972, 1–8.

CRANE, DWIGHT B., and WILLIAM L. WHITE, "Who Benefits from a Floating Prime Rate?" *Harvard Business Review,* 50 (January–February 1972), 121–29.

HALEY, CHARLES W., and ROBERT C. HIGGINS, "Inventory Control Theory and Trade Credit Financing," *Management Science,* 20 (December 1973), 464–71.

HAYES, DOUGLAS A., *Bank Lending Policies,* 2nd ed. Ann Arbor: University of Michigan Press, 1977.

LAZERE, MONROE R., "Swinging Swindles and Creepy Frauds," *Journal of Commercial Bank Lending,* 60 (September 1977), 44–52.

QUILL, GERALD D., JOHN C. CRESCI, and BRUCE D. SHUTER, "Some Considerations about Secured Lending," *Journal of Commercial Bank Lending,* 59 (April 1977), 41–56.

REED, EDWARD W., RICHARD V. COTTER, EDWARD K. GILL, and RICHARD K. SMITH, *Commercial Banking,* 2nd ed. Englewood Cliffs, N.J.: Prentice-Hall, 1980.

SCHWARTZ, ROBERT A., "An Economic Analysis of Trade Credit," *Journal of Financial and Quantitative Analysis,* 9 (September 1974), 643–58.

SILVERS, J.B., "Liquidity, Risk and Duration Patterns of Corporate Financing," *Financial Management,* 5 (Autumn 1976), 54–66.

STONE, BERNELL K., "The Cost of Bank Loans," *Journal of Financial and Quantitative Analysis,* 7 (December 1972), 2077–86.

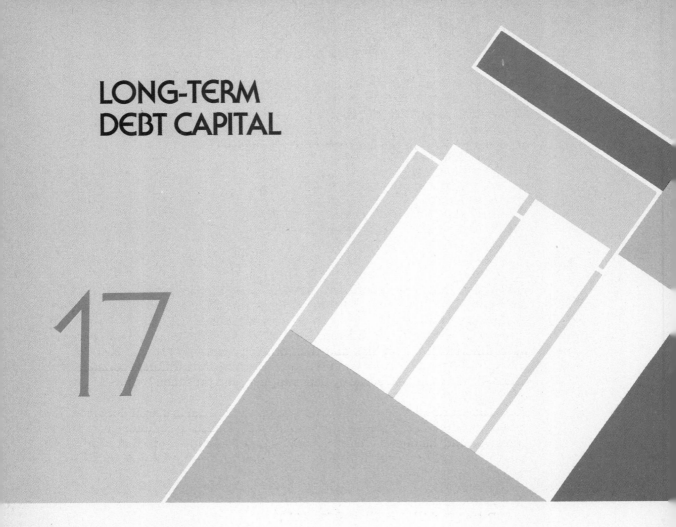

# LONG-TERM
# DEBT CAPITAL

## 17

## INTRODUCTION

Following the format established in the preceding chapter for short-term debt capital, this chapter provides information about the various types of long-term debt capital and develops guidelines for making choices among the alternatives. We will show that there is a wide range of medium- and long-term capital-acquisition options open to the firm. The firm can choose among term loans, leasing, mortgage bonds, and debentures. Each of these alternatives can be tailored to meet the specific needs of the firm. We will examine each of them in terms of their effect on the firm's expected cash flows, riskiness, and stockholder wealth.

The conceptual framework for long-term-debt decisions is similar to that employed when making asset-acquisition decisions. Using equation 17–1 as a background for discussion, we can see that there are three basic ways in which different mixtures of long-term-debt capital can affect stockholder wealth. If stockholder wealth is to be affected by financing alternatives, one of the three terms (dividends, required rate of return, or expected growth) in the equation must be changed.[1]

$$PV_s = \frac{D_1}{k_s - g}$$

(17-1)

## BONDS

A bond is a long-term promissory note issued by a business firm. Firms use bonds to raise the major portion of long-term debt capital. There is a tendency to think of all bonds as being the same, but in fact, each bond issue tends to be unique. Even different bond issues of the same corporation can have different levels of risk and thus different costs ($k_d^*$) to the firm. For example, different bond issues of the same firm may have different collateral. This will affect the risk borne by debt suppliers and thus their required rates of return ($k_d$).

The precise nature of each bond issue is spelled out in a legal document called an *indenture agreement*, which is in essence a contract between borrower and lender. Included in each bond indenture agreement is the basic information relating to the bond. Some of the items that must be included are these:

1. Coupon interest rate
2. Dates on which interest must be paid
3. The value of the bond at the maturity date (par value)
4. The maturity date
5. The designation of an independent trustee to enforce the provisions of the indenture agreement (for bonds sold to the general public)

Most indenture agreements also contain certain provisions relating to:

6. The seniority of the bondholders' claims in the event of liquidation
7. The collateral, if any, supporting the bond issue
8. Limitations on the freedom of management to take certain actions while the bonds are outstanding

These provisions included in the indenture agreement permit the debt

---

[1] We will use the constant-growth valuation model for common stock as a framework for our discussion. Other models could have been selected and the conclusions would be similar.

supplier to assess the risk associated with the purchase of a bond and to minimize uncertainty with respect to these crucial points. Thus, the indenture agreement spells out in great detail the contractual obligations of the firm as well as the avenues open to the bondholders to enforce the agreement.

## COLLATERAL

There are three basic types of bonds: mortgage bonds, chattel mortgage bonds, and debentures. Mortgage bonds use real property such as land and buildings as collateral. Chattel mortgage bonds are backed by claims on personal property, such as furniture and equipment. Debentures have no specific collateral; their holders are general creditors of the firm. In the event of liquidation, holders of mortgage and chattel mortgage bonds receive the proceeds from the specified assets used as collateral. Only the liquidation proceeds for these specified assets that are in excess of the mortgage and chattel mortgage claims are available to debenture holders. The riskiness of both the mortgage and chattel mortgage bonds will depend upon the adequacy of the property held as collateral for these bonds. Other things being equal, however, a firm's debentures are riskier than its mortgage and chattel mortgage bonds, since the debentures are not backed by specific collateral. Thus, the required rates of return on debentures and the cost of debenture capital will be higher than the corresponding rates for mortgage and chattel mortgage bonds.

## SENIORITY OF CLAIMS

The indenture agreement frequently specifies that the bonds being issued are subordinated to other debt claims against the firm. For example, debentures are on occasion subordinated to the firm's notes payable. This means the holder of a debenture bond agrees in advance that, in case of the liquidation of the firm, the holders of notes payable are to be completely compensated before any compensation is paid to debenture holders. New issues of debenture bonds are frequently subordinated to prior issues of debentures. The nature of subordination is such that subordinated debenture holders are taking higher risks than if the bonds were unsubordinated. Subordination increases the risk borne by the purchaser of new bonds, increases the required rate of return of the bondholders, and thus makes the cost of new subordinated debt issues relatively high.

Of course, management would prefer not to use the subordination feature, since it increases the cost of new debt. Its use exists only because the holders of notes payable or prior bond issues insist upon such a provision. In effect, creditors of the firm are able to minimize their risk by insisting that new debt claims against the firm be subordinated. Thus, the risk of new subordinated debt tends to be higher than the risk of the older debt.

## LIMITATIONS ON MANAGEMENT

Frequently the indenture agreement also protects the interest of debt suppliers by placing certain restrictions on management. For example, the indenture may require that the firm limit the use of debt in the future, or maintain certain levels of liquidity. Such restrictive provisions of indenture agreements are designed to reduce the risk borne by debt suppliers. For the stockholder, the advantage of restrictive provisions is to reduce the cost of debt capital, which in turn tends to increase profits and possible cash flows to stockholders. On the other hand, restrictive indenture provisions may deter the firm from taking actions that would be beneficial to stockholder wealth. In some cases, the indenture agreement even restricts the payment of dividends to stockholders pending the fulfillment of specified conditions. Restrictive provisions in the indenture agreement should not be treated lightly, since they may have a profound effect on the future of the firm.

## SINKING FUNDS

Some bond issues carry *sinking-fund* provisions. In effect, sinking funds are used to make periodic reductions in the principal amount of the loan outstanding. The reduction in debt reduces the risk of the remaining outstanding bonds.

For example, assume that the JG Corporation sold a $100-million, 20-year bond issue on February 1, 1980. If no sinking fund was employed, JG Corporation will have to redeem the entire $100 million in bonds on February 1, 2000. This large cash flow on a single date may cause uncertainty and increase the riskiness of the firm. If a sinking-fund provision is included in the JG indenture agreement, periodic payments will be used to reduce the total maturity-date obligation of this bond issue. For example, the agreement may call for JG to retire $8 million in bonds each February 1, beginning in 1991. In this case, JG makes nine payments of $8 million, and then a final payment of $28 million on February 1, 2000. The sinking-fund procedure reduces the need for a large cash payment on the maturity date.

Since sinking funds reduce the risk borne by the supplier of debt capital, the required rate of return on debt is reduced. But the advantage of lower debt costs may be offset by reduced flexibility on the part of the firm. Generally speaking, firms would prefer not to be encumbered by sinking-fund requirements. Instead, they would prefer to allow the bond issue to mature and, at or near the date of maturity, offer a new bond issue, the proceeds of which would go to retiring the outstanding bond issue. Remember, the firm does not want to reduce the debt to zero. To the contrary, stockholder-wealth maximization calls for maintaining optimal debt ratios. Optimal-debt-ratio maintenance calls for issuance of new debt to replace old debt (other things remaining equal). The use of sinking funds requires that the firm enter the market for long-term debt on a continuing basis. In the absence of sinking funds, the firm can make one large bond issue, which may result in substantial cost reductions. In a sense, then, sinking funds may have the hidden disadvantage of higher debt-issuance and debt-management costs.[2]

The typical sinking-fund provision gives the firm a choice in the method used to retire the bonds. On the date the sinking-fund payment is due, the firm can provide the trustee with bonds purchased on the open market and having a face value equal to the sinking-fund payment. As an alternative, the firm may provide the trustee with the funds necessary to buy the bonds from the bondholders. In this case, bonds are selected randomly, and the owners of those bonds must tender them for redemption, since no further interest payments on the bonds will be made. Neither the firm nor the bondholder has a choice once the process is set in motion.

The alternative chosen by the firm to meet the sinking-fund obligation will depend on the existing market price of the outstanding bonds. If current interest rates are higher than the rates that prevailed at the date of issue, the market price of the bonds will be lower than their face value. In such cases, the firm should purchase on the open market and deliver the bonds to the trustee. If present interest rates are lower than the interest rates at issuance, bonds will be selling at prices higher than face value. In such cases, the firm should deliver funds to the trustee. The trustee will buy back the bonds at their face value. Since the face value is below the market value, the firm is in effect acquiring an asset below its market costs. This increases stockholder wealth.

## CALL PROVISIONS

Most bonds (not all) have a call provision. The call provision gives the corporation the right to retire bonds before the specified maturity date. Note that the sinking fund *requires* early bond retirement, and the call provision *permits* it. The call provision can be used by management only if such use is specified in the indenture agreement. It tends to be used when interest rates fall and bond prices rise. In the typical case, the firm will sell new bonds at the new lower interest rates. The proceeds of the new bond issue can be used to buy back (call) the older higher-interest bond issue. The bondholder receives the face value of the bond plus a call premium as specified in the indenture agreement. The call premium usually declines as the bond

---

[2]A rapidly growing firm that plans to increase its long-term debt every two or three years finds the sinking-fund provision less burdensome, since the reduction in debt due to sinking-fund payments can be offset by increases in the scheduled borrowing amounts.

approaches maturity and is expressed as a declining percentage of the maturity value of the bond.

An example will illustrate the use of the call provision. Assume that in 1980, the Christine Corporation issued a 20-year bond (face value $1,000) with a coupon interest rate of 10 percent. The indenture agreement included a postponed call provision with a declining call premium. First, exercise of the call provision is not permitted until 1984.[3] The indenture agreement specified that if the bonds are called in 1984, the bondholder is entitled to the par value of the bond plus an 8 percent call premium ($1,080). The indenture agreement further specified that the call premium will be reduced by ½ of 1 percent in each successive year (7½ percent in 1985, and so on). Thus, the cash premium received by the supplier of debt capital is reduced as the bond approaches maturity.

It should be noted that the call provision can only work to the detriment of bondholders. If interest rates fall, the call provision permits the issuing corporation to redeem the bonds. In such a case, the bondholder is forced to give up a financial asset yielding a rate of return higher than available elsewhere at the current time. The bondholder gives up the bond, receives cash, and invests that cash elsewhere *at a lower rate*.

Obviously, bondholders would prefer bonds without call provisions, since the call provision introduces additional risk. Callable bonds, therefore, carry higher required rates of returns and costs to the firm. If the firm is able to forecast the downward movement of interest rates, the inclusion of the call provision in the indenture agreement may lead to increases in stockholder wealth.[4] If no such declines in interest rates take place, the firm has increased the cost of debt and reduced stockholder wealth. This situation once again illustrates management's need for knowledge about events taking place outside the firm (in this case, interest-rate changes).

## CONVERTIBLE BONDS

The convertible bond is a special type of bond that allows the holder to exchange the bond for a specified number of shares of common stock. For example, assume that the National Steel Corporation issued a 20-year convertible bond in 1980. The bond can be exchanged at any time between 1980 and 2000 for 50 shares of common stock.[5] The number of shares that can be obtained in exchange for one bond is called the *conversion ratio*. The

---

[3]In 1979, most industrial bonds carried a ten-year postponement. This is very high by historical standards, and it is not known whether the length of required postponement will be shortened in the future.

[4]The mechanics of a refunding situation are presented in Appendix 17A.

[5]The conversion provision may specify different conversion ratios during the life of the bond. For example, the convertible bond of National Steel might be exchangeable for 50 shares up to 1985, and for only 40 shares from 1985 to 2000.

*conversion price* is the price paid for each share of common stock if the bond is converted. In the case of National Steel, the conversion price at the time of the original issue of the bond would be:

$$\text{Conversion price} = \frac{\text{Par value of the bond}}{\text{Conversion ratio}} = \frac{\$1,000}{50} = \$20 \text{ per share}$$

The conversion price (usually 15 to 20 percent above the existing market price) and conversion ratio are specified in the indenture agreement. The firm commonly sets a conversion price *above* the current market price of common stock. For example, the common stock of National Steel may have a current market price of $15. Thus, it would not be advantageous to pay $1,000 for the bond and convert it immediately into 50 shares of National's common stock, since these 50 shares can be purchased today for only $750 ($15 × 50).

The advantage to the investor in convertible bonds is that they permit participation in future increases in the market price of common stock. Let us assume, for example, that in the year 2000, the common stock of National Steel sells for $30 per share. The investor can then convert the bond for 50 shares. But, you may say, the gain realized would have been greater if the investor had acquired the 50 shares for $750 in 1980. The answer lies in the lower degree of risk in the purchase of the convertible bond than in the purchase of 50 shares of common stock. If the market price of common stock in the year 2000 is only $10 per share, *the investor is not required to convert the bond*. The bonds are convertible at the option of the bondholder. Thus, if the price is only $10, the bonds will not be converted, and the full par value of the bond ($1,000) will be realized upon maturity.

This advantage to the bondholders allows the firm to pay a lower interest rate than the required rate of return of the bondholders ($k_d$) for similar bonds without the convertibility provision. Thus, the cost to the firm of issuing convertible bonds is lower than the cost of issuing bonds with the same maturity but not convertible. There is, however, one potential disadvantage to the firm of issuing convertible bonds. If the bonds are converted into common stock, the number of shares outstanding will increase, resulting in a dilution of earnings per share.

On occasion, firms design the convertible-bond issue in such a way that there is a high probability of conversion at a future date. Firms are attracted to this strategy when the common-stock price is expected to rise in the future. That is, the firm acquires debt capital with the expectation that common-stock price will increase and the debt will be converted to equity. In a sense, such strategies amount to selling stock at a rate (price) higher than that prevailing in the market at the present time. Of course, the attractiveness of convertible bonds to the potential buyer will depend on his or her evaluation of future common-stock prices. If they are not expected to increase, capital suppliers will be unwilling to accept the lower rate of return associated with convertible bonds.

# TERM LOANS

Financial institutions, usually commercial banks, extend credit to business firms for periods longer than one year through what are normally called term loans.[6] Term loans have the following common characteristics: (1) The maturity of the loan is usually between two and six years, although a few term loans may have a maturity of ten years; (2) payments are made on a monthly, quarterly, semiannual, or annual basis; (3) the borrowed amount is amortized over the life of the loan; (4) collateral may be required for the loan; and (5) the lender may impose certain restrictions on the financial activities of the firm.

First, let us illustrate the repayment methodology of a term loan. The AnnCa Corporation desires to borrow $20,000 over a five-year period. The Second National Bank is willing to make a $20,000 term loan under the following conditions: (1) The annual interest rate of the loan is 10 percent,[7] and (2) five equal annual payments are required to fully amortize the loan. The annual payment necessary under these conditions will be:

$$PV_5^{10\%} = A(3 \text{ Coef.}_5^{10\%})$$

$$\$20,000 = A(3.791)$$

$$A = \frac{20,000}{3.791} = \$5,275.65$$

Thus, five equal annual payments of $5,275.65 will fully pay the interest and principal of the $20,000 term loan.[8] Table 17–1 shows the loan amortization schedule. Note from the table that the entire debt (both principal and interest) is repaid to the Second National Bank over the five-year period.

Banks may require collateral on term loans. The amount, type, and restrictions of the collateral will depend on the creditworthiness of the borrower. Firms with excellent credit ratings may not have to pledge any assets as collateral for a term loan, but firms with lower credit ratings may be required by the lender to pledge certain assets.

The term-loan agreement commonly includes certain covenants specifying actions that the borrower must perform and others that the borrower must not undertake. For example, the agreement may require the borrower to provide financial statements to the lender on specified dates, or to maintain cash balances above a specific amount. These provisions are called *affirma-*

---

[6]Medium-term loans made for the purchase of a specific asset are called installment loans. These loans differ to some degree from term loans. This chapter, however, will give the same treatment to installment and term loans.

[7]In many cases, the interest rate charged is variable. Usually the contract will call for a certain rate above the prime rate, with both a maximum and a minimum interest rate (collar).

[8]See Chapter 3 for a discussion of the computations required to determine the payments on term loans.

TABLE 17-1

LOAN AMORTIZATION SCHEDULE

| Year | Payment | Interest[a] | Principal repayment | Debt outstanding |
|------|---------|-------------|---------------------|------------------|
| 1 | $5,275.65 | $2,000.00 | $3,275.65 | $16,724.35 |
| 2 | ' | $1,672.44 | $3,603.21 | $13,121.14 |
| 3 | ' | $1,312.11 | $3,963.54 | $ 9,157.60 |
| 4 | ' | $ 915.76 | $4,359.89 | $ 4,797.71 |
| 5 | ' | $ 479.77 | $4,795.88 | [b] |

[a]Interest is always 10% of the debt outstanding at the end of the preceding year.

[b]The oustanding balance was not reduced to zero in year 5 due to rounding errors present in Table 3–3.

tive covenants. *Negative covenants*, on the other hand, specifically forbid the firm to do certain things unless the borrower approves. For example, the borrower may be prohibited from selling specified assets, or from increasing its debt ratio above a certain level. These covenants, affirmative and negative, are included in the loan agreement for the protection of the lender. They reduce the risk taken by the lender and lower the required rates of return.

The advantages and disadvantages of medium-term loans to the borrower fall somewhere between those for short- and long-term debt. To the lender, medium-term loans are riskier than short-term loans and less risky than long-term bonds. The cost of medium-term loans also tends to fall between those of short- and long-term loans. Medium-term loans are especially important to smaller firms with limited access to the bond markets. These firms use medium-term loans to finance fixed assets. In some cases, medium-term loans constitute the longest maturities available to small borrowers.

## LEASES

The firm may also raise debt capital by entering into lease arrangements. There are two types of leases: financial leases and service leases.[9] Since the evaluation techniques used depend on the type of lease, it is important that you be able to distinguish between the two types.

A financial lease is a lease that (1) is fully amortized, (2) is not cancelable, and (c) does not include maintenance or other services. Full amortization means that the lessor (the person providing the leased asset) is ensured the entire cost of the item in lease payments. For example, a bank may buy a jet aircraft and lease it to an airline. The airline agrees to pay the

---

[9]The analysis of real estate leases is not covered in this book.

bank a series of lease payments adequate to cover the entire cost of the aircraft plus a fair profit for the bank. This aircraft lease is fully amortized. Not all leases are fully amortized (hence, not all are financial leases). For example, closed-end automobile leases are not fully amortized. Assume that the lessee (the person acquiring the use of the leased asset) is provided a car with a market value of $6,000. In return, the lessee agrees to pay the lessor $125 a month for 36 months. This lease is not fully amortized, since the sum of the payments ($4,500) is less than the cost of the asset plus a fair return for the lessor. Leases that are not fully amortized may still be profitable to the lessor, since the lessor reclaims and sells the asset at the end of the lease period.

Financial leases are not cancelable, thus ensuring that the lessor will receive the full series of payments. Some leases are cancelable (hence, they are not financial leases). For example, rapidly changing equipment needs encourage firms to enter into cancelable leases for such items as computers, office copying equipment, and telephone equipment.

Financial leases do not include services such as maintenance or repair of equipment. Under a financial lease, the lessee must pay for maintenance and repairs. If the machine breaks down or fails, lease payments must still be maintained. The lessor's only obligation is to provide the equipment in an initially acceptable condition. Subsequent developments do not alter the lessee's payments.

Note well that the responsibilities of the firm leasing equipment under a financial-lease agreement are exactly the same as if the firm purchased the equipment. Whether the firm buys the equipment or signs a financial lease for its use, the entire cost of the equipment must be covered, and the firm assumes the risk of breakdown and premature obsolescence.

On the other hand, when a firm enters into a service lease for a piece of equipment, it gets something more than the service that is provided directly by the equipment—more service than it would get if it purchased the equipment or entered into a financial lease for its use. For example, compare the differences in services received under a service lease for a computer and an outright purchase or financial lease of exactly the same computer.[10] If the firm's equipment needs change, the service lease provides for the replacement or removal of the existing equipment. If the firm had purchased the computer, it would have had to dispose of it and acquire new equipment (a costly development). The lessor under the service lease provides the service of assuming this risk, as well as the risk of technological obsolescence (as when a new generation of computers is born) and the risk of breakdown.

Service leases are substantially different from financial leases. When a firm must decide between entering a financial lease and buying, it is choosing between financing methods, since exactly the same services are received in both cases.

---

[10]The computer service lease being discussed here is a common form but not the only form of computer lease.

# FINANCIAL LEASES

**Decisions Relating to Financial Leases**

Before the firm enters a financial lease, two decisions must be made. First, the firm must evaluate, by means of capital-budgeting techniques, the attractiveness of acquiring the use of the asset. Second, the firm must decide on how to raise the cash needed to pay for the asset.

The cost of financing the particular asset does not enter into the decision relating to the acquisition of its use. As discussed in Chapters 7 and 9, each asset acquired by the firm is viewed as being financed partly by equity and partly by debt (the financial lease is a type of debt). Thus, the capital-budgeting process uses the asset-specific cost of capital as the measure of the cost of funds regardless of whether the particular acquisition is financed by common stock, long-term debt, or financial lease.

The second decision the firm makes before it enters a financial lease involves the choice of financing to employ at the time the asset is acquired. The firm should have already decided to acquire the use of the asset before the financing decision is made. By searching for the least expensive financing alternative, the firm will be minimizing its cost.

The fact that debt capital is available in the form of lease financing only when special types of equipment are acquired should not obscure the fact that lease financing is a special type of debt financing. The evaluation of leases is essentially a comparison of the advantages and disadvantages of lease financing with the advantages and disadvantages of other types of financing. At this point, it is possible to say two things about financial leases:

1. Since equipment leases tend to have maturities similar to those of term loans, the riskiness of these two alternative financing strategies is approximately the same. On the other hand, leasing tends to be more risky than the use of bonds and less risky than the use of short-term debt.
2. Since term loans and leases have approximately the same risk, the choice between these two alternatives should be based on cost. Stockholder wealth will be maximized by choosing the alternative financing mode with the lowest cost.

In this section we will present a methodology for comparing financial-lease financing with medium-term debt financing. However, keep in mind that the analysis of short-term loans and bonds as an alternative financing strategy should be considered. (Such analysis should follow the conceptual frameworks presented in Chapter 16 and earlier sections of this chapter.) For such comparisons, it is best to view leasing as a type of medium-term loan.

As we compare financial leases to medium-term financing, the student should recognize the importance of taxes in the lease-financing evaluation. As you will see, benefits associated with leasing are derived from the tax laws. This is not to say that financial leasing is usually attractive; there is a substantial reservoir of opinion that it is advantageous only in special tax situations. Such arguments hold that in a competitive market for capital with neutral tax laws, there is no reason why financing from leasing companies should be less expensive than financing through banks or insurance-company loans.

Evaluation of a<br>Financial Lease—An<br>Example

Let us illustrate the procedures involved in financial-lease evaluation through the use of an example. Assume that the Gerhard Corporation has completed its capital-budgeting analysis and has decided to acquire a new electronic testing machine. This decision was made after carefully considering all other possible asset acquisitions. The net-present-value technique used in the framework of the capital budget has resulted in the positive decision about the electronic tester. That is, the asset-specific cost of capital for the electronic tester was used to discount the cash flows associated with the tester and has resulted in a positive net present value.

We will also assume that the Gerhard Corporation has already signed a contract with the American Electronics Corporation for acquisition of the machine. Gerhard must now raise the capital required to pay for the machine. The capital can be raised in the following ways:

1. Enter into a long-term debt agreement with an insurance company.
2. Borrow on a five-year term-loan basis.
3. Enter into a five-year financial-lease arrangement with the American Electronics Corporation.

Gerhard Corporation examines its capital structure and decides that the maintenance of an optimal capital structure necessitates the acquisition of medium-term financing. Additional short-term debt will increase the riskiness of the firm to an unacceptable level, and long-term-debt rates are viewed as being too high. The Gerhard Corporation recognizes that medium-term capital can be obtained in either of two ways, a term loan or financial leasing. Since the financial risk associated with these alternative financing strategies is approximately the same, the management of Gerhard plans to analyze the present value of the costs associated with each alternative and to choose the alternative with the lowest cost.

The term-loan alternative involves borrowing $100,000 at a 10 percent rate of interest. Repayment must be made in the form of five equal annual payments, beginning at the end of the first year. If the firm uses this method of raising capital, it will obtain legal title to the equipment and will maintain possession of the machine after the loan has been repaid. However, the equipment is expected to be worthless at the end of the five-year period.

As shown in Table 17–2, the annual payment associated with the term loan will be $26,378.26, which includes both interest and principal repayment. Note that the interest portion of the payment declines as the outstanding principal is reduced.

TABLE 17-2

GERHARD CORPORATION:
AMORTIZATION SCHEDULE FOR A $100,000 TERM LOAN USED
TO FINANCE EQUIPMENT (interest rate = 10%)

| Year | Total Payment[a] | Interest Portion of the Payment[b] | Portion for Repayment of the Principal[c] | Principal Outstanding[d] |
|---|---|---|---|---|
| 0 | 0 | 0 | 0 | $100,000.00 |
| 1 | $26,378.26 | $10,000.00 | $16,378.26 | $83,621.74 |
| 2 | $26,378.26 | $8,362.17 | $18,016.09 | $65,605.65 |
| 3 | $26,378.28 | $6,560.57 | $19,817.69 | $45,787.96 |
| 4 | $26,378.26 | $4,578.80 | $21,799.46 | $23,988.50 |
| 5 | $26,378.26 | $2,398.85 | $23,979.41 | $9.09[e] |

[a]$PVA = A(3 \text{ Coef.}_n^i) = A(3 \text{ Coef.}_5^{10\%})$

$$A = \frac{PVA}{(3 \text{ Coef.}_5^{10\%})} = \frac{\$100,000}{3.791} = \$26,378.26$$

[b]Annual interest equals the interest rate (10%) times the principal outstanding at the beginning of the year.

[c]Principal repayment equals the total payment minus the interest portion of the payment.

[d]The principal outstanding equals the principal outstanding at the end of the previous period minus repayment of the principal during the period.

[e]The final amount does not equal zero because of rounding errors in the present-value tables.

Although the Gerhard Corporation is required to make annual payments of $26,378.26, the actual cash outflow is less than this amount. This is because the acquisition of legal title to the equipment and the use of the term-loan alternative permit Gerhard to deduct interest expense and depreciation from taxable income, thus reducing the firm's income taxes. As shown in Table 17–3, the net cash outflow associated with a $26,378.26 loan

TABLE 17-3

GERHARD CORPORATION:
After-Tax Cash Flows Associated with a Term Loan for Financing Equipment

| Year | Total payment on term loan | Tax-deductible expenses Interest | Depreciation[a] | Total | Tax savings[b] (Deductions × Tax rate) | Net cash Outflows[c] |
|---|---|---|---|---|---|---|
| 0 | 0 | 0 | 0 | 0 | 0 | 0 |
| 1 | $26,378.26 | $10,000.00 | $20,000.00 | $30,000.00 | $12,000.00 | $14,378.26 |
| 2 | $26,378.26 | $8,362.17 | $20,000.00 | $28,362.17 | $11,344.87 | $15,033.39 |
| 3 | $26,378.26 | $6,560.57 | $20,000.00 | $26,560.57 | $10,624.23 | $15,754.03 |
| 4 | $26,378.26 | $4,578.80 | $20,000.00 | $24,578.80 | $9,831.52 | $16,546.74 |
| 5 | $26,378.26 | $2,398.85 | $20,000.00 | $22,398.85 | $8,959.54 | $17,418.72 |

[a]We have used the straight-line method of depreciation and assumed no salvage value for the equipment at the end of five years.

[b]The marginal tax rate of the Gerhard Corporation is 40%.

[c]The net cash outflows equal the total payment made on the term loan minus the tax saving.

amortization payment is substantially lower than that amount. It is the net cash outflow rather than the total loan payment that is relevant for the evaluation of the term-loan alternative.

Gerhard can also acquire the asset by entering into a financial lease with American Electronics. The lease arrangement calls for five annual payments of $26,817.90, commencing at the end of the first year. As shown in Table 17–4, these payments are tax-deductible. Thus, the actual after-tax cash outflow to Gerhard is only $16,090.74 per year.

**TABLE 17–4**

GERHARD CORPORATION:
After-Tax Cash Flows Associated with the Financial Lease

| Year | Before-tax lease payment | tax savings[a] | After-tax cash outflows[b] |
|---|---|---|---|
| 0 | 0 | 0 | 0 |
| 1 | $26,817.90 | $10,727.16 | $16,090.74 |
| 2 | $26,817.90 | $10,727.16 | $16,090.74 |
| 3 | $26,817.90 | $10,727.16 | $16,090.74 |
| 4 | $26,817.90 | $10,727.16 | $16,090.74 |
| 5 | $26,817.90 | $10,727.16 | $16,090.74 |

[a]The tax saving to Gerhard equals the amount of the annual lease payments times the tax rate (40%).

[b]The after-tax cash flows equal the actual lease payments minus the tax saving.

The appropriate procedure for comparing a financial lease with a term loan calls for discounting the cash outflows for each alternative and choosing that alternative for which the present value of the cash outflows is lower. Since the risk associated with each alternative is the same, minimizing costs will maximize stockholder wealth. In the Gerhard Corporation case, the present value of the cash outflows associated with the term-loan alternative is lower than that associated with the financial-lease alternative. The computations are presented in Table 17–5. Thus, the term-loan alternative will maximize stockholder wealth.

**Discount Rate in Financial-Lease Evaluations**

Note that the required rate of return on debt (before-tax cost of debt) was used as the discount rate in the financial-lease evaluation. This reflects the fact that the cash flows are known with a high degree of certainty, as compared to cash flows associated with an asset acquisition for which an asset-specific cost of capital is used.[11]

---

[11]Considerable controversy surrounds the selection of the appropriate discount rate. Traditionally, the after-tax rather than the before-tax cost of debt was used. For a more detailed explanation, see James C. Van Horne, *Financial Management and Policy*, 5th ed. (Englewood Cliffs, N.J.: Prentice-Hall, 1980), Chap. 19; or Myron J. Gordon, "A General Solution to the Buy or Lease Decision: A Pedagogical Note," *The Journal of Finance*, March 1974, pp. 245–50.

TABLE 17–5

GERHARD CORPORATION:
Present Value of Cash Flows Associated with Financial Leasing
and Term Loans as Means of Financing the Asset

| | TERM LOAN | | FINANCIAL LEASE | |
|---|---|---|---|---|
| Year | After-tax cash outflows | Present value[a] | After-tax cash outflows | Present value[a] |
| 0 | 0 | 0 | 0 | 0 |
| 1 | $14,378.26 | $13,069.84 | $16,090.74 | $14,626.48 |
| 2 | $15,033.39 | $12,417.58 | $16,090.74 | $13,290.95 |
| 3 | $15,754.03 | $11,831.28 | $16,090.74 | $12,084.15 |
| 4 | $16,546.74 | $11,301.43 | $16,090.74 | $10,989.98 |
| 5 | $17,418.72 | $10,817.03 | $16,090.74 | $9,992.35 |
| | | $PV_{outflows} = $59,437.16 | | $PV_{outflows} = $60,983.91 |

[a]The present value is obtained using the present-value-of-$1 table, or:

$$PV = FV(2\ Coef._n^i)$$

The present value of the lease can also be obtained by using the present-value-of-an-annuity table, or:

$$PV = FV(3\ Coef._n^i)$$

For both the term loan and the lease, the discount rate is the before-tax cost of debt to the firm, or 10%.

## SERVICE LEASES

As noted earlier, service leases are leases that include something other than financing. Consider a situation in which the lease payments are such that the cost of the equipment is not fully amortized. That is, at the end of the lease period, the equipment is expected to have a positive salvage value. If the firm leases the equipment, the salvage value will be captured by the lessor.[12] On the other hand, a firm using term-loan financing will own the equipment at the end of the period. The firm must compare the attractiveness of acquiring the salvage rights to the alternative of passing such rights on to the lessor. Since there is bound to be some uncertainty associated with salvage values, the firm minimizes this uncertainty by leasing. The uncertainty will, of course, be reflected in the size of lease payments. Lessors will expect to be compensated for taking such risk.

The same type of analysis can be applied to the risks of breakdown and early obsolescence. If the firm enters a service-lease agreement, such risks may be borne by the lessor, and the lessor will demand compensation for assuming them. The firm must determine whether the additional payment to

---

[12]The situation described here is similar to a "closed-end" automobile lease.

a lessor is justified by the reduction in risk. Such analysis must be conducted on a case-by-case basis; there is no general solution to the problem.

## ADVANTAGES OF LEASING

There are several reasons why a firm may find it attractive to enter into a lease arrangement. For one thing, tax laws may place the lessor in a better position to take advantage of the investment tax credit and the depreciation charges associated with the asset. For example, a firm with a low level of taxable income may be unable to capture the full tax benefit of asset ownership. In such cases, these tax benefits can in effect be "sold" to a lessor.

In other cases, the lessor may be able to provide services at a lower cost than available elsewhere. For example, computer-leasing firms may be able to service the equipment more cheaply and efficiently than the lessee. The same can be said for dealing with the problem of obsolescence. Computer-leasing firms may be in a better position to find new users for old equipment. Therefore, lessors may have a lower risk of obsolescence than lessees.

These special capabilities of lessors, combined with the corporate income tax laws, apparently make leasing very attractive to a large number of firms. It is estimated that in 1979, $30 billion in equipment was leased by American corporations. However, it should be noted that there is no general advantage to leasing. That is, although in some cases the advantages of leasing may be so great as to encourage its use, in most cases the firm finds it more attractive to use more conventional methods for financing asset acquisitions. Lease arrangements must be evaluated on a case-by-case basis in order to determine their attractiveness to the firm.

## ACCOUNTING TREATMENT OF LEASES

Raising capital through the use of leases creates an opportunity for the firm to use what is known as "off-balance-sheet financing." Since firms are required to include term-loan obligations on the balance sheet but are not required to include service leases as part of the capital raised by the firm, it is possible for the firm to underreport the total debt claims against it.

Today, financial leases must be "capitalized" and carried on the balance sheet as both an asset and a liability. The capitalized value of the lease payments is computed by taking their present value. Thus, today, the accounting treatment afforded financial leases and term loans would be virtually the same. There should be no major "balance-sheet advantage" of using financial leasing as opposed to term-loan financing.

Service leases are treated differently and may represent an opportunity for "off-balance-sheet financing." Since service-lease payments constitute payments for capital and payments for services (maintenance), it would be unreasonable to treat the full amount of the lease payment as a payment for capital. Capitalizing service-lease payments would tend to overreport the total indebtedness of the firm. The exclusion of service-lease payments, on the other hand, underreports the firm's indebtedness. Current accounting practice does not include the capitalized value of service leases as a balance-sheet item. Instead, such lease payments are usually reported in footnotes to financial statements. To the extent that service-lease payments represent payments for capital, this practice represents off-balance-sheet financing.

SUMMARY        The particular type of long-term-debt capital used by the firm will affect stockholder wealth because different types of long-term debt have different effects on the stock's expected dividends and/or risk. Three major categories of longer-term capital were discussed in this chapter: bonds, term loans, and financial leases. Each of these categories was evaluated in terms of risk–return implications.

Long-term bonds tend to be a relatively costly and less risky type of longer term debt capital. The characteristics of particular bond issues can vary greatly in terms of collateral, subordination, callability, convertibility, limitations on management, and sinking-fund requirements. Various combinations of these factors will affect the risk and thus the required rates of return for particular bond issues. It is quite possible for different bond issues of the same firm to have different required rates of return, owing to differences in their features.

Term loans usually have maturities of between two and six years. They tend to have lower required rates of return than bond issues and also tend to be repaid in installments. Term-loan agreements usually restrict management activities and require collateral. Term-loan financing is especially important to smaller firms.

Today, leases are an important source of longer-term capital. Financial leases and debt are for all practical purposes identical. Service-lease payments constitute both payments for capital and payments for services, so they cannot be directly compared to debt. The evaluation of the attractiveness of financial leases relative to debt requires the computation of the after-tax cash flows associated with the various financing alternatives and the computation of the present values of financing costs. Stockholder wealth can be maximized by minimizing financing cost when risk is constant.

QUESTIONS
FOR
DISCUSSION

1. What is an indenture agreement? What is included in such an agreement? Why is the indenture agreement important to both bondholders and the firm?
2. Describe the three different types of bonds and the risk–return characteristics of each.
3. Describe how a sinking fund operates and how it affects the risk–return characteristics of bonds.

4. Describe the nature of the call provision associated with bonds and explain how it affects the risk–return characteristics of bonds.

5. Describe the nature of convertible bonds and explain how convertibility provisions affect the risk–return characteristics of bonds.

6. What are term loans, and what are the advantages and disadvantages of such loans?

7. Explain the differences between financial and service leases.

8. Why are financial leases viewed as a method of raising capital?

9. Describe the sequence of events involved in evaluating a financial lease.

10. What are the advantages and disadvantages of leasing?

11. Explain why service leases should be evaluated differently from financial leases.

**PROBLEMS**

1. The Dennbo Corporation requires $50 million in debt financing. This financing will be needed for the foreseeable future (50 years). The firm has two alternatives: first, to obtain a ten-year loan from an insurance company with an annual interest rate of 10%; second, to issue 25-year bonds paying an annual interest rate of 12%. Both these alternatives will require refinancing in the future. The effect of these alternatives on the firm will be as follows:

| Insurance-Company Loan (refinanced) | Long-Term Bonds (refinanced) |
|---|---|
| $D_1 = \$3.50$ | $D_1 = \$3.00$ |
| $g = 6\%$ | $g = 6\%$ |
| $k_s = 20\%$ | $k_s = 19\%$ |

Which method of long-term financing is more beneficial to the firm? Explain your answer.

2. The American Space Corporation issued a 30-year bond in 1980. The bonds can be exchanged at any time between 1980 and 2010 for 25 shares of common stock. Each bond has a par value of $1,000.
   a. Calculate the conversion price.
   b. Assuming that the market price of the common stock of the corporation reaches $50 by year 2010, would the bonds be converted?
   c. Assuming that the market price of the common stock of the corporation reaches $30 by year 2010, would the bonds be converted?

3. Imperial Wineries is negotiating a term loan with a commercial bank. The firm wants to borrow $100,000. The bank is willing to provide a five-year term loan with an annual interest rate of 12%. The firm must make five equal annual payments to fully amortize the loan. Prepare a loan-amortization schedule for this loan.

4. Intercontinental Airlines has decided to acquire a Boeing 747. The firm is comparing two alternative financing plans: first, to purchase the plane and finance it with a term loan with an annual interest cost of 12%; second, to lease the plane under a financial-lease arrangement with American Leasing. The after-tax cash outflows associated with the two alternatives are as follows:

| | Costs (in millions) | |
|---|---|---|
| Year | Term loan | Financial lease |
| 0 | 0 | 0 |
| 1 | $10 | $12 |
| 2 | $11 | $12 |
| 3 | $12 | $12 |
| 4 | $13 | $12 |
| 5 | $14 | $12 |
| 6 | $15 | $12 |
| 7 | $15 | $12 |
| 8 | $15 | $12 |
| 9 | $15 | $12 |
| 10 | $15 | $12 |

    a. Calculate the present value of the cash flows associated with the term loan.

    b. Calculate the present value of the cash flows associated with the financial lease.

    c. Which alternative method of financing should be accepted by Intercontinental? Explain your answer.

**5.** Reliable Trucking has decided to purchase new trucks. These trucks have an expected life of four years and no salvage value at the end of four years. The total purchase price of the trucks is $400,000. The firm has two alternative methods of financing the acquisition: First, it can obtain a term loan from a commercial bank for the entire $400,000. The term loan has two provisions: (1) an annual interest rate of 10%, and (2) full amortization of the loan over four years, with four equal annual payments. The second alternative is to obtain a financial lease. The lease payments are $130,000 every year for four years. Reliable Trucking has a marginal tax rate of 40%, and uses the straight-line method of depreciation.

    a. Calculate the present value of the cash flows associated with the term loan.

    b. Calculate the present value of the cash flows associated with the financial lease.

    c. Which alternative method of financing should be accepted by Reliable Trucking? Explain your answer.

# APPENDIX 17A
# Bond Refunding

This appendix deals with the procedures used to compute the effect on stockholder wealth of the interest-rate cost reductions associated with bond refunding. Specifically, we will develop a decision rule for deciding whether or not a firm should refund an outstanding bond issue when interest rates have fallen below those that prevailed at the time the bonds were issued.

First, it is important to recognize that refunding a bond issue can increase stockholder wealth only when interest rates have fallen *and* a call provision is in existence. In the absence of a call provision, bond prices will rise as interest rates fall. Under such conditions, there is no advantage to refunding, since the advantage of lower interest rates is offset by higher bond prices. Refunding is attractive only because the call provision permits the firm to purchase the bonds at prices below those prevailing in unrestricted markets. In effect, the call provision permits management to shift wealth from bondholders to the stockholders of the firm.

The procedures used to evaluate the effect of refunding on stockholder wealth are best explained through the use of an example. Assume that the Annie Corporation sold a $20-million callable bond issue in 1975. These bonds had a 25-year maturity and carried a coupon interest rate of 10 percent. The flotation cost involved in issuing the bonds, $2.5 million, has been amortized on a straight-line basis and currently has a book value of $2 million.

Today (1980), interest rates are lower than they were in 1975, and the Annie Corporation can sell new bonds maturing in 20 years at an effective rate of interest of 8 percent. In order to sell such bonds, the firm will incur $3 million in new flotation costs. In addition, the firm will be required to pay a call premium of 8 percent. Management must decide whether or not the possible cost reduction associated with the lower interest rates is great enough to offset the outlays associated with the flotation cost and call premium.

The computation of the 1980 net cash outflow required for refunding is presented in Table 17A–1. The firm will experience a change in cash flows in 1980, since a call premium of $1.6 million (8 percent of $20 million) must be paid. The firm will also incur $3 million in flotation costs for the new issue. Table 17A–1 summarizes the cash flows in 1980. Note that the after-tax cash outflows of the call premium are only $960,000, because this expense is deductible for tax purposes (a tax rate of 40 percent is assumed). The after-tax cash outflows of the flotation costs of the new issue ($3 million) are identical to the before-tax cash outflows. Flotation costs cannot be deducted by the firm in the same year they are incurred, but must be amortized over the entire life of the bond issue. Thus, the firm will be allowed to deduct $150,000 ($3 million/20 years) every year for 20 years as an amortization expense.

There is an additional effect on the cash outflows of the firm in 1980. Since the firm is planning to retire the old bond issue, it will be permitted to write off as a tax deduction the unamortized flotation costs ($2 million) of the retired bond issue. This will reduce the tax payments of the firm by $800,000 (40 percent of $2 million). Thus, if the firm decides to refund the old bond issue, the total cash outflows in 1980 for the Annie Corporation will be $3,160,000.

The advantage to the firm of refunding is due to the anticipated savings in interest expenses. The current annual interest payments of the firm are $2 million (10 percent of $20 million). The annual interest payments of the new bond issue will be only $1.6 million (8 percent of $20 million). Thus, if the bonds are refunded, the Annie Corporation will have annual savings of

### ANNIE CORPORATION:
### Cash Outflow at 1980, Bond Refunding

| Type of cash flow | Before-tax amount | After-tax amount |
|---|---|---|
| Call premium[a] | $1,600,000 | $ 960,000 |
| Flotation cost[b] | $3,000,000 | $3,000,000 |
| Tax reduction due to recognition of amortized flotation cost on old issue[c] | ($2,000,000) | ($ 800,000) |
| | Net cash outflow | $3,160,000 |

[a]Firm pays bondholders $1,600,000. This reduces taxes by $640,000 ($1,600,000 × 0.4). The after-tax cost is $960,000 ($1,600,000 − $640,000).

[b]Not tax-deductible at $t_0$; must be amortized.

[c]The firm is now permitted to recognize an expense of $2,000,000. This reduces taxable income by $2,000,000 and taxes by $800,000 ($2,000,000 × 0.4).

Note: In addition to the cash flows listed here, there is typically a short period during which the firm must pay interest on both the old and new issues.

$400,000 every year for 20 years. In addition, the firm will increase its annual amortization expense. The annual amortization expense of the old bonds was $100,000 ($2.5 million/25 years). The annual amortization expense of the new bonds will be $150,000 ($3 million/20 years). Thus, the firm will increase its annual amortization expense by $50,000 every year for 20 years. Table 17A–2 shows the estimation of the periodic cash flows caused by the decision to refund the bond issue. The firm will have a positive cash flow of $260,000 every year for 20 years.

It should be noted that the total riskiness of the firm tends to be unaffected by the bond refunding.[18] Note also that the cash flows in a

### ANNIE CORPORATION:
### 20-Year Periodic Cash Inflows Due to the Bond Refunding

| Annual changes | Amount |
|---|---|
| Δ Interest payment | ($400,000) |
| Δ Amortization of flotation costs | 50,000 |
| Change in earnings before taxes = | $350,000 |
| − Tax increase | (140,000) |
| Change in earnings after taxes = | $210,000 |
| + Noncash expenses (Δ Amortization) | 50,000 |
| Change in periodic cash flows | $260,000 |

bond-refunding situation are known with greater certainty than the cash flows usually associated with asset acquisitions. This is attributable to the fact that call premiums, flotation costs, amortization changes, and interest savings are known with perfect certainty. Changes in corporate income tax rates introduce the only uncertainty associated with refunding cash flows.

The discount rate to be used in discounting bond refundings is the subject of considerable controversy. The most recent analysis suggests that the before-tax cost of debt should be used in situations involving the maintenance of the existing optimal capital structure.[14] The before-tax cost of new debt is lower than the firmwide cost of capital, reflecting the lower relative risk associated with bond-refunding cash flows as compared to those of asset acquisitions. Thus, stockholder wealth is maximized when the firm computes the net present value associated with bond refunding by computing the present value of cash inflows, using the before-tax cost of new debt as the discount rate. The net present value is computed by subtracting cash outflows from the present value of inflows. The firm should refund whenever the net present value is positive.

The computations for the net present value of bond refunding in the Annie Corporation illustration are shown in Table 17A–3. Note that the net present value is a negative $607,320. This is the reduction in stockholder wealth associated with refunding. In other words, the firm is not pursuing policies consistent with stockholder-wealth maximization by spending $3,160,000 in order to increase its annual cash flows by $260,000 every year for 20 years. Obviously, had the cash outflows been lower or the cash inflows higher, the net present value could have been positive. Positive net present values call for the refunding of the bond issue.

TABLE 17A–3

ANNIE CORPORATION:
NET PRESENT VALUE OF BOND REFUNDING

Present value of cash inflows = $260,000 (3 $\text{Coef.}_{20}^{8\%}$) = $2,552,680

Net present value = $PV_{\text{inflows}}$ − Outflows
           = $2,552,680 − $3,160,000 = ($607,320)

PROBLEM    1. California Gas & Electric is investigating the possibility of refunding a bond issue. California Gas sold a $100-million callable bond issue in 1970. These bonds, when originally issued, had a 40-year maturity and carried a coupon

---

[13]There is actually a tendency for the firm's debt ratio to decline (remember that market values are used to compute the debt ratio). This may cause a further increase in stockholder wealth.

[14]See G. Leber, "Implications of Discount Rates and Financing Assumptions for Bond Refunding Decisions," *Financial Management*, Vol. 8, No. 1 (Spring 1979), 7–12.

interest rate of 13%. The flotation costs involved in issuing these bonds were $4 million. These flotation costs have been amortized on a straight-line basis and have a current book value of $3 million. The bonds have a call premium of 8% of par value.

At the present time (1980), interest rates are lower than in 1970. California Gas can sell new bonds maturing in 30 years at an effective rate of interest of 10%. The flotation costs of the new issue ($100 million) are $6 million.

Should California Gas & Electric refund the existing bond issue if the firm's marginal tax rate is 40%? (Show the effect of refunding on stockholder wealth.)

**SELECTED BIBLIOGRAPHY**

ANDERSON, PAUL F., and JOHN D. MARTIN, "Lease vs. Purchase Decisions: A Survey of Current Practice," *Financial Management,* 6 (Spring 1977), 41–47.

BLACK, FISCHER, and JOHN C. COX, "Valuing Corporate Securities: Some Effects of Bond Indenture Provisions," *The Journal of Finance,* 31 (May 1976), 351–67.

BULLINGTON, ROBERT A., "How Corporate Debt Issues are Rated," *Financial Executive,* 42 (September 1974), 28–37.

GORDON, MYRON J., "A General Solution to the Buy or Lease Decision: A Pedagogical Note," *The Journal of Finance,* 29 (March 1974), 245–50.

KRAUS, ALAN, "The Bond Refunding Decision in an Efficient Market," *Journal of Financial and Quantitative Analysis,* 8 (December 1973), 793–806.

MIDDLETON, J. WILLIAM, "Term Lending—Practical and Profitable," *Journal of Commercial Bank Lending,* 50 (August 1968), 31–43.

MORRIS, JAMES R., "On Corporate Debt Maturity Strategies," *The Journal of Finance,* 31 (March 1976), 29–37.

REED, EDWARD W., RICHARD V. COTTER, EDWARD K. GILL, and RICHARD K. SMITH, *Commercial Banking,* 2nd ed. Englewood Cliffs, N.J.: Prentice-Hall, 1980.

ROBINSON, ROLAND I., and DWAYNE WRIGHTSMAN, *Financial Markets: The Accumulation and Allocation of Wealth,* 2nd ed. New York: McGraw-Hill, 1980.

VAN HORNE, JAMES C., "The Cost of Leasing with Capital Market Imperfections," *Engineering Economist,* 23 (Fall 1977), 1–12.

———*Financial Management and Policy,* 5th ed. Englewood Cliffs, N.J.: Prentice-Hall, 1980.

WHITE, WILLIAM L., "Debt Management and the Form of Business Financing," *The Journal of Finance,* 29 (May 1974), 565–77.

WISHNER, MAYNARD I., "Coming: Significantly Larger Roles for Secured Corporate Financing," *Financial Executive,* 45 (May 1977), 18–23.

YAWITZ, JESS B., and JAMES A. ANDERSON, "The Effect of Bond Refunding on Shareholder Wealth," *The Journal of Finance,* 32 (December 1977), 1738–46.

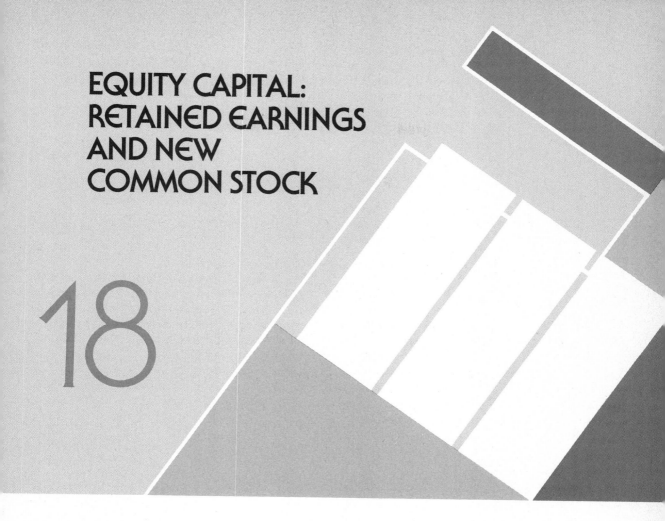

# EQUITY CAPITAL: RETAINED EARNINGS AND NEW COMMON STOCK

## 18

## INTRODUCTION

The last two chapters discussed the various types of debt capital available to the firm, and the effect of each on stockholder wealth. We now turn our attention to equity as a source of capital to the firm. Although our discussion will focus on corporate equity (stockholder wealth), it is also applicable to the ownership interest in sole proprietorships and partnerships. In both situations, *equity* refers to the claim by the owners of the firm on its assets.

## TERMINOLOGY

Before proceeding with a discussion of equity capital, it is necessary to define certain terms. First, the words *common stock*, *net worth*, and *equity* are often used interchangeably. They all refer to the claims of the common stockholders on the assets of the firm. On the balance sheet, the three entries that indicate the level of ownership by common stockholders are "common stock" (also called "capital stock"), "capital surplus" (also called "paid-in surplus") and "earned surplus" (also called "retained earnings"). These three items combined represent the book value of common stockholders' ownership in the firm.

*Preferred stock* is a type separate and distinct from common stock. Typically, preferred stockholders have no vote and do not participate in the earnings of the firm beyond dividends. In most cases, preferred stock has greater similarities to debt than to common stock, since the returns on it (the dividends) are fixed by contract. Outstanding preferred stock is usually considered part of the firm's equity base, since failure to make dividend payments to preferred stockholders cannot force the firm into bankruptcy. Thus, because the claims of preferred stockholders are subordinated to those of debt-capital suppliers, preferred stock provides part of the equity "cushion" that supports the debt issued by the firm. From the debt suppliers' point of view, preferred stock is similar to common stock insofar as it reduces the risk assumed by debt-capital suppliers. From the point of view of common stockholders, preferred stock is similar to debt, since the common stockholders cannot receive dividends until the claims of both debt-capital suppliers and preferred stockholders have been fully met.

However, the issue as to whether preferred stock should be considered part of the total equity base or part of debt capital is really irrelevant, because preferred stock is seldom used today as a means of raising capital. The fact that preferred-stock dividends are not tax-deductible (and interest payments to debt suppliers *are* tax-deductible) has led to a management preference for the use of debt rather than preferred stock. This is consistent with the stockholder-wealth-maximization strategy of the firm.

Owing to the factors above, we confine a more detailed explanation of preferred stock to Appendix 18A. In the body of this chapter, we will assume that the firms under discussion have no preferred stock outstanding and are not likely to use this source of capital in the future.

Among the other balance-sheet terms that require definition is *par value*, an arbitrary value assigned to each share of common stock that, for practical purposes, has no financial significance.[1] In the Sanders Corporation balance sheet presented in Table 18–1, the par value of each share of common stock is $5, only because the corporate charter of the corporation specifies this arbitrary value. The charter could have specified a par value of $1, or $10, or even no par value. The only potential informational use of the par value of common stock is to determine the number of shares outstanding. The number of shares outstanding is equal to the dollar value of the common-stock account, divided by the par value of a single share. For the

---

[1] If management sells common stock to stockholders at a price below par value and the corporation later fails, the owners of the shares purchased below par value could be liable for an additional investment up to par value.

Sanders Corporation, the number of shares outstanding is 20 million ($100 million/$5).

TABLE 18-1

SANDERS CORPORATION:
Balance Sheet (In Millions)

| | | | |
|---|---|---|---|
| Current assets | $500 | Current liability | $200 |
| | | Long-term debt | 300 |
| | | Stockholder equity: | |
| | | Common stock ($5 par value) | 100 |
| | | Capital surplus | 400 |
| | | Retained earnings | 1,000 |
| Fixed assets | 1,500 | Total stockholder equity | $1,500 |
| Total assets | $2,000 | Total liabilities and equity | $2,000 |

It is important to differentiate between the number of shares of common stock *authorized, issued,* and *outstanding.* The number of shares that management is permitted to sell to the public is specified in the corporate charter and is called the number of shares authorized. The number of shares that have actually been sold to the public at any time is called the issued shares. The outstanding shares are those currently in the hands of the public. The difference between issued and outstanding shares is the number that have been repurchased by the corporation (*treasury stock*).

*Book value* of common stock is a term for the "accounting" value of each share. It is computed by dividing the total dollar value of common stockholders' equity by the number of shares outstanding. For the Sanders Corporation, the book value of each share of common stock is $75 ($1,500 million/20 million shares). Keep in mind that the book value of a share of common stock is an *accounting concept* and is not equal to the market price. Book values do not take into consideration the market values of the assets of the firm, the current market value of the debt of the firm, or the expected future dividends and their growth, nor do they reflect the riskiness of the firm.

*Capital surplus* ("paid-in surplus") refers to the price paid for common stock in excess of par value. Thus, if the Sanders Corporation sells 1 million shares of common stock at $60 per share, the common-stock account increases by $5 million (1 million shares × $5 par value), and the capital-surplus account increases by $55 million (1 million shares × [$60 market price − $5 par value]). The significance of the capital surplus is that the firm is not allowed to pay dividends if such payments cause a reduction in this account. Reductions in this account correspond to a repayment of the original capital contributions rather than a distribution of earnings.

Finally, *retained earnings* ("earned surplus") refers to prior income of the firm that was not distributed to the stockholders. The corporation laws of most states require that dividends be paid out of current earnings or prior undistributed earnings.[2] Note that retained earnings *do not* constitute a reservoir of cash. The entry only signifies a claim by the stockholders on the assets of the firm.

Students are often confused by the fact that stockholder equity is distributed over several different accounting entries. While other entries in the right-hand side of the balance sheet refer to distinct types of claims against the firm, the three equity entries refer to a single type of claim. Thus, the book value of stockholder equity is the sum of these three entries. In this context, a single entry has no special meaning of its own. Similarly, the market value of stockholder equity (price of common stock times the number of shares outstanding) is the market value of all three accounts (a single type of claim). It is not possible to talk about the market value of the capital surplus as distinct from that of retained earnings. The market places a value on the total equity claim, not on each of its components.

## COMMON STOCK

### CLAIMS ON INCOME AND ASSETS OF THE FIRM

Common stockholders are the actual owners of a corporation. They assume the largest degree of the risk associated with the enterprise and are thus rewarded with the profits of the firm. The earnings of the firm, after payment of all other obligations, belong to the stockholders; that is, stockholders have a *residual* claim on the income and the assets of the corporation.[3] The corporation must meet all its contractual obligations before stockholders can benefit from either the income or the liquidation of the assets of the firm. Thus, all other suppliers of capital (short-, medium-, or long-term debt, preferred stock, and so on) must be compensated *before* stockholders can receive any return on their investment. Therefore, the risk borne by stockholders is greater than that borne by other suppliers of capital.

On the other hand, stockholders are not limited as to potential rewards. If the corporation is extremely successful, bondholders and holders of preferred stock (in almost all cases) will not receive additional returns, but those to stockholders are unlimited.[4]

### CONTROL OF THE FIRM

Stockholders of large, publicly traded corporations do not participate directly in the management of the firm. However, they participate indirectly,

---

[2]When distributions to stockholders result in a negative balance for retained earnings, the firm is involved in the repayment of capital rather than the payment of dividends.

[3]In this chapter, the word *stockholders* refers to the common stockholders of the firm.

[4]This statement, of course, can be constrained by restrictions imposed by society. The oil industry is an excellent example. Stockholders of oil corporations have not received the full benefit of recent increases in the price of oil, since society has decided to limit the profits of oil companies.

through their right to choose the board of directors of the corporation, which acts as their representative. The board of directors does not actually run the corporation on a day-to-day basis. Its responsibility is to select, oversee, and if necessary replace the actual managers of the firm. The indirect nature of the control by stockholders over the corporation is summarized in Figure 18–1.

The voting procedure used by stockholders in electing the board of directors is delineated in the corporate charter.[5] There are two common voting procedures: (1) majority voting, and (2) cumulative voting. Let us illustrate the differences between these two systems.

The Irene Corporation has 1 million shares of common stock outstanding, and there are fifteen positions on the board of directors, all of which are up for election. Under majority voting, a stockholder has one vote for each share owned and must vote for each board position open for election; that is, each share can vote fifteen times, but only once for any position on the board. Let us assume that the stockholders of the Irene Corporation are divided into two opposing factions: Group A owns 600,000 shares and Group B owns the remaining 400,000 shares. Under majority voting, Group A could elect the *entire board of directors* by casting 600,000 votes for each director. Group B will not be able to elect *any* directors, since it can cast only 400,000 votes for each position on the board. Therefore, each choice of Group B would be defeated by the choice of Group A. This method of voting reduces minority representation on the board of directors.

---

[5]Some corporations—the Ford Motor Company is a classic example—have two different types of common stock, of which one class (usually called "class B stock") has a greater voting power than the other. We will assume in this chapter, however, that the voting rights of all common stockholders are proportional to the number of shares owned.

**FIGURE 18–1**

Indirect Control
of the Firm
by the Stockholders

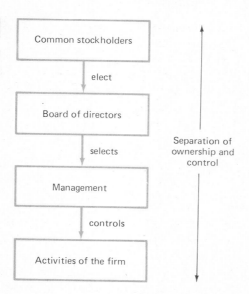

Cumulative voting has developed as an alternative to majority voting in order to give minority stockholders a greater voice in the affairs of the corporation. Under cumulative voting, stockholders are able to concentrate their votes on any one director. In our previous example, Group B has 6 million votes (400,000 shares × 15 directors being elected). With cumulative voting, Group B can allocate its total voting power in such a way as to ensure the election of six members of the board of directors. Instead of 400,000 votes for each of the fifteen director positions, Group B can cast 1 million votes for each of six positions. Each share of stock still has fifteen votes, but each share may vote more than once for the same candidate. Group A has a total of 9 million votes (600,000 shares × 15 directors being elected). If Group A decided to place 900,000 votes for each of ten candidates, it would still elect only nine members of the board.[6]

Even though the cumulative voting procedure ensures minority representation on the board of directors, the extent to which a minority of stockholders can influence management policy is exaggerated by the previous example. In most widely held corporations, the ownership of 40 percent of the voting stock would virtually guarantee the election of the entire board. In addition, most stockholders do not attend the annual meetings and do not vote directly for the board of directors. Usually, stockholders assign their rights to vote to another person or persons, usually the current management of the firm, by signing a document called a *proxy*. If there is widespread dissatisfaction with current management, a *proxy fight* may occur. This is a situation in which a group of stockholders competes with current management by soliciting the proxies of all other stockholders of the corporation. This alternative is rarely used, owing to the high expense and low success rate of proxy fights; however, the possibility is always present, and management must always consider the effect of its actions on the stockholders of the firm.

## EQUITY SOURCES

### DIVIDEND POLICY

A corporation desiring to raise equity has two basic choices: (1) retain some of the earnings of the firm, or (2) sell new common stock. This section of the chapter focuses on retained earnings as a source of equity. Later we will

---

[6]The minimum number of shares of common stock necessary to ensure the election of a certain number of directors can be computed as follows:

$$\frac{\text{Total number of} \atop \text{shares outstanding} \times \frac{\text{Number of directors} \atop \text{desired}}{\text{Total number of directors} \atop \text{being elected} + 1} + 1$$

In many occasions, stockholders fail to vote. Thus, the number of shares required to elect directors may be smaller than the number suggested by the formula.

analyze raising equity funds outside the firm through the issuance of new common stock.

Retained earnings is a residual concept. A corporation has a certain amount of earnings available to common stockholders; these earnings may be paid out to them in the form of dividends or retained by the firm. Retained earnings is the amount left over (the residual) after dividends have been paid to the stockholders.

Table 18–2 shows a hypothetical balance sheet for the Roberts Corporation. The amount of retained earnings of the Roberts Corporation is a function of the earnings after taxes, the amount of dividends that must be paid on preferred stock, and the amount of dividends paid to the common stockholders.[7] The key is the relationship between the earnings available to common stockholders and retained earnings. Note that the Roberts Corporation had $8 million available for common stockholders, of which $3 million was paid out in dividends and $5 million retained by the firm.

The Roberts Corporation could have declared a common-stock dividend of $8 million, thus paying out all available earnings in dividends and reducing the change in retained earnings for 1980 to zero. Or the corporation could have reduced the common dividend to zero, in which case retained earnings would have increased by $8 million during 1980. The board of directors determines the amount of dividends to be paid to common stockholders. Usually, the board adopts a dividend policy that it follows over a period of years. The increase in equity capital due to retained earnings is what is left over after this dividend policy has been executed. In a sense, dividend policy and retained-earnings policy are two ways of looking at the same thing.

As discussed in Chapter 6, the theory of finance makes two important statements about dividend/retained-earnings policy. First, the theory suggests that stockholder wealth will be maximized by raising equity through retention of earnings rather than the sale of new common stock, since income received in the form of dividends is taxed at a higher rate than income received in the form of higher stock prices (capital gains). This implies that firms in need of new equity capital should cut back on dividends and thus increase earnings retention.[8] The actual behavior of firms has been consistent with the theoretical proposition. Specifically, more than 80 percent of all equity raised by nonfinancial corporations from 1960 to 1975 was raised through the retention of earnings; less than 20 percent of the increase in equity resulted from the sale of new common stock.

The theory of finance also suggests that, to the extent that corporations do pay dividends, the dividends should follow a well-defined and publicized policy (a consistent dividend policy). A consistent dividend policy will permit stockholders to select stocks in such a fashion as to minimize

---

[7]See Appendix 18A for a discussion of the legal obligation to pay preferred dividends.
[8]Assuming that the firm has asset-acquisition alternatives with positive net present values.

TABLE 18–2

ROBERTS CORPORATION:
Balance Sheet and Income Statement

BALANCE SHEET AS OF DECEMBER 31, 1979
(In Millions)

|  |  |  |  |
|---|---|---|---|
|  |  | Total liabilities | $10 |
|  |  | Preferred stock | $20 |
|  |  | Common stock | $10 |
|  |  | Capital surplus | $15 |
|  |  | Retained earnings | $45 |
|  |  | Total liabilities |  |
| Total assets | $100 | and equity | $100 |

INCOME STATEMENT FOR 1980
(In Millions)

| | |
|---|---|
| Earnings after taxes | $10 |
| *less:* Dividends on preferred stock | ($2) |
| = Earnings available to common stockholders | $8 |
| *less:* Dividends paid to common stockholders | ($3) |
| = Increase in retained earnings | $5 |

BALANCE SHEET AS OF DECEMBER 31, 1980
(In Millions)

|  |  |  |  |
|---|---|---|---|
|  |  | Total liabilities | $10 |
|  |  | Preferred stock | $20 |
|  |  | Common stock | $10 |
|  |  | Capital surplus | $15 |
|  |  | Retained earnings | $50 |
|  |  | Total liabilities |  |
| Total assets | $105 | and equity | $105 |

personal income tax liabilities and brokerage fees, thus maximizing stockholder wealth.

But the preference for the use of retained-earnings financing (as opposed to the sale of new common stock) and a consistent dividend policy may conflict with each other. For example, suppose that a corporation with earnings available to the stockholders of $35 million has been following a policy of paying dividends at a rate of $25 million per year. Now the firm is unexpectedly presented with very favorable asset-acquisition alternatives, and to acquire such assets, $60 million in capital is needed. In order to maintain the firm's optimal capital structure, $20 million must be raised in the form of additional equity. Existing dividend policy, however, will permit the firm to raise only $10 million in retained earnings ($35 million in earnings available to common stockholders less $25 million in dividends). Since the asset-acquisition alternatives are so favorable, the firm must choose between selling new common stock and changing its dividend policy. This situation is not unusual. Many corporations, including such economic giants as American Telephone & Telegraph, frequently sell stock and pay dividends simultaneously. It would appear that in general, firms choose to maintain consistent dividend policies even if new common stock must be sold to the public in order to meet new equity-capital needs.

Most firms adopt one of three dividend payout policies and maintain that policy unless some major unforeseen event interferes. The most frequently followed policies are (1) a stable-dividend policy, (2) a constant-payout-ratio policy, and (3) a policy calling for a low regular dividend plus a bonus under certain circumstances. These policies are described below.

The most widely followed dividend policy is that of paying *stable dividends*, regardless of the fact that earnings of American corporations fluctuate from year to year. The earnings of automobile manufacturing firms, for example, increase dramatically during periods of prosperity and decline during periods of recession.

An illustration of the stable-dividend policy pursued by the hypothetical Intercontinental Airline Corporation is presented in Table 18–3. Note that stable dividends do not imply constant dividends. In the case of Intercontinental Airlines, dividends have increased gradually during the ten-year period reviewed. Note also that the dividends of the firm are considerably less volatile than earnings. As shown in the table, a stable-dividend policy implies that dividends are maintained even when earnings become negative, as in 1973. Stability of dividends also implies that dramatic increases in earnings are not accompanied by proportional increases in dividends—that is, dividends vary less than the earnings of the firm for the same time

TABLE 18–3

INTERCONTINENTAL AIRLINES:
Stable-Dividend Policy

| Year | Earnings per share | Dividends per share | Payout ratio, dividends/earnings |
|------|--------------------|---------------------|----------------------------------|
| 1970 | $5.00 | $2.60 | 52% |
| 1971 | $7.00 | $2.70 | 39% |
| 1972 | $4.00 | $2.70 | 68% |
| 1973 | ($1.00) | $2.70 | - |
| 1974 | $9.00 | $2.90 | 32% |
| 1975 | $12.00 | $3.10 | 26% |
| 1976 | $7.00 | $3.10 | 44% |
| 1977 | $5.00 | $3.20 | 64% |
| 1978 | $3.00 | $3.20 | 106% |
| 1979 | $8.00 | $3.30 | 41% |
| Total | $59.00 | $29.50 | 50% |

period—and that the percentage of earnings paid out varies greatly from year to year.[9]

A *constant-payout-ratio* policy is another dividend policy that is sometimes followed by American corporations. Under this policy, the firm will pay a constant percentage of its earnings in dividends. Table 18–4 illustrates a constant payout ratio for Intercontinental Airlines. It is assumed that the firm desires to pay dividends equal to 50 percent of its earnings. Note that the total earnings, total dividends, and thus total retained earnings for the entire ten-year period remain the same as under the policy of stable dividends; but the dividends exhibit a much greater volatility.

TABLE 18–4

INTERCONTINENTAL AIRLINES:
CONSTANT PAYOUT RATIO
(50% of Earnings)

| Year | Earnings per share | Dividends per share |
|------|--------------------|---------------------|
| 1970 | $5.00 | $2.50 |
| 1971 | $7.00 | $3.50 |
| 1972 | $4.00 | $2.00 |
| 1973 | ($1.00) | 0[a] |
| 1974 | $9.00 | $4.00 |
| 1975 | $12.00 | $6.00 |
| 1976 | $7.00 | $3.50 |
| 1977 | $5.00 | $2.50 |
| 1978 | $3.00 | $1.50 |
| 1979 | $8.00 | $4.00 |
| Total | $59.00 | $29.50 |

[a]In order to obtain comparable results, we have assumed that the "deficit" in 1973 is made up in 1974.

Another dividend policy calls for the firm to pay *low regular dividends, plus a "bonus"* dividend during very good years. This is a compromise between the stable-dividend and constant-payout-ratio policies. Table 18–5 illustrates such a policy for Intercontinental Airlines. Note that this results in a higher volatility of dividends than for a stable-dividend policy, but a lower volatility than for the constant payout ratio. Nevertheless, the total dividends received by stockholders are the same under each of the three dividend policies discussed.

The bonus portion of the dividend is often anticipated by stockholders, and they may interpret unfavorably any failure to pay such a bonus. For example, General Motors Corporation follows a policy of low regular dividends plus a bonus. In 1979, despite high earnings, GM decided to

---

[9]A ten-year horizon is used for illustrative purposes in our discussion of the various dividend policies. In practice, firms usually use shorter periods.

TABLE 18–5

INTERCONTINENTAL AIRLINES:
LOW REGULAR DIVIDENDS PLUS BONUS

| Year | Earnings per share | Regular dividend | + | Bonus dividend | = | Total dividend |
|------|------|------|---|------|---|------|
| 1970 | $5.00 | $2.00 | + | 0 | = | $2.00 |
| 1971 | $7.00 | $2.00 | + | $1.00 | = | $3.00 |
| 1972 | $4.00 | $2.00 | + | 0 | = | $2.00 |
| 1973 | ($1.00) | $2.00 | + | 0 | = | $2.00 |
| 1974 | $9.00 | $2.00 | + | $2.00 | = | $4.00 |
| 1975 | $12.00 | $2.00 | + | $3.50 | = | $5.50 |
| 1976 | $7.00 | $2.00 | + | $1.00 | = | $3.00 |
| 1977 | $5.00 | $2.00 | + | 0 | = | $2.00 |
| 1978 | $3.00 | $2.00 | + | 0 | = | $2.00 |
| 1979 | $8.00 | $2.00 | + | $2.00 | = | $4.00 |
| Total | $59.00 | $20.00 | | $9.50 | | $29.50 |

forego the bonus on the grounds that it needed the capital for proposed asset acquisitions. The next day, the price of GM common stock fell dramatically.

**Evaluation of Dividend Policies**

Empirical evidence suggests that most American corporations follow a stable-dividend policy. Table 18–6 shows the earnings after taxes and actual dividends paid by American nonfinancial corporate businesses. From 1967 to 1972, earnings after taxes fluctuated between a low of $27.9 billion and a high of $42.2 billion. Dividends paid during the same period exhibited a lower degree of fluctuation, a high of $21.6 billion and a low of $18.8 billion. American corporations tend to increase dividends only when they have the confidence that a higher permanent level of earnings has been attained. They do not like to reduce dividend payments unless major economic factors force them to.

The willingness of corporations to pay dividends while at the same time selling new common stock is presumably based upon the assumption that a reduction in dividends will have a greater negative effect on stock prices (stockholder wealth) than will the sale of new common stock. There are several reasons for believing that this assumption may be valid:

1. First is the *informational content of dividends*. A sharp reduction in the dividends paid by the firm may carry a negative connotation to market participants. The announcement of a cut in dividends may signal the market that management anticipates a permanent decline in earnings. Thus, corporations attempt to maintain dividend payments even when earnings have declined or new common stock must be sold. A corporation maintaining dividends in the aftermath of an earnings decline is signaling the market that the decline is only temporary and that it expects earnings to recover to previous levels.

TABLE 18–6

## DIVIDEND POLICY OF NONFINANCIAL CORPORATION BUSINESSES
### (In Billions)

| Year | Profits after tax | Dividends paid | Payout ratio (dividends as a percentage of earnings) |
|------|-------------------|----------------|------------------------------------------------------|
| 1967 | $37.7 | $18.8 | 50% |
| 1968 | $38.3 | $20.7 | 54% |
| 1969 | $35.1 | $20.6 | 59% |
| 1970 | $27.9 | $19.8 | 71% |
| 1971 | $33.4 | $20.0 | 60% |
| 1972 | $42.2 | $21.6 | 52% |
| 1973 | $52.6 | $23.8 | 45% |
| 1974 | $60.2 | $25.9 | 43% |
| 1975 | $60.4 | $28.3 | 47% |
| 1976 | $77.2 | $32.9 | 43% |
| 1977 | $83.9 | $37.0 | 44% |
| 1978 | $97.3 | $41.6 | 43% |
| Total | $646.2 | $311.0 | 48% |

Source: Board of Governors of the Federal Reserve System, *Flow of Funds Accounts*, various issues.

2. A large number of investors have a *preference for current income*. For example, retired people may count on dividends for current consumption. Such people would have a "built-in" preference for a firm that has a high degree of dividend stability. The stockholder can, of course, sell the stock in order to obtain funds. This alternative, however, may be less desirable, owing to brokerage costs and the aversion to reductions in capital. The corporation encourages income seekers to buy its stock by maintaining stable dividends. This will have a positive effect on stock prices.

3. Certain institutional investors (for example, pension funds) are required to invest their funds in stocks included in a *legal list* developed by regulatory bodies. One of the characteristics of stocks included in such lists is an uninterrupted pattern of dividend payments over time. Thus, firms that pursue a stable-dividend policy have a greater probability of being included on such legal lists. This should have a positive effect on stock price.

The following points summarize our discussion on dividend policy and retained earnings:

1. Nonfinancial corporations raise more than 80% of new equity capital by retaining earnings. Less than 20% of new equity is raised by selling new common stock.
2. Approximately half the earnings of nonfinancial corporations are retained and the other half paid out in the form of dividends.

3. The dividends paid by the firm tend to be disbursed under a stable-dividend policy. Such a policy calls for maintaining dividend levels despite changes in earnings or the need for new equity capital.

4. In order to maintain the price of common stock, firms frequently pay dividends (reduce potential retained earnings) while simultaneously selling new common stock.

Assets acquired with additional capital must be justified in terms of earning returns in excess of the asset-specific cost of capital (positive net present values). Only firms with asset-acquisition alternatives having positive net present values require additional capital. The decision to retain earnings (as well as to sell new common stock or increase debt) must ultimately be justified in terms of the assets' ability to increase stockholder wealth. In the extreme cases, a firm with no attractive asset acquisitions would retain no earnings. Earnings should not be retained automatically.

## REPURCHASE OF COMMON STOCK AS AN ALTERNATIVE TO PAYING CASH DIVIDENDS

A corporation may find itself with excess cash and no acceptable investment opportunities in the foreseeable future. One alternative open to the firm is to maintain such excess funds in marketable securities; but at best, this is a temporary solution, since the returns will be quite low. Stockholder wealth would be improved if, in the absence of acceptable investment opportunities, the firm distributes excess funds to the stockholders. Stockholders, however, may not want cash dividends. This will be the case when stockholders have high marginal tax rates and/or high transaction costs. As an alternative, the corporation could use the excess funds to purchase its common stock in the open market. The repurchase will decrease the number of shares outstanding. Thus, the expected earnings and dividends per share (assuming the same payout ratio) will increase. This should result in an increase in the market price of the common stock of the firm.

The advantage of repurchase is that it allows the stockholders to receive the benefits of stock ownership in the manner most beneficial to their financial position. Stockholders in high income brackets or with a preference for postponement of consumption would keep their higher-priced shares, benefitting by the increase in the market price of common stock. Those stockholders that prefer current income can sell part of their stock holdings. They would benefit because only the gain on the sale will be taxed, and perhaps at a lower effective tax rate than the rate applied to dividend income.

The firm can repurchase its stock in either of two ways: It can purchase the stock in the open market, or it can make a tender offer for a specified number of shares at a specified price, usually slightly higher than the current market price.

A word of caution on repurchases: The Internal Revenue Service scrutinizes stock repurchases, especially in the cases of closely held corporations, and it will investigate a corporation repurchasing its stock on a continuous basis. This procedure for distributing earnings may be viewed by the IRS as a means of evading the tax liability on cash dividends. Under normal circumstances, a one-time stock repurchase due to special economic conditions would not be challenged by the IRS, but repetitive stock repurchases may be challenged, because of the reduction in the tax liabilities of the stockholders.

## SELLING NEW COMMON STOCK

Under normal circumstances, corporations prefer to raise equity funds through earnings retention rather than new issues of common stock. However, various factors limit the ability of the firm to retain funds within the enterprise. These factors include (1) the firm's dividend policy, (2) diminished earnings during a certain period, or (3) very large investment opportunities. Such factors may force the firm to raise equity funds through the issue of new common stock.

If the management of a corporation decides that equity will be raised through the sale of new common stock, a choice must be made among a number of different sales strategies: The stock may be sold to the public through an investment banker, through a rights offering, or through a dividend reinvestment program. Each of these sales strategies has advantages and disadvantages, which will be discussed in the following sections of the chapter.

**The Role of the Investment Banker**

As we saw in Chapter 15, the investment banker facilitates the flow of capital from savers to investors. When a firm utilizes an investment banker to sell a new issue of common stock to the public, the firm essentially sells the new issue to the investment banker and, in turn, the banker sells the new issue to the public. The services provided by the investment banker include (1) the assumption of the risk associated with declines in stock prices during the period that the stock is being sold to the public; (2) the marketing and distribution of the issue; (3) advice and counsel to the firm relative to price, marketing, and other strategies; and (4) assistance in meeting the requirements of the Securities and Exchange Commission and other regulatory agencies.

The investment banker expects to be compensated for providing these services. Typically, such compensation is received in the form of a discount on the stock price. That is, the investment banker pays less for the stock than the price paid by the public. The discount plus certain other costs constitute the cost of floating the stock issue. For a large, well-known, low-risk corporation, flotation costs may be as low as 2 percent. For smaller, more risky corporations, they can run to 10 percent or more.

The major advantage of using investment bankers to sell new common stock is that the marketing expertise of these organizations frequently enables the firm to gain access to new capital suppliers, thus expanding and diversifying the ownership of the firm. The primary disadvantage of the use of investment bankers is that the costs of their services are frequently higher than the costs of selling new common stock through rights offerings or dividend reinvestment plans.

**Rights Offerings** Corporate charters frequently include provisions requiring that new stock issues be offered to existing stockholders before they can be offered to the general public. That is, existing stockholders have a *right* to maintain their proportional share of a corporation by purchasing a proportional share of the newly issued common stock. For example, a person owning 5 percent of a corporation's outstanding stock would be entitled to buy 5 percent of the newly issued stock, thus maintaining a 5 percent ownership interest in the corporation.

The mechanics of a rights offering are rather complicated. To illustrate them, we will assume that the Eloco Corporation plans to raise an additional $10 million in equity by selling new shares of common stock through a rights offering. The firm currently has 1 million shares of common stock outstanding, and each stockholder receives a piece of paper, called a *right*, for each share of common stock owned. For example, a stockholder with 100 shares of common stock will receive 100 rights. These rights, plus a specified amount of cash, can be used to purchase the firm's common stock at a price lower than existing market levels. In the Eloco Corporation example, the firm specifies that four rights plus $40 will buy one share of common stock. The current market price of the common stock of the Eloco Corporation is $50. The discount offered on the new shares encourages their purchase and thus makes it easier for the firm to raise new equity capital.

The number of rights needed to purchase one share will depend on the number of new shares to be issued and the existing shares outstanding. In the Eloco Corporation example, 250,000 shares will be sold ($10 million/$40). Since there are 1 million shares outstanding (1 million shares of existing common stock), four rights will be needed to acquire a new share at the discount price, as shown in equation 18–1:

$$\frac{\text{Number of rights needed}}{\text{to buy a share of stock}} = \frac{\text{Outstanding shares}}{\text{Newly issued shares}}$$

$$= \frac{1,000,000}{250,000} = 4 \text{ rights} \tag{16-1}$$

Since the holder of rights is entitled to purchase common stock at a price below those prevailing in the market, each right has a value of its own. In a general sense, we can see that the possession of four rights entitles the bearer to a $10 discount on the purchase of one share of common stock of the Eloco Corporation.[10]

It is not necessary for an existing stockholder to use the rights received. As an alternative, the stockholder can sell the rights to another person who is interested in purchasing the stock of the corporation. In fact, it is quite easy to sell rights, and stockholders frequently do it. When rights are sold, the stockholder is reducing his or her percentage of equity owned. Note, however, that such a reduction is accompanied by a cash inflow to the stockholder (the proceeds from the sale of the rights).

In most rights-offering situations, the subscription price is between 10 and 20 percent below the prevailing market price. The size of the discount will affect the number of new shares issued and the future price of the common stock. A large discount will result in a relatively high number of shares being sold to raise the same amount of capital. The relatively high number of new shares tends to reduce the expected earnings and dividends per share and, other things being equal, to reduce the market price of the common stock. This price reduction is commonly called the *dilution effect* of rights offerings. For example, if the Eloco Corporation had established the subscription price at $20 rather than $40, the firm would have had to sell 500,000 shares rather than 250,000 in order to raise the $10 million. The resulting larger number of shares outstanding would tend to drive the price of common stock down. Of course, stockholders who use the rights to acquire new shares would be compensated for the reduction in market price per share by being able to purchase more shares. Those stockholders selling rights are compensated for the lower market price of common stock by receiving higher prices for their rights. So the effect of the size of the discount on stockholder wealth appears to be neutral.

The utilization of rights offerings tends to increase stockholder wealth by reducing the cost of selling new common stock. The flotation costs involved in a rights offering are much lower than those involved in a public offering. Other things being equal, this lower cost with no additional risk should increase stockholder wealth.

---

[10]The theoretical value of the right can be computed using the following equation:

$$R_0 = \frac{P_0 - S}{N + 1}$$

where $R_0$ = value of one right

$P_0$ = market price of one share of common stock selling *with* the right (rights-on)

$S$ = subscription price of the new shares

$N$ = number of rights needed to acquire one new share

For the Eloco Corporation illustration, the computation would be as follows:

$$R_0 = \frac{\$50 - \$40}{4 + 1} = \$2.00 \text{ per right}$$

For a more detailed explanation of rights, see James C. Van Horne, *Financial Management and Policy*, 5th ed. (Englewood Cliffs, N.J.: Prentice-Hall, 1980), pp. 592–99.

**Dividend Reinvestment Plans**

A number of large American corporations have given their stockholders the option to participate in a dividend reinvestment plan. Under such a plan, the corporation pays a cash dividend, but the stockholder has the option of receiving the cash or using it to purchase from the firm additional shares of common stock.

Let us illustrate the dividend reinvestment plan with a hypothetical example. California Telephone pays a $5 dividend per share of common stock. The current market price of the stock is $100. California Telephone offers its stockholders the following options: (1) to receive the $5 dividend per share, or (2) to reinvest the dividend. If the dividend is reinvested, the price of each share is usually below the current market price. Let us assume that California Telephone offers a 5 percent discount on reinvested dividends. Thus, the stockholder would pay only $95 for each share acquired.

Therefore, a stockholder owning 190 shares of California Telephone stock has two options: (1) to receive a $950 cash dividend from the firm, or (2) to receive ten shares of common stock.[11] At first glance, this policy appears beneficial to both the firm and the stockholder. The firm can raise equity funds without incurring significant flotation costs and, furthermore, can pay a high cash dividend. The stockholders, on the other hand, appear to benefit from two provisions of the plan: (1) They do not incur brokerage costs to acquire new shares of common stock, and (2) they can purchase the stock at a "bargain" price. In addition, this plan allows those stockholders with a preference for current consumption to elect the cash dividend.

The key factor that makes the dividend reinvestment plan somewhat negative toward maximizing stockholder wealth is the tax law. The stockholder must pay a personal income tax on the dividend received regardless of the reinvestment decision. Thus, our hypothetical stockholder must pay taxes on the $950 received from the firm whether he or she elects to receive the cash dividend or the ten shares of common stock, because the IRS interprets the $950 as income whether it is reinvested or not. Therefore, stockholder wealth would be reduced by the amount of taxes on the $950 dividend received.

Let us continue our hypothetical California Telephone example. Assume that *all* stockholders elect to fully participate in the dividend reinvestment plan. In this situation, the entire "dividend" will remain within the firm; stockholders will maintain the same proportional ownership interest they had before; and each stockholder will have a tax liability equal to the dividend "received" times the individual's marginal tax rate.

As an alternative, California Telephone could elect to pay *no dividends* and retain the earnings. Thus, the firm would have the *same amount of funds* as if all the dividends had been reinvested; the stockholders would maintain

---

[11]The stockholder can elect to reinvest only a certain percentage of the dividend—for example, to receive $475 and five shares.

the same proportional ownership in the firm; and the stockholders would *not have to pay any taxes* on their stock unless they sold some of it.[12]

There are, however, some advantages to the dividend reinvestment plans. First, they allow stockholders an easy choice between current consumption (elect the cash dividend) and postponement of consumption (reinvest the dividend) without incurring brokerage costs. Second, they allow savings to the firm by reducing flotation costs. Third, they allow the firm to pay stable and high dividends, thus permitting a stable-dividend policy without large cash outflows. Finally, in some cases, the major disadvantage of such plans—taxes—may not be as large as discussed in this section. If the stockholders of the firm are exempt from taxation (foundations, pension funds, or the like), are at a very low marginal tax rate (retired stockholders), or are very small stockholders (paying no taxes on the dividend owing to the dividend exclusion provision of $100 or $200), the negative effect on stockholder wealth of tax payments may be more than offset by the reduction in brokerage and flotation costs.

## STOCK DIVIDENDS AND STOCK SPLITS

On occasion, a corporation may pay a stock dividend instead of a cash dividend. In such a situation, the board of directors gives stockholders additional common stock rather than cash as a dividend. The accounting treatment of a stock dividend is illustrated below. Table 18–7 shows the balance sheet of the Invicta Corporation before and after a 10 percent stock dividend is declared. The current market price of the common stock of the corporation is $50 per share. Thus, a 10 percent stock dividend will increase the number of shares outstanding from 10 million to 11 million. The market value of such an increase is equal to $50 million (1 million shares × $50 per share). This $50 million is entered into the balance sheet as follows: (1) $10 million in the common-stock account (1 million shares × $10 par value), and (2) the remaining $40 million ($50 million market value less $10 million in the common-stock account) in the capital surplus. The increase in these two accounts is accompanied by a reduction in retained earnings. A stock dividend results in a shift in funds among the equity accounts; total equity is not changed.

Note that nothing has happened that will affect the total dividends paid to stockholders. No new assets have been acquired, no costs have been reduced. All that has happened is that the number of shares of common stock outstandifg has increased. Since total earnings and dividends are expected to remain the same, dividends per share and the price of common stock should fall.

---

[12]See the beginning of Chapter 6 for a review of the effect of dividends compared to that of retained earnings on stockholder wealth.

TABLE 18-7

INVICTA CORPORATION:
EQUITY ACCOUNTS OF THE BALANCE SHEET[a]

| BEFORE STOCK DIVIDEND | |
|---|---|
| Common stock ($10 par value) | $100 million |
| Capital surplus | 300 million |
| Retained earnings | 500 million |
| Total stockholder equity | $900 million |
| Number of shares outstanding = 10 million | |

| AFTER 10% STOCK DIVIDEND | |
|---|---|
| Common stock ($10 par value) | $110 million |
| Capital surplus | 340 million |
| Retained earnings | 450 million |
| Total stockholder equity | $900 million |
| New number of shares outstanding = 11 million | |

[a]Stock price before = $50 per share

With a stock dividend, current stockholders maintain the same proportional ownership in the firm. For example, the shares of a stockholder owning 5 percent of the outstanding shares will increase from 500,000 to 550,000, but the stockholder will have exactly the same ownership interest as before, 5 percent. In a competitive market, the price of the stock would decline in a proportional manner. Thus, for the Invicta Corporation, the market price should decline from $50 per share before the stock dividend to $45.45 after it. Our hypothetical stockholder's wealth would be $25 million ($50 × 500,000) before and $25 million ($45.45 × 550,000) after the stock dividend. The reason for the decline in the market price of the stock is that even though *the financial situation of the firm* (total earnings, total dividends, and so on) *remains the same*, the benefits of the firm are divided among a larger number of shares.

Some financial practitioners state that stock dividends are beneficial to stockholder wealth, owing to two factors: (1) The stock will trade at a lower, more "popular" price, and (2) the announcement of the stock dividend tends to produce a favorable psychological reaction. These two arguments basically assume an imperfect market. The first implies that stockholders will pay a premium for lower-priced stock; the second that the market will not recognize good news about the firm unless stock dividends are declared.

The *stock split* has certain similarities to the stock dividend, although it has a different accounting treatment. Table 18–8 shows a 2-for-1 stock split for the Invicta Corporation. Note that the only change in the balance sheet is in the par value per share (reduced from $10 to $5) and the number of shares outstanding (increased from 10 million to 20 million). The dollar value of each equity account remains unchanged, as does the total value of equity.[13]

INVICTA CORPORATION:
EQUITY ACCOUNTS OF THE BALANCE SHEET

| | |
|---|---|
| *BEFORE 2-FOR-1 STOCK SPLIT* | |
| Common stock ($10 par value) | $100 million |
| Capital surplus | 300 million |
| Retained earnings | 500 million |
| Total stockholder equity | $900 million |
| Number of shares outstanding = 10 million | |
| *AFTER 2-FOR-1 STOCK SPLIT* | |
| Common stock ($5 par value) | $100 million |
| Capital surplus | 300 million |
| Retained earnings | 500 million |
| Total stockholders equity | $900 million |
| Number of shares outstanding = 20 million | |

Does a stock split affect stockholder wealth? The answer to this question and the basic arguments pro and con are the same as those for stock dividends.[14] The stock split does not change the proportional ownership interest of current stockholders; thus, stockholder wealth should remain unchanged in a competitive market. It is generally believed, however, that the major positive feature of stock splits and dividends is to bring the stock price into a better price range, making it more attractive to a larger number of buyers and increasing the interest in the stock. This increased interest may have a slightly positive effect on the total value of the firm's equity.

It is crucial to recognize that stock dividends and stock splits are in no way comparable to cash dividends. On occasion, one gets the impression that corporate management attempts to mislead stockholders on this issue.

## DEBT OR EQUITY: THE OPTIMAL CAPITAL STRUCTURE

The general relationship between the proportion of capital raised through the use of debt and stockholder wealth was discussed in Chapter 5. There,

---

[13]The corporation can also declare a reverse split. In such a case, the number of shares outstanding is reduced. For example, if the Invicta Corporation made a 1-for-2 reverse split, the par value would increase to $20, and the number of shares outstanding would decline to 5 million.

[14]From the stockholder's point of view, there is no significant difference between a stock dividend and a stock split. The New York Stock Exchange classifies any distribution of stock of less than 25% of that outstanding to be a stock dividend. A distribution over 25% is considered a stock split.

we noted that stockholder wealth tends to increase as the relative use of debt increases, because the tax deductibility of interest payments results in a cost/risk advantage to debt. That is, the cost savings associated with debt are large enough to offset the increased riskiness borne by common stockholders. Within the context of common-stock valuation equations, it is easy to see what happens as small amounts of debt are used:

$$PV_s = \frac{D}{k_s} \text{ (no growth)}$$

(2-7)

$$PV_s = \frac{D_1}{k_s - g} \text{ (constant growth)}$$

(2-9)

Although both dividends ($D$) and the required rate of return ($k_s$) increase as the amount of debt used increases, the beneficial aspects of the increase in dividends tend to dominate. Thus, the price of common stock, and stockholder wealth, increase.

As also noted in Chapter 5, the firm can reach a debt ratio at which stockholder wealth begins to decline. At this higher level of debt, expected bankruptcy costs, personal income taxes, and market imperfections result in a situation in which the required rate of return ($k_s$) dominates and thus market price (and stockholder wealth) is decreased.

These propositions may be visualized in the graphical analysis presented in Figure 18–2. If the debt ratio ($\theta$) is zero, the firm has a certain required rate of return on debt ($k_{d(0)}$) and equity ($k_{s(0)}$). As the debt ratio increases, the required rate of return on debt increases because of the higher risk assumed by the debtholders. In addition, the required rate of return of the stockholders increases owing to the higher risk borne by the stockholders. The cost advantage of debt (interest tax subsidy) outweighs the stockholders' increased risk. Thus, the firmwide cost of capital declines. This situation is shown in Figure 18–2. The firm can reduce its firmwide cost of capital by increasing $\theta$ up to point A. Once the debt ratio exceeds point A, the expected bankruptcy costs, differential income tax rates, and market imperfections outweigh the lower-cost advantage of debt, and the firmwide cost of capital increases.

The graph in Figure 18–2 illustrates one, and only one, optimal debt ratio. Many financial scholars contend that the optimal debt ratio is actually a range rather than a single value. This proposition is illustrated in Figure 18–3. Note that the firmwide cost of capital is almost the same over a debt-ratio range from point B to point C. Thus, in order to maximize stockholder wealth, a firm should attempt to maintain its debt ratio within this optimal range.

SUMMARY    This chapter was devoted to an examination of the roles of common equity capital and common stockholders in the modern corporation. With respect to common stockholders, two important points were made:

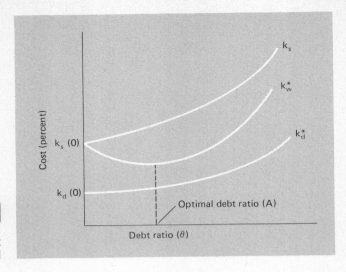

**FIGURE 18–2**

The Firmwide Cost
of Capital

1. Stockholders exercise only *indirect* control over the corporation's activities, and
2. Cumulative voting procedures may enable minority stockholders to gain representation in the firm's board of directors.

In any case, the ability of an individual stockholder or even groups of stockholders to participate in management is limited by the fact that in the modern large American corporation, existing management is often able to control the outcome of elections to the board of directors by controlling the proxy voting process.

The corporation can raise equity capital either by selling new common

**FIGURE 18–3**

The Firmwide Cost
of Capital
(optimal range)

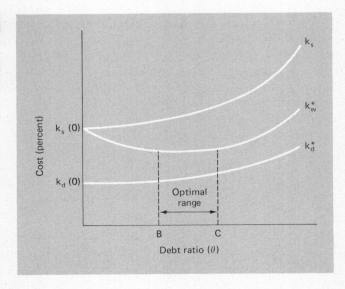

stock to the public or by retaining earnings. The structure of U.S. corporate income tax laws is such that it is advantageous to the stockholder if the firm pays stable dividends and raises new equity capital by retaining earnings (as distinct from selling new common stock). When these two preferences clash, there is a tendency for management to maintain dividends. Thus, it is not uncommon for firms to pay dividends and sell new common stock at the same time.

New common stock can be sold to the public in several ways. Most frequently, firms use an investment banker to market the stock. Another frequently used procedure for selling new common stock is the rights offering. In addition, dividend reinvestment plans are increasing in popularity.

This chapter also described stock dividends and stock splits, and noted that these do not represent increases in equity capital, so their use has minimal effect on stockholder wealth.

QUESTIONS<br>FOR<br>DISCUSSION

1. Define and explain the importance of the following:
   a. Par value of common stock
   b. Number of shares of common stock (1) authorized, (2) issued, and (3) outstanding
   c. Book value of common stock
   d. Capital surplus

2. "It is not possible to talk about the market value of capital surplus." True or false? Explain your answer.

3. Discuss the process through which stockholders control the corporation.

4. Describe how cumulative voting takes place to elect the board of directors of a corporation. What are the advantages of cumulative voting?

5. Why does a right have value? How is the value of a right related to stockholder wealth?

6. What are the two important statements made by the theory of finance about dividend/retained-earnings policy? How do these positions conflict?

7. Describe the following dividend policies, and explain how they relate to stockholder-wealth maximization:
   a. Stable-dividend policy
   b. Constant-payout-ratio policy
   c. Policy of low regular dividends plus a bonus

8. Corporations sometimes pay dividends and sell new common stock simultaneously. How does this policy relate to stockholder-wealth maximization?

9. How does the repurchase of common stock affect stockholder wealth? How does a repurchase strategy compare to a strategy calling for the payment of cash dividends?

10. Describe the role of the investment banker in the sale of a new issue of common stock.

11. What are the advantages and disadvantages of dividend reinvestment plans to (a) the stockholder, and (b) the corporation?

12. Stock dividends and stock splits represent an important way of distributing the

earnings of the firm and usually lead to substantial increases in stockholder wealth. True or false? Explain your answer.

13. What is a voting proxy? Why are proxies important to American corporations?

14. Describe the relationship among debt, equity, and the optimal capital structure.

**PROBLEMS**

1. The balance sheet of the Sandman Corporation is as follows (in thousands):

| | | | |
|---|---|---|---|
| Current assets | $8,500 | Current liabilities | $1,400 |
| | | Long-term debt | $12,100 |
| | | Stockholder equity: | |
| | | Common stock ($5 par value) | $3,500 |
| Fixed assets | $17,000 | Capital surplus | $2,300 |
| | | Retained earnings | $6,200 |
| | | Total stockholder equity | $12,000 |
| Total assets | $25,500 | Total liabilities and equity | $25,500 |

   a. Calculate the number of shares outstanding.
   b. Calculate the book value of each share of common stock outstanding.

2. The Christine Corporation has 5,000,000 shares of common stock outstanding. The stock of the corporation is divided into two voting blocks. The majority group controls 3,400,000 shares. The minority group controls 1,600,000 shares. The entire board of directors (12 members) of the Christine Corporation is up for election.
   a. How many directors could the minority group elect if the corporation used majority voting?
   b. How many directors could the minority group elect if the corporation used cumulative voting? *Hint:* This requires "trial and error" and the use of the equation in footnote 6.

3. The AnnCa Corporation is considering three alternative dividend policies: (1) stable dividends, (2) constant payout ratio, and (3) low regular dividends plus a bonus. The corporation wants to pay dividends equal to 40% of all earnings during the five-year forecast period. Management makes the following forecast of EPS for the next five years:

| Year | EPS |
|---|---|
| 1981 | $5.00 |
| 1982 | $8.00 |
| 1983 | ($2.00) |
| 1984 | $12.00 |
| 1985 | $7.00 |

   Prepare a forecast of dividends to be paid by the AnnCa Corporation for the five-year period under the three alternative dividend policies.

4. William Manufacturing Corporation is planning to issue new common stock using a rights offering. The firm has 20 million shares outstanding at the present time. The current market price of the common stock is $60. The subscription

price of the new stock, however, is only $50. William Manufacturing wants to raise $100 million in new equity capital.

    a. How many rights will be needed to purchase *one* new share of common stock?

    b. What will be the theoretical value of one right? (*Note:* Use the equation shown in footnote 10.)

5. National Steel has declared a 10% stock dividend. The current market price of the common stock of the corporation is $38. The par value of the common stock is $10.

    a. Show the effect of the stock dividend on the balance sheet of the corporation:

*Equity Accounts before Stock Dividend*

| | |
|---|---|
| Common stock ($10 par value) | $500 million |
| Capital surplus | 300 million |
| Retained earnings | 2,000 million |
| Total stockholder equity | $2,800 million |

    b. Would the price of the common stock remain at $38 per share after the stock dividend? Explain your answer.

6. The Donegal Corporation plans to declare a 4-for-1 stock split. The current market price of the common stock of the corporation is $42. The par value of common stock is $10.

    a. Show the effect of the stock split on the balance sheet of the corporation:

*Equity Accounts before Stock Split*

| | |
|---|---|
| Common stock ($10 par value) | $350 million |
| Capital surplus | 150 million |
| Retained earnings | 200 million |
| Total stockholder equity | $700 million |

    b. Calculate the number of shares outstanding before and after the stock split.

    c. Would the price of the Donegal common stock remain at $42 per share after the stock split? Explain your answer.

# APPENDIX 18A
# Preferred Stock

Preferred stock is a difficult security to categorize. It is often called a *hybrid* security, with some of the characteristics of bonds and some of common stock. Preferred stockholders earn a *fixed dividend* return, which is stated as a percentage of the par value of the preferred stock (usually $100). This feature is similar to the fixed annual interest payments on bonds. There is, however, one significant difference: The firm has a legal obligation to make interest payments, regardless of its financial situation, but it may be able to skip dividend payments on preferred stock. This represents a significant advantage to the firm. Given a difficult financial situation, the firm can reduce its cash outflows by eliminating its preferred dividend. The dividend will eventually have to be paid; but the firm may be in a better financial position in the future, and the ability to postpone preferred dividends diminishes the probability of bankruptcy.

Therefore, the uncertainty of future cash flows of preferred stockholders is greater than that of the bondholders but lower than that of the common stockholders. Thus, the riskiness of future cash flows assumed by preferred stockholders is between that assumed by bondholders and that assumed by common stockholders.

The ability of the firm to stop paying dividends on preferred stock is limited. First, no dividends can be paid to common stockholders if dividends on preferred have been skipped. Second, a very high percentage of preferred stock has a *cumulative provision*. This provision requires that all past unpaid preferred dividends be fully paid *before* any dividends are paid to common stockholders. Thus, preferred stockholders have a high probability of receiving dividends, since common stockholders can receive nothing until past and present preferred dividend payments are made.

Preferred stock, when compared to common stock, has a *senior claim* on the assets of the firm. Preferred-stock claims, however, are subordinated to the claims of all the creditors of the firm. Thus, in the event of liquidation, the claims of all the creditors must be fully satisfied before preferred stockholders receive compensation, and preferred-stock claims must be fully satisfied before common stockholders receive any of the proceeds from liquidation. Therefore, the risk assumed by preferred stockholders is again between that assumed by bondholders and that of common stockholders.

The additional risk assumed by preferred stockholders as compared to that assumed by bondholders usually results in a higher required rate of return on preferred stock.[15] This situation is illustrated by the security-market line shown in Figure 18A–1. Using preferred stock instead of debt increases the firm's cost of capital.

There is an additional feature of the tax laws that has greatly reduced the use of preferred stock as a means of raising capital by modern corporations. Preferred dividends *are not a deductible tax expense to the corporation*. Thus, the after-tax cost to the corporation of preferred stock is the same as the before-tax cost. This is significantly different from the tax treatment given to interest payments made by the firm. For example, if the

---

[15]Corporations owning preferred stock of other corporations may have a lower required rate of return on preferred stock than on debt. The explanation for this apparent discrepancy lies in the tax laws. Interest received by a corporation is fully taxed. Corporations, however, are allowed an 85% exclusion (up to 100% if a consolidated return is filed) on dividends received from other domestic corporations. Thus, the after-tax return to a corporation may be higher on preferred dividends than on interest receipts.

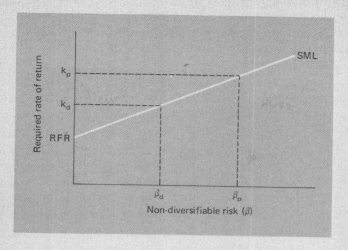

**FIGURE 18A–1**

Security-Market Line

Williams Corporation pays 10 percent interest to bondholders ($k_d$) and an 11 percent dividend to preferred stockholders ($k_p$), its after-tax cost of debt and preferred stock would be as follows:

*After-Tax Cost of Preferred*        *After-Tax Cost of Debt*

$$k_p = 11\% \qquad k_d^* = k_d(1 - T) = 10\%(1 - 0.46) = 5.4\%$$

Thus, the advantages to the firm of issuing preferred stock are more than offset by the fact that the after-tax cost of preferred stock tends to be approximately twice the after-tax cost of debt.[16]

There are some special provisions that may be present in preferred stock sold in the marketplace. These provisions are not always used, and only some (or none) may be included in a particular issue of preferred stock. These special features are (in order of their frequency) as follows:

1. *Convertibility.* Preferred stock may be convertible into a specified number of shares of common stock. The use of this provision has increased in recent times.
2. *Voting rights.* In some special cases, preferred stockholders are given limited voting rights in the election of the board of directors of the corporation. This

---

[16]The tax laws, interestingly enough, encourage the use of preferred stock in the event of mergers or acquisitions. The method of payment for the acquisition determines the tax liabilities of the owners of the acquired firm. If payment is in the form of cash or bonds, these owners have realized a long-term capital gain. If payment involves an exchange of stock (preferred stock is considered stock), the owners of the acquired firm can defer long-term capital gains. The acquiring firm can "buy out" the old owners by giving them common stock in the acquiring corporation. This procedure, however, may be desirable to neither the acquiring firm nor to the owners of the acquired firm. The acquiring firm may find the use of common stock as payment unattractive because it gives the owners of the acquired firm a significant voice in the management of the acquiring firm. Furthermore, the owners of the acquired firm may not desire to continue their involvement in management, and may prefer to receive constant (dividends on preferred stock) rather than uncertain (dividends on common stock) future cash flows.

provision is usually conditional upon the failure of the firm to pay dividends on preferred stock.

3. *Maturity.* Preferred stock usually has no maturity date. Thus, its value is computed in the same manner as the value of perpetual bonds. But in the event that the preferred does have a maturity date, the determination of its value is similar to that of a bond.

4. *Call provision.* Preferred stock may have a call provision that is similar to the call provision of long-term bonds.

**SELECTED BIBLIOGRAPHY**

BACON, PETER W., "The Subscription Price in Rights Offerings," *Financial Management*, 1 (Summer 1972), 59–64.

BLACK, FISCHER, and MYRON SCHOLES, "The Effects of Dividend Yield and Dividend Policy on Common Stock Prices and Returns," *Journal of Financial Economics*, 1 (May 1974), 1–22.

DOUGALL, HERBERT E., and JACK E. GAUMNITZ, *Capital Market and Institutions*. Englewood Cliffs, N.J.: Prentice-Hall, 1980.

ELTON, EDWIN J., and MARTIN J. GRUBER, "The Effect of Share Repurchases on the Value of the Firm," *Review of Economics and Statistics*, 41 (May 1959), 99–105.

———, "Marginal Stockholders' Tax Rates and the Clientele Effect," *Review of Economics and Statistics*, 52 (February 1970), 68–74.

GORDON, MYRON J., "Dividends, Earnings and Stock Prices," *Review of Economics and Statistics*, 41 (May 1959), 99–105.

———, *The Investment, Financing and Valuation of the Corporation*. Homewood, Ill.: Richard D. Irwin, 1962.

KEANE, SIMON M., "Dividends and the Resolution of Uncertainty," *Journal of Finance and Accounting*, 1 (Autumn 1974), 389–93.

MILLAR, JAMES A., and BRUCE D. FIELITZ, "Stock-Split and Stock-Dividend Decisions," *Financial Management*, 2 (Winter 1973), 35–45.

NELSON, J. RUSSELL, "Price Effects in Rights Offerings," *Journal of Finance*, 20 (December 1965), 647–50.

NORGAARD, RICHARD, and CORINE NORGAARD, "A Critical Examination of Share Repurchase," *Financial Management*, (Spring 1974), 44–50.

PETTWAY, RICHARD H., and R. PHIL MALONE, "Automatic Dividend Reinvestment Plans of Nonfinancial Corporations," *Financial Management*, 2 (Winter 1973), 11–18.

STEWART, SAMUEL S., JR., "Should a Corporation Repurchase Its Own Stock?" *Journal of Finance*, 31 (June 1976), 911–21.

VAN HORNE, JAMES C., *Financial Market Rates and Flows*. Englewood Cliffs, N.J.: Prentice-Hall, 1978.

WATTS, ROSS, "The Informational Content of Dividends," *Journal of Business*, 46 (April 1973), 191–211.

# FINANCIAL
# ANALYSIS

# Introduction to PART FOUR

Part four of this book comprises only one chapter. The intent of the chapter is to provide guidelines and techniques that will be helpful in estimating the future financial prospects of the firm. The chapter deals with methods and procedures for estimating the firm's future cash flows and riskiness.

# ANALYSIS OF THE FIRM'S FUTURE FINANCIAL PROSPECTS

## 19

## INTRODUCTION

The financial position of the firm is of special interest to a number of groups. The suppliers of capital to a firm attempt to analyze the risks and the cash flows associated with supplying that capital. Labor unions try to evaluate the firm's ability to pay higher wages and benefits. Government regulatory agencies establish rates and regulations based upon an analysis of the financial position of a given firm. Finally, the management of the firm may analyze itself in order to identify the potential strengths and weaknesses of the firm.

    The most frequent users of financial-position analysis are capital suppliers. Their dilemma is summarized in Figure 19–1. Note that the process of supplying capital implies the creation of uncertain future cash receipts in exchange for the present capital contribution. For example, consider the following situations:

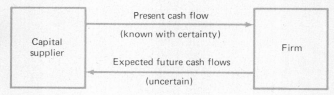

1. An individual decides to purchase new common stock issued by a firm on the basis of *expectations* of the future cash flows associated with the stock.
2. The King Corporation decides to extend credit to the Queen Corporation on the basis of the *expectation* that the Queen Corporation will make a payment at a later date.
3. The California Pension System decides to purchase new bonds issued by the Peters Corporation. This decision is based on the *expectation* that the Peters Corporation will make future interest and principal payments.

Note that in each situation, the cash flow to the capital supplier is a future, expected, and uncertain cash flow.

Capital suppliers attempt to minimize the risk associated with future expected cash flows by carefully analyzing the financial position of the firm acquiring the capital. They search for indicators of (1) the probable size of future payments to capital suppliers, (2) the probable timing of future payments to capital suppliers, and (3) the riskiness of future cash flows to capital suppliers. The analysis is designed to reduce the uncertainty associated with supplying capital and maximize the overall returns gained by the capital supplier.

The information necessary for analyzing the financial position of a firm comes from a number of sources. Among the most useful sources of information for predicting the amount, timing, and riskiness of future cash flows are the following:

1. The financial statements of the firm acquiring capital often provide important information. The capital supplier would typically analyze the statements for a number of years in the recent past. Income statements, balance sheets, and statements of changes in financial condition are all important for this purpose.

2. In addition to the financial statements of the firm acquiring capital, capital suppliers frequently analyze recent payments made by the firm to other capital suppliers. For example, the supplier of trade credit is interested in the firm's record of meeting prior trade-credit commitments. Suppliers of long-term-debt capital are interested in the actions of the firm relative to prior debt issues.

3. A third important source of information relative to the amount, timing, and riskiness of cash flows to capital suppliers is the security markets themselves. By looking at the required rates of return being demanded by the security market for other capital raised by a particular firm, the new capital supplier can estimate the collective judgment of the security market relative to new capital raised by the same firm. Thus, for example, if the risk premium associated with existing debt is very high, the new debt should also carry a high risk premium. And even though an individual analyst may disagree with the security market's consensus, only a foolhardy person would fail to place *any* importance on this valuable information.

These three types of information—(1) financial statements, (2) recent payment experience, and (3) security-market consensus—provide the informational foundation for the analysis of a firm's financial prospects. Although different types of capital suppliers emphasize different elements, and not all informational elements are available for all firms, in an ideal situation each element would play at least some role in the analytic procedure.

Now, notice the very important fact that the information used by the analyst tends to be backward-looking (historical) rather than future-looking. The assumption is, for example, that past financial statements of the firm will give some indication of a future financial event (a cash flow to capital suppliers). It goes without saying that the past is not a perfect predictor of the future. Unforeseen events, either favorable or unfavorable, are likely to occur and may result in future cash flows at levels different from those expected. At best, historical data furnish only a rough guide to probable future conditions. As in the case of almost all business decision making, the financial analysis of a firm requires skilled judgments based upon experience and perhaps a little luck. It is not a mechanical process, and there is no magic formula that provides unambiguous answers. Even the most sophisticated computer is unable to extend the past into the future with perfect certainty. However, just as in the case of other business judgments discussed in this book, a sound conceptual framework and careful attention to detail can improve the accuracy and efficiency of the analysis of the financial position of a given firm.

## ANALYSIS OF FINANCIAL STATEMENTS

As noted previously, the past performance of the firm as reflected in its financial statements may be useful in projecting the firm's performance into the future. However, the task of analyzing financial statements is relatively complex and time-consuming. In this section, we present a conceptual framework that is useful to analysts in searching through financial statements. The methodology presented here is only one of several that could be employed; but it is one of the more effective and widely used.

## RATIO ANALYSIS

The general procedure in ratio analysis involves the selection of two items from the firm's financial statements and division of one item into the other, thus forming a ratio. This ratio is then compared to some standard, perhaps an industry average for the ratio, and a judgment is made of the current financial position of the firm.[1] For example, the analyst may be interested in how well the firm is managing its assets. Accordingly, one of the assets considered is inventory. The analyst would compute the firm's *inventory-turnover ratio* for a number of years by dividing inventories (a balance-sheet item) into sales (an income-statement item) for each year. The resulting inventory-turnover ratios would then be compared to a standard (perhaps an industry average) and a judgment made as to how well the firm has been (note the emphasis on the past) managing its inventories. Generally, if no troublesome developments are indicated by the historical data, the analyst assumes that the firm will continue to manage these assets adequately in the future. Thus, adequate ratios (historical) are usually interpreted as indicating adequate future performance.

**Ratio Categories**    Since any two items in the balance sheet or income statement can be used to form a financial ratio, the analyst is forced to select from the thousands of possible ratios available. In order to facilitate the selection process, four ratio categories are used, each representing a different aspect of the firm's performance:

1. *Liquidity ratios.* These ratios measure the firm's ability to meet its maturing short-term obligations. This is a combined measure of the business and financial risk of the firm.
2. *Leverage ratios.* These measure the extent to which the firm is financed by debt and indicate the firm's financial risk.
3. *Profitability ratios.* These measure the extent to which the firm has been able to generate profits. They give some indication of the size of potential cash flows to capital suppliers. The extent to which profitability changes from year to year is an indicator of business risk. The level of profits may indicate how well the firm is being managed.
4. *Activity ratios.* These ratios measure the ability of the firm to manage its resources. They are another indicator of the business risk associated with the firm.

A hypothetical firm, the AMA Corporation, will be used to illustrate the ratio computation and analysis procedures. The income statement for the AMA Corporation is presented in Table 19–1; the balance sheet is shown in Table 19–2; and a summary of the various ratios, the formulas used for their

---

[1]Comparisons to industry averages must be made with caution. It is essential that the firm being analyzed is identified as belonging to the appropriate industry. In addition, if the analyzed firm uses accounting methods different from those employed by the industry, a distorted picture may emerge.

TABLE 19–1

THE AMA CORPORATION:
1979 Income Statement

| | | |
|---|---:|---:|
| Net sales | | $9,000,000 |
| *Less:* Cost of goods sold[a] | | 7,740,000 |
| *Equals:* Gross profits | | $1,260,000 |
| *Less:* Selling and administrative expenses[a] (operating costs) | | 270,000 |
| *Equals:* Gross operating income | | $990,000 |
| *Less:* Depreciation | | 300,000 |
| *Equals:* Net operating income | | $690,000 |
| *Plus:* Other income | | 45,000 |
| *Equals:* Earnings before interest and taxes | | $735,000 |
| *Less:* Interest on notes | $24,000 | |
| Interest on first mortgage | 75,000 | |
| Interest on debentures | 36,000 | $135,000 |
| *Equals:* Earnings before taxes | | $600,000 |
| *Less:* Federal income taxes | | 240,000 |
| *Equals:* Earnings after taxes | | $360,000 |

[a]In addition, total lease payments made by the firm during 1979 were $200,000.

computation, and the actual values of the ratios for the AMA Corporation are given in Table 19–3. (The computations for these ratios are discussed in greater detail in Appendix 19A). Note that there are several ratios in each category. This suggests that there is more than one way of measuring liquidity, profitability, and so on. Several ratios are used because each gives a different dimension of these factors. The computation of financial ratios is a reasonably straightforward process. A basic knowledge of accounting and simple arithmetic skills are all the analyst needs.

## ANALYSIS OF FINANCIAL RATIOS

**Industry Standard**  Simply computing the financial-statement ratios provides little insight into the past performance or future prospects of the firm. In the AMA illustration, for example, there is no indication of whether profits have been very high or too low. Nor is there any method of projecting past performance into the future. Clearly, what is needed in order to solve this dilemma is adequate standards for comparison. The analyst must be able to compare the ratios of the AMA Corporation to something. A judgment about the adequacy of past performance and a projection of future performance can be based on such a comparison. Table 19–4 makes such a comparison for the AMA Corporation, using industry averages as the standard for comparison.

In the AMA Corporation illustration, the following observations can be made on the basis of financial ratio analysis:

TABLE 19–2

THE AMA CORPORATION:
BALANCE SHEET
(December 31, 1979)

| | | |
|---|---:|---:|
| Cash | | $150,000 |
| Marketable securities | | 450,000 |
| Accounts receivable | | 600,000 |
| Inventories (at cost) | | 900,000 |
|   Total current assets | | $2,100,000 |
| Gross plant and equipment | $5,400,000 | |
| *Less:* Accumulated depreciation | − 1,500,000 | |
|   Net plan and equipment | | $3,900,000 |
| Excess of cost over net assets of | | |
|   businesses purchased (goodwill) | | 500,000 |
|   Total assets | | $6,500,000 |
| | | |
| Notes payable to bank (8%) | | 300,000 |
| Accounts payable | | 180,000 |
| Accrued current liabilities | | 30,000 |
| Income taxes | | 390,000 |
|   Total current liabilities | | $900,000 |
| First mortgage bond (5%) | | 1,500,000 |
| Debentures (6%) | | 600,000 |
|   Total long-term liabilities | | $2,100,000 |
| Common stock (1,800,000 shares) | | 1,800,000 |
| Retained earnings | | 1,700,000 |
|   Total net worth | | $3,500,000 |
|     Total liabilities & net worth | | $6,500,000 |

1. *Liquidity.* The firm's present ability to meet short-term maturing obligations appears to be equal to the industry average. This implies an average level of risk.
2. *Leverage.* The proportional amount of debt employed by the AMA Corporation is approximately the same as the industry average. This implies an average level of financial risk.
3. *Profitability.* The profitability of the AMA Corporation is relatively high. This implies an ability to meet current payments to capital suppliers.
4. *Activities.* Most of the firm's assets appear to be very well managed. Accounts receivable appear to be well below the industry averages (a relative low average collection period), which may indicate a lower-than-average business risk. Costs are in line with industry averages.

As we have shown in this example, financial ratios combined with industry averages can be used to formulate judgments about the riskiness of the firm. Once again, note that the process is judgmental and not mechanical.

TABLE 19-3

## THE AMA CORPORATION: COMPUTATION OF RATIOS[a]

*Liquidity Ratios*

1. Current ratio $= \dfrac{\text{Current assets}}{\text{Current liabilities}} = \dfrac{\$2,100,000}{\$900,000} = 2.33$ times

2. Quick ratio $= \dfrac{\text{Cash + Marketable securities + Receivables}}{\text{Current liabilities}}$

$$= \dfrac{\$150,000 + \$450,000 + \$600,000}{\$900,000} = 1.33 \text{ times}$$

*Leverage Ratios*

1. Debt ratio $= \dfrac{\text{Total debt}^{b}}{\text{Total assets}} = \dfrac{\$3,000,000}{\$6,500,000} = 46\%$

2. Debt to tangible net worth $= \dfrac{\text{Total debt}}{\text{Tangible net worth}}$

$$= \dfrac{\$3,000,000}{\$3,500,000 - \$500,000(\text{goodwill})} = 100\%$$

3. Times interest earned $= \dfrac{\text{EBIT}}{\text{Total interest}} = \dfrac{\$735,000}{\$135,000} = 5.4$ times

4. Fixed-charges coverage[c] $= \dfrac{\text{EBIT + Lease payments}}{\text{Interest + Lease payments}} = \dfrac{\$735,000 + \$200,000}{\$135,000 + \$200,000}$

$$= 2.8 \text{ times}$$

*Activity Ratios*

A. Turnover ratios:

1. Total asset turnover $= \dfrac{\text{Annual sales}}{\text{Total assets}} = \dfrac{\$9,000,000}{\$6,500,000} = 1.38$ times

2. Fixed-asset turnover $= \dfrac{\text{Annual sales}}{\text{Net fixed assets}} = \dfrac{\$9,000,000}{\$3,900,000} = 2.3$ times

3. Inventory turnover $= \dfrac{\text{Annual sales}}{\text{Inventories}} = \dfrac{\$9,000,000}{\$900,000} = 10$ times

4. Average collection period $= \dfrac{\text{Accounts receivable}}{\text{Sales per day}} = \dfrac{\$600,000 \times 360}{\$9,000,000} = 24$ days

B. Cost ratios:

1. Cost-of-goods-sold ratio $= \dfrac{\text{Cost of goods sold}}{\text{Annual sales}} = \dfrac{\$7,740,000}{\$9,000,000} = 86\%$

2. Operating-cost ratio $= \dfrac{\text{Operating costs}}{\text{Annual sales}} = \dfrac{\$270,000}{\$9,000,000} = 3\%$

*Profitability ratios*

1. Return on total assets $= \dfrac{\text{Earnings after taxes}}{\text{Total assets}} = \dfrac{\$360,000}{\$6,500,000} = 5.5\%$

*Table 19–4 continued*

2. Return on sales $= \dfrac{\text{Earnings after taxes}}{\text{Annual sales}} = \dfrac{\$360,000}{\$9,000,000} = 4\%$

3. Return on net worth $= \dfrac{\text{Earnings after taxes}}{\text{Total net worth}} = \dfrac{\$360,000}{\$3,500,000} = 10.3\%$

4. Return on tangible net worth $= \dfrac{\text{Earnings after taxes}}{\text{Tangible net worth}}$

$$= \dfrac{\$360,000}{\$3,500,000 - \$500,000} = 12\%$$

5. Earnings per share $= \dfrac{\text{Earnings after taxes}}{\text{Number of shares outstanding}} = \dfrac{\$360,000}{1,800,000}$

$$= \$0.20 \text{ per share}$$

[a]For a more detailed explanation of the financial ratios, see Appendix 19A.

[b]Total debt is equal to current liabilities plus long-term debt.

[c]The firm may have an additional financial obligation—sinking-fund payments. Thus, the fixed-charge coverage may have to be modified. Such payments are not deductible for tax purposes. Thus, the fixed-charges-coverage ratio would be computed as follows:

$$\text{FCC} = \dfrac{\text{EBIT} + \text{Lease payments}}{\text{Interest} + \text{Lease payments} + \dfrac{\text{Sinking-fund payments}}{(1 - \text{Tax rate})}}$$

*Sources of Information on Industry Averages.* Industry-average ratios are available from a number of sources. Selected ratios for a limited number of industries (usually characterized by larger firms) are published in *Dun's Review* in the fall of each year. These are known as the Dun & Bradstreet ratios and are limited in number and industry coverage; that is, not all ratios and not all industries are covered in this source.

Perhaps the best source of financial ratios for large, publicly traded corporations is the Compustat computer tapes published by Standard & Poor's Corporation. These tapes include detailed financial information filed with the Securities and Exchange Commission both annually and quarterly. The tapes are widely available and permit the analyst to compute virtually any ratio and to define industries in a variety of ways. "Canned programs" make it possible for even beginning business students to develop up-to-date financial information in a relatively short time.

Averages for industries characterized by smaller firms (automobile dealers, dentists, and so on) are presented in the annual *Statement Studies*. This publication is compiled by Robert Morris Associates, which is the national association of bank lending officers, and covers more than 100 different lines of business.

**Historical Standards** Historical standards can be used as a substitute for, or a supplement to, industry standards. The user of historical standards evaluates the trend in a firm's financial ratios. For example, the financial ratios for the W.T. Grant Company covering the period from 1967 to 1972 are presented in Table 19–5. For many years, W.T. Grant operated a chain of department stores. The firm went bankrupt and was liquidated in the 1970s. As shown in Table 19–5, the

TABLE 19–4

THE AMA CORPORATION:
COMPARISON OF FINANCIAL RATIOS WITH INDUSTRY AVERAGES

|  | AMA Corporation | Industry averages |
|---|---|---|
| Liquidity ratios: | | |
| 1. Current ratio | 2.33 times | 2.5 times |
| 2. Quick ratio | 1.33 times | 1.0 times |
| Leverage ratios: | | |
| 1. Debt to total assets | 46% | 45% |
| 2. Debt to tangible net worth | 100% | 98% |
| 3. Times interest earned | 5.4 times | 5.0 times |
| 4. Fixed-charges coverage | 2.8 times | 3.0 times |
| Activity ratios: | | |
| A. Turnover ratios: | | |
| 1. Total asset turnover | 1.38 times | 1.1 times |
| 2. Fixed-asset turnover | 2.3 times | 2.0 times |
| 3. Inventory turnover | 10 times | 11.0 times |
| 4. Average collection period | 24 days | 36 days |
| B. Cost ratios: | | |
| 1. Cost-of-goods-sold ratio | 86% | 87% |
| 2. Operating-cost ratio | 3% | 2% |
| Profitability ratios: | | |
| 1. Return on total assets | 5.5% | 4.6% |
| 2. Return on sales | 4.0% | 4.2% |
| 3. Return on net worth | 10.3% | 8.4% |
| 4. Return on tangible net worth | 12.0% | 10.0% |
| 5. Earnings per share | $0.20 | |

deterioration of the firm was indicated by the trend in its financial ratios. The historical trend analysis shows deteriorating liquidity, profitability, and management of assets, as well as increased reliance on debt as a source of funds. The extension of the past trend into the future would have suggested that by 1970, the W.T. Grant Company was a risky investment for capital suppliers.

## DECISIONS BASED ON RATIO ANALYSIS

The major purpose of financial-statement analysis is to assist in the decision-making process and not merely to evaluate the future prospects of the firm for academic purposes. For example, the supplier of trade-credit capital (another business firm) must decide whether the future financial situation of the buyer (borrower) is sufficiently attractive to warrant the extension of trade credit. The acquirer of capital (borrower) does not have to be perfect, just good enough to present a profit-making opportunity to the

### TABLE 19-5

## W. T. GRANT COMPANY: FINANCIAL RATIOS

|  | 1967 | 1968 | 1969 | 1970 | 1971 | 1972 |
|---|---|---|---|---|---|---|
| *Liquidity ratios:* | | | | | | |
| 1. Current ratio | 2.60 | 2.70 | 2.50 | 2.20 | 2.00 | 1.75 |
| 2. Quick ratio | 1.26 | 1.29 | 1.20 | 1.10 | 1.00 | 1.12 |
| *Leverage ratios:* | | | | | | |
| 1. Debt to total assets | .56 | .54 | .53 | .57 | .61 | .64 |
| 2. Debt to tangible N.W. | 1.38 | 1.25 | 1.18 | 1.29 | 1.47 | 1.71 |
| 3. Times interest earned | 6.27 | 5.29 | 5.49 | 5.36 | 3.83 | 3.74 |
| *Profitability ratios:* | | | | | | |
| 1. Return on total assets | 6.16% | 5.98% | 6.14% | 5.92% | 4.90% | 3.73% |
| 2. Return on sales | 3.39% | 3.32% | 3.46% | 3.44% | 3.14% | 2.55% |
| 3. Return on tangible N.W. | 15.05% | 13.81% | 13.39% | 14.38% | 13.10% | 10.81% |
| 4. Earnings per share | 2.48 | 2.50 | 2.72 | 3.01 | 2.86 | 2.49 |
| *Activity ratios:* | | | | | | |
| A. Turnover ratios: | | | | | | |
| 1. Total asset turnover | 180 | 178 | 176 | 171 | 155 | 136 |
| 2. Fixed-asset turnover | 1920 | 2065 | 2225 | 2196 | 2036 | 1786 |
| 3. Inventory turnover | 5.29 | 5.36 | 5.25 | 5.47 | 4.81 | 4.61 |
| 4. Collection period | 89 | 100 | 103 | 109 | 120 | 125 |
| B. Cost ratios: | | | | | | |
| 1. Cost of goods sold | 68.4 | 68.2 | 67.5 | 67.3 | 67.0 | 67.6 |
| 2. Operating-cost ratio | 24.8 | 25.1 | 25.2 | 25.3 | 26.1 | 27.1 |

capital supplier. Thus, firms with less-than-perfect financial prospects are able to obtain trade credit, borrow from banks, sell stock, and sell bonds. Presumably, the suppliers of capital to these firms believe that the rates charged for the funds compensate them for the risk undertaken.

Within the context of this discussion, it is easy to visualize the complexity of the decision-making process and the difficult task facing the financial analyst. The discovery of weak points in a firm's financial statements does not automatically eliminate the firm from consideration as a potential recipient of capital funds. It is all a question of degree and judgment. Does the financial weakness of the firm acquiring capital generate risks above the level acceptable to the capital supplier? Can a higher rate of return paid to the capital supplier compensate for the added risk? What rate of return should be required by the capital supplier? As suggested by these questions, the end result of financial-statement analysis is not simply the placing of "good" or "bad" labels on the firm. Based upon the analysis, capital-acquiring firms are, for example, (1) placed in different trade-credit-risk categories, (2) assigned different interest rates on loans or bond issues, and (3) required to have different amounts and types of collateral for loans.

The amount of capital that can be acquired and the terms for the acquisition may be based upon the financial-statement analysis.

## STATISTICAL MODELS OF FINANCIAL-STATEMENT ANALYSIS

In recent years, financial statements have come under increased statistical scrutiny, and statistical models have been incorporated into decision models. The intent has been to reduce the amount of subjective judgment involved in the decision process and to develop precise probabilistic measures of the risks undertaken when specific decisions are made. It is beyond the scope of this book to develop detailed statistical models for financial decision making; however, the following example is presented to help the student understand the promise, prospects, and difficulties associated with the application of statistical models to financial-statement data.[2]

For purposes of illustration, let us examine Fischer's model for estimating the risk premium associated with corporate bond issues.[3] The steps in the analytical concept are these:

- *Step 1.* Fischer selected a cross section of firms that issued bonds. For each of these firms, financial statements and other financial information were gathered. In addition, information on the bond's interest rate was obtained.
- *Step 2.* Based upon the data collected, Fischer developed a multiple-regression (least-squares) model that has high explanatory powers. The bond-risk premium was found to be explained by four variables:
  a. The variability of net income over a nine-year period ($X_1$)
  b. The age and reliability of the firm ($X_2$)
  c. The debt ratio of the firm ($X_3$)
  d. The marketability of the bonds ($X_4$)
- *Step 3.* The statistical model employed is:

$$\text{Bond-risk premium} = 0.987 + 0.307X_1 - 0.253X_2 - 0.537X_3 - 0.275X_4$$

Note that computing the various ratios and substituting them into the model permits a specific numerical estimate of the bond-risk premium. This is quite different from the probable result of the more traditional ratio analysis, which would have been largely a rough estimate, a guess. Note also that the statistical procedures, utilizing the concept of standard error, permit the analyst to assign specific probability to the errors in estimates of various sizes.

Statistical techniques have also been used in such business decision-making situations as the extension of trade credit and the establishment of the terms of bank loans. In each case, a statistical information base must be

---

[2]For a detailed discussion of this topic, see Baruch Lev, *Financial Statement Analysis: A New Approach* (Englewood Cliffs, N.J.: Prentice-Hall, 1974). Particular attention should be paid to Chapters 7 through 11.

[3]L. Fischer, "Determinants of Risk Premiums on Corporate Bonds," *The Journal of Political Economy*, 67 (June 1959), 221.

established. In the trade-credit situation, the financial information and payment records of many firms must be analyzed. From this search, a general statistical pattern may emerge and be used by the firm in the decision-making process.

The disadvantages of statistical models are threefold: (1) cost, (2) inflexibility, and (3) difficulties in understanding them. Large amounts of time and effort are involved in constructing statistical models, and their development cost can be very high. The inflexibility is reflected in the fact that models may become obsolete owing to a basic change in the environment—for example, a change in the tax laws. There is no easy way to incorporate such changes in many models. Thus, a firm can spend a great deal of time and money on a model that has limited usefulness, with the costs outweighing any potential benefits.

But it is the lack of management understanding of statistical techniques rather than strict cost-benefit considerations that limits the use of statistically oriented decision models. Today, models that can be justified on a cost/benefit basis are often rejected because of the inability of management to use them correctly. Perhaps this will change slowly over time as statistical competency improves.

## THE DUPONT RATIO ANALYSIS MODEL

The Dupont Ratio Analysis Model, modified to include the use of debt (DRAM-D), provides an interesting insight into the relationship among financial ratios and often suggests reasons for a firm's poor or superior performance. As shown in Figure 19–2, DRAM-D focuses on the book value of return on stockholder equity. Note that the return on stockholder equity (net worth) can be increased either by increasing the return on assets or by reducing the percentage of assets financed by equity (increasing the debt ratio). Equation 19–1, which is a mathematical summary of Figure 19–2, is useful in identifying the fundamental causal relationship underlying a specific return on stockholder wealth.

$$\text{Return on net worth} = \frac{\text{Percentage return on assets}}{\text{Percentage of assets financed by net worth}} \quad (19\text{–}1)$$

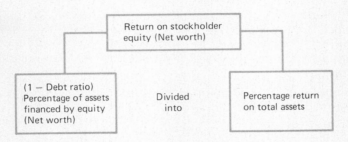

**FIGURE 19–2**

Dupont Ration Analysis Model, with Debt (Dram-D)

For example, a low return on net worth may be attributable to insufficient use of debt. That is, the percentage of assets financed by stockholder equity may be too high. On the other hand, a low return on net worth may be attributable to operating factors such as poor cost controls or poor asset management. This second situation would be reflected in a low return on total assets. Thus, the analytical usefulness of Figure 19–2 lies in its ability to focus the analyst's attention on the two major categories of forces affecting return on stockholder equity. It helps answer questions such as, "Is the low return on stockholder equity due to inadequate use of leverage or to deficiencies in operations?" Such questions can be answered by combining DRAM-D with the previously discussed industry and historical financial-ratio comparisons.

This analytic procedure applied to the AMA Corporation case is shown in Table 19–6. The information in this table has been taken from Table 19–4 and shows that AMA's relatively high return on net worth is attributable to its relatively high return on assets rather than the use of additional debt. That is, it is AMA's operations rather than the use of debt that is generating the relatively high profits of the firm.

TABLE 19–6

DRAM-D APPLIED TO AMA CORPORATION AND TO INDUSTRY AVERAGES

| | Return on net worth | = | Return on assets | ÷ | Percentage of Assets financed by net worth |
|---|---|---|---|---|---|
| AMA Corporation | 10.3% | = | 5.5% | ÷ | 54% |
| Industry averages | 8.4% | = | 4.6% | ÷ | 55% |

A more complete version of DRAM-D is presented in Figure 19–3. Note that the additional detail is designed to highlight the fundamental relationships that determine the firm's return on total assets. The major thrust of the additional detail is to isolate the effect on return on assets of cost-control factors and asset-utilization factors. As shown in equation 19–2, return on total assets is the product of return on sales and the asset turnover.

$$\text{Return on assets} = \text{Return on sales} \times \text{Asset turnover} \qquad (19\text{–}2)$$

Equation 19–2, when applied to a particular firm and industry standards, can yield important insights into the operation of the firm. For example, the AMA Corporation and the industry averages are compared in Table 19–7. This table suggests that the superior performance of AMA rests on its superior utilization of assets. If we continue to work down the table and continue our comparison with industry averages, it is possible to identify accounts-receivable management as a particularly strong point of AMA's operations.

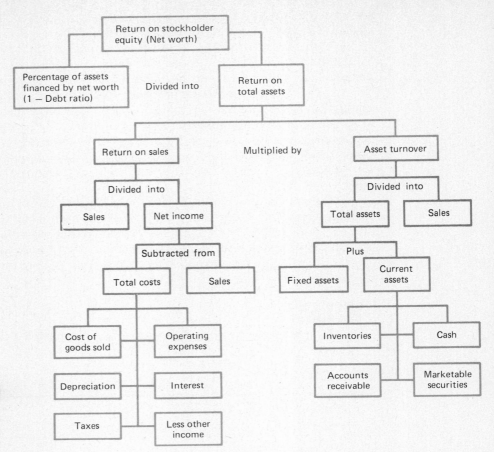

Dupont Ratio Analysis
Model With Debt
(Dram-D)

Thus, the Dupont Ratio Analysis Model modified for the use of debt (DRAM-D) provides a convenient conceptual framework for analyzing the relationships among the various financial ratios. This technique, when combined with industry or historical comparisons, can provide a more meaningful and coherent understanding of the firm's performance. The major deficiency of the model is its focus on book rather than market values for debt and equity. Stockholders are concerned with the return on the market value of their equity contribution. To the extent that book values

**TABLE 19–7**

DRAM-D APPLIED TO THE AMA CORPORATION AND TO INDUSTRY AVERAGES

|  | Return on assets | = | Return on sales | × | Asset turnover |
|---|---|---|---|---|---|
| AMA Corporation | 5.5% | = | 4.0% | × | 1.38 |
| Industry averages | 4.6% | = | 4.2% | × | 1.10 |

provide inconsistent indicators of market values, the model may lead to erroneous conclusions.

## STATEMENTS OF SOURCES AND USES OF CAPITAL

Constructing a statement of sources and uses of capital will frequently provide an insight into the future prospects of the firm.[4] Such a statement is constructed by comparing the balance sheets of the firm over time and determining exactly which types of capital have been raised by the firm and which types of assets have been acquired with that capital. The statements can highlight unusual buildups of certain assets and unusual methods of acquiring capital. These developments may have significant implications for the future financial prospects of the firm.

As an illustration, consider the balance sheets of the MS Corporation, shown in Table 19–8. Note that over the one-year period covered, the balance sheet has changed considerably. The changes are classified as either sources or uses of capital:

1. *Uses of Capital.* There are two possible uses of capital: First, capital can be used to acquire assets; second, a firm may repay capital suppliers. Accordingly, uses of capital are indicated by either:
   a. Increases in asset accounts, or
   b. Reductions in liability or equity accounts.
2. *Sources of Capital.* There are two possible sources of capital: First, the firm can acquire capital directly from capital suppliers; second, the firm can sell assets, which in turn will release capital for other uses. Accordingly, sources of capital are indicated by either:
   a. Increases in liability or equity accounts, or
   b. Reductions in asset accounts.

Note that the sources and uses of capital as computed for the MS Corporation in Table 19–8 are consistent with these definitions. Accumulated depreciation, although it appears on the left-hand side of the balance sheet as a negative asset, is best treated as a liability. Thus, increases in depreciation make funds available for other uses. Note also that the total sources of capital must *exactly* equal the total uses of capital. This follows from the fact that if two balance sheets balance, the changes in the balance sheets must also balance.

The sources and uses of capital computed in Table 19–8 are rearranged and presented as a sources and uses of capital statement in Table 19–9. The percentage distribution of sources and uses of capital provide a convenient summary of the firm's activities during the period. In the case of the MS Corporation, the primary uses of capital were in the areas of inventory and

---

[4]Sources and uses of capital statements are similar to accounting statements appearing under the names of "Sources and Applications of Funds Statements" and "Statement of Changes in Working Capital Position."

TABLE 19-8

MS CORPORATION:
COMPARATIVE BALANCE SHEETS
(millions of dollars)

|  | 12/31/1978 | 12/31/1979 | Source | Use |
|---|---|---|---|---|
| Assets |  |  |  |  |
| Cash | 45 | 21 | 24 |  |
| Marketable securities | 33 | 0 | 33 |  |
| Accounts receivable | 66 | 90 |  | 24 |
| Inventories | 159 | 225 |  | 66 |
| Gross fixed assets | 225 | 450 |  | 225 |
| (Accumulated depreciation) | (78) | (123) | 45 |  |
| Total assets | 450 | 663 |  |  |
| Liabilities and equity |  |  |  |  |
| Accounts payable | 45 | 54 | 9 |  |
| Notes payable | 45 | 9 |  | 36 |
| Other current liabilities | 21 | 45 | 24 |  |
| Long-term debt | 24 | 78 | 54 |  |
| Common stock | 114 | 192 | 78 |  |
| Retained earnings | 201 | 285 | 84 |  |
| Total liabilities & equity | 450 | 663 | 351 | 351 |

fixed-assets acquisition. The firm raised capital from many different sources. The analyst could use this information to evaluate the firm's policies toward capital structure and asset acquisitions. When viewed over a period of five or ten years, the sources and uses of capital statement also provides important information on the strength, weakness, and financial prospects of the firm.

## RECENT PAYMENT EXPERIENCE AS A SUPPLEMENT TO FINANCIAL-STATEMENT ANALYSIS

Decisions made by suppliers of capital almost always involve the use of financial-statement data and some additional information. For example, financial institutions and suppliers of trade credit frequently rely on information supplied by credit reporting agencies, such as Dun & Bradstreet or TRW, as well as many other smaller credit reporting firms. Among the pertinent information these credit reports usually include are:

1. Names of the firm's bank(s)
2. Names of the firm's suppliers
3. Status of recent payments

The capital supplier can use these reports as the basis for a decision, or

TABLE 19-9

MS CORPORATION:
SOURCES AND USES OF CAPITAL STATEMENT
(in millions of dollars)

|  |  | Percentage |
|---|---|---|
| **Sources** | | |
| Assets: | | |
| Decrease in cash | $24 | 6.8% |
| Decrease in marketable securities | $33 | 9.4% |
| Liabilities and equities: | | |
| Increase in depreciation | $45 | 12.8% |
| Increase in accounts payable | $9 | 2.6% |
| Increase in other current liabilities | $24 | 6.8% |
| Increase in long-term debt | $54 | 15.4% |
| Increase in common stock | $78 | 22.2% |
| Increase in retained earnings | $84 | 23.9% |
| Total sources | $351 | 99.9%[a] |
| **Uses** | | |
| Assets: | | |
| Increase in receivables | $24 | 6.8% |
| Increase in inventories | $66 | 18.8% |
| Increase in gross fixed assets | $225 | 64.1% |
| Liabilities and equities: | | |
| Decreases in notes payable | $36 | 10.3% |
| Total uses | $351 | 100.0% |

[a]Does not equal 100% owing to rounding error.

augment them with information provided by the firm's banks and/or suppliers.

## PUBLISHED FINANCIAL INFORMATION ABOUT INDIVIDUAL FIRMS

There are a substantial number of published reports that are helpful in evaluating the future financial prospects of a firm. These reports are generally based upon a detailed analysis of financial statements and other information. Analysts frequently interview the firm's management, competitors, and bankers, among others. In addition, the industry in which the firm operates is studied closely, and recent stock and bond price movements are analyzed. The following annotated list includes some of the more useful sources of information about particular firms:

1. *Value Line Investment Survey.* Analyzes approximately 1,500 firms and rates them from several perspectives. This source contains information on the betas

for particular stocks (indicating riskiness) and information on estimated annual yields (dividends/price) for common stocks.

2. Standard and Poor's *Stock Reports*. Analyzes approximately 3,700 firms. Each report contains a brief analysis of the firm's financial prospects as well as recent developments.

3. *Moody's Handbook of Common Stocks*. Information on the financial prospects and recent developments of approximately 900 firms.

4. Standard and Poor's *Industry Surveys*. Convenient source for background information about the industry in which the firm operates. Included in the *Industry Surveys* is information about historical development, recent events, and future prospects for the industry as a whole.

In addition to these sources, there are specialized reports providing information on firms in specific industries, such as public utilities firms, banks, and transportation companies. In general, there is a tremendous amount of information and opinions available about particular firms. This material can be used as a supplement to financial-statement analysis and individual investigation.

**SUMMARY**  Good decision making often calls for estimating the future financial prospects of the firm. The historical financial statements of the firm, payment experience, and market information should be incorporated into such analysis whenever possible. Financial statements can be analyzed using ratio analysis, statistical models, the Dupont Ratio Analysis Model, or a sources and uses of capital statement. Data on recent payment experiences of the firm are available from a number of sources. In addition to stock and bond price information, the security market provides many reports that are useful to the financial analyst.

The wealth of information available and the number of options open to the financial analyst highlight the fact that there is no one correct method for analyzing the financial prospects of a particular firm. Judgment, analytical skills, and effort are required to achieve success in this area.

**QUESTIONS FOR DISCUSSION**

1. Describe the problems associated with using historical data to analyze the firm's future financial prospects.

2. Describe the major ratio categories and explain what each type of ratio measures.

3. Describe the sources of information useful in analyzing the future financial prospects of a firm.

4. Explain why financial ratios must be compared to something in order to make them useful, and describe the comparisons that can be made.

5. A firm with a financial weakness should automatically be excluded from consideration as a potential recipient of capital funds. True or false? Explain your answer.

6. Describe the advantages and disadvantages of using statistical models in financial-statement analysis, using examples whenever possible.

7. Give a verbal description of the Dupont Ratio Analysis Model (with debt), and explain the major limitations of its use.

8. Give a verbal description of how the sources and uses of capital statement are constructed, and explain how this statement can be used.

9. What is meant by "recent payment experience information," and how can such information be used in analyzing the future financial prospects of the firm?

10. List some of the important sources of published information about a firm, and explain how such information can be incorporated into an analysis of the firm's future financial prospects.

**PROBLEMS**

1. The California Retirement Plan is considering the purchase of securities of the Donegal Corporation. An analysis of the financial prospects of the firm is necessary before such a decision is made. The income statement and balance sheet of the Donegal Corporation and the appropriate industry ratios are presented below:

DONEGAL CORPORATION:
INCOME STATEMENT FOR 1979 (in millions)[a]

| | |
|---|---:|
| Net sales | $2,000 |
| − Cost of goods sold | − 1,370 |
| = Gross profits | $630 |
| − Selling and administrative expenses | − 300 |
| = Gross operating income | $330 |
| − Depreciation | − 22 |
| = Earnings before interest and taxes | $308 |
| − Interest payments | − 48 |
| = Earnings before taxes | $260 |
| − Federal income taxes | − 104 |
| = Earnings after taxes | $156 |

[a]In addition, total lease payments for 1979 were $50 million.

DONEGAL CORPORATION:
BALANCE SHEET AS OF DECEMBER 31, 1979 (in millions)

| Assets | |
|---|---:|
| Cash | $50 |
| Marketable securities | 30 |
| Accounts receivable | 150 |
| Inventories | 140 |
| Total current assets | $370 |

| | |
|---|---:|
| Gross fixed assets | 870 |
| Less: accumulated depreciation | 70 |
| Net fixed assets | $800 |
| Excess of cost over net assets of businesses purchased (goodwill) | 10 |
| Total assets | $1,180 |
| **Liabilities and equity** | |
| Notes payable (12%) | $150 |
| Accounts payable | 83 |
| Accrued wages and taxes | 56 |
| Total current liabilities | $289 |
| Debentures (10%) | 300 |
| Common stock (2,000,000 shares) | 10 |
| Retained earnings | 581 |
| Total net worth | $591 |
| Total liabilities and equity | $1,180 |

| Ratios | Industry Averages |
|---|:---:|
| Current ratio | 1.3 times |
| Quick ratio | 0.7 times |
| Debt ratio | 30.0% |
| Times interest earned | 8.0 times |
| Fixed-charges coverage | 7.0 times |
| Total asset turnover | 1.6 times |
| Fixed-asset turnover | 2.4 times |
| Inventory turnover | 14.0 times |
| Average collection period | 30.0 days |
| Cost-of-goods-sold ratio | 70% |
| Operating-cost ratio | 14% |
| Return on total assets | 13% |
| Return on sales | 8% |
| Return on net worth | 18% |

a. Compute the financial ratios of the Donegal Corporation.

b. Compare these ratios to the industry averages. Review the liquidity, leverage, utilization of assets, and profitability of the Donegal Corporation.

c. Assuming that similar returns could be earned on the bonds of other firms in the industry, would you recommend the purchase of Donegal's bonds to the California Retirement Plan?

d. Would you give the same answer if the California Retirement Plan were considering the purchase of Donegal common stock?

2. The Winston Manufacturing Corporation has requested a financial analysis from United Consultants, Inc. The financial statements of Winston Manufacturing and the appropriate industry averages obtained by United Consultants are provided below:

## WINSTON MANUFACTURING CORPORATION: INCOME STATEMENT FOR 1979 (in thousands)[a]

| | |
|---|---:|
| Net sales | $300,000 |
| − Cost of goods sold | − 205,000 |
| = Gross profits | $95,000 |
| − Selling and administrative expenses | 18,000 |
| = Gross operating income | $77,000 |
| − Depreciation | 14,000 |
| = Earnings before interest and taxes | $63,000 |
| − Interest | 13,000 |
| = Earnings before taxes | $50,000 |
| − Federal income taxes | 20,000 |
| = Earnings after taxes | $30,000 |

[a]In addition, total lease payments for 1979 were $10 million.

## WINSTON MANUFACTURING CORPORATION: BALANCE SHEET AS OF DECEMBER 31, 1979 (in thousands)

| Assets | |
|---|---:|
| Cash | $3,470 |
| Marketable securities | 8,640 |
| Accounts receivable | 82,560 |
| Inventories | 115,320 |
| Total current assets | $209,990 |
| Gross fixed assets | 415,280 |
| Less: Accumulated depreciation | 106,170 |
| Net fixed assets | $309,110 |
| Excess of cost over net assets of businesses purchased (goodwill) | 0 |
| Total assets | $519,100 |

| Liabilities and equity | |
|---|---:|
| Notes payable (10%) | $50,000 |
| Accounts payable | 37,500 |
| Accrued wages and taxes | 15,650 |
| Total current liabilities | $103,150 |
| Long-term debt (8%) | 100,000 |
| Common stock (2,500,000 shares) | 25,000 |
| Retained earnings | 290,950 |
| Total net worth | $315,950 |
| Total liabilities and equity | $519,100 |

| Ratios | Industry Averages |
|---|---|
| Current ratio | 1.5 times |
| Quick ratio | 1.0 times |
| Debt ratio | 40% |
| Times interest earned | 4.9 times |
| Fixed-charges coverage | 4.9 times |
| Total asset turnover | 0.7 times |
| Fixed-asset turnover | 1.0 times |
| Inventory turnover | 5.0 times |
| Average collection period | 97 days |
| Cost-of-goods-sold ratio | 70% |
| Operating-cost ratio | 5% |
| Return on total assets | 7.2% |
| Return on sales | 10.3% |
| Return on net worth | 12% |

a. Compute the financial ratios of Winston Manufacturing.

b. Compare these ratios to the industry averages. Review the liquidity, leverage, asset utilization, and profitability of Winston Manufacturing.

c. What areas should be targeted for an in-depth analysis by United Consultants?

3. The American Radio Corporation has computed its financial ratios from 1975 to 1979. These ratios are as follows:

| | 1975 | 1976 | 1977 | 1978 | 1979 |
|---|---|---|---|---|---|
| *Liquidity* | | | | | |
| Current ratio (times) | 1.80 | 1.80 | 1.81 | 1.82 | 1.81 |
| Quick ratio (times) | 1.00 | 1.00 | 0.98 | 1.02 | 1.03 |
| *Leverage* | | | | | |
| Debt ratio (%) | 37 | 39 | 43 | 46 | 50 |
| Times interest earned (times) | 8.5 | 8.3 | 8.0 | 7.9 | 7.9 |
| Fixed-charges coverage (times) | 8.5 | 8.3 | 8.0 | 7.9 | 7.9 |
| *Activity* | | | | | |
| A. Turnover: | | | | | |
| Total asset turnover (times) | 8.0 | 7.9 | 7.6 | 7.5 | 7.5 |
| Fixed-asset turnover (times) | 10.1 | 10.0 | 10.0 | 10.0 | 10.1 |
| Inventory turnover (times) | 30.0 | 29.0 | 27.0 | 30.0 | 28.0 |
| Average collection period (days) | 18 | 20 | 23 | 26 | 30 |
| B. Cost: | | | | | |
| Cost-of-goods-sold ratio (%) | 67 | 69 | 72 | 73 | 74 |
| Operating-cost ratio (%) | 6 | 6 | 7 | 6 | 7 |
| *Profitability* | | | | | |
| Return on total assets (%) | 6.0 | 5.8 | 5.6 | 5.5 | 5.4 |
| Return on sales (%) | 8.0 | 7.8 | 7.6 | 7.5 | 7.5 |
| Return on net worth (%) | 10.3 | 10.7 | 9.8 | 9.5 | 9.0 |
| Earnings per share ($) | 1.57 | 1.50 | 1.38 | 1.30 | 1.25 |

a. Analyze the historical trend of the ratios of American Radio. Review the liquidity, leverage, asset utilization, and profitability of the firm.

b. Would this analysis be in error if no adjustments have been made for major changes in the accounting system of the firm in 1977? (For example, changes in depreciation methods, in valuation of inventories, etc.) Do not attempt to make any calculations.

4. The Gerhard Manufacturing Corporation wants to prepare a sources and uses of capital statement for the 1980 calendar year. The appropriate financial statements are as follows:

BALANCE SHEET (in millions)

|  | Dec. 31, 1979 | Dec. 31, 1980 |
|---|---|---|
| Cash | $350 | $430 |
| Marketable securities | $178 | $90 |
| Accounts receivable | $680 | $680 |
| Inventories | $530 | $600 |
| Total current assets | $1,738 | $1,800 |
| Gross fixed assets | $3,830 | $5,200 |
| Less: Accumulated depreciation | $715 | $800 |
| Net fixed assets | $3,115 | $4,400 |
| Total assets | $4,853 | $6,200 |
| | | |
| Notes payable | $210 | $200 |
| Accounts payable | $340 | $420 |
| Accrued wages and taxes | $160 | $165 |
| Total current liabilities | $710 | $785 |
| Mortgage bonds | $500 | $500 |
| Debentures | $1,400 | $1,800 |
| Total long-term debt | $1,900 | $2,300 |
| Common stock | $1,500 | $2,300 |
| Retained earnings | $743 | $815 |
| Total net worth | $2,243 | $3,115 |
| Total liabilities and equity | $4,853 | $6,200 |

a. Prepare a sources and uses of capital statement, similar to that shown in Table 19-9.

b. Discuss the information obtained in the sources and uses of capital statement.

5. Using the financial statements of the Donegal Corporation (problem 1), analyze the firm using the Dupont Ratio Analysis Model with debt (DRAM-D).

6. Using the financial statements of the Winston Manufacturing Corporation (problem 2), analyze the firm using the Dupont Ratio Analysis Model with debt (DRAM-D).

Most business students have already been exposed to the computation of financial ratios in accounting courses. For this reason, financial ratios were not discussed in detail in the body of the chapter. This appendix provides the reader with an opportunity to review the computations and the informational content of financial ratios. We will compute a number of financial ratios for the AMA Corporation, whose balance sheet and income statement were presented in Tables 19–1 and 19–2. As discussed in the chapter, financial ratios are commonly divided into four major categories: (1) liquidity ratios, (2) leverage ratios, (3) activity ratios, and (4) profitability ratios.

## LIQUIDITY RATIOS

The *current ratio* is the most common liquidity ratio used in financial analysis. The current ratio is computed by dividing current assets by current liabilities. It measures the ability of the firm to maintain solvency over the short run. Current liabilities are, by definition, obligations maturing within one year. Thus, the analyst can review the extent to which the firm can "cover" such liabilities with current assets. For the AMA Corporation, the current ratio can be computed as follows:

$$\text{Current Ratio} = \frac{\text{Current assets}}{\text{Current liabilities}}$$

$$= \frac{\$2,100,000}{\$900,000} = 2.3 \text{ times}$$

The *quick* or *acid-test ratio* is used because the liquidity of all current assets is not the same. Cash and marketable securities are highly liquid. Accounts receivable have less liquidity, since they must be collected before they can be used to cover current liabilities. However, receivables, unless of poor quality, would be easily converted into cash. On the other hand, inventories commonly possess a lower degree of liquidity. Finished-goods inventories must first be sold and the proceeds collected before they are converted into liquid funds. Raw-materials and work-in-progress inventories are even less liquid. And other current assets—for example, prepaid insurance—may have even less liquidity.[5] Therefore, the quick ratio is computed by dividing liquid current assets by current liabilities. For the AMA Corporation, the computation would be as follows:

$$\text{Quick ratio} = \frac{\text{Liquid current assets}}{\text{Current liabilities}} = \frac{\text{Cash} + \text{Securities} + \text{Receivables}}{\text{Current liabilities}}$$

$$= \frac{\$150,000 + \$450,000 + \$600,000}{\$900,000} = 1.3 \text{ times}$$

Generally speaking, firms with liquidity ratios higher than those of the industry show a strong liquidity position. This statement, however, should not be construed as implying that management should attempt to maximize the liquidity ratios of the firm. As discussed in Chapter 11, holding current assets carries a cost to the firm. From the point of view of the supplier of short-term capital, high liquidity ratios provide greater protection, *all other things being equal.*

## LEVERAGE RATIOS

The *debt ratio* ($\theta$) measures the extent to which the firm uses debt to finance asset acquisitions. This ratio has been used to analyze the optimal capital structure of the firm, and has been discussed in considerable detail throughout the book. The debt ratio is computed by dividing the total debt by the total assets of the firm. For the AMA Corporation, the computation would be:

$$\text{Debt ratio} = \frac{\text{Total debt}}{\text{Total assets}}$$

$$= \frac{\$900,000 + \$2,100,000}{\$6,500,000} = 46\%$$

It should be noted that this method uses book rather than market values as the measure of the firm's debt. As we saw in Chapter 13, the market value of the debt is a better indicator of the firm's true level of debt, but book values are easier to compute. Book values are frequently used as proxy measures of market values in ratio analysis, since there is apt to be some stability in a ratio of book-to-book values.

*Debt to tangible net worth* is obtained by dividing the total debt by the tangible net worth. This ratio gives a better picture of the true financial leverage used by the firm. Intangible assets are subtracted from net worth in order to arrive at the tangible net worth of the firm. Intangible assets are

---

[5]Some current assets, such as an expected income tax refund, should be considered highly liquid and thus included in the quick ratio. The analyst must make the decision after an evaluation of the asset.

presumed to be of questionable value and are thus excluded from the "protection" for debt suppliers in the event of liquidation. In the AMA Corporation, there is one intangible asset, the excess of cost over net assets of businesses purchased (goodwill). Thus, the ratio can be computed as follows:

$$\text{Debt to tangible net worth} = \frac{\text{Total debt}}{\text{Net worth} - \text{Intangibles}}$$

$$= \frac{\$3,000,000}{\$3,500,000 - \$500,000} = 100\%$$

Financial analysts are also interested in the ability of the firm to meet their fixed interest-payment obligations out of current earnings. The *times-interest-earned ratio* is obtained by dividing the earnings before interest and taxes by the total interest payments made by the firm during the same period. This ratio measures the number of times interest payments are earned by the firm and thus serves as an indication of the degree of protection to capital suppliers in the event of an earnings decline. Note that the amount of earnings before interest and taxes (EBIT) is used because interest payments are deductible for tax purposes. For the AMA Corporation, the times interest earned is computed as follows:

$$\text{Times interest earned} = \frac{\text{Earnings before interest and taxes}}{\text{Interest payments}}$$

$$= \frac{\$735,000}{\$135,000} = 5.4 \text{ times}$$

As discussed in Chapter 17, leases are commonly used as a means of financing assets. Lease payments are legal obligations of the firm. Thus, the financial analyst is interested in evaluating the ability of the firm to meet *all* its financial obligations out of current earnings. The *fixed-charges-coverage ratio* is obtained by dividing the total funds available from current earnings by the total contractual financial obligations of the firm. The numerator of this equation is equal to the earnings before interest and taxes plus any lease payments made during the same period. The reason for adding back the lease payments is that such payments have already been included once as expenses in either cost of goods sold or selling and administrative expenses. For the AMA Corporation, it can be computed as follows:[6]

---

[6]Some analysts advocate the inclusion of other financial obligations, such as sinking-fund payments (discussed in Chapter 17), in this ratio. However, it would be difficult to obtain this information, especially for comparison purposes. In addition, depreciation cash flows could be used to meet current financial obligations and thus could be included in the ratio. However, the use of depreciation cash flows may impair the ability of the firm to maintain plant and equipment.

$$\text{Fixed-charges coverage} = \frac{\text{EBIT} + \text{Lease payments}}{\text{Interest} + \text{Lease payments}}$$

$$= \frac{\$735,000 + \$200,000}{\$135,000 + \$200,000} = 2.8 \text{ times}$$

## ACTIVITY RATIOS

Activity ratios measure how well the firm utilizes its assets. These ratios are commonly divided into two subgroups: turnover and cost ratios. Turnover ratios measure the level of sales that is supported by the assets. The *total asset turnover* measures how many dollars of sales are supported by each dollar in total assets. Normally, the higher the ratio, the better the utilization of total assets. This turnover ratio is obtained by dividing the annual sales by the total assets of the firm.[7] For the AMA Corporation, it would be computed as follows:

$$\text{Total asset turnover} = \frac{\text{Annual sales}}{\text{Total assets}}$$

$$= \frac{\$9,000,000}{\$6,500,000} = 1.4 \text{ times}$$

The *fixed-asset turnover* is similar, except that the firm desires to investigate the utilization of fixed assets (plant and equipment). This ratio is computed by dividing the annual sales by the net fixed assets of the firm. For the AMA Corporation, the computation would be:

$$\text{Fixed-asset turnover} = \frac{\text{Annual sales}}{\text{Net fixed assets}}$$

$$= \frac{\$9,000,000}{\$3,900,000} = 2.3 \text{ times}$$

The analyst would also be interested in the firm's utilization of current assets. The *inventory-turnover ratio* measures the level of sales supported by the inventories of the firm. This ratio is computed by dividing annual sales by inventories. For the AMA Corporation, the computation would be:

$$\text{Inventory turnover} = \frac{\text{Annual sales}}{\text{Inventories}}$$

$$= \frac{\$9,000,000}{\$900,000} = 10 \text{ times}$$

---

[7]For precision, the denominator should be the weighted average of the total assets owned by the firm during the period. For example, if the firm made a large asset acquisition on the last day of the year, it would give the wrong impression on utilization of assets. This comment applies to all turnover ratios.

The number of days that accounts receivable of the firm are outstanding is of significant interest. The *average collection period* measures the number of days that it takes to collect the average receivable. As discussed in Chapter 11, this measurement depends on the credit terms and collection policies of the firm. The ratio is obtained by dividing the accounts receivable outstanding by the sales made per day. Special attention must be placed on using the correct figure for accounts receivable. For example, the ratio would not be representative if it were computed in periods of seasonally low or high receivables. For the AMA Corporation, the computation of the average collection period would be as follows:[8]

$$\text{Average collection period} = \frac{\text{Accounts receivable}}{\text{Sales per day}} = \frac{\text{Accounts receivable}}{\text{Sales/360}}$$

$$= \frac{\text{Accounts receivable} \times 360}{\text{Sales}}$$

$$= \frac{\$600,000 \times 360}{\$9,000,000} = 24 \text{ days}$$

There are two ratios used to measure the effect of costs on the sales of the firm. The *cost-of-goods sold ratio* (which is related to the gross profit margin) is computed by dividing cost of goods sold by the sales made during the period. The *operating-cost ratio* is computed by dividing sales and administrative expenses (operating expenses) by the sales made during the period. Both these ratios measure the ability of the firm to control its costs. For the AMA Corporation, the computation of these ratios would be as follows:

$$\text{Cost-of-goods-sold ratio} = \frac{\text{Cost of goods sold}}{\text{Annual sales}}$$

$$= \frac{\$7,740,000}{\$9,000,000} = 86\%$$

$$\text{Operating-cost ratio} = \frac{\text{Selling and administrative expenses (operating cost)}}{\text{Annual sales}}$$

$$= \frac{\$270,000}{\$9,000,000} = 3\%$$

## PROFITABILITY RATIOS

There are four common ratios used to measure the profitability of the firm. The *return on total assets* measures the return of the firm on the total assets owned. It is computed by dividing the earnings after taxes by the total assets

---

[8] A 360-day year is used for ease of computation.

of the firm. For the AMA Corporation, the return on total assets ratio is computed as follows:

$$\text{Return on total assets} = \frac{\text{Earnings after taxes}}{\text{Total assets}}$$

$$= \frac{\$360,000}{\$6,500,000} = 5.5\%$$

The *return on sales* measures the profitability of each dollar of the firm's sales. It is obtained by dividing the earnings after taxes by the annual sales of the firm. For the AMA Corporation, it is computed as follows:

$$\text{Return on sales} = \frac{\text{Earnings after taxes}}{\text{Annual sales}}$$

$$= \frac{\$360,000}{\$9,000,000} = 4\%$$

The stockholders, however, are more interested in the return received per dollar invested. *Return on net worth* is obtained by dividing earnings after taxes by the total net worth (stockholders' equity) of the firm. Stockholders of the firm are entitled to the entire earnings after taxes. The firm may pay dividends or retain earnings; but all funds belong to the stockholders. Net worth includes common stock, paid-in surplus, and retained earnings. The total figure represents the total investment made by the stockholders in the firm. For the AMA Corporation, it is computed as follows:

$$\text{Return on net worth} = \frac{\text{Earnings after taxes}}{\text{Net worth}}$$

$$= \frac{\$360,000}{\$3,500,000} = 10.3\%$$

*Return on tangible net worth* is another frequent measure of profitability. Intangible assets are subtracted from net worth in order to arrive at tangible net worth. Intangible assets are presumed to be of questionable value and are thus eliminated from the profitability computation. Thus, return on tangible net worth is a relatively more conservative measure of profitability. In the case of the AMA Corporation, there is only one intangible asset, the excess of cost over net assets of businesses purchased (goodwill). The return on tangible net worth is obtained by dividing earnings after taxes by tangible net worth. For the AMA Corporation, it is computed as follows:

$$\text{Return on tangible net worth} = \frac{\text{Earnings after taxes}}{\text{Tangible net worth}}$$

$$= \frac{\text{Earnings after taxes}}{\text{Net worth} - \text{Intangible assets}}$$

$$= \frac{\$360,000}{\$3,500,000 - \$500,000} = 12\%$$

*Earnings per share* is the final measure of profitability to be discussed in this appendix. Earnings per share is computed by dividing the earnings after taxes of the firm by the number of shares of common stock outstanding. For the AMA Corporation, it is computed as follows:

$$\text{Earnings per share} = \frac{\text{Earnings after taxes}}{\text{Number of shares of common stock outstanding}}$$

$$= \frac{\$360,000}{1,800,000} = \$0.20 \text{ per share}$$

**SELECTED BIBLIOGRAPHY**

ALTMAN, EDWARD I., "Financial Ratios, Discriminant Analysis and the Prediction of Corporate Bankruptcy," *Journal of Finance*, 23 (September 1968), 589–609.

BENISHAY, HASKELL, "Economic Information in Financial Ratio Analysis," *Accounting and Business Research*, 2 (Spring 1971), 174–79.

BIERMAN, HAROLD, JR., "Measuring Financial Liquidity," *Accounting Review*, 35 (October 1960), 628–32.

DEAKIN, EDWARD B., "A Discriminant Analysis of Predictors of Business Failure," *Journal of Accounting Research*, 10 (Spring 1972), 167–79.

FOSTER, GEORGE, *Financial Statement Analysis*. Englewood Cliffs, N.J.: Prentice-Hall, 1978.

HELFERT, ERICH A., *Techniques of Financial Analysis*, 4th ed. Homewood, Ill.: Richard D. Irwin, 1977.

LEV, BARUCH, *Financial Statement Analysis: A New Approach*. Englewood Cliffs, N.J.: Prentice-Hall, 1974.

MURRAY, ROGER, "Lessons for Financial Analysis," *Journal of Finance*, 26 (May 1971), 327–32.

O'CONNER, MELVIN C., "On the Usefulness of Financial Ratios to Investors in Common Stock," *Accounting Review*, 48 (April 1973), 339–52.

REILING, HENRY B., and JOHN C. BURTON, "Financial Statements: Signposts as Well as Milestones," *Harvard Business Review* (November–December 1972), pp. 45–54.

SEITZ, NEIL, *Financial Analysis: A Programmed Approach*. Reston, Va.: Reston Publishing Company, 1976.

# EPILOGUE

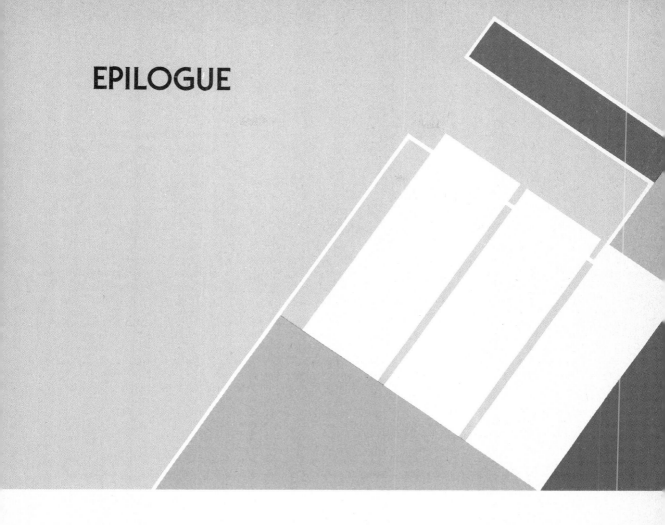

## INTRODUCTION

Even though most of the readers of this book will pursue careers in business-administration specialties other than finance (marketing, management, and so on), we hope that we have provided all of them with a general introduction to the way in which financial decisions should be made. The conceptual framework we have provided is useful for the analysis of many different decisions facing today's business firms, and therefore it is important to all managers, regardless of their specialties.

The theme of the book is that the basic objective of management should be the maximization of stockholder wealth. We have noted that this objective is constrained by social and technological factors, but that within these constraints, each financial alternative facing the firm should be evaluated in terms of its effect on stock price (stockholder wealth). Since stock prices are going to be determined by the expected amount, timing, and riskiness of the cash flows to stockholders, management must pay special attention to the implications of each business alternative for these three factors. Management must recognize that, in a sense, the decisions of the firm are monitored by a competitive stock market, and that it is apt to be difficult to mislead this market for very long.

The book discussed dozens of techniques that can be applied to many different situations. We went to great pains to show that the techniques discussed can be used in such a way as to make decisions consistent with stockholder-wealth maximization. There are, of course, hundreds of techniques currently in use by business firms, and no one book can possibly cover all of them. Some of the techniques we have not covered can be used to make decisions consistent with stockholder-wealth maximization; others are clearly misleading. The reader of this book should be in a position by now to look at almost any technique and evaluate how it fits in with the goal of stockholder-wealth maximization. At any rate, the techniques we have presented are among the most widely used, and certainly among the easiest to understand. Always remember that every technique should relate in some manner to the dividends and riskiness of common stock. This is the essence of stockholder-wealth maximization.

## FURTHER STUDIES IN FINANCE

This is an introductory book to finance, comparable to a first-level book on European history or economics. It is an introduction to the discipline, organized around the conceptual framework of stockholder-wealth maximization. Just as in the case of history or economics, there are other books that deal on a more advanced level with the topics covered in this book.

In terms of the conceptual framework itself, Boudreaux and Long's presentation *Basic Theory of Corporate Finance* is a more detailed, rigorous, and precise analysis.[1] Copeland and Weston's *Financial Theory and Corporate Policy* is a step closer to the frontiers of current knowledge.[2] This book contains extensive discussions of controversial points in the theory of finance and is an excellent introduction to scholarly journals in finance.

Because there is an extensive time lag between the writing of a book and the time it reaches the student, almost all new developments in financial theory have first appeared in scholarly journals. These new ideas are then

---

[1]Kenneth J. Boudreaux and Hugh W. Long, *The Basic Theory of Corporate Finance* (Englewood Cliffs, N.J.: Prentice-Hall, 1977).

[2]Thomas E. Copeland and J. Fred Weston, *Financial Theory and Corporate Policy* (Reading, Mass.: Addison-Wesley, 1979).

evaluated, discussed, subjected to critical review, and perhaps modified before they are included in textbooks. The most widely read and followed journals in finance are *American Economic Review, Financial Management, Journal of Finance,* and *Journal of Financial and Quantitative Analysis.*[3] A good mathematical background is a *must* before the articles in these journals can be understood. In addition, the student must have a fairly complete understanding of financial theory before attempting to review these articles.

It should be noted that the references cited above deal primarily with the conceptual (theory) framework of finance. There are many second-level textbooks that deal extensively with the techniques of financial management. The two dominant books in this area are Van Horne's *Financial Management and Policy,* and Weston and Brigham's *Managerial Finance.*[4] These books combine theory and techniques, with an emphasis on techniques. Both books require a greater competence in mathematics than that demanded by this book. In addition, both these second-level books are somewhat flawed by failing to justify the use of particular techniques in the context of financial theory. Both, however, are remarkable in their breadth of coverage and their clear writing style.

In conclusion, we would like to refer once again to the history analogy presented at the beginning of this epilogue. All of us recognize that it is impossible to master the history of Western civilization by reading only one book. A single book may provide an overview, but not an in-depth coverage of the topic. In the area of the history of Western civilization, there are books and articles devoted to such topics as the fall of Rome, the French Revolution, or the American Civil War. These topics are covered only briefly in a single book on Western civilization.

In a similar fashion, a number of topics have only been touched upon in this book, and others omitted entirely. Some of the topics that students may wish to pursue independently are noted below, and suggestions for readings in each topic are footnoted.

1. Institutional practices in security markets[5]
2. Dealing with risk associated with commodities[6]
3. Forecasting[7]

---

[3]There are other scholarly journals in specialized areas of finance, such as real estate, insurance, investments, etc. Many of the new developments in these specialized fields, however, are first presented in the four aforementioned journals.

[4]James C. Van Horne, *Financial Management and Policy,* 5th ed. (Englewood Cliffs, N.J.: Prentice-Hall, 1980); and J. Fred Weston and Eugene F. Brigham, *Managerial Finance,* 6th ed. (Hinsdale, Ill.: The Dryden Press, 1978).

[5]Robert C. Coates, *Investment Strategy* (New York: McGraw-Hill, 1978).

[6]For a description of the commodities market, see Richard J. Teweles, Charles V. Harlow, and Herbert L. Stone, *The Commodity Futures Game* (New York: McGraw-Hill, 1974). In addition, actual transactions and prices are published in the *Commodity Year Book* (New York: Commodity Research Bureau, Inc., latest issue).

[7]Spyros Makridakis and Steven C. Wheelwright, *Forecasting Methods and Applications* (New York: John Wiley, 1978).

**4.** Mergers and acquisitions[8]

**5.** Bankruptcy[9]

## SOME FINAL WORDS

Several areas of the theory of finance are the subject of considerable controversy. Among such controversies are (1) the maximization of stockholder wealth within the context of efficient and competitive markets, (2) the applicable discount rate in the leasing/buying decision, (3) the exact advantage of the use of debt and its effect on the cost of capital of the firm, and (4) the optimal dividend policy. These controversial areas emphasize one important point: Finance is a dynamic field undergoing constant change. No one person has all the answers.

Many beginning students complain that finance courses take a theoretical rather than a practical approach. They prefer an actual description of current business practice. Remember, however, that today's students will be responsible for the management of businesses in the future, and so the student should come to grips with the future as well as the present. For example, net present value was not widely used by American corporations during the early 1950s. Continuous exposition in our universities of the inherent analytical advantages of net present value brought this tool into practice by the business community. Many large, medium, and even small firms today accept net present value as the best method by which to evaluate asset-acquisition alternatives. The theory of finance will provide a means of understanding and applying new techniques in the future. Businesses will be able to visualize new methods to help them make correct decisions.

---

[8]See Uwe E. Reinherdt, *Mergers and Consolidations: A Corporate Finance Approach* (Morristown, N.J.: General Learning Press, 1972); and J. Fred Weston and Sam Peltzman, *Public Policy towards Mergers* (Pacific Palisades, Cal.: Goodyear, 1969).

[9]Edward I. Altman, *Corporate Bankruptcy in America* (Lexington, Mass.: Heath Lexington Books, 1971).

# APPENDICES

# APPENDIX A
## Selected Answers to Numerical Problems

**Chapter 2**
  **1.** a. $1,158  b. $1,331  c. $1,521
  **2.** a. $2,723.38  b. $2,486.85  c. $2,283.46
  **3.** a. $431.78  b. $375.66  c. $328.73
  **4.** a. $110.25  b. $121  c. $132.25
  **5.** a. $90.70  b. $82.64  c. $75.61
  **6.** a. $82.64  b. $93.11
  **7.**   $1,250
  **8.**   $100
  **9.** a. Declines to $66.67  b. Increases to $200
  **10.** a. 5%  b. $1,666.67, $500, $333.33
  **11.** a. $133.33  b. $100  c. $80
  **12.** a. $110  b. $30

**Chapter 3**
  **1.** a. $1,469  b. $1,611  c. $1,486  d. $1,480
  **2.** a. $621  b. $211.70  c. $85.30
  **3.** A. $3,405  B. $3,000
  **4.** a. $36,800  b. $80,050  c. $52,540  d. $8,163
  **5.** a. $1,327.04  b. $999.60  c. $875.48
  **6.**   $14,903.13
  **7.**   12%
  **8.**   12%
  **9.** a. A. $8,301.20  B. $8,386
  **10.** a. $1,000.44  b. $1,229.60  c. $830.12
  **11.** a. $65,905  b. $72,435  c. $79,685
  **12.**   $1,880.23

**Chapter 4**
  **1.** a. 0.75  b. 1.2  c. 1.5
  **2.** a. 0.6  b. 0.8  c. 1.4
  **5.** a. $k = 8\% + (14\% - 8\%)\beta$  b. $k = 10\% + (16\% - 10\%)\beta$  c. $k = 8\% + (16\% - 8\%)\beta$
  **6.** a. 13.2%  b. 8.4%  c. 12%  d. 15.2%
  **7.** a. $889  b. $606  c. $727, $526  d. $800, $513
  **8.** a. $641, $800
  **9.** a. $35.71  b. $31.25  c. $41.67
  **10.** a. $55.56  b. $45.45  c. $71.43
  **11.** a. $43.75  b. $52.50  c. $35
  **12.**   Without: $26.50, with: $24

| | | |
|---|---|---|
| **Appendix 4A** | **1.** | 109.5 |
| | **2.** | $3,162.30 |
| | **3.** | 0.75 |

| | | |
|---|---|---|
| **Chapter 5** | **1.** | a. 11.2%   b. 12.8%   d. 6.72% |
| | **2.** | Present: $59.52; proposed: $65.22 |
| | **4.** | a. 11%, 4.4%, 6.6% |
| | **5.** | 31.4% |

| | | |
|---|---|---|
| **Appendix 5A** | **1.** | 20% |

| | | |
|---|---|---|
| **Chapter 6** | **1.** | a. $62.50   b. $60 |
| | **2.** | a. $700   b. $880 |
| | **3.** | b. $53,000 and $54,200 |

| | | |
|---|---|---|
| **Appendix 6A** | **1.** | a. $14,778   b. $392   c. $490   d. $196 |
| | **2.** | a. $139,678   b. $6,860   c. $7,000   d. $2,800 |

| | | |
|---|---|---|
| **Chapter 7** | **1.** | a. 20%   b. 12.5%, 15%, 25%   c. 2.0 |
| | **2.** | 11.6% |
| | **3.** | 14.8% |
| | **5.** | a. $157,025   b. Increases by $7,025, decreases by $2,975 |
| | **6.** | a. 9%   b. $217,995   c. +$17,995 |

| | | |
|---|---|---|
| **Chapter 8** | **1.** | $27,141.67 |
| | **2.** | a. $9,250   b. $26,750   c. $72,750   d. $4,580,750 |
| | **3.** | a. $702   b. $2,745   c. $9,366   d. $18,698 |
| | **4.** | a. $215,350   b. $222,750 |
| | **5.** | $281,250 |
| | **7.** | a. $300,000   b. $287,500   c. $200,000 |
| | **8.** | $394,750 |
| | **9.** | $1,559,250 |
| | **10.** | a. $37,087   b. $57,130 |

| | | |
|---|---|---|
| **Appendix 8A** | **1.** | a. $20,000   b. $33,333, $26,667, $20,000, $13,333, $6,667   c. $40,000, $24,000, $14,400, $10,800, $10,800 |
| | **2.** | a. $33,000 + salvage   b. $34,800, $33,600, $32,400, $31,200 + salvage |

| | | |
|---|---|---|
| **Chapter 9** | **1.** | $6,675 and 18.6% |
| | **2.** | ($7,660) and 10.1% |
| | **3.** | a. $90,000   b. $15,600 + salvage   c. $9,722 and 12.4% |
| | **4.** | NPV = $47,064 |
| | **5.** | NPV = ($2,589,000) |
| | **6.** | NPV = $11,450   IRR = 14.05% |
| | **7.** | NPV = $1,843 |

**8.** a. $58,000   c. NPV = +$15,421

**9.** a. $1,600,000   b. $160,000 + salvage   c. ($155,760)

**Appendix 9A**   **1.** a. $1,496,620   b. $272,000 + land and equipment   c. $238,912

**Appendix 9B**   **1.** a. 4.39   b. 14.2%

**Appendix 9C**   **1.**   15.13%
   **2.**   18.66%

**Chapter 10**   **1.** a. Both: $3,439,500   b. First: $2,027,500
   **2.** a. $30 million   b. $26 million
   **3.** a. and b. $7,345,000
   **4.** c. Trucks and control system NPV = $4,401,000
   **5.** b. Trucks and control system NPV = $4,401,000

**Chapter 11**   **1.** a. $300,000   b. $400,000   c. $500,000
   **2.** a. $10,000,000   b. $80,000
   **3.** a. $889   b. $667; Yes, to both cases
   **4.** a. $25,000, $33,333   b. ($816,067)
   **5.** A. +$898,000   B. ($375,000)
   **6.**   +$341,000
   **7.** a. 600   b. 500
   **8.** a. 100,000   b. 90,000   c. 100,000
   **9.**   200

**Appendix 11A**   **1.**   $4,250, $3,300, $3,000
   **2.** a. In thousands: $60, $50, $50, $50, $320, $280

**Chapter 12**   **1.** a. $500,000   b. $520,000   c. $510,000   d. $530,000
   **2.** a. $3,500,000, $500,000, $3,000,000   b. $2,500,000, 0, $2,500,000
   **3.** a. $2,100,000, $400,000, $1,700,000   b. $2,100,000, $300,000, $1,800,000
   **4.** a. $2,400,000, $1,000,000, $1,400,000   b. $2,400,000, $600,000, $1,800,000
   **5.** a. NPV = ($1,546,400)
   **6.** a. NPV = +$2,148,000   b. NPV = ($88,151)

**Chapter 13**   **1.**   11.94%
   **2.**   10%
   **3.**   10%
   **4.** a. Book weights: 8%, 17%, 8% and 67%;   b. market weights: 9.4%, 15.1%, 7.5%, 67.9%
   **5.** b. 12.13%
   **6.** 14%, 13.44%, 14.76%, 16.88%, 17.52%

Chapter 14    **1.** a. 6%  b. 0  c. 2%

          **2.** a. 9%  b. 5.4%

          **3.** a. 10%  b. 6%

          **4.** a. 10%  b. 10%

          **5.** a. 10%  b. 15.5%  c. 11.1%, 17.22%

          **6.** 24.3%

          **7.** 13% to 15%

          **8.** 14% to 16%

          **9.** a. 0 and 6%  b. 15%, 14% to 16%  c. 11.475%

          **10.** a. 4.8% and 5.4%  b. 14%, 13% to 15%  c. 10.04%

          **11.**    $NPV = +\$130,000$

          **12.** 12%

Appendix 14A    **1.** a. $k = 10\% + (16\% - 10\%)\beta$  b. 1.33  c. 18%

          **2.** a. $k = 8\% + (13\% - 8\%)\beta$  b. 1.43  c. 15.15%

Chapter 16    **1.** a. 12%  b. 13.64%  c. 8.4% and 9.55%

          **2.** a. $1,117,647  b. $134,118  c. 13.41%

          **3.** a. $432,500  b. 10.4%

          **4.** a. $49,208.30  b. 15.54%

          **5.** a. 14.7%  b. 37.1%  c. 18.2%  d. 18.8%

          **6.** $61,000

          **7.** a. $900,000  b. 12%

          **8.** a. 8½%

Chapter 17    **1.**    $25 and $23.08

          **2.** a. $40

          **4.** a. $73,122,000  b. $67,800,000

          **5.** a. $238,487  b. $247,260

Appendix 17A    **1.**    +$7,745,680

Chapter 18    **1.** a. 700,000 shares  b. $17.14

          **2.** b. 1,538,462.5 shares; thus they can elect 4 directors

          **4.** a. 10 rights  b. $0.91

Chapter 19    **4.** a. Total sources = Total uses = $1,530 million

# APPENDIX B
Compound and Present-Value Tables

# COEFFICIENTS FOR FUTURE VALUES OF $1

$$1 \text{ Coef.} = (1 + i)^n$$

| To be held until the end of Period | 1% | 2% | 3% | Interest Rate 4% | 5% | 6% | 7% |
|---|---|---|---|---|---|---|---|
| 1 | 1.010 | 1.020 | 1.030 | 1.040 | 1.050 | 1.060 | 1.070 |
| 2 | 1.020 | 1.040 | 1.061 | 1.082 | 1.102 | 1.124 | 1.145 |
| 3 | 1.030 | 1.061 | 1.093 | 1.125 | 1.158 | 1.191 | 1.225 |
| 4 | 1.041 | 1.082 | 1.126 | 1.170 | 1.216 | 1.262 | 1.311 |
| 5 | 1.051 | 1.104 | 1.159 | 1.217 | 1.276 | 1.338 | 1.403 |
| 6 | 1.062 | 1.126 | 1.194 | 1.265 | 1.340 | 1.419 | 1.501 |
| 7 | 1.072 | 1.149 | 1.230 | 1.316 | 1.407 | 1.504 | 1.606 |
| 8 | 1.083 | 1.172 | 1.267 | 1.369 | 1.477 | 1.594 | 1.718 |
| 9 | 1.094 | 1.195 | 1.305 | 1.423 | 1.551 | 1.689 | 1.838 |
| 10 | 1.105 | 1.219 | 1.344 | 1.480 | 1.629 | 1.791 | 1.967 |
| 11 | 1.116 | 1.243 | 1.384 | 1.539 | 1.710 | 1.898 | 2.105 |
| 12 | 1.127 | 1.268 | 1.426 | 1.601 | 1.796 | 2.012 | 2.252 |
| 13 | 1.138 | 1.294 | 1.469 | 1.665 | 1.886 | 2.133 | 2.410 |
| 14 | 1.149 | 1.319 | 1.513 | 1.732 | 1.980 | 2.261 | 2.579 |
| 15 | 1.161 | 1.346 | 1.558 | 1.801 | 2.079 | 2.397 | 2.759 |
| 16 | 1.173 | 1.373 | 1.605 | 1.873 | 2.183 | 2.540 | 2.952 |
| 17 | 1.184 | 1.400 | 1.653 | 1.948 | 2.292 | 2.693 | 3.159 |
| 18 | 1.196 | 1.428 | 1.702 | 2.026 | 2.407 | 2.854 | 3.380 |
| 19 | 1.208 | 1.457 | 1.754 | 2.107 | 2.527 | 3.026 | 3.617 |
| 20 | 1.220 | 1.486 | 1.806 | 2.191 | 2.653 | 3.207 | 3.870 |
| 25 | 1.282 | 1.641 | 2.094 | 2.666 | 3.386 | 4.292 | 5.427 |
| 30 | 1.348 | 1.811 | 2.427 | 3.243 | 4.322 | 5.743 | 7.612 |

| Period | 8% | 9% | 10% | 12% | 14% | 15% | 16% |
|---|---|---|---|---|---|---|---|
| 1 | 1.080 | 1.090 | 1.100 | 1.120 | 1.140 | 1.150 | 1.160 |
| 2 | 1.166 | 1.186 | 1.210 | 1.254 | 1.300 | 1.322 | 1.346 |
| 3 | 1.260 | 1.295 | 1.331 | 1.405 | 1.482 | 1.521 | 1.561 |
| 4 | 1.360 | 1.412 | 1.464 | 1.574 | 1.689 | 1.749 | 1.811 |
| 5 | 1.469 | 1.539 | 1.611 | 1.762 | 1.925 | 2.011 | 2.100 |
| 6 | 1.587 | 1.677 | 1.772 | 1.974 | 2.195 | 2.313 | 2.436 |
| 7 | 1.714 | 1.828 | 1.949 | 2.211 | 2.502 | 2.660 | 2.826 |
| 8 | 1.851 | 1.993 | 2.144 | 2.476 | 2.853 | 3.059 | 3.278 |
| 9 | 1.999 | 2.172 | 2.358 | 2.773 | 3.252 | 3.518 | 3.803 |
| 10 | 2.159 | 2.367 | 2.594 | 3.106 | 3.707 | 4.046 | 4.411 |
| 11 | 2.332 | 2.580 | 2.853 | 3.479 | 4.226 | 4.652 | 5.117 |
| 12 | 2.518 | 2.813 | 3.138 | 3.896 | 4.818 | 5.350 | 5.926 |
| 13 | 2.720 | 3.066 | 3.452 | 4.363 | 5.492 | 6.153 | 6.886 |
| 14 | 2.937 | 3.342 | 3.797 | 4.887 | 6.261 | 7.076 | 7.988 |
| 15 | 3.172 | 3.642 | 4.177 | 5.474 | 7.138 | 8.137 | 9.266 |
| 16 | 3.426 | 3.970 | 4.595 | 6.130 | 8.137 | 9.358 | 10.748 |
| 17 | 3.700 | 4.328 | 5.054 | 6.866 | 9.276 | 10.761 | 12.468 |
| 18 | 3.996 | 4.717 | 5.560 | 7.690 | 10.575 | 12.375 | 14.463 |
| 19 | 4.316 | 5.142 | 6.116 | 8.613 | 12.056 | 14.232 | 16.777 |
| 20 | 4.661 | 5.604 | 6.728 | 9.646 | 13.743 | 16.367 | 19.461 |
| 25 | 6.848 | 8.623 | 10.835 | 17.000 | 26.462 | 32.919 | 40.874 |
| 30 | 10.063 | 13.268 | 17.449 | 29.960 | 50.950 | 66.212 | 85.850 |

| Period | 18% | 20% | 24% | 28% | 32% | 36% |
|--------|-----|-----|-----|-----|-----|-----|
| 1 | 1.180 | 1.200 | 1.240 | 1.280 | 1.320 | 1.360 |
| 2 | 1.392 | 1.440 | 1.538 | 1.638 | 1.742 | 1.850 |
| 3 | 1.643 | 1.728 | 1.907 | 2.067 | 2.300 | 2.515 |
| 4 | 1.939 | 2.074 | 2.364 | 2.684 | 3.036 | 3.421 |
| 5 | 2.288 | 2.488 | 2.932 | 3.436 | 4.007 | 4.653 |
| 6 | 2.700 | 2.986 | 3.635 | 4.398 | 5.290 | 6.328 |
| 7 | 3.185 | 3.583 | 4.508 | 5.629 | 6.983 | 8.605 |
| 8 | 3.759 | 4.300 | 5.590 | 7.206 | 9.217 | 11.703 |
| 9 | 4.435 | 5.160 | 6.931 | 9.223 | 12.166 | 15.917 |
| 10 | 5.234 | 6.192 | 8.594 | 11.806 | 16.060 | 21.647 |
| 11 | 6.176 | 7.430 | 10.657 | 15.112 | 21.199 | 29.439 |
| 12 | 7.288 | 8.916 | 13.215 | 19.343 | 27.983 | 40.037 |
| 13 | 8.599 | 10.699 | 16.386 | 24.759 | 36.937 | 54.451 |
| 14 | 10.147 | 12.839 | 20.319 | 31.961 | 48.757 | 74.053 |
| 15 | 11.974 | 15.407 | 25.196 | 40.565 | 64.359 | 100.712 |
| 16 | 14.129 | 18.488 | 31.243 | 51.923 | 84.954 | 136.97 |
| 17 | 16.672 | 22.186 | 38.741 | 66.461 | 112.14 | 186.28 |
| 18 | 19.673 | 26.623 | 48.039 | 85.071 | 148.02 | 253.34 |
| 19 | 23.214 | 31.948 | 59.568 | 108.89 | 195.39 | 344.54 |
| 20 | 27.393 | 38.338 | 73.864 | 139.38 | 257.92 | 468.57 |
| 25 | 62.669 | 95.396 | 216.542 | 478.90 | 1033.6 | 2180.1 |
| 30 | 143.371 | 237.376 | 634.820 | 1645.5 | 4142.1 | 10143. |

| Period | 40% | 50% | 60% | 70% | 80% | 90% |
|--------|-----|-----|-----|-----|-----|-----|
| 1 | 1.400 | 1.500 | 1.600 | 1.700 | 1.800 | 1.900 |
| 2 | 1.960 | 2.250 | 2.560 | 2.890 | 3.240 | 3.610 |
| 3 | 2.744 | 3.375 | 4.096 | 4.913 | 5.832 | 6.859 |
| 4 | 3.842 | 5.062 | 6.544 | 8.352 | 10.498 | 13.032 |
| 5 | 5.378 | 7.594 | 10.486 | 14.199 | 18.896 | 24.761 |
| 6 | 7.530 | 11.391 | 16.777 | 24.138 | 34.012 | 47.046 |
| 7 | 10.541 | 17.086 | 26.844 | 41.034 | 61.222 | 89.387 |
| 8 | 14.758 | 25.629 | 42.950 | 69.758 | 110.200 | 169.836 |
| 9 | 20.661 | 38.443 | 68.720 | 118.588 | 198.359 | 322.688 |
| 10 | 28.925 | 57.665 | 109.951 | 201.599 | 357.047 | 613.107 |
| 11 | 40.496 | 86.498 | 175.922 | 342.719 | 642.684 | 1164.902 |
| 12 | 56.694 | 129.746 | 281.475 | 582.622 | 1156.831 | 2213.314 |
| 13 | 79.372 | 194.619 | 450.360 | 990.457 | 2082.295 | 4205.297 |
| 14 | 111.120 | 291.929 | 720.576 | 1683.777 | 3748.131 | 7990.065 |
| 15 | 155.568 | 437.894 | 1152.921 | 2862.421 | 6746.636 | 15181.122 |
| 16 | 217.795 | 656.84 | 1844.7 | 4866.1 | 12144. | 28844.0 |
| 17 | 304.914 | 985.26 | 2951.5 | 8272.4 | 21859. | 54804.0 |
| 18 | 426.879 | 1477.9 | 4722.4 | 14063.0 | 39346. | 104130.0 |
| 19 | 597.630 | 2216.8 | 7555.8 | 23907.0 | 70824. | 197840.0 |
| 20 | 836.683 | 3325.3 | 12089.0 | 40642.0 | 127480. | 375900.0 |
| 25 | 4499.880 | 25251. | 126760.0 | 577060.0 | 2408900. | 9307600.0 |
| 30 | 24201.432 | 191750. | 1329200. | 8198500.0 | 45517000. | 230470000.0 |

# COEFFICIENTS FOR PRESENT VALUE OF $1

$$2 \text{ Coef.} = \frac{1}{(1 + i)^n}$$

To be
received at
the end of

Discount Rate

| Period | 1% | 2% | 3% | 4% | 5% | 6% | 7% | 8% | 9% | 10% | 12% | 14% | 15% |
|---|---|---|---|---|---|---|---|---|---|---|---|---|---|
| 1 | .990 | .980 | .971 | .962 | .952 | .943 | .935 | .926 | .917 | .909 | .893 | .877 | .870 |
| 2 | .980 | .961 | .943 | .925 | .907 | .890 | .873 | .857 | .842 | .826 | .797 | .769 | .756 |
| 3 | .971 | .942 | .915 | .889 | .864 | .840 | .816 | .794 | .772 | .751 | .712 | .675 | .658 |
| 4 | .961 | .924 | .889 | .855 | .823 | .792 | .763 | .735 | .708 | .683 | .636 | .592 | .572 |
| 5 | .951 | .906 | .863 | .822 | .784 | .747 | .713 | .681 | .650 | .621 | .567 | .519 | .497 |
| 6 | .942 | .888 | .838 | .790 | .746 | .705 | .666 | .630 | .596 | .564 | .507 | .456 | .432 |
| 7 | .933 | .871 | .813 | .760 | .711 | .665 | .623 | .583 | .547 | .513 | .452 | .400 | .376 |
| 8 | .923 | .853 | .789 | .731 | .677 | .627 | .582 | .540 | .502 | .467 | .404 | .351 | .327 |
| 9 | .914 | .837 | .766 | .703 | .645 | .592 | .544 | .500 | .460 | .424 | .361 | .308 | .284 |
| 10 | .905 | .820 | .744 | .676 | .614 | .558 | .508 | .463 | .422 | .386 | .322 | .270 | .247 |
| 11 | .896 | .804 | .722 | .650 | .585 | .527 | .475 | .429 | .388 | .350 | .287 | .237 | .215 |
| 12 | .887 | .788 | .701 | .625 | .557 | .497 | .444 | .397 | .356 | .319 | .257 | .208 | .187 |
| 13 | .879 | .773 | .681 | .601 | .530 | .469 | .445 | .368 | .326 | .290 | .229 | .182 | .163 |
| 14 | .870 | .758 | .661 | .577 | .505 | .442 | .388 | .340 | .299 | .263 | .205 | .160 | .141 |
| 15 | .861 | .743 | .642 | .555 | .481 | .417 | .362 | .315 | .275 | .239 | .183 | .140 | .123 |
| 16 | .853 | .728 | .623 | .534 | .458 | .394 | .339 | .292 | .252 | .218 | .163 | .123 | .107 |
| 17 | .844 | .714 | .605 | .513 | .436 | .371 | .317 | .270 | .231 | .198 | .146 | .108 | .093 |
| 18 | .836 | .700 | .587 | .494 | .416 | .350 | .296 | .250 | .212 | .180 | .130 | .095 | .081 |
| 19 | .828 | .686 | .570 | .475 | .396 | .331 | .276 | .232 | .194 | .164 | .116 | .083 | .070 |
| 20 | .820 | .673 | .554 | .456 | .377 | .312 | .258 | .215 | .178 | .149 | .104 | .073 | .061 |
| 25 | .780 | .610 | .478 | .375 | .295 | .233 | .184 | .146 | .116 | .092 | .059 | .038 | .030 |
| 30 | .742 | .552 | .412 | .308 | .231 | .174 | .131 | .099 | .075 | .057 | .033 | .020 | .015 |

| Period | 16% | 18% | 20% | 24% | 28% | 32% | 36% | 40% | 50% | 60% | 70% | 80% | 90% |
|---|---|---|---|---|---|---|---|---|---|---|---|---|---|
| 1 | .862 | .847 | .833 | .806 | .781 | .758 | .735 | .714 | .667 | .625 | .588 | .556 | .526 |
| 2 | .743 | .718 | .694 | .650 | .610 | .574 | .541 | .510 | .444 | .391 | .346 | .309 | .277 |
| 3 | .641 | .609 | .579 | .524 | .477 | .435 | .398 | .364 | .296 | .244 | .204 | .171 | .146 |
| 4 | .552 | .516 | .482 | .423 | .373 | .329 | .292 | .260 | .198 | .153 | .120 | .095 | .077 |
| 5 | .476 | .437 | .402 | .341 | .291 | .250 | .215 | .186 | .132 | .095 | .070 | .053 | .040 |
| 6 | .410 | .370 | .335 | .275 | .227 | .189 | .158 | .133 | .088 | .060 | .041 | .029 | .021 |
| 7 | .354 | .314 | .279 | .222 | .178 | .143 | .116 | .095 | .059 | .037 | .024 | .016 | .011 |
| 8 | .305 | .266 | .233 | .179 | .139 | .108 | .085 | .068 | .039 | .023 | .014 | .009 | .006 |
| 9 | .263 | .226 | .194 | .144 | .108 | .082 | .063 | .048 | .026 | .015 | .008 | .005 | .003 |
| 10 | .227 | .191 | .162 | .116 | .085 | .062 | .046 | .035 | .017 | .009 | .005 | .003 | .002 |
| 11 | .195 | .162 | .135 | .094 | .066 | .047 | .034 | .025 | .012 | .006 | .003 | .002 | .001 |
| 12 | .168 | .137 | .112 | .076 | .052 | .036 | .025 | .018 | .008 | .004 | .002 | .001 | .001 |
| 13 | .145 | .116 | .093 | .061 | .040 | .027 | .018 | .013 | .005 | .002 | .001 | .001 | .000 |
| 14 | .125 | .099 | .078 | .049 | .032 | .021 | .014 | .009 | .003 | .001 | .001 | .000 | .000 |
| 15 | .108 | .084 | .065 | .040 | .025 | .016 | .010 | .006 | .002 | .001 | .000 | .000 | .000 |
| 16 | .093 | .071 | .054 | .032 | .019 | .012 | .007 | .005 | .002 | .001 | .000 | .000 | |
| 17 | .080 | .060 | .045 | .026 | .015 | .009 | .005 | .003 | .001 | .000 | .000 | | |
| 18 | .069 | .051 | .038 | .021 | .012 | .007 | .004 | .002 | .001 | .000 | .000 | | |
| 19 | .060 | .043 | .031 | .017 | .009 | .005 | .003 | .002 | .000 | .000 | | | |
| 20 | .051 | .037 | .026 | .014 | .007 | .004 | .002 | .001 | .000 | .000 | | | |
| 25 | .024 | .016 | .010 | .005 | .002 | .001 | .000 | .000 | | | | | |
| 30 | .012 | .007 | .004 | .002 | .001 | .000 | .000 | | | | | | |

# COEFFICIENTS FOR PRESENT VALUE OF A $1 ANNUITY

$$3 \text{ Coef.} = \sum_{n=1}^{n} \frac{1}{(1 + i)^n}$$

Received at
the end
of each
period for:                          Discount Rate

| Period | 1% | 2% | 3% | 4% | 5% | 6% | 7% | 8% | 9% | 10% |
|---|---|---|---|---|---|---|---|---|---|---|
| 1 | 0.990 | 0.980 | 0.971 | 0.962 | 0.952 | 0.943 | 0.935 | 0.926 | 0.917 | 0.909 |
| 2 | 1.970 | 1.942 | 1.913 | 1.886 | 1.859 | 1.833 | 1.808 | 1.783 | 1.759 | 1.736 |
| 3 | 2.941 | 2.884 | 2.829 | 2.775 | 2.723 | 2.673 | 2.624 | 2.577 | 2.531 | 2.487 |
| 4 | 3.902 | 3.808 | 3.717 | 3.630 | 3.546 | 3.465 | 3.387 | 3.312 | 3.240 | 3.170 |
| 5 | 4.853 | 4.713 | 4.580 | 4.452 | 4.329 | 4.212 | 4.100 | 3.993 | 3.890 | 3.791 |
| 6 | 5.795 | 5.601 | 5.417 | 5.242 | 5.076 | 4.917 | 4.766 | 4.623 | 4.486 | 4.355 |
| 7 | 6.728 | 6.472 | 6.230 | 6.002 | 5.786 | 5.582 | 5.389 | 5.206 | 5.033 | 4.868 |
| 8 | 7.652 | 7.325 | 7.020 | 6.733 | 6.463 | 6.210 | 5.971 | 5.747 | 5.535 | 5.335 |
| 9 | 8.566 | 8.162 | 7.786 | 7.435 | 7.108 | 6.802 | 6.515 | 6.247 | 5.995 | 5.759 |
| 10 | 9.471 | 8.983 | 8.530 | 8.111 | 7.722 | 7.360 | 7.024 | 6.710 | 6.418 | 6.145 |
| 11 | 10.368 | 9.787 | 9.253 | 8.760 | 8.306 | 7.887 | 7.499 | 7.139 | 6.805 | 6.495 |
| 12 | 11.255 | 10.575 | 9.954 | 9.385 | 8.863 | 8.384 | 7.943 | 7.536 | 7.161 | 6.814 |
| 13 | 12.134 | 11.348 | 10.635 | 9.986 | 9.394 | 8.853 | 8.358 | 7.904 | 7.487 | 7.103 |
| 14 | 13.004 | 12.106 | 11.296 | 10.563 | 9.899 | 9.295 | 8.745 | 8.244 | 7.786 | 7.367 |
| 15 | 13.865 | 12.849 | 11.938 | 11.118 | 10.380 | 9.712 | 9.108 | 8.559 | 8.060 | 7.606 |
| 16 | 14.718 | 13.578 | 12.561 | 11.652 | 10.838 | 10.106 | 9.447 | 8.851 | 8.312 | 7.824 |
| 17 | 15.562 | 14.292 | 13.166 | 12.166 | 11.274 | 10.477 | 9.763 | 9.122 | 8.544 | 8.022 |
| 18 | 16.398 | 14.992 | 13.754 | 12.659 | 11.690 | 10.828 | 10.059 | 9.372 | 8.756 | 8.201 |
| 19 | 17.226 | 15.678 | 14.324 | 13.134 | 12.085 | 11.158 | 10.336 | 9.604 | 8.950 | 8.365 |
| 20 | 18.046 | 16.351 | 14.877 | 13.590 | 12.462 | 11.470 | 10.594 | 9.818 | 9.128 | 8.514 |
| 25 | 22.023 | 19.523 | 17.413 | 15.622 | 14.094 | 12.783 | 11.654 | 10.675 | 9.823 | 9.077 |
| 30 | 25.808 | 22.397 | 19.600 | 17.292 | 15.373 | 13.765 | 12.409 | 11.258 | 10.274 | 9.427 |

| Period | 12% | 14% | 16% | 18% | 20% | 24% | 28% | 32% | 36% |
|---|---|---|---|---|---|---|---|---|---|
| 1 | 0.893 | 0.877 | 0.862 | 0.847 | 0.833 | 0.806 | 0.781 | 0.758 | 0.735 |
| 2 | 1.690 | 1.647 | 1.605 | 1.566 | 1.528 | 1.457 | 1.392 | 1.332 | 1.276 |
| 3 | 2.402 | 2.322 | 2.246 | 2.174 | 2.106 | 1.981 | 1.868 | 1.766 | 1.674 |
| 4 | 3.037 | 2.914 | 2.798 | 2.690 | 2.589 | 2.404 | 2.241 | 2.096 | 1.966 |
| 5 | 3.605 | 3.433 | 3.274 | 3.127 | 2.991 | 2.745 | 2.532 | 2.345 | 2.181 |
| 6 | 4.111 | 3.889 | 3.685 | 3.498 | 3.326 | 3.020 | 2.759 | 2.534 | 2.339 |
| 7 | 4.564 | 4.288 | 4.039 | 3.812 | 3.605 | 3.242 | 2.937 | 2.678 | 2.455 |
| 8 | 4.968 | 4.639 | 4.344 | 4.078 | 3.837 | 3.421 | 3.076 | 2.786 | 2.540 |
| 9 | 5.328 | 4.946 | 4.607 | 4.303 | 4.031 | 3.566 | 3.184 | 2.868 | 2.603 |
| 10 | 5.650 | 5.216 | 4.833 | 4.494 | 4.193 | 3.682 | 3.269 | 2.930 | 2.650 |
| 11 | 5.938 | 5.453 | 5.029 | 4.656 | 4.327 | 3.776 | 3.335 | 2.978 | 2.683 |
| 12 | 6.194 | 5.660 | 5.197 | 4.793 | 4.439 | 3.851 | 3.387 | 3.013 | 2.708 |
| 13 | 6.424 | 5.842 | 5.342 | 4.910 | 4.533 | 3.912 | 3.427 | 3.040 | 2.727 |
| 14 | 6.628 | 6.002 | 5.468 | 5.008 | 4.611 | 3.962 | 3.459 | 3.061 | 2.740 |
| 15 | 6.811 | 6.142 | 5.575 | 5.092 | 4.675 | 4.001 | 3.483 | 3.076 | 2.750 |
| 16 | 6.974 | 6.265 | 5.669 | 5.162 | 4.730 | 4.033 | 3.503 | 3.088 | 2.758 |
| 17 | 7.120 | 5.373 | 5.749 | 5.222 | 4.775 | 4.059 | 3.518 | 3.097 | 2.763 |
| 18 | 7.250 | 6.467 | 5.818 | 5.273 | 4.812 | 4.080 | 3.529 | 3.104 | 2.767 |
| 19 | 7.366 | 6.550 | 5.877 | 5.316 | 4.844 | 4.097 | 3.539 | 3.109 | 2.770 |
| 20 | 7.469 | 6.623 | 5.929 | 5.353 | 4.870 | 4.110 | 3.546 | 3.113 | 2.772 |
| 25 | 7.843 | 6.873 | 6.097 | 5.467 | 4.948 | 4.147 | 3.564 | 3.122 | 2.776 |
| 30 | 8.055 | 7.003 | 6.177 | 5.517 | 4.979 | 4.160 | 3.569 | 3.124 | 2.778 |

## COEFFICIENTS FOR FUTURE VALUES OF ANNUITIES

$$4 \text{ Coef. } \frac{\%}{n} = \sum_{n=0}^{n-1} (1-i)^n$$

| To be deposited each Period | 1% | 2% | 3% | 4% | 5% | 6% |
|---|---|---|---|---|---|---|
| 1 | 1.000 | 1.000 | 1.000 | 1.000 | 1.000 | 1.000 |
| 2 | 2.010 | 2.020 | 2.030 | 2.040 | 2.050 | 2.060 |
| 3 | 3.030 | 3.060 | 3.091 | 3.122 | 3.152 | 3.184 |
| 4 | 4.060 | 4.122 | 4.184 | 4.246 | 4.310 | 4.375 |
| 5 | 5.101 | 5.204 | 5.309 | 5.416 | 5.526 | 5.637 |
| 6 | 6.152 | 6.308 | 6.468 | 6.633 | 6.802 | 6.975 |
| 7 | 7.214 | 7.434 | 7.662 | 7.898 | 8.142 | 8.394 |
| 8 | 8.286 | 8.583 | 8.892 | 9.214 | 9.549 | 9.897 |
| 9 | 9.369 | 9.755 | 10.159 | 10.583 | 11.027 | 11.491 |
| 10 | 10.462 | 10.950 | 11.464 | 12.006 | 12.578 | 13.181 |
| 11 | 11.567 | 12.169 | 12.808 | 13.486 | 14.207 | 14.972 |
| 12 | 12.683 | 13.412 | 14.192 | 15.026 | 15.917 | 16.870 |
| 13 | 13.809 | 14.680 | 15.618 | 16.627 | 17.713 | 18.882 |
| 14 | 14.947 | 15.974 | 17.086 | 18.292 | 19.599 | 21.051 |
| 15 | 16.097 | 17.293 | 18.599 | 20.024 | 21.579 | 23.276 |
| 16 | 17.258 | 18.639 | 20.157 | 21.825 | 23.657 | 25.673 |
| 17 | 18.430 | 20.012 | 21.762 | 23.698 | 25.840 | 28.213 |
| 18 | 19.615 | 21.412 | 23.414 | 25.645 | 28.132 | 30.906 |
| 19 | 20.811 | 22.841 | 25.117 | 27.671 | 30.539 | 33.760 |
| 20 | 22.019 | 24.297 | 26.870 | 29.778 | 33.066 | 36.786 |
| 25 | 28.243 | 32.030 | 36.459 | 41.646 | 47.727 | 54.865 |
| 30 | 34.785 | 40.568 | 47.575 | 56.805 | 66.439 | 79.058 |

| Period | 7% | 8% | 9% | 10% | 12% | 14% |
|---|---|---|---|---|---|---|
| 1 | 1.000 | 1.000 | 1.000 | 1.000 | 1.000 | 1.000 |
| 2 | 2.070 | 2.080 | 2.090 | 2.100 | 2.120 | 2.140 |
| 3 | 3.215 | 3.246 | 3.278 | 3.310 | 3.374 | 3.440 |
| 4 | 4.440 | 4.506 | 4.573 | 4.641 | 4.770 | 4.921 |
| 5 | 5.751 | 5.867 | 5.985 | 6.105 | 6.353 | 6.610 |
| 6 | 7.153 | 7.336 | 7.523 | 7.716 | 8.115 | 8.536 |
| 7 | 8.654 | 8.923 | 9.200 | 9.487 | 10.089 | 10.730 |
| 8 | 10.260 | 10.637 | 11.028 | 11.436 | 12.300 | 13.233 |
| 9 | 11.978 | 12.488 | 13.021 | 13.579 | 14.776 | 16.085 |
| 10 | 13.816 | 14.487 | 15.193 | 15.937 | 17.549 | 19.337 |
| 11 | 15.784 | 16.645 | 17.560 | 18.531 | 20.655 | 23.044 |
| 12 | 17.888 | 18.977 | 20.141 | 21.384 | 24.133 | 27.271 |
| 13 | 20.141 | 21.495 | 22.953 | 24.523 | 28.029 | 32.089 |
| 14 | 22.550 | 24.215 | 26.019 | 27.975 | 32.393 | 37.581 |
| 15 | 25.129 | 27.152 | 29.361 | 31.772 | 37.280 | 43.842 |
| 16 | 27.888 | 30.324 | 33.003 | 35.950 | 42.753 | 50.980 |
| 17 | 30.840 | 33.750 | 36.974 | 40.545 | 48.884 | 59.118 |
| 18 | 33.999 | 37.450 | 41.301 | 45.599 | 55.750 | 68.394 |
| 19 | 37.379 | 41.446 | 46.018 | 51.159 | 63.440 | 78.969 |
| 20 | 40.995 | 45.762 | 51.160 | 57.275 | 72.052 | 91.025 |
| 25 | 63.249 | 73.106 | 84.701 | 98.347 | 133.334 | 181.871 |
| 30 | 94.461 | 113.283 | 136.308 | 164.494 | 241.333 | 356.787 |

| Period | 16% | 18% | 20% | 24% | 28% | 32% |
|--------|-----|-----|-----|-----|-----|-----|
| 1 | 1.000 | 1.000 | 1.000 | 1.000 | 1.000 | 1.000 |
| 2 | 2.160 | 2.180 | 2.200 | 2.240 | 2.280 | 2.320 |
| 3 | 3.506 | 3.572 | 3.640 | 3.778 | 3.918 | 4.062 |
| 4 | 5.066 | 5.215 | 5.368 | 5.684 | 6.016 | 6.362 |
| 5 | 6.877 | 7.154 | 7.442 | 8.048 | 8.700 | 9.398 |
| 6 | 8.977 | 9.442 | 9.930 | 10.980 | 12.136 | 13.406 |
| 7 | 11.414 | 12.142 | 12.916 | 14.615 | 16.534 | 18.696 |
| 8 | 14.240 | 15.327 | 16.499 | 19.123 | 22.163 | 25.678 |
| 9 | 17.518 | 19.086 | 20.799 | 24.712 | 29.369 | 34.895 |
| 10 | 21.321 | 23.521 | 25.959 | 31.643 | 38.592 | 47.062 |
| 11 | 25.733 | 28.755 | 32.150 | 40.238 | 50.399 | 63.122 |
| 12 | 30.850 | 34.931 | 39.580 | 50.985 | 65.510 | 84.320 |
| 13 | 36.786 | 42.219 | 48.497 | 64.110 | 84.853 | 112.303 |
| 14 | 43.672 | 50.818 | 59.196 | 80.496 | 109.612 | 149.240 |
| 15 | 51.660 | 60.965 | 72.035 | 100.815 | 141.303 | 197.997 |
| 16 | 60.925 | 72.939 | 87.442 | 126.011 | 181.87 | 262.36 |
| 17 | 71.673 | 87.068 | 105.931 | 157.253 | 233.79 | 347.31 |
| 18 | 84.141 | 103.740 | 128.117 | 195.994 | 300.25 | 459.45 |
| 19 | 98.603 | 123.414 | 154.740 | 244.033 | 385.32 | 607.47 |
| 20 | 115.380 | 146.628 | 186.688 | 303.601 | 494.21 | 802.86 |
| 25 | 249.214 | 342.603 | 471.981 | 898.092 | 1706.8 | 3226.8 |
| 30 | 530.312 | 790.948 | 1181.882 | 2640.916 | 5873.2 | 12941.0 |

| Period | 36% | 40% | 50% | 60% | 70% | 80% |
|--------|-----|-----|-----|-----|-----|-----|
| 1 | 1.000 | 1.000 | 1.000 | 1.000 | 1.000 | 1.000 |
| 2 | 2.360 | 2.400 | 2.500 | 2.600 | 2.700 | 2.800 |
| 3 | 4.210 | 4.360 | 4.750 | 5.160 | 5.590 | 6.040 |
| 4 | 6.725 | 7.104 | 8.125 | 9.256 | 10.503 | 11.872 |
| 5 | 10.146 | 10.846 | 13.188 | 15.810 | 18.855 | 22.370 |
| 6 | 14.799 | 16.324 | 20.781 | 26.295 | 33.054 | 41.265 |
| 7 | 21.126 | 23.853 | 32.172 | 43.073 | 57.191 | 75.278 |
| 8 | 29.732 | 34.395 | 49.258 | 69.916 | 98.225 | 136.500 |
| 9 | 41.435 | 49.153 | 74.887 | 112.866 | 167.983 | 246.699 |
| 10 | 57.352 | 69.814 | 113.330 | 181.585 | 286.570 | 445.058 |
| 11 | 78.998 | 98.739 | 170.995 | 291.536 | 488.170 | 802.105 |
| 12 | 108.437 | 139.235 | 257.493 | 467.458 | 830.888 | 1444.788 |
| 13 | 148.475 | 195.929 | 387.239 | 748.933 | 1413.510 | 2601.619 |
| 14 | 202.926 | 275.300 | 581.859 | 1199.293 | 2403.968 | 4683.914 |
| 15 | 276.979 | 386.420 | 873.788 | 1919.869 | 4087.745 | 8432.045 |
| 16 | 377.69 | 541.99 | 1311.7 | 3072.8 | 6950.2 | 15179.0 |
| 17 | 514.66 | 759.78 | 1968.5 | 4917.5 | 11816.0 | 27323.0 |
| 18 | 700.94 | 1064.7 | 2953.8 | 7868.9 | 20089.0 | 49182.0 |
| 19 | 954.28 | 1491.6 | 4431.7 | 12591.0 | 34152.0 | 88528.0 |
| 20 | 1298.8 | 2089.2 | 6648.5 | 20147.0 | 58059.0 | 159350.0 |
| 25 | 6053.0 | 11247.0 | 50500.0 | 211270.0 | 824370.0 | 3011100.0 |
| 30 | 28172.0 | 60501.0 | 383500.0 | 2215400.0 | 11705000.0 | 56896000.0 |

# Index

References to definitions of important terms and concepts appear in boldface.